T0319492

2023

THE BEDFORDSHIRE
HISTORICAL RECORD SOCIETY

Contact details for the Society are on its website
http://www.bedfordshirehrs.org.uk

THE PUBLICATIONS OF THE BEDFORDSHIRE
HISTORICAL RECORD SOCIETY
VOLUME 98

BEDFORDSHIRE PROBATE INVENTORIES BEFORE 1660

Edited by
Barbara Tearle

THE BEDFORDSHIRE HISTORICAL RECORD SOCIETY

THE BOYDELL PRESS

First published 2024

A publication of
Bedfordshire Historical Record Society
published by The Boydell Press
an imprint of Boydell & Brewer Ltd
Bridge Farm Business Park, Top Street, Martlesham, IP12 4RB
and of Boydell & Brewer Inc.
668 Mt Hope Avenue, Rochester, NY 14620, USA
website: www.boydellandbrewer.com

ISBN 978-0-85155-085-5

ISSN 0067-4826

The Society is most grateful for financial support from The Wixamtree Trust and the James Dyer and Colin Muris bequests which have helped make the publication of this volume possible.

Details of previous volumes are available from Boydell & Brewer Ltd

A CIP record for this book is available from the British Library

Contents

Illustrations

Figures

Tables

In memory of
Sir Samuel Whitbread KCVO, FSA, 1937–2023

Following in his father's and grandfather's footsteps, Samuel Charles Whitbread became President of the Bedfordshire Historical Record Society in 1979, a post that he held to his death in 2023. He was an active president and as chair of the Annual General Meeting he always ensured that everyone was able to contribute while at the same time keeping meetings to the point.

In 1986 he headed the Society's appeal for funds for the Record Office (Bedfordshire Archives) to acquire the important archive of the Orlebar family of Hinwick Hall.

On 12 June 2012 at the Society's centenary garden party, which he generously hosted at his family home of Southill Park, he said, 'Bedfordshire is fortunate to have had such a galaxy of historians, who between them have established the pre-eminent position among archive societies in the country .... As the Society moves into its hundredth year, may the Society continue to make available original sources for many years to come.'

Sam had a long career in public service in Bedfordshire, including as a county councillor, High Sheriff and, from 1991 until 2012, Lord Lieutenant. As a county councillor he was Chairman of the Leisure Committee, which managed the Record Office in which his family's older documents were housed. His particular interest in the Whitbread family of Southill led to him to publish his excellent family history *Plain Mr Whitbread* in 2006.

Sam's enthusiasm for the Society and the warmth of friendship he had with its members will long be remembered.

Acknowledgements

These volumes could not have been produced without the help of many people. Staff at Bedfordshire Archives, Lincolnshire Archives, Huntingdonshire Archives, Hertfordshire Archives and Local Studies and The National Archives provided digital images and answered my questions, some giving exceptional help beyond what could be expected, especially Pamela Birch whose support and readiness to discuss the project has been greatly appreciated. My friends in the Oxfordshire Probate Group encouraged me throughout and helped by checking transcriptions, reading sections of the introduction, correcting mistakes and providing information. Friends in Bedfordshire Historical Record Society provided similar support and help with checking. My academic reviewers Dr Adrienne Rosen, Dr Heather Falvey and Dr Peter Doyle read the Introduction at different stages and their comments led me to rethink and produce what I hope is a better analysis of the inventories. Several specialists generously answered questions. Tom Jaine of Prospect Books, Professor William Sayers of Cornell University and Caroline Davidson, author of *A Woman's Work is Never Done*, discussed kitchen equipment with me. Elise Naish of the Culture Trust Luton went to great trouble during covid-19 lockdown to supply the information I requested about the painted cloths owned by the Trust. I am particularly grateful to Dr Joan Schneider and Dick Pilkinton of Markyate for access to the marvellous inventory of Edward Catherall, now in Bedfordshire Archives. I am grateful to Alan Higgs for allowing the use of his re-creation of Toddington town centre for the cover design, bringing to life the now-faded Agas map of 1581, and to Mel Jefferson for producing a clear map of the distribution of surviving inventories.

The hiatus in life during the covid-19 pandemic allowed more time for background research using internet resources, online databases and the ever-helpful catalogue and Community Histories pages of Bedfordshire Archives. Pandemic or not, these resources are a boon to researchers.

I am grateful to Bedfordshire Historical Record Society for accepting the proposal for this volume with enthusiasm and to the general editor Nicola Avery for encouragement, help (to the extent of visiting Lincolnshire Archives with me), advice, patience and seeing it through to publication. As usual, many thanks to Boydell & Brewer who have produced a beautiful volume.

Acknowledgement is made to Alan Higgs for permission to reproduce his painting of Toddington on the cover and to Lincolnshire Archives for permission to reproduce the image of William Hobeme's inventory (MISC WILLS K101). Permission to publish transcriptions of inventories in their collections is acknowledged to Bedfordshire Archives, Hertfordshire Archives and Local Studies, Huntingdonshire Archives, Lincolnshire Archives and The National Archives (for © Crown copyright. Licensed under the Open Government Licence v3.0).

Barbara Tearle
November 2022

Editorial conventions

Order

The inventories are arranged in the order in which they were made, to reflect the agricultural year. Undated inventories have been inserted between the date of burial and exhibition or the most likely date based on other evidence.

Dates

The date in the transcription is as it appears in the inventory. Where it falls in the January to 25 March period, the new style year has been used in the editorial heading, notes and introduction.

Editorial headings

The first three lines for each document is an editorial heading. It gives the name, place of residence and occupation of the deceased and the date of making (new style). Where an inventory is undated, dating information has been taken from other sources. The second line gives the record office holding the document and the reference. An optional third line comments on the condition of the document as it affects the completeness and accuracy of the transcription.

Inventory text

The body of the inventory has been presented line by line as it is in the original inventory, except that the formal opening lines naming the deceased, date and appraisers and the closing lines recording the appraisers' names and signatures have been presented as continuous texts.

Exhibition clauses

The exhibition clause added by court officials at the foot of the inventory is missing from many inventories. Where it appears, it is normally abbreviated. They have been summarised in the transcriptions and printed in italics as an editorial addition.

Layout

Several conventions have been adopted to make the transcriptions easy to read, while preserving as much faithfulness to the original as possible. The practice in many inventories of placing the name of the room in the centre of the line has been retained and the headings emboldened. A few inventories put this heading in the left margin; these have been centred. A few inventories have been written as continuous text with values interspersed; they have been re-formatted to the standard layout.

Pagination

Many inventories are on two or more pages. Pages have only been noted where it is necessary to understand the sequence of text or the presence of totals.

Spelling and unusual terms

Many unusual spellings can be worked out by slowly pronouncing the words aloud. Unusual words and spellings are explained in the glossary.

Punctuation

Punctuation has been transcribed as it was in the original inventory, except that commas have been added between the names of the appraisers at the beginning and end of the inventories.

Values

Values have been transcribed as they appear in Roman or arabic numerals. In most inventories the abbreviations *li*, *s* and *d* follow the values. For clarity, values have been set out in columns headed £ s d.

Totals

All totals and sub-totals have been checked and corrections added in brackets in italics.

Notes

Other documents with a bearing on the deceased have been noted and the most relevant facts giving additional information about the inventory have been summarised. The principal documents used have been parish registers, wills, glebe terriers, church court proceedings and clergy career sources. For a list of the sources, see the Abbreviations.

Transcription conventions

[*?*] preceding a word	doubtful transcriptions
[...]	text lost through damage. In a value column it means the value in that column is missing.
[*illeg.*]	text which is too faint or badly formed to read. In a value column it means the value in that column is illegible.
[*value illegible*] or [*value missing*]	means that the whole of the value is illegible or missing
[*word deleted*]	means that the deleted word is illegible. Where the deleted word is legible, it has been included and crossed through.
[*words in italics*]	editorial additions: 1. a comment on the state of the document; 2. an interpretation of a difficult spelling; 3. letters or words obliterated in the document by blots or holes but are obvious from the context; 4. corrected values, sub-totals and totals.

Some common words have been abbreviated in a variety of different ways in the inventories. They have been transcribed in full, without abbreviation. They are:

Anno Domini, implements, Imprimis, Item, Master, Mistress, quarter, summa totalis, Thomas, William, which, with

Words with contemporary standard marks of omission or contraction have been transcribed in full, without enclosing missing letters in brackets. They are:

'	er, ir
' in place of the last letter in a word	m, n, um
¯ indicating the omission of a letter	mm, m or en [e.g. tenement], u [e.g. sum], a [e.g. that]
3	et or us or left as 3 where the appropriate transcription is unclear
als with a line	alias
con with a line over it	cion
me[moran]d[um] and similar contractions	memorandum
p3	patet
r	er, or, ur
ꝑ	per, par
p^{3}	pre, pri, prae, prai
ꝓ	pro

Abbreviations

als	alias
Alumni Oxon	Joseph Foster, ed., *Alumni Oxonienses 1500–1714* (Oxford 1891), online at https://www.british-history.ac.uk/search/series/alumni-oxon
BHRS	Bedfordshire Historical Record Society publications
BPR	*Bedfordshire Parish Registers* (Bedford, 1931–1989), 80 vols
Beds Archives	Bedfordshire Archives Service
CCEd	Clergy of the Church of England database
Cal. S.P. Dom Jas I	*Calendar of State Papers, Domestic series of the reign of James I 1603*[*–1625*] *preserved in the State Paper Department of Her Majesty's Public Record Office* (London, 1857–9), 5 vols
Cal. S.P. Dom Chas I	*Calendar of State Papers, Domestic series of the reign of Charles I 1625*[*–1649*] *preserved in the State Paper Department of Her Majesty's Public Record Office* (London, 1858–98), 23 vols
Forman and Napier, case no.	see Kassell in the list of Books and Articles
Forman and Napier's *Casebooks*	see Kassell in the list of Books and Articles
HALS	Hertfordshire Archives and Local Studies
Hunts Archives	Huntingdonshire Archives
Lincs Archives	Lincolnshire Archives
np	no place of publication
ODNB	*Oxford Dictionary of National Biography*
OED	*Oxford English Dictionary*
TNA	The National Archives
Venn/ACAD	see Venn in the list of Books and Articles

Introduction

This collection of inventories provides rich evidence for historians of many different specialisms for life in Bedfordshire in the period from 1550 to 1660. Readers will come to the collection with varying degrees of knowledge of the place, period, probate procedure and material. This introduction provides background information to fill in these different lacunae.

The first half of the introduction is about structure. It discusses what inventories were; their survival rate in Bedfordshire; the character of the county in the sixteenth and seventeenth centuries; the Bedfordshire people for whom inventories were made; and how the inventories reflect the procedures of the probate system. The second half of the introduction is about their contents. It highlights issues about farming, housing, household and personal possessions in order to alert readers to features that need to be recognised to understand the inventories.

Probate inventories were the lists of a deceased person's goods, with their values, which were required to be made and produced in the church courts as part of the process of obtaining probate of a will (or letters of administration in the case of intestacy).[1] Their purpose was to prevent fraud by the executor, creditors, debtors, heirs and beneficiaries and also to protect them, especially minor children, from fraud. One copy of the inventory was kept by the church courts and a second copy was returned to the executor.[2]

Throughout the country as a whole, many thousands of inventories have survived and are held amongst diocesan records, most deposited with county record offices. However, for Bedfordshire only a few hundred have survived for the period before 1660. Bedfordshire Historical Record Society (BHRS) has already published 181[3] and this book complements them with a further 432, one of which was made in 1497 and the others between 1550 and 1659. A few more survive in fragments and have been omitted.

The county and the Archdeaconry of Bedford were almost coterminous. The exceptions were the two parishes making up the peculiars of Biggleswade and Leighton Buzzard and the extra-parochial area of Colworth; they were administered separately from the Archdeaconry. The area covered by this volume includes the peculiars and

1 For the sake of brevity, the two processes (probate for wills and administration for intestacy) have often been referred to as probate in this introduction.

2 See Appendix 2 for more on the purpose of the inventory and a summary of the formal procedure and p. xxxvii below for its application in Bedfordshire.

3 F. G. Emmison, 'Jacobean Household Inventories', BHRS vol. 20 (Aspley Guise, 1938), pp. 1–143 and C. E. Freeman, 'Elizabethan inventories' in *Harrold Priory: a Twelfth Century Dispute and other articles*, BHRS vol. 32 (Streatley, 1952), pp. 92–107. Hereafter cited as BHRS vol. 20 and BHRS vol. 32.

Figure 1 Survival rate for Bedfordshire inventories before 1660.

Table 1 The publication of Bedfordshire inventories before 1660 by decade

	Where published			
Decade	**In this volume**	**BHRS 32**	**BHRS 20**	**Totals by decade**
pre-1550	1			1
1550s	21			21
1560s	29	1		30
1570s	39	1		40
1580s	34	12		46
1590s	42	1		43
1600s	30		1	31
1610s	111		122	233
1620s	87		43	130
1630s	23			23
1640s	6			6
1650s	9			9
Totals	**432**	**15**	**166**	**613**

BHRS 32: C. E. Freeman, 'Elizabethan Inventories', BHRS vol. 32 (1952), pp. 92–107.
BHRS 20: F. G. Emmison, 'Jacobean Household Inventories', BHRS vol. 20 (1938), pp. 1–143.

all parishes which have at any time been part of the county. Four hundred and twenty inventories are among the records of the diocese of Lincoln, the archdeaconries of Bedford and Huntingdon, the Prerogative Court of Canterbury and the Court of Civil Commission of the 1650s. The remaining twelve inventories are the copies which were retained by the executors and are in private deposits in Bedfordshire Archives. The inventories in this volume are held at Lincolnshire Archives (338), Bedfordshire Archives (67), Huntingdonshire Archives (17), Hertfordshire Archives and Local Studies (1) and The National Archives (9).

Four inventories, those of James Woodward (*1*), William Grey (*114*), Edward Catherall (*260*) and Christopher Crouch (*395*), have been published before.[4] They are included here because the earlier publications may not be easily accessible and because it has been possible to make a few corrections. A few documents in this volume are not standard probate inventories but have been included because they deal with administering the estate or were accepted by the church courts for probate purposes:

- Daniel Payne 1558 (*20*) who had three documents: a list of livestock and crops made seven years before his death; an undated list of household goods, probably a draft; and a list made after his death of goods divided between his executors (Beds Archives, OR 1036, 1917, 1918).

4 For Woodward, see Margaret McGregor, ed., *Bedfordshire Wills proved in the Prerogative Court of Canterbury 1383–1548*, BHRS vol. 58 (Bedford, 1979), pp. 41–2; for Grey and Crouch see 'A Sixteenth Century Inventory' and 'An Inventory of the XVIIth Century', *Bedfordshire Notes & Queries* vol. 3 (1893), pp. 252–4 and 276–8 respectively; for Catherall, see Joan Schneider, 'An Inventory of 1612/1613: a Luton Brewer' and J. J. Hayes 'The Malting and Brewing Process', *Manshead Archaeological Society Journal* no. 19 (1969), pp. 30–41.

- John Francklyn of Burystead, Thurleigh 1581 (*100*) whose inventory lists the value of a lease and money owed to him. It is among an eighteenth-century summary of family documents at Bedfordshire Archives (FN 1248).
- Henry Gale 1591 (*126*) who was living in Southoe, Hunts, when he died. He has been included because his will identifies him as from Knotting.
- William Brace of Millbrook 1610 (*197*) whose document is a record of payments rather than the usual form for an inventory or a probate account. It is highly informative about the work of administration.
- John Willson of Warden Abbey 1622 (*331*) whose ten page document dated one year before his burial opens with the words 'A true Inventorye of all *my* linnen'. Some marginal notes and the value of the goods are in a different hand. Probably the appraiser added valuations to a pre-existing inventory. The document was exhibited and accepted.
- John Cooper of Tempsford (*336*) whose undated list, made between 1617 and 1622, is a mixture of prices obtained on the sale of his goods, money received from his creditors and valuations of items as yet unsold. It is neither an inventory nor a probate account.
- Susan and Thomas Carter of Bedford (*425*) whose inventory is listed in probate indexes under his name. He died in 1638, but it is a list of the possessions of his widow which were sold by her son at her death in 1652. It is among Bedford Archdeaconry probate records together with court proceedings and deeds.

Although the publication of all currently-known Bedfordshire inventories before the Restoration has been completed by this volume, more may come to light.

Much can be learnt about contemporary life from probate inventories but, for a broader understanding, it is essential to look at other documents. Thus, relevant material has been referred to and summarised at the end of many transcriptions. Documents cited include wills, commissions, deeds, church court proceedings and glebe terriers from amongst the Lincoln Diocesan and Bedford Archdeaconry records; transcriptions of burial registers;[5] information from the Clergy of the Church of England database (CCEd);[6] the online version of *Alumni Oxoniensis*;[7] the Cambridge University online version of Venn's *Biographical Register of the University of Cambridge to 1751*;[8] Forman and Napier's casebooks of medical and astrological consultations;[9] and information from Bedfordshire Archives' ever-helpful online catalogue and Community Histories' pages.[10]

5 *Bedfordshire Parish Registers*, published by Bedfordshire County Record Office, 1931–1989. 80 volumes. Hereafter *BPR* and volume number.

6 Clergy of the Church of England database https://theclergydatabase.org.uk hereafter CCEd.

7 Joseph Foster, ed., *Alumni Oxonienses 1500–1714* (Oxford 1891), 4 vols, online at https://www.british-history.ac.uk/search/series/alumni-oxon hereafter *Alumni Oxon*.

8 John Venn, *Alumni Cantabrigienses ... from the earliest times to 1751* (Cambridge, 1922–27), 4 vols, online as *ACAD: A Cambridge Alumni Database* https://venn.lib.cam.ac.uk hereafter Venn ACAD.

9 Lauren Kassell, Michael Hawkins, Robert Ralley, John Young, Joanne Edge, Janet Yvonne Martin-Portugues, and Natalie Kaoukji, eds, *The casebooks of Simon Forman and Richard Napier, 1596–1634: a digital edition*, https://casebooks.lib.cam.ac.uk.

10 https://bedsarchives.bedford.gov.uk/ArchivesAndRecordOffice.aspx.

Bedfordshire in the sixteenth and seventeenth centuries

Before discussing the inventories, the county and period need some explanation to show the context in which they were made.

Bedfordshire is a small inland county to the north of London and surrounded by the counties of Buckinghamshire to the west, Northamptonshire and Huntingdonshire on the north and east, and Cambridgeshire and Hertfordshire on the east and south-east. It is approximately thirty miles from north to south and twenty-five miles from west to east and has an area of about 300,000 acres (c.1214sq km). It had some 135 parishes, the largest being Luton in the south of the county at 15,000 acres (61sq km). Many parishes had dispersed settlements, some of which are named as the places of residence in the inventories.

Estimating sixteenth and seventeenth century population is beset with difficulties.[11] The figures on which estimates are based derive from sources that were collected for other purposes, such as taxation, communicants and parish registers. Returns in some sources were in round figures. Others have not survived for the county or part of it. Many may be under-recorded. They should be taken as *indicative* of magnitude only. On that basis, the population of Bedfordshire in 1563 has been estimated at about 27,000.[12] In 1603 it might have been approaching 35,000.[13] The Protestation returns of 1641–1642 have not survived for Bedfordshire but a generation later, there are two sets of population figures: the 1671 hearth tax returns and the 1676 Compton Census. Both are subject to problems of omission and interpretation. Lydia Marshall calculated that the population of Bedfordshire from the hearth tax returns was slightly over 41,000, by multiplying the number of houses by 4.25.[14] Anne Whiteman has subjected the Compton census and the hearth tax to careful scrutiny. She has suggested that the population of Bedfordshire in 1676 could have been 38,037, or 42,475 or 46,336, depending on the multiplier used for adding in those aged under sixteen.[15] These two sets of calculations are not inconsistent. To put this into perspective, these figures for the *county* in the sixteenth and seventeenth centuries scarcely reach a quarter of the population of Bedford *borough* in the 2021 census (185,000).[16]

Bedfordshire had one borough, Bedford, and several other parishes described in contemporary accounts as market towns: Ampthill, Biggleswade, Dunstable, Leighton Buzzard, Luton, Potton, Shefford,[17] Toddington and Woburn. Of these,

11 For a thorough account, see A. Dyer and D. M. Palliser, eds, *The Diocesan Population Returns for 1563 and 1603* (Oxford, 2005). For a discussion of population statistics for a contiguous county see L. Munby, *Hertfordshire Population Statistics 1563–1801*, 2nd ed. by Heather Falvey (np, 2019), Hertfordshire Record Society.

12 The number of families in the parishes as recorded by Dyer, *Diocesan Population Returns*, multiplied by 4.75.

13 Communicant families, and non-communicant and recusant individuals or families. Dyer and Palliser question the adequacy of a multiplier of one third to account for children and suggest at least 45% to allow for all omissions (Dyer, *Diocesan Population Returns*, p. lxxii).

14 Lydia M. Marshall, *The Bedfordshire Hearth Tax Returns for 1671*, BHRS vol. 16 (Aspley Guise, 1934, repr. 1990).

15 Anne Whiteman and Mary Clapinson, eds, *The Compton Census of 1676: a critical edition* (London, 1986), Appendix D, pp. xcviii–xcii, and p. cx. The three sets of figures are derived from the assumption that those under 16 formed 33%, 40% or 45% of the population.

16 https://www.ons.gov.uk/visualisations/censuspopulationchange.

17 Shefford was included in the parish of Campton.

Bedford, Biggleswade, Ampthill and Dunstable were also listed as amongst the principal fairs in England.[18] The main routes through Bedfordshire were Watling Street on the south west; the Ermine Street section of the Great North Road on the east; a route from St Albans entering the county in Luton and running to Bedford where it joined roads going west, north-west and east; and an east-west route from Bristol to Cambridge crossing Bedfordshire from Newport Pagnell to Gransden via Bedford.[19] These routes put Dunstable on the ten mile stretch of Watling Street on the third day of travel to or from London. It was well served with inns for these travellers, and an inventory for the Crown Inn survives (*176*).[20] Only three other inventories for innkeepers survive and this total of four fails to do justice to the number of inns that would have been necessary in the county for local and the large passing trade.

A contemporary view of the agriculture of the county is provided by William Camden who reported that:

> The Aire here is very temperate and pleasant bringing both delight and health to the Inhabitants. The Soile is rich and fertile, but especially where the Riuer *Ouse* by the moistening of her bankes makes the meadowes send forth their increase in abundance. And although the other parts of the Shire are somewhat more barren, being for the most part a Champion, yet by the industrious Inhabitants it is well stored with Barly, and plenty of Pasturage, and is not wanting for some store of Woods.[21]

Later surveys report 'Every soil and every mixture of soil, commonly seen on high land in the united kingdoms, may be found in this county, from the strongest clay to the lightest sand'.[22] The *Agrarian History of England and Wales* characterised late seventeenth century farming in bands running south-west to north-east as corn and sheep in the south including Luton, corn and cattle from Leighton Buzzard to Henlow, market gardening from Woburn to Sandy and corn and cattle around and to the north of Bedford.[23]

There was some enclosure by agreement (voluntary or otherwise) and Bedfordshire was one of the counties investigated in 1607 after the Midland Revolt during which participants had protested against the enclosure of open fields and common land and engrossment of holdings during the later decades of the sixteenth century.[24]

18 Richard Grafton, *A Briefe Treatise Conteinyng Many Proper Tables and easie Rules, etc.* (London, 1573), unpaginated; John Chartres, ed., *Chapters from the Agrarian History of England and Wales, volume 4: Agricultural Markets and Trade 1500–1750* (Cambridge, 1990), pp. 138–41.

19 Neatly shown on CamPop's map 'Ogilby's Principal Roads, 1675: After A map of XVIIth century England, Ordnance Survey 1930 with additions' https://www.campop.geog.cam.ac.uk/research/projects/occupations/onlineatlas/ogilby1675.png (accessed on 1 November 2019).

20 For inns in Dunstable see Vivienne Evans, *Historic Inns of Dunstable* (Dunstable, 2002).

21 William Camden, *The abridgement of Camden's Britannia* (London, 1626).

22 Thomas Batchelor, *General View of the Agriculture of the County of Bedford* (London, 1808), p. 4.

23 Joan Thirsk, ed., *The Agrarian History of England and Wales* (Cambridge, 1984) vol. 5, pt 1, p. 241. There is no evidence of market gardening in the inventories, although gardens and orchards are mentioned.

24 Edwin F. Gay, 'The Midland Revolt and the Inquisitions of Depopulation of 1607', *Transactions of the Royal Historical Society* vol. 18 (n.s.) (1904), pp. 195–244.

Nevertheless, Bedfordshire was primarily a mixture of open field cultivation and some closes, which are mentioned in several inventories (e.g. *107*, *235*), until Parliamentary enclosure began in the middle of the eighteenth century.[25]

The weather during the period was changeable and often poor throughout the country, with a catalogue of harsh winters, frozen rivers, severe thunderstorms, poor summers and some droughts resulting in frequent poor harvests. Famines occurred nationally in 1556, 1597, 1631 and 1649.[26] Prices of wheat and wool fluctuated in those and other years, causing hardship to farmers. The varying prices for agricultural produce in the Bedfordshire inventories bear this out. In the years of bad harvests preceding the famine of 1597, the price of barley doubled from Raynold Ireland's inventory in 1594 (*143*) to John Place's in 1596 (*151*).

In common with other counties, Bedfordshire suffered from recurrent waves of plague, the resultant deaths around the county being recorded in some of the parish registers. The first plague victim in Dunstable in July 1593 was a visitor from London, whose burial was followed by another fifty-nine between then and May 1594. None of these victims are among the people for whom inventories are extant. More than seventy people were buried at Cardington in 1604, including Christopher Bennet (*177*), in comparison with around a quarter of that number in each of the two years before and after 1604, indicating plague or another epidemic.[27]

Other disasters such as fires occurred e.g. Woburn in 1595, Houghton Regis in about 1605 and Leighton Buzzard in 1645.[28] The river Ouse flooded in Bedford in 1579. None of these events nor similar catastrophes are obvious from the inventories, but they may have had an impact on the lives of some decedents and their communities.

Bedfordshire played its part in national military matters during the second half of the sixteenth century. Mobilisation, evidenced by militia musters, included impressment for service in Ireland in the 1590s and early 1600s (which claimed Humfrey Gregorie from the family of Ambrose Gregorye of Eversholt, *146*). The county had increasing difficulty meeting the demands for supplies and horses during the 1580s and exhibited growing resistance to musters during the early seventeenth

25 Enclosure by agreement is recorded in Stanbridge in 1624 (Beds Archives, AD 3787) and in Dean in 1626 (Beds Archives, PA 59). For an overview of early enclosures and an account of a contested attempt at enclosure, see Steve Hindle, 'Persuasion and Protest in the Caddington Common Enclosure Dispute 1635–1639', *Past & Present* no. 158 (1998), pp. 37–78.

26 J. M. Stratton, *Agricultural records AD220–1968*, edited by Ralph Whitlock (London, 1969).

27 Figures derived from Bedfordshire Parish Registers, vol. 44 (Dunstable) and vol. 8 (Cardington). Godber notes epidemics based on burials in thirteen parishes in 1557–1560 and other plague deaths (J. Godber, *History of Bedfordshire 1066–1888* (Bedford, 1969), pp. 221, 261).

28 *A short, yet a true and faithfull narration of the fearefull fire that fell in the towne of Wooburne, in the countie of Bedford, on Saturday the 13 of September last, Anno. 1595 Together with a Christian admonition as to the particular people of that place* (London, 1595); R. Simpson, *Memorials of St John at Hackney, Part III* (Guildford, 1882), p. 41 records the collection of 8s for the relief of Houghton Regis's fire in 1605; and the petition to Parliament from Leighton Buzzard noted on 25 July 1645, *Journal of the House of Lords: Volume 7, 1644* (London, 1771), p. 508.

century.[29] The presence of weapons in some inventories may be a relic of time in the militia. There was opposition to the imposition of ship money in Bedfordshire and other inland counties, with the sheriff making an example of the men of Tilsworth and of John Gregory of Eversholt in 1638 (another of Ambrose Gregorye's family).[30]

Men were recruited from the county to both sides in the civil war, 150 being supplied for the New Model Army in 1645. There were no major encounters in Bedfordshire but the county experienced billeting, taxation, skirmishes and the passage of troops of both sides.[31] Several thousand Royalist soldiers captured at Naseby in 1645 were marched to London, passing through Bedford, Dunstable and Luton.[32] A few months later in November between 1000 and 1500 Royalist cavalry from Oxford and Banbury passed through Leighton Buzzard on their way towards the Eastern Association forces[33] and plundered Robert Staunton's house at Birchmore (*428*).[34] On the religio-political front, the Westminster Assembly of Divines of 1643 had several Bedfordshire members. One of the first ministers to be nominated to the Assembly was Edmund Staunton (brother of Robert Staunton of Birchmore, *428*)[35] and another member was Oliver Bowles, rector of Sutton who had been an appraiser of the goods of John Durrant, rector of the neighbouring parish of Cockayne Hatley in 1625 (*381*).[36]

Bedfordshire people had many contacts beyond the county. Boys were apprenticed to trades in London and elsewhere (e.g. the son of Edward Edwyn (*419*) in 1650) and boys from other counties came to Bedfordshire. Some boys obtained their education at the Inns of Court, went on to highly successful careers, remembered their origins and returned to family estates or to buy land and endow charities, such as George Francklin who left money for the education of poor children (*306*). The county had strong ties with the University of Cambridge and sons of gentry, clerical and yeoman families matriculated there. Others obtained their education at Oxford University (e.g. *334*).

Diverging religious views existed, sometimes dividing minister from congregation. More than thirty incumbents were ejected in the 1640s and 50s.[37] Dissent also lead to the departure of Peter Bulkeley ('a discreet nonconforming clergyman'),[38] his son, their families and some of the Odell parishioners for the New World in 1635. The Bulkeley family had been rectors of Odell for two generations and the blacksmith David Towler who died in 1625 would have been one of his

29 Nigel Lutt, ed., *Bedfordshire Muster Rolls 1539–1831*, BHRS vol. 71 (np, 1992), pp. 56–8.

30 *Cal. S.P. Dom. Charles I*, vol. 12 (1637–1638), p. 432.

31 More on Bedfordshire and the civil war is to be found in Ross Lee, *Law and Local Society in the time of Charles I: Bedfordshire and the Civil War*, BHRS vol. 65 (np, 1986) and Godber, *Bedfordshire*, pp. 247–50.

32 Civil War Petitions database https://www.civilwarpetitions.ac.uk/blog/the-wounded-of-naseby/.

33 *Cal. S.P. Dom. Charles I*, vol. 21 (1645–1647), p. 239.

34 Beds Archives, Community Histories, Woburn during the English Civil War.

35 'Edmund Staunton 1600–1671' by John Gurney, *ODNB*.

36 Mentioned in his son's *ODNB* entry ('Edward Bowles 1613–1662' by Stephen Wright, *ODNB*).

37 Edwin Welch, 'The Geography of Dissent in Bedfordshire', in *Bedfordshire Historical Miscellany: Essays in Honour of Patricia Bell*, BHRS vol. 72 (np, 1993), pp. 54–60.

38 'Peter Bulkeley 1583–1659' by Michael McGiffert, *ODNB*.

congregation (*348*). Another emigrant to the New World with possible connections to these inventories was Thomas Dickerman, who may have been the son of George Dickerman (*270*).

Members of Parliament for the county and the borough of Bedford were drawn from local families. Prominent among the county MPs were the St Johns and Lukes, to whom Oliver (*181*) and Nicholas Luke (*337*) were related. The borough was also represented by local families including John Burgoyne of Sutton whose servant was Ralph Briten (*149*) and Sir Humphrey Winch of Everton whose sister-in-law, Mary Onslow, lived in his household and died there in 1627 (*389*). These and other families also provided the commissioners who were charged with administering the county (e.g. *428*).

Being only two or three days' journey from London, the county was not only a route to and from more distant counties but also a place for country estates and visiting royalty, who no doubt caused a stir, but the greater impact on the neighbourhood would be accommodating and supplying their entourages.[39] Grand houses were built or rebuilt, such as Toddington Manor in the 1540s–60s; Harrold Hall by Francis Farrer in 1608–1610;[40] Houghton House before 1621; Marston was probably built in the late sixteenth century by the incomer Thomas Snagge.[41] Warden Abbey where Robert Gostwick died in 1562 was rebuilt by the St Johns in the early seventeenth century and rented by John Willson in 1622 (*331*).[42]

These, then, were the times in which the decedents and their appraisers lived and which coloured their lives.[43] The county was active, thriving, well off and engaged with the world beyond its border. The inventories should never be seen in isolation from surrounding events and, no doubt, other connections between people and events will emerge with more background research.

About the inventories

An inventory of the goods at death of all adult males, widows and single women (the people who qualified for the probate process) should have been taken. An estimate of the potential number can be made based on data from a few sample parishes where the burial registers note sufficient family information to eliminate children and wives from the totals. At Wilden, there were 450 burials in the years 1550 to 1650, of which 212 were for qualifying people, in contrast to the five surviving inventories.

39 Queen Elizabeth I stayed at Woburn Abbey in 1572 and Toddington manor in 1563 (Godber, *Bedfordshire*, p. 176); James I was a frequent visitor to the St Johns at Bletsoe at least seven times during his reign and at Toddington in 1614; his wife stayed at other houses nearby (James Collett-White, *Inventories of Bedfordshire Country Houses 1714–1830*, BHRS vol. 74 (Bedford, 1995), p. 165); and Arbella Stuart was at Wrest in 1603 (Mary S. Lovell, *Bess of Hardwick: first lady of Chatsworth, 1527–1608* (London, 2005), p. 445).

40 John Weaver, 'The Building Accounts of Harrold Hall', in *Miscellanea*, BHRS vol. 49 (np, 1970), pp. 56–80.

41 Godber, *Bedfordshire*, p. 245, where other building in the late sixteenth century is also listed.

42 Robert Gostwick's inventory is in Freeman, 'Elizabethan inventories', p. 102.

43 See Godber, *Bedfordshire* for many more local events.

At Toddington in the shorter period 1581 to 1640, there were 810 burials, of which 398 were for qualifying people and only six inventories have survived.[44] If this is a reliable indication of the number of qualifying decedents, the potential number of inventories for the 135 or so parishes would have been many thousands (even accounting for failures to carry out procedure), in contrast to the six hundred-odd that have actually survived and comparable to the thousands that have survived for some other counties.[45]

The main reason for such a low survival emerges from an administrative history of transfer and neglect.[46] Describing the first accession of Bedford Archdeaconry material, Bedfordshire Archives' catalogue says that they appear to have been 'originally kept in a room over the south porch of St. Paul's church' and 'it is alleged that many were used to light the fire.'[47]

Analysis by parish and decade of the 432 inventories in this volume and the 181 in BHRS volumes 20 and 32 shows how haphazard the distribution is (Figure 1 and Appendix 1). Inventories survived from more than one hundred parishes including the five parishes in the borough of Bedford. Only twelve parishes have ten or more inventories. Some have only one and there are none for sixteen parishes.[48] The greatest number is for the parishes of the borough of Bedford (33). The other market towns have varying numbers: Ampthill (4), Biggleswade (1), Dunstable (11), Leighton Buzzard (3), Luton (18), Potton (16), Shefford (5), Toddington (7) and Woburn (2). Blunham, Eaton Socon and Sandy also stand out with 16, 19 and 17 respectively. Notable amongst the market towns with few inventories are the peculiars of Biggleswade and Leighton Buzzard and its four hamlets (Billington, Eggington, Heath and Reach and Stanbridge). Their ecclesiastical records were kept by the prebends and, being small jurisdictions, their records were more liable to loss and few have survived.

While nine of the twelve decades have more than twenty surviving inventories, the 1610s and 20s stand out with 232 and 129 (of which 111 and eighty-six respectively are published in this volume).

Between 750 and eight hundred Bedfordshire testators had their wills proved in the Prerogative Court of Canterbury before 1660 (or the Court of Civil Commission for the 1650s). They were not only the wealthy and middling sort such as the Earl of Bedford, local gentry, clergy and officials but also humbler people such as yeoman

44 Figures have been derived from the transcribed series of Bedfordshire Parish Registers.

45 Arkell puts the survival of inventories in England and Wales for the long seventeenth century at one million 'or so' (Tom Arkell, 'Interpreting probate inventories', in Tom Arkell, *When Death Do Us Part*, p. 72). An estimate of survival in the diocese of Durham from 1540s to 1720 is 13,000 (J. Linda Drury, 'Inventories in the Probate Records of the Diocese and Durham, *Archaeologia Aeliana* vol. 28 (2000), pp. 177–91.

46 The administrative history of the Bedfordshire probate records of the Diocese of Lincoln and Archdeaconries of Bedford and Huntingdon has been described by Chris Pickford in the introduction to *Index of Bedfordshire Probate Records 1484–1858*. British Record Society, *Index Library* vol. 104 (London, 1993), pp. vii–xiv, xviii.

47 http://bedsarchivescat.bedford.gov.uk/Details/archive/110003054.

48 Aspley Guise, Battlesden, Eggington, Farndish, Harlington, Heath and Reach, Higham Gobion, Hockliffe, Holwell, Kensworth, Little Barford, Lower Gravenhurst, Salford, Stanbridge, Totternhoe, Upper Stondon.

and widows (who may have been among the élite and wealthy, of course).[49] However, inventories for only nine of those testators have survived.[50]

Neither the 432 inventories published here, nor the 613 overall, provide sufficient data for analysis to establish an in-depth picture of the county as a whole in this period, as has been possible with larger collections for other areas.[51] It is possible, nevertheless, to extract many examples pointing to broad trends in the traditional themes of house design, use of rooms and type of agriculture. The concentration of inventories in the 1610s and 1620s could provide snapshot overviews of the county for those decades. Many of the inventories contain details of distinctive aspects of life, enabling an exploration of themes such as the clergy (there are inventories for thirteen clergymen), debt, how widows managed and provision for old age and retirement. Despite the random nature of survival, inventories survive for several members of the same families, such as the two ploughwrights from the Bull family in Riseley (*130*, *167*), the Newolds of Kempston (*51*, *430*) and others.

The decedents[52]

The essential information about the decedents is set out in Appendix 3 and Tables 2 to 5: name, place of residence and date of inventory; sex and marital status; social status and occupations; and inventory values.[53] These are the basic data for putting individual decedents into their contemporary context.[54]

The 432 inventories were for 373 men (86%) and fifty-nine women (14%). By adding information from parish registers and wills, it has been possible to determine the marital status of almost two thirds of them (61%). Nearly half the men were married (and probably many in the 'status not known' category as well). Twenty-six men and the majority of women were widowed and there were twenty-four singles of both sexes. The information on marital status facilitates a better understanding of the lives presented by these inventories. Henry Foster of Thurleigh, a yeoman who died in 1625 (*352*), is a good example. The initial impression from his inventory is of a prosperous farmer with £95-worth of animals, crops and farming equipment, somewhat light on household goods but possessing books. This would suggest an established, family man. However, behind the superficially standard, male, farming inventory is a very different stage in his life: his will shows that he was single, that he intended to marry and had probably been helped by his father with the lease to the land he farmed.[55]

There are three occurrences of a husband and wife dying within days of each other. The inventories of Thomas and Annes Semer (*28*, *29*) were made by the same

49 Figures derived from PROB lists in the catalogue of The National Archives.
50 In TNA, PROB 2.
51 Arkell, 'Interpreting probate inventories', pp. 72–102.
52 From this point in the Introduction, figures and comments refer to the inventories published in this volume only.
53 See pages ciii for Appendix 3 and xxiv–xxvii for the tables.
54 For an account of domestic, social and economic interdependence and society at this period, see Keith Wrightson, *Earthly Necessities: economic lives in early modern Britain*, 1470–1750 (Penguin, 2002).
55 For setting up sons, see Wrightson, *Earthly Necessities*, pp. 60–1.

Table 2 Sex and marital status of the decedents

Inventories per decade	Men				Women			
	single	mar	wid	nk	single	mar	wid	nk
pre-1550 (1)				1				
1550s (21)		2	2	16			1	
1560s (29)		4		23			2	
1570s (39)		4	1	29			4	1
1580s (34)		5	1	23			5	
1590s (42)	2	9	2	22	1		6	
1600s (30)	4	12	2	7			5	
1610s (111)	7	65	7	18			14	
1620s (87)	7	37	9	22	2		10	
1630s (23)		14		4	1		3	1
1640s (6)		5	1					
1650s (9)		4	1	1			3	
Totals (432)	**20**	**161**	**26**	**166**	**4**		**53**	**2**

mar = married; wid = widowed; nk = marital status not known.
Column 1: the bracketed figure is the total number of inventories for the decade.

appraisers, exhibited on the same day in 1560 and have four items in common. Their burial records have not survived but he died first because an inventory was made of her goods, as well as his, signalling that she outlived him. Thomas Elmar and his wife were both buried in Shillington on 6 September 1611 (*242*). Thomas's son and executor did not seek administration of her goods, indicating that she died first. Richard and Agnes Hancock's inventories were made on 23 September 1611, and it is clear from hers that he died first (*246*, *247*).

The combined information from inventories, parish registers and wills establishes the status or occupations of about two-thirds of the decedents (Tables 4 and 3, column 1). They are predominately from the middling to low ranks of Bedfordshire inhabitants. By a further addition of the evidence of crops and livestock (columns 2–5), the extent of farming as a main or subsidiary occupation among all groups emerges. Only sixty-eight of the 432 inventories (16%) lack animals and crops. The inventories themselves show that 90% of the yeoman, husbandmen and labourers were farming and that many in the other categories were combining farming with a trade, clergy status or widowhood. The 364 inventories with crops and animals encompass farming at many levels, ranging from those whose crops and animals are a substantial part of their possessions to people with a couple of acres and a few pigs.

A few inventories lack totals because they are incomplete or damaged or are more like accounts and do not record the value of decedents' possessions (e.g. *13*, *20*, *197*). The remainder range in value from £1 5s to £877 3s and two exceptionally high valuations of £2245 (*428*) and £4471 (306).[56] Table 4 shows how they relate to social status and occupations and Table 5 shows the valuations by decade.

56 See Appendix 3 for an alphabetical list of inventories and their values.

Table 3 Occupations, status, and farming

Occupation or status and number in each category	farming			no crops or animals
	animals & crops	**animals only**	**crops only**	
Gentry (19)				
gentleman (14)	9	3		2
esquire (3)	1	1		1
spinster (1)				1
widow (1)	1			
Clergy (13)	10	2		1
Yeoman (54)	41	5	2	6
Husbandman (45)	40	4		1
Labourer (28)	12	10	1	5
Shepherds (3)	1	1		1
Clothing (19) (dyer, fuller, glover, shearman, shoemakers, tailors, weavers)	4	9	2	4
Food preparation (17) (baker, brewer, butchers, maltmen & maltsters, millers)	7	5	1	4
Tradesmen (21) (blacksmith/smiths, carpenters, fletcher, ploughwrights, ropemaker, stringer, tanners, teler,* turner)	15	5		1
Services (6) (barber, cook, innholder/keepers)	4	1		1
Servants (5)	1	1		3
Women (57)				
widows	18	15	1	18
singles and status not known	5	1		4
gentlewomen see gentry above				
Occupation of men unknown (145)	97	32	3	13
Totals (432)	**261**	**95**	**10**	**66**

Column 1: occupations are as stated in the inventories or found in parish registers, wills, other documents and a few from internal evidence in the inventory. The dual occupations of some men, especially in the yeoman group, are not listed. The bracketed figure is the number of inventories in the group.
* Indicates meaning unknown.

Table 4 Status, occupations and inventory values

Occupation or status and number in each category	no. of inventories with totals	inventory values		
		lowest	highest	median
Gentry (19)				
esquire (3)	3	£49	£4471	£2245
gentleman (14)	12	£45	£877	£269
gentlewomen (widow 1, single 1)	2	£104	£248	
Clergy (13)	13	£20	£490	£126
Yeoman (54)	49	£18	£797	£103
Husbandman (45)	45	£9	£448	£45
Labourer (28)	28	£1	£110	£11
Shepherd (3)	3	£4	£25	£15
Clothing trades (19) (dyer, fuller, glover, shearman, shoemakers, tailors, weavers)	19	£5	£186	£17
Food preparation (17) (baker, brewer, butchers, maltmen & maltsters, millers)	15	£5	£537	£33
Tradesmen (21) (blacksmith/smiths, carpenters, fletcher, ploughwrights, ropemaker, stringer, tanners, teler,* turner)	21	£3	£426	£17
Services (6) (barber, cook, innholder/keepers)	6	£37	£302	£148
Servants (5)	5	£1	£37	£4
Women (57)				
widows	52	£4	£244	£22
singles and status not known	5	£4	£41	£17
gentlewomen see gentry above				
Occupation of men unknown (145)	143	£1	£444	£26
Totals (432)	**420**			

This table shows the lowest, highest and median values in each occupation or status group for 420 inventories where totals survive.

Column 1: occupations are as stated in the inventories or found in parish registers, wills, other documents and a few from internal evidence in the inventory. The dual occupations of some men, especially in the yeoman group, are not listed. The bracketed figure is the number of inventories in the group.

Columns 3–5: all values have been rounded to the nearest £.

* Indicates meaning unknown.

Table 5 Summary of inventory values by decade

Inventories per decade	**no. of inv. with totals**	**lowest value**	**highest value**	**median**
pre-1550 (1)	1	£13 10s		
1550s (21)	19	£4 6s	£231	£12 10s
1560s (29)	29	£5 3s	£216 1s	£29
1570s (39)	39	£3 14s	£165 7s	£26
1580s (34)	34	£4 16s	£171 15s	£28
1590s (42)	42	£1 5s	£432 1s	£57
1600s (30)	30	£4	£494 10s	£52
1610s (111)	108	£1 5s	£568 8s*	£32
1620s (87)	85	£2 12s	£877 3s	£42
1630s (23)	20	£4 8s	£173 7s	£39 10s
1640s (6)	5	£15 6s	£133 19s	£34
1650s (9)	8	£17	£432 17s*	£88
Totals (432)	420			

Column 1: the bracketed figure is the total number of inventories for the decade.
Columns 3 and 4: totals have been rounded to the nearest pounds and shillings.
Columns 5: totals have been rounded to the nearest pound or exact 10 shillings.
* The highest totals in these two decades (£4471 and £2245 respectively) have been excluded from these calculations.

The period of these inventories coincided with the highest inflation for several centuries before and after. Modern tables compiled for the period show that prices more than doubled between 1550 and 1660.[57] These tables show averages, based on a range of crops and livestock, taken from a wide geographical area and fluctuating widely from year to year. Insufficient data for other commodities have survived to provide a wider, contemporary 'basket of consumables' to compare with a modern one. The majority of items in the inventories are not of agricultural products with a current market price, but of goods acquired over a lifetime, which have variable second hand values depending on age and condition. Accordingly, assessing the inventory values against the overall rate of inflation is problematic and no attempt in this introduction has been made to do so. The existence of inflation, however, must be remembered when looking at the inventories over the decades.

Excluding the inventory from 1497, low valuations at or below £5 occur for twenty-six inventories and persist throughout the decades until the 1640s. Two of them are for family men in Cople in 1616, who were described in the burial register as paupers. Their valuations at around £5 provide a contemporary view of poverty

57 For a very detailed price list for agricultural produce and an account of prices and inflation, see Peter J. Bowden, ed., *Chapters from The Agrarian History of England and Wales volume 1: Economic Change: prices, wages, profits and rents 1500–1750* (Cambridge, 1990), pp. 13–69 and Statistical Appendix, pp. 116–72. Lionel Munby, *How much is that worth?* (Chichester, 1989) published for the British Association for Local History, pp. 29–30 summarises issues around inflation for the local historian and includes several price indexes.

(*283*, *284*). Most of the other low value inventories are for single or widowed people at the beginning or end of their lives, whose circumstances varied and may or may not have reflected real poverty. Nevertheless throughout the period administrators or executors of poor people considered it necessary to observe the probate process and make inventories for even the poorest. It is not until the 1640s and 1650s that a significant increase in the lowest valuations occurred with a jump to £15 and £17, although that might merely reflect the small number of inventories surviving in those decades.

The highest valuations in each decade fluctuate widely in five bands: the 1550s and 60s, then a drop in the 1570s and 80s, a jump and rise decade by decade in the 1590s to 1620s, another substantial drop in the 1630s and 40s, ending with a rise in the 1650s (Table 5, column 4). This is too small a sample on which to base wider conclusions and no attempt is made to do so. The median values also fluctuate considerably and do not mirror the highest valuations in each decade. Possibly they provide a more realistic view of the prosperity of the majority and a benchmark against which to measure individual prosperity. Inventory values can be highly misleading about a person's wealth, possessions and social position, as some of the examples later in this introduction will show.

Gentry

None of the aristocracy and élite of the county – the earls of Bedford and Kent, the St Johns, the Cheneys and Wentworths – are among the inventoried decedents. Their probate administration was more likely to be before the Prerogative Court of Canterbury than the Bishop of Lincoln and their inventories have not survived. At the highest social level in these inventories, there are nineteen from the ranks of Bedfordshire gentry,[58] about half of whose families were recorded in the heralds' visitations.[59]

Of the three esquires, the two wealthiest and most prominent were George Francklin of Mavourn in Bolnhurst valued at £4471 in 1618 (*306*)[60] and Robert Staunton of Birchmore, Woburn valued at £2245 in 1656 (*428*). Both came from Bedfordshire yeoman families who were upwardly mobile during the sixteenth century, Francklins in the north and Stauntons in the south. Both attained office as high sheriff or justice of the peace and Robert Staunton actively supported Parliament in the civil war and Commonwealth period. Almost three-quarters of Francklin's wealth was in ready money and gold (£107), money owed to him (£2808) and debts forgiven in his will (£300). While his inventory values his household and farming goods at around £1200, it is not detailed. Ninety percent of Staunton's inventory value is in money owed to him. Footnotes to Staunton's transcription identify some of the debtors, providing an idea of the range of his commercial activities. In contrast, the possessions of Nicholas

58 For an exploration of the concept and practice of gentry see Felicity Heal and Clive Holmes, *The Gentry in England and Wales, 1500–1700* (London, 1994).

59 *The Visitations of Bedfordshire annis domini 1566, 1582 and 1634*, Publications of the Harleian Society vol. 21 (London, 1884). Inclusion or absence was not conclusive evidence of status as visitations were infrequent, would miss families whose presence was fleeting and those who did not present themselves for inclusion.

60 For an account of the Francklin family see the introduction and deeds in Beds Archives, FN and FN 999; and *Visitations of Bedfordshire*, p. 120.

Luke, also an esquire, were valued at less than £50 (*337*). He has animals valued at £11 and clothing at £2, but no money. By comparison with other groups, this puts him at the median point for husbandmen, yet he was sufficiently wealthy to leave £400 to his daughters in his will.[61] This emphasises the point that inventory values are misleading indicators of a person's overall wealth. Presumably much of his was tied up in land and marriage settlements. Nicholas Luke and his brother Oliver (*181*), the other member of the prominent Luke family in these inventories seem to have been minor members of the family, not office holders.

On the rung below esquires were the gentlemen and the three gentlewomen. The gentlemen's inventories were valued in a range, the upper limit of which was only slightly above the yeomen's, although the median point was more than double, indicating a greater proportion of higher valuations for gentlemen than for yeomen. The distinguishing features are the higher value of their clothing, the possession of silverware and books, and the amount of money owed to them on bonds, attesting to an accumulated wealth that could be used for display or deployed outside the home. (This is a generalisation as some from the yeoman group exhibit similar characteristics, e.g. *173*, *231*.) The anomaly amongst the gentlemen is Robert Jones of Steppingley whose inventory was valued at £45 in 1631, very low for a gentleman, yet he had several unusual items (knobs and perfume pan, aquavita bottles, books and a pair of gold weights) that suggest cultivated interests (*405*). He is difficult to identify and may have been a younger son of the Lidlington family, recorded in the heralds' visitations.[62]

The three gentlewomen, Joan Mayes widow of Sutton (or Everton) 1577 (*86*); Dionisia Norton widow of Streatley 1628 (*394*); and Mary Onslow spinster of Everton 1627 (*389*) present three contrasting pictures. Joan Mayes' first husband and their son, who was her administrator, were gentlemen. Her second husband was a yeoman. Her house seems comfortably, if modestly, furnished and she owns silverware valued at 50s. Dionisia Norton had a much larger and more valuable establishment, including crops and animals which made up half her inventory value of £104. Her clothing was valued at £4 (above the average) and she had a horse and a side saddle. Her husband William Norton had held at least 160 acres in Streatley which were increased by later generations whose prosperity was based on London trade as well as property.[63] Mary Onslow was also from a prosperous, well-established family. Her father and brother-in-law were lawyers and members of Parliament. Her connection with Bedfordshire was through her sister Cicely, the widow of Sir Humphrey Winch of Everton. She may have been living permanently with Cicely when she died, as she appointed Cicely and Cicely's daughter as her executrices. She only had £15-worth of household goods (mainly soft furnishings which reinforces the impression of living in someone else's household), but £10-worth of clothes, £20 in money and £200 owed to her.

These examples show that the disparity in lifestyle and wealth within the group of gentry could be considerable, although as with the other groups, it must be remembered that the inventory only accounts for part of a person's wealth.

61 TNA, PROB 11/140.
62 *Visitations of Bedfordshire*, p. 120.
63 Beds Archives, SM 14.

Clergy

The clergy are the best documented group.[64] Francis Dillingham, one of several clerical sons of a north Bedfordshire yeoman family, stands out as the wealthiest with an inventory value of £490 (*349*). He was also the most distinguished, being a Hebrew scholar and a member of one of the Cambridge commissions preparing the King James Bible. Dillingham was minister at Wilden for twenty-five years and, indeed, most of the clergy served in Bedfordshire parishes for decades. The exception to holding a cure for many years was John Durrant, rector of Cockayne Hatley, who died in 1625 after only a few years in the parish (*381*). He had been curate to Thomas Crabtree (vicar of Potton for twenty-six years) and followed him as vicar there for three years before being appointed to Cockayne Hatley. Many of the clergy were Cambridge graduates, one was an Oxford graduate but several were non-graduates or cannot be satisfactorily identified in the Cambridge and Oxford sources (*90*, *142*, *158*, *291*, *280*, *328*). Most of the clergy seem to have comfortable yeoman-like farming households. The exception is William Foxcroft whose parish of St Cuthbert's was the smallest and poorest in Bedford and who was greatly in debt. Several clergy were licensed to preach in their parish and two (Dillingham and Crabtree) were licensed to preach throughout the Diocese of Lincoln. Dillingham's sermons, including one before the King, and instructions to his parishioners were published. The outstanding feature of several clergy inventories is the value of their books, two reaching £70–80 (*328*, *349*).[65] The inventory information about clergy houses can be supplemented by descriptions in the glebe terriers, many taken in 1607, that add details of room arrangement, materials and roofing and thus provide a broader picture than the inventories alone. Some of the houses were substantial, others were described as poor (*233*).

Yeomen

The classic definition of the status of yeoman was that he held about 100 acres or more and had freehold land worth at least 40s p.a., entitling him to vote for a knight of the shire and that he was content with his lot. Recent ideas challenge this rigidity and show that in practice he was a substantial farmer who might have more or less land, which might be leased or copyhold as well as freehold, regularly employed non-family labour and had a large surplus of produce above his household needs.[66] The Bedfordshire yeomen's inventories bear out this diversity and the desire for advancement is illustrated by the backgrounds of some of the gentry, who rose from yeoman origins.

64 Most are recorded in CCEd, *Alumni Oxon.*, Venn ACAD, Beds Archives' *Fasti* and the Church's glebe terriers (Beds Archives and Lincs Archives). For comparison with clergy elsewhere, see Annabelle Hughes, ed., *Sussex Clergy Inventories, 1660–1750*, Sussex Record Society vol. 91 (Lewis, 2009).

65 For the education and training of contemporary clergy elsewhere and their possession of books, see Joan Dils, 'The books of the clergy in Elizabethan and Early Stuart Berkshire', *The Local Historian* 36 (2006), pp. 92–105.

66 Christopher Clay, ed., *Chapters from the Agrarian History of England and Wales, volume 2: Rural society: landowners, peasants and labourers* (Cambridge, 1990), pp. 66–71; Wrightson, *Earthly Necessities*, p. 34.

The inventory values of the goods of landholding yeomen range from quite poor (*14*) to more prosperous than some gentlemen and clergy. Most of those above the median point (and some below) had large, well-furnished houses. Most were farming but many were also engaged in commerce or trade, such as William Chambers of Potton, who described himself in his will as a yeoman but whose inventory included almost £100-worth of leather and equipment for tanning as well as crops and livestock (*214*). Other inventories value leases and even manors or premises in other parishes (*151*, *355*); show evidence of improvements such as a new dairy or squared timbers ready for building (*177*, *179*); include expensive clothing or luxury items such as silver and books (*374*, *193*, *352*); and reveal moneylending (*224*).

Evidence of farming is lacking in some yeomen's inventories, indicating that the term was used more widely for status as well as occupation (e.g. *168*, *213*, *326*, *393*).[67] The outstanding example of this usage is Ralph Briten, who was described as a yeoman and servant of John Burgoyne, esquire of Sutton (*149*). He had few possessions other than his clothing which was more lavish than most men's.[68] Other yeomen whose inventories show no evidence of farming may have been retired, such as Nicholas Chappell of Wrest with sufficient goods for living in one room but about £40 owing to him (*213*).

Husbandmen

With few exceptions, the households of all the husbandmen were similar: a house with three or more adequately furnished rooms and service rooms, and mixed farming of crops and livestock (Table 3). Nearly all had sheep amongst their livestock, with most of the wealthier husbandmen having thirty or more. At the lowest inventory values, husbandmen are little different from many labourers (*19*, *223*) and at the highest inventory values, their level of housing and farming is in the yeoman bracket (Table 4). However, the majority were near the median value of £45 and were worth less than half the median value of yeomen. The exceptions to these generalisations are two husbandmen whose inventory values are predominantly in money owed to them, possibly indicating retirement from active farming (*161*, *318*). Only one husbandman is recorded with debts, although others may also have been in debt (*101*).[69]

The hazy boundaries between gentry and yeomen and yeomen and husbandmen rely to some extent on how their neighbours and appraisers saw them, e.g. Timothy Warde of Wilden was described as a yeoman in the burial register, but his appraisers called him a husbandman, despite an inventory valuation of £189 in 1598 (*163*).

Labourers

Most of the labourers had small, two or three roomed houses, minimal and low value furniture and furnishings, a few animals and a few acres. Some lacked even

67 The dictionary definition of a yeoman is a senior servant in a royal or noble household; an attendant or assistant to an official; a man holding a small landed estate; a freeholder under the rank of a gentleman; hence *vaguely*, a commoner or countryman of respectable standing, *esp.* one who cultivates his own land (*OED*).

68 For a brief biography of John Burgoyne, see History of Parliament Trust https://www.historyofparliamentonline.org/volume/1558-1603/member/burgoyne-john-1538-1605.

69 It was not obligatory to record decedents' debts, although they are listed in approximately fifty inventories (see below p. lxxxv).

that level of provision. One or two had better accommodation (e.g. *256*) and several had woollen and linen wheels and hemp. The inventory values of the labourers are distorted by four people whose totals are boosted by money owed to them (*172, 143, 196, 311*). If those men are ignored, the top value of the labourers' possessions is £45, and the median £9, better reflecting the level of this group (Table 4). This diversity is a reminder of the position of labourers; they were not wholly dependent on wages nor able to sustain themselves from a small amount of land, a few animals and 'cottage' industry.[70]

Tradesmen and services

Those engaged in clothing, food, trade and services make up only 14.5% of the inventories (Table 4). They have been identified from occupations assigned to them by their appraisers and/or the contents of their inventories (e.g. tanned and untanned leather and 'implementes belongeinge to the tanneres trade', *214*) as well as from their wills and the burial registers. Although Bedfordshire was a rural county, Bedford and the market towns were not lacking in trades. Thus the total of sixty-six men in these groups seems low in number and deficient in variety of occupations, considerably under-representing the county's commercial activities.[71]

With the exception of services, the groups have low median inventory values and there is little to distinguish those at the bottom of the ranges from husbandmen or better-off labourers. Most of the Bedfordshire tradesmen at all valuation levels had some crops, a little land and a few animals (e.g. *321*, *344*), except the very poorest and most of those who lived in the urban centres, Bedford, Leighton Buzzard, Luton and Dunstable. The combination of trade and farming was easier to manage if the latter was animal rather than arable husbandry, because animals required tending at specific times, leaving the remainder of the day for the craft; arable required continuous work.[72]

There is a jump in wealth from the majority of tradesman who were at a low level to a few prosperous individuals at the top of each category. Some of the wealthiest tradesmen were also successfully farming (*267*, *214*) and one had most of his wealth in money owing to him (*376*). At the top of the wealth range there are some notable inventories, such as William Ireland, called a miller by his appraisers and a wealthy man by the standards of the 1550s, who farmed and had both a fulling mill 'shop' with appropriate equipment and also corn mills (*5*). Another tradesman with two occupations was Robert Austin, described as a barber – and indeed his inventory values shaving cloths and barbering tools – but he also owned four looms and other weaving equipment (*385*). It is difficult to decide if Thomas Harbert of Leighton Buzzard was a butcher, based on the slaughter house in his back yard, or an innkeeper, based on the large quantity of pots, barrels, malt and ready-brewed ale (*365*). Lacking explanation is the description of George Dickerman as a cook: he was farming and his possessions lacked evidence of his profession (*270*).

70 Wrightson, *Earthly Necessities*, p. 35.

71 See Godber, *Bedfordshire*, pp. 272–5 for an overview of trades and crafts.

72 Mark Overton, *Agricultural Revolution in England: the Transformation of the Agrarian Economy, 1500–1850* (Cambridge, 1996), p. 18.

The largest trade group is the maltsters and brewers, who all lived in the south and south-east of the county – in a crescent from Dunstable to Luton, Barton and Shillington then north to Potton. They belonged to the long-established group of middlemen from predominantly south Bedfordshire and neighbouring Hertfordshire who were suppliers of malt to London.[73] The group became progressively wealthier over the period of these inventories (with one exception). Only three of their inventories list goods used for malting and brewing, possibly because much of the equipment might have been built into the fabric of the buildings and thus not recorded in the inventory. Three inventories stand out for the detailed insight they provide to the malting business. Thomas Abraham alias Bolnest had half his wealth in malt and related items (£42) in 1610 (*209*). Edward Catherall had a mill and brewhouse and his inventory of 1613 has a detailed list of malting and brewing equipment (*260*). Edward Edwyn's inventory of 1641 lists £71 owed to him for 'mault and other thinges' (*419*).

The other occupations which stand out as uniformly wealthy are the innholders and innkeeper. James Duckington had a large and well-appointed inn at the regular stopping point of Dunstable on the main route from London to the north and north-east (*176*). It compares with the best in similarly well-located towns elsewhere in the country.[74]

Widows

Widows' inventories exhibit distinct characteristics. Some were farming, presumably carrying on the farming work of their gentry, yeomen, husbandmen or labourer husbands (Table 3; e.g. *73*, *148*, *264*). Many widows, however, had a reduced quantity of household goods. Some were cooking for themselves; others had no cooking equipment. This suggests that they were living in a very small house or in one or two rooms with family. On the other hand, at least sixteen had money owing to them on bond or other specialty. A few had clothing worth more than £2 or had gold and silver items, maybe reflecting a previous high standard of living when they were married (e.g. *122*, *248*). Some had no visible support – no money owing, no livestock, no produce. Possibly they were being entirely supported by their family or were receiving a small annual sum under their husband's will, as was the case of Alice Brace the widow of William (*197*) and Phoebe Horne (*379*).

A few examples further illustrate the variety of widows' situations:

- Bridget Francklin, who had a bed, coffers, cooking equipment, a woollen wheel, wool and poultry, was probably living independently as she owed rent. Her goods were valued at £5 4s, yet in the burial register she was described as the wife (i.e. widow) of Master Francklin, who would have been a well-respected figure to be accorded that title (*293*).
- Elizabeth Purratt, whose labourer husband William died in 1619 with an inventory value of £143 of which £121 was in bonds and bills owed to him

73 Chartres, *Agricultural Markets and Trade*, pp. 57 for Luton and Dunstable as suppliers of malt to London; F. J. Fisher, 'The London Food Market, 1540–1640', *The Economic History Review* vol. 5 (April 1935), p. 61.

74 For example, Robert Palmer's inn at St Albans in 1612 had a similar number of rooms, furnishings and linen at a comparable valuation (Pat Howe and Jane Harris, eds, *Wills, inventories and probate accounts from St Albans, 1600–1615*, Hertfordshire Record Society vol. 32 (np, 2019), p. 270).

(BHRS vol. 20, p. 130), was reduced to about £3 of household goods and clothing and had £41 owed to her (*361*).

- Susan Carter lived in a small house in Bedford, where she retained the marital household goods for her life and had an income from the sale of two houses to bring up her children. By the time of her death fourteen years after her husband's, she still had a comfortable home (*425*).

Single people

The six people described as single or as bachelor servants had clothing and a coffer to hold it, but little else. Five had money or money owing to them and one also had some livestock (*237*). The inventory of only one of this group was valued at more than £7 (at nearly £16, *401*). All of this group seem to have been either starting out in life or established in a dependent role.

The unmarried status of other men, as either never married or widowers, sometimes emerges through accompanying documents and other records. Some were established in their occupations, such as Henry Raulins of Thurleigh (*358*); others were starting out and probably unmarried, e.g. William Searle of Dunton (*205*); or at the end of their life and widowers e.g. Henry Merrill of Cople valued at £2 16s in 1625 (*380*).

Families

In such a small group as 432 inventories, drawn from three-quarters of the county and spread over 110 years, it is perhaps surprising to find family relationships emerging among at least sixty people. Many are noted in this introduction and at the end of their inventories. The same surname may show a relationship and have a bearing on the understanding of other inventories, such as the Searles (*205*, *207*), but cannot be assumed to do so, as in the case of the three Kippests (and variant spellings) who do not appear to be related (*110*, *287*, *408*).

Appraisers and writers

As described in Appendix 2, appraisers should number at least two and preferably more. Administrators and executors in Bedfordshire preferred to use more than two appraisers. Of the 396 inventories naming appraisers, only ninety-three (23%) employed the minimum number of two. The majority had between three and four and 49 inventories used five or more appraisers. The number does not seem to have been influenced by the value of the inventory, as some of the poorest had four or more appraisers.

Appraisers were to be drawn from a) creditors, b) beneficiaries, or c) other honest persons, with preference given to kin.[75] The identification of most is difficult or inconclusive; nevertheless of the 1300 or so appraisers, 208 have been *tentatively* identified and fall within one or more of the specified categories.[76]

75 See Appendix 2 and Cox, 'Probate inventories: the legal background', pp. 134–5.

76 Information on status has been taken from the transcribed Bedfordshire Parish Register series, the Clergy of the Church of England database, the Bedfordshire Archives online catalogue and volumes in the Bedfordshire Historical Record Society publications.

Table 6 Identity of appraisers in 137 inventories

Identity of appraisers	no. of appraisers
creditors	9
beneficiaries	not checked
family	62
honest people	
churchwardens	55
clergy	41
gentry	12
yeomen	13
Master	8
schoolmasters	4
husbandmen	2
parish clerk	1
neighbour	1
Total	208

Note that some appraisers fall into more than one category and some were appraisers for more than one inventory.

As it was not obligatory for inventories to list a person's debts (although many Bedfordshire inventories did so), the presence of nine creditors identifiable amongst appraisers is likely to be much lower than actually occurred. The largest, discernible group were those having a family relationship with the decedent. Thus, several of the appraisers in each of the Negus and Dillingham inventories in Shelton, Dean and Wilden were family members (*134*, *138*, *173*, *231*).[77] As well as blood relations, those through marriage were also appraisers, e.g. Evans King's father-in-law (*397*) and no doubt many more would emerge with some research. A relationship to the decedent may usually be assumed where the appraiser's surname is the same, although the relationship may not be close.

The remaining appraisers who would fall within the category of honest men were predominantly the local churchwardens and clergy. Only thirty-five of the 208 appraisers were from the prosperous and high status groups of the gentry, yeomen and those addressed as Master. There are several examples of gentry appraising gentry, such as Oliver Boteler who appraised the long and valuable inventory of John Willson who leased Old Warden in 1622 (*331*). However, the gentry were not confined to appraising decedents of their own status. They also served as appraisers for people of much lower levels of wealth, such as the two gentlemen who appraised the inventory of the labourer William Hobeme in 1597 (*154*).

All appraisers have been identified in ten inventories and reinforce heavy dependence on clergy and churchwardens (Table 7). Although the decedents were

77 The two families were also related to each other through the marriage of Alice Dillingham and John Negus; see the will of Thomas Negus of Shelton in 1615 (TNA, PROB 11/132/657).

Table 7 Status of appraisers in ten sample inventories

Inv. no.	Decedents	Date	Inventory value	no. of appraisers	Status of appraisers
72	Edmund Hare of Houghton Conquest	1574	£21	3	the rector; 2 future churchwardens
111	Robert Cartere of Northill	1585	£12	3	2 family members; the curate who wrote the inventory
173	John Dillingham of Dean, yeoman	1604	£281	4	4 family members, one of whom later became a churchwarden
195	Alexander Hopkin of Wrestlingworth	1609	£24	2	the rector; 1 former churchwarden
307	Thomas Wood of Milton Bryan, labourer	1619	£9	2	both former or future churchwardens, 1 of whom was called Master
310	Thomas Younge of Langford, labourer	1620	£8	4	1 family member; 1 current churchwarden; 2 former churchwardens
325	Richard Hall of Pertenhall	1622	£22	2	2 former churchwardens
331	John Willson of Old Warden, gentleman	1622	£877	4	2 esquires; 2 clergy, one being the vicar of Old Warden
364	Thomas Symons of Eversholt	1625	£140	4	1 current churchwarden; 3 former churchwardens
384	Thomas Hawkynes of Houghton Regis, yeoman	1625	£44	2	the vicar; 1 future churchwarden

from varying social levels and wealth, some or all of the appraisers for each person were clergy or churchwardens (past, present or future).

Although women as widows were often executors or administrators, none were appraisers, even for other women's inventories where the nature of the goods (often mainly clothing) might suggest it. Expert appraisers also seem to be lacking, even for high value specialist goods such as the large quantities of books owned by clergymen (*328*, *349*) and a tanner's stock (*214*). One inventory with an appropriately qualified appraiser was Edward Catherall's (*260*). He had a malting and brewing business and one of the appraisers was another local maltster, John Pilgryme. Appraisers were usually from the same or neighbouring parishes, with a few exceptions such as the short list of leases and creditors of John Francklyn in 1581 made by two men who were probably fellow Middle Templars (*100*) and family from Cottesbatch (Leics), Keysoe and Clipston who were drawn upon to appraise the goods of John Dillingham of Dean (*173*). The voice of the appraisers may sometimes be heard. In listing the debts owed to Thomas Mason, the vicar of Souldrop, his son who was one of the appraisers lists 'things lent to *my* sister' valued at 1s (*280*). Another appraiser included several items for which he or the executor was responsible: '*I* owe to Master Joye vijs' (*309*).

It seems that Bedfordshire administrators and executors pressed into service the designated groups of people as appraisers, who, probably, saw the task as in their or their family's interests or as a community duty.

It is unusual for the writer of an inventory to be named and it occurs less than a dozen times in these inventories. Francis Rollenson says that he is 'the writer thereof' (*220*) and Oliver Smith signs himself 'the writer of the same' (*269*). When the named writers can be identified, they were usually the local minister (e.g. *111*, *189*), the parish clerk (*269*), a schoolmaster (*302*) or scriveners (*80*, *109*, *338*).[78] The remainder are difficult to identify, such as Henry Kettle and Richard Sam, who were appraisers and signed the inventories as 'by me' or 'per me' and may have written them (*238*, *239*).

Among the anonymous writers of the majority of the inventories are people with a wide range of writing and spelling skills. Most followed the set pattern, or a limited number of variations, in writing the inventories. A few had less idea of established patterns, such as the writer of John Gale's inventory in 1611 (*223*). His writing skills and spelling were poor and he did not use the normal opening formula, yet he knew roughly how to set it out. Were the majority of inventory writers who followed a set pattern practising scriveners (which suggests a strong local profession) or were they local men who had some education and a sufficient knowledge of procedure to turn their hands to producing the basic documentation needed in everyday life? The inventories provide insufficient data to pursue this matter but it is of significance to the operation of local business.[79]

Form of the inventory

The 1529 Act and subsequent commentaries merely note that inventories were to list 'goods, cattels, wares, merchandises'. West's precedent shows household goods first and recommends either a room by room arrangement *or* by commodity.[80] Both orders were used in the Bedfordshire inventories. However, at least eighty-seven (20%) of the 432 inventories ignore both orders and begin with the livestock or crops, clearly demonstrating the priority of many appraisers in this very agricultural county.[81] It is also common in other counties.[82] One inventory went as far as ignoring household goods entirely and only listing agricultural goods (*222*).

78 Scriveners and notaries in London were regulated by the Scriveners' Company but it did not have jurisdiction beyond the London area. They learned their trade through apprenticeship.

79 The question of practical administrative and legal education (including the transmission of documentary formulas) is discussed in relation to scriveners and the common law in an earlier period by Kitrina Bevan, 'Legal Education in Late Medieval England: how did provincial scriveners learn their law?' in M. Korpiola, *Legal Literacy in Premodern European Societies* (Basingstoke, 2018), pp. 19–41. She focuses on apprenticeship, on-the-job training, self-teaching and business schools, in particular one at Oxford but not part of the university, but the article does not tackle the question of how writers of inventories from other occupations learnt the appropriate formulas.

80 William West, *Symboleography which may bee termed the art, description or image of instruments, extra-judicial, as covenants, contracts, obligations, conditions, feffements, graunts, wills, etc Or the paterne of presidents. Or the notarie or scrivener ... The first part, newly corrected and augmented by William West of the Inner Temple gentleman* (London, 1598), unpaginated, section 796.

81 For a discussion of the developing format of inventories, see D. Spaeth, '"Orderly made": re-appraising household inventories in seventeenth-century England', *Social History* vol. 41 (2016), pp. 417–35.

82 M. A. Havinden, *Household and Farm Inventories in Oxfordshire, 1550–1590*, Oxfordshire Record Society vol. 44 (London, 1965); Lionel M. Munby, *Life & Death in King's Langley,*

It was necessary to present two indented copies of the inventory to the church court, that is copies written twice on the same sheet of paper then separated by a wavy cut. The indentations can be seen on many of the inventories but many more were on separate sheets of paper, either fair copies or probably copies made by the church court scribes.

A few inventories appear, from the handwriting and layout, to be drafts. Although Elizabeth Field's inventory bears the exhibition clause, it is clearly a draft as the first few lines of an indented fair copy is preserved with it among the Lincoln Archives records (*202*). Some documents were exhibited and accepted although they were not in the standard format for an inventory. The factor that is likely to have made them acceptable was that the goods were priced. An example is Alice Hunt's goods, which are listed in 1612 as being given to different people; they are, nevertheless, valued in the document and accepted as an inventory (*254*). Helen Drawsworth's deed of gift in 1620 looks like a nuncupative will except for the addition of valuations (*313*). Other documents resemble a running commentary on the administration of the decedents' goods, falling short of a formal probate account. A very long list of the goods of John Cooper of Tempsford 1617–1622 (*336*) which had been sold by his administrator ends with a shorter list of items still unsold and their values (including twenty pairs of sheets and other linen at £8). The administrator was aware that he was not producing an inventory as he headed the undated document 'A note of such of the goodes of John Cooper late of Temsford deceased as were sold by John Cooper of Barkford administrator of the same.' It was accepted and has a full exhibition clause at the foot. The administrator for William Brace of Millbrook c. 1611 produced a list of payments he had made (*197*), dividing it into three parts: nearly £200 paid to twenty-one people to whom Brace owed money on specialty and £112 10s to Alice Brace, the widow; a second list of more than £70 still to be paid; and the last part lists legacies that had been paid out.

Despite these examples of the latitude permitted by the church courts, the great majority of the inventories were written in the prescribed form.

Procedure for exhibiting

The formal directions for making inventories are set out in Appendix 2. The practice in Bedfordshire is described in the following sections of the Introduction, so that theory and practice may be compared.

The executor or administrator was supposed to present the will and inventory in person and swear an oath to administer the estate properly. No doubt this happened on many occasions but allowance was made for those who could not do so. Instead a commission was issued to a local clergyman to administer an oath to the executor or administrator. The oath was a standard, mass-produced, usually handwritten document with spaces for the date and names of people. One of the few commissions surviving amongst the Archdeaconry records illustrates the obligations they imposed. It was issued to John Orme, rector of Bletsoe and William Tapp, curate,

Wills and Inventories 1498–1659 (King's Langley, 1981); Honor Lewington, *Stoke Mandeville wills and inventories 1552–185*, Buckinghamshire Record Society vol. 38 (Aylesbury, 2019).

to administer an oath to Judith, wife and executrix of William Sherley of Bletsoe in 1612 (*252*). The commission was in Latin; the oath in English read:

> You shall swear that so farre forthe as you doe knowe, the will by you exhibited is the true & laste will of William Sherley your husband departed & that according to the trust unto you committed, you will performe as neare as you can, all thinges theyrin contained that you will paye his debtes and legacies so farre forthe as by lawe you are bounde: and that the Inventarie also by you exhibited is the true Inventarie so farre forthe as you doe alraddie knowe of all his goodes and that yf anie of his goodes shall come unto your knowledg hearafter you will adde them unto the Inventarie and informe the Commissare of Bedford shuer for the time being thearof so God helpe you in Jesus Christe.

Taking the will and inventory to the church court to obtain probate was not always the end of the process. From the surviving court proceedings, it seems that witnesses were called to explain the circumstances of nuncupative wills (*60*, *262*).[83] The court could also investigate the circumstances and content of the will or inventory if either were questioned (*273*). A bond for proper administration of the estate was often demanded, especially in the case of intestacy (e.g. *49*). Where details of the bond survive, the normal amount of twice the value of the inventory was applied (e.g. *30*, *407*). Surviving documentation for these processes has been summarised in the notes at the end of the inventories. They can throw light on family disputes and decedents' circumstances: the case of William Brace has already been mentioned (*197*).

At the end of the probate and exhibition process, the court officials took their fee. The amount has been noted on a few inventories, such as that of Henry Gale, whose executor paid 5s 2d on an estate valued at £6 9s 6d in 1591: 3s 6d for the probate, 8d for sealing and 6d for signing (*126*). Similarly a note on Henry Ingram's inventory of 1611 states the fees as 2s 6d for administration and 1s 10d for signing the bond, giving a total of 4s 4d on an estate worth £6 6s 4d (*251*). These figures are in line with the scale set out in the 1529 Act.

The last step in the process was to produce an account of the administration. No formal accounts for Bedfordshire for this period have survived, although several inventories look like interim statements of account, as noted above.

Time and place of exhibiting

There was no explicit requirement for an inventory to be presented on the same day as probate was sought. The official position was that administration could not commence before probate was granted and that an inventory listing all the decedent's goods was pre-requisite to administering an estate. Dates for probate and exhibition have been found for about one hundred decedents and are the same for 80%, showing that the practice in Bedfordshire, as elsewhere, was for inventories to be exhibited on the same day as probate was obtained. It would seem that Bedfordshire executors were well aware of the court's requirements and adopted the practical approach of making only one visit to the court.

83 For circumstances surrounding the making of nuncupative wills and subsequent challenges in the church courts during the plague in Newcastle in 1636, see Keith Wrightson, *Ralph Tailor's Summer: a scrivener, his city and the plague* (New Haven, 2011), pp. 84–6, 131–43.

Where delays between probate and exhibition occurred, some may be explained by a challenge to the will in the church court (e.g. *273*, *337*); by the procedure of the Prerogative Court of Canterbury and the Court of Civil Commission in London where most inventories were exhibited a day or two after the will was proved (e.g. *429*); and possible scribal errors in dates on documents (e.g. *430*). The exhibition of Robert Staunton's inventory ten years after his death in 1656 stands out as an exceptional delay, possibly caused by the uncertainty of the period or by the difficulty in drawing up a full list of everyone who owed him money (*428*).

The length of time that executors or administrators took to deal with the formalities of probate and exhibition can be calculated for 205 (47%) of the 432 inventories in this volume, where the relevant dates of burial, making the inventory, exhibiting it and obtaining probate are available. Three-quarters were made within twenty-eight days of the burial and two-thirds were made and exhibited within three months.[84] This looks like people getting on with what was required after a person's death and fitting it around the responsibilities of daily life and the effort of travelling to exhibit the inventory.

However, not all inventories fit this pattern. Several were dated so close to the exhibition that the timescale for making, writing, travelling and exhibiting the inventory seems improbable or even impossible. Eight were dated before the day of burial (e.g. *133, 405*) and five on the day itself. These were not all simple inventories requiring little work. One or two days before burial is feasible as there might be a delay between death and burial, but five days (*60*) looks as if the burial date in the parish register might be wrong or some planning in anticipation of death was taking place, in the form of an inventory being taken, possibly with the agreement of the person dying as part of the preparation for death.

Forward planning also looks likely when there were only a few days between burial and exhibiting the inventory, as in the case of Richard Ebbes of Sandy (*203*). He was buried on 10 March 1610, his inventory was dated 12 March and exhibited at Potton on 14 March. Greater speed was displayed by Agnes Ventam who had her husband's goods appraised the day after his burial and exhibited the following day (*273*). These timescales suggest not only forward planning but also that people were well aware of the location and dates of church court sittings.

At the other end of the scale, a few inventories were made more than a year after the death. Were the executors or administrators avoiding their duty or were there other circumstances? The case of Thomas and Susan Carter (*425*), referred to above (p. xxxiv), may not be so unusual and other exhibitions of inventories may also have been deferred until after the death of the widow.

Between these two extremes, there is great variety in the speed with which the different stages of the process were carried out. The shearman John Storer was buried on 1 March 1621, his inventory was made within a fortnight but his will and inventory were not taken to the court for another two months (*314*). The inventory of Robert Clapham, rector of Tilbrook, was not made until five months after his

84 A similar timetable has been found by Stephen Porter in a survey of 125 inventories, which showed 86% made within twenty-eight days of death, noting the likely consequences of thoroughness and accuracy of the inventory (Stephen Porter 'The Making of Probate Inventories', *The Local Historian* vol. 12 (1976), p. 36–7).

burial, his will was proved two months later and the inventory exhibited a further four months afterwards (*292*).

When an inventory was exhibited, it was subscribed with the date, place and name of the court official, reference to the person presenting it and sometimes signed by a notary public. Two-thirds of the inventories in this volume lack the exhibition clause and most of the remainder merely have a brief scribbled note on the copy retained by the court, the clause probably being written in full on the copy retained by the administrator or executor.[85] Where the place of exhibition was noted, it generally met the criteria of being a convenient location for the executor, as the courts were held around the county at towns or markets – Ampthill, Bedford, Bromham (once), Dunstable, Leighton Buzzard, Luton and Potton.[86] Some court sittings at Bedford and Dunstable coincided with fairs (e.g. *304*, *356*).

Administrators or executors did not always take advantage of such convenience and no doubt there were discrete circumstances for taking inventories from Haynes, Shillington and Stotfold to exhibit at Dunstable; from Tempsford and Stotfold to be exhibited at Ampthill; from Cranfield to Hitchin; and from Roxton, Ravensden and Shelton to Buckden despite there being church court sittings much nearer the decedents' parishes. Possibly the executor or his attorney lived nearer the place of exhibition than the decedent's home.

The majority of inventories, for which the place of exhibition was recorded, were exhibited in the Archdeaconry of Bedford. However, thirty-one were exhibited elsewhere:

- sixteen in towns in the Archdeaconry of Huntingdon (Baldock and Hitchin, Herts; Huntingdon and St Neots, Hunts)
- three at Buckden, Hunts, which was the bishop's seat and a peculiar of Lincoln Cathedral
- one in the Archdeaconry of Lincoln at Stamford, Lincs (for Nicholas Luke of Eaton Socon (*337*), whose low value inventory has already been noted)[87]
- and eleven in London at the PCC (or the Court of Civil Commission during the 1650s)

Inventory totals

The central reason for an inventory was to find out the value of a decedent's goods so that his debts could be paid and the distribution of his goods carried out in accordance. It is therefore curious that greater care was not taken to total the inventories correctly. Around 130 (30%) were incorrectly added up, roughly half to more than the correct totals and half to less.[88] This is a high error rate to attribute solely to arithmetical

85 The scribbled and abbreviated clauses mean that it has not been possible to determine where or in which court (archdeaconry or bishop's) the inventory was presented.

86 See R. B. Outhwaite, *The Rise and Fall of the English Ecclesiastical Courts 1500–1860* (Cambridge, 2006), p. 7 for convenient places for exhibiting inventories.

87 See pp. xxviii xxix and the notes following the transcription of his inventory. Note that his will was proved in the PCC, but the inventory exhibited at Stamford after much delay.

88 This compares with an error rate of 0.8% in Havinden, *Household and Farm Inventories*; 21% in Munby, *Life & Death in King's Langley*; and 27% in Howe and Harris, *St Albans*.

error on the part of the person writing the inventory. Sometimes the total was only wrong by a few pence with 4d being a common error, probably resulting from the values ending in 4d and 8d in so many items. Errors crept in where the valuation was expressed in marks, which were then converted incorrectly to shillings and pence (e.g. *3*, where 4 marks was converted to £2 10s instead of £2 13s 4d). Another reason for error may be that a line or more was missed in making the copy. This is especially likely where the inventory total was substantially different from the corrected total. Such a shortfall (of £4 17s 4d) occurred in Thomas Ryseleye's inventory (*171*). However it is difficult to account for the difference of £135 0s 8d between the recorded and corrected totals of Ralph Place's inventory (*217*) and there are others with similarly large discrepancies. It is strange that neither the appraisers nor church court officials noticed such significant omissions, especially as it is clear that addition was sometimes checked (e.g. *414*).

The inventory of Thomas Farre in 1564 provides an insight to the method of producing an inventory and explains how easy it would be to make mistakes (*36*). The inventory, which looks like a draft, was written as a continuous text interspersed with the values, some only being expressed as unit prices. It would be easy to make a mistake in preparing a fair copy from such notes. Occasionally the appraisers admit to possible errors. William Rechford's appraisers ended with the statement 'the hole some is or tharabouts': in fact it was correct (*423*).

Appraisers were charged with making a market valuation of the goods. The repetition of certain values is noticeable and suggests that appraisers often used standard prices for many goods but there is no evidence that the church courts challenged these 'standard price' values and they may indeed have represented normal pricing. One standard was the mark (13s 4d) and many goods were valued at a mark or a fraction or multiple (i.e. 3s 4d, 6s 8d, 26s 8d, 33s 4d, etc.). The other standard was 10s and its multiples (£1, £1 10s etc.). A good example of the use of non-standard values is the inventory of John Smythe of Everton in 1591 (*127*), where more effort seems to have been taken to produce distinct, rather than rounded, values.

In summary, Bedfordshire administrators and executors generally acted quickly and followed accepted probate procedures, although there were noticeable exceptions to some of the individual requirements of the process.

Understanding the inventories

On the surface, inventories appear to be a snapshot of a person's possessions and often their home at the time of death, but this is a misleading perception as there are many factors which affected the content – and thoroughness – of an inventory. As already noted, most inventories were taken more than one week after the death and in some cases several months later. The longer the delay, the less accurate would be the inventory as a reflection of the home and possessions as they were in the decedent's lifetime.[89]

89 For detailed examinations of omissions from inventories, see Margaret Spufford, 'The limitations of the probate inventory', in John Chartres and David Hey, eds., *English Rural*

Many items were deliberately or accidentally omitted. Some had already been given away during the decedent's lifetime or immediately after death. Occasional glimpses of these missing items may be seen. William Shreeve's inventory in 1611 records the value of 'his apparell *left ungiven*' (editor's italics) before his death at £3 (*220*). Some goods were disposed of by will and might – or might not – have already been given to beneficiaries before the inventory was taken. John Place's will in 1596 returns the household goods which his wife brought to the marriage and the inventory lists and values them, nearly £30-worth of goods out of an inventory value of £432 (*151*). Frequently clothing was not listed and shoes and boots were rarely mentioned. Similarly, food was normally omitted, with the exception of preserved stores. Terms such as 'other lumber', 'trash', 'trifles', 'implements', 'trumpery' and 'utensils' were used for small or low value items which were not individually listed. Sometimes a picture can be built up from other inventories of what such phrases as 'all his working tools' might include. Appraisers were aware of likely omissions and might cover themselves by including a small sum for 'all things unprised and forgotten' (*183*).

Freehold and copyhold land was not part of the personal estate nor were certain crops such as grass, fruit and vegetables, so their omission was deliberate. Confusion existed about whether certain items were to be included or not and may reflect the transition of moveable luxuries to permanent fixtures. In 1598 the appraisers of Timothy Warde of Wilden noted at the beginning of the section on household goods 'Imprimis the glasse & waynescotte excepted as standers to the howse' (*163*), but other inventories included them (e.g. *158*, *183*). Fixtures such as ovens or brewing equipment were omitted because they were built into the fabric of the house. Inventories were not required to list what the decedent owed, yet around 10% of the inventories list their debts, usually giving the creditors' names.[90] The debt culture will be discussed below and it is worth noting here that many more decedents are likely to have owed money. The omission of land and debts could seriously distort the understanding of a person's wealth.

In inventories listing goods by room, rooms not containing any of the decedent's goods would not be mentioned (e.g. if they were occupied by other independent members of the family or lodgers) and this omission affects the perception of the size of a house.

All these possible omissions make the inventory, in Margaret Spufford's words, 'a seriously misleading document.'[91] Nevertheless, the inventories contain a wealth of detail about the many possessions of these people so that, with caution and the addition of other sources, a lot may be gleaned about Bedfordshire people's material culture and individual life style. The following sections discuss the houses and main categories of goods, providing some quantification and illustrations of their occurrence.

Society 1500–1800: Essays in Honour of Joan Thirsk (Cambridge, 1990), pp. 139–74 and Lena Cowen Orlin, 'Fictions of the early modern English probate inventory', in Henry Turner, ed., *The Culture of Capital: Property, Cities, and Knowledge in early modern England* (New York, London, 2002), pp. 51–83.

90 This is greater than debts listed in other collections: 6% in Havinden, *Household and Farm Inventories*; 0% in Lewington, *Stoke Mandeville*; 5.5% in Munby, *Life & Death in King's Langley*; and c. 6% in Howe and Harris, *St Albans*.

91 Spufford, 'Limitations of the probate inventory', p. 144.

Houses

It was not necessary for appraisers to include much, if anything, about houses in order to produce an inventory of goods. Indeed, about one third of the inventories do not mention the house or its rooms. The reasons were varied. Sometimes the decedent was living with someone else (e.g. *49*, *335*). In other inventories, the appraisers took the thematic approach, listing goods without attributing them to a place or room.[92] More frequently they adopted a mix of room surveys and thematic listings. Where rooms and their contents are listed, it is sometimes clear from the quantity and variety of goods that there were more rooms than named; for example Edward Slowe of Studham whose 1598 inventory was valued at £214, and who had five bedsteads and 'their furniture' at the high value of £5 13s 4d, but whose inventory only named the hall (*159*). As already mentioned, rooms were omitted if they contained nothing belonging to the decedent or so little that the contents were included in one of the catch-all phrases 'and other trumperie'.

Most of the two-thirds of the inventories where rooms and their contents are listed seem to be moderately complete as a systematic survey of the house's contents room by room, with considerable detail in some inventories about the relationship of rooms to each other, such as 'the loft over the hall' and 'the chamber over the entry'. It is a matter of judging the descriptions in each inventory to decide how complete a picture of the house has been presented. Bearing in mind these limitations, it is possible to learn a little about housing and house construction and a lot more about the size and layout of the houses, although caution must be exercised in attempting a full-scale reconstruction of their layout.

Rural and urban houses

As previously noted, Bedfordshire was predominantly a rural county with several small market towns and some differences between rural and urban houses can be observed in the inventories.

Village houses varied greatly in their size and the configuration of rooms. By comparing them with other evidence and other places in the region, houses in the inventories look to be typical of housing in Bedfordshire generally.[93] A useful contemporary source for information is the glebe terriers, as many rural houses in these inventories are similar to Bedfordshire vicarages.[94] Several survive for 1607, providing a second source for descriptions of both well-off and poor clergy houses,

92 For the room-based format, see Spaeth, '"Orderly made"', pp. 423–4.

93 For information about house construction in Bedfordshire, see John Bailey, *Timber Framed Buildings: a study of medieval timber buildings in Bedfordshire and adjoining counties* (np, 1979) and articles by John Bailey and others in the *Bedfordshire Archaeological Journal* vol. 12 (1977), pp. 57–106 (David H. Kennett and Terence Paul Smith 'Crowhill Farm, Bolnhurst, Bedfordshire: a timber-framed building and its history', pp. 57–84; J. M. Bailey, 'Rowe's Cottage: a 'Wealden' House at Little Barford, Bedfordshire', pp. 85–98; J. M. Bailey, 'Lower Roxhill Farm, Marston Moretaine: a measured survey of a timber-framed building', pp. 99–106). Historic England's listings include many late sixteenth and early seventeenth century Bedfordshire houses of all sizes https://historicengland.org.uk.

94 Beds Archives, ABE 1.

such as the well-appointed house of Samuel Fulke at Barton (*328*) and the poor house of Augustine Topcliffe at Willington (*233*).

Inventory descriptions of some houses in the market towns are similar to those in the villages or are inconclusive about their layout. Several from Bedford show the long, narrow arrangement of a burgage plot, with rooms fitting together to make the most of the space. Joan Williamson's house in 1583 is well-defined as a town house, with a jettied upper floor (or floors) and rooms in line (*109*). Although, as usual, her inventory begins with the hall, the presence of a long parlour next to it with a little parlour below, indicates that the hall and long parlour were on the first floor and wider than the ground floor and were over the passage from the street to the back of the property. The chamber 'over the street' was probably a jettied front room on the first floor. The ground floor had a shop probably under the jettied chamber and the buttery and cellar were under the hall. The kitchen and brewhouse were beyond them and the cellar may have been beyond or underneath. This might have been a two-storey house or possibly three. This is a typically urban layout fitting into a burgage plot, but most urban houses in these Bedfordshire market towns show a layout similar to houses in the villages. This illustrates Bailey's comments about urban houses being dependent on the street frontage, with some having narrow-fronted burgage plots and others having a wider street frontage.[95]

House construction

According to William Harrison, writing in the 1570s and quoting old men, house styles had changed greatly in the recent preceding years. One change was in building materials: from timber to brick and stone:

> The ancient manors and houses of our gentlemen are yet and for the most part of strong timber … Howbeit such as be lately builded are commonly either of brick or hard stone, or both, their rooms large and comely, and houses of office further distant from their lodgings.[96]

The only newly-built gentry house in these inventories is Warden Abbey, leased by John Willson, who died in 1622. Assuming that it can be identified with the house built by Robert Gostwick in the 1560s, Warden Abbey fell into Harrison's description of new houses being brick-built.[97]

Surveys of surviving dateable houses in Bedfordshire show that the homes of ordinary people were of timber construction throughout most of the county, with the exception of houses in the north-western parishes, which were of coursed limestone rubble.[98] Building materials are mentioned in several inventories, for example, squared and unsquared timber, boards and other wood at £3 6s 8d in 1596 (*152*),

95 Examples in Dunstable are given in Bailey, *Timber Framed Buildings*, p. 24.

96 *Harrison's Description of England in Shakespere's Youth: being the second and third books of his Description of Britaine and England*; edited by Frederick J. Furnivall (London, 1877), p. 239, spelling modernised.

97 Historic England https://historicengland.org.uk/listing/the-list/list-entry/1222165. For a description of the building see Bernard B. West, 'A note on the post suppression remains at Warden Abbey Farm', *Bedfordshire Archaeological Journal* vol. 2 (1964), p. 69.

98 Many buildings survive from the late sixteenth and seventeenth centuries and have been listed (Historic England https://historicengland.org.uk).

timber ready sawn at £20 in 1607 (*179*) and 1150 laths in 1598 (*158*). There is no clue to their intended use nor to that of the lime and bricks in the inventory of the vicar of Chalgrave, John Bellamie in 1622 (*334*).

Other inventories refer to new rooms: a new chamber and building timber in 1596 (*151*); a new dairy house in 1605 (*177*); a new parlour and loft in 1611 (*225*); a new house (parlour, hall, buttery and kitchen) and rooms over them in 1622 (*327*); and a new loft in 1628 (*394*). In these new buildings, materials other than timber are rarely mentioned. There is an incomplete reference to 'streng beames and stones' in 1557 although it is not clear if they were building materials (*8*). Glebe terriers describe some buildings as built partly of stone, for example Thomas Mason's parsonage at Souldrop, in the north-west of the county (*280*). Only roofing material for outside buildings such as hovels is mentioned in the inventories (e.g. *301*). If the glebe terriers of the clergy are an indication of general building practice, roofing was normally either thatch or tile.

From these inventories, it can be seen that timber, laths, some stone, bricks, thatch and tiles were used in the construction of Bedfordshire houses. In short, they confirm but add little about new features and building materials used in the county's housing stock to what is already known from other sources.[99]

Chimneys were among innovations claimed as a sixteenth-century phenomenon by Harrison with a 'multitude of chimneys lately erected [where previously] each one made his fire against a reredos in the hall, where he dined and dressed his meat'.[100] These inventories contain few direct references to chimneys, because they were part of the building and thus did not need to be accounted for. Where they are mentioned, it is usually in relation to other features, such as chimney chambers (e.g. *90*), or more often an iron bar in the chimney, chimney irons and 'other implements in the chimney for the fier' (*234*), although no firebacks occur. There is indirect evidence for chimneys in about two hundred inventories in the form of the proliferation of fire irons, spits, cobirons, andirons and iron bars used in heating and cooking. Several inventories list fire shovels, tongs and bellows in rooms where there is no evidence of cooking, implying heated rooms and chimneys. Indeed, some houses had several heated rooms (e.g. *64, 217, 331, 428*). It is noticeable that the inventory for James Duckington's inn at Dunstable in 1604 did not list fireplaces or any fire equipment, despite luxurious furnishings (*176*) (surely an unintended omission or a decision to concentrate on the larger items in each room), whereas four years later William Ordwaye's house in Dunstable had heating in the hall and buttery (*193*).

The insertion of chimneys in what had been the screens passage separating the hall from a service room altered the layout of many houses. It created an entry lobby inside the front door with doors to rooms on the left and right, either or both

99 Alan Cox, *Brickmaking: a history and gazetteer* (London, 1979) in the RCHM Survey of Bedfordshire series for the location of brickworks; Barbara Tearle, *The Accounts of the Guild of the Holy Trinity, Luton 1526/7–1546/7*, BHRS vol. 91 (Woodbridge, 2012) for house repairs in the Luton area in the early sixteenth century; Bailey, *Timber Framed Buildings*; and house surveys in the *Bedfordshire Archaeological Journal* vol. 12 (1977) pp. 57–106.

100 *Harrison's Description of England*, pp. 239–40, spelling modernised. For their application to Bedfordshire houses see *Bedfordshire Archaeological Journal*, vol. 12, 1977, for descriptions of four houses of different types and sizes, including David H. Kennett and Terence Paul Smith 'Crowhill Farm, Bolnhurst, Bedfordshire: a timber-framed building and its history', *Bedfordshire Archaeological Journal* vol. 12 (1977) pp. 57–84.

of which might be heated. There are thirteen inventories referring to entries, usually in terms of 'the loft [or chamber] over the entry'. Most are short on details of room layout and names, such as the urban house of the Carters in Bedford in 1652 (*425*). A couple of inventories are specific. Between the hall and the parlour, both of which were heated, in the gentleman John Colbeck's house in 1573 was 'the entry by the hall' which contained a cupboard covered by a cupboard cloth (*64*). Ralph Place of Eaton Socon, another gentleman, had a chamber over the entry in 1611. The detailed account of the contents of his hall, parlour and the best chamber over the parlour lists fire irons (*217*). Architectural investigation shows that a late sixteenth-century house in Leighton Buzzard was either built with a chimney or in such a way that a chimney could be inserted, which was done a few years later.[101] These houses (and probably others where the descriptions are inconclusive) had been modernised with a chimney and entry.

The evidence for chimneys, whether inserted and creating an entry or newly built, is insufficiently detailed to say more than that Bedfordshire was likely to be amongst Harrison's 'multitude of chimneys'. Certainly more than a decade after the last of these inventories, the hearth tax return in 1671 recorded the widespread presence of chimneys and that even people exempt because of poverty had them.[102]

Like chimneys, stairs are rarely mentioned unless they are a point of reference, such as Jonas Offam's 'chamber above stares' (*421*). Several inventories show the stairhead used for storage of an old coffer (*97*) and bacon and baskets (*327*). Robert Stanton of Pertenhall had a cupboard under the stairs in 1597 (*156*).

Imprecise as the evidence for chimneys and stairs often is, the evidence for inserting a floor above the hall is almost non-existent, yet this was a common practice in the period. The inserted floor was so new in Richard and Agnes Hancocke's house in 1611 (and regarded as moveable by his appraisers) that his inventory includes 'the bord and Joyces over the hall' at 13s 4d (*246* and notes to *247*).

Gatehouses are mentioned in passing in four inventories in the context of describing the location of rooms such as 'the chamber (or shop) next the gatehouse' and did not have any inventoried contents. They occurred in three farms and a Dunstable inn (*176, 190, 260, 394*). From instances elsewhere, a gatehouse seems to be typical of rural farms and many urban houses, often inns, providing access to a courtyard and barns or accommodation.[103] Gatehouses may have been a far more common feature of Bedfordshire houses than their infrequent mention in these inventories would suggest.

Other features which began as movable novelties and then gradually became standards, and ignored by appraisers, are wainscot as a wall covering and glass in the windows.[104] As early as 1573 John Colbeck provided in his will that 'all my Glasse wyndowes shall remayne & be taken as heireloomes Incydent & necessarye to & for the howsse as they now Stande'. They are not mentioned in his inventory (*64*).

101 Maureen and Paul Brown, *Leighton Buzzard's Tudor House: the story of 17 to 21a Hockliffe Street* (Leighton Buzzard?, 2016?), p. 47–8.

102 Marshall, *Bedfordshire Hearth Tax Returns*.

103 Examples of gatehouses elsewhere show people in St Albans from different social and financial backgrounds and with both large and small houses having gatehouses (Howe and Harris, *St Albans*, pp. 56, 117, 170, 267, 272); and a Banbury alderman valued at £58 (Havinden, *Household and farm inventories*, p. 265).

104 Oak, either native or imported, was used to line interior walls and also for furniture.

A generation later in 1606, William Ordwaye of Dunstable directed in his will that the glass and wainscot, together with some furniture, were to remain in the house and they, too, were excluded from his inventory (*193*). In contrast, other appraisers up to the 1610s included wainscot, such as the lining of the walls of nine rooms in James Duckington's inn in 1604 (*176*) and the wainscot in the hall of Rodger Burden in 1610 (*208*). After this date it is not easy to determine whether the few references to wainscot are to furniture or wall covering.

Similarly glass windows and casements quickly became standards and are rarely listed. An exception is the glass for windows and casements listed with building materials in the work being done for William Ridge, vicar of Southill in 1598 (*158*). Including them in his inventory was appropriate as they had not been installed at that time. Like wainscot, the presence of glazed windows can probably be assumed in many houses, especially when window curtains are listed. A few houses had lattices, although it is not clear if they were infill for unglazed windows or used for a different purpose (e.g. *175*).

Omission from the inventories should not be taken as lack of presence and, in fact, many of the houses should probably be interpreted as having wainscoted walls and glazed windows.

House size

Using the names of rooms for domestic spaces (hall, chamber, parlour, kitchen, buttery, loft, entry, 'ladrye', 'pastrye', 'soller' and house), an estimate of the size of 270 houses, almost two thirds of the inventories, can be attempted. Other inventories name some rooms but are clearly incomplete and have been omitted from Table 8. Seven houses only had one room and, at the other end of the scale, fourteen had more than ten rooms. A quarter of the houses only had three rooms. Looked at more broadly, the majority of houses (56%) had between two and four rooms and a third (35%) had between five and nine rooms.

By the way in which the inventories have been expressed, the quantity of household goods and the inventory totals, it seems likely, although by no means certain, that the seven houses identified as one-roomed were indeed one-roomed (*7, 13, 99, 289, 293, 309, 310*). The room is called the hall or dwelling house and the decedents' household goods are often meagre, although several decedents have crops and animals (*7, 13, 99, 310*) and one is bringing up a young family (*310*). Two are widows whose goods are valued at £6 13s and £5 in 1616 and 1617 (*289, 293*). These seven houses may have had a sleeping platform over part of the hall, which the appraisers did not think worth mentioning as the location of beds or mattresses. The most likely one roomed house was Thomas Alen's in 1620 (*309*). His inventory lists a minimal number of items and only in quantities of one or two, e.g. 'wone olde bed' 'tooe olde stoles' 'wone brase bole' 'tooe partere dyches' 'vj dyches and toe spones' etc. coming to a value of 52s.

Those inventories with houses that appear only to have two rooms call them hall and chamber or parlour or, in one instance, hall and buttery. They predominate in the period up to the 1620s. These inventories, like those for the one-roomed houses, may also have omitted a sleeping platform.

The rooms in three-roomed houses were usually called hall, chamber *or* parlour, kitchen *or* buttery, with a few variations such as hall, chamber, lower house/little house. The development in three-roomed houses was a room designated for food

Table 8 Size of houses measured by number of rooms

	Rooms											Total	
Inventories per decade	**1**	**2**	**3**	**4**	**5**	**6**	**7**	**8**	**9**	**10–12**	**13–15**	**n**	*%*
pre-1550 (1)												0	*0*
1550s (21)	2	4	5	3			1					15	*71*
1560s (29)		7	4	3	2		1					17	*59*
1570s (39)		7	5	2	2	2	3					21	*54*
1580s (34)	1	4	5	2	3		2		1	1		19	*59*
1590s (42)		3	7	3	2	2	3	1			1	22	*52*
1600s (30)		3	1	4	2	2	3	1	1	1	1	19	*63*
1610s (111)	2	9	13	6	9	5	5	4	4	3	1	61	*55*
1620s (87)	2	11	13	11	7	4	4	4	5	1	3	65	*75*
1630s (23)		2	7	3	1	2		3	1			19	*82*
1640s (6)			1	2			1	1				5	*83*
1650s (9)			3		1				1	1	1	7	*77*
Totals (432)	7	50	64	39	29	17	23	14	13	7	7	270	*63*
% of 270	*3*	*19*	*24*	*14*	*11*	*6*	*9*	*5*	*5*	*3*	*3*		

The rooms counted are: hall, chamber, parlour, kitchen, buttery, loft over any of these rooms, entry, 'ladrye', 'pastrye', 'soller', house.
Column 1: the bracketed figure is the total number of inventories for the decade.
Last two columns: the total number of houses with 1, 2, 3 etc. rooms and as a *percentage of the total inventoires for each decade*.
Penultimate line: the total number of houses with 1, 2, 3 etc rooms
Last line: the column totals in the previous line as *a percentage of the 270 houses with an identifiable complement of rooms*.
Percentages have been rounded to the nearest whole number.

preparation or cooking in addition to, or in substitution for, the hall. These small, one-, two- and three-roomed houses make up almost half (44%) of the inventories enumerating rooms.

Larger houses up to nine rooms occur throughout the period, especially from the 1570s. The extra rooms tend to be described as more chambers (often with descriptions such as servants' chamber), a parlour (sometimes more than one) and a kitchen *and* buttery. This is a further development of food preparation and cooking spaces and a greater division into public and private spaces (see p. li for use of parlours and chambers).

At the other end of the scale, the owners of the fourteen houses with ten or more rooms were among the gentry (*152, 181, 287, 300, 331, 394, 428*), clergy (*327, 328*), an innkeeper and maltsters (*176, 235, 260*) and two whose status is not known (*98, 427*). Two were widows, Dionisia Norton a gentlewoman (*394*) and Ann Fisher (*427*). Excluding the inn because the rooms were for accommodating travellers, these houses have both a greater number of chambers and a range of specialist rooms, e.g. studies (*328, 427*), dining chamber, 'lardry' and 'pastry' (*287*), more than one kitchen or buttery (e.g. *328, 235*). Several also have a great chamber or parlour, as well as chambers and a parlour, which, from their furnishing, shows the development of formal public rooms.

The identification of storeys is beset with uncertainty as many inventories omitted reference to vertical locations and in others, descriptions are ambiguous. As already mentioned, some of those apparently with minimal rooms on a single storey may have had a sleeping platform above an open hall. Nearly a dozen houses with more than eight rooms appear to be on one level, which can either be disproved (e.g. *331*) or is unlikely (e.g. *337, 428*). Each inventory should be assessed carefully to determine the probability of a one or more storey arrangement. The evidence for additional floors – basements and spaces above the second storey – is small and often inconclusive. Only four garrets and cock lofts occur (*306, 320, 428, 395*). Fewer than twenty inventories list cellars, the location of which is often ambiguous (e.g. *277, 301*). However, their use is not ambiguous as they were all for storage, mainly for hogsheads and other beer or ale containers.

This assessment of rooms and storeys should not be taken as a conclusive configuration of the living space in houses. Rooms could be omitted for many reasons. Second storeys or underground cellars might not have been necessary descriptors for the appraisers. Table 8 and the general descriptions should be notionally adjusted to reflect more rooms in many houses, and more houses of two or more storeys. Nevertheless, it is a rough indication of the type of properties in the county.

Rooms

With a very few exceptions, the hall (or hall house or house) is the first room to be named and, probably, the first room on entering a house. An exception is Joan Williamson's house in Bedford in 1583 where the hall was on the second storey and a parlour seems to have been the first room entered (*109*). The furnishings show that the hall was normally used as the reception room and in many houses for eating and cooking. Typical reception use is demonstrated by the furnishings of the hall of the yeoman John Brewtye in 1605: tables, cupboard, stools, chairs, forms, painted cloths and cushions (*178*). Several inventories list cooking equipment in the hall in the form of pot hangers and iron bars and the kitchen was also equipped for cooking (e.g. *141*, *151*, *385*, *399*).

Almost forty of the parlours were used as mixed reception and sleeping rooms, being furnished with both beds, bedding and chests and also tables, chairs and cupboards. Twenty-five were furnished exclusively as sleeping rooms and a similar number as reception rooms only with tables and chairs. A few houses had two parlours, the second being distinguished by terms such as 'little parlour' or 'chamber parlour', one usually furnished with tables and chairs, the other with beds. Several parlours were heated. Few were used for storage, although William Knight's parlour had cheese in it (*183*). Exceptionally, Susan Carter was cooking in her parlour in 1652 (*425*).

The overwhelming majority of chambers on the ground and first floors were furnished as sleeping rooms. Only a few had any sign of reception room furniture (i.e. table, chairs, stools, cupboards, benches) and where they did it might include a display of pewter on a cupboard (e.g. *287*). Second and subsequent chambers and upstairs chambers tended to contain less variety of furniture (e.g. *204*).

In addition to sleeping, chambers were used for storage for such items as barrels (e.g. *161*), churns and tubs (e.g. *164*), linen and woollen wheels (*252*), armour for a horseman (*263*) and a drink stall (a stand for barrels) in the servants' chamber (*175*). About twenty second-storey chambers were used solely for storage: wool, apples and hops (*211*) and bacon, laths, hemp, grain and lime (*369*).

The sleeping room of the decedent was sometimes identified as 'his chamber', 'lodging chamber' or 'the chamber where he [or she] lay'. The word bedchamber is only used once, for a room in the five- or more roomed house of Rodger Burden in Silsoe (*208*). The term 'guest chamber' occurs once, with a full complement of beds, bedding, chests, a chair, pewter, a table and a cupboard (*138*); this was in the house of one of the Dillinghams, a wealthy yeoman and clergy family.

Descriptive names or locations for chambers and lofts in larger houses are standard (such as the maids' chamber, the chamber over the hall). Lofts are frequent in all sized houses and just as likely to contain beds as to be used for storage, or both. Other names occurring occasionally for upper rooms in large houses are 'soller', used for sleeping or storage (*79*, *156*), and room at the stairs head (*327*).

Distinctive names were applied to chambers and parlours in a few houses. Warden Abbey had a 'Courte Parlour' (*331*); although furnished with a bed and bedding and a cupboard, it might, at one time, have been a room in which to hold manorial courts or transact business. Rooms named after colours (presumably denoting the decorative scheme) occur as green and blue rooms in gentry houses (*331*, *405*, *428*). It was normal practice to name rooms in inns, and the Crown Inn run by James Duckington in Dunstable was no exception.[105] He had eleven rooms furnished with beds, bedding, chairs and tables and six had unusual names (Gratious Parlour, Tabatt Chamber, Gatehouse Chamber, Butlers Chamber, Crown Chamber, and Paradise Chamber), all names common to inns. The furnishings for each room were valued between £5 and £24, significant sums in 1604.

105 The Crown Inn was in High Street South, next to The Star. I am grateful to John Buckledee of Dunstable and District Local History Society for sharing this information from the late Joan Curran's notes.

In the larger houses, separation of functions, due to a growth in specialisation and privacy, is reflected in the descriptions or names given to rooms. Most descriptors were added to chamber, parlour and buttery, and identified a function or location, such as dining chamber; guest chamber; nursery chamber; (long) parlour within the hall; drink buttery; servants', maids', men servants' or folks' chamber.

Most inventories list dining furniture – tables, chairs, stools and cupboards – in the hall, which was the main public area, or in a multi-purpose chamber or parlour. A change was occurring during the period of these inventories and rooms dedicated to dining were coming into fashion;[106] they can be identified with some confidence in twenty inventories, belonging to the wealthiest decedents. They are styled parlours and only contain tables, chairs, cupboards and sometimes fire irons. Where occupations are known, they belong to an esquire (*337*), gentlemen (e.g. *64*, *217*, *300*), clergy (e.g. *328*, *349*, *381*), yeomen (*95*, *125*) and the tanner of Potton (*214*). All have five or more rooms in their houses (that is hall, chambers, parlours, kitchen and buttery and other indoor rooms) and the inventories of nearly half were valued above £100 (eight were over £400). The poorest people in this group are the esquire, a gentleman and a vicar, valued at between £45 and £55 (*334*, *337*, *405*). Their use of a room dedicated to dining may reflect the number of rooms they had or a desire to maintain their status. Only one person, William Kippest a gentleman of Northill, has a room *described* as a dining chamber and a chamber within it which contained several cupboards (*287*).

'Nether' was used to describe four rooms in Marston Moretaine, presumably on the ground floor (*253*). The house had a hall, then the farther nether room (with salting trough), the nether room (a bed and chests), and two outer nether rooms (boards, scythes, banking irons, a molestaple, pitchforks, woollen and linen wheels). The adjective may have been an idiosyncrasy of the family or appraisers or it may have been a locational description of a house with an unusual configuration.

As already noted, kitchen or buttery was frequently the name given to one of the extra rooms in houses that had more than two ground floor rooms. It was often a single-storey addition to a house or even a separate building. Possibly the kitchens in these inventories, where they are the third room in a small house, were built on, but there is no evidence for this. Today the kitchen is thought of as the place for cooking and the buttery for the complementary function of storing drink, food, kitchen utensils and tableware but in the sixteenth and seventeenth centuries there was flexibility in the use of kitchen, buttery and hall and the kitchen was not always the primary cooking room.

The room in which cooking took place can be established in 190 inventories (44%) (Table 9) by the presence of andirons, cobirons, bars, hooks, hangings, spits and cooking vessels. In just over half, cooking occurred in the hall and in 39% in the kitchen. This bias in favour of the hall replicates findings for the first half of the seventeenth century in Kent where 53% of cooking was in halls and 32% in kitchens, and a small sample in the parish of Ewelme in Oxfordshire with 52% cooking in halls and 19% in kitchens.[107]

106 Chinnery, *Names for things: a description of household stuff, furniture and interiors 1500–1700* (Wetherby, 2016), p. 104. In contrast the 'dining parlour' of Robert Palmer of St Albans in 1612 was a mixed use room (Howe and Harris, *St Albans*, p. 272).

107 For Kent see Mark Overton and others, *Production and Consumption in English Households 1600–1750* (London, 2004), p. 128 and Table 6.5. The information for Ewelme is an

Table 9 Location of cooking

Decades	Cooking in hall	kitchen	elsewhere
pre-1550 (1)			
1550s (21)	3	6	
1560s (29)	8*	1*	chamber
1570s (39)	5	8	buttery
1580s (34)	3	8	chamber
1590s (42)	4	10	parlour; nether house; kitchen & buttery
1600s (30)	7	5	buttery; parlour
1610s (111)	30	22	little house; buttery
1620s (87)	31	10	buttery
1630s (23)	11	1	buttery
1640s (6)	1	1	
1650s (9)	1	3	parlour
Totals (432)	104	75	11

Column 1: the bracketed figure is the total number of inventories for the decade.
* Includes inventories with evidence of cooking in hall and kitchen.

The majority of kitchens were, in fact, used for some form of food preparation and many inventories provide detailed lists of food-related utensils and equipment (e.g. *155*, *168*). Some kitchens also contain kneading troughs, moulding boards, bolting vessels, mashing vats, salting troughs, churns, cheese vats and presses – all large equipment for the wholesale preparation or preservation of food.

In a few inventories where the kitchen was an all-purpose room, this may have been a product of individual circumstances. Nicholas Bryde's kitchen has a bed with tester and the bedding, a table and chairs, woollen and linen wheels, a kneading trough and arks, a churn, bowls and pails as well as pots, pans and pothangers and fire-related items. The house also has a hall, parlour, buttery and milkhouse, so it does not lack other rooms for the bed and non-cooking items (*170*). Thomas Stanbridge's use of rooms is different: the kitchen holds the 'wooden stuff' (whatever that might have been), the butteries house barrels and a salting trough and the hall (called a hall house) has two tables, seating, andirons and spits, kettles and pots (*393*).

These inventories show that the kitchen and buttery are used in a variety of ways and could often be interchangeable. The use of butteries and other rooms for cooking may be a mixture of individual circumstances and the names people chose for their rooms.

In this period, closets were often private spaces used for writing or prayer; however only one closet might have been used in that way (*152*) while the remaining few closets in these inventories seem to have been used for storage (e.g. *231*, *337*); they

unpublished analysis produced by the Oxfordshire Probate Group for the South Oxfordshire Project, courtesy Heather Horner.

may have been large walk-in cupboards rather than rooms. The closet at Warden Abbey might have been off the long entry as it is listed after the great chamber and long entry and is used for storing a trunk, boxes and glasses (*331*). Storage does not preclude a private area but the appraisers' focus was on content rather than personal use.

Nine houses have studies. In the five clergy houses, as might be expected, they contain books and appropriate furniture (*280*, *328*, *349*, *381*) including shelves (*301*). The 1607 glebe terrier for Barton confirms the longstanding existence of the study of Samuel Fulke, who died in 1622 (see notes to *328*). The study of Robert Jones, whose inventory was of comparatively low value for a gentleman, is similarly equipped with a desk and books (*405*) but the rooms designated as studies in the houses of two widows are dumping grounds for boxes – maybe they had contained books during their husbands' lifetimes (*234*, *394*) – and one is furnished with a bed and bedding (*427*).

The glebe terrier for Barton lists a house of office (a privy) attached to Samuel Fulke's house (*328*). It is not recorded in his inventory nor are privies in any other inventories, although possibly some of the little houses occasionally listed may have been privies. According to Harrison they were common for newly built houses but they were unlikely to contain moveable items, which accounts for their omission from inventories.[108]

Most of the twenty-three shops are in the inventories of artisans living in market towns who may have been working in, and selling from, the shop. The term is also used for the work space used by blacksmiths (e.g. *174*, *249*) and by the fletcher (*208*). Two weavers have their looms 'and the furniture' in a shop (*275*, *385*), although the spaces housing looms in other inventories are not given specific names (e.g. *321*, *403*). 'Shop' is also used for a general work space without any obvious trade (e.g. *351*). Other shops are mentioned in passing as in 'the chamber over the shop'. Where no goods are listed, the shop might have been let out to someone else (e.g. *98*, *236*).

The identification of 'sellers', 'cellars' and 'sollers' in these inventories is hampered by variations in spelling. The only space described as a cellar is indeed a storage area located off the closet in Warden Abbey and used for storing glasses (*331*). The majority of the spaces referred to as 'sellers' are also storage areas for tubs, vats, barrels and other containers for drink. They were often listed near the buttery or kitchen (e.g. *193*). It is not clear whether they were at ground floor level or a storage area at a lower level.

Two of the 'sellers' are furnished as sleeping rooms, one above the hall (*156*) and the other called the 'Seller Parlour' in James Duckington's inn, the furnishings of which were valued at £8 (*176*). In these inventories, the 'sellers' were probably a spelling variant of 'soller', a term used in Thomas Cater's house in Sandy (*79*) where his two 'sollers' were over the hall and the parlour. These rooms were worthy of the older name of 'solar' (a private room) as they were fitted out as comfortable sleeping rooms with beds and tables and chairs. From its furnishings and fire place, the 'soller' over the parlour in Thomas Cater's house was probably his own room.

108 *Harrison's Description of England*, p. 238.

Service rooms, yards and outbuildings

The activity of turning agricultural produce into food (baking, brewing, butter and cheese making, preserving meat) was essential to the lives of the great majority of these people. Much of the work required large pieces of equipment and a third of the inventories list separate service rooms for these purposes, although some of the functions also took place within the house in kitchens, butteries and halls.

Harrison says that service rooms were separate structures close to newly built houses.[109] It is rarely possible to determine from the wording of inventories whether they were separate structures or under one roof with the living rooms. Exceptionally, a few inventories strongly suggest that they were part of the house, for example that of John Durrant, rector of Cockayne Hatley (*381*). The sequence of his ground floor rooms and then the loft over the parlour, followed by the loft over the milkhouse (both furnished with beds, bedding and chests) then the study with his books makes it most likely that the milkhouse was part of the house. However, most inventories are uninformative about the location of service rooms.

Many service rooms had little content, denoting that equipment such as ovens, brewing vessels and kilns for drying hops, might be built in and would not, therefore, be listed in inventories. Where equipment is listed in detail, it provides an informative account of what was used in the processes (e.g. *64*). Occasionally equipment is at variance with room names, such as the cupboard, salting trough and boards in Henry Wolhed's milkhouse in 1571 (*58*) and the ox yokes and a new cart body in John Wye's malt house in 1625 (*355*). The overall impression, however, is that the majority of service rooms were used for the expected purpose, while some of the remainder were used for multiple purposes and some for general storage.

The spellings 'backhouse' and 'bakehouse', applied indiscriminately in twenty-one inventories, present a particular problem. Were they used to designate purpose or place? The contents of these rooms help to answer the question and also show that spelling did not really matter. Some were equipped for baking with a bolting trough, moulding boards etc. (e.g. *230 backhouse*, *297 bakehouse*); some used for other purposes (e.g. a *backhouse* used for storage (*26*) or a *bakehouse* for brewing (*64*)). Even the baker's room with its moulding boards, arks and trough is called a *backhouse* (*357*).

Looked at overall, only one third of the inventories mention or list the contents of service rooms. This is probably an under-recording of such rooms and may be due to the frequent omission of the location of goods in inventories, the use of 'and other trash' or 'lumber' and the practice of building in some equipment, all of which might lead to rooms being missed out.

More than half the inventories refer to yards and outside buildings (Table 10). Most of the latter are barns mentioned with their contents or hovels which were moveable, although only two are described as on pattens (*365*). Hovels might be large, such as the four bays of 'hovelling' belonging to William White of Biddenham (*339*). Other outside buildings illustrate the wide range of farming and household activity: a coach house (belonging to Robert Staunton, *428*), cowhouses, granaries, henhouses, hogsties, oxhouse, sheepcotes, a slaughter house (*365*), stables, a tithe barn (belonging to William Kippest of Northill, *287*), a woathouse (*278*), a woodhouse and little houses (already mentioned, as possibly privies). Three gardens, an orchard

[109] *Harrison's Description of England*, pp. 237–8.

Table 10 Houses per decade having service rooms, and yards and outbuildings

Inventories per decade	Houses with service rooms		Houses with yards and outbuildings	
	n	%	n	%
pre-1550 (1)	0		0	
1550s (21)	4	*19*	6	*28*
1560s (29)	4	*14*	18	*62*
1570s (39)	13	*33*	22	*56*
1580s (34)	8	*24*	19	*56*
1590s (42)	11	*26*	23	*55*
1600s (30)	13	*43*	19	*63*
1610s (111)	40	*36*	68	*61*
1620s (87)	32	*37*	51	*59*
1630s (23)	6	*26*	15	*65*
1640s (6)	5	*83*	5	*83*
1650s (9)	6	*67*	6	*67*
Totals (432)	142	*33%*	252	*58%*

Service rooms include backhouses, bakehouses, brewhouses, boulting houses, dairy houses, kiln houses, larder houses, malt houses, milk houses, mill houses, shops, store houses, wagon house and wash houses. Yards and outbuildings include barns, hovels and stables.
Column 1: the bracketed figure is the total number of inventories for the decade.
Columns 3 and 5: percentages are of the total number of inventories for that decade.

and a horse pond are also mentioned and there are glimpses of palings and gates relating to outside spaces.

Premises elsewhere

A handful of inventories are for people who had more than one house (e.g. *355*) or who were storing goods elsewhere (e.g. *319*). Nicholas Taillour of Stevington (*6*) had two establishments, one in Stevington and the other at Wellingborough (Northants). The provisions of his will suggest that the house in Wellingborough, which he left to his wife, might have been her home and the one in Stevington, which he left to his son, was his home. John Wye, a yeoman of Southill, had another house at Biggleswade (*355*). Laurence Gerie had crops, farming and household goods in several houses in Potton, where he and his wife Sarah had lived, holding land there and in neighbouring parishes for several decades, yet he was living at Stukeley (Hunts) at his death in 1623 (*340*).[110]

Amongst the gentry, only Robert Staunton's inventory shows goods in more than one house. He is described in the inventory as of Birchmore 'but for two yeares last past of St John the Evangelist in Watling streete London'. Most of his goods were at Birchmore and others were being kept by other people in their houses (*428*). It is surprising that other wealthy gentry, such as George Francklin, were not noted as having houses elsewhere (*306*).

110 For landholding in Potton and neighbouring parishes see Beds Archives, X222/11, 12, 13, 18 and 19.

The inventories show local arrangements for storing goods in other people's houses or barns or, in the case of two vicars, in the church porch and the school house (*301*, *334*). They are a reminder of the domestic and commercial arrangements that were part of many people's lives.

In summary, almost all houses were the homes of the middling or poorer sort. Several of the yeoman and clergy houses were large, well furnished and provided with extensive outbuildings. By combining inventory descriptions with the surviving glebe terriers, a more detailed picture of vicarages may be built up than that provided by inventories alone (see the notes following the inventories).

Only a few houses stand out as different, special or fashionable. James Duckington's inn at Dunstable was very well furnished and typical of inns in having named rooms, although the inventory raises questions, including which room was used by James and his wife (*176*). William Kippest's house is the most fashionable with its dedicated dining room furnished with dining table, chairs and cupboards and its larder and pastry (*287*). John Willson's is probably the only newly built, grand house and his inventory is extraordinarily detailed in its description of household linen, childbed linen and furnishings, although disappointing in its description of the rooms (*331*).

It is easy to focus on the houses of the better off, but there are many inventories of the poorer sort and people at different stages of their lives. With detailed analysis, they reveal much about housing for the poor, especially when read in combination with other evidence, such as wills and church court depositions.

Furniture, furnishings and household stuff

Having identified the varied usage of different rooms, much detail of their furniture and furnishing can be found in the inventories. The hall was typically furnished with a minimum of a table and frame, form, bench, benchboard, stools, chairs, cupboards, another table and painted cloths. If it was the main living room it would also have cooking utensils and a fire (e.g. *23*), although another room might be used for food preparation. The chamber or parlour had beds and bedding (i.e. mattresses, pillows, bolsters and coverings), chests, coffers and boxes and often a table and stools or a form. Sometimes items such as spinning wheels or farming or trade implements might also be stored in them. Bed linen was usually listed separately in the inventories, only rarely being specifically noted as in coffers and chests in a named room. Additional ground floor chambers and many of the upstairs lofts and chambers had similar contents (beds, chests and stored household items). The kitchen typically contained pots and pans, kettles, a frying pan and other cooking equipment, plates and dishes and often a table, form or stools. The kitchen or the room used for cooking had ironware for the fireplace: an iron bar for the chimney, spits, andirons, gridirons, pot hangers and pot hooks, tongs, fire shovels and a dripping pan (essential for catching fat from roasting meat). The buttery nearly always housed the troughs, boards and other items for food preservation. Sometimes it also had cooking utensils, brass and pewter. An exception was Ralph Pratchett's buttery in Flitwick in 1635 which was predominately a storage room for linen and woollen products (*413*).

These were the typical contents of the living rooms, although many other items can be found. As part of the task of listing and valuing them, appraisers often provided a description (e.g. '3 ioyned stooles & a Matted chaire', *220*) or a comment on its condition ('certeyn sorry lynnen', *229*), from which a wider picture of the household can be built up.

Wall coverings

According to Harrison, wall coverings were a common domestic insulating and decorative feature by the late sixteenth century:

> The walls of our houses on the inner sides in like sort be either hanged with tapestries, arras work, or painted cloths, wherein either diverse histories, or herbs, beasts, knots, and such like are stained, or else they are ceiled with oak of our own, or wainscot brought hither out of the east countries, whereby the rooms are not a little commended, made warm, and much more close than otherwise they would be.[111]

In the period to 1620, between half and three quarters of inventories in each decade included some form of wall covering: wainscot, painted cloths or wall hangings.[112] More frequently listed than wainscot were textile wall coverings because they were portable.[113] The inventories use three terms – painted cloths, hangings and hallings. In places the terms may have been used interchangeably, as seen in the phrase 'hangings or painted cloths' (*217*) but the terms may also have been used deliberately to distinguish between hangings in different places in the house or of different types. For example John Dalington's appraisers referred to two painted cloths in the hall and to all the hangings about the chamber in 1610 (*204*). There are similar examples (e.g. *110*, *168*, *170*), but insufficient descriptions or valuations of hangings to reach any conclusion about the distinction. Painted cloths could either be fixed to batons nailed to the wall or hang loosely. They could cover the upper part of the wall above the wainscot or the whole wall. As they were usually made of linen or canvas, the use of parchment for painted cloths and testers in one of the five rooms of Edward Hawton of Bedford in 1574 was unusual (*76*).

Painted cloths were recorded in Bedfordshire as early as 1506 in the will of William Wodill of Marston Moretaine.[114] By the late sixteenth and early decades of the seventeenth centuries, they were ubiquitous for people in every social and financial group. The shoemaker Thomas Browne with an inventory value of £7 had them in both his rooms in 1552 (*4*) and the gentleman Ralph Place still had them in his two public rooms in 1611 (*217*).[115] Valued at a unit price of between 3d to 1s per yard in the sixteenth century, they were cheap to buy and were generally considered of low value.[116] Valuations for cloths in Bedfordshire inventories range

111 *Harrison's Description of England*, p. 235, spelling modernised.

112 For wainscot in the inventories, see pp. xlvii–xlviii.

113 Nicholas Mander, 'Painted Cloths' in *The Cambridge Guide to the Worlds of Shakespeare* (Cambridge, 2015), pp. 461–70.

114 A. F. Cirkett, ed., 'English Wills 1498–1526', BHRS vol. 37 (Streatley, 1957), p. 29.

115 Of those people with goods valued at more than £800, only three lacked painted cloths and any other wall coverings (*306*, *331*, *374*).

116 Mander, 'Painted Cloths' p. 461.

from 4d (*160*) to 20s (*85*), which would take age, condition, size and the number of painted cloths into account. The valuations are noticeably high in the 1570s to 1590s, which Mander identifies as the beginning of their heyday. Some painted cloths may have lasted for many years, been sold (*336*) or inherited, decreasing in value as they became older. The decline in their popularity, as seen in inventories from the 1620s, is in line with national decorative trends,[117] although another explanation may be that they had become regarded as fixtures in many houses and therefore were not listed.

Irrespective of the type of hangings or the material, the effect was to provide not merely draught-proofing but also colour and pictures. Designs were taken from Biblical stories or other religious and classical themes. They were large, bold and colourful. The 1506 painted cloth referred to above had a crucifix design. Bedfordshire is amongst the few places that can boast surviving painted cloths in public ownership. A set of six cloths was discovered by the local historian F. G. Gurney in an attic in an old house in Church Street, Luton and bought in 1916. They are now in the care of The Culture Trust, Luton. Five of the six are 7ft 6in. (2.3m) in height and from 15ft 9in. (4.8m) to 2ft 6in. (0.8m) wide. The sixth is 3ft (0.9m) by 7ft 9in. (2.4m). Four are scenes from the Old Testament (the meeting of Solomon and Sheba; Elijah's ascent to heaven; Balaam and the ass; and the finding of Moses); the other two are landscapes. Each has a border of leaves and fruit sewn around it. In its day the colours, which included scarlet, bright green and brown, would have brightened and enlivened the rooms. The cloths have been identified as probably early seventeenth century and apparently from the same hand or workshop as the painter of the 85ft (25.9m) frieze panel from Brandeston Hall, Suffolk (Lincoln Museum).[118] They may have been typical of painted cloths recorded in many of the inventories.

Window curtains

The inventories give little indication as to how many houses had glazed windows as they are only mentioned occasionally. Other sources suggest that many windows were glazed.[119] Six inventories mention window curtains specifically, notably James Duckington's inn at Dunstable in 1604 (*176*) and Warden Abbey the home of John Willson in 1622 (*331*) which were both lavishly supplied with them. At a modest social level, Edward Jones, a dyer, had a window curtain in his chamber over the shop in Luton in 1611 (*236*). In many of the inventories, it is difficult to tell whether curtains refer to windows or to bed hangings.

[117] Mander, 'Painted Cloths', p. 465; Anne Buck, 'Clothing and textiles in Bedfordshire inventories, 1617–1620', *Costume* no. 34 (2000), pp. 32–3.

[118] I am grateful to Elise Naish, Head of Heritage & Collections, The Culture Trust, Luton for information from the Trust's catalogue, and additional notes and extracts from F. G. Gurney's diary (The Culture Trust 254/51).

[119] Glass windows in Richard Dermer's house in 1533 (Tearle, *Luton guild accounts*, p. 83); glass as a fixture not to be removed according to the will of Thomas White of Cranfield 1556 (Beds Archives, ABP/R 13/64); and conveyances containing conditions that wainscot, glass, doors and locks were included in the sale, e.g. Cranfield in 1580; Clapham in 1594; Clophill in 1601; Elstow in 1604 (Beds Archives, X 86/322, S/AM 24, L4/8 and AD 346/9).

Wooden furniture

With a few exceptions for wicker chairs (e.g. *252*) furniture was made of wood but only occasionally was the type of wood – cypress, fir, oak, spruce and walnut – described. The main table in the hall, described as a table with a frame or as a long table, is frequently first on the list, showing its central importance. Any other table was also described and was clearly a secondary item, for example a round or folding table (e.g. *44*). The description of furniture as 'joined' indicates that it was of better quality and attracted a higher value than carpenters' work. The distinction is most noticeable with stools and bedsteads. The use made of cupboards in the hall is occasionally described as, for example, 'with pewter upon it' (e.g. *53*, *109*, *209*) and one 'with a press in it and a desk upon it' (*355*). A few people had shelves and cases to display glass, such as the widow Alice Negouse who had a glass case with glasses in her parlour in 1593 and George Negusse who had 'a glasscase, a frame for glasses' in his hall in 1611 (*134*, *231*). They may have been the same items if George were her son and had inherited her glass case.

A range of wooden storage containers – chests, coffers, boxes, forcers and trunks – were housed in parlours and chambers. They differed in shape or size and a few had further descriptions such as a 'carved chest' and a 'barred chest' (both in the hall, *151*) and two chests 'barred with iron' in a bed chamber (*409*). Some presses and press cupboards for hanging clothes are listed (*373*).

Beds

In the chamber or parlour, beds and their 'furniture' are described in great detail. Today's beds were then called bedsteads and came in a bewildering array of designs: with uprights and a tester over them from which curtains were suspended, a field bed which was also curtained,[120] a trundle or truckle bed that could be wheeled under another bed, a trussing bed that could be dismantled.[121] After the bedstead some inventories merely record 'and their furniture' or 'the bedding' but others give careful descriptions of mattresses (often also called beds and filled with feathers, wool, flock, or straw), pillows, bolsters, blankets, carpets, coverlids, coverings, quilts and rugs.[122] One inventory even notes the weight of the featherbed at 45lb (20.4kg) and of three bolsters and seven pillows at 83lb (37.6kg) (*345*). Their age and quality are commented on as they affected value. New items are noted, such as the new bolster on one of the beds in Katherine Clarke's house (*276*), but it was more common to note that an item was old. In an extreme case the terms 'sorry' and 'rotten' were used (e.g. *322*). A few inventories record beds that had an accompanying footpace or steps to facilitate climbing into it, for example Robert Mayes' widow Susan reclaimed two footpaces with other items that she had brought to the marriage (*199*).

The bed of the head of many households (and sometimes other beds in the house) was well-equipped and a few were luxuriously furnished (e.g. *331*). Many had a tester, with a valance around the top and curtains or hangings on rods around the sides (*250*, *337*). Most hangings in chambers are listed in close association with beds

120 Originally a portable or folding bed (Chinnery, *Names for things*, p. 117).

121 Chinnery, *Names for things*, p. 257.

122 Carpets and rugs were woollen coverings, often decorated, that went on top of a bed, table or cupboard, not on the floor as today.

and bedding and should probably be interpreted as bed hangings rather than wall hangings. They had a similar function in excluding draughts and providing greater comfort and privacy, especially in rooms with more than one bed; however they appear surprisingly infrequently with barely a fifth of inventories in each decade mentioning them.

Bedding, bedlinen and household linen

Bedlinen and other household linen was often kept in chests in the best furnished chamber (what would today be called the master bedroom). Many inventories list bedlinen in great detail: sheets, undersheets and pillowcases (known then as pillow-bears), in addition to the heavier coverings noted above. The majority of households had between one and twenty pairs of sheets, roughly commensurate with household sizes from one person to a farmer with family and servants. However twenty-three households had between twenty-one and sixty pairs of sheets. Most, as can be expected, belonged to gentry, wealthy yeomen and clergy whose goods were valued at more than £100, although three in the 1560s and 1570s were valued at less (*37*, *51*, *71*). The widow Elizabeth Anglesey, whose goods were valued at £40 in 1631 (after deducting money owed to her) had twenty-three pairs of sheets; possibly she had retained the bedlinen appropriate to her former household, although at the time of her death she was probably living in someone else's house (*409*). Explanations for unexpectedly large numbers of sheets could be that, as expensive items, they were looked after and passed on to family and friends, as can be seen in so many wills of the period. They were also hard wearing and durable. Nevertheless, the sixty pairs of sheets of the bachelor rector of Wilden stands out as exceptional (*349*).

Most inventories abound in other household linen. In some houses every surface was covered by table cloths or cupboard cloths and every activity had its towels, napkins and table napkins, the latter sometimes counted by the dozen. Inventories often distinguish between different quality linen: lawn, holland, flaxen, hemp tare, hemp towe and harden. The different grades can be seen in a few inventories where they have been valued separately (e.g. *252*). Fourteen inventories include a *spere* cloth amongst the household linen, or in one instance a *spere* towel. In one inventory, it is listed separately and priced at 6s, a considerable sum in 1571 (*60*) and far higher than in any other, later, inventory. Its rarity and, in this one instance, its value suggest that *spere* cloths were significant items.

Iron, brass, pewter and latten ware

Like bedding and household linen, metal goods were also expensive to purchase and valued accordingly in the inventories. All the fire and cooking apparatus were iron. Many of the cooking vessels were brass. In 1497, James Woodward's brassware at 1½d and 2d per pound weight (*1*) was valued at 9s out of his £14 10s-worth of goods. Wooden plates and dishes were being joined or replaced by pewter plates and dishes. Latten ware (an alloy of copper, tin and a little lead, resembling brass) was also owned and is associated with basins, candlesticks, chaffing dishes, ladles and mortars. Glassware was not uncommon, but was of sufficient value to be displayed in cases (e.g. *134*, *199*, *231*) or on designated shelves (*333*, *407*). While most display cases were owned by wealthy people, John Gybson of Swineshead, whose inventory was valued at £45 and who may only have had three rooms, also had a glass case in 1633 (*410*).

Comfort and style

Throughout the period, the inventories reveal many Bedfordshire people living in comfortable homes. Many had separated domestic functions and daily living from the hall into specialist rooms. Cooking and brewing had gone into kitchens, butteries and specialist outbuildings; daily living and sleeping into chambers and parlours, although many of these rooms were still multi-functional. In addition to specialisation and privacy, such things as warmth, draught exclusion and the general comfort provided by soft furnishings were standard. Comfort is noticeable in the profusion of painted cloths, cushions and cloths covering tables and cupboards that proliferated in the halls, parlours, chambers and some of the additional chambers.

The colourful decoration of painted cloths has already been discussed. The colours and fabrics of bed hangings and curtains are sometimes mentioned, especially those belonging to the gentry, and red and green predominate. John Colbecke of Tempsford had curtains and room hangings of say (a light, twilled, woollen fabric) and a tester 'payned' with damask and velvet (i.e. in sections) on a bed in another chamber in 1596 (*152*). Francis Marsh, gentleman of Eaton Bray, had a valance of red and green silk wrought with gold and with a silk fringe and five silk curtains in 1611 (*250*). John Willson of Warden Abbey had a bed with a valance of fugurato (a figured material) and a silk fringe and green say curtains fringed with green and orange silk; another with a valance and curtains of crimson mockado (a material resembling velvet) and green silk fringe; and his own bed with valance and curtains of green and yellow in 1622 (*331*). Even at the poorer end of society, some people had a bed with tester and curtains of red and green say (*5*), painted hangings round the bed (*94*) or a painted tester (*170*).

Sanitary provision is evident in the presence of basins and ewers and the abundance of chamber pots and John Willson's necessary stools at Warden Abbey (*331*).

Heating, cooking and food

Food and cooking have been touched upon in connection with chimneys, fires, kitchens and butteries. This section focusses on food and its preparation.

Food was included in inventories because it had a sale value as well as being produced for consumption. Indeed, William Barcock's inventory of 1597 includes 'Grane thresshed and other provision for housekepinge' at 40s (*153*) and West's precedent of 1598 lists 'wine, oyle, beere, ale' among the examples of goods to be included in an inventory.[123] In rural areas in the sixteenth and seventeenth centuries, much food would have been produced seasonally in bulk both for sale and for use during the year. It is possible to see the transition of agricultural produce to edible or saleable goods: store pigs to flitches of bacon; grain in the fields to harvested barley; barley to malt to ale; milk to cheese and butter; and bees to honey. They are the most frequently listed foodstuffs, often in substantial quantities. The yeoman, Robert Hanscombe, had butter and cheese worth £7 in 1625 (*374*). Quantities of grain at various stages of processing and contained in hutches and meal tubs are commonly listed.

123 West, *Symboleography* (1592), section 707.

Fruit and vegetables, apples and onions are also common. Warden pears and melons were among William Kippest's foodstuffs in 1616 (*287*).[124] Less easily understood as worthy of inclusion in an inventory are the six loaves of bread and four apple pasties in William Grey's house in 1587 but they were valued at 16d, which makes them more valuable than his chair and spinning wheel (*114*).

A noticeable omission is direct reference to salt. It occurs as equipment used for salting, as salt 'sellers' and as a box for salt in William Gore's inventory in 1626 (*386*) but is not listed separately although it was essential and, presumably, had a re-sale value.

As well as where and what people cooked, the inventories reveal how people cooked and heated their homes. More than 60% of the inventories include firewood, used for heating, cooking, baking and brewing. A few inventories refer to coal, the contemporary term for charcoal. What is now called coal was usually known at that time as seacoal and only one inventory specifically mentions it, that of the maltster Edward Catherall in 1613 (*260*). He was using it for heating in his hall and in the malt shop. John Willson, who lived at Warden Abbey, had a 'range to hold up coles' (*331*) and three other inventories had 'cole rakes' or pans (*64*, *142*, *291*); they may have referred to charcoal or seacoal. The evidence is slight but it appears that coal in the modern sense had hardly reached householders in the county and was not used in cooking.

Inventories list spits to be laid on andirons or cobirons in front of the fire to roast meat and the accompanying dripping pans beneath the spits to catch the fat and juices; pot hangers for a variety of pots to suspend over the fire from the iron bar in the chimney; gridirons and trivets for pots to stand over the fire; chafing dishes to keep food warm or for slow cooking for people who did not have equipment for roasting or boiling. The range of cooking utensils – pots and pans, kettles (large pots, not like our kettles for boiling water), posnets and frying pans – was appropriate for boiling, roasting, simmering, frying and keeping food warm.

The only evidence of baking is the occasional listing of peels (bread shovels). This is because ovens were part of the fabric and not a moveable item. Other equipment for food preparation might also be built in and similarly omitted from inventories, such as kilns, furnaces and table work surfaces for food preparation.

Two unexplained kitchen items are also mentioned: *treddes* and *bayards*. They both occur in proximity to cooking irons around the fire. The word *tredde* probably derives from 'tread' with the connotation of using the foot. Possible explanations are a foot-operated spit-turning device or a small stool for standing on to reach cooking pots or things in the fireplace. Another possibility is a local term for a jack or the turnspit operated by a dog, neither of which words is common in these inventories.[125] The *OED* definition of *bayard* is a bay horse (which can be discounted because of context) or a hand barrow. In eight of the ten occurrences in these inventories, a

124 Melons, known as millions, had been grown in England since at least the Elizabethan period, when their cultivation was described by Thomas Hill (*OED*).

125 I am indebted to Tom Jaine of Prospect Books, Professor William Sayers of Cornell University and Caroline Davidson, author of *A Woman's Work is Never Done*, for discussing possible explanations of *tredde* with me. The conclusions are my own and may not represent their views.

bayard is associated with fire shovels, pothangers and other fire irons and could be a hand barrow for bringing wood for the fire. The other instances are in the context of bedding, coffers and hall furniture. Another explanation was offered by the Rev. J. E. Brown, who thought it might be a clothes horse.[126] Both words occur in the same context in other Bedfordshire documents but have not been found elsewhere, leading to the conclusion that they were local Bedfordshire terms, meanings still uncertain.

Personal possessions

Other than clothing, only a few inventories list personal possessions, such as books, weapons and recreational items. It is likely that some personal possessions, such as the gold ring left to his son by William Sherley (*252*), were given to the intended recipient before the inventory was taken, although William Doe's silver hooks, pins and rings which he left to his daughters are accounted for in his inventory (*71*).

Books

Forty inventories contain books. Six people kept them in their study. Others had books in the parlour, the hall, the decedent's chamber, other chambers and the loft. Twenty-six inventories valued the books separately and they ranged from 2s to £80 with nine of them at less than £1. (It is difficult to be precise about values because some books were included with clothing or furniture.)

Thirteen Bibles were specifically mentioned, belonging to eleven people (ten men and one woman), none of them clergy, although no doubt all the clergy had Bibles. The first Bible occurs in an inventory of 1610 (*199*), a year before the publication of the new King James Authorised Version (which cost 10s to buy, unbound). Only four other religious books are named: Calvin's *Institution of Christian religion* (Francis Marshe, gentleman of Eaton Bray 1611, *250*); Calvin's *Harmonye upon the four Evangelists*, Wolfgang Musculus' *Common places of Christian religion*; and Zacharias Ursinus' *The summe of Christian religion* (William Foxcroft, rector of Bedford St Cuthbert's 1625, *383*). Although these books fit into the county's Puritan tendency, they are too few to draw any conclusions about religious beliefs in Bedfordshire at this period. Possibly the people who had Bibles in the hall or parlour either used them frequently or were making a public statement about their piety and ability to read.

The only non-religious book was Rastell's *Abridgement of the Statutes* owned by Edward Catherall, a brewer in Luton (*260*). Books of statutes were published throughout the period including several editions by John Rastell or his son William from 1519 onwards. If Catherall's book was indeed by one of the Rastells (and not a later collection with Rastell's name on it), it would have been out of date by 1613. What practical use Catherall had for it is a puzzle.

It is surprising that only eleven out of the fourteen clergymen were recorded as owning books, most of which were valued between £5 and £8.[127] To provide an idea

126 Rev. J. E. Brown, 'An Inventory of Household Goods, 1612', *The Antiquary* vol. 42 (1906), pp. 27–9.

127 Most values were similar to those in Berkshire for the same period, where the range was from 6s 8d to £30 (Dils, 'Books of the clergy', pp. 101–2).

of what these values represented, the £5-worth of books owned by William Ridge, vicar of Southill, in 1598 were quantified as more than sixty-eight books 'xxij books in folio with forty six of another sort with certaine paper books and other old books of small value' (*158*). Two clergymen stand out above the others. Samuel Fulke, parson of Barton (*328*) and Francis Dillingham, rector of Wilden (*349*) had substantial libraries, valued respectively at almost £80 and £70. Fulke's brother was William Fulke, Cambridge scholar and religious controversialist[128] and Dillingham was a noted Hebrew scholar and a member of one of the Cambridge commissions which prepared the King James Bible.

Book ownership was concentrated among the clergy and better off but several of the poorer sort had books. At the poorest level in 1616 John Rule, a smith from Tempsford, had one book amongst his possessions which were valued at £3 9s 2d (*286*) and seven others whose inventories were below £50 also had books, including William Foxcroft, rector of Bedford St Cuthbert's, who seems to have been in financial difficulties. In contrast, the wealthy esquire George Francklin, had books and maps worth £16 3s 4d (*306*). The unanswered question is who valued the books, especially those of Fulke and Dillingham. Books were specialist items. None of the appraisers appear to have any expertise in books and Fulke and Dillingham's inventories were made within days of death. There was no time for a specialist stationer to have been called in to value them and so maybe these appraisals are an example of forward planning with the decedent obtaining a valuation during his lifetime.

Weapons

In addition to the bows and arrows of the fletcher Rodger Burden which were his stock in trade (*208*),[129] weapons and armour were owned by twenty people of all social ranks and predominantly reflect the weapons required by those who were picked for service in the musters. Nationally, there was a gradual change from bows, arrows and bills needed by archers and billmen during Henry VIII's time, first to calivers (light muskets), swords and daggers in Elizabeth's reign (and specified for men impressed for service in Ireland in 1591) and then to muskets, swords and headpieces in the early seventeenth century.[130] The presence of bows and arrows, swords and daggers in these inventories reflects these changing requirements. The halberd and two black bills in 1596, 1601 and 1622 may have been retained long after their useful life; references to other bills are, from their context, more likely to have been agricultural implements than weapons.

As well as labourers, servants and yeomen who had weapons, several gentlemen had arms and armour, usually with little detail and valued between 30s and £5 (*64*, *181*, *331*, *428*). However, the value of George Francklin's armour and 'furniture for service' in 1618 at £22 6s 8d is in a different league and may indicate his position in the county administration as a justice of the peace and sheriff in 1602 (*306*). Clergy

128 'William Fulke 1536/7–1589' by Richard Bauckham, *ODNB*.

129 Although bows and arrows had been overtaken by other weapons by the late sixteenth century, training in their use continued and they were still in use in the Civil War. The occupation of fletcher continued to occur for Bedfordshire testators until the 1630s (Beds Archives, online catalogue).

130 Lutt, *Bedfordshire Muster Rolls*, p. 41–2.

were required to be under arms with their bishop's consent and were reported as such by the Earl of Kent in 1615.[131] Three clergymen's inventories between 1618 and 1625 contain arms and armour which may be this equipment. All three had a headpiece; two had swords; two had calivers; and one also had a dagger (*301*, *334*, *381*).

A different type of weapon was owned by the second John Colbecke of Tempsford whose rapier was worth 3s 4d in 1596 (*152*). This was a gentleman's accessory and says much about the status he wanted to project. The lack of fowling pieces is noticeable. Only Robert Staunton of Birchmore has one, listed with his armour and other guns in 1656 (*428*). Three are recorded in the 1610s in other inventories published by Bedfordshire Historical Record Society: John Mayes of Sandy in 1617, Richard Fisher a yeoman of Milton Ernest and Henry Richardson of Blunham both in 1619.[132]

Valuables

Valuables and the more unusual items that throw light on a person's status or leisure are not abundant.

More than forty people owned gold or silver items. The gold was in money or, in a few cases, as rings. Not all of those who had gold rings were wealthy; one ring, valued at 19s, belonged to a yeoman of modest means (*362*). Exceptionally, George Francklin had a gold chain, jewels and plate (valued at £174 10s) as well as £107 in gold and silver coins (*306*). Silver items were commonly spoons and salt 'sellers' and less frequently cups, bowls, masers and pins, hooks and rings. Gold and silver were usually found in gentry, clergy, yeomen's and widows' households: the majority of those people had inventories valued at more than £100, although inventory values for several of the widows were far below that level, possibly reflecting the remains of their previous married status. The silver spoons of at least one yeoman, who had no farming or occupational goods and a low overall inventory total of £29 pointing to retirement, suggests a previously more affluent life-style (e.g. *168*).

Other valuable items included a perfume pan, aquavita bottles, gold weights, looking glasses, hour glasses and a clock. Except for the ten inventories (three of them inns) which contain playing tables or a pair of tables (for backgammon), the only other evidence of social recreational activity is the treble 'violen' of William Peirce, a yeoman of Toddington, in 1622 (*326*).

Clothing

Despite being a universal possession, only 322 inventories (75%) mentioned clothing; only 283 (65%) provided valuations; and fewer than seventy-five listed individual garments. Delving further offers explanations into the practical approach made by appraisers to clothing. This section looks at these issues then considers the actual clothing. Only the clothing of the decedent should have been included in an inventory, not his wife's or other family members', as their clothing belonged to them, but there are a few exceptions here where the wife's clothing is included (and, in one inventory,

131 *Cal. S.P. Dom. James I*, vol. 2, 1611–1618, p. 319.
132 BHRS vol. 20, pp. 51, 75 and 101 respectively.

that of an adult daughter, *345*). In most instances, parish registers show that they had died shortly before the person for whom the inventory was being made.

Table 11 Value of clothing by decade

Inventories per decade	inventories with clothing valued				lowest value	highest value	median
	men	women	total	%			
pre-1550 (1)	1		1		10s		
1550s (21)	4	1	5	*24*	6s	£4	13s 4d
1560s (29)	12	2	14	*48*	3s 4d	£2	16s 8d
1570s (39)	16	2	18	*46*	6s 8d	£5 5s 4d	£1 4s
1580s (34)	6*	1	7	*21*	14s 8d	£4 3s 4d	£1
1590s (42)	21	4	25	*60*	6s 8s	£7	£1 14s
1600s (30)	21*	4	25	*83*	5s	£7 10s	£1 10s
1610s (111)	76*	11	87	*73*	5s	£58 13s 4d	£1 10s
1620s (87)	64*	10	74	*86*	3s 4d	£34	£2
1630s (23)	16	4	20	*87*	10s	£6 13s 4d	£2 10s
1640s (6)	4	0	4	*67*	10s	£3	£1 10s
1650s (9)	3	0	3	*33*	£2	£11 10s	£6
Totals (432)	244	39	283	*66*	3s 4d	£58 13s 4d	£1 10s

This table only includes inventories where clothing is listed and valued separately.
Column 1: the bracketed figure is the total number of inventories for the decade.
Column 5: % is of inventories with clothing as a percentage of all inventories in the decade.
Columns 5–7: are the *overall* lowest, highest and median values of clothing in the decade.
* Indicates inventories where a wife's clothing was listed with her husband's.

Omissions and low valuations

A few appraisers declared that clothing had been bequeathed or given away in the decedent's lifetime or before the inventory was taken.[133] This may have been common practice and would explain the lack of clothing in some inventories. It might also explain the presence of old clothes at a low value which occurred in many inventories throughout the period, such as Nicholas Fyssher who had goods worth £34 but his 'old apparel' was only valued at 3s 4d (*46*).

As well as clothes in general, shoes, boots and hats were routinely ignored. Only twelve inventories mention shoes and six mention boots, all in men's inventories. Only seventeen include hats, four being women's clothing. In view of the social importance of wearing a hat and the laws requiring it, everyone would have had at least one hat or cap. Possibly shoes, boots and hats were regularly included in all-inclusive terms such as 'his/her apparel', or were amongst miscellaneous items or had been given away before the inventory was taken. Some appraisers combined clothing with other items, such as money, rings, silverware, books and painted cloths,

133 'Memorandum That the Saide Wylliam Irelande didde gyve by his lyff tyme unto his Chilldren all hys Apparrell therfor hit is nott praised' (*5*); and 'Item his apparell lefte ungiven before his death £3' (*220*).

and one inventory even lists wearing apparel 'with other trash' and another with 'other goods not remembered'.

Another cautionary note in interpreting the valuations is the predominance of round figures, either as fractions or multiples of a mark (13s 4d) or as multiples of 10s. This stands out in the lowest and median values (Table 11). The use of round figures may imply that many appraisers approached the task of valuing clothing as a unit to which a notional scale of standard rates was applied. Where clothing is itemised, more attention to actual value is evident, for example Elizabeth Bacon's clothes at 11s 4d in 1552 (*3*) and John Brimsall's extensive wardrobe at 37s in 1563 (*34*).

The summary of decadal clothing values in Table 11 ranges from a low of 3s 4d (a quarter of a mark) to a high of nearly £60. From the 1590s onwards, the percentage of inventories listing and valuing clothing increases significantly, probably showing a greater attention to detail by the appraisers. The lowest valuations are less than £1 until the last decade and these continuing low valuations may reflect the omissions referred to above. The median values show a slow increase over the decades, albeit with some setbacks, and it may give a better view of how much the majority of people's clothing was worth.

The highest valuation in each decade fluctuates wildly, showing the affluence of some decedents. Only eighteen of the inventories valued clothing at more than £6 (the highest decadal median value) and of these only nine at £10 or more: Humfrey Mee a carpenter and farmer at £10 in 1614 (although £4 of the clothing may have belonged to his wife, *267*); Thomas Grene, baker of Bedford, in 1625 (*357*) and Robert Staunton, esquire, in 1656 (*428*) both at £11 10s; William Sherley, miller or yeoman, at £12 in 1612 (*252*); Samuel Fulke, clergyman, at £13 6s 8d in 1622 (*328*); John Willson, gentleman, in 1622 (*331*) and Mary Onslow, gentlewoman, in 1627 (*389*) both at £20; and Francis Dillingham, rector, at £34 in 1625 (349). George Francklin esquire was by far the most expensively dressed at £58 13s 4d in 1618 (*306*). The five highest valuations were for gentry or clergy, as might be expected, but it is noticeable that the clothing of some yeomen and tradesmen was valued more highly than that of some other gentry and clergy.

In view of omissions, round figures and the persistently low values for some people throughout the period, the lists of clothing and valuations must be viewed as indicative of minimum clothing, not as an exact statement of a person's clothes at their death.

Wearing apparel and linen apparel

Instead of listing items individually, the appraisers in almost half the inventories employ a group of standard descriptions for clothing. The general term is 'his/her apparel' but they also use 'wearing apparel', 'all his wearing apparel', 'wearing linen' and 'linen apparel'. At first sight, these merely look like variations of a general description and are not distinguished in the *OED* nor in current glossaries of terms for local historians. On closer examination distinct meanings emerge, which affect the way lists of clothing should be interpreted.

Some inventories have separate entries for wearing apparel and linen apparel, such as Agnes Hurst who had woollen apparel at 40s and linen apparel at 20s (*57*). William Whootton's appraisers listed 'all his weareing apparrell woollen & linnen' at 26s 8d (*322*). This separation of wearing apparel and linen apparel occurs elsewhere.

At Merton in Oxfordshire in 1585, Katherine Doylye's very detailed inventory listed 'her wearing linnen' at £3 and 'woollen apparrell' at £20, and at King's Langley, Hertfordshire in 1640 Elizabeth Dowse's inventory listed 'all the smalle wearing linen' at 10s and 'the wearing aparill shee left un givne' at 6s 8d.[134]

A few inventories spell out what was meant by these two descriptions, 'wearing apparel' and 'linen apparel'. William Ridge's appraisers itemised 'all his waringe apparrell as gownes, dublettes, cotes, hose etc.' (*158*). Anne Style had 4 gowns, 4 petticoats, 1 cloak and 'other wearing clothes' as well as wearing linen and a stuff apron (*234*). Richard Thompson had 3 shirts and 4 bands as well as 'an old cloake and his wearing apperrell' (*196*). Joan Mayes has 'her wearing apparel' at 46s 8d and smocks, neckerchewes, sleeves, kerchewes, rayles and an apron listed with 3 pillowbears at 16s altogether (*86*). Other inventories also include wearing linen with household linen.

The distinction is between outer wear (cloaks, coats, jerkins, doublets, breeches, gowns, hose, stockings, petticoats and safeguards) described as wearing apparel and items worn next to the body (smocks, shirts, bands, sleeves, kerchers, neckerchers) described as linen apparel. A practical difference was that wearing apparel was generally woollen (or leather), probably made by a tailor and kept clean by brushing, and linen apparel was made at home and was washable.

Was this distinction the contemporary understanding of the terms 'wearing apparel' and 'linen apparel'? Was it routinely observed in inventories but only occasionally spelled out? If so, a reassessment of the evidence for the quantity and value of people's clothing is necessary. To every statement of a person's 'wearing apparel' or a list of outer garments should be added a notional sum for wearing linen if it is not mentioned separately.

Clothes

Only seventy-four inventories list garments by name. This number, spread over 110 years, is insufficient for an in-depth survey of fashion trends in the county or the extent to which sumptuary laws were observed but it is sufficient to pick out common garments and some more unusual items.[135]

The gentry and clergy would be expected to dress according to their status, but unfortunately their inventories provide little information about their actual clothes. Both groups (sixteen gentry and fourteen clergy) had clothes valued within a wide spectrum from a low of £2 and £1 10s to a high of £58 13s 4d and £34 respectively, which shows a wide disparity (*162*). Little more can be gleaned as only the clothing of two men in these groups has been itemised. Gerrard Fittesgeffreie had 2 doublets, 2 pairs of hose and 2 pairs of stockings at £2, although as his inventory was valued at £183, his dearth of clothing may be due

134 Havinden, *Household and Farm Inventories*, pp. 196–7; Munby, *Life & Death in King's Langley*, p. 102.

135 The clothing appropriate to every level of society was highly regulated by an act of Henry VIII in order to keep people in their place and support English industries. Elizabeth I reinforced this law by proclamations several times during her reign. In these sumptuary laws, clothes and materials marked out people's position in society, proclaiming their status or profession (Apparel Act, 1533, 24 Hen. 8 c.13 (*Statutes of the Realm*, vol. 3, p. 430); Frederic A. Youngs, *Proclamations of the Tudor Queens* (Cambridge, 1976), pp. 161–70).

to its dispersal before the inventory was taken (*162*). The debts of the clergyman William Foxcroft almost cancelled out his inventory value of £20 (*383*). The careful itemisation of a doublet, pair of breeches, other old apparel, boots, shoes, linen and woollen valued at £1 10s may have been an attempt to list as many assets as possible and may therefore be nearer to the clothing he possessed than Gerrard Fittesgeffreie's. Given the number of clergy amongst these inventories and the controversy in many parishes about the minister wearing a surplice, it is not surprising, that only one, Henry Watts, parson of Potsgrove, has a surplice. It was valued at 4s in 1594 (*142*).

Occupation might also require a high standard of clothing. The young innkeeper James Duckington's clothes are described as two cloaks, three doublets 'and the rest' and valued at £5 which is high for that date (1604) and may represent appropriate dress for the keeper of a lavishly furnished inn on a major route to and from London (*176*).

A person's 'wardrobe'

Bearing in mind these difficulties in interpretation, can anything useful be learned about a 'normal' wardrobe? Where garments have been listed individually and valued at one of the standard rates, the inventories help to identify the quantity of clothing that rate would provide at second hand values.

Several examples from inventories valuing clothing up to 20s show a basic number of outer garments. Examples for men are:

- a coat, a doublet and a pair of hose at 10s in 1560 (*25*);
- a cloak, a coat, a jerkin and a pair of hose at 10s in 1574 (*67*) and the same items at 13s 4d in 1591 (*126*);
- a cloak, a coat, two leather doublets, a leather jacket, a pair of breeches and a hat at 13s 4d in 1609 (*194*).

In comparison, the cloak, two jerkins, a truss (a body garment) and a pair of hose of John Smythe of Everton priced at 8s in 1591 (*127*) and the coat, doublet and pair of hose of William Haines of Sutton at 5s in 1611 (*218*) are so much lower in value that the garments may have been old or very poor quality.

At the slightly higher value of £1 5s, the clothing of William Gray alias Butler in 1569 includes linen and more outer wear: 2 coats, 1 jerkin, 2 doublets, 3 pairs of hose, 4 shirts, 2 pairs of ruffs and 1 hat (*49*).

At a valuation between £1 10s and £2, a far greater number of garments occur:

- 3 coats, 2 cloaks, 4 jerkins, 2 pair of hose, 2 petticoats (a small coat worn beneath a doublet), 7 shirts, 2 hats and 2 nightcaps at £1 17s in 1563 (*34*).
- 3 doublets, 1 frieze jerkin, 1 Spanish leather jerkin, 3 pairs of breeches, 2 hats, 4 pairs of stockings, 2 cloaks and 2 shirts valued at £1 14s in 1596 (*152*).
- 1 cloak, 2 doublets, 2 pairs of breeches, hats, shirts, bands, etc. at £2 in 1610 (*209*).
- 2 cloaks, 1 doublet, 1 pair of hose, his old clothes, shirts, bands, boots, shoes and a hat at £1 16s in 1611 (*244*).

Nicholas Chappell's unspecified 'wearing apparel' in 1610 valued at 40s is amplified in his will where he bequeathed 'his working day sute of apparrell … a jerkin lined with furr … his best suite of apparrell … a gown … two pairs of shoes' to different family members (*213*).

These examples show that men with clothing valued at £2 had a far greater range of clothing. They look credible as a set of working clothes and another for best.

Examples of the clothing included in these price ranges for women are more scarce:

- Elizabeth Bacon's gown, 3 kirtles, a petticoat (the skirt or part of a dress, worn to be seen beneath an open gown), and 6 kerchiefs were valued at 11s 4d and she also had 4 aprons unpriced in 1552 (*3*).
- Alice Philyppes' coat and gown was valued at 10s and she had 2 smocks and 1 kercher (unpriced) in 1563 (*35*).
- Margaret Laine (whose inventory was published in BHRS vol. 20, p. 77), had 2 gowns, 2 petticoats, 2 waistcoats, 2 hats, hose and shoes at 22s in 1620.
- Ellen Feild (BHRS vol. 20, p. 74) had neckerchiefs, cross clothes and other wearing linen, 2 waistcoats, 2 gowns, 4 petticoats and 2 hats valued at £2 5s in 1620.

These descriptions show that women could have working clothes and a change for best wear at low valuations.

At valuations of more than £2, fewer than twenty of the inventories identify sufficient garments to give a convincing account of what people were wearing. One example of a modest wardrobe in 1640 is William Rechford's £3-worth of clothing comprising 2 doublets, 2 jerkins, 2 cloaks, 2 pairs of breeches, 2 pairs of hose, 2 pairs of shoes, 2 hats and 3 shirts (*423*). He had a wider range of garments than men twenty or thirty years before but still only two of each, except shirts.

It is worth noting that clothing is itemised for the poor more often than for those with moderate means and the clothing of the really wealthy is not itemised: perhaps appraisers were trying to make the most of meagre possessions.

Material and colour

The great majority of inventories only refer to the fabric of clothing as linen and woollen: linen was worn next to the body and woollen was outer clothing. It can be assumed that much of the clothing was plain and durable. Unlike linen for sheets, there are no descriptions of types or quality of linen for clothing, except William Hoge's 'dublas' jerkin which was probably dowlais (a coarse calico) (*67*). Types of wool are described in a few inventories: durance was used for aprons (*166*), worsted for a nightcap (*54*) and aprons (*57*, *86*), russet for a cloak (*194*), and frieze (a heavy duty wool) for coats, cloaks and jerkins (*121*, *152*, *194*). Leather was used for jerkins (*80*), jackets and doublets (*194*). Occasionally inventories described fabrics in order to distinguish between two garments, e.g. two types of aprons (*166*); two types of jerkins (*152*); and two types of coats, one blue and one frieze (*121*).

Several inventories provide a glimpse of finer or more expensive material, e.g. John Colbecke's jerkin of Spanish leather (*152*) and Ralph Briten's hat band of cyprus, a fine silk/linen weave (*149*). Silk was an element in several materials and is evident in some people's clothing, such as George Adams' velvet girdle (*235*) and John Dillingham's apron of rich taffeta at 10s (presumably his wife's) (*173*).

Similarly, among the itemised garments, there are few clues to their colour. Only two people are recorded as having black clothes: George Adams had a black cloak and a black coat amongst his £3 10s-worth of clothing (*235*); and a singlewoman of Roxton has a black damask apron and a black durance apron (*166*). John Wynche, a maltman of Luton, has 12 yards of black russet cloth in 1571 valued at 16s. Black could be either a standard colour that faded quickly or a sign of expensive clothing when a strong, lasting dye was used. These examples are likely to be for the good quality black clothing. The other colours are red, a common colour especially for women's petticoats (*122*, *166*) and blue, a cheap dye for ordinary clothes (*121*).

Types of clothing

The basic linen garments of smocks for women and shirts for men are frequently listed, as are the various linen cloths with which women covered their heads and shoulders.

A few people – women especially – had more linen than might be expected, such as Agnes Smithe, a widow, who had about £4-worth of clothing in 1588 (*122*). Besides outer garments, she had 11 smocks, 15 aprons, 6 kerchers, and 2 neckerchers. Ellen Cawne, another widow who died in 1611, had a similar collection of clothing: including 13 aprons, 10 smocks, wearing kerchiefs and neckerchiefs (*243*). Were these normal quantities of wearing linen which stand out because they were itemised whereas others were not?

By the late sixteenth century, women were moving from kirtles (a gown) to separates – half kirtles and a pair of bodies, a fashionable garment like a corset, usually boned with reeds but in the only example here (in 1598) boned with whalebone (*166*). It belonged to a singlewoman whose clothing is valued at £3 13s 4d out of her inventory's total of £4 3s 8d. Another early fashion of 1577 can be seen in the four sleeves belonging to Joan Mayes although by that time separate sleeves were going out of fashion (*86*). They could be pinned to the armholes of a kirtle, allowing variety in appearance. The newer fashion for separates is visible by 1611 in Ellen Cawne's inventory: she had four waistcoats and five petticoats (*243*).

A doublet with hose (a full length waist-to-toes garment) was worn by men in the 1560s and continued to be worn by poorer men into the 1610s (e.g. *186*, *218*). The doublet teamed with breeches (a knee length garment) and hose or stockings (from the knee to foot) is first listed in 1598 (*162*) and then frequently after 1609 (*194*). Five pairs of venetians (a style of breeches to the knee and fashionable from about 1570 to 1620) were owned by Ralph Briten in 1594 (*149*). A suit, that is matching doublet and breeches and fashionable from the late sixteenth century, was an expensive set of garments. It is only listed once, belonging to William Sherley in 1612, who in fact had two suits, valued at £4 (*252*). Henry Linnis's will shows that he had a suit, which he bequeathed to his sons: his other clothing was probably dispersed soon after his death in 1624 because his apparel was only valued at 5s (notes to *344*). Looking at other sources, the new suit belonging to the labourer Thomas Robinson of Cardington was valued at 16s in 1620 (BHRS vol. 32, pp. 61–2). The paucity of suits in these inventories makes an assessment of their adoption difficult.

The most valuable individual items of clothing in these inventories are gowns, usually worn as best wear by both men and women and often highly priced. Several are listed in women's inventories including the singlewoman Ward who had two gowns, priced at 26s 8d in 1598 (*166*), which are surpassed by Ellen Musgrave's one gown at 30s in 1624 (*345*). Gowns were also formal outer wear for men and were usually more highly valued than a coat or cloak. Thomas Grene's gown worth £7 in 1625 was an exceptional amount for one garment (his other clothing was valued at

£4 10s) and it was undoubtedly special (*357*). If such a gown denotes an officer of Bedford borough, the surviving records are insufficient to identify him. His is the most valuable gown but the others are also expensive items in comparison with other garments: an old sleeveless coat and an old gown at 46s 8d (*54*); a cloth gown at 13s 4d (*76*) and a long gown at 30s (*252*). Long gowns were worn by professional men and older men of substance. The owner of the long gown was William Sherley of Bletsoe, a yeoman and miller whose estate was valued at £205 in 1611, with clothing valued at £12.

Two men had livery cloaks, a uniform worn by a retainer, servant or official or the distinctive dress worn by liverymen of a guild or London livery company. The inventories of both only contain itemised clothing and a coffer or trunk, with the addition of weapons and a saddle for one and a nag and mare for the other. Ralph Briten was a servant of John Burgoyne of Sutton who, while not having a high profile public career, was of gentry rank from which county officials and MPs were drawn (he sat once for Bedford); Ralph as his servant was appropriately clothed (*149*). Nathan Scarrett's occupation is not given, and he has not been traced in other records, but his goods were so similar to Ralph Briten's that it is probable he was also a servant in a gentry household (*244*). Although made fifteen years apart, the livery cloaks of both men were valued at 13s 4d, as much as the value of some people's complete wardrobe.

Three inventories included safeguards – an outer skirt or covering to protect women's clothes when riding. Only the wives of men with horses would ride and need a safeguard.[136] Here, two of the three are listed among the goods of wealthy men, whose wife (and daughter in the case of Peter Musgrave, *345*) had predeceased them (*173*). The third is in a man's inventory, also wealthy but with no obvious explanation of its owner (*267*). The goods of all three were valued at more than £250.

Other than bearing sheets or blankets (christening robes or sheets used in childbirth) only one inventory contains children's clothing. They are what would have been called a layette in the mid-twentieth century and are in a gentry inventory, that of John Willson of Warden Abbey. The exceptionally detailed list, spreading over two pages, includes fine, decorated bed linen for mother and child and shirts, bibs, biggins (caps) and more for the child (*331*). They may not have been new when he died as he had three children under seven as well as the child expected at the time of his death in 1622.

Cloth

As well as clothing, fifty-four of the inventories list new cloth, suitable for clothing or household use. Substantial quantities were owned by a few people. Besides linen, which might have been intended for household items or clothing, other types of new cloth were wool, kersey, linsey-woolsey and russet – all good country materials – and say (a light, twilled wool). Colours were white, grey, black, blue, red and red and green for the say.

Henry Dillingham's twenty-nine ells[137] of tare, harden and flaxen linen could have been used for sheets, pillowbears, table cloths and towels and for smocks, shirts and kerchiefs for various members of the family (*138*). Thomas Wallin alias Poulter had

136 Buck, 'Clothing and textiles in Bedfordshire inventories', p. 29.

137 An ell was usually 45in., so that 29 ells measured 36¼ yards (33m).

linen and woollen cloth valued at £6 13s 4d in 1631 (*400*). Ellen Cawne, the widow whose clothing is described above, also had hemp and woollen cloth valued at 27s (*243*). While most of the owners of new cloth were wealthy, not everyone was. In 1624 the goods of Stephen Mumforde, a labourer or cottager, were valued at about £16, his clothing was only worth £1 6s 8d yet he was able to make provision for new clothes or household linen for himself or his family to the extent of 10 ells of linen (about 12½ yards or 11.75m) valued at 10s. A few inventories record the purpose of the fabric. The labourer William Hobeme had cloth for a shirt (*154*) and William Whootton, a shepherd, had coarse woollen cloth for blanketing (*322*). In 1594, the vicar of Potsgrove had a piece of cloth for a cloak valued at 26s 8d (*142*). Thomas Cater, a wealthy yeoman, had 12 yards (11m) of red and green say in the 'soller' over the parlour (*79*), probably intended for bed curtains, as it was a fabric and colour used elsewhere for that purpose.

Disappointingly, only one of the eight tailors has any cloth in his inventory and that is only a small quantity of silk and fustian (*302*).

Land and farming[138]

Three hundred and seventy-two of the 432 inventories include growing crops or livestock (Table 12). This encompasses the whole range of 'farming' from those who had one pig or a couple of acres at their death (e.g. *185*, *316*) to those such as Robert Hanscombe who had 228 acres under cultivation, 32 cattle, 15 horses and 200 sheep (*374*). Several inventories refer to the decedents' half share in land, crops, animals or equipment but the nature of the arrangements is not explained in the inventory or other surviving documentation (e.g. *148*, *404*). The inventories contain a significant quantity of data providing overall evidence for farming practices in the county such as the crops being grown, use of fallow, inter-mixing of crops in the same field, sheep, and use of cattle for dairy and draught and horses as draught animals, although there are insufficient inventories to enable agricultural changes to be charted systematically at the parish or county level.

Many factors have been identified as contributing to an agricultural revolution in early modern England.[139] The outstanding factor emerging in these inventories is the presence of leguminous crops. They are specified as peas and beans, lentils, tares, a solitary reference to clover and the catch-all term vetches. The detailed listing of plough parts may also assist in identifying the kind of ploughs being used on the varying types of Bedfordshire soil.

Acreage

Land itself was not to be included in inventories because it belonged to the heir, not the executor, or was subject to local copyhold arrangements, although the value of a

138 For an account of farming in the sixteenth and seventeenth centuries see Overton, *Agricultural Revolution in England*, especially chapter 2, and J. H. Burgess, *The Social Structure of Bedfordshire and Northamptonshire 1524 1674* (University of York, Ph.D. thesis, 1978), 2 vols.

139 For a brief overview see Overton, *Agricultural Revolution in England*, chapter 1.

Table 12 Type of husbandry

	number	% of all 432 inventories	% of 372 farming inventories
Growing crops	285	*66*	*77*
Cattle	306	*71*	*82*
Horses	186	*43*	*50*
Sheep	230	*53*	*62*
Pigs	249	*58*	*67*
Poultry	171	*40*	*46*
Bees	49	*11*	*13*

lease was to be included.[140] These restrictions did not apply to growing crops. Thus, land holding in almost 40% of the inventories is recorded and described in terms of the acreage of crops under cultivation or of land prepared for planting (Table 13). A large majority of these inventories were made in the spring and summer months before harvest and they give a credible account of acreage under cultivation (and the range of crops) (e.g. *120*, *271*). Those taken at other times of year record the acreage of tilth as well as growing crops.

These descriptions enable an estimate of the *minimum* size of holdings to be made for many of the decedents, but the occupation of more land is highly likely for many of them. A few inventories are also specific about holdings in the common fields (*184*, *413*) and one seems to show a three-field system with 21 acres of barley and wheat, 22 acres of oats and peas and 20 acres of tilth (*239*). Table 13 records acreage in bands from less than five to more than two hundred acres *and* the crops grown in each band. The size of a yardland in Bedfordshire is unknown, but the table indicates that almost three quarters of the holdings were at or below the common yardland size of between twenty and thirty acres. It also shows that most holdings were small or moderate: only three people held more than 100 acres.

As noted above, it would be erroneous to conclude that these acreages of crops represent all of a person's land. The figures would not account for much unsown acreage, land used for pasture, or copyhold land surrendered during the decedent's last illness, to give three examples. Further information about the size of estates for comparison with acreages recorded in inventories can be found in other sources. For example, John Stalford of Sundon had sixty-three acres under cultivation at his death in 1611 (*239*). He may be identified with John Stalworth of Sundon who obtained a customary messuage, three closes and 140 acres of land in Sundon by enfranchisement in 1610, indicating that he held more than double the amount of land that is recorded in his inventory.[141] The land devised in Edward Fremane's will in 1617, his house in Stotfold called Frenches with two orchards, closes and a cottage to his wife and another house with ten acres to his son might match the thirteen or more acres in his inventory made in March 1618, but the acreage does not match the

140 Swinburne, 1591, fol. 218r and v.

141 See the notes following the transcription for this identification and Beds Archives, T 42/82 for his landholding.

Table 13 Recorded acreage and growing crops

	No. of inventories		
Acres	**n**	**%**	**Growing crops**
under 5	50	*30*	wheat, barley, rye, peas, beans, oats, vetch, hemp
5–9	25	*15*	wheat, barley, rye, maslin, peas, beans, oats, vetches, grass, lentils
10–19	31	*18*	wheat, barley, rye, peas, beans, oats, vetch, lentils, hemp
20–29	16	*10*	wheat, barley, rye, peas, oats
30–39	15	*9*	wheat, barley, rye, white grain, peas, beans, oats, vetches, meadow
40–49	12	*7*	wheat, barley, rye, peas, beans, oats, meadow, hemp
50–59	8	*5*	wheat, barley, rye, peas, beans, bullimonge, oats, meadow
60–69	3	*2*	wheat, barley, rye, peas, vetches, oats, grass
70–79	2	*1*	wheat, barley, rye, peas
80–89	1	*0.5*	wheat, barley, peas, oats
90–99	2	*1*	wheat, barley, rye, peas, oats
100–200	2	*1*	wheat, barley, rye, peas, oats, drage, tares, hemp
over 200	1	*0.6*	wheat
Total	**168**	*100%*	

Acreage and the crops under cultivation are given in 168 of the 285 inventories listing growing crops.
Column 1: acres in bands.
Column 2: the number of inventories in each band.
Column 3: the numbers in col. 2 as a percentage of the 168 inventories with acreage.
Column 4: the crops recorded in inventories where the acreage under cultivation was specified.

produce stored in barns remaining over the winter nor the land for grazing sixty sheep (*300*). Thus, acreages recorded here should be viewed with extreme caution and, to reiterate, be seen as a record of a decedent's *minimum* land holding.

Crops

Almost 40% of all inventories had growing crops, either named (Table 13) or described by the general terms crops, corn or grain. The same crops are described as harvested crops, with the frequent addition of hay, straw and chaff. Three inventories record hops and claver (probably clover) (*138*, *260*, *366*). Many decedents were growing four, five or six different crops but wheat, barley and peas predominate. The narrower range of crops within the bands above seventy acres may be accounted for by the small number of inventories (eight out of 168) and may not be representative of farming on that scale. It is also possible that appraisers were less detailed when recording crops on larger acreages.

Despite being exempt from listing, grass and meadow acreage are included in a few inventories and harvested hay is ubiquitous. Where hay is the only crop in an inventory, it might have been grown by the decedent or bought in to feed horses or cattle, e.g. John Phillips, an innkeeper in Shefford (*407*) and Raynolde Savyge who had several animals to feed (*21*).

The relative quantities of different crops under cultivation varied, depending on the time of year the inventory was taken. It might also depend on crop rotation in the common fields, on whether the decedent had closes that he could cultivate outside the common field system and whether he had animals to feed. High acreages of barley are noticeable in many inventories, such as Thomas Farre of Henlow (*36*), half of whose 129½ acres were sown with barley in May 1564. Some may be examples of commercial growing, as maltmen operated especially in the south of the county and supplied malt to London (although none of the brewers, maltsters and maltmen in these inventories are recorded as growing barley).[142] Large quantities of peas, beans and vetches are also noticeable, often equalling the barley (e.g. *6*, *90*, *171*). In some instances, 50% or more of the crops were being grown for animal feed and soil improvement, such as Timothy Warde who had fifty acres of his 97 down to peas and oats, which would have been fodder for his twenty-four cows and calves and seven horses (*163*).

Hemp was widely cultivated and is recorded as a crop in fifty inventories, with a few noting hemplands amongst the acreage, e.g. George Ellys of Sandy had one hempland as well as forty-seven and a half acres (*55*).[143] The use of flax and hemp for sheets, clothes and household linen is ubiquitous in the inventories.

The single reference to underwood 'new fallen' may mean that it was intended as a cash crop (*352*).

Animals

Animal husbandry was practised extensively on a large and small scale (Table 14). Almost three hundred inventories list cattle. They are described as beasts, bullchins, bullocks, bulls, calves, cows, heifers, kine, mylch beasts/cattle/kine, oxen, steers and further as being dry, gest, weaners, yearlings and once as *shootes* (*301*). These specialised descriptions focus on productivity for milk and the age of the animals. The context of the inventory helps to explain whether they were kept for work, meat, and dairying or for fattening and selling on. Descriptions in nearly three-quarters of the inventories are in terms explicitly or probably describing dairy animals and between half and three-quarters of the inventories had dairies and milk houses or milk churns and cheese-making equipment. Although there is little doubt about the five inventories that contained drawing and draught steers (*31*, *165*, *355*), plough or draught oxen (*1*, *79*), the descriptions of most of the other cattle are too general to be certain about their use. Many were probably plough animals. All the cattle might also have had dual purposes, being fattened and sold for meat after their useful milking or ploughing days.

About half the cattle owners had five or fewer animals and the smaller the number, the clearer is their description as dairy animals. The largest dairy herds were sixteen (*181*), twenty-two (*374*) and twenty-six (*231*). Some people were engaging in significant production. In 1579 Thomas Nyxe, the rector of Bletsoe, who had eight cows, had forty cheeses valued at 6s 8d (i.e. 2d each) (*90*). Fourteen years later in November

142 Chartres, *Agricultural Markets and Trade*, p. 57; Fisher, 'London Food Market', p. 61.

143 While hemp was a practical crop for the purpose of providing the raw material for some textiles, its cultivation was ordered by Henrician and Elizabethan legislation to bolster home production, especially of rope. A quarter of an acre (later one acre) per sixty acres of land held by everyone was to be used for flax and hemp (Flax and Hemp Act 1532, 24 Henry VIII c.4, *Statutes of the Realm*, vol. 3, p. 421; Maintenance of the Navy Act 1562, 5 Eliz. I c.5, s. xix, *Statutes of the Realm*, vol. 4, pp. 425–6).

Table 14 Livestock

Animals	Number of animals										Total	*% of 372 farming inventories*
	1–5	6–10	11–20	21–30	31–40	41–60	61–80	81–100	100+	nk		
Cattle	164	69	45	13	5			1		9	306	*82*
Horses	147	27	4		1					7	186	*50*
Sheep	50	38	50	21	11	13	13	11	11	12	230	*62*
Pigs	127	53	25	3	1					40	249	*67*
Poultry	20	27	26	8	3	2	1			84	171	*46*
Bees*	24	15								10	49	*13*

The Totals column is the number of inventories with each type of animal.
nk means inventories with an unspecified number of animals.
* Bees are counted as stocks or hives.

1593, Henry Dillingham had a herd of twelve cows, with calves being bred to take their place, and a stock of thirty cheeses and 50lb of butter (*138*). While some of the produce may have been for home consumption over the winter, most was probably for sale. Some people who combined a trade with husbandry also had a good number of animals, e.g. Rodger Burden, a fletcher, who had five beasts and twenty-four cheeses worth 10s (5d each) in June 1610 (*208*).

Several inventories list cattle, often in large numbers, but no mangers or dairying equipment (e.g. *20*, *65*). It is unlikely that they lacked these essentials. Their absence may be due to the brevity of some inventories, which concentrated on the main and most valuable possessions, or to the use of all-embracing terms such as 'all other such stofe' (*65*) and 'things tending to that use' (*203*) or to the cattle being grazed and fattened before being sold on. A few people, such as William Peirce (*326*), had dairying or cheese making equipment but no cows, maybe the remnants of household goods after a change in circumstances.

From the frequency of spits, dripping pans and salting troughs in household goods, many people were eating meat of one sort or another. Two of the decedents (*97*, *399*) and several appraisers were butchers and one man had a slaughterhouse (*365*). Other than that, the inventories contain little to identify meat production, with the exception of John Gibbes who had eight 'fatting kine' in 1598 (*165*), nor the local or regional market that might have been served. However, it is probably safe to say that some people were buying cattle for fattening and selling to the London market.[144]

Horses are listed in half the farming inventories (Table 13), most recording between one and five horses (Figure 2). Above that number, ownership dropped off dramatically. Horses were the most valuable of the animals. Identifying the purposes for which they were kept helps understand people's priorities. A handful of inventories specify cart horses and many more list horse harnesses for cart and plough, horse collar harnesses and fetters and locks for use on plough horses (e.g. *5*, *90*, *141*, *235*), showing that many farmers used horses as draught animals for ploughing and carting.[145] Some inventories list both horses and oxen as draught animals (e.g. *79*, *165*). There is plenty of evidence for comparing the use of horses or oxen for these tasks.

Some horses were kept for a specified purpose, such as the miller Richard Spenly alias Newald who used his two as mill horses (*241*). A few were for riding, e.g. Dionisia Norton's one horse in 1628 for which she had a side-saddle (*394*). George Francklin, esquire, had a coach but coach horses were not distinguished from his 'oxen milche beastes gueldinges and other Catell' valued together at £191 6s 8d in 1618 (*306*). The use of the horses by several people with non-agricultural trades and without land, crops or carts is less obvious (*80*, *236*). Other uses were similarly varied or lacking.

Browsing through the inventories, it is quite clear that many people had sheep, sometimes only one or two, sometimes exceptionally large flocks. This impression is confirmed by Table 14 which shows 230 sheep owners out of 372 farming inventories (62%). Yet more than half these people had fewer than twenty sheep, denoting that keeping only a few sheep was common. The table also shows a rapid decrease in

144 Fisher, 'London Food Market', p. 51.

145 The use of horses for ploughing in Caddington in the 1630s was noted by Hindle, 'Caddington Common Enclosure Dispute', p. 57.

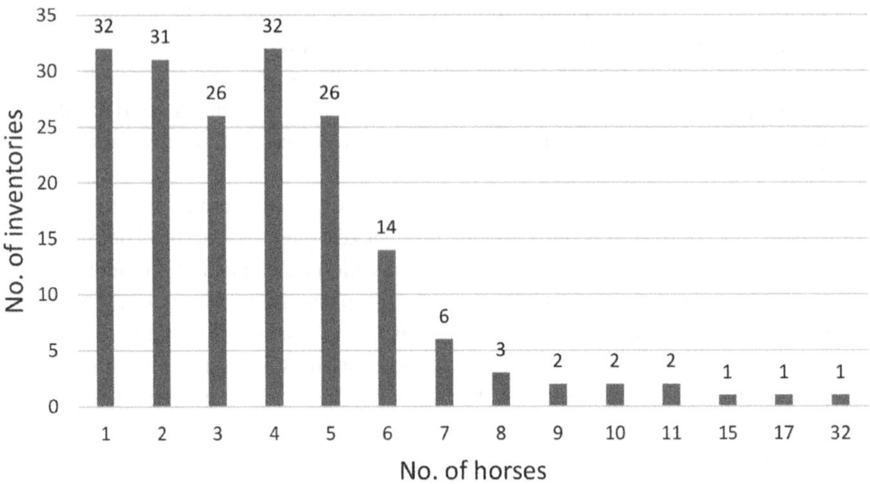

Figure 2 Ownership of horses.

Showing the number of inventories listing ownership of between one and thirty-two horses. Two decedents who owned two and three horses each also had a share in another one.

the number of people with flocks of more than thirty sheep: only eleven people had sizeable flocks of more than 100.

The importance of even a few sheep is clear from the detail in which they were recorded by appraisers. Although the great majority called them sheep, couples, ewes or lambs, other terms referring to their age or their breeding capability were used especially with smaller flocks (hoggerels, lambhogs, shearhogs, tegs, theaves, wethers, dry, gest and shotes). Ambrose Gregorye of Eversholt, who died in 1594, had one ewe, one lamb and one teg (*146*); and John Squier of Ampthill, who died in 1625, had 2 ewes, 2 lambs and 1 dry sheep (*371*). At the other end of the scale John Freeman of Dean, who died in 1566, had 23 ewes, 23 lambs, 14 lambhogs and 6 shearhogs (*39*); and Humfrey Mee of Shelton, who died in 1614, had 23 couples and 39 sheep, weathers and lambhogs (*267*). The descriptions 'shorn' and 'woolled' should relate to the time of year, before or after shearing. From the prevalence of wool and woollen wheels in the inventories, it is probable that, at the level of a few sheep, many people were keeping the wool for home use. During the sixteenth century the production of cheese from sheep's milk declined nationally in favour of cows' milk: these Bedfordshire inventories reflect this change when they specifically refer to 'mylch kine', although possibly people with a couple of ewes might still be making their cheese from sheep's milk.

The highest proportion of inventories recording sheep were made during the first five decades (1550–1600), exceeding three-quarters of inventories in the 1560s. There was a decline in the following four decades, although the proportion is still between 42% and 52% of the inventories for those decades. Without more information, it is difficult to decide whether this is a chance result of the sample or whether it reflects a change from sheep farming.

The eleven largest flocks of more than 100 sheep were located in ten parishes spread across the county. There were three large flocks in Podington and Shelton on the north west border with Northamptonshire; one in each of Milton Ernest and Eaton Socon in the north east, the adjacent parishes of Potton and Sandy in the east, Southill and nearby Meppershall also in the east, Streatley in Luton in the south, and Toddington in the south central area. These parishes are not located in the areas described above as more likely to be sheep country (p. xviii) nor is there a concentration in specific parishes, so from these inventories no region in the county stands out as sheep country. The largest flock, 579 sheep, belonged to Daniel Payne of Podington who died in 1558 (*20*). He is an example of an upwardly mobile Elizabethan yeoman who gradually accumulated leases of property in and beyond his native Higham Ferrers in Northamptonshire, as well as in Podington. His large flock may have been spread over all his properties.

Almost half the pig owners had between one and five animals (Table 13). The appraisers call them pigs, hogs and sows, or shoats (shots or shotes – young weaned pigs) with a few boars and occasionally swine. Many are more specifically described as stores, that is animals for fattening. That description, coupled with the flitches of bacon found in many inventories, suggests the main purpose for keeping pigs was domestic food production. Twenty-nine inventories, however, contain herds of eleven or more pigs, with Thomas Farre having thirty-one pigs or hogs in 1564 (*36*). Herds of that size (and some of the smaller ones) were probably in excess of domestic consumption for all but a few households and surplus animals were for sale.

Scarcely 40% of the 432 inventories include poultry and that only rises to 50% of those inventories with evidence of farming, so apparently there was no ubiquitous keeping of a few hens and a pig in the backside (Table 13). Noticeably high numbers of poultry were owned by a few people in such quantities as to be principally for the sale of eggs, chickens and feathers, or indicating large households with high domestic consumption. Thomas Farre had sixty-two poultry and, as already noted, thirty-one pigs and a large acreage of barley (*36*); similarly William Watson, who died in 1560, had forty-one poultry and twenty store pigs amongst an otherwise modest holding of livestock (*27*). Most poultry is listed collectively as pullen, but types of poultry such as ducks, geese and turkeys as well as hens occur frequently. Turkeys were introduced into England during the early part of the sixteenth century and can be found in the region by the late sixteenth century,[146] but they do not appear in the inventories until the early seventeenth century, when Edward Fremane had three amongst his 43 poultry in 1618 and Nicholas Luke had eleven amongst his 28 poultry in 1622 (*300*, *337*). Both were gentry, which may indicate that turkeys were still the preserve of the élite.

Bees are described as hives or stocks and once as a swarm. Forty-nine inventories list them, ranging from one person with only one stock (Annys Prior a widow of Barton, *262*) to William Amerye of Biddenham (*43*), who has ten beehives (Table 13). Only three people assessed at less than £10 had bees, implying that, like poultry keeping, beekeeping was not a part of the lives of the poorest. They are normally found in households with diverse livestock and which fall into the moderate (£20-£100) and higher valuation categories (more than £100).

[146] In Stoke Mandeville, Buckinghamshire in 1607 (Lewington, *Stoke Mandeville*, p. 48), and in tithe cases in Oxfordshire: Hethe in 1572 and Bodicote in 1612 (Jack Howard-Drake, *Oxfordshire Church Court Depositions 1570–1574* (Oxford, 1993), p. 46 and *Oxfordshire Church Court Depositions 1609–1616* (Oxford, 2003), p. 26).

Farming equipment

The inventories frequently provide elaborate details of farming equipment, showing how important these items were considered to be as part of a person's goods. They list troughs and mangers, hurdles and hovels. Hovels are ubiquitous and clearly portable because they would not have been listed if they were fixed. Barns were rarely valued because they were fixed buildings and belonged to the lessor but they are frequently mentioned as holding crops. Exceptionally, the stables, barns and slaughterhouse of Thomas Harbert of Leighton Buzzard stood on pattens, which makes them moveable; these buildings were valued at £40 in 1625 (*365*).

There were several types of carts (long carts, dung carts and tumbrels) and cart gear and one inventory with waggons (*328*). Shod wheels or pairs of wheels are frequently listed separately.[147] Ploughs and plough gears with the component parts of ploughs being named are frequent: axetrees (and many variant spellings), plough beams and plough teams (the latter is part of the plough not the team of horses or oxen pulling it), coulters, copsoles or coppes, foot teams, ox teams (chains), chains, handells, neckes and sheaths, shears, swingletrees, teathers and tyes, traces, tugg withes, whiple trees, wrystes or reshes and yokes. Rolls and rakes were common and there are three inventories with a seeding plough, for which the *OED* has no reference before 1767.[148] There are also specialist bills and other equipment. The inclusion of such detail for these items underlines both their practical and monetary value.

Farming was the main occupation in the county. Its trading dimension is not obviously visible but undoubtedly existed. Several farmers' inventories list large flocks of sheep and tods of wool (e.g. *60*, *106*), others list large quantities of grain (e.g. *138*) or animals (e.g. *319*). In the absence of specific statements, the presence of bushels and other measuring containers, a large quantity of grain or number of animals and the use of barns for storage outside the decedents' own property, might be indicators of agricultural produce being grown for sale as well as domestic use.

Commerce and craftsmen

Some commercial, non-farming, activities are visible in the inventories. Sixty-three are for people who can be identified as engaged in a trade or providing services (Table 3) and more may be surmised from inventory contents. The detailed online catalogue of Bedfordshire Archives and other general sources show that tradesmen were far more common throughout the county than these inventories suggest.[149] Most

147 Carts were two-wheeled vehicles and waggons had four wheels. Wheels were detachable and listed separately from the cart.

148 They were discussed in seventeenth century books on farming, although in such a way to suggest that the idea of a combined plough for ploughing, harrowing and seeding was still experimental in the 1650s (Walter Blith, *The English improver improved or the survey of husbandry surveyed*, 3rd ed. (London, 1652), pp. 219–20). The 1726 edition by Nathan Bailey of John Worlidge, *Dictionarium Rusticum, Urbanicum & Botanicum, Or a Dictionary of Husbandry, Gardening, Trade, Commerce, and all Sorts of Country-Affairs* (London, 1726) has an entry for a corn setting engine which describes it in great detail.

149 See also Godber, *Bedfordshire*, pp. 207–9.

trades were clearly aimed at a local market, such as shoemakers and the barber (*385*); some have an obviously wider market, especially the maltmen and innkeepers.

Inventories containing retail goods are sparse. One shoemaker has four and a half dozen pairs of shoes (*4*) and the fletcher has ready-made bows and arrows for sale (*208*). There are no inventories for mercers or any other shops such as have survived elsewhere.[150] There are, however, plenty of inventories for tradesmen that provide information about their tools, materials and, sometimes, customers. The malting and brewing equipment of the wealthy brewer and maltster Edward Catherall (*260*) stands out for its detail and high value. He had brewing equipment valued at £40; malting equipment; £18-worth of malt at various stages of preparation; and 12s-worth of hops. The list of people to whom he owed money may include some from whom he had bought barley because it is clear that he did not grow sufficient barley for his business.

In many inventories tools of the trade are merely noted collectively as working tools, but sometimes more detail is provided, e.g. Thomas Albrite's tailoring tools and a little material (*302*). Although only four inventories are for people identified as weavers, eight inventories list looms and their equipment (e.g. *370*, *385*). Inventories for other tradesmen contain glovers' and tenters' materials (*227*, *299*). At his death in 1556, the fellmonger Nicholas Taillour of Stevington had £53-worth of fells (animal hides still bearing hair or wool) and another 300 fells at £18 elsewhere, which together made up almost 30% of his inventory value (*6*). Similarly William Chambers the tanner (*214*) had £98 of leather and tanners' tools, amounting to almost a quarter of his inventory value of £426.

The out-county area within which one group of tradesmen were doing business may be glimpsed in the inventories of three Luton maltmen, Edward Catherall (*260*), John Wynche (*54*) and Thomas Androw (*80*). If their debtors and creditors can be equated to *customers*, they were trading in Middlesex (Holborn and Edmonton) and Essex (Waltham Abbey) as well as closer to home in Hertfordshire (Markyate, St Albans and Pirton).

For a county that was a through route to other parts of the country, held large fairs in several of its market towns each year, and is known to have possessed many inns, the number of innkeepers and innholders in this collection is disappointing.[151] Only one of them, the Crown in Dunstable, provided accommodation (*176*). The quality of its furnishings singles it out as an elegant place to stay on the route along Watling Street traveling north-west from London.

The 'hidden' trade in so many inventories is the production of hemp and spinning. Many inventories record hemp at most stages of production, from hemp sheaves which have not yet been processed, to the finished product as slips of yarn after spinning. They occur in households at most levels of wealth. More inventories contain woollen or linen wheels and some have cards and other equipment. It is unclear how much was being produced for domestic consumption and how much for sale. Other trades may also be hidden within inventories where farming predominates.

[150] e.g. Howe and Harris, *St Albans*, p. 104.

[151] The Community Histories pages of Bedfordshire Archive's website contain much information about inns.

Financial transactions

Money is referred to in just over half the inventories (53%); the other 47% of decedents either have no money, or it is overlooked. Sometimes it is not listed separately but with clothing or other goods. The inventories account for money in distinctive ways: cash and money owed to the decedent through different types of transactions.

Eighty-five inventories record money in the house (20%), calling it money in his/her purse or ready money. The amounts range from a few pennies to the £200 in ready money possessed by John Willson, whose inventory totals £877 (*331*). The innholder James Duckington had £30 in cash; this might be appropriate for a thriving business including passing trade (*176*). The median amount of cash and ready money is much lower for the majority of men, at around £4. Ready money or cash in the purses of women was less than men's, which may only reflect the fewer number of women's inventories and their lower level of wealth.

About 120 inventories record money owed to decedents, sometimes by one person, sometimes by several.[152] The amounts range from a few shillings to more than £3000 owed to George Francklin (*306*), with a median of about £21. Money owed was for purchases, wages, rent and loans.

Different loan procedures can be seen in these inventories. Greatest security for lending was obtained by using formal arrangements termed 'specialty', which included obligations, bills and bonds. A handful of inventories refer to loans without specialty or name a witness to the loan (e.g. *152*, *261*). Just under fifty men and women were lending by way of these secured and unsecured transactions. A minority of inventories itemise the loans, allowing their size to be seen. Most were for a few shillings or pounds. A few were in the range of £20 to £50 rising to £100 (*250*). The impression given is that most people lent less than £20 to each debtor, with only a few loans standing out above this level. Exceptionally, the dates of repayment are given for two bonds of £100 due to William Shreeve and seem to have been part of an arrangement to lease land (*220*). Some unspecified debts were stated as being for money lent by the decedent but without citing a formal arrangement. Two such occurrences relate to lending within the family, where widows lent money to sons (*122*, *243*).

About seventy inventories either recorded other reasons for money due to the decedent or gave no reasons. A few were for household or trade goods already sold such as animals (e.g. *261*), grain (*68*) or wool (*237*). John Rule, a smith, had 'scores oweing to hime at the day of his death 13s 4d' (*286*). A vicar's inventory noted debts due in his Easter book, but gave no details of the amounts or people who owed them (*334*). Outstanding rent occurred a few times (e.g. *392*). An unusual debt, which was not based on lending, was recorded in the inventory of John Smythe of Everton who had obtained a judgment against Christopher Fanscrafte for £3 6s 8d, which was still outstanding (*127*). Desperate debts (debts that were unlikely to be repaid) were recorded in fourteen inventories, the largest amount being £123 owed

152 An examination of moneylending based on probate accounts but relevant to the evidence in these inventories is provided by Peter Spufford, 'Long-term Rural Credit in Sixteenth- and Seventeenth-century England: the Evidence of Probate Accounts', in Arkell, *When Death Do Us Part*, pp. 213–28.

to a widow (*427*), but most were for a few pounds. The phrase referring to money 'in the hands of others' occurred a few times (e.g. *347*), explained by Spicksley as meaning literally money being looked after for safe-keeping by someone else who would pay interest.[153]

Some of the unspecified debts were probably part of the decedent's business dealings, such as the £9 owed to the maltman Thomas Androw of Luton from people in Hertfordshire and Middlesex (*80*). A shoemaker had sperate debts of £5 10s (i.e. debts likely to be repaid) and desperate debts of £4 (those unlikely to be repaid) (*369*). No shopkeeper's or tradesman's inventory with a detailed account of outstanding sales and purchases has survived to throw light on trade and retail in the county, although by this period tradesmen, retailers and merchants were well-established in the villages as well as the larger centres of Bedford, Biggleswade, Leighton Buzzard, Luton and Potton.[154] Money was owed to several servants probably in wages (e.g. *216*). The largest amount in this category of unspecified money due is the £2808 owed to George Francklin for which, disappointingly, no details are given (*306*). If many of these unspecified debts were in fact for money lent rather than delayed payment for goods or services, the volume of moneylending would be far greater than at first appears.

Decedents' debts were recorded in almost fifty inventories, three of them for women.[155] As debts were not required to be listed, these fifty are undoubtedly only a fraction of the decedents who owed money. Most reasons for owing money were the same as for being owed it, such as the credit extended to Richard Yerill for household goods and services. He owed just over £18 to eight named people, including a wheelwright, a smith and a tailor (*101*). Other reasons for debts were sometimes given. John Colbecke owed 5s 10d for the subsidy in 1596 (*152*) and Thomas Mason, rector of Souldrop, owed £3 6s 8d in London where he had been staying at the time of his death (*280*). Unpaid legacies occur in three inventories (*50, 197, 381*). The £18 owed by William Foxcroft, rector of St Cuthbert's, Bedford, to a dozen people, his son and others, including 44s to the churchwardens, reduced the value of his possessions to £2 and raises questions about why he was one of the poorest clergyman in these inventories (*383*). Was it due to a low income from his parish or his own improvidence? In four inventories the cost of burials were noted, one with the explanation that the decedent's 30s in cash had been used for his funeral (*36*).[156]

Where a debtor's or creditor's place of residence was stated, most fall within a circle of three or four parishes from the decedent. The trade area of Luton maltsters was wider, as already mentioned, and no doubt other debtors from a wider area would be found if all debts had been recorded. An atypical inventory for more distant

153 Judith M. Spicksley, '"Fly with a duck in thy mouth": single women as sources of credit in seventeenth-century England', *Social History* vol. 32 (2007), p. 194–5. Although this article focusses on the experience of single women as creditors, it discusses the range of credit activities available to men and women.

154 In contrast, see, for example, the inventory of Robert Wolley the elder, draper of St Albans, drawn up in 1605, which values numerous types of cloth in his shop, either by the yard or the ell (Howe and Harris, *St Albans*, p. 101–5).

155 It is difficult to be precise about the number of inventories because of damage to some and uncertainty in a few whether money was owed by or to the decedent.

156 Funeral costs should have been listed in probate accounts, not inventories.

contacts is Robert Staunton's; his debtors, where they can be identified, came from Essex, Cambridgeshire, Surrey and Somerset. His involvement with the Protectorate government and his life in London were the focus of much of the money owed to him (*428*).

These inventories present sufficient information about credit and debt to provide an insight into the importance of moneylending for people's finances. In an economy with no banks for ordinary people, coinage in short supply and many in rural areas dependent on the agricultural cycle for money and income, moneylending was important to keep the economy moving. Usury was theoretically forbidden but practice and legislation from the late sixteenth century permitted it, with a cap on interest rates at 10% per annum in 1571, reducing to 8% in 1623 and 6% in 1651.[157]

The capital needed in order to lend could be acquired even by ordinary people such as the majority of these Bedfordshire decedents. Wills often left the residue of a man's estate to his widow outright, or made provision for children's portions payable on marriage or at a given age, or gave small sums to godchildren, family and friends (see notes to *310*, *297*, *254*). This allowed young people to build up capital. Similarly older people were using moneylending to provide them with an income during retirement. This provision for widows or old age is most noticeable in inventories where the decedents had mainly bonds but otherwise very few possessions.

Thus in several ways people of all ages and levels of society might have sums of money available to them for investment. Attempts to estimate the extent of moneylending vary in their conclusions. Spicksley estimated that 40% of wills have signs of moneylending.[158] Spufford's examination of East Kent probate accounts shows that around 25% had signs of moneylending.[159] The much smaller group of fifty decedents in these Bedfordshire inventories who were lending money on some form of security was only 11% of the 432 inventories. However, if many of the other seventy decedents who were owed money for unspecified reasons where engaged in lending rather than just extending credit for goods or services, then the Bedfordshire percentage of loans might approach the Kent figure of 25%. These three sources (Spicksley, Spufford and Bedfordshire) are not directly comparable as they use documentation from different stages in the probate process (wills, accounts and inventories). What they do show is a noticeable level of secured money lending and that the Bedfordshire findings from inventories may underestimate the extent of the practice.

Of these 120 inventories recording money owing on specialty and for unspecified reasons, nine men lent more than £100 to one or more people (ranging from £108 to £322). They were all gentry or successful tradesmen. The largest loans to individuals were for £100 by Francis Marshe of Eaton Bray (*250*) and £75 by John Colbecke

157 Usury Act 1571, 13 Eliz. 1 c.8 (*Statutes of the Realm*, vol. 4, p. 542–3), Usury Act 1623, 21 Jas 1 c.17 brought into force in 1625 (*Statutes of the Realm*, vol. 4, pp. 1223–4) and 'August 1651, Act for prohibiting any person to take above six pounds for loan of one hundred pounds by the year' (*Acts and Ordinances of the Interregnum 1642–1660* vol. 2, pp. 548–50). Usury is discussed by Spufford, 'Long-term rural credit', pp. 219–21 and Spicksley, 'Fly with a duck in thy mouth', p. 201.

158 Spicksley, 'Fly with a duck in thy mouth', p. 190.

159 Spufford, 'Long-term rural credit', pp. 215–19.

which was secured by statute and defeasance (*152*).[160] Where loans are itemised below this level, the overwhelming majority are for £10 or less, with only sixteen between £10 and £75, including a weaver who lent £65 in bonds (*370*).

As the ten women lenders and borrowers are spread over a long period, it is not possible to test the wider conclusions that have been drawn about women being frequent lenders.[161] The Bedfordshire instances merely provide isolated examples. The largest sums range between £18 and £52, lent to six individuals (two of whom were probably family members), and the remainder range between £1 10s and £11. There is only one instance of a woman lending to another woman (one of Susan Underwood's debtors, *354*). The highest lender is Agnes Rawlins of Bolnhurst, who was owed £88 on specialty by ten people in 1611 and who, in turn, owed £18 to one person (*248*). After deducting the money she was owed from her inventory value, her goods were worth £28 14s: it would appear that she had a comfortable household and probably maintained herself through moneylending.[162]

Lending within the family was not uncommon. Agnes Smyth was owed £52 by Richard Smith, probably a family member (*122*); Ellen Cawne was owed £26 by her son (*243*); Elizabeth Child owed £39 mainly to family members (*175*); and Robert Spufforde was owed money by his brother and owed money to his daughter (*224*). Research into the named debtors and creditors in these inventories would probably uncover a far more complex relationship among them and with the decedent from whom they borrowed than these examples show.[163]

Taking debts, credits and moneylending into account reveals a different picture of decedents' circumstances and wealth at the end of their lives than often appears at first glance from their inventories. After payment of debts, the value of the estates of all fifty decedents who owed money changed, some significantly, and three were in deficit. John Wynche a maltman of Luton had an inventory value of £50 but he owed £75 in several transactions (*54*); Edward Jones, a dyer of Luton, had a comfortable house and an inventory valued at £33 but had over-extended himself by borrowing £35 from six men (*236*); and similarly Oliver Aspland, a miller of Bletsoe, had an inventory valued at £32 but owed £44 to twelve men, his rent of £2 5s and the cost of two burials at £2 (*308*). It is noticeable that they were all tradesmen. Their debts may be indicative of cash flow and the necessity to borrow to maintain a business. This explanation might also apply to farming (*188*) but the occupation of many of those in debt is unknown.

A significant and unusual drop in wealth was in the estate of John Durrant, the rector of Cockayne Hatley (*381*). His estate was valued at £177 but he owed £171, mainly to the Crabtree family, attributable to his responsibility for administering the estate of the widow of the vicar Thomas Crabtree (see notes following *301*). At the lowest inventory totals, some people only owed a few shillings or a pound, but, if

160 Statute and defeasance was a bond and collateral deed enrolled in a staple or borough court and the first debts to be paid after taxes (Spufford, 'Long-term rural credit', p. 217).

161 See Spicksley, 'Fly with a duck in thy mouth', pp. 187–207.

162 £88 lent out at 8% would have given her an annual income of £7, assuming that it was paid on time.

163 Both Spicksley and Spufford note the high percentage of borrowers being related by blood or marriage to the lender or a wider network based on those relationships (Spicksley, 'Fly with a duck in thy mouth', p. 198; Spufford, 'Long-term rural credit', p. 223–4).

paid, it would bring their overall wealth to less than £2 (e.g. *15*, *359*). The wives or children of these and other decedents would have been left with very little when all debts were satisfied.

Looking at decedents as moneylenders, most people only lent a few shillings or pounds and the social group to which they belonged does not seem to have influenced the practice of lending. Of greater interest is what moneylending says about life-style, especially by those decedents who had average or above average inventory values but few possessions and large sums owed to them (e.g. *52*, *347*), suggesting a different stage in their life cycle: they may have 'retired' and were living, possibly with family, off the interest of money lent out on bonds. There is plenty of similar evidence in these inventories to go beyond the normal assessment of people's material surroundings and investigate their financial arrangements.

* * *

This introduction has sought to bring out the immense detail of the inventories, while acknowledging their omissions and deficiencies. Bedfordshire emerges as a county of prosperous people of the middling sort, many making a good living, mainly from farming. A few are very poor, with some designated in parish registers as paupers. Most are comfortable, some are quite prosperous and two are outstandingly wealthy, although not at the level of the great landowners and merchants of the country. The inventories contain much about levels of material comfort, which are high for many people. They are a rich source for the social and economic history of the individuals and the county. By delving below the surface and using other documents, they also reveal information about families, life cycles, provision for old age, the debt culture, business networks and social contacts.

Appendix 1

Distribution of inventories by parish and decade

Appendix 1 tabulates the number of inventories in this volume and BHRS volumes 20 and 32 for each parish and decade.

Figures presented as e.g. 5 are the number of inventories in this volume for the parish. Figures presented as (5) are the number in BHRS volumes 20 or 32. Volume 32 covers the years 1562 to 1591; and volume 20 covers the two decades from 1610 to 1630. The two undated inventories from Kempston are in volume 20.

Parish	1490s	1550s	1560s	1570s	1580s	1590s	1600s	1610s	1620s	1630s	1640s	1650s	no date	Parish totals	Grand totals
Ampthill								(2)	2					2 (2)	**4**
Arlesey								1 (2)						1 (2)	**3**
Aspley Guise														0	**0**
Astwick								(1)						0 (1)	**1**
Barton	1					(1)		2 (2)	1					4 (3)	**7**
Battlesden														0	**0**
Bedford				3	2 (1)		1	5 (5)	7 (8)			1		19 (14)	**33**
Biddenham			1						1 (1)					2 (1)	**3**
Biggleswade				(1)										0 (1)	**1**
Billington									1					1	**1**
Bletsoe				2				2 (2)	1					5 (2)	**7**
Blunham			4		1 (1)	1		4 (3)	1 (1)					11 (5)	**16**
Bolnhurst		1	1		1			2 (3)						5 (3)	**8**

Parish	1490s	1550s	1560s	1570s	1580s	1590s	1600s	1610s	1620s	1630s	1640s	1650s	no date	Parish totals	Grand totals
Bromham						1		1 (3)						2 (3)	**5**
Caddington					2		2	1	1					6	**6**
Campton and Shefford					1 (1)		1	(1)		1				3 (2)	**5**
Cardington		1	1	1			1	(2)	1 (4)					5 (6)	**11**
Carlton			1									1		2	**2**
Chalgrave								(1)	1 (1)					1 (2)	**3**
Chellington			1					(2)						1 (2)	**3**
Chicksands				1										1	**1**
Clapham									1					1	**1**
Clifton						1		1 (2)		1				3 (2)	**5**
Clophill								(1)						0 (1)	**1**
Cockayne Hatley					(1)			(1)	1					1 (2)	**3**
Colmworth			1	1			1		1					4	**4**
Cople								5	3					8	**8**
Cranfield			1	2				2 (3)	1					6 (3)	**9**
Dean			1		1	1	1		1 (1)	1	1			7 (1)	**8**
Dunstable							3	4 (2)	1		1			9 (2)	**11**
Dunton								3 (1)						3 (1)	**4**
Eaton Bray						1		2	1 (1)	1				5 (1)	**6**
Eaton Socon				1	3 (1)	2	3	2 (2)	3 (1)	1				15 (4)	**19**
Edworth					(1)									0 (1)	**1**
Eggington														0	**0**
Elstow						1	1	(4)	2					4 (4)	**8**
Eversholt					1	2		(1)	1					4 (1)	**5**

Parish	1490s	1550s	1560s	1570s	1580s	1590s	1600s	1610s	1620s	1630s	1640s	1650s	no date	Parish totals	Grand totals
Everton						1		3	2	2	1			9	**9**
Eyeworth			1					1 (1)						2 (1)	**3**
Farndish														0	**0**
Felmersham		1				1	1	2 (1)						5 (1)	**6**
Flitton		1						2 (2)	2					5 (2)	**7**
Flitwick					(1)			(3)		1				1 (4)	**5**
Goldington		1						(4)	(1)	1				2 (5)	**7**
Great Barford					1			1 (2)						2 (2)	**4**
Harlington														0	**0**
Harrold									1					1	**1**
Haynes			1					1	(1)					2 (1)	**3**
Heath and Reach														0	**0**
Henlow		2	1	1							1			5	**5**
Higham Gobion														0	**0**
Hockliffe														0	**0**
Holcot									(1)					0 (1)	**1**
Holwell														0	**0**
Houghton Conquest				1				(2)						1 (2)	**3**
Houghton Regis				1			1	2	3					7	**7**
Husborne Crawley								1	1	1				3	**3**
Kempston			1		3 (1)			(2)	1			2	(2)	7 (5)	**12**
Kensworth														0	**0**
Keysoe			1	1		1				1				4	**4**
Knotting						1						1		2	**2**

Parish	1490s	1550s	1560s	1570s	1580s	1590s	1600s	1610s	1620s	1630s	1640s	1650s	no date	Parish totals	Grand totals
Langford			1		1		1	1 (1)	1					5 (1)	**6**
Leighton Buzzard		1							2					3	**3**
Lidlington				1				(1)	(2)			1		2 (3)	**5**
Little Barford														0	**0**
Little Staughton					(1)	1		1						2 (1)	**3**
Lower Gravenhurst														0	**0**
Luton		1		2	1			8 (3)	(2)	1				13 (5)	**18**
Marston Moretaine				2	(1)			4 (2)	1 (1)					7 (4)	**11**
Maulden								(1)						0 (1)	**1**
Melchbourne		1				1		(2)						2 (2)	**4**
Meppershall								(1)	2					2 (1)	**3**
Millbrook								1	(1)	1				2 (1)	**3**
Milton Bryan								1 (1)						1 (1)	**2**
Milton Ernest		1			1	1	1	(1)						4 (1)	**5**
Northill					1			1 (2)						2 (2)	**4**
Oakley								1 (2)	(2)					1 (4)	**5**
Odell									1					1	**1**
Old Warden			(1)	1				(1)	1					2 (2)	**4**
Pavenham					1	1		(1)	(2)					2 (3)	**5**
Pertenhall		1			1	1			1					4	**4**
Podington		1	1		1									3	**3**
Potsgrove						1								1	**1**
Potton					1	1	1	8 (1)	3	1				15 (1)	**16**
Pulloxhill				1			1		1 (2)			1		4 (2)	**6**

Parish	1490s	1550s	1560s	1570s	1580s	1590s	1600s	1610s	1620s	1630s	1640s	1650s	no date	Parish totals	Grand totals
Ravensden						2	1	(1)	(1)					3 (2)	**5**
Renhold								(1)	(1)					0 (2)	**2**
Ridgmon								(1)						0 (1)	**1**
Riseley				3		2	2	(2)						7 (2)	**9**
Roxton						1	1			1				3	**3**
Salford														0	**0**
Sandy			1	4	1	1		3 (5)	2					12 (5)	**17**
Sharnbrook		1						(1)						1 (1)	**2**
Shefford see Campton and Shefford															
Shelton						2		2 (1)	1					5 (1)	**6**
Shillington			1					2 (2)	1	2				6 (2)	**8**
Silsoe see Flitton															
Souldrop				2			1	2						5	**5**
Southill				1		1		1 (3)	1 (2)					4 (5)	**9**
Stagsden				2	1				1					4	**4**
Stanbridge														0	**0**
Steppingley										1				1	**1**
Stevington		1			(1)									1 (1)	**2**
Stotfold		1					1	5	1	1				9	**9**
Streatley								(1)	1					1 (1)	**2**
Studham			1			1		1 (2)	2					5 (2)	**7**
Sundon								1						1	**1**
Sutton				1		2	1	2 (2)						6 (2)	**8**
Swineshead								1	5	1	1			8	**8**

Parish	1490s	1550s	1560s	1570s	1580s	1590s	1600s	1610s	1620s	1630s	1640s	1650s	no date	Parish totals	Grand totals
Tempsford			1	1		2	2	2 (2)		2				10 (2)	**12**
Thurleigh					1			1	3					5	**5**
Tilbrook								2 (2)						2 (2)	**4**
Tilsworth									1					1	**1**
Tingrith								1						1	**1**
Toddington						1		1 (1)	4					6 (1)	**7**
Totternhoe														0	**0**
Turvey		1	1		1 (1)			1						4 (1)	**5**
Upper Gravenhurst									(2)					0 (2)	**2**
Upper Stondon														0	**0**
Westoning									1					1	**1**
Whipsnade								1	1					2	**2**
Wilden				1	1	2		(1)	1					5 (1)	**6**
Willington			1	2				2	2 (3)					7 (3)	**10**
Wilshamstead			1	1		2		1 (3)	1					6 (3)	**9**
Woburn								1				1		2	**2**
Wootton		1			2	1			1	1				6	**6**
Wrest see Flitton															
Wrestlingworth			1		1		1	1 (1)				1		5 (1)	**6**
Wymington						1								1	**1**
Yelden		1			2									3	**3**
Parish not identified		2	2					1 (6)	(1)		1			6 (7)	**13**
Total for decades	1	21	29 (1)	40 (1)	34 (12)	42 (1)	30	111 (121)	86 (43)	23	6	9	(2)	432 (181)	**613**

Appendix 2

Making the inventory – law and procedure

The obligation to produce an inventory of a deceased person's goods as part of the procedure for obtaining probate or letters of administration developed during the medieval period.[1] Some aspects were formalised in legislation by the Probate Fees, Inventories etc. Act 1529, which was not repealed until 1925 by which time the practice of producing an inventory had fallen out of use.[2] Although the 1529 Act did not give a reason for making an inventory, later commentators explained it as to prevent fraud, principally by the executor, and to protect creditors and anyone else having a claim on the estate. It is quaintly explained by Swinburne as 'least the executor be disposed to deale unfaithfully, shoulde defraude the creditors or legataries, by concealing the goods of the deceased.'[3]

Diocesan officials, proctors and notaries public who practised in the church courts in the sixteenth and seventeenth centuries and earlier and the scriveners who worked for some decedents probably had formularies or notes to guide them with the documentation. How the laity who helped people with wills and inventories gained the knowledge of procedure and the formulas to use is not known and there were no printed law books to guide either group until the end of the sixteenth century. The process is described here to inform the reader of the different requirements and enable a comparison with Bedfordshire practice.[4]

The framework for making inventories set out in the 1529 Act focussed on curbing excessive fees, setting the scale for proving wills and exhibiting inventories (which remained unchanged throughout the period covered by this volume) and setting out who had priority for appointment as administrator in cases of intestacy.[5]

1 The early fifteenth century procedure as used in the archdiocese of Canterbury is described in the introduction to *The Register of Henry Chichele, Archbishop of Canterbury, 1414–1443*, ed. by E. F. Jacob, Canterbury and York Society vol. 42 (Oxford, 1937), vol. 2, pp. xxix–xxxiii.

2 This is the modern short title. The original title in full was An Act concerning fines and sums of money to be taken by the ministers of bishops and other ordinaries of Holy Church for the probate of testaments (21 Henry VIII c.5. *Statutes of the Realm*, vol. 3, pp. 285–8). Referred to hereafter as the 1529 Act.

3 Henry Swinburne, *A briefe treatise of testaments and last wills* ... (London, 1591), fol. 217v.

4 For an introduction to inventories and their role in probate see Heather Falvey, 'The probate process in medieval England and Wales and the documents which it generated', *The Local Historian* vol. 52 (2022), pp. 8–26; Nancy and Jeff Cox, 'Probate inventories: the legal background – Part 1', *The Local Historian* vol. 16 (1984), pp. 133–45, and Part 2 pp. 217–27; and Tom Arkell and others, *When Death Do Us Part: understanding and interpreting the probate records of early modern England* (Oxford, 2000).

5 Margaret Bowker has investigated the pre-1529 fees made in Lincoln diocese ('Some Archdeacons' Court Books and the Commons' Supplication against the Ordinaries', in D. A. Bulloch and R. L. Storey, *The Study of medieval records: essays in honour of Kathleen Major*

The framework was commented on and developed in books published later in the sixteenth and seventeenth centuries. The detailed procedure has to be teased out of these sources.[6]

William Lyndwood's *Provinciale*, made in the previous century, gathered together orders and procedures that governed the church. It was printed in an English translation in 1534 and was later cited by Swinburne.[7] Henry Swinburne, who practised in the church courts of York, published a *Brief Treatise on Testaments* in 1591 with editions in 1611, 1635 and 1640.[8] West's *Symboleography*, 1598 was a precedent book on all subjects.[9] The Canons of the Church of England 1604, produced by the Bishop of London were concerned with doctrine and procedure from the church's standpoint.[10] Thomas Wentworth's *The office and duty of executors* 1641 focused on wills but summarised executors' duties in relation to inventories.[11]

To prevent fraudulent dealing with the decedents' goods, the executor or administrator could not administer the goods until an inventory had been made. The executor was expected to decide whether to accept the duty within a year, preferably within one or two months, of the death. At the time of the application for probate or administration, the church court was to ask whether the deceased had goods valued at £5 in any other diocese within the province. If so, probate or administration was to be referred to the Archbishop of Canterbury's court. Where there was no executor named or the executor refused to act, and on intestacy, the *grant of administration* was to be made to the widow or next of kin. The executor or administrator had to appear in person before the church court to swear to administer the estate properly. A substitute could not swear in his or her place. If the person could not appear because of age or sickness or other good cause, a commission could be issued by the court to a cleric to administer the oath (Canons of the Church of England 1604 no. 132).

The fees payable to the church courts for granting probate or letters of administration were:[12]

(Oxford, 1971), p. 300–2). Even after the 1529 Act, some church courts charged more than the standard fees, see Robert Peters, *Oculus episcopi: administration in the Archdeaconry of St Albans 1580–1625* (Manchester, 1963), p. 80 for the fees charged in the Archdeaconry of St Albans.

6 Despite its title, the Executors' Act of the same year had little bearing on inventories as it dealt with power to sell land designated for sale in a will (21 Henry VIII c.4 An Act concerning Executors of laste Willes and Testamentes, *Statutes of the Realm*, vol. 3, p. 285).

7 William Lyndwood, *Provinciale Constitutions p[ro]uincialles, and of Otho, and Octhobone, translated in to Englyshe* (London, 1534).

8 Swinburne (1591). This was the standard textbook on wills running into seven editions during the next 200 years.

9 William West, *The first part of symboleography, which may bee termed The art or description of instruments and presidents* (London, 1598).

10 Constitutions and Canons Ecclesiastical of the Church of England 1604 no. 125 and 92 (https://www.anglican.net/doctrines/1604-canon-law/ viewed on 21 June 2020).

11 Thomas Wentworth, *The Office and Dutie of executors, or, A treatise of wills and executors, directed to testators in the choise of their executors and contrivance of their wills, with direction for Executors in the execution of their Office, according to the law …* (London, 1641) and later editions.

12 1529 Act; Lyndwood (1534), p. 42; Swinburne (1591) fol. 225–8; Wentworth (1641), p. 61.

- none for estates under £5, except 6d to the scribe 'for writing of the probate of the Testament' or for the 'commission of mynistration'. Church court officials could not refuse to grant probate;
- for estates valued between £5 and £40, the fee was 3s 6d, of which 2s 6d went to the church court officials and 1s to the scribe for registering the will;
- for estates valued at more than £40, the fee was 5s, of which 2s 6d went to the church court officials and 2s 6d to the scribe for registering the will or 1d per ten lines of 10 inches at the scribe's choice.

The detailed procedure for producing and exhibiting inventories can be identified as:

- an executor must *make or cause an inventory to be made*, prove the will, pay the testator's debts and legacies and make an account (and presumably an administrator also, although this is not specified);[13]
- a *surety (a bond)* could be taken for the true administration of the goods;[14]
- the church court officials could decide when an inventory was to be made and exhibited, 'so soon as conveniently may be after the parties death'[15] taking into account 'the distance of the place where the goodes remaine, being more or lesse, together with other circumstances'[16] and church courts were to be *held in convenient places* for those who were to attend and at times so that people could return home afterwards;[17]
- the executor or administrator had to *take an oath* to the truth of the inventory;[18]
- the executor or administrator was to appoint *two appraisers at least*[19] or *four appraisers or more*[20] from amongst the following groups of people, chosen in this order:
  - two at least of the decedent's creditors,
  - or two at least of the beneficiaries,
  - or in default, two other honest persons with preference to the next of kin. The provision in the Act of 'at least' was not repeated for this group
- the executor or administrator was *to make or have made* 'a true and perfect Inventory of all the goods, cattels, wares, merchandises, as well moveable as not moveable';[21]
- the inventory was to be made in the *appraisers' presence*;[22]
- a list of goods was not sufficient; it was to be *valued and priced* 'by some honest and skilfull persons, to be the just value thereof in their judgements and consciences, … at such price as the same may be solde for at that time';[23]

13 Swinburne (1591) fol. 217–18.
14 1529 Act; Swinburne (1591) fol. 225.
15 West, *Symboleography* (1592), section 707.
16 Swinburne (1591) fol. 219.
17 Canons of the Church of England, 1604.
18 1529 Act; Wentworth (1641), p. 62.
19 1529 Act; Swinburne (1591) fol. 219; Wentworth (1641), p. 62.
20 West, *Symboleography* (1592), section 707; later quoted in Cowell's *Interpreter* (1607), unpaged (John Cowell, *The Interpreter or booke containing the Signification of Words ... as are mentioned in the Law Writers of Statutes of this ... Kingdom ...* (Cambridge, 1607)).
21 1529 Act; Swinburne (1591) fol. 219.
22 1529 Act, Swinburne (1591) fol. 219; Wentworth (1641), p. 62.
23 Swinburne (1591) fol. 220r.

- the *order of the inventory* was as 'in ancient time' of moveables (household stuff, corn and cattle), immoveables (leases) and then debts due to the deceased;[24]
- the goods in the inventory were presumed to be *in the hands of the executor and to have belonged to the deceased*; no more goods were presumed to exist;[25]
- a creditor or beneficiary who claimed that more goods existed had to prove the claim;[26]
- the church court officials *could not refuse* to accept the inventory;[27]
- the inventory was to be *indented*, and one part taken by the executor or administrator to the church court officials, who were to keep it. The other part was to be kept by the executor or administrator;[28]
- if anyone *required a copy*, the church court officials were to provide it without delay on payment of the same fee as for registering the will or inventory;[29]
- an inventory was to *include*
  - 'goods, cattels, wares, merchandises, as well moveable as not moveable'[30]
  - moveable goods were spelled out as household stuff, corn on the ground, cattle and rights belonging or due to the deceased;[31]
  - immoveables such as leases of land or tenements.[32] (Swinburne noted that usually this requirement was observed and condemned the occasions when leases were omitted);
  - *debts due to* the deceased;[33]
  - the deceased's wife's jewellery, bed and bedding;[34]
- an inventory was to *exclude*
  - the value of land designated for sale in the will;[35]
  - the land, tenements and hereditaments and the appurtenances that belonged to the heir;[36]
  - grass and growing trees, items fixed to the freehold, land and tenements were not to be included because they belonged to the heir;[37]
  - glass and wainscot, because they belonged to the freehold, even if the lessee had paid for their installation and, by extension, anything else fixed to the house or ground;[38]

24 Swinburne (1591) fol. 220.
25 Swinburne (1591) fol. 220v–221r.
26 Swinburne (1591) fol. 220v–221r.
27 1529 Act; Swinburne (1591) fol. 220.
28 1529 Act; Swinburne (1591) fol. 219–220; Wentworth (1641), p. 62.
29 1529 Act; Swinburne (1591) fol. 227; Wentworth (1641), p. 62.
30 1529 Act; Swinburne (1591) fol. 218r.
31 Swinburne (1591) fol. 218r and v.
32 Swinburne (1591) fol. 218r.
33 Swinburne (1591) fol. 218.
34 Swinburne (1611) fol. 254.
35 1529 Act; Executors Act 1529 (*Statutes of the Realm*, vol. 3, pp. 285–8); Swinburne (1591) fol. 218v; Wentworth (1641), p. 62.
36 Swinburne (1591); Wentworth (1641), p. 62.
37 Swinburne (1591) fol. 218.
38 Swinburne (1611) fol. 253.

- the deeds of the property and the box in which they were kept; fish in ponds and doves in dovecotes;[39]
- the deceased's wife's 'convenient apparrell, agreeable to her degree' although other items she brought to the marriage and her jewels etc. became her husband's and should be listed in his inventory;[40]
- *debts owed by* the deceased. If they were included, the church court officials ought to investigate them. The provision to exclude his debts was aimed at preventing a record of false obligations and was part of the concern that executors could defraud the widow and children;[41]

• officials dealing with probate might 'convent' the executors and administrators to bring inventories in all other respects as before the Act was made (i.e. that other pre-1529 probate and inventory rules were to continue).[42]

West's *Symboleography*, 1592 includes a 'precedent for an inventory' which is quoted here in full, as it is the model for so many of the inventories in this volume:[43]

> AN Inventorie is a description or Repertorie orderly made of all dead mens goods and chattels prized by fower credible men, or more, which every Executor and Administrator ought to exhibite to the Ordinarie, at such time as he shall appoint the same. And Inventaries ought to be made so soone as conveniently may be after the parties death, least the goods be imbesiled, and for the most part they are made thus:
>
> The Inventarie of the goods and cattels of A. B. of D. in the Countie of C. yeoman deceased, made and prooved by C. D., E. F., G. H. and I. K. the second day of May, in the xxxvi yeere of the raigne of our Soveraigne Queene Elizabeth &c 1592.
>
> - *Inprimis*, in ready Money x £
> - His Apparell xl[s]
> - Item in his bed Chamber two standing beds with testors iiii £
> - Item fower Fetherbeds, and one downe bed x £
> - Item fowerteene Blankets xxx[s]
> - Item eight paire of Sheetes xl[s]
> - Item sixe Coverlets, and two Coverings vii £
>
> In like maner every thing, as woollen, linnen, wine, oyle, beere, ale, corne, and graine, hey, wooll, flaxe, wood, coales, iron, lead, houshold stuffe of all sortes: as tables, hangings, chaires, cushions, chestes, pots, pannes, pewter vessell, brewing vessels, implements of husbandrie, leases, debts due to the dead man, or by him due to any other, corne vpon the ground, horses, oxen, kine, sheepe, swine, pullen &c. And for the houshold stuffe either to set downe what is in every severall roome: as every parler, chamber, studie, shop, buttery, seller, panterie, hall, deirie, kitchyn, brewhouse, backhouse, laundrie, barne, stable, oxehouse, cowhouse, doovehouse, slaughterhouse, milkehouse, and every other house. Or els (which seemeth better) to sort all thinges of one kind together: as all brasse together, all pewer, together, all bedding together &c. prising every thing severally by it selfe. And then to subscribe the same Inventarie with the names of the same praisers, in

39 Swinburne (1611) fol. 253.

40 Swinburne (1611) fol. 253–4.

41 Swinburne (1591) fol. 218v.

42 1529 Act.

43 West, *Symboleography* (1592) section 707. To make it more readable, the text has been slightly amended by substituting *v* for *u* and *£* for *l*, deleting some full stops and inserting some commas.

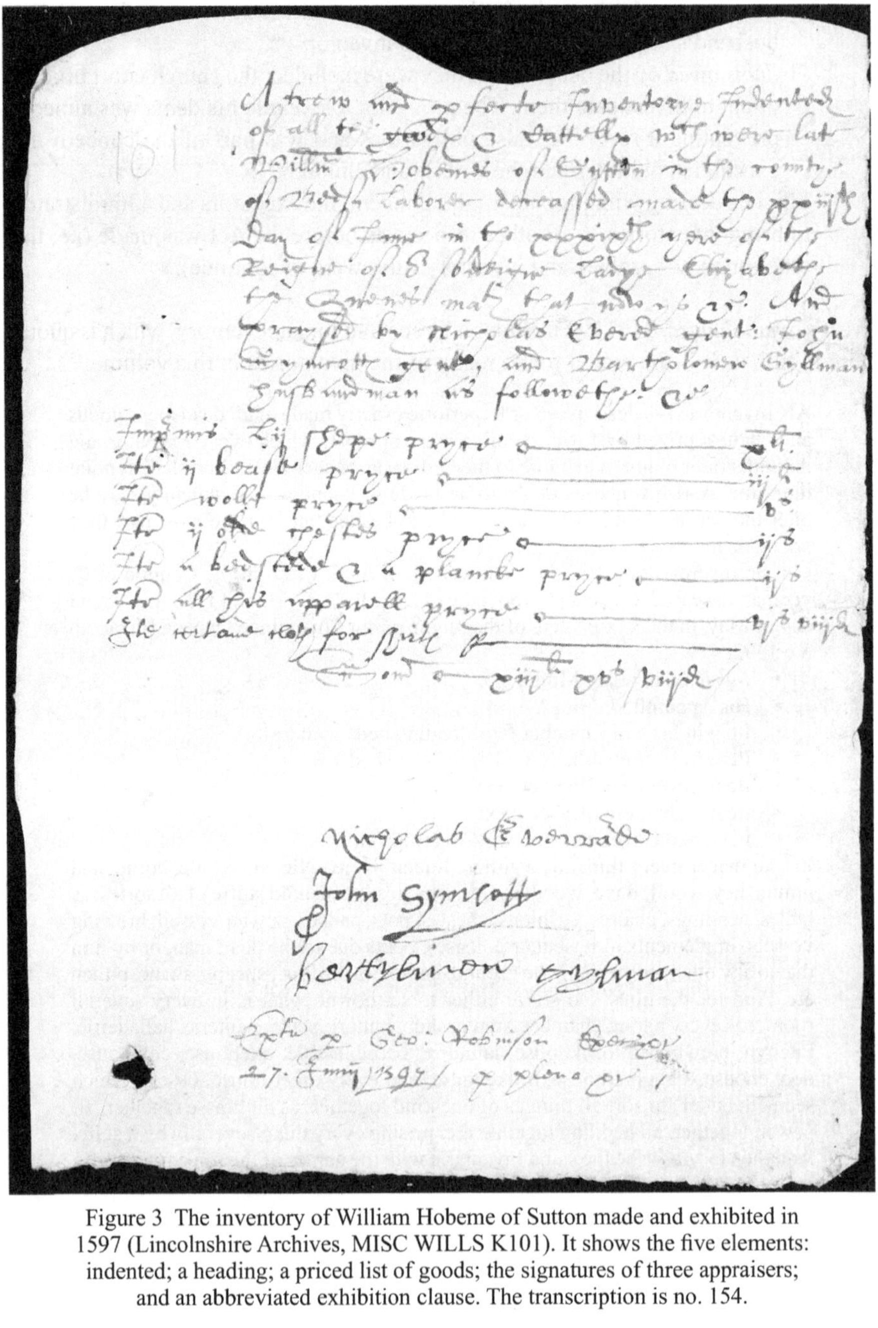

Figure 3 The inventory of William Hobeme of Sutton made and exhibited in 1597 (Lincolnshire Archives, MISC WILLS K101). It shows the five elements: indented; a heading; a priced list of goods; the signatures of three appraisers; and an abbreviated exhibition clause. The transcription is no. 154.

> the presence of sufficient witnesses. And this ought to be done with great diligence, care, and sinceritie, that the true value of every thing may be knowen, to the end that the mans children or kinsfolkes, his legatories and creditors may have their owne, without such fraudulent concealing, as in like cases is daily committed.
>
> Per nos A. B., C. D., E. F., G. H.

Although there are some differences among these sources, the procedure for preparing and exhibiting inventories is clear. The main variations are that the 1529 Act, Swinburne and Wentworth specified two appraisers and West, four or more; and that West recommended that the inventory listed goods by type rather than their location in the house and other buildings. There was no direction that an inventory was to be exhibited at the same time as the grant of probate or administration nor was a time frame for taking it laid down. However the practical requirements (probate or administration being obtained before dealing with the estate; church court officials enquiring into the value of goods in another diocese; and making an inventory before administering the estate) makes simultaneous probate and exhibiting the most convenient and usual arrangement.

Well before West was writing there was a recognised layout for an inventory with several well-established elements:

- a formal heading identifying the document as an inventory, giving the name, place of residence and occupation or status of the decedent, the date the inventory was taken and the names of the appraisers (the second paragraph of West's precedent beginning 'The Inventarie of the goods and cattels');
- the body of the inventory listed the goods with their valuations and the total value;
- the signatures or marks of the appraisers;
- an exhibition clause added by the church court officials.

The inventory was frequently indented, that is written twice on the same sheet of paper, then separated with a wavy cut so that the two parts could be fitted together again to confirm the authenticity of the two parts, one being kept by the church court and the other by the executor or administrator.

How the procedures worked in practice in Bedfordshire is demonstrated by the inventories in this volume and the wills and other documents referred to in the notes following them.

Appendix 3

Alphabetical list of Bedfordshire inventories published in this volume and in BHRS volumes 20 and 32

Column 1 Published: Simple numbers, e.g. 272, refer to the inventory number in this volume. Compound numbers, e.g. 20/133 and 32/14, refer to inventory numbers in BHRS vols 20 or 32.

Column 6 Year: This is the year in which the inventory was made (New Style).

Column 7 Value: For inventories in this volume, the values are as they appear in the inventories (or corrected where the addition was wrong) or as it was recorded in the grant of probate or supplied by the editor where they were not totalled. For inventories in BHRS vols 20 and 32, the value is as given in the volume. Values in square brackets are minimum, where damage precludes a reliable total, or where dubious.

Published	First name	Surname	Place	Occupation	Year	Value
272	John	ABBICE	Bedford		1614	£12–01–02
20/133	Richard	ABBOTT	Chellington		1619	£46–11–08
20/94	Daniel	ABBOTTS	Bletsoe	labourer	1619	£16–03–04
209	Thomas	ABRAHAM als BOLNEST	Potton	maltster	1610	£81–04–00
235	George	ADAMS	Luton	yeoman	1611	£192–03–02
302	Hugh	ALBRITE	Dunstable	tailor	1618	£81–09–00
309	Thomas	ALEN	Bedford St Mary		c.1620	£2–12–07
20/49	Richard	ALLCOCKE	Bolnhurst	husbandman	1619	£577–08–08
20/148	Henry	ALLINGHAM	Tilbrook	husbandman	1619	£84–06–00
277	William	ALLYN	Sandy	yeoman	1614	£216–00–00
43	William	AMERYE	Biddenham		c.1568	£9–04–00

Published	First name	Surname	Place	Occupation	Year	Value
20/19	John	AMIAS	Southill	husbandman	1620	£194–12–08
80	Thomas	ANDROW	Luton	maltman	c.1577	£54–01–08
409	Elizabeth	ANGLESEY	Keysoe	widow	1631	£92–13–08
20/40	William	ARCHER	Lidlington	yeoman	1620	£175–13–08
20/20	William	ARDON	Pavenham	freemason	1620	£20–02–00
136	Thomas	ARROWSMITH	Elstow		1593	£1–05–00
20/162	Edward	ASHBY	Luton	weaver	1619	£28–19–00
20/56	Francis	ASHBY	Goldington		1619	£16–10–00
255	William	ASMOND	Turvey	husbandman	1612	£34–07–00
308	Oliver	ASPLAND	Bletsoe	miller	1620	£32–13–04
20/67	Stephen	AUCOKE	Eaton Socon, Duloe	labourer	1619	£27–14–08
200	Alice	AUSTIN	Potton	widow	1610	£14–14–08
318	Robert	AUSTIN	Tilsworth	husbandman	1621	£88–03–08
385	Robert	AUSTIN	Potton	barber	1626	£126–08–06
249	John	AYNSWORTH	Potton		1611	£4–00–00
3	Elizabeth	BACON	Goldington	widow	1552	£7–09–00
125	Thomas	BAIE	Tempsford	yeoman	1590	£98–09–00
179	Anthony	BALLARDE	Elstow	yeoman	1607	£68–15–06
23	Thomas	BAMFORD	Blunham		1560	£24–15–08
20/35	Robert	BARACLE	Upper Gravenhurst		1620	£8–03–02
368	Abraham	BARBER	Pulloxhill?	yeoman	1625	[£29–13–04]
20/81	Bartholomew	BARBER als ENTERDEWCE	Kempston	butcher	1617	£46–16–08
153	William	BARCOCK	Little Staughton	husbandman	1597	£113–06–04
20/99	Richard	BARKER/BAKER	Felmersham, Radwell		1618	£30–11–02

Published	First name	Surname	Place	Occupation	Year	Value
373	Jane	BARNET	Stotfold	widow	1625	£4–03–00
399	William	BARRE	Tempsford	butcher	1631	[£30–05–00]
20/143	Ralph	BATE	Flitwick	vicar	1619	£6–18–10
424	Michael	BEAMENT	Wrestlingworth	yeoman	1651	£279–10–08
188	Joan	BEAMOND	Pulloxhill	widow	1608	£34–02–00
20/5	Thomas	BEARD als FARMER	Sutton	gentleman	1617	£237–10–06
20/153	John	BECHE	Bedford	glover	1619	£21–03–04
83	Jone	BEDCOTE	Lidlington	widow	c.1577	£8–04–04
334	John	BELLAMIE	Chalgrave	vicar	1622	£55–05–00
77	Edward	BENET	Riseley	yeoman	c.1572	£101–13–04
112	Thomas	BENET	Bolnhurst		c.1587	£93–11–03
177	Christopher	BENNET	Cardington, Cotton End	yeoman	1605	£121–03–08
369	William	BENNITT	Potton	shoemaker	c.1625	£77–03–04
32	William	BESOWTHE	Studham	husbandman	1563	£29–03–04
257	William	BEYSTON	Bletsoe	yeoman	1612	£92–06–08
20/113	John	BLYTH	Bolnhurst	yeoman	1619	£9–13–02
95	Richard	BLYTHE	Eaton Socon, Begwary	yeoman	1580	£75–03–00
197	William	BRACE	Millbrook	yeoman	1610	
178	John	BREWTYE	Sutton	yeoman	1605	£36–14–00
34	John	BRIMSALL	Sandy, Girtford		1563	£40–17–10
149	Raphe	BRITEN	Sutton	yeoman, servant	1595	£4–07–10
363	John	BRITTAN	Flitton, Silsoe	husbandman	1625	£30–19–07
20/59	Warine	BRITTINE	Blunham	labourer	1619	£8–06–04
20/103	John	BROUNE	Bedford		1619	

Published	First name	Surname	Place	Occupation	Year	Value
275	Edward	BROWNE	Stotfold		1614	£31–09–00
20/58	John	BROWNE	Bedford St Paul	mason	1620	£19–12–08
4	Thomas	BROWNE	Leighton Buzzard	shoemaker	1552	£7–03–00
20/166	William	BROWNE	Melchbourne		1619	£254–10–06
170	Nicholas	BRYDE	Tempsford		1601	£9–19–04
38	William	BRYTAYNE	Blunham		1566	£20–02–00
128	Nicholas	BUCHER als SIBTHORPE	Felmersham	labourer	1591	£4–11–09
227	George	BUCKE	Luton, Leagrave	glover	1611	£10–05–10
167	Edward	BULL	Riseley	ploughwright	1601	£149–19–00
130	John	BULL	Riseley	ploughwright	1591	£50–10–00
20/160	Nicholas	BULL	Cardington, Cotton End	husbandman	1618	£43–18–00
240	William	BULL	Dunstable	labourer	1611	£21–05–04
20/108	Edward	BULMER	Ravensden	husbandman	1619	£183–06–02
68	Simon	BULMER	Riseley		1574	£25–05–00
404	William	BUNDEY	Roxton, Chawston	yeoman	1631	[£88–10–10]
285	Oliver	BUNKER	Tingrith	husbandman	1616	£119–14–08
208	Rodger	BURDEN	Silsoe, Flitton	fletcher	1610	£80–03–10
20/53	William	BURDEN	Silsoe	yeoman	1619	£513–03–06
185	Richard	BURDSEY	Dunstable	turner	1607	£6–15–07
44	William	BURELL	Chellington		1569	£5–03–02
20/9	Thomas	BURGER	Cardington, Fenlake	carpenter	1620	£3–19–02
228	Thomas	BURTHOLL	Luton, Stopsley		1611	£21–16–00
281	Thomas	BURTON	Felmersham		1615	£85–16–08
20/132	George	BUTTON	Maulden	gentleman	1619	£27–02–00

Published	First name	Surname	Place	Occupation	Year	Value
416	Alice	CADWELL	Everton	widow	1637	£12–01–00
20/117	Nicholas	CANON	Barford	labourer	1619	£27–03–08
56	Robert	CAPON	Bedford St Paul		1571	£9–08–06
17	John	CARTAR	Wootton		1558	£12–10–09
221	Mathew	CARTAR	Shillington	yeoman	1611	£25–13–04
20/105	John	CARTE	Studham, Markyate	wheelwright	1619	£8–01–04
20/101	Michael	CARTEIR	Houghton Conquest		1619	£17–19–04
425	Susan & Thomas	CARTER	Bedford St Paul	widow; glover	1652	£22–18–02
20/91	Thomas	CARTER	Studham, Markyate		1619	£31–06–00
111	Robert	CARTERE	Northill		1585	£12–11–10
79	Thomas	CATER	Sandy		1574	£165–07–06
260	Edward	CATHERALL	Luton	brewer	1613	£537–11–10
20/95	William	CATLINE			1619	£22–07–04
243	Ellen	CAWNE	Wilshamstead	widow	1611	£36–04–08
20/77	Joan	CHALKELEY	Luton	widow	1619	£12–09–00
359	John	CHAMBERLAYNE	Bedford St Paul		1625	£8–00–00
214	William	CHAMBERS	Potton	yeoman	1610	£426–10–07
213	Nicholas	CHAPPELL	Flitton, Wrest	yeoman	1610	£60–05–02
160	Thomas	CHARGE	Toddington	labourer	1598	£7–12–04
175	Elizabeth	CHILD	Roxton	widow	1604	£134–12–08
292	Robert	CLAPHAM	Tilbrook	rector	1617	£142–16–04
20/137	Christopher	CLARE	Riseley		1619	£6–09–08
192	Grace	CLARKE	Potton	widow	1608	£50–12–04
20/51	John	CLARKE	Pulloxhill		1620	£81–13–00

Published	First name	Surname	Place	Occupation	Year	Value
276	Katherine	CLARKE	Stotfold	widow	1614	£13–19–02
20/26	Peter	CLARKE	Marston Moretaine		1620	£322–11–04
20/69	William	CLARKE	Goldington		1619	£11–15–04
20/97	Barnaby	CLARKE als THOMASIN	Wrestlingworth	yeoman	1619	£114–08–08
375	John	COCKINE	Westoning	husbandman	1625	£13–19–00
64	John	COLBECK	Tempsford	gentleman	1573	£136–10–02
152	John	COLBECKE	Tempsford	gentleman	1596	£177–12–04
20/52	John	COLLENS	Husborne Crawley	yeoman	1620	£239–15–10
20/104	Mary	COLLIN[S]	Elstow		1619	£2–14–02
25	William	COLMANE	Shillington	maltman	1560	£28–15–00
91	Henry	COMES	Stagsden		c.1580	£62–06–04
131	Alice	COOKE	Eaton Bray	widow	1591	£11–02–08
20/116	Luke	COOKE	Bedford	malt miller	1619	£10–18–00
20/65	Roger	COOKE	Cranfield		1619	£9–03–04
20/88	Thomas	COOKE	Elstow	yeoman	1619	£31–19–00
336	John	COOPER	Tempsford	husbandman	c.1622	£110–04–01
206	Francis	COPER	Potton		1610	£8–00–04
258	William	COSTE	Marston Moretaine, Pillinge	labourer	1612	£5–18–04
20/13	Richard	COVINGTON	Pavenham		1620	£6–15–08
69	John	COWPER	Willington		1574	£53–18–00
2	Robert	COWPER	Cardington, Harrowden	husbandman	1552	£34–14–08
426	Stephen	COX	Kempston	weaver	1654	£88–06–00
391	John	COXE	Stagsden	yeoman	1628	£63–12–10
172	Thomas	COXE	Eaton Socon	labourer	1603	£110–03–02

Published	First name	Surname	Place	Occupation	Year	Value
301	Thomas	CRABTREE	Potton	vicar	1618	£260–13–04
396	Thomas	CRANFILD	Tempsford		1631	£28–15–02
20/130	Edward	CRASH als BAXTER	Bedford	baker	1619	£46–03–08
107	Richard	CRAWLEY	Luton, Otebridge	yeoman	1583	£171–15–10
20/87	William	CRIPSEE als BARNERDE			1619	£56–00–00
395	Christopher	CROUCH	Potton	innholder	1630	£174–07–00
32/14	Ralph	CULCHETH	Stevington	minister	1589	£13–18–11
20/76	John	CUMBERLAND	Northill, Caldecote		1619	£421–19–04
429	Thomas	CURFEY	Lidlington	labourer	1657	£19–15–08
20/12	John	CURTIS	Dean	husbandman	1620	£53–04–08
204	John	DALINGTON	Tempsford	husbandman	1610	£168–01–10
63	Thomas	DARLYNG	Bletsoe		1573	£42–11–10
32/6	Robert	DAVE/DAUE	Little Staughton		1587	£1–17–04
274	William	DAVYE	Dunstable	maltster	1614	£4–17–08½
20/66	John	DAWES	Chellington	labourer	1619	£18–01–10
20/32	John	DAWESWORTH	Bedford St Mary		1620	£15–13–04
264	Alice	DAY	Tilbrook	widow	1614	£17–18–04
31	William	DECONS	Wilshamstead		1562	[£51–01–08]
360	Simon	DICKENSON	Leighton Buzzard	miller	1625	£41–19–00
270	George	DICKERMAN	Marston Moretaine	cook	1614	£147–05–06
138	Henry	DILLINGHAM	Shelton		1593	£264–09–08
173	John	DILLINGHAM	Dean	yeoman	1604	£281–14–04
349	Francis	DILLYNGHAM	Wilden	clerk, rector	1625	£490–14–04
71	William	DOE	Cranfield		1574	£41–01–02

Published	First name	Surname	Place	Occupation	Year	Value
261	Abraham	DOGGAT	Bedford		1613	£45–11–04
313	Helen	DRAWSWORTH	Bedford St Mary	widow	c.1620	£3–15–00
176	James	DUCKINGTON	Dunstable	innholder	1604	£302–12–04
20/102	Richard	DURDENT	Eyeworth		1619	£113–05–10
381	John	DURRANT	Cockayne Hatley	rector	1625	£177–16–00
219	Richard	DYER	Luton, Stopsley	labourer	1611	£14–10–00
203	Richard	EBBES	Sandy		1610	£35–09–00
12	Thomas	EBETT	Pertenhall		1558	£16–12–10
324	William	EDWARDES	Dean, Nether Dean		1622	£94–04–04
20/63	George	EDWARDS	Wilshamstead, Cotton End	yeoman	1619	£68–06–04
30	John	EDWARDS	Carlton		1561	£16–00–04
11	Thomas	EDWARDS	Turvey		1557	£138–12–02
32/10	Thomas	EDWARDS	Bedford		1588	£6–15–00
419	Edward	EDWYN	Dunstable	maltster	1641	[£345–12–02]
191	John	ELLIS	Souldrop	tailor	1608	£6–17–00
55	George	ELLYS	Sandy		1571	£44–06–01
242	Thomas	ELMAR	Shillington	yeoman	1611	£38–07–08
20/109	Robert	ELMER	Shillington		1619	£67–09–06
20/36	John	ENSAME als BORROWE	Haynes		1620	£652–09–04
316	Gilyon	ENTERDWSE	Kempston		1621	£40–06–00
20/152	Henry	ETHERIDGE	Flitwick	husbandman	1619	£178–19–00
105	William	ETHROPE	Sandy		1583	£25–03–00
347	Johan	EVERETT	Sandy	widow	1624	£29–02–04
20/114	John	FANNE	Wilshamstead	singleman	1619	£59–10–01

Published	First name	Surname	Place	Occupation	Year	Value
36	Thomas	FARRE	Henlow		1564	[£216–01–02]
376	George	FARYE	Toddington	cordwainer	1625	£186–07–08
20/43	Ellen	FEILD	Luton	widow	1620	£16–08–04
190	Lucy	FEILD	Shefford	widow	1608	£89–13–10
320	Robert	FEILD	Studham	yeoman	1621	£332–16–08
202	Elizabeth	FIELD	Luton	widow	1610	£53–10–08
187	Robert	FISH	Riseley	husbandman	1608	£30–16–00
427	Ann	FISHER	Carlton	widow	1655	£213–00–08
20/27	Ralph	FISHER	Goldington	yeoman	1620	£15–04–00
20/47	Richard	FISHER	Milton Ernest	yeoman	1619	£74–06–10
162	Gerrard	FITTESGEFFREIE	Ravensden	gentleman	1598	£181–19–00
282	Edward	FLETCHAR	Houghton Regis		1616	£4–08–08
216	Walter	FOREST	Sutton		1611	£40–18–06
18	Richard	FORTUNE	Henlow		1558	£22–05–06
189	George	FOSSEY	Houghton Regis, Bidwell	husbandman	1608	£36–15–04
352	Henry	FOSTER	Thurleigh	yeoman	1625	£123–04–08
383	William	FOXCROFT	Bedford St Cuthbert	rector	1625	£20–09–04
315	John	FRANCKE	Eaton Socon, Wyboston	husbandman	1621	£67–11–00
65	Thomas	FRANCKELYN	Marston Moretaine		c.1574	£123–00–00
293	Bridgete	FRANCKLIN	Potton	widow	1617	£5–04–00
306	George	FRANCKLIN	Bolnhurst	esquire	1618	£4471–15–03
100	John	FRANCKLYN	Thurleigh		1581	£86–14–04
32/4	Robert	FRANKLIN	Marston Moretaine		1587	£8–10–00
210	Edward	FREEMAN	Stotfold	gentleman	1610	£411–02–06

Published	First name	Surname	Place	Occupation	Year	Value
39	John	FREMAN	Dean, Nether Dean		1566	£42–03–00
300	Edward	FREMANE	Stotfold	gentleman	1618	£706–03–04
328	Samuel	FULKE	Barton	rector	1622	£244–10–00
26	John	FYSHER	Tempsford	husbandman	1560	£45–12–06
46	Nicolas	FYSSHER	Blunham, Moggerhanger		1569	£34–10–08
414	George	GALE	Husborne Crawley	yeoman	1635	£71–12–08
126	Henry	GALE	Knotting; Southoe, Hunts	labourer	1591	£6–09–06
223	John	GALE	Oakley	husbandman	1611	£16–15–08
20/50	Robert	GALE	Oakley		1620	£148–12–08
284	Nicholas	GALLIGAN	Cople		1616	£5–10–01
237	John	GARDENER	Barford	singleman	1611	£9–02–08
32/7	Matthew	GARDNER	Blunham	husbandman	1587	£18–11–08
321	Nicholas	GATES	Dunstable	weaver	1621	£17–00–04
289	Margaret	GAYTON	Cople	widow	1616	£6–13–03
340	Laurence	GERIE	Potton; Gt Stukeley, Hunts		1623	[£19–02–06]
165	John	GIBBES	Eversholt	yeoman	1598	£198–16–00
20/147	John	GIGGELL	Meppershall		1619	£8–08–00
66	Thomas	GILLION	Riseley		c.1574	£27–03–04
20/16	Edward	GLOVER	Bedford St Cuthbert		1620	£1–02–04
133	Francis	GODFREYE	Sandy, Girtford		1592	£101–14–00
194	Thomas	GOLDSMITH	Eaton [?Socon]	shepherd	1609	£4–00–03
32/11	Robert	GOODDYE	Kempston		1588	£4–18–04
10	Thomas	GOODES	Luton		1557	£5–04–06
20/83	John	GOODIN	Flitton, Greenfield	yeoman	1619	£25–15–00

Published	First name	Surname	Place	Occupation	Year	Value
137	Edward	GOODWYN	Clifton		1593	£38–00–00
417	Alice	GOODY	Goldington		1638	£16–13–06
386	William	GORE	Swineshead		1626	£26–02–08
32/1	Robert	GOSTWICK	Old Warden		c.1562	£12–06–04
41	Jarratt	GRANTT	Eyeworth		1566	£36–11–08
40	Thomas	GRAY	Blunham, Moggerhanger		1566	£26–08–08
49	William	GRAY als BUTLER	Langford		1569	£5–12–02
20/126	Richard	GREEN	Dunton		1619	£28–06–00
108	William	GREENE	Langford		1583	£36–14–10
356	William	GREENE	Husborne Crawley	weaver	1625	£39–13–02
146	Ambrose	GREGORYE	Eversholt	yeoman	1594	£64–02–02
357	Thomas	GRENE	Bedford St Paul	baker	1625	£99–18–08
157	Thomas	GRENHEFFE	Blunham		1597	£173–13–08
114	William	GREY	Eaton Socon	husbandman	1587	[£36–06–09]
20/30	Nicholas	GROOME	Chalgrave, Wingfield	labourer	1620	£43–11–08
20/119	Lawrence	GRYMSON	Shefford		1619	£9–03–04
390	John	GURRIE	Swineshead	husbandman	1627	£59–02–08
410	John	GYBSON	Swineshead		1633	£47–04–06
59	John	GYLLAT	Eaton Socon, Staploe		c.1571	£16–07–08
269	John	HALL	Caddington	labourer	1614	£1–05–06
20/64	John	HALL	Potton	baker	1619	£225–04–00
325	Richard	HALL	Pertenhall	labourer	1622	£22–03–04
186	Henry	HALSEY als CHAMBER	Caddington, Cantlow	yeoman	1608	£94–06–08
20/46	Thomas	HAMMOND	Cardington	shepherd	1620	£5–10–00

Published	First name	Surname	Place	Occupation	Year	Value
370	William	HAMMOND	Shillington	weaver	1625	£74–17–02
247	Agnes	HANCOCKE	Blunham, Moggerhanger	widow	1611	£6–19–04
246	Richard	HANCOCKE	Blunham		1611	£14–04–04
53	Robert	HANGER	Souldrop		1571	£23–10–00
374	Robert	HANSCOMBE	Meppershall	yeoman	1625	£797–16–08
20/37	William	HARBERDE	Eaton Bray	freemason	1620	£112–02–04
365	Thomas	HARBERT	Leighton Buzzard	butcher	1625	£154–04–04
291	John	HARDEN	Dunton		1617	£32–18–02
420	John	HARDING	Henlow		1643	£22–00–04
329	William	HARDINGE	Eaton Bray	ploughwright	1622	£13–14–02
72	Edmund	HARE	Houghton Conquest		1574	£21–09–08
169	Thomas	HARPER	Bedford St Peter Merton	servant	1601	£37–07–01
263	Hugh	HARRIS	Studham, Markyate Street	yeoman	1613	£56–08–02
32/9	Richard	HART	Edworth		1588	£4–07–04
20/158	Joan	HARTE	Elstow	widow	1619	£2–17–06
245	Leonard	HARWOOD	Little Staughton	servant, bachelor	1611	£7–16–04
20/154	Henry	HASTER	Bromham	shepherd	1619	£34–04–06
60	Richard	HAWKINS	Houghton Regis, Thorne		1571	£99–07–06
332	Anthony	HAWKYNES	Houghton Regis		1622	£101–03–04
384	Thomas	HAWKYNES	Houghton Regis	yeoman	1625	£44–00–02
76	Edward	HAWTON	Bedford	tailor	1574	£13–15–06
20/146	Richard	HAYNES	Bolnhurst	labourer	1619	£24–11–06
218	William	HAYNES	Sutton		1611	£10–11–10
432	Joan	HEWETT	Knotting	widow	1659	£17–00–00

Published	First name	Surname	Place	Occupation	Year	Value
132	Joane	HEWETT	Melchbourne	widow	c.1591	£31–17–00
22	Richard	HEWETT	Melchbourne	husbandman	1559	£25–04–10
20/155	Robert	HILL	Clophill	shoemaker	1619	£99–17–08
87	Thomas	HILL	Chicksands		1577	£91–00–00
20/78	Thomas	HILL	Lidlington		1619	£164–16–04
335	William	HINDE	Cardington	singleman	1622	£4–02–02
154	William	HOBEME	Sutton	labourer	1597	£13–15–08
330	John	HODDLE	Elstow	yeoman	1622	£80–09–10
20/34	Thomas	HODLE	Renhold	husbandman	1620	£102–19–04
67	William	HOGE	Souldrop		1574	£16–15–09
351	John	HOLLOWAY	Cople	husbandman	1625	£24–13–10
180	John	HOPHAM	Felmersham, Radwell End	husbandman	1607	£31–05–08
195	Alexander	HOPKINS	Wrestlingworth		1609	£24–10–06
211	John	HORNE	Whipsnade	husbandman	1610	£103–16–08
338	Miles	HORNE	Whipsnade		1622	£19–12–10
379	Phoebe	HORNE	Houghton Regis	widow	1625	£22–00–00
103	Thomas	HORNE	Kempston		c.1583	£11–15–04
98	John	HORSLEYE	Campton, Shefford		1580	£52–06–10
350	Peter	HUNNILOVE	Bedford	tailor	1625	£32–10–00
254	Alice	HUNT	Southill, Stanford	widow	1612	£53–15–00
57	Agnes	HURST	Henlow		1571	£26–06–08
251	Henry	INGRAM	Blunham	labourer	1611	£6–06–04
143	Raynold	IRELAND	Wilshamstead	labourer	1594	£71–09–08
5	William	IRELAND	Milton Ernest	miller	1555	£30–04–03

Published	First name	Surname	Place	Occupation	Year	Value
20/14	Joane	JACKSON	Bedford St Paul	widow	1620	£2–00–00
20/120	Richard	JACKSONNE	Ridgmont	husbandman	1619	£50–13–10
32/5	William	JARVIS	Eaton Socon, Begwary		1587	£76–09–00
366	William	JEAYSE	Colmworth	husbandman	1625	£176–08–00
20/138	John	JEYES	Cardington	labourer	1619	£23–01–10
222	William	JOHNSON	Cranfield, Bornend	husbandman	1611	£83–10–10
236	Edward	JONES	Luton	dyer	1611	£33–00–10
405	Robert	JONES	Steppingley	gentleman	1631	£45–15–04
20/140	William	JUDGGE	Cranfield	labourer	1619	£6–14–00
297	Robert	JUGGINS	Cranfield		1617	£126–14–00
20/55	Robert	KEFFORD	Sandy		1619	£38–17–05
283	Edward	KELKE	Cople	tailor	1616	£4–18–04
431	Thomas	KENT	Pulloxhill	yeoman	1657	
19	William	KENTT	Felmersham	husbandman	c.1558	£9–04–00
408	John	KEPPEST	Eaton Socon		1631	£4–08–06
97	William	KERBEY	Bedford	butcher	1580	£15–00–00
401	Elizabeth	KIDGELL	Eaton Bray	singlewoman	1631	£15–13–04
333	John	KILLINGWORTH	Wilshamstead	yeoman	1622	£38–15–04
20/18	John	KING	Ravensden	carpenter	1620	£78–10–08
397	Evans	KINGE	Stotfold		1631	£36–15–08
20/25	John	KINGE	Blunham	husbandman	1620	£163–16–08
20/107	Robert	KINGE	Shelton	husbandman	1619	£216–06–00
287	William	KIPPEST	Northill	gentleman	1616	£568–08–04
81	George	KNIGHT	Wilden		1576	£12–09–00

Published	First name	Surname	Place	Occupation	Year	Value
183	William	KNIGHT	Colmworth		1607	£56–09–04
20/74	Dorothy	KYNG	Bromham	widow	1619	£25–00–06
62	Margery	KYNGE	Pulloxhill	widow	1573	£16–11–00
48	William	KYNGE	Wrestlingworth		1569	£35–04–00
110	John	KYPPIS	Eaton Socon, Duloe		1585	£41–17–00
150	Richard	KYRCKE	Potton	labourer	1596	£4–03–08
20/48	Margaret	LAINE	Biddenham	widow	1620	£26–19–00
20/17	John	LAMBERT	Bedford St Peter		1620	£6–03–02
82	William	LAMBERT	Stagsden		c.1577	£37–00–00
20/106	Thomas	LANDER	Barton	weaver	1619	£39–08–06
8	Christopher	LANGDON	Henlow		c.1557	£11–17–02
20/84	John	LANGLEY	Sandy	weaver	1619	£33–19–02
89	Gilbert	LAPIDGE	Southill		1579	£14–03–02
298	Henry	LARGE	Everton		1617	£22–09–04
78	Peter	LARKYN	Sandy		1574	£7–09–02
139	Henry	LATTIMER	Riseley		1594	£6–09–00
32/13	Robert	LEAY	Flitwick	servant	1588	£3–08–05
20/22	Robert	LENTON	Southill	yeoman	1620	£20–14–08
422	Phinees	LEVERIDGE	Swineshead		1647	£43–17–08
20/31	John	LEWES	Bedford St Paul		1620	£16–16–00
20/44	William	LINGERD	Lidlington	husbandman	1620	£35–18–08
344	Henry	LINNIS	Meppershall	tailor	1624	£11–03–00
230	Edward	LOCKKEY	Bedford St John		1611	£59–07–08
20/156	Ann	LONG	Chalton (Blunham or Toddington?)		1618	£98–05–00

Published	First name	Surname	Place	Occupation	Year	Value
337	Nicholas	LUKE	Eaton Socon, Begwary	esquire	1622	£49–09–00
181	Oliver	LUKE	Eaton Socon, Begwary	gentleman	1607	£494–10–00
20/110	Thomas	LUNS	Cranfield		1619	£34–04–02
20/10	Andrew	LYCET	Millbrook	labourer	1620	£1–05–00
145	Oliver	LYNFORDE	Bromham		1594	£70–00–10
20/15	Thomas	MAN	Willington	labourer	1620	£4–00–00
15	John	MANNYNG	Flitton		1558	£7–04–00
279	John	MANTON	Willington		1615	£33–18–08
266	Humfrey	MARGATE	Wrestlingworth	servant	1614	£1–05–04
388	Lucy	MARSHALL	Everton	widow	1627	£112–17–00
250	Francis	MARSHE	Eaton Bray	gentleman	1611	£273–17–08
296	Henry	MARSHE			1617	£15–04–00
174	Richard	MARTIN	Caddington	blacksmith	1604	£12–01–06
280	Thomas	MASON	Souldrop	rector	1615	£126–06–08
20/61	William	MASON	Willington	husbandman	1620	£36–00–04
20/165	William	MASON	Bedford St John	tailor	1620	£19–15–02
305	Simonde	MASSANE	Everton		1618	£33–05–04
116	Walter	MAYE	Potton		c.1587	£24–03–10
86	Joan	MAYES	Everton	widow	1577	£24–00–04
20/4	John	MAYES	Sandy		1617	£15–07–08
199	Robert	MAYES	Sandy		1610	£246–10–09
99	Thomas	MAYNERD	Wootton		1580	£28–13–00
378	Thomas	MEANORD	Bedford	bachelor	1625	£8–06–00
267	Humfrey	MEE	Shelton	carpenter	1614	£259–05–00

Published	First name	Surname	Place	Occupation	Year	Value
380	Henry	MERRILL	Cople	labourer	1625	£2–16–04
288	Walter	MERRILL	Cople	carpenter	1616	£16–11–04
229	Thomas	MILLER	Potton	carpenter	1611	£6–08–08
20/135	Thomas	MILLWARD	Bletsoe	yeoman	1619	£192–16–06
20/38	James	MILLWARD als SMYTH	Cardington	labourer, singleman	1620	£50–10–03
20/112	Anne	MISSELDINE	Flitwick	widow	1619	£2–10–00
294	Mathew	MONTAGUE	Everton		1617	£7–00–08
20/125	William	MORGAN	Goldington		1619	£90–03–04
20/41	Robert	MORRIS	Luton, Westhide	labourer	1619	£132–10–00
135	Christopher	MORRYCE	Pavenham	blacksmith	c.1593	£15–16–02
411	John	MOXE	Dean		1633	£20–16–09
342	Stephen	MUMFORDE	Clapham	labourer	1624	£16–03–04
345	Peter	MUSGRAVE	Swineshead	yeoman	1624	£267–08–02
134	Alce	NEGOUSE	Shelton	widow	1593	£31–14–04
20/118	Thomas	NEGUSS	Melchbourne		1619	£3–10–00
231	George	NEGUSSE	Shelton	yeoman	1611	£467–16–05
73	Elizabeth	NEWMAN	Colmworth	widow	1574	£76–08–01
51	Reginald	NEWOLD	Kempston		1569	£51–18–02
430	William	NEWOLD	Kempston	yeoman	1657	£432–07–02
20/28	Thomas	NEWTON	Bedford St Peter		1620	£7–03–06
20/128	Robert	NICKOLLS	Tilbrook	husbandman	1619	£121–02–08
394	Dionisia	NORTON	Streatley, Sharpenhoe	widow	1628	£104–02–04
13	William	NUMAN als NEWMAN	Bolnhurst		1558	
90	Thomas	NYXE	Bletsoe	rector	1579	£35–01–06

Published	First name	Surname	Place	Occupation	Year	Value
33	John	ODELL	Cranfield		1563	£19–11–00
75	John	ODELL	Cranfield		1574	£36–07–04
421	Jonas	OFFAM	Everton	husbandman	1645	£133–19–08
389	Mary	ONSLOW	Everton	spinster	1627	£248–02–04
20/139	Elizabeth	ORDWAY	Dunstable	widow	1619	£152–02–02
193	William	ORDWAYE	Dunstable	yeoman	1608	£111–17–00
377	Thomas	OSMOND	Willington		1625	£72–01–00
20/79	Jeffrey	PALMER	Ampthill	gentleman	1619	£520–06–08
119	Joan	PARKER	Yelden	widow	1588	£6–17–00
290	William	PASSELL	Cople		1617	£12–06–08
32/3	Fulke	PATERNOSTER	Campton		1587	£5–08–10
20	Daniel	PAYNE	Podington	yeoman	1558	
124	Alice	PEACOCKE	Kempston	widow	c.1588	£14–00–00
20/1	Thomas	PEARCE	Marston Moretaine	yeoman	1617	£150–13–04
402	William	PEARSON	Shillington	yeoman	1631	[£155–04–04]
326	William	PEIRCE	Toddington	yeoman	1622	£222–11–06
304	Thomas	PETCHET	Stotfold		1618	£25–15–00
117	Joan	PETTET	Podington	widow	1588	£10–06–08
16	Hugh	PEYCOCK	Sharnbrook		1558	£11–05–00
418	Jeffery	PHILIPES	Dean, Nether Dean	shepherd	1640	£15–06–08
184	Katherine	PHILLIPE	Stotfold	widow	1607	£87–03–04
407	John	PHILLIPPES	Campton, Shefford	innkeeper	1631	£149–05–04
35	Alice	PHILYPPES	Cardington, Harrold	widow	1563	£9–11–10
20/60	Anthony	PIMORE	Old Warden	singleman	1619	£55–16–08

Published	First name	Surname	Place	Occupation	Year	Value
151	John	PLACE	Eaton Socon	yeoman	1596	£432–01–00
217	Raphe	PLACE	Eaton Socon	gentleman	1611	£537–08–06
96	Richard	PLOMMER	Eversholt		1580	£17–06–08
20/11	Edward	PLUMMER	Holcot	rector	1620	£99–06–04
412	William	PORTER	Luton, Brach Mill	miller	1634	£14–14–00
413	Raphe	PRATCHETT	Flitwick	husbandman	1635	£42–04–06
262	Annys	PRIOR	Barton	widow	1613	£36–08–02
20/29	Thomas	PRUDDON	Streatley	husbandman	1620	£159–06–08
20/111	Nicholas	PRYER	Barton	householder	1619	£51–17–08
372	Thomas	PUDDIPHAT als HILLE	Studham	husbandman	1625	£71–12–04
278	Robert	PURNEY	Bedford St Peter		1615	£39–10–06
361	Elizabeth	PURRATT	Toddington, Fancot	widow	1625	£43–19–08
20/141	William	PURRATT	Toddington, Fancot	labourer	1619	£143–08–06
37	William	PURRYAR	Turvey		1565	£40–14–04
20/96	Philip	PURSER	Wilshamstead	husbandman	1619	£134–13–04
32/2	John	RACHFORD	Biggleswade	husbandman	1575	£100–03–10
118	Reynald	RADWELL	Kempston		1588	£13–16–00
20/142	John	RANDALL	Southill		1619	£9–02–00
403	Edmund	RANDELL	Clifton		c.1631	£25–19–02
20/123	Joan	RANDELL	Clifton	widow	1618	£3–18–02
20/42	Henry	RANDOLL	Upper Gravenhurst	smith	1620	£34–12–02
52	Thomas	RANESHAWLLE	Old Warden		1570	£69–13–04
358	Henry	RAULINS	Thurleigh	yeoman	1625	£32–11–00
248	Agnes	RAWLINS	Bolnhurst	widow	1611	£116–19–00

Published	First name	Surname	Place	Occupation	Year	Value
140	Henry	RAYNER	Keysoe	carpenter	1594	£13–18–10
20/134	Elizabeth	RAYNOLDS	Eaton Socon	widow	1619	£51–12–00
92	William	READ	Turvey		c.1580	£42–12–00
423	William	RECHFORD	Oakley	husbandman	1648	£33–12–00
20/75	Henry	RETCHFORDE	Blunham, Moggerhanger	labourer	1619	£7–04–08
20/122	Sarah	RICHARDS		wife of Laurence	1617	£25–15–04
20/80	Henry	RICHARDSON	Blunham		1619	£17–18–06
317	John	RICKETT	Elstow	labourer	1621	£4–19–06
158	William	RIDGE	Southill	vicar	1598	£67–00–00
148	Elizabeth	ROBINSON	Ravensden	widow	1595	£110–07–02
93	John	ROBINSON	Pavenham		1580	£17–05–04
20/21	Thomas	ROBINSON	Cardington, Cotton End	labourer	1620	£18–08–00
319	Thomas	ROFFE	Shelton	husbandman	1621	£447–19–04
20/92	Gerard	ROGERS	Sharnbrook		1619	£3–10–00
20/145	Henry	ROGERS	Southill	carpenter	1613	£19–15–04
20/100	John	ROGERS	Chalgrave	husbandman	1619	£26–06–06
20/23	Thomas	ROGERS	Tempsford	butcher	1619	£22–19–02
387	Alice	ROSE	Cople	widow	1627	£4–13–02
20/24	Francis	ROSSILL	Willington	labourer	1620	£29–02–10
353	Thomas	ROZELL	Willington		1625	£27–16–08
20/159	John	RUD	Pavenham		1619	£34–04–00
286	John	RULE	Tempsford	smith	1616	£3–09–02
147	John	RUSHE	Wilden	labourer	1594	£21–13–03
113	Robert	RUSSELL	Yelden	tailor	1587	£11–17–00

Published	First name	Surname	Place	Occupation	Year	Value
47	John	RYCHARD	Keysoe		1569	£85–01–06
171	Thomas	RYSELEYE	Ravensden	yeoman	1602	£102–19–06
406	William	SAME	Millbrook		1631	£13–01–00
20/150	Thomas	SAMON	Tempsford	weaver	1619	£25–02–08
271	Thomas	SAMUEL	Blunham	husbandman	1614	£113–11–08
299	Robert	SAVIDGE	Bromham	fuller	1618	£26–19–00
21	Raynolde	SAVYGE	Eaton Socon		1559	£10–13–08
20/6	Henry	SCARBORROWE	Kempston		c.1606	£10–03–00
244	Nathan	SCARRETT	Haynes		1611	£22–03–02
20/8	Robert	SCOTT	Eaton Socon, Duloe	yeoman	1620	£570–15–02
312	Widow	SEARE	Caddington	widow	1620	£6–13–06
207	Robert	SEARLE	Dunton, Milloe		1610	£13–03–06
205	William	SEARLE	Dunton		1610	£27–13–04
29	Annes	SEMER			c.1560	£5–03–10
28	Thomas	SEMER			c.1560	£9–04–00
212	Thomas	SEXTON	Eaton Socon, Wyboston	labourer	1610	£18–18–00
20/115	William	SHADBOLT	Sandy	labourer	1619	£7–17–00
232	Robert	SHARP	Clifton		1611	£99–08–08
252	William	SHERLEY	Bletsoe	yeoman	c.1612	£205–18–04
220	William	SHREEVE	Toddington		1611	£444–08–02
311	John	SIMPSON	Blunham	labourer	1620	£31–05–04
85	John	SKELLITER	Sandy, Girtford		1577	£20–02–06
159	Edward	SLOWE	Studham	husbandman	1598	£219–15–00
74	Thomas	SMALLWOOD	Willington	carpenter	1574	£23–01–08

Published	First name	Surname	Place	Occupation	Year	Value
182	John	SMITH	Milton Ernest	yeoman	1607	£53–08–06
20/33	Michael	SMITH	Bedford		1617	£17–04–08
88	Thomas	SMITH	Keysoe	labourer	1577	£6–13–08
122	Agnes	SMITHE	Wilden	widow	1588	£73–00–08
20/161	Henry	SMITHE	Dunstable	tailor	1619	£40–00–08
20/144	Annis	SMYTH	Sutton	widow	1619	£179–02–02
94	Oliver	SMYTH	Milton Ernest	tanner	1580	£27–12–11
238	Thomas	SMYTH	Husborne Crawley	tanner	1611	£19–03–10
20/57	Elizabeth	SMYTHE		widow	1620	£10–12–03
20/121	George	SMYTHE	Arlesey	labourer	1619	£8–08–00
127	John	SMYTHE	Everton	husbandman	1591	£35–10–04
20/3	John	SMYTHE	Ampthill		1617	£14–08–00
20/54	John	SMYTHE	Renhold	husbandman	1619	£50–08–04
20/136	John	SPARKS			1619	£28–08–00
241	Richard	SPENLY als NEWALD	Bedford	miller	1611	£12–15–00
70	John	SPENSER	Bedford	tanner	c.1574	£30–10–00
20/157	John	SPRIGNELLS	Arlesey	weaver	1618	£4–18–04
224	Robert	SPUFFORDE	Luton, Stopsley	yeoman	1611	£138–00–09
371	John	SQUIER	Ampthill	tailor	1625	£5–09–00
382	Henry	SQUIRE	Thurleigh		1625	£3–12–02
20/93	William	SQUIRE	Astwick		1619	£21–05–00
14	John	SQUYRE	Stotfold	yeoman	1558	£18–09–01
20/86	Thomas	STACIE	Cockayne Hatley	gentleman	1619	£55–01–10
239	John	STALFORD	Sundon	husbandman	1611	£95–10–00

Published	First name	Surname	Place	Occupation	Year	Value
104	Richard	STANBRIDGE	Wootton	husbandman	1583	£15–00–00
393	Thomas	STANBRIDGE	Wootton	yeoman	1628	£22–09–00
106	Richard	STANTON	Pertenhall		1583	£100–02–06
156	Robert	STANTON	Pertenhall	yeoman	1597	£300–10–00
168	Thomas	STAPLE	Tempsford	yeoman	1601	£28–16–08
428	Robert	STAUNTON	Woburn, Birchmore; London	esquire	1656	£2245–18–11
20/151	John	STEVENS	Northill, Thornecote		1619	£5–02–01
20/7	William	STEVENSONE			1610	£57–08–09
20/39	Richard	STOKES	Oakley		1620	£22–06–08
20/73	Thomas	STOKES	Oakley		1619	£15–04–00
314	John	STORER	Eaton Socon	shearman	1621	£7–00–00
161	William	STORER	Eaton Socon	husbandman	1598	£98–01–00
42	William	STRATTON	Podington		c.1566	£16–19–10
20/163	Thomas	STRINGER	Houghton Conquest	labourer	1619	£16–18–10
234	Anne	STYLE	Woburn	widow	1611	£31–03–00
123	William	SWAN	Dean, Nether Dean	husbandman	1588	£45–02–00
164	Margerie	SWANNE	Dean, Nether Dean	widow	1598	£21–05–00
253	John	SWIFT	Marston Moretaine, Shelton		1612	£5–13–10
20/98	Thomas	SYMONS	Eversholt		1619	£110–11–07
364	Thomas	SYMONS als SEAMAN	Eversholt	yeoman	1625	£140–07–02
6	Nicholas	TAILOUR	Stevington; Wellingborough, Northants	yeoman	1556	£231–00–00
201	Thomas	TAPPE	Felmersham, Morend		1610	£17–07–02
323	Silvester	TAVERNER	Marston Moretaine	gentleman	1621	£56–19–00
20/124	Robert	TETTRINGTON	Wilden	labourer	1619	£4–17–00

Published	First name	Surname	Place	Occupation	Year	Value
20/62	John	THOMPSON	Riseley	clerk, vicar	1619	£209–05–04
196	Richard	THOMPSON	Langford	labourer	1609	£40–05–04
343	Roger	THROSTLE	Swineshead	labourer	1624	£5–00–00
341	William	THROSTLE	Swineshead		1623	£18–16–04
20/71	Robert	THURGOOD	Southill		1619	£30–04–10
215	Richard	TIPLADY	Dunstable		1611	£1–14–04
20/129	Elizabeth	TITTE	Marston Moretaine		1619	£6–12–00
268	John	TOMPKINS	Houghton Regis, Bidwell	husbandman	1614	£44–05–06
233	Augustine	TOPCLYFFE	Willington	vicar	1611	£64–00–00
346	John	TOUNESEND	Billington	yeoman	1624	£47–09–09
348	David	TOWLER	Odell	blacksmith	1625	£12–17–02
155	Edward	TURNER	Milton Ernest	gentleman	1597	£264–19–04
415	John	TYBBALL	Everton	husbandman	1636	£44–13–00
20/164	Thomas	TYNGAIE	Clifton	singleman	1619	£40–06–08
20/127	Joan	UNDERWOOD	Langford	widow	1619	£22–10–04
354	Susan	UNDERWOOD	Sandy	widow	1625	£48–16–00
303	Lawrence	UNDERWOODE	Arlesey	stringer	1618	£46–17–06
20/68	John	VALLETT	Goldington	carpenter	1619	£20–14–06
273	John	VENTAM	Eaton Bray	husbandman	1614	£29–05–11
7	John	VERDER	Chalton	ropemaker	1557	£13–17–00
362	John	VINCENT	Toddington	yeoman	1625	£77–12–02
20/89	William	WAKEFIELD	Kempston	labourer	1619	£6–12–00
50	William	WALL	Willington	husbandman	1569	£33–19–04
20/72	Joan	WALLIN als POULTER	Shillington		1619	£19–02–04

Published	First name	Surname	Place	Occupation	Year	Value
400	Thomas	WALLIN als POULTER	Shillington	yeoman	1631	£146–10–04
166	[blank]	WARD	Roxton, Chawston	singlewoman	1598	£4–03–08
265	Alice	WARDE	Marston Moretaine	widow	1614	£4–02–08
163	Timothy	WARDE	Wilden	husbandman	1598	£189–14–04
45	Thomas	WARNAR	Colmworth		1569	£86–02–08
115	John	WARNER	Caddington		1587	£4–16–08
392	Richard	WASSE	Ampthill	labourer	1628	£6–05–04
121	John	WATKINS	Caddington		1588	£9–19–08
27	William	WATSON	Bolnhurst		c.1560	£23–09–00
142	Henry	WATTES	Potsgrove	clerk, rector	1594	£46–14–05
144	Robert	WATTES	Wymington	husbandman	1594	£68–00–00
102	Thomas	WENNAM	Wrestlingworth		c.1583	£60–03–04
24	John	WHAULEY	Haynes	husbandman	1560	£41–12–00
120	William	WHEELER	Great Barford	husbandman	1588	[£88–07–06]
20/149	Joan	WHITE	Kempston	widow	c.1619	£13–19–10
339	William	WHITE	Biddenham	'teler'	1623	£16–19–10
322	William	WHOOTTON	Harrold	shepherd	1621	£25–16–04
256	Thomas	WHYSSON	Langford	husbandman	1612	£20–08–04
32/12	Robert	WHYTEHED	Turvey		1588	£9–11–00
20/82	William	WIANTE	Elstow		1619	£9–03–04
109	Joan	WILLIAMSON	Bedford	widow	1583	£11–03–08
331	John	WILLSON	Warden Abbey	gentleman	1622	£877–03–08
20/131	Richard	WILSHER	Sandy, Beeston		1619	£11–05–06
20/70	William	WILSHIRE	Barford	yeoman	1619	£169–19–02

Published	First name	Surname	Place	Occupation	Year	Value
20/2	William	WINCH	Luton	yeoman	1620	£32–02–06
226	Annis	WINE	Eyeworth	widow	1611	£5–00–08
398	Elizabeth	WITT	Wootton	widow	1631	£130–15–08
58	Henry	WOLHED	Marston Moretaine		c.1571	£21–15–00
84	John	WOLHED	Wilshamstead		1577	£36–06–06
327	Richard	WOOD	Flitton	vicar	1622	£189–02–05
307	Thomas	WOOD	Milton Bryan	labourer	1619	£8–19–02
1	James	WOODWARD	Barton	maltman	1497	£14–10–11
32/15	Mathew	WOODWARD	Barton		1591	£40–17–06
367	Robert	WOODWARD	Cranfield	yeoman	1625	£123–19–04
225	John	WOODWARDE	Barton	innholder	1611	£37–14–00
129	Elsabeth	WOOLLET	Wilshamstead	widow	1591	£15–14–08
20/45	Lawrence	WRIGHT	Oakley	tailor	1619	£7–10–08
141	Thomas	WRIGHT	Wootton		1594	£144–12–00
32/8	Nicholas	WRITE	Cockayne Hatley		1587	£61–18–04
355	John	WYE	Southill	yeoman	1625	£433–13–06
9	Henry	WYLDE	Yelden		c.1557	£4–06–00
54	John	WYNCHE	Luton	maltman	1571	£50–11–10
61	Henry	WYNGAR	Cardington	servant	1573	£3–14–08
259	Henry	YARWELL	Souldrop		1612	£28–12–08
295	John	YDOLL	Swineshead		1617	£56–08–00
101	Richard	YERILL	Blunham, Chalton		c.1582	£45–09–04
198	Thomas	YOUNG	Thurleigh	labourer	1610	£21–00–00
310	Thomas	YOUNGE	Langford	labourer	1620	£7–19–00

The Inventories

1 James Woodward of Barton, maltman made 30 November 1497

The National Archives, PROB2/128

The document is discoloured, especially the top half where there are also four large holes. Some text is missing.

A true [...] all the good & Catalles of Jacob Woodward maltman late of Barton in the [...] of Bedford praised by William Swayn, William Child, Thomas Jeffrey & Richard [...] Barton aforeseid by the oversight of [*illeg.*] [*?*]Harmer the last day of November [...] lord M^{l}CCCClxxxxvij and the xiij [*yere of the*] Reigne of king Hen[*ry*] [...]

		£	s	d
Stuffe of the kechyn				
In primis ij pottes of bras poiȝ[1] xxxviij ^{lb} at j^{d} ob Sum			iiij	ix
Item ij pannes of bras poiȝ xxvij ^{lb} at ij^{d} Sum			iiij	vj
Item a Skyllet [...] of bras pricd				xvj
	Sum		x	vij
In the [...] in the servantes Chamber				
Item in matteres [...] paier of blankettes and iij olde Coverlettes [...]			xvj	viij
	Sum		xvj	viij
Catall				
Item iiij plowgh Oxyn price			xxxij	
Item ij olde kyne price			x	iiij
Item the plowgh harnes price			iij	iiij
	Sum		xlv	viij
Corne				
Item in whete barley malt & benys xl quarters at ij^{s} viij^{d}			Cvj	viij
	Sum		Cvj	viij
[...] money				
Item in Redey mone[*y*]			lxxiij	iiij
	Sum		lxxiij	iiij
Gownys with oder Stuff				
Item a old blew gowne and Russet gowne price			x	
Item iij payer of Shetys price			v	
	Sum		xv	
Sperat Dettes				
Item John Freer of London			xxiij	
	Sum		xxiij	
Sum to[ta]les of the praisyd goodes Corne Catall Redy money and Sperat Dettes		xiiij	x	xj

1 Probably a contraction for *ponderat*, which may be translated in this context as *weighing*.

Fynerall Expensys

		£	s	d
Item paid to preestes Clerkes Ryngyng of belles hys leistow lynnyn Clothe with oder necessaries & youen [*given*] in Almes to pore peopill			xliij	iiij
	Sum		xliij	iiij

The probat of the testament

Item paid for the probat of the testament with all oder thinges that longeth thereto [*no sum entered here*]

[*No exhibition clause*]

Notes: James Woodward's burial has not been found. He made his will on 24 September 1497. He left more than £11 to Barton church and for other charitable uses. He made his wife Alice his residual legatee and appointed her and their son Robert as his executors. The will was proved by Robert Woodward in the Prerogative Court of Canterbury on 24 November 1497 (TNA, PROB11/11). In 1516 James and Alice Wodward were posthumously admitted to the Luton Guild with Robert and Anne Wodward of Barton (from the manuscript list of admissions to the Luton Guild prepared by John Lunn).

2 Robert Cowper of Harrowden, Cardington, husbandman made 23 September 1552

Lincolnshire Archives, MISC WILLS L/29

The document is faded and damaged down the right side.

Thys Inventory followyng of all suche goodes as weere of latet [*sic*] Robart Cowpers of Hrowden In the parrysche of Cardyngton husbandman nowe dyssessyd vewyd & praysyd the xxiij daye of September Anno 1552 by the vew & price [*?*]feat

	£	s	d
Inprimis iij horses the pryce		liij	iiij
Item iiij kyyn the price		xlvj	viij
Item ij steeres and a hecfor of ij ere of Age		xxv	
Item xxviij scheepe		xlvj	viij
Item iij hogges for bacon		x	
Item vj stoorres		x	
Item a sow and viij sockyng pygges		v	
Item for wheete and Rye		xl	
Item for the croppe of barly	x		
Item for the croppe of peese		xx	
Item for the croppe of oytes		x	
Item for haye		xl	
Item for ij payyr of schoode wheeles and ij cart boddes		xxvj	viij
Item for harnes for v horses		v	
Item for a plow and that longtherto		vj	viij
Item for the woode in the yearde		xxxiij	iiij
Item for ij syythys		ij	viij
In the chamber			
Item a fetherbed withe bolster		vj	viij
Item ij coverlettes		x	
Item iij payre of flaxyn scheetes		xij	
Item v payre of hardden scheetes		x	

Item ij tabull clothys & iij towels		iiij	
Item j grete cooffer & ij lesse coffers		viij	
Item the hankynges			xij
Item iij peyelows of tycke			xij
Item iij slyppes of arine			xx
Item iij bedsteeyddes		ij	

In the hall

Item an old cowber		vj	viij
Item an old folddyng tabull		v	
Item a tabull standdyng apon the benche			xx
Item a turnyd cheyer & ij formys			xij
Item a banker and ij coosschyns			xx
Item ij old hankyns			ij
Item ij byrgar [*bigger*] brasse pootes and ij lesse		x	
Item iij brasse pannys		xiij	iiij
Item a pottel pan and a skyllett			xij
Item vij pewter platters old and new		iiij	viij
Item a pewter pot and ij salt sellers			x
Item ij bell candelstykes and one other candelstyke			xx
Item a lattyn bassin and a chaffyngdysche			xvj
Item a payre of cobyron and a spyytt			xij
Item a payyr of pothookes a poot hankyns for a poot and a gredyron & a trevet			xx
Item a steypyng fat & an elyng tub and ij dryngkyn tubbys		v	
Item an old knedyng trohe & an old kylet			viij
Summa	xxxv		x
[*Corrected total*	*£34*	*14s*	*8d*]

The namys of the praysars of thys Inventory by thes John Batman: Henry Cowper: Edmond Perrett: and John Bawdwyn: Inhabiters of the sayd parrysche

Thes be the dettes that Robart Cowper dothe owe

Inprimis to Robart Patn[*?am*]	iij	vj	viij
Item to Edmond Perrett		xxxiij	iiij
Item owyng for a quarter of barly		vij	
Item owyng for a xij busschelles of barly		xj	
Item owyng for vj busschelles of ootes		vj	
Summa	vj	iiij	

[*No exhibition clause*]

Notes: Robert Cowper's burial has not been found.

3 Elizabeth Bacon of Goldington, widow

made 27 September 1552

Lincolnshire Archives, MISC WILLS L/32

Thys Inventary takyn of the goodes of Elsabeth Bacon wyddoo late deseysyd In the paryche of Goldyngtone and presentytt by Master Jonson, Wyllyam Berde, Jorge Monyngham, Wyllyam Gale, Thomas Kyng, Thomas Fyscher the xxvij day of Septembr Anno domini 1552[2]

2 The date has been written in a different ink and hand.

	£	s	d
Fyrst A coobert the pryse		v	
Item ij bake chers			vj
Item A tabull and a forme with a backe borde			xiiij
Item a cobert a bedested with a pented cloth		ij	iiij
Item a cradell a [*?*]toowbe ij bordes			xij
Item a pane v keteles ij pottes a fryng pane		xix	
Item ix pesys of pweter		vj	
Item a chafyng desche ij candylstykes a salte a peyre of peper quyrns		ij	
Item for ij coffers & ij beddesteddys a forme iij bordes and iiij pentyd clothes with a lynnen tester		viij	
Item a matras ij bolsters iij pyllowys		ij	
Item ij coverletes			xij
Item a gowne iij kyrtylles & a pedecote		vij	iiij
Item iij peyre of shetes		ix	iiij
Item one shetes a tabell cloth ij towelles and a naperne		ij	
Item vj carchaffes		iiij	
Item iij apernes a hande towell with iij peces of lynene			xij
Item In moyne		xxiiij	

Summa iiij^{l} xv^{s} viij^{d}

[*The following lines are in a different ink and hand*]

	£	s	d
Summa	iiij	xv	viij
Item a howse iiij markes ~~viij li~~		[*53*	*4*]
~~Summa~~	~~xij~~	~~xv~~	~~viij~~
Summa	vij	v	viij
[*Corrected total for the goods and the howse*	*£7*	*9s*	*0d*]

[*No exhibition clause*]

Notes: Elizabeth Bacon's burial has not been found.

4 **Thomas Browne of Leighton Buzzard, shoemaker** made 4 October 1552

Lincolnshire Archives, MISC WILLS L/31

Damage at the foot of the document. Some words or values are missing.

The Inventorie of the goodes of Thomas Browne of Leighton Bossard in the Cowntie of Bedford shomaker made the fourth daye of Octobre in the yere of our lorde god MCCCCCLij & in the syxte yere of the Reinge of oure soveraynge lorde kyng Edwarde the vjth praysed by Nycholas Wryght, Robart Scrogges, John Parson & Thomas Sanders

	£	s	d
In the halle			
Inprimis a folden tabyll & ij formys		ij	viij
Item a nolde tabyll & a backe stoylle			vj
Item a cupborde & iiij bedstedes		iij	iiij
Item iij brasse pannys & ij kettylles		x	
Item three puter platters a puter dycshe & ij sawsers		ij	
Item ij puter pottes & too cruettes			xviij
Item too candylstyckes & ij salte sellowrs		ij	ij
Item a basson a laver & a chesse dyshe			xx

Item a speet & a pare of bellowys			vj
Item a trevett ij pare of pott hangylles a Irone hoycke a fryinge panne and a brasen ladyll		ij	
Item iiij bordes & three shelve bordes			viij
Item foure dossen ~~pare par~~ and vj pare of shoys		xl	vj
Item vj stockes of bees		xij	
Item xvj qwarttes of honye		x	
Item foure pownde waxe & an halfe		ij	viij
Item a brasse pott & too postnettes		iiij	
In the chambre			
Item an nolde feddare bede & a bolster		v	
Item iij pare of sheettes		iij	
Item three coffers a huche & an olde arke		viij	viij
Item fyve ~~coffers~~ paynted cloythys			xx
Item too tubbes a repynge hoyke a axe & iij Irone wedgys			xx
Item a malte qwerne and too planckes		v	iiij
Item foure werynge garmenttes		vj	
Item iij dossen lastes & other thynges belongynge therto		iij	iiij
Item a berynge byll & an olde lynen weell			vj
Item a coke iiij hennys & v chekkens		ij	
Item iij loyde woode		viij	
Item cheyne a buckett & anyarne spyndyll			xx
~~Summa totalis~~	~~vij~~	~~iij~~	~~iiij~~
[*Corrected total*	*£7*	*3s*	*0d*]
Thes be the dettes that Thomas B[*row*]ne do awe			
Item to Gorge Bannester [*illeg.*]		[...]	viij
Item for howse rent [...]	[...]	viij	
Summa totalis [*goods less his debts*]	v		vj

[*No exhibition clause*]

Notes: Thomas Browne's burial has not been found.

5 William Ireland of Milton Ernest, miller made 5 April 1555

Hertfordshire Archives and Local Studies, A25/183

This is a beautifully written, fair copy on parchment. There is slight damage and loss of a few letters on the right side.

This Inventory made the vth daye of Aprill in the yere of our Lorde gode m^{l} CCCCC lv^{ne} at Mylton Ernes in the count[*y*] of Bedford and In the yere of the reigne of our moost gracious & victorius Philipe and Mary by the grace of god king and Quene of Englande fraunce Naples Jerusalem and Irelande defenders of the faith prynces of Spayne and Cicilie Archedukis of Austria Dukes of Mylayne Burgundie & Brabande Counties of Hasburge Flaunder[*s*] And Tyrole[3] the first and Seconde all moveable goodes and Cattalles pertenyng unto Wylliam

3 The full royal title used to date the document by regnal year occurs in some of the inventories in this volume but is more common in wills. Philip and Mary's royal titles are more elaborate than other sovereign's because of Philip's multiple titles.

Irelande late of Mylton afforsaide in the countie afforsaide miller and nowe deceased as Followith

		£	s	d
All the Croppe				
First of wheat tooe Acres praesed at			x	
Item of Rye tooe Acres and haulff at			viij	iiij
Item of Barly ix[ne] Acres prased at			xl	
Item of peaslande ix[ne] Acres at			xxx	
	Summa	iiij	viij	iiij
Catalle				
First Sevyn kyne prased at		iiij	xiij	iiij
Item A Bulle at			x	
Item thre Heckffordez at			xxx	
Item tooe yerling bullockis praysed at			x	
Item thre C[...]s praised at			vj	
Item iiij[e] C[...] horse at		v		
Item thre Leane maers praised at			xxx[ti]	
Item iij[e] yerling foolles and one foole of ij yeres ould at			xiij	iiij
Item one Eywe sheape with hir Lambe and one other Theave Sheape at			iiij	
Item tooe Hogges praised at			iij	iiij
	Summa	xv		
Cartis and Carte gayers with plough and therto belongyng				
First one Shodde Carte praised at			xx	
Item tooe dung Cartis at			vj	viij
Item horse harnes and horse gaires bothe for the plough & Carte praised at			x	
Item one plough with a Cullter and the Share & all therto belongyng at			v	
Item ij paire of fettars with tooe horse Lockis & tooe keys at				xij
	Summa		xlij	viij
The fulling myll Shoppe				
First a Shearbord praised at				iiij
Item tooe payre of fullers shears at			v	
Item xij paire of fullers Handilles at				iiij
Item one paire of fullers nyppars at				j
Item of flockis in the fulling mill Beyng a pounde waight at				ij
	Summa		v	xj
Memorandum That the Saide Wylliam Irelande didde gyve by his lyff tyme unto his Chilldren all hys Apparrell therfor hit is nott praised at			nullis	
The Corne mylles				
Imprimis First one Arke of made [*sic*] to putt corne into hit priased at			iij	
Item A gynne with a gable roope and all othir thinges therto belongyng			v	
	Summa		viij	

In the haulle place

First one Joyned forme praised at			xij
Item a Joyned kubbord at		vj	viij
Item a foulding table with a shorte carpit therto belonging at		iij	iiij
Item iiij^{e} Buffytt stoolis at			xij
Item one nywe Chear of wyckars and one other being tornyd at		ij	
Item a wodden benche withe a borde against the waull & a banckir cloth of wullen at			xx^{ti}
Item iij paynted clothes in the same haull at			xij
Item iij Shelves of bordes in the same haull at			xij
Item Sixe pewtir dysshis one pewtir bason and on Latyn basone too pewter plattirs		iiij	x
Item too sault Sellers vj Sawcers iij latyn Candyll stickis & too Candill stickis of Tyne or pewtir		ij	viij
	Summa	xxv	ij

In the Chamber next the haull

First one borded Bedstead and one lytle Bedsted for Chilldren one ould fetherbed with a boulster a pilloe a blanckit a covirlit of carpit worke praysed at		xiij	iiij
Item xj paire of flexyn sheatis at		xx^{ti}	
Item iij table clothes of lynyn beyng of harden clothe and praised at		iiij	
	Summa	xxxvij	iiij
Also belongyng unto the [?]waukter [*?water*] one boote at		x	

In the kychyn & the ovir howce

First Syxe brasse pannes Smalle & great at		xxvj	viij
Item iiij^{e} kettilles smalle & great at		iiij	
Item iij brasse pottes Smalle & great at		x	
Item too brasse possenyttes at		ij	
Item too plattirs v potyngers too sawcers of pewtir praysed at		iij	iiij
Item one Chafyng dysshe of lattyn at			xij
	Summa	xl^{ti}vij	

[*end of first side of the sheet*]

In the kychyn and the ovir Howce

Also A Joyned bedstead withe a testor and the Curtyns of Redde Saye and greane A flock bedde & a boulster a Blanckyt a Covirlit of Tapstery worke praysed		xiij	iiij
Item a Trunndilbed undre the Joyned bead praysed at			xij
Item a Long Borde at			iiij
Item a masshingfatt & vj tobbes at		ij	iiij
Item A paire of smale Iren cobbierns at			viij
Item a firepanne with a paire of tonges at			vj
Item too Spittes & one trevytt at			x
Item too nywe Skeppis at			iiij
Item a Rounde Table at			xx^{ti}

Item thre meele bowlles at				iiij
Item A Tornyd Cubberd named a penne at			vj	viij
	Summa		xxviij	

In the bullting Howce

First A Joyned bedsted A paynted Tester a mattres a boulster one ould covirlit of tapstery a Thrombe Covirlit all at			vj	viij
Item A Trundelbed praysed at				xij
Item v[ne] kymnelles at				xvj
Item a Chease presse with a boulting vessell at				viij
Item a Bearing [*?brewing*] kowlle at				iij
Item a great vessell named A tunne at				vj
Item A kneding Trough at				iiij
Item a nyw Carte roope at				x
Item a Spennyng wheale				iij
	Summa		xj	x
The totall somme of thies parcelles within and this Syde is		xxx	iiij	iij

The Namez of the Inhabitantes in Mylton Afforsaide whiche didde praise thies goodez and Cattalles mensioned in this saide Inventory the daye and yere above wryten In the presence of Sir Robert Thowould vicar of the same towne Frauncys Lewys gent, Thomas Tappe, Robert Nevyll, Richard Veele, Richard Smyth, John Churche, William Riddell
[*No exhibition clause*]

Notes: William Ireland, miller, was buried at Milton Ernest on 31 March 1555. His will was made in 1555, in which he requested burial at St Albans (HALS, 305AW11, 3AR63). Robert Thewold or Thorrold was vicar of Milton Ernest 1554–72 (CCEd).

6 Nicholas Tailour of Stevington

made 17 and 24 April 1556

The National Archives, PROB2/263
The heading is stained and smudged on the left side.

[*illeg.*] off the goodes & cattalls off [*illeg.*] Tailour [*illeg.*] Stevinton in the [*illeg.*] ….borough within the dyoces of [*illeg.*] xvij [*illeg.*] Aprell in the yere off our Lord [*illeg.*] Hatley, Roberte Tailour, George [*illeg.*] & [*illeg.*] Tarlyng

		£	s	d
[*illeg.*] at Stevinton [*illeg.*] Felles		xv		
At Wendleingborough [*?*]sevin [...] Felles		[*?*]xviij		
	Summa	Liij		
In the [*illeg.*]			viij	
A table			ij	
wolle			[*?*]v	
	Summa		xv	
In the Stable caled the hackney stable				
The graye horse			xl	
In the carte stable iij horses & a coult		vij		
Cart harnes			x	
Haye in the hay barne			[*?*]xx	
	Summa	x	x	
In the Barly barne viij quarters barley		vj	xiij	iiij
Thre quarters wheat		iij		

vij Quarters pease		v		
wodde in the y[*ar*]de			xiij	iiij
In the barly loft vj quarters barley		iiij		
Two quarters wheat			xl	
	Summa	xxj	vj	viij
In the malthous Thre hundreth Felles		xviij		
In the mault loft vij quarters mault		v		
One [*sic*] the kyll two quarters mault			xxviij	
In the yarde hennes & other pullyn			iiij	
woode in the woodyarde			xl	
four cartes		iiij		
Two plowes			vj	viij
Elevyn beastes		xij		
Thre yerlynges			xxx	
vij shyepe			xxx	
	Summa	xlv	xviij	viij
In the kytchyn foure brasse pottes				
fyve skylletes [*?*]Five postnettes				
a Furnes panne a ledde in the furnasse			xl	
iij Spyttes a payr off Rackes				
Two Tables Two payles with other trashe			xij	
	Sum		lij	
In the yelyinge hous iiij pannes				
a lyttell Fatt iij ale tubbes				
a Saltinge troffe ij buffett stoles				
four bordes ij lyttell fourmes			xxxiij	iiij
a Fryeng panne ij gost pannes a verges				
barrell two lyttell brasse pannes				
sevintyne pyeces off peughter			xl	
	Sum	iij	xiij	iiij
In the Chyese lofft thre bordes a bedstedde				
a matteres sertayn ploutymber			vj	viij
In the chamber over the kytchyn a Bedstede				
a table a coverlet woll yarne			xxvj	viij
In the haule a Table a fourme Two cheares				
four buffett stoles an ambry a lattyn laver				
a lyttell table a payr off cobyrons a barre				
off Iren Two potthangers a painted				
hangynge a payr off Tonges			xx	
	Sum		liij	iiij
In the parlour a Foulden Table a fourme				
a cubborde ij cheares a standyng bedde				
a trundell bedde ij mattresses a fetherbedde			xxx	
ij boulsters a pyllowe a Quylt a payr				
off blanckettes a russett coverlett vj cusshyns				
a curtyn			xxx	
	Sum	iij		
In the lesser chamber over the parlour a trusse				
bedstedde thre curtyns a matteres a fetherbedd				
a payr off whyght blanckettes two coverlettes				
a coffer a chare			xxx	

In the great chamber over the parlour a standynge bedd			
a matteres a Fetherbedd a boulster a coverlet		xxvj	
iiij coffers ij chestes a presse xx^{ti} pair of shyetes	iij		
iiij table clothes iij towelles ij napkyns			
iiij pyllowebyers a spynnynge whyele & a			
payre off cardes		xviij	
Sum	vj	xiiij	
Sum totalis	Cxlix	xjx	
[*Corrected total*	*£126*	*6s*	*0d*]

Certayne goodes at Wendlyngborough within the dyoces off Peterborough aforsayde beinge N Taylores aforsaide vallued & praysed the xxiiijth off Aprell in the yeare off our lord MDLvj by John [*?*]Denyt, Raulfe Cushow, Robert Tarlynge & Henry Davy

	£	s	d
In the haule			
a Table a Counter four cheares a forme		xj	viij
viij buffet Stoles Ten Cusshyns		vij	iiij
Thre Towelles a carpett a tableclothe		vij	iiij
a Latten Lavor			xij
Sum		xxvij	iiij
In the chamber above the parlour ij fetherbeddes		xxvj	viij
[*?*]v mattresses Two stondynge beddes one trussbedde		xxxviij	iiij
vij Cusshens vij coverynges Thre blanckettes		lvij	
viij pyllowis Ten pyeces off peughter		xv	iiij
Two Coverynges four curteyns foure boulsters		viij	
One Tredd Two coffers		vij	viij
Sum	vij	xiiij	
[*Corrected sub-total*	*£7*	*13s*	*0d*]
In the yelyng hous			
Two pannes Two Tubbes a Kymnell		xj	viij
a yelyng boule			ij
Sum		xj	x
In the buttrey			
Twelve platters Two pewghter basons		xiiij	
four peughter deshes v peughter porryngers		v	x
four peughter pottes fyve saucers		iiij	
syx Latten basons Two ewers		xiij	
Thre Chaffyngdyshes a morter		iiij	
a [*?*]St[*illeg.*]pytt viij Candelstyckes		v	
Two Fryeng pannes one skumer			xvj
a latten Ladell Two Iron wedges			xvj
Sum		lviij	vj
[*Corrected sub-total*		*48s*	*6d*]
In the loft above the yelynge hous			
Two pannes		xxx	
one Iron [*?*]bare			xvj
Sum		xxxj	iiij
In the parlour			
One Stondynge bedde one Fetherbedde		xvj	viij
one matteres iij Redd blanckettes		ix	iiij
Thre whyght blancketes one curteyn one cheare		iiij	[*?*]x
one Russett Blancket one cubbord		viij	

nyntyne payr off shyetes viij tableclothes		v		iiij
vj towelles xij pyllowbyers v table napkyns			xiiij	iiij
v coffers			vj	viij
	Sum	vij	xjx	iiij
The kytchen parlor				
A Table a fourme foure brasse pottes			xxj	ij
iij brasse pannes one Iron barre a payre off				
Andyrons a fyer shovyll a payr of [*?*]cobyrons			vij	x
a tredd a fyer fork a boultyng tobbe a kymnell			iiij	iiij
	Sum		xxxviij	x
	[*Corrected sub-total*		*33s*	*4d*]
In the kytchen four kettelles Two brasse pottes			xj	
a tredd four tubbes Two leddes			xiij	iiij
	Sum		xxiiij	iiij
In the outer yarde a pease hovell				
by estymacion two quarters			xxvj	viij
a shodde carte			xxvj	viij
Two weanyng calves			vj	viij
Two quarters barly			xxx	
In the shoppe				
a certayn tryen ware Two chestes			xj	viij
In the chamber above the shope				
four Quarters Rye		iiij		
In the work house Two Fattes			vj	viij
a certayn tryn boules			vj	viij
four bease one geldyng		viij	vj	viij
	Sum	xviij		xx
Corne in the fyelde at Stevinton				
xviij acres barley		vj	vj	viij
xx acres pease		vj	vj	viij
four acres wheate			xl	
	Sum	xiiij	xiij	iiij
In reddy money			xl	
Desperate dettes that [*ap*]eare owinge to Master Taylor				
Henry Clarke allias Sumner		viij		
John Vyrgylett		v		
William Wheler allias Newman		iij		
Thomas Barcoll			xl	
Thomas Wyndo[*illeg.*]			xx	
Henry Faxton			xxxiij	
Henry Gorman			xx	
	Sum	xxxiij	xiij	
	[*Corrected sub-total*	*£21*	*13s*	*0d*]
Deptes that N Tailour dyd owe				
[*most of text has been lost where the two sheets were sewn together*]				
allias Smyth		vj		
[...]			lvij	viij
[...]				[*?*]vj
	Sum Totall of this Inventary	CCxlij		iiij
	[*Corrected total*	*£231*	*0s*	*0d*]

[*Exhibited by John Stephenson in London on 16 March 1558*]

Notes: Nicholas Taillour's burial has not been found. He made his will on 31 August 1555, making charitable bequests to the church in Stevington and the nearby highways and bridges. He directed the fells at Wellingborough to be sold to discharge an obligation. His wife Margaret was to occupy his Stevington house for one year unless she and Peter, his second son, agreed to her moving out earlier. She was given malt and an annual payment of 40s for five years and her own goods at Wellingborough. Peter was given the house and land in Stevington; he was the residual legatee. The third son Richard was given another house and land in Stevington, carts, horses, cows, some household goods and £40 when he came out of his apprenticeship. Daughter Elizabeth was given 40s. Sons Peter and Richard were appointed executors. Probate was granted to his three sons, John, Peter and Richard Tailor in London on 27 April 1556 (TNA, PROB 11/38/22).

7 John Verder of Chalton, ropemaker made in 1557

Lincolnshire Archives, INV/26/296

[*illeg.*] 1557 Inventorie Jhon Verder prisers Wyllyam Ward, Robert Smalwod

	£	s	d
In primis a coberde & [?]ti[m]bre ware in the hall		vj	viij
Item brasse pottes & pans		xiij	
Item peuter & laten		v	iiij
Item in Iren ware		ij	
Item in bedstedes		v	
Item in beddyng		x	
Item in apern ware		xx	
Item in cofers		v	
Item in tubbes & troffes		vj	viij
Item in whete barle & rye		xl	
Item iij horses		xx	
Item a cart & cart geyres a plough & plough geires		xx	
Item Instrumentes for making of Roppes			xvj
Item hey		vj	viij
Item wode		v	
Item v besse	iij	vj	viij
Item iiij bullokes		xxvj	viij
Item hogges & shootes		xij	
Item in poltre		v	
Summa	xiij	17	
Dettes that I owe		xiij	iiij
Suma remanes	13	3	8

[*No exhibition clause*]

Notes: John Verder's burial has not been found. Both Toddington and Blunham had hamlets called Chalton. It has not been possible to identify which parish John Verder lived in.

8 Christopher Langdon of Henlow undated; probably 1557

Lincolnshire Archives, INV/1/153

The inventory is badly damaged and some words have been lost.

An Inmentory taken at Henloo of the goodes viz the movables etc [...] Langdon lat dessessd by the presentment Thomas Recford, Richar[*d*] [...] ~~Recford~~ Hemynge, Larance Underwod, Wylliam Brytten & other [...] praysed by the parties a bove sayd as followethe

	£	s	d
In primis vj pesses of gold viz ij riouls & on angell & iij Ingles croune [...]	v	v[4]	
Item on brone [*brown*] cow praysid at			[...]
Item of grayn iij quarters & a halfe prised at		xxj	[...]
Item on hog prised		[*illeg.*]	iiij
Item of streng beames & stones ther to be longe prised at		iij	viij
Item on fan the prise			[...]
Item on other croawne of gold delivered to Ric Hemmyng			[...]
linyne			
of shetes iiij payre of shetes ij tabell clothes & on bolster & ij pillos prised			[...]
Item ij coverledes & on pese of ruset clothe praysed			[...]
Item iiij pewter disshis & on old coffer prise at			[...]
Item of old brase v pesies & on saltinghe & on old cher prise			[...]
Item ij plankes a strang forme & a hemstocke & a forme			[...]
Item of shep vj praysed at			[...]
Item the goodes in the hale		xx	[...]
Item the goodes in the chamber		xx	[...]
Item on cow praysed		xx	[...]
Summa totalis	vj	xij	ij
[*Total of gold and goods*	*£11*	*17s*	*2d*]
[*Fyrste*] to John Berrer		ij	ij
[...] to Ric[*hard*] Clarke			xviij
[...] to Nicolas Bayrfot			viij
[...] Wylliam Wacfeld			[*?*]xv
[...] Titmarse		v	[...]
[...] cotton his wyffes son		[*?*]ij	[*?*]vj
Suma		xiij	x

[...] distributid alredy acording to the wyll in the p[*?resence*] [...] [*?of*] bothe the executors Ric[*hard*] Hemyng & Wylliam [...] agreid that the nobeles ohill [*?will*] be by & by [*?*]dis[*?tributed*]

[*on the verso*] by the executors & by the over sitt of the sayd Rich[*ard*] Hemyng this thurd daye [*n*]ext be fore therone sunday [*letter deleted*] her his [*here is*] nothinges of movabelles but it is gyffe[*n*] by the wyll all redy therefore her [*here*] is no profit to the pore

[*No exhibition clause*]

Notes: Christopher Langdon's burial has not been found.

4 The sum of £5 5s is at the beginning of the next line. It would seem to refer to the value of the gold and has been moved to the values' columns accordingly.

9 Henry Wylde of Yelden undated; 1557

Lincolnshire Archives, INV/1/107

The document is damaged along both sides.

The Inventorye of Henrye Wylde of Yelden late deceased of all his goodes moveable & unmovable praised by John Logsden & Thomas [*?*]Felding

	£	s	d
The hall			
In primis a table [*?*]form & an olde paynted clothe			xx
Item ij brasse pottes ij litell pannes & a Cittell		x	
Item viij dishes of pewter olde [*?*]warne & vj candelstikes		iij	iiij
Item an olde awmbre & an old chere			xij
[...] the chamber			
Item ij olde fether beddes ij coverlettes blankett & ij bolsters		xx	
Item iiij coffers ij olde materis		iij	iiij
[...] kyne			
Item ij kyne & a bullocke & ij hogges		xl	
Item ij hennes v duckes			xvj
Item ij shepe & one lambe		iiij	
Item iij tubbes			xvj
Summa	iiij	vj	vij
[*Corrected total*	*£4*	*6s*	*0d*]

[*No exhibition clause*]

Notes: Henry Wylde's burial has not been found.

10 Thomas Goodes of Luton made 21 March 1557

Lincolnshire Archives, INV/224/21

There is some damage down the right side.

An Inventrie made the xxj day of March in the thyrde & iiijth yere of the Reyne of King Phelipe & quyne Marie of Tho Goodes his goodes of Luton in the com' of Bedf

	£	s	d
In primis iiij cobbardes pric[*e*]		xiij	iiij
Item a table a frame a chayire & ij trestelles		iiij	
Item iiij quesheis & a benche bord			xiiij
Item vj peuter pottes		iij	iiij
Item viij candelstelstekes a chafinge dishe a laver		iiij	
Item xvij peces of pewter iij saucers iij saltes old stuffe all		vj	viij
Item xv old brasse pottes & hookes posnet iij panes & ij old broches		xiijj	iiij
Item a fetherbed a bolster an old coverlet a blankett ij pillowes & a mattres		x	

		£	s	d
Item xj pare of shietes			xx	
Item iiij old coffers			iij	viij
also vj silver spones a broken maser			[?]xx	
Item certeyn peynted clothes & a certen [*illeg.*] [*illeg.*]			iiij	
	Sum	v	iiij	vj

preysed by Richard Presten & [?]Geirge Feils
[*No exhibition clause*]

Notes: Thomas Goodes' burial has not been found.

11 Thomas Edwards of Turvey made 21 September 1557
The National Archives, PROB2/275
The inventory is faded and damaged down the right side. Some values may be incomplete.

The Inventory of all the goodes & cattelles of Tho[*mas*] Eddardes thelder late of Turvey in the county of Bedford decesse praysed by Wylliam Lyon, [?]Thomas [?]Lawrence, [*illeg.*] Stevynson & othere the xxj day of [?]September [*illeg.*] Philippe & Marie dei Gra Regis & Regine [*illeg.*]

	£	s	d
Inprimis one hundreth of Chesys		[?]xxx	
Fyftene peire of Shetes		[?]xxx	
Thre Coverlettes		vj	[?]viij
All the brasen vesselles as pottes pannes & kettylls		[?]xxx	
xvij peces of pewter		x	
Fyve Candelstyckes		iij	
one Cubberde in the Hall		x	
one rounde Table & two benchebordes			[?]xviij
Two leades in the bakhouse		x	
All the trene & Woodyn brewynge vesselles		vj	
Thre bedstedes xij^{d} and thre coffers v^{s} in to[*tal*]		vj	
Two Fetherbeddes xiij^{s} iiij^{d} and two mattressez ij^{s} iiij^{d}		[*15*	*8*]
ploughe Tymber		vj	
xij bordes		vj	
Sixe lodys of Wood		xij	
Sixe busshelles of malte		xiij	iiij
Two Spyttes, two Cobyrons j Gradyron j Trevett and one peire of pothokes		vj	viij
Tenne cartehorses	xij		
Tenne peire of harnessez for the same		xiij	iiij
Fyve Shodde Cartes	[?]v		
Two plowes with all the yrons belongynge to them		vj	viij
Foure horselockes & iiij peire of Fetters		iiij	
Twelve mylche kyne	xvj		
vij Bullocks breeders wherof ij beynge ij yeres olde & thother yerelynges	xxx		
Fyftene grete hogges & Stores		xxxij	
iiij^{xx}x Shepe	x		
All the barley whete pease & ootes & the hey	xl		

		£	s	d
Thre Toddes of Wolle			xl	
Werynge Raimentes of lynnen & Wollen		iiij		
	Suma totalis	Ciij	xiiij	x
	[*Corrected total*	*£131*	*18s*	*10d*]
Also of desperate dettes		vj	xiij	iiij
	[*Corrected total*	*£138*	*10s*	*2d*]

[*The exhibition clause has faded but seems to say that the inventory was exhibited by John Edwards on 21 January but the year is illegible*]

Notes: Thomas Edwards' burial has not been found. He made his will on 7 August 1557, giving £20 to his wife Margaret and his goods for life, which were to be divided among his children after her death. He left £20 each to sons John and Robert, and £15 to son Thomas. He appointed his wife as executrix. The will was proved in London on 29 November 1557 by his sons Thomas and Robert, Margaret having died (TNA, PROB11/39).

12 Thomas Ebett of Pertenhall undated; 1558

Lincolnshire Archives, INV/26/284

The document is damaged along the lower left side. A few letters and words are missing.

Anno domini 1558. The Invytory of Thomas Ebett off Perttnall

		£	s	d
Inprimis iiij kyne	v markes		[*66*	*8*]
Item iij horse			xxx	
Item xij sheppe			xxx	
Item v hogges			x	
Item ij wenynge Calves			iiij	
Item ij Cockes & xvj hennes			iij	
Item vij quarteres of barley			xxviij	
Item ij quarteres off wheatt & Rye			x	
Item in haye			iij	iiij
Item in pease			ij	
Item x acares Sowne in the Felldes off all maner of grayne			xl	
Item Cartte & Cartt geres plowe & plowe geres			xxvj	viij
Item the woode in the yearde			vj	viij
Item in the haule ij Tables ij Formes ij Chayres one Cubborde and payntyde Clothes			xiij	iiij
Item in the Chamber one Fetherbeed ij bollssteres ij Coverlettes [...] blankettes x payre of shettes one coffer ij beddestedes and [*t*]he hangyns in the Chamber			xxxvj	viij
[*Item*] in brasse & pewter Splitt Cobyrns Trevytt [...] hengles tonges Fyer shulf			xx	
[...] lynnyne as table Clothes towelles & napkyns			ij	vj
	Summa	xvj	xij	x

and praysseres hereoff Walter Graye, Wylliam Reve, Thomas Sheppard, Thomas Wendevor paryter

[*No exhibition clause*]

Notes: Thomas Ebett's burial has not been found.

13 William Numan alias Newman of Bolnhurst made after 1 January 1558
Lincolnshire Archives, INV/224/59
This inventory is creased and badly damaged, especially on the lower right side.

[*T*]hys ys a true Inventory of all the goodes off William Numan off [*B*]olnehyrst wyche departyd owt off thys world the fyrst daye [*o*]ff January & In the yere off owre lord god a M CCCCC & lvij praysyd [*by*] Thomas Rolt, Henry Coke, Thomas Wyndon with other

	£	s	d
Inprimis iiij horses	iiij		
Item iiij key [*kine*]	iiij		
Item ij calvys		x	
Item xx shepe		xl	
Item vj pygges & a sowe		x	
Item vj gese & a gander		ij	
Item ij duckes			vj
Item xij hennys & a cocke		iiij	
Item cart & cart gerys plow & plow gerys		[...]	
whete In the barne iij quarters & a halfe		[...]	
Corne In the barne xiiij quarters		[...]	
Item peyce iiij quarters		xxv	viij
Item whete sowne & the tylthe		[...]	
Item hey		[...]	
Item the whoode In the yerd		[...]	
Item all the pewter & brasse & a cubbord In the halle		[...]	
Item a fether bedde iij matterewys v coverlettes & a quilt		[...]	
Item v coffers iij bolsters & a pillowbere & iij tabull [*?cloths*]		[...]	
[*Item*] vj payre off shetes & a halfe a cubbord & forme [...]		[...]	
[*Item*] all hys Rayment		[...]	
[...] the Implementes [...]		[...]	
Summa totalis		[...]	

[*No exhibition clause*]

Notes: William Numan alias Newman's burial has not been found. He made his will on 16 November 1557. He had two houses, one in Bolnhurst, the other in Little Staughton. Sons Walter and Robert were given the Bolnhurst house for six years provided they brought up his other children. After six years the house was given to son William and the Little Staughton house to Walter and Robert provided they gave 8 nobles to son John. Son George was given animals and a great pan. Sons Walter and Robert were given his looms. The residue was to be divided equally between sons Thomas and Henry. The executors were sons William and Walter, to whom probate was granted in April 1558 (Beds Archives, ABP/W 1558/222).

14 John Squyer of Stotfold, yeoman made 10 January 1558
Lincolnshire Archives, INV/26/277
The second page is a fragment only. The handwriting is very poor and names are particularly difficult to read.

The Inventory of all gondes [*sic*] & cattelles of John Sqyer lat of Stotfold in the countye of Bedford yoman prysyd the tenthe daye of January in the yere off our lord god 1557 by Thomas ~~prtt~~ Pratt, Thomas Shottboltt, Crystofer [*?*]Tr[*um*]pton, Robert [*?*]Edynbrasse & Huhe Squer

	£	s	d
In the hall			
Inprimis xj pewter platteres		vj	viij
Item viij pewter dyshes		ij	viij
Item vj sauceres & ij pot[n]ygeres			xx
Item vj peuter pottes & iij sauceres		iij	
Item vj candylstygh		ij	
Som		xvj	vj
[*Corrected sub-total*		*16s*	*0d*]
In the kechyng			
Item iiij brasse pottes		x	
Item [*?*]xiij kettylles & ij pannes		xvj	
Item a frying pane a chaffyng dyshe a skomer			xx
Item ij spyttes ij andyrones ij pare of pott hokes iij trevettes a grydyron a fyre shovyll		viij	
Item one old cobord		vj	viij
Item one tabyll a Furme a [*?*]banker iij kyssynges ij tressylles		x	
Sum		xlviij	iiij
[*Corrected sub-total*		*52s*	*4d*]
In the chamber			
Item iij fether bedes		xxj	
Item ij mattres		iiij	
Item iij coverlettes		x	
Item v bolsters		v	
Item ix pyllowys		iij	
Item iiij blankettes		iiij	
Item iiij old coffers		iij	
Item xiiij payr of shettes		xviij	
Item vj pyllow beres		vj	
Item iij cottes a Jakett a old [*?*]g[*one*]		xiij	iiij
Item iij bedstedes & the longes therto [*belongs to them*]		vj	viij
Sum	iiij	xiiij	
In the lofte			
Item iiij pycheforckes ij bylles a bushell a crowe of Iron & other old Iron		iij	iiij
Sum		iij	iiij
In the barne			
Item in the barne in barly ij quarters		xiiij	
Sum		xiiij	
Item ij geldynges iiij markes		[*53s*	*4d*]
Item one cowe		xvj	
Item ij pyges		ij	vj
Sum	iiij	iiij	iiij
[*Corrected sub-total*	*£3*	*11s*	*10d*]
[*second page*]			
Item in Redye money	v	vj	
Sum	v	vj	
dettes desperatt			
Item of Robertt Gere		v	iiij
Item of [*?*]Tomsone		iij	ij

		£	s	d
Item of Robertt Bettellshaw			iij	
	Sum		xj	vij
	Sum totalis	xix	viij	j
	[*Corrected total*	*£18*	*9s*	*1d*]

dettes that he houghe

Item to Edward Freman			v	x
Item to Crystofer Haryson smyth				xviij
Item to the lord worden[5] for a hole yeres rentt			xvj	iiij
Item for a quarter off [*illeg.*]				xviij
	Sum		xxv	ij

[*No exhibition clause*]

Notes: John Squyer's burial has not been found.

15 John Mannyng of Flitton undated; after 20 January 1558

Lincolnshire Archives, INV/26/297

The Inventory of all the goodes of John Mannyng of Fletton which decessed the xx[ti] day of Januarij in Anno domini 1557 dwely valued by John House, Thomas Busse, John Wheteley

		£	s	d
In the hall				
Item j table j forme j chere j cupbord j henpen			iiij	
Item iij brasse pottes iij pannes iiij candelstickes & iiij peces of pewter			viij	
In the chambr				
Item j coverled j mattres j bolster iiij pyllos			vj	viij
Item ij coffers iiij shettes			vij	
In the kytchen				
Item j bryndyren j spitt j par pott hengles				xvj
Item I[*n*] the yarde ij ladders & wode			iij	viij
Item cartt & cartt geres plow & plowgers			x	
Item iij Mayres j lytle horsse & j fele			xl	
Item j cowe & iij bullockes			xxx	
Item the cropp in the Feild			xxxiij	iiij
	Summa	vij	iiij	
Debttes thatt the Testator oeth				
Item to Robertt Hutchyn		iij		
Item to Welles of Newton			xxxvj	viij
Item to Mannyng of Walton			viij	
Item to Auste[n] of Allarton [*Harlington*]			iij	viij
Item to John Coke of Fletton			ij	
Item to John Hutchyn of All[e]rton			ij	
Item to Annys Chapman			iij	viij

5 The Lord Warden has not been identified.

Item to John Grenehall		iij	
Summa	v	xviij	iiij
[*Corrected total of debts*	*£5*	*19s*	*0d*]
the summa the debttes allowed is		xxiiij	viij

[*No exhibition clause*]

Notes: John Mannyng's burial has not been found.

16 Hugh Peycock of Sharnbrook made 3 February 1558

Lincolnshire Archives, INV/224/28

Thys inventory made the iij day of februarij in the yere of owr lord god m cccc lvij of all the goodes late Hugh Peycockes of Sharebrok presyd be Wylliam Cobbe, Wylliam Wodhin the yonger & Ric Meryell

	£	s	d
Fyrst the hall			
A table aforme acupbord Apen & the hallyng		vj	
iiij brasse pottes ij pannys & ij kettyllys		xxvj	viij
xij peces of pewter a chaffyng dysche & a Candylstyck		vj	
In the chamber			
viij pere of scheyttes ij bordclothys iij towelles		xx	
ij mattrys ij coverlettes v pelows & v pelowberys		x	
ij bedstedes iiij Coffers with other trasche		vj	
In the kytchyn			
iij kymlyns atable ij spyttes a peyr of cobhyerns			
ij tablys a ȝelyng fatt & serten plowȝe tymber		x	
In the barne			
serten barley whete & pese		xxxiij	iiij
In the ȝeard			
iij kiyn ij bullockes & a horsse	iiij	x	
a old cart ij ladders iij pygges & serten pultre		xiij	iiij
dettes that the seyd Hugh had howyng hym			
Ric Hull of Hygam Ferrys		iij	viij
Sum	xj	v	
dettes that the seyd Hugh Peycock owthe at the day of hys deathe			
fyrst To Ric Peycock		xxxiij	iiij
Wylliam Cobbe		v	
Ric Meryell		ij	
Ph Cowper of Bedford			xij
Sum		xlj	iiij
Summa totalis de claro	ix	iij	viij

[*No exhibition clause*]

Notes: Hugh Peycock's burial has not been found.

17 John Cartar of Wootton made 16 February 1558

Lincolnshire Archives, INV/38/85

The right hand edge is damaged and some figures may be missing. The handwriting is very poor and some of the figures in particular are difficult to read.

This is the true Inmytorye of the goodes of Jhon Cartar [*in the*] paryshe of Wotton lat dissesed & mayd the xvjth daye of Feberyarye in the yaere of owr lord god 1557

		£	s	d
Inprimes in the hall [*?*]vij tabulles a forme a cobord a cheare			[*?*]vj	[*?*]
Item iiij barse potes ij panes ij ~~kettles~~			[*?*]xiij	[*?*]
Item ~~vij~~ iiij platres ij pouwte dyshes iij scaltes ij cawcers iiij canstykes a chaffyng dyshe a skale			iiij	
Item a spet a pare cobirnes a grydirne a p[*ai*]r pot haynges				viij
in the chamber				
Item in the chamber a matres on[*e*] coweryng iij badstedes ij coffers ij bolsters the hanynges abowt the bades			v	
Item a coffer in the loft with other trase				xij
Item vj pare shetes a tabull clothe & towell			xij	
Item in the boltyng howse a uanbe[*r*] [*?aumbry*] with trase				xij
Item in the chykchen [*?*]trase in the ij howsen			iij	iiij
Item what barly & pease & haye		iiij	vj	viij
Item iij kyne			l	
Item iiij horse	a marke		[*13*	*4*]
Item vj shepe			xij	
Item ij cart & geres plos & geres			[*?*]xl	
Item [*?*]vj henes & ducke				xviiij
	Somme	xij	x	ix

[*in a different hand*] xiij die mensis octobris Anno domini 1560 apud Bedford

Thes be the prisers names William Borne, Robart Walles, Thomas Rydge with other mo[*re*]

[*Exhibited at Bedford on 13 October 1560. Another exhibition clause at the bottom of the document has been crossed out and is mainly illegible.*]

Notes: John Cartar's burial has not been found.

18 Richard Fortune of Henlow made 18 March 1558

Lincolnshire Archives, INV/26/350

A Inventori of all the goods and catall of Rychard Fortune layte of Henlow praysed by Nycolas Barforth, John Gedyng, Wylliam Oost, Thomas Yonge Anno domini 1557 the xviij day of March

	£	s	d
fyrst iiij horses plo and plo gere & carte gere	iij		
Item ij cartes		xxvj	viij
Item iiij quarters Rye		xxiiij	
Item The hay		vj	viij
Item Barle in the barne		xv	
Item wood in the yard		viij	

Item iij pytcheforkes			vj
Item iij kyne & iij bullockes	iij	vj	viij
Item in the fyld all corne sowen pric[*e*]	viij		
Item a Tabyll a forme stoles the hangyng in the hall brasse & pewter in the hall		xx	
Item in the chambers bedyng and howsehold stofe pric[*e*]		xl	
Item a Sow and Seven pygges and henes		viij	
Summa Totalis	xxij		vj
[*Corrected total*	*£22*	*5s*	*6d*]

[*No exhibition clause*]

Notes: Richard Fortune's burial has not been found.

19 William Kentt of Felmersham, husbandman

undated, c. 1557

Lincolnshire Archives, INV/1/106

The Invitarye of the goudes of William Kentt husbandman of Felmersham late departed praised by these men folowyng [*Christopher*] Smyght, Morgayn Leache, Robert Otway, Rycharde Leache the yonger

	£	s	d
In the halle			
In primis a table a furme a cupburde		iiij	
Item ix puder dishes on sauser a chaffyng deshe ij candelsteckes ij salte sellers		iiij	
Item iij brasse pottes iiij kettells and a panne with a possenett		ix	
Item a chare iij [*?*]stoulles with a furme			viij
Item a friyng panne			iiij
In the parlar beneigh the halle			
Item iij coffers iijs iiijd Item iij berdes with ~~that~~ hang gyngs xs Item vj payr of shettes xs		[*23*	*4*]
Item In the kechyng a knedyng trought with other Im plementes and with a spett cobyornes pott hockes and a [*?*]trede		v	
Item for iij olde ~~Jades~~ horses		xx	
Item ij kyne iij bullockes		xl	
Item iiij acres of wheat and rye		xiij	iiij
Item xj acres of barle		xxij	
Item viij acres of pease		xvj	
Item a shode carte		xiij	iiij
Item ploweght and ploweght geare		v	
Item an eve and a hoggrell		iij	iiij
Item ij store pigges		iij	iiij
Item jj [*word rubbed out*] hennes and a cocke			xvj
[*Total*	*£9*	*4s*	*0d*]

[*The inventory ends at this point. There is no exhibition clause.*]

Notes: William Kentt's burial has not been found.

20 Daniel Payne of Podington, yeoman

undated; after 18 August 1558

Bedfordshire Archives, OR 1036, 1917, 1918

The first document (OR 1036) is an inventory made by the deceased in 1551 during his lifetime; the second (OR 1917) is an undated list, probably a draft, and is reproduced here for comparison with the following document; the third (OR 1918) is an undated list of his goods as divided between his executors.

Thys Inventory made of the goodes & cattell of Danyell Payne the xij daye of July in the fythe yere of our sovereynge lorde kinge Edward the vj[th] [*1551*]

	£	s	d
Item xxj kyne pric[*e*]	xxj		
Item on boll pric[*e*]		xx	
Item xiiij sterys & hayffers	x	vj	viij
Item vij yerlynges and wenyinge calvys		xlvj	viij
Item iiij marys	vj		
Item iiij horses	xij		
Item a olde horsse		v	
Item a yonge geldynge	iiij		
Item a horcolte [*sic*] in the [*?*]Fennys		vj	viij
Item a ~~mare~~ colte with Crystofer [*?*]Kettes		x	
Item iij ~~ga~~ cartes with all the geres ther to belonngynge	v		
Item viij score & x scheype	xxij		
Item lvij lambes	v		
Item [*blank*] Syver sponys	iij		
Item [*?*]iiij fethur bedes and all thynys ther to be lonnginge	vj		
Item all maner of howssold stoff	x		
Item my crope apon the grounde	xl		
Item vj acurs of whete	vj		
Item corne in the garners	x		
Item iiij kyne with Nycholas [*?*]Burbaye price	v		
Item the seyd Nycholas doethe ow me	iiij		
Summa totallis	Clxxiij	xv	

The second document (OR 1917) is an undated list of household goods without values, probably a draft. It is set out in two columns, reproduced here as a continuous list. It is written in two inks, possibly by two people as the formation of the letters differs.

Goodes remaynyng with Robert Payne Wyff Whyche Were Danyell Payne his brother

First column

Fyrst ~~vj~~ iij Cussyn

Item one Stole

~~Item one Carpett~~

Item one rele [*illeg.*]

Item one carpet

Item one banker ofer wyndowe
Item one mantell
Item [*illeg.*] Red sayes
Item ij ~~one~~ pyllowes
Item [*word deleted*] iiij bosters
Item ij coverynges
Item iiij platters
Item ~~iiij~~ v peuter dysshes
Item iij porren gers [*sic*]
Item iiij sausers
Item one sautseller
Item ij ewers
Item one chafynge dysshe
one tyne bottell
one tyne goblet
iij peuter potes
ij candel styckes
iij ~~pot~~ bras potes
v sylver sponnes
ij dobnetes
iij bras pones
iij bras kettels
one basone
one branderd
second column
Item iij blanketes one fether bed
Item iij cussyns
Item ij matteres
~~Item x shipe~~
a tabull
cattell
Item xij shipe xx
Item ~~iiij~~ v bese
viz ij kene ij heyfer
& a stere
the one haulfe [*sic*]
Item x pere of shetes iij tabell clo[*thes*]
iiij tabule napkenes one touell
Item one hempen tabell clothe
vjij pere & a haulf of hempen
shetes ~~iij tabelclotes~~

The third document (OR 1918) is undated and lists the division of his goods between his executors. It is badly damaged on the lower right side and many values are missing.

These parcell of goodes & catells here after folowyng whyche were Danyell Paynes late decessed and were devyded betwene Robert Payne & George Payne executors of the seyd Danyell

	£	s	d
fyrst wolle	v		
Item nyne mylche kyne			
thre bulles & thre steres	xij		
Item eleven yerlynges	iij	xvij	
Item seven calffes		xij	
Item eyght cart horsses	viij		
Item a ambulyng geldyng & one			
ambulyng horse		xxxiij	iiij
Item xvij[ten] skore shippe	xxxiiij		
Item xix[ten] hogges		l	vi[...]
Item thre bee hyves		ij	[?]viij
Item gyes hennes & duckes		v	[?]
Item whet			[...]
Item Rye			[...]
Item barley			[...]
Item beanes & peyes			[...]
Item ottes			[...]
Item hey			[...]
Item one other carte & cart gey[*re*] [...]			[...]
Item too ploughes & plough g[*ear*] [...]			[...]
Item a peire of harrowes			[...]
Item threy ladders			[...]
Item a gryndelston			[...]
Item fyre wood			[...]
Item three Sythes pycforkes spades [*missing*]			[...]

On the verso, in a different hand:
[*illeg.*] for Higham mills [*word deleted*] and other writynges concernigne [*sic*] Higham
[*No exhibition clause*]

Notes: Daniel Payne's burial has not been found. His date of death on 18 August 1558 can be established from the grant of wardship of his son William to Thomas Cobbe and an annuity from his death (*CPR, Elizabeth*, vol. 1, p. 341). His will, dated 20 March 1558, provided for his son William to be a royal ward until aged 21, because Podington parsonage and lands were held in chief; one-third of the lands being in royal hands, and two-thirds in the hands of executors during his heir's minority. William also received land in Worcestershire; £20; household goods; and clothing. His son Francis received land and money and his two daughters, money and furniture. The residue of his goods were left to Stephen Hodges and wife Joan 'at reasonable price'. He appointed his brothers Robert and George Payne as his executors and Thomas Cobb of Souldrop and John Pyrwyne of Higham as overseers (Bedfordshire Archives, OR 731, and a copy at OR 732).

The rectory and advowson of Podington had belonged to Canons Ashby Priory and were leased by Daniel Payne of Higham Ferrers, Northants, from the Crown after their dissolution in 1539 (*VCH Bedford*, vol. 3, p. 87).

21 Raynolde Savyge of Eton Socon made 4 February 1559
Lincolnshire Archives, INV/23/32

Anno Domini 1558. This is the trewe Inventorye Of all suche goodes as ware Raynolde Savygies of Eton athe Daie of his Deathe Prysid the fourte Daie of Fabruary By Androo Cater of Eton, John Wight of the Same And Thomas Wyndon

	£	s	d
Inprimis			
Fyve kyne and a Bullucke	vj		
Item fower Ewies		xiij	iiij
Item two Lamhogges		v	iiij
Item a pygge			xx
Item haye		ij	iiij
Item the wood		v	
Item thre pewter dissheis			xij
Item two pare of Hardyn shetes & a table clothe & a flaxin shete		v	
Item two coferres a coverlatt with one bolstare & a pyllowe		iij	iiij
Item a bedstead & thre yerdes of cloithe & his Rayment		vj	viij
Item a greate brasse pann & two kettyls		viij	
Item a tabyll an Awmbre & a backe bord			xij
Item a hallinge a chayre & ~~a backe borde~~ gyrdIyerne			xij
Deptes awinge unto the Same R Savyghe			
Nic[o]lus Greneleave		xx	
Item John [*?*]Curbye		xx	
Summa Totalis	x	xv	viij
[*Corrected total*	*£10*	*13s*	*8d*]

[*No exhibition clause*]

Notes: Raynolde Savyge's burial has not been found. His place of residence was probably Eaton Socon as the appraiser Andrew Cater appears as a witness to the will of John Barker, priest, of Eaton Socon in 1547 (Beds Archives, ABP/R12/3d).

22 Richard Hewett of Melchbourne, husbandman made 23 November 1559
Lincolnshire Archives, INV/38/140

The inventorye of all the goodes cattles & movables of Rychard Hewett of Melcheburn in the cont[*y*] of Bedf husbandman Lattlye desessed praysed the xxiij^{ti} day of Novembr in the yere of our Lord god a thowsand fyvehunderthe ljx^{ti} by Thomas Logsden, Ryc Buttler, Thomas Whest with other

	£	s	d
Chambr			
In primis ij mattres		vj	viij
Item iiij Coverlettes		viij	
Item iij of flaxen shettes		vj	
Item vij pere of harden		x	
Item iij bolsters		ij	
Item iiij pylloos		iij	iiij
Item ij Coffers		iiij	

The hall			
Item a penteyd clothe		ij	
Item a table & a forme			xvj
Item a Cher & a Longe forme			vj
Kyechen			
Item ij brasse poottes		ij	iiij
Item ij brasse pannes		x	
Item ij brasse kyettles		ij	viij
Item ij brasse posnettes			x
Item a spytt ij Cobyrons			xiiij
Item a grydyron			iiij
The yard			
Item iiij hors	iiij		
Item viij melche beys	iiij		
Item ij yerlynges		iiij	
Item ij hecforsse		iiij	
Item ij shodcarttes		xxvj	viij
Item iiij peyre of Carttgeyres		ij	viij
Item ij plooes ij temes		v	
Item v hogges vj pygges		xx	
Item vj shottes		xiij	iiij
Item a fram hovell		vj	viij
Item the wood		viij	
The barne			
Item a quartter of whet		xiij	iiij
Item viij quartter of barlye	iij		
Item v quartter of peys		xl	
Item xlvij[ti] shepp	iiij		
Summa totalis	xxiiij	iiij	x
[*Corrected total*	*£25*	*4s*	*10d*]

[*No exhibition clause*]

Notes: Richard Hewett's burial has not been found.

23 Thomas Bamford of Blunham made 27 April 1560

Lincolnshire Archives, INV/38/109

Document creased near the top and damage at the bottom left corner resulting in some loss of text.

The true Inventorie of all the goodes and cattalles of Thomas Bamford of Blunham in the countie of Bedf deceassed made the xxvij[th] daye of Apryle 1560 Robert Fyssher, Thomas Whyte, Richard Thorpe & Thomas Pecke praysers therof

	£	s	d
Inprimis in the halle a foldynge table a cupbord a forme iij chayres & a stole		viij	
Item a pene iij pottes vj kettles a panne a posnet a skellet & a fryeing panne		xxiiij	
Item a bason a chafindysshe vj candlestyckes & xx[ti] peces of pewter		x	

	£	s	d
Item a hatchell bowlles dysshes & platters		ij	
Item paynted clothes iiij mattresses ij coverletes & ij blanketes		xx	
Item a pottehangle & ij spyttes a paire of tonges & a payer of cobIrones		ij	
In the chamber			
Item vij payre of shetes v kerchieffes iij table clothes a towell iij pyllowebeares		xxiij	iiij
Item iij bedstedes ij bolsters hangynges of the bed a forme & a trestle		vij	
Item v cofers & a forcer		xij	
In the lofte			
Item a chese racke old Iron & bourdes & ij bottles		vj	
Item all his apparell		xxj	
Item v flytches of bacon		ix	
In the chamber beneth the halle			
Item a table a troughe iiij bourdes & a fourme		vij	
Item ij hatchelles an old churne			xij
In the bakehouse			
Item ij old troughes & bourdes		iij	iiij
In the stable			
Item iij horses	iij		
Item a carte & plouyghe with carte & plough gayrs		xxj	
Item a hovell & fyr wod a rolle & ploughtymber		xx	
Item vj hogges		xvj	
[...] shepe & iiij lambes		xviij	
[...] kyne & iij bullockes	iiij	x	
[...] the corne & grayn sowen			
[...]cres & a half at vj^{s} viij^{d} the acre[6]	v	x	
[...] all the pultrey		v	
Summa totalis	xxiiij	xv	viij

[*Exhibited at Bedford on 12 October 1560*]

Notes: Thomas Bamford's burial has not been found.

24 John Whauley of Haynes, husbandman made 18 June 1560

Linconshire Archives, INV/38/151

An Inventorie of Jhon Whaulers goodes husbonne man of Haunes

	£	s	d
Item v horse	iij	vj	viij
Item a cart, plow, & carte & plow geares		xx	
Item v kynne & ij bullockes	vj		
Item xxx^{ti} coples of shepe	iij		
Item xx^{ti} shepe		xxxiij	iiij
Item vj hogges & ij pyges		xiij	iiij

6 At 6s 8d per acre, the acreage was sixteen and a half.

	£	s	d
Item in pultrie		ij	
Item haulf a quarter of rye		iiij	
Item vj busshels of malt		vj	
Item in whoale timber		xxx	
Item in brasse & pewter		xx	
Item in stufe in the halle		xiij	iiij
Item stufe in the chambers		xxx	
Item in stowles, payels		xiij	iiij
Item in corne in the fyled	xx		
Summa totalis	xlj	xij	

Prayse the xviij[th] day of June anno domini 1560
by Willam Hyckeman, Willam Jhonson, Richard Gogen, Jhon Ampes
[*Exhibited at Dunstable on 17 October 1560*]

Notes: John Whauley's burial has not been found.

25 William Colmane of Shillington, maltman — made 3 October 1560

Lincolnshire Archives, INV/38/54
The document is badly creased with loss of some words, lines and figures.

The Invitorye of all the goods & cattalls of William Colmane late of Shetlington maltman deceased praysed the iij of October Anno domini [*blank*] by Richard Ashton, Thomas Colman, Thomas Clarke with other

	£	s	d
Inprimis a table with a frame & a forme		x	
Item one owld Rownd table			viij
Item a Cobard		vj	viij
Item a bench bord with a nould hawling			xij
Item iij shelfe bords and a nowld Joyned Stole			viij
Item a pare of Irone drafftes			xvj
In the chamber			
Item a bedsted			viij
Item ij underclothes & ij owld boustars ij blankytes and ij coverlettes		xiij	iiij
Item iiij owld paynted clothes			xx
Item a cofer		ij	iiij
Item iij caldelstekes a chafin dyshe x peces of puter ij saltes		ix	
Item one smale brase pott one kettell with ij other smale kettels a skillitt		viij	
Item a fruinge pan a lytell tobe a botle and one pale a pare of pothokes a spyte & a pare of Andirons a nowld spaid & a basket		v	

	£	s	d
Item a cotte a doblett and a pare of hosse		x	
Item v pare of owld course harden shetes and a berynge shette a table clothe a pillober and ij handtowels		xv	
Item ij owld bedsteds a powdrynge troughe with a cover a wollen and a [...] laynen whell		v	
Item an owld arke a mattoke a owld sawe a pare of bodey trases iij pare of plene trases & ij Rige wythes a Ridinge pannell		iij	iiij
Item xl ^{li} of hempe		iij	iiij
Item a nowlde [*illeg.*]			iiij
Item drafte [*illeg.*]			xij
Item a [*illeg.*]			viij
Item in [*illeg.*] [*?*]houses vij lode of haye & one lode of [*illeg.*] estimacon		xl	
Item in the barne iiij lode of feches [*illeg.*]		xx	
Item corne in the same barne [*illeg.*] by estimacon vij quarters	iiij	iiij	
Item iij sowes vij stores & a bore		xl	
Item a Cowe		xij	
Item all the horses	x		
Item peasen by estimacon vij acers & a halfe	iiij		
Summa totalis	xxviij	xv	

[*Exhibited at Bedford on 12 October 1560*]

Notes: William Colmane was buried at Shillington on 14 September 1560.

26 John Fysher of Tempsford, husbandman made 10 October 1560

Lincolnshire Archives, INV/38/110

The page is damaged and some words at the foot of the first side and the top of the second side are missing.

This is the Inventory indentid made the xth day of October the second yere of the reigne of Elizabeth by the grace of god of England Fraunce & Ireland quene defender of the feithe etc of all the goodes Cattalles & dettes of John Fyssher of Temysford in the County of Beds husbondman decessid praysed by Richerd Maye of Beston husbondman, Richerd Parkyn, Thomas Bayes & Henr[y] Parkyn of Temysford aforsed husbondmen

	£	s	d
In primis xij payer of shetes wherof thre be of Flexon price		xxviij	
Item Thre table Clothes price		iiij	
Item fyve kyrcheyffes price		iiij	
Item Two Coverlettes price		iij	
Item Two blankettes price		v	iiij
Item fyve pyllowes two bolsters with the tyckes price		v	iiij
Item two matteresses price		vj	viij
Item nyne peynted Clothes hanging about the Chamnber price		viij	

Item Thre Bedstedes price		iij	iiij
Item Thre Coffers price		v	
Item one ambery price		iij	iiij
Item xv pewte platters a pewte pott fower Candylstyckes & two sawsers price		xvj	iiij
Item all his weryng rayment price		xx	
Item one table a benche bourde & thre formes price		ij	viij
Item one foult table in the hall price		x	
Item all the Cheses price		x	
Item one olde hallyng & one old peynted Clothe price		iij	iiij
Item sixe ketles one old pan & thre brasse pottes price		xxxiij	iiij
Item a spitte two cobyernes pothookes pothangilles & a gredyerne price		ij	viij
Item two peyer of harrowes price		iij	iiij
Item a bason price			xij
Item a dozen hurdelles price		iij	
Item one forme & a troff with a borde over yt price		ij	iiij
Item certeyn hempe price			xx
Item xv pound of wollen yarne beyng wevers wayte price		x	
Item one wollen whele a mattocke fower old Sythes & all other ymplementes & trasshe in the Backhowse price		ij	viij
Item a saltyng troffe a Cherme certeyne tubbs & all other ymplementes & trasshe in the Butterey price		vj	viij
Item two Cheres & two Stoles price			xij
Item a byll an axe & a hachett price			xij
Item two bottelles price			xvj
Item two shudde Cartes & a ~~ma~~ mucke Carte price		xl	
Item fower horsses price	iij	vj	viij
Item horsse harnes Collers & trace price		iij	iiij
Item two ploughes thre Coulters two Sharrs two oxe teamys & tortrees price		viij	
Item fyve duckes & a Drake price			xviij
Item ~~Item~~ xij hens & Chekyns price		ij	
Item one sedcodde one Scuttle one skeppe & one Fan price			xx
Item fower hogges & sixe pygg[*es*] price		xxvj	viij
Item fyve bullockes price		xl	
Item one wenyng Calff price		v	
[...] mylchebeas two oxon & two hecfors price	ix	vj	viij
[...] score Shepe price	ix	vj	viij
Item certe[*yne*] tymber & other Ploughe woode price		vj	viij
Item xvj acres of Tylthe price		xlviij	
Item certeyne hey price		xx	
Item xij quarters of Barly price	v	viij	
Item ten quarters of otes price		~~xliij~~ liij	iiij
Item viij quarters of peas & fetches price		~~vj~~ liij	~~viij~~ iiij
[*Total*	*£45*	*12s*	*6d*]

[*Exhibited at Bedford on 12 October 1560*]

Notes: John Fysher's burial has not been found.

27 William Watson of Bolnhurst undated; c. 1559–1560

Lincolnshire Archives, INV/38/106

The document is stained and faded along the lower right side. Some figures near the end of the inventory are barely legible.

Thys ys a true Inventory of all the goodes of William Watson of Bolnehurst late deceasyd valuyd & prasyd by Thomas Halkot, Whyllyam Newton, John Rawlyn, Raffe Virqilat with other

	£	s	d
In primis iiij horsys	iiij	xiij	viij
Item vij Key & iij bullockes	vj		
Item xx storys		x	
Item xxv gese		vj	viij
Item xvj hennes & cockes		iiij	
Item ij quarters of whete		xl	
Item the corne In the barne	iiij	vj	
Item the ootes & peyse		xxxiiij	
Item the heye		xiiij	
Item plow & plow geres cart & cart geres		xxj	
Item the chamber		[?]xx	
Item the halle		xiij	
Item the chychyn		vj	viij
Summa totalis	xxv		
[*Corrected total*	*£23*	*9s*	*0d*]

[*Exhibited at St Neots on 11 October 1560*]

Notes: William Watson's burial has not been found. On the verso of the inventory are notes of the grant of administration to Katherine Watson, his widow, and a bond for £40 taken by William Cotton, rector of Bolnhurst from her and Hyway (whose first name missing), a husbandman of Bolnhurst. It is undated and damaged. William Cotton was rector of Bolnhurst 1555–65 (Beds Archives, Fasti/1/Bol; not in CCEd).

28 Thomas Semer undated; before October 1560

Lincolnshire Archives, INV/38/52

Thys ys the Invitore of Thomas Semers goods praysed by John Martyne, William Barbar & John Tomsine

	£	s	d
In primis his howsald Stuffe		xxx	
Item the Rye		xxvj	viij
Item the barley		ix	vj
Item a hogge		ij	viij
Item a table		v	
Item ij lowmes with certene geres therto belongynge		liij	iiij
Item hys Apparell		xl	
Item ij doe skynes		v	
Item a bowe and shaftes		x	

	£	s	d
Item lynnen yarne			xxij
Summa	ix	iiij	

[*Exhibited at Bedford on 12 October 1560*]

Notes: No place of residence or burial has been found for Thomas Semer. His inventory has been tentatively attributed to Bedfordshire in Lincolnshire Archives catalogue. The next document is the inventory of Annes Semer, probably his wife as it is almost identical at the beginning and the appraisers were the same.

29 Annes Semer — undated; before October 1560

Lincolnshire Archives, INV/38/77

This ys the Invitorye of Annes Semers ~~goods~~ housald Stowffe prayssed to the somme of xxxs

	£	s	d
Item for the Rye		xxvj	viij
Item barley		ix	vj
Item hempe		ij	viij
Item the Firewood in the yard		x	
Item one hogge		vj	viij
Item a table		v	
Item her Apparell		xiij	iiij
Sum	v	iij	x

praysed by Johne Martyne, William Barbar and Johne Tomsyn
[*Exhibited at Bedford on 12 October 1560*]

Notes: No place of residence or burial has been found for Annes Semer. The inventory has been tentatively attributed to Bedfordshire in Lincolnshire Archives catalogue. The previous document is the inventory of Thomas Semer, probably her husband as it is almost identical at the beginning and the appraisers were the same.

30 John Edwards of Carlton — undated; probably 5 February 1561

Lincolnshire Archives, INV/1/89

The inventory is badly damaged and only the centre of the document survives. It is also poorly written and some words and values are indecipherable. All values, except the two sums of £5, are unclear.

The Inviatory [*remainder of this line and the beginning of the next one is missing*] the fyfte day of February [...]

	£	s	d
Item a fetherbede A matrys two bolstars			
two blancates two pere of shetes		x	
with bras & peuter a tabull		[*?*]x	[*illeg.*]
Item [*?*]Fyfftene quarters of barly whete			
& Rye pees	v	[*illeg.*]	[*illeg.*]
Item Fore hors		xxiij	[*illeg.*]
Item fyve bees	v	[*illeg.*]	[*illeg.*]

Item a shod cart		x	[*illeg.*]
Item tene shepe		xvij	[*illeg.*]
Summa	xvj		iiij

praysyd by Rychard Mychyll, William [*?*]Byree & Thomas Rudde the helder & Thomas Rudde the yonger
[*No exhibition clause*]

Notes: John Edwards was buried at Carlton on 29 October 1560. A loose document filed with the inventory notes a bond for £30 was taken from Agnes Edwards, administratrix, William [*?*]Pyrrwine of Turvill, Bedfordshire (maybe Turvey) and John [*?*]Pyrrionre of Hardmead, Buckinghamshire, husbandmen.

31 William Decons of Wilshamstead — made 30 September 1562

Lincolnshire Archives, INV/42/61
The foot of the inventory is missing.

The Invytory of all suche goodes and cattelles as one William Decons laite of Wilshamsted deceased died seased of made the laste daye of September in the forthe yeare of the Raign of our sovereagne lady Elyzabeth by the grace of god Quene of England Fraunce and Iralond etc in the yeare of our lord god 1562

	£	s	d
in the halle			
Item in primis in the halle one Table and Settell a forme a chare fyve stoles & a chosse chare		x	
Item a Cubbard & a Settill for pewter		vj	viij
Item the hangins in the hawle		iij	
the parler			
Item in the parler a Cownter Table the forme to the same a chare		vj	viij
Item a Cubbard & iij Coffers		x	
Item the Bedde in the said parler as yet [*it*] stand ther		xx	
Item the hangins on the said parler and fower Cusshins		v	
in the loffte over the parler & the other loffte			
Item the Bedde in the loffte as it stand		iij	iiij
Item for the Bedde in the other loffte as it stand		vj	viij
Item ~~the~~ a greate cheste in the same lofte		iij	iiij
in the chamber next the halle			
Item in the chamber next the hawle iij Beddes as they stand		xxvj	viij
Item for iij Coffers in the chamber		vij	
the brasse & pewter			
Item all the Brasse		xxvj	viij
Item all the pewter		xx	

	£	s	d
Item certen other stuff bequethid by the said will to Francis Decons as appereth by the said will	iiij	vj	viij
Item ~~the~~ all trene wayre		iij	iiij
the napry			
Item all the Naprye		xxvj	viij
the playte			
Item one silver sault & viij sponnes		xxx	
in the yard and the closses			
Item the woode on the yard		x	
Item ij cartes		xiij	iiij
Item all the calves being weners		xxx	
Item all the hogges on the yard		xxvj	viij
Item xvij beasst and bullockes	xvij		
Item vj drawing stearres	x		
Item v[th] horsses & coltes	v		
Item plowgh gearres & carte gea[...] other such [...]			
~~Item~~			
The remainder of the inventory is missing.			
[*The total is at least*	*£51*	*1s*	*8d*]

[*No exhibition clause*]

Notes: William Decons' burial has not been found. The will mentioned in the inventory has not survived.

32 William Besowthe of Studham, husbandman made 6 March 1563

Lincolnshire Archives, INV/42/47

Slight damage at the top right corner. The document is written in a cramped court hand.

An Inventory of all the goodes & Cattaylles late Wylliam Besowthes of Studh[a]m in the Coun[...] Hertf husbandman decessed taken the vj[th] daye of Marche Anno Domini 1562 and praysed by John [...] Belfeld, John Beaymonde, John Barrett, John [*?*]Cameler, Thomas [*?*]Hess, John Barton & others

	£	s	d
Inprimis Wheate in the Barne unthreshed iij quarters praysed at	iiij		
Item in ottes unthreshed iiij quarters prised at		xl	
Item peyse & hay prised at		x	
Item Wheate growynge in diverse feyldes xij acars prised at	vj		
Item iiij horses, plowe & plowegeres cartes & carte harnes etc	vj		
Item j Cowe ij hekefers & ij Calves		xlvj	viij
Item xx[ti] shepe of all sortes		liij	iiij
Item viij hogges & shottes		xiij	iiij
Item beache & ashe tymber for Whealles		xl	
Item the howshold Stuff with the pultre & hys wearynge apparrelles		lx	
Sume	xxix	iij	iiij

[*No exhibition clause*]

Notes: William Besowthe's burial has not been found.

33 John Odell of Cranfield made 20 May 1563

Lincolnshire Archives, INV/42/51A

An Invetory of the Godes of John Odell of Cranfeild dysseaced mayd & praysed by Wylliam Sylbys, Thomas Wheler, Henry Doo, John Mowse & with others the xx[ti] of May 1563

		£	s	d
Inprimis ij horses at	iiij markes		*[53s*	*4d]*
Item ij kyen & iij bullokes at		v		
Item xiiij shepe at			xxx	
Item one hogg & ij ~~stokes~~ stores at			x	
Item one shoyd cart at			xx	
Item iij half acres of wheat at			xxvj	viij
Item iij acres of barlye at			xxx	
Item iiij acres of pease at			xx	
Item wodd in the yard at			xx	
Item an old panne of brasse at			vj	viij
Item a brasse pott & vj pewder dysshes at			x	
Item a mattres ij coverlettes ij blaketes vj payre of sheites			xxij	
Item one chare & ij stoles at				xx
Item a table & fowrme			ij	iiij
Item a plowghe with harnes to horsse			x	
Item plowgh tymber			xiij	iiij
Item a hovell with pease at			xv	
	Summa	xix	ij	iiij
	[Corrected total	*£19*	*11s*	*0d]*

[*No exhibition clause*]

Notes: John Odell's burial has not been found.

34 John Brimsall of Girtford, Sandy made 5 July 1563

Lincolnshire Archives, INV/42/50 and INV/42/78

These are identical copies of John Brimsall's inventory. Both are damaged. The transcription has been made principally from INV/42/50 with doubtful readings or additional information supplied from the other copy.

This is a true Inventorye of all the goodes that were John Brimsalles Late deseased of Gyrthforthe in the parishe of Sandye at the day of his Death which was the fyfte day of Julye in the yere of our Lorde god a thousande fyve hundreth lxiij in the fyfte yere of the Reigne of our most gratious sovereigne Ladye quene Elizab[*eth*] prised by William Edroppe, John Symons, Edward Brittan, John Underwoode & John Yarway Julij nono

	£	s	d
In primis a table a forme & a benchborde			xvj
Item a Cubborde		v	
Item 3 chaires			xij
Item the hallynge & paynted clothes		iij	iiij
Item 4 Cusshins			xij
Item a basen a chaffyndyshe & 3 litle candlestickes			xx
Item xv pece of pewter 3 sasers & 2 litle saltes		viij	

Item one pewter pott				ij
Item 5 earthen Cruses				v
Item 4 Coverlettes			x	
Item 4 blankettes			vj	viij
Item 3 mattresses			vj	viij
Item 3 bolsters & 3 pillowes ticke			iiij	
Item 9 payre of shetes			xx	
Item 6 pillowberes			ij	
Item 4 table clothes			iiij	
Item 4 table napkyns				viij
Item 3 pottes & one posnett			x	
Item 2 olde pannes & 3 litle kettles			vj	viij
Item 5 tubbes 2 kymmelles 2 barrelles & one cherme			iiij	
Item one saltinge troughe				viij
Item 2 dosan dyshes				viij
Item 2 dosan trinchers				iiij
Item 2 dosan wodden spones				iij
Item 4 milke boules				viij
Item 6 chesfattes				xij
Item 2 spetes & one paire of Cobirons				xvj
Item one gridirone treddes & a paire of potthoukes				xij
Item one fryinge panne & a fyer forke				viij
Item 5 olde bedsteades			ij	
Item 5 Coffers & one litle fosser			x	
Item painted clothes in the chamber			v	
Item 3 coates			x	
Item 2 clokes & 4 girkyns			x	
Item 2 paire of hose & 2 petticotes			v	
Item 7 shirtes			x	
Item 2 hattes & 2 nightcappes			ij	
Item 2 dosan pounde of wollen yarne			iiij	
Item 2 carte bodyes & 2 paire of shudd wheles		iij		
Item cart harnes & plow harnes			x	
Item 2 Carte Ropes			ij	
Item fyre wodde & other wodde a litle			v	
Item 2 draweng Rakes & 13 other			ii	
Item 5 horse & a coult		vj		
Item 4 kyne		v		
Item 2 oxen	fouer markes		~~xxxiij~~	~~iiij~~[7]
	[*Corrected value*		*53s*	*4d*]
Item 3 yearyng bullockes & a litle stere	v nobles[8]		xxxiij	iiij[9]
Item one dosan shepe			xx	
Item 6 hogges & 2 litle pigges			xiij	iiij
Item 2 acars wheat			xiij	iiij
Item 3 acers Rye			xx	
Item a dosan acars barley		vj		

7 In INV/42/50 only.
8 In INV/42/78 only.
9 In INV/42/50 only.

Item 6 acars peasone	fyve nobles[10]		xxxiij	iiij[11]
Item 2 bushelles wheat			vj	
Item 2 quarters malt			xxx	
Item Rye & barley eight bushelles			xv	
	Summa totalis ut supra	xlj	iiij	vj
	[*Corrected total*	*£40*	*17s*	*10d*]

[*No exhibition clause*]

Notes: John Bromsalle (the usual spelling in the parish register) was buried at Sandy on 7 July 1564. In view of the dating problem in the registers for the periods 1558–64 and 1568–74, this may be an error for 1563 (*BPR*, vol. 6, pp. Ai and A83).

35 Alice Philyppes of Harrold, Cardington, widow made 15 July [1563]
Lincolnshire Archives, INV/42/48

An Invitarie taken the xv[th] daie of Julij of all such goodes and cattell as was Alce Philyppes of Harrod ~~It~~ in the parych of Cardyngton In the Counte of Bedford widow lately deseaced as foloweth

	£	s	d
Fyrst in the chamber ij ollde bedstedes		ij	
Item ij fetherbedes ij bollsters		xx	
Item ij cuverynges		vj	
Item iij coffers And one fosser		v	
Item a table and ij tressells			xij
Item one other olde bedsted			vj
Item the hangyng over the bede			viij
Item ij paye of shetes and one shete		vj	viij
Item ij olde cottes of hyrs and a gowne		x	
Item ij smokes iij pellowberes one table clothe j cherchew		v	
In the halle			
Fyrst the hangyng in the halle		ij	
Item ij platters ij pewter dysshes		ij	
Item ij pewter poottes iij porryngers a salt			xx
Item a latten basin a chafyngdich ij canstykes		iij	
Item ij brasse pottes ij spytes		vij	
Item one kettell		ij	
Item ij ollde tubbes			xij
of cattell In the yard			
Fyrst ij myllch kene		xl	
Item xx[ti] sheppe and x lambes	iij	xvj	iiij
Summa	ix	xj	x

All thes goodes and cattell valuwed and presed by thes men John Berde, John Leie, Harrye Coper, John Crumpe, Harrye [*illeg.*], Nycolas Coper with other
[*No exhibition clause*]

Notes: Alice Philyppes' burial has not been found. The inventory is dated to 1563 in Lincolnshire Archives online catalogue.

10 In INV/42/78 only.
11 In INV/42/50 only.

36 Thomas Farre of Henlow — made 10 May [1564]

Lincolnshire Archives, INV/42/30

This document is badly damaged, being torn along the fold lines. Much of the list has been written as a continuous text, not set out with values on the right of the page. In the interests of clarity, the text has been put into the normal format. Where values have only been expressed as prices per unit, they have been calculated and inserted in the right hand columns. The statement naming the deceased and the appraisers has been moved from the foot of side three to the end of the inventory. No text has been omitted.

First side

The Invytori of all the movables of Tomas Farr

	£	s	d
Fyrst in myddlefyld of pese teres & otes xviij acres & di prise	vj	xiij	iiij
In dogditchfyld of Dradge v acres iij acres prise l^{s}		[*?50*]	
& in the Same fylde of whete xvij acres prise xiij^{s} iiij^{d} ac[*re*]	[*11*	*6*	*8*]
In northfyld x acres of pese with teris & barley pryse	v		
In northfyld of rye xv acres prise xiij^{s} iiij^{d}	[*10*	*0*	*0*]
In northfyld in berley lx & ~~v~~ iiii acres & in dogditchfyld both to			
gether prise for everi acre xv^{s}	[*48*	*0*	*0*]
Item ix horssis & ij gyldynges prise	xvij		
all plow harnis & carthernis ~~prise~~ with haulters cartsadeles prise		xx	
a lytle porsion of haye prise		x	
Item iiij payer of Shodd wheles ij long cartes & ij doung cartes with			
a lytell cart to carri tythe pryse v^{li} with the cartlades	v		
Item vj coultes prise	viij		
Item vij wenid caulves & a calff that Sucketh		xxvj	viij
Item ~~to~~ iij plowes with v herrowes & iiij iren rakes & ij ox yokes			
with the plow chaynes & whipletres coulters & Shers all to gether		xxxij	
Item Sithes axes bylles pitchforkes pesehokes & a doung forke with			
to dounge hokes all to gether		v	
Item xv bese & ij steres prise to gether	xxv	x	
Item x bullokes prise	vij	x	
Item xvj hoges & stores & ~~p~~ xv wenyd pyges fyve marke	[*3*	*6*	*8*]
Item Shepe at the xth daye of maye xxvj prise	iiij	vj	viij
Item Shepes skyns xv viij calves skyns & a horse Skyn all to gether		xij	vj
Item fell woull by estimation xiiij pounde prise ~~vj^{s}~~		v	ij
Item xxvj henns & vj capons & xxx duxx prise		xx	
Item in barle xiiij quarteres by estimation prise	x	x	
Item in whete & rie by estimation v quarteres prise	v		
Item iiij Ropes too Fannes & a bushell price of all together		iiij	
Item viij tobbes iiij barrelles iij Fates viij bowells v trovis j [*?*]Irs			
peill [*?iron pail*] a cherme a powddring toobbe vj cheis molles all			
together		xxvij	
Item too tables in the hawll ij formes iij chaires altogether		vj	viij
Second side			
[*Item*] [...] paynited clothes in the hawll		iij	
Item a panne & a kettell		xij	
Item ~~iiij~~ v kettelles & olde panne iij bras pottes ij friing pannes			
a posnet ij peire of potte hookes ij peir of andyerns			
a Spytt ij Chafyng dyshes ij gredyerns [*?*]ij [*?*]peir			

of pott hanggynges too trevettes ij latten morters price of all to gether		xxxv	vj
Item xix peces of pewter too porringers v sawcers vj pewters spones price altgether		xx	
Item in the hawll j coubbard		vj	viij
Item in the parlor			
~~Item a folded table~~			
Item a table & a carpet iij chaires		vj	
Item too coffers		viij	
Item a coubbord		xiij	iiij
Item xij peices of pewter		xij	
Item iij candelstyckes			[...]
Item iij saltes of pewter			xij
a coubberd cloth			xij
Item the peyncted clothes in the parlor		v	
Item a bedsted a fether bed a matteres a bolster a coverlett ij pyllowes price alltogether		xxvj	viij
Item in the lowft over the parlor j bedsted a fether bed, a coverled a bolster with a tester over the bed price		xiij	iiij
Item one other bedsted a coverlet a bolster		iiij	
Item iij old coffers		iij	
Third side			
Item vij peyr of flaxen sheittes		xl	
Item xvj peyre of towen sheittes		xxxij	
iiij towelles		iij	iiij
iiij table clothes price		v	
Item ~~viiij~~ v pyllobeires		v	
Ittem his apparell unbequested		xiij	iiij
Item in a nether chamber iij bedstedes iij coveringes iij bolsters price		x	
[*line deleted and illegible*]			
Ittem certeyne of [*illeg.*] & [*?*]steill			xx
Ittem in Redy mony xxx[s] which was bestowed uppon the funeralles		xxx	
Item xx [*?*]salt cheses price		vj	viij
Item a grynston ij ladders		iiij	
Item certeyn hempe land sowen		x	
Item vj flytchis bacon		vj	viij
Fourth side			
Item iiij sackes		v	
Item v bottelles price		v	
Item the Lease of the Fearme	xx		
Item a bucket with a cheine			xvj
Item xiiij[li] of hempe		iij	
Item vj skaynes of lynen yarne		iij	iiij
Item j wollen wheill & ij lynen wheilles		iij	
Summa	ijCxiiij	xiij	ij
[*Corrected total is at least*	*£216*	*1s*	*2d*]

Item This Invytory taken of all theis goodes the xth of Maye by Henry Hurst, George Clarke, Thomas Underward, William Geding, Thomas Agas, William Hurst, William Tylly
[*No exhibition clause*]

Notes: Thomas Farre was buried at Henlow on 19 April 1564.

37 William Purryar of Turvey made 27 May 1565
Lincolnshire Archives, INV/45/28

The Inventorye of all suche goodes & Cattelles as late were Willia[m] Purryar of Turvey decessed prased the xxvij of Maye the yere of our lord god 1565 by Robert Skevyngton, Raffe Carpenter, George [*?*]Lawte & John Stevensonn of the same towne of Turveye

	£	s	d
iiij horses prised at	iij	vj	viij
The horse geyres & Carte geyres		vj	viij
v kyne prised att	vj		
iij Bullockes att		xxvj	viij
ij Cartes & One bodye		liij	iiij
iiij store hogges		xvj	
One pese hovell		xxxiij	iiij
vj coples		xxiiij	
The hovelles		xiij	iiij
The wooll		xxxiij	iiij
The plowghe Tymber & bordes		xx	
The Iron & plowghes		xiij	iiij
One drawght Rak			xx
The brasse pottes & pannes		xxxiij	iiij
The pewter		xiij	iiij
The Table One forme ij cheyres stoles One Amberye		vj	viij
One Spytt One payre of Cobyrons One payre of hookes		iij	
One payre of Tonges and Trevett			viij
One Tubbe one Saltyngtrowghe ij meylles		iiij	viij
All the paynted clothes		vj	viij
Three cofers		vij	
Three bedstedes		iij	
One matterys three coverlaydes		xij	
Three bolsters iij pyllowes with thre Beers		ix	
xxij payre of Shetys iij Table clothes iij Towelles iij Table napkyns	iij	vj	viij
xxij ~~& di~~ Acres & di barleye Otes wheat at vj^s^ viij^d^ the Acre	vij	x	
malte xij bus & di barley vij quarters vj bus Rye & wheat vj bus	iij	x	
[*Total*	*£40*	*14s*	*4d*]

[*Exhibited at Bedford on 1 July 1566*]

Notes: William Purryar's burial has not been found.

38 William Brytayne of Blunham made 21 March 1566

Lincolnshire Archives, INV/45/34

Some damage on the top right hand side. The final figures in the pence column of some values may be missing, making the total wrong.

An Inventorie of the goodes & catalles of William Brytayne of Blun[*ham*] in the countie of Bed deceassed made & pryesed the xxj[th] daye of Marche 1566 by Robert Osburne, Robert Wotton, Robert Gardyner & William Crane inhabitantes of Blunham

		£	s	d
Fyrst in the halle a table a forme a chaire & a long settell			ij	vj
Item in the chamber a cupbord & iij cofers			viij	[...]
Item ij bedstedes a bolster ij pylowes & a coverlet			vj	[...]
Item v paynted clothes			ij	[...]
Item x peces of pewter			vj	viij
Item iij candelstyckes a sawcer iij saltes & a porynger			ij	iiij
Item ij curtaynes & a blanket			vj	
Item v payre of shetes			xx	
Item iij pylow beares				xx
Item vij yardes of clothe whyghte gray & a yard of carsey			xij	
Item one blanket a cote ij Jerkyns & ij payer of hose			viij	
Item a cloke & a paire of bote hose			iij	
Item iij shertes & an old payr of shetes			iiij	
Item a saltynge troughe & a kymnell				xx
Item a paire of cobyrons & a spyt			ij	vj
Item a brasse panne & ij litle tubbes			iij	
Item in bieffe & bacon in the ruffe			vj	viij
Item in haye & vitches			x	
Item ij kyne & a calfe			xl	
Item iij loade of wood			vj	viij
Item halfe a quarter of wheat & muney for wheat			xvj	
Item iij bussheles rye			vj	
Item x bussheles barley			xv	
Item iij hogges			vj	viij
Item in all kynd of grayne iiij acres & an halfe			xxxiij	iiij
Item xviij shepe	iiij markes		[*53s*	*4d*]
Item xxx[ti] shepe sold unp[*ai*]d for		v		
In debtes to hym				
Robert Gardyner oweth hym			xix	vj
	[*Total*	*£20*	*2*	*0*]
he oweth as Followeth				
To John Brytayne his brother			xxvj[ti]	viij
to Henrie Parkyn of Temsford			xiiij	ij
to John Kyrbye for rent			xv	
to Agnis Spencer for iij shepe			vij	
to Robert Wotton			iij	iiij
	[*total he owed*	*£3*	*6*	*2*]
	Sum totall the debtes alowed	xv	xvij	iiij

[*Exhibited at Bedford on 2 July 1566*]

Notes: William Brytayne's burial has not been found. A note on the verso of the inventory records the grant of administration to his widow Elizabeth.

39 John Freman, junior, of Nether Dean, Dean made 16 April 1566
Lincolnshire Archives, INV/45/90

Thys Inventory Indentyd of all the goodes Cattalles & howsholde of one John Freman late of Netherdean junior deceast taken the xvjth daie of Apryll anno regni domine nostre regine Elizabeth octavo by Rychard Neall senior gent, Wylliam Eston, John Bole, Thomas Marshall & Thomas Dawson Fol[low]ȝ [?]sig

	£	s	d
Fyrst in the hall a table a forme a Settell one chere six great buffytt Stoles iij lesser buffytt stoles a turned pen		x	
more there a chafyng dyshe ij Candelstyckes a brasse pott iij lyttle kettelles a posnett a lyttle pan a spyse mortar a [?]teme a bentche borde & a cradell		xiiij	viij
more in the parlar a Cubbarde 5 platters 4 pewter dyshys 6 porrengers 3 Sawcers 2 Salt sellers & a Cubberd clothe		xxx	
more there a Framed bedsted a Fetherbedd a mattres 2 keverlettes 3 tycke pyllowes 5 pyllowe beres one paire of shete a Coffar & the hangeinges there		xl	
more there 4 payre of Flexson shetes 13^{s} 4^{d} 6 paire of harden shetes 13^{s} 4^{d} a baryng shete 3^{s} 4^{d} ij Flexson bordeclothys 3^{s} 4^{d} iiij harden bordeclothes 4^{s} syx table napkyns of myddell harden 2^{s} 6^{d} a lyttle Fossar 8^{d}		xl	vj
more in a Chamber a pair of blanketes [...] turned presse 3 lyttle barrelles a lyttle black [?]wooll iij Flexson sleppes of yarne ij ravelles & a bowltar		viij	
more in the loft a bedstad a bushell a chese racke ij chese bordes a newe hyve		ij	
more in the kytchyn 2 kettelles a Sawcer one pewter dyshe 3 chessefates a mele a cheseprese a wolle whele a lynnen whele a [?]thele iij endes of [?]slabbes		vj	viij
more in the chamber by the kytchen 16 bushelles malt 24^{s} a hogg in Salt iij^{s} iiij^{d} olde Iron there xij^{d} Foure hogges in the Roofe xiij^{s} iiij^{d}		xlj	iiij
[*Corrected value*		*41*	*8*]
more in the Stable iij horses 2 coltes iiij^{li} 13^{s} 4^{d} iiij paire of olde cart geres ijs 4 pair of plowghe geres viijd ij pyckforkes a pece of an old Cart rope & 4 mullyn halters viij^{d} & ij Sackes ij^{s}	iiij	xviij	viij
more 7 myltchebeaste two thre yere old bullockes one two yere old bullocke & ij yerenges vj^{li} 13^{s} 4^{d} one Sowe ij pygges & viij lyttle Stores 13^{s} 4^{d} xxiij ewes & 23 lambes iiij^{li} 14 lambhogges xxviij^{s} Syx sherehogges xx^{s}	xiij	xiiij	viij

more in the barne u[*n*]threshe by estymaciun ij quarters of barley xxiiij^{s} two bushelles of Rye iij^{s} vj^{d} one role xij^{d} ij sydes for a cart xvj^{d} one Ryddell one Ryeing Syve ij lyttle ladders ~~xxvj^{s} viij^{d}~~ one long cart one payre of wheles with tyer a muckcart body one harrowe 26s 8d		lv	vj
[*Corrected value*		*56*	*6*]
more a sedyng plowghe & certeyn plowghe tymber vj^{s} viij^{d} a shep rack and certeyn wood in the yarde 4s		x	viij
more 13 hennes 2 Cokes 9 duckes 2 drakes 2 geyse one gander 2 beyhyves		vj	viij
more 17 akers of barley v^{li} xiij^{s} iiij^{d} 5 rodes of otes vj^{s} 3 rodes of wheat viij^{s} a 15 akers of pease & Fetches iij^{li} xv^{s}	x	ij	iiij
Sum	xlj	xviij	
[C*orrected total*	*£42*	*3s*	*0d*]

R[*ichard*] N[*eale*], William Eston, Thomas Dawson
[*Exhibited at Bedford on 1 July 1566*]

Notes: John Freman's burial has not been found.

40 Thomas Gray of Moggerhanger, Blunham made 4 June 1566
Lincolnshire Archives INV/45/156

The Inventorie of the goodes & cattalles of Thomas Gray of Muggerhanger in the paryshe of Blunh[a]m in the countie of Bed deceased made & praised the iiijth daye of June 1566 by William Fyssher, Nicolas Fyssher & William Chamber inhabytantes ther

	£	s	d
In primis in the halle an old cupbeurd		ij	
Item iiij brasse pottes		xv	
Item ij brasse pannes & a lytle posnet		viij	
Item xij peces of pewter and ij candlestyckes		xv	
Item a benchebord a banker a forme & a chayr		vj	
In the chamber			
Item ij coverletes a matres ij bolsters ij pylowes a bedsted		xvij	
Item a cofer & hanginges of paynted clothes		x	
Item iij flaxen shetes		x	
Item two paire of shetes ter of hempe		x	
Item iij payre & one shet of herden shetes		x	
Item ij table clothes & ij old towelles		iiij	
Item an old bedsted & ij old pylowes		ij	
Item an old cart		xx	
Item all the Fyrewood		xlvj	viij
Item iij old troughes		iij	
Item a horse		xxxiij	iiij
Item iij kyne	iiij		
Item viij ewes & lambes & an od shepe		xl	
Item xv acrs of corne sowen	ix		

Item in money gyven for a cofer			iij	iiij
Item all his apparll			xiij	iiij
	Sum totall	xxvj	viij	viij

[*No exhibition clause*]

Notes: Thomas Gray's burial has not been found.

41 Jarratt Grantt of Eyeworth made 15 June 1566

Lincolnshire Archives, INV/45/147

the Inventore of all the goodes and cattelles moveable and unmo[v]able late Jarrott Grantt of Eyworth decessed made by the vewe and preysement of Renold Robyns[o]n, Henri Colyke the xv[th] daye of June in the yere of our lord god a thousand fyve hundred threre scoore and vj

		£	s	d
the Implementes in or of the hall				
Fyrst paynted clothes			iij	
Item a coberde price			vij	
Item ij ~~cheyess~~ cheares				xij
Item on spynnynge whele				viij
Item for pewther			xl	
Item for brasse			xx	
Item for iij brasse potes			x	
Item iij coffers			x	
Item iij coverlettes			xvj	
Item for paynted clothes in the chamber			iiij	
Item iij par of lynyn shetes			xviij	
Item vj par of hempe shetes			xx	
Item ij tabull clothes			ij	viij
Item a saltynge trowffe				xvj
Item ij tubbes				xvj
Item ij baryles			ij	
Item a kymnel				vj
Item in the yarde vj hogges			xij	
Item for hennes cokkes & chekynes			iij	iiij
Item dysshes and spoyns				vj
Item tylthe in the Felde xl acres price		x		
Item vj in arcres ~~barle~~ berleye		iij		
Item iiij hors[es]			xl	
Item v mylche bees		v		
Item vj yerynges calffes			xl	
Item xx[th] shepe price		iij		
Item ij cartes			xxxiij	iiij
Item Fyer wode in the yarde				xij
Item in the chamer iij bedstedes			iiij	
Item iij mattres with bostares and pelos			xx	
	Sum	xxxv	iiij	viij
	[*Corrected total*	*£36*	*11s*	*8d*]

[*Exhibited at Baldock on 8 July 1566*]

Notes: Jarratt Grantt was buried at Eyworth on 13 November 1565.

42 William Stratton of Podington undated; before July 1566
Lincolnshire Archives, INV/45/41

The Invitory of goods & cattells of William Stratton decessed prised by Sartaine honest men as folowth videlict

	£	s	d
Item fyrste the hawle a table a frame one Chere and Stoles			xx
Item one old ambrey and a pen		ij	
Item ij Toubes ij Stopes and other trene waire			xvj
Item towe brase pootes A porsnet towe brase pannes a kettell & Skilleat		xiij	iiij
Item thre pewtter platters iiij disshes iiij Sawsores towe kandlestekes ij Sawltes A Chavingdishe prise		v	
Item A littell bare of Iron over the fyer and hangles of Iron A treveat and A greydyoren			xx
Item the Chamber iij bedstedes			xij
Item towe Coveres vallewed		ij	
Item one matterease ij booulsteres one of teike one of clothe ij pillowes towe coverleates		vj	viij
Item thre paire of flexon Shettes thre paire of harden Shetes towe table Clothes		x	
Item the Stable iij horse ij mayres vallowed at xiij^s iiij^d the pece	iij	vj	viij
Item fyve Bease at x^s the peac thre bullockes at v^s the pece and one wenyned Calfe at xx^d [*illeg.*]	iij	vj	viij
Item xv Shepe vallowed at ij^s the pec		xxx	
Item one Sowe and v Stores at xvj^d the pece		viij	
Item one Cart and one pair of old wheles vallowed		xxvj	viij
Item one plow and plow geres with the Carte geres		iij	iiij
Item ij Akres & A halfe of whette at v^s the Akre		xij	vj
Item vj quarteres of barley at viij^s the quarter		xlviij	
Item vj quarter of peac at v^s the quarte		xxx	
Item iij old hovelles vallowed		iij	iiij
Summa totalis	xvj	xix	x

[*Exhibited at Bedford on 1 July 1566*]

Notes: William Stratton's burial has not been found.

43 William Amerye of Biddenham undated; c. 1568

Lincolnshire Archives, INV/48/207

The document is damaged on the right side and some words and values are missing.

Thys ys the true Invitorye of all the goods and Catells of Wylliam Amerye of Byddenham in the Countye of Bedforde late dissese[*d*]

	£	s	d
Inprimis in the hall a Coubborde x pece of pewter a saltt a [...] iij Candilstyckes ij bras pootes ij bras ketyles a tabull a four[*m*] a setyll a benche borde a hallyng a testor a payll dysshe [...] trenchers spones iij stoles presed at		xxiij	iiij
Item in the Chamber a Cofer iij bedsteds ij Keverledes ij bl[*?ankets*] j bolster iij pelowes iiij payr of shettes		xiij	iiij
Item in grayne v boshells of malt v bosheles of barlye ij boshells [...] pryse		xiij	iiij
Item ij horses xs j cowe xiijs iiijd a yearlyng bolocke [...]	[*value missing*]		
Item in the kechyn a boltyng arke a kymnell a trought [...] trasshe		iiij	
Item all the woode in the yeard		xv	
Item x behyves		xx	
Item a Cart & Cart geares plowe & plowe geares		xiij	iiij
Item x hennes & a Coke ij geyse & a gander & vj gosselynges		[*ij*]	
Item x akers of grayne in the Feld	iij		[...]
Summa totalis	ix	iiij	

Theys be the names of the presers Robert Alyne, Thomas [...], Wylliam Harper of the parsonage, Wylliam Harper [...]

[*No exhibition clause*]

Notes: William Amerye's burial has not been found. The inventory is dated c. 1568 on Lincolnshire Archives online catalogue.

44 William Burell of Chellington made 23 January 1569

Lincolnshire Archives, INV/48/199

Anno Domini 1568: 23 of Januarij. An Imentory of such goodes and cattayles moveables & unmoveables thatt perteined[12] unto William Burell of Chelingto[*n*] in the county of Bedford diseased taken and praised bi Thomas Smith, William Quarell, George Frelove, Robert Rudd, John A barne & Henry Allin curatt thear the dai & year above writin

	£	s	d
Inprimis in the hall one grediron one paire of fire tonges one fire shovell			vj
Item all the brasse		iiij	
Item the pewter & iiij candelstikes		iij	
Item one cubbord		vj	

12 Changed from *perteinithe.*

	£	s	d
Item one old aumbry		ij	
Item one frame table vj buffet stoles		v	
Item one folden table ij bordes with other formis & stoles & two chaires		vij	
Item in the parlor ij bedstedis ij coveringes of listes one matris ij bolsters one presse of bordes ij cofers iij pair of shetes		xiij	iiij
Item iiij milch kine one yerling calfe		xl	
Item ix shepe		xij	
Item the wodd		vj	
Item ij pigges & the poltrey vj hense one cokk		ij	viij
Item all other thinges not namid			xx
Summa totalis	v	iij	ij

[*No exhibition clause*]

Notes: William Burell's burial has not been found.

45 Thomas Warnar of Colmworth made 15 March 1569

Lincolnshire Archives, INV/48/177

Some damage on the lower right side.

The Invintorye of all the goodes & cattaylle of Thomas Warnare of Colmorth in the co[u]nty of Bedford and in the dyocesse of Lyncolne madde the xv[th] daye of march anno domini 1568 & praised by theise indyfferent men Nycolas Dycons gentleman, Wylliam Kyng & Thomas Judd the yonger

	£	s	d
Inprimis two yo[u]ng horses	iiij	xiij	iiij
Item iij othere horses	iiij	xiij	iiij
Item one bawld horse		x	
Item one bay horse		xxxiij	iiij
Item two coltes		xxvj	viij
Item one greye nagg		x	
Item plowghs & plowgh boott carts & cart boott	iij	vj	viij
Item pannylls & gyrthes			xvj
Item v neatt	iij		
Item barly and wheat	iij	xiij	iiij
Item pease		v	
Item peason and oates sown	vij		
Item vj acres of wheatt & rye	iij		
Item xxiiij acres of tylth	iiij		
Item at Mowlsworth corne & cattayll	xix	xiij	iiij
Item fyve score shyppe	xv		
in the parlare			
Item viij pare of shetts		xvj	
Item amatteryse		ij	vj
Item a cubbord		viij	
Item hys rayment		xx	
Item two coffers		iiij	
Item pewter		vj	viij

in the lytle parlar			
Item a cubbord		x	
Item a fetherbedd		x	
Item a bedsted		vj	viij
Item a coffere		iij	
Item fower buffytt stolls		ij	
in the chamber			
Item ij bedsteds			xvj
Item fower coffors		v	iiij
Item an olde fatt & a trunck		ij	
Item a Jacke		iij	iiij
in the old Chamber			
Item rye and mawlt		xvij	
Item other stuffe in the same chamber		v	
Item stuffe in the neyther chamber		v	
in the mawlt howse			
Item a stepyng fatt		v	
Item raw mawltt		xx	
Item iij sythes		iiij	
Item aquyrne		v	
Item abowltyng tubb kymnells & amowldyng bord		iij	[...]
Item all thyngs in the buttry		iij	iiij
Item all thyngs in the mylck hows		ij	
Item all thyngs in the hall		xx	
Item bacon		xij	
Item two hovells		xl	
Item a grynston		v	
Item a hoggstrowgh & tymber		v	
Item ladders			xij
Item stores & pyggs		xx	
Item syxe hennes & a cocke			xx
Item fowre ducks & a drak			xiiij
somme	lxxxvj	ij	viij

[*No exhibition clause*]

Notes: Thomas Warnar's burial has not been found.

46 Nicolas Fyssher of Moggerhanger, Blunham made 26 March 1569

Lincolnshire Archives, INV/48/186

There is damage on the right side but no values have been lost. The scribe has written e *in several places where* o *would be expected.*

An Inventorie of the goodes & catalles of Nycolas Fyssher of ~~the paryshe~~ Muggerhanger of the paryshe of Blunham in the countie of Bedf deceassed viewed & praysed the xxvj[te] daye of Marche 1569 by Them[a]s Grey, Robert Them[a]s, ~~Thomas Angell~~ Robert Pecke[13] & William Them[a]s Inhabytantes there

[13] Robert Pecke has been written above the deleted name of Thomas Angell.

	£	s	d
In the halle			
Inprimis a standinge framed table & a forme		viij	
Item a table on the benche			xvj
Item a cupbeurd		vj	viij
Item ij old chairs & a gowse penne			xvj
Item ix peces of p[*ew*]ter		vj	viij
Item a lytle pot a panne & iiij old ketles		xij	
Item iij old quysshyons		ij	
Item iij old candlestyckes & dysshes of wood			xij
Item ij cofers & a cradle		v	
Item iij old bedstedes		ij	
Item a matresse iij bolsters & iij pylowes		xij	
Item iij coverletes		x	
Item paynted clothes in the halle & chamber		vij	
Item a lytle yarne		ij	
Item x payre of shetes		xxvij	
Item in old strakes of yron		x	
Item his old apparell		iij	iiij
Item vj old horse	iiij	xij	
Item x beastes & calves	v		
Item xij shepe		xxiiij	
Item in rye & corne ix quarters	iiij		
Item hogges & gese & hennes		xiiij	
Item plough horse gayres & ploughgaires		xiij	iiij
Item in all manner grayne sowen xxv[ti] acrs	xij	x	
Sum totallis	xxxiiij	x	viij

[*No exhibition clause*]

Notes: Nicolas Fyssher's burial has not been found.

47 John Rychard, senior, of Keysoe made 19 April 1569

Lincolnshire Archives, INV/48/205

The right side is damaged and two figures may be missing.

The Inventory of all the moveable goodes of John Rychard late of Caysho decessyd made the xix daye of Apryll in the yere of our lord god M[l]CCCCC lxix praysyd by Henry SeyntJohn gentylman, Rychard Talbot, Henry Reyner, Thomas Slade & Henry Rychard

	£	s	d
In the hall & kechyn			
Fyrst xviij peysses of pewter platters & dysshes & iij pewter sawsers iiij salttcellers & halff a dosyn of tynne spones		xvj	
Item iij lattyn candelstyckes & a Chayffyngdysshe		ij	
Item iij brasse pannes iiij brasse pottes iiij kettelles & a skomer		xl	
Item iij spyttes a payr of CobbeIernes a fryeng panne ij Treddes & the potte hangelles		vj	viij
Item one olde Cupbord a Tabull a forme a Chayre & benchebord		x	

Item iiij Cussyones a bankecar a hallyng and other payntyd clothes in the hall		vj	viij

In the Chambers

Item a fetherbed a matresse a bolster a pyllowe a blanket & Coveryng		xxvj	viij
Item ij matresses a bolster a pyllowe and iij Coverynges		xiij	iiij
Item v Coffers smalle & grett		x	
Item xvj peyr of sheyttes Flaxen & hardyn	iij	vj	viij
~~Item vj Tabulclothes~~			
Item vj Tabulclothes & twoo towelles		xvj	
Item iiij olde bedsteyddes with the testers & peyntyd hangynges		vj	viij
Item viij Tubbes grett & smalle iij paylles a stantte a stoppe a kymnell iiij bolles ij dosyn of dysshes twoo dosyn of ~~th~~ trenchers & dosyn of spones		x	
Item xij yardes of Roset vij yardes of Caffey & iiij yardes of graye pleyn		xlj	
Item his waryng Rayment		xx	

The stabull

Item vij horse & Coltes	xiij	vj	viij
Item xiiij beysse & bullockes iiij yerelyng Calves & iiij wenyng Calves	xiiij		
Item iiij^{xx} [*80*] shepe	x		
Item ij sowes & vij Stores		vj	[...]
Item vj bee hyves		vj	[...]
Item ij shood Cartes & donge Carte & peyr of parers unshoyd with the Carte geares	iiij		
Item ij plowes & one oxe teame and oxe yokes with the plowe geares plowe tymbe & carte tymber		xxx	
Item other square tymber in the yarde twoo Framyed hovylles & iij ladders		xxvj	viij
Item one mattocke with pyckeforkes shovylles & donge Forkes		ij	vj
Item a saltyng troffe iiij bordes & ij theylles		v	
Item vj quarters of maltte vj quarters of barley Fowre quarters of wheyt & ij quarters of peysse	x		
Item one Ierne harowe & one Ierne Rake		vj	viij

The Croppe in the Feld

Item iij acres & a halff of wheyt in the feld xvj acres of barley & xxiij acr[es] of peysse & Otes	xv		
Summa totalis[14]	iiij^{xx}v		xviij

[*on verso*] The Inventorye of John Rychard the elder of Caysho
[*No exhibition clause*]

Notes: John Rychard's burial has not been found.

14 i.e. £85 1s 6d.

48 William Kynge of Wrestlingworth made 20 April 1569
Lincolnshire Archives, INV/48/191

Jesus Anno 1569 11 regina Elyzabeth 20 Aprell
an Inventory of William Kyngs goods lately deceassed in Wrastlyngworth being truly prysed by Thomas Wanam, John Warwick, Ryc Squyer, Antony Eltam

	£	s	d
Inprimis for brass & pewter with all other thinges in the house		xx	
Item all the lynnen at		xx	
Item beddes and beddyng, in the chambers with chestes		xx	
Item a trofe with a few tubbes		v	
Item for iiij horse		xl	
Item carte geares with all other thyngs in the stable		vj	viij
Item a carte		xx	
Item ij oxen		liij	iiij
Item for vj bullockes and beastes	iij		
Item for xx^{ty} shepe		xl	
Item xl acres of grayne sowne	xxj		
Summa totalis	xxxv	iiij	vij
[*Corrected total*	*£35*	*4s*	*0d*]

[*No exhibition clause*]

Notes: William Kynge's burial has not been found.

49 William Gray alias Butler of Langford made 22 April 1569
Lincolnshire Archives, INV/48/193
The inventory is torn along the right side and text is missing. The ink has bled through the paper making it difficult to read.

A true Invytory of the goodes of William Gray other wayse Butler decesed anno salutis 1569 in & uppon 22 of Apryll

	£	s	d
Item a cofer the price			xx
Item ij cottes & a yerkynge		jx	
Item ij dubletes		ij	
Item iij pare of hose		v	iiij
Item iiij shyrtes		vij	viij
Item ij pare of roffes & a hatt			xx
Item a booe & viij shaftes			x
Item on heowe & a lame		iiij	
Item a bullocke		xiij	iiij
Item Thomas Harmer oveth v markes		[*66*	*8*]
Sum	iij	xij	ij
[*Corrected total*	*£5*	*12s*	*2d*]
Item detes to be payd to Mr Vicker of Langford		[*value missing*]	
Item dett to the shepird			iiij

The presers Thomas Hemmy[...], Henrye Hemmyng, Edmonde Underw[...], Jhon Grene
[*No exhibition clause*]

Notes: William Gray's burial has not been found. On the verso of the inventory is a note that he died intestate and that his brother John Gray alias Butler, a labourer of Baldock, was granted administration and bound in the sum of £10 to administer the estate. The other bondsmen were Henry Hemming, husbandman of Langford, and Henry Smith, yeoman of Caddington. Master Vicker of Langford may have been William Dymbylton, who had been appointed vicar of Langford in 1541. However, neither CCEd nor Beds Archives, Fasti/1/Lang are clear about the identity of the vicar in 1569.

50 William Wall of Willington, husbandman made 25 April 1569

Lincolnshire Archives, INV/48/198

This ys the true Invitorie of all the goodes and cattell of William Wall of Willington husbandman in the countie of Bedforde Late deacesed and valued praysed the xxv[th] of Aprill in the xj[th] yere of the Rayne of owr soveraigne Ladye Quene Elizabeth praysed by Thomas Shatbolt, John Ryselie, John Clayton, Robert Osmunt and John Cowper with others

	£	s	d
In primis in the halle a table a forme twoe chayres		iij	iiij
Item A Cubborde a hene pene		x	
Item all the pewter & the Lattyn		xiij	iiij
Item the pott braysse & the payn brasse		x	
Item the hangings in the hall		ij	viij
Item in the chamber iiij coffars		vj	viij
Item iij olde borded bedes ij matterises twoe coveringes ij olde blanckets		vij	
Item the hanginges in the same chamber		iij	
Item vj payre of Sheites vj table clothes one dossen of table Napkyns iiij bolsters iij pyllowes		xxx	
Item in the Lofte one olde fetherbed A blanckett a coverlet a coffer		vj	viij
Item A trevett ij Spyttes ij CobbeIornes A gredIorne a pott hangell ij Iornes to bare uppe the woode		v	
Item his wereynge apparll		iij	iiij
Item iiij quysshyns			viij
Item in the kytchyn vj tubbes a fatt and a busshell		x	
Item iij Troves a cheise prest and A borde and a payn		ix	
Item in the yarde twoe olde cart bodies and one payre of wheles		xx	
Item in the stabull fyve horse	vj		
Item Carte harnes & plowe harnes		iij	iiij
Item plowe tymber & Carte tymber		iiij	
Item vj mylche kyne iiij bullockes	v		
Item twoe Sowes fyve stores		xiij	iiij
Item the plowe teme & harrowes and a Roole		ij	viij

	£	s	d
Item xxx[ti] Shepe		liij	iiij
Item ij Ladders		ij	
Item all the Croppe groweinge in the feylde	xij		
Summa totalis	xxxiij	xix	iiij

Wherof the executrix dothe crave allowance for certeyne Legacies bequethed by his father and other dettes that he dyd owe at the hower of his death which dothe drawe the some of [...]

	£	s
Sum	xiiij	xvj

[*No exhibition clause*]

Notes: William Wall's burial has not been found.

51 Reginald Newold of Kempston made 25 April 1569

Lincolnshire Archives, INV/48/183

The inventory is badly damaged along the lower part of the right side. Many values are missing.

The trw Inventory of all the goodes & cattells of Reginald Newold of Kempston in the countie of Bedd Late desessed praised by Roger Crawley, Renold Newolde thelder, William Fowler and William Boutton the 25 of Aprill 1569

	£	s	d
Imprimis in the Hall ij folden tabulls		viij	
Item one coborde		xvj	
Item one benche borde one forme fyve cheires & x stowles		xij	viij
Item the paynted clothes & the Iorne abowte the fyer		xiij	iiij
Item coshins one carpyte & one cobord cloth		xj	viij
Item the pewter & candelstikes & other lattyn thinges		xxv	
Item one lytell cobbord in the chamber		vj	viij
Item one morter & pestill		ij	
Item ij bedstedes iij cofers & one forser		xxxiij	iiij
Item ij fetherbedes & ij bowlstrs		xlvj	viij
Item ij materis ij bolsters iij coveringes ij blancketes And the paynted [*cl*]othes in the chamber		xl	
Item xij payre of flaxen shetes & xviij payre of other harden shetes	v		
Item xij tabull clothes towells pelowbeares & kerchewes	iij		
Item iiij cofers one forster x pelowes one bedstede one bowlster one materis & ij carpites		xxx	[...]
Item one dozen trenchers ij dozen pewter spownes and ij dozen trene dishis		ij	ij
Item one fetherbed one coverlet one blancket one bolster one cobord and one coffer		xx	[...]
Item vij yardes of harden cloth & the paynted clothes		vj	[...]
Item ij Iorne wedgis one bill & one bedsted one forme		ij	v[...]
Item vij brasse potes		xxx	
Item ij brasse pannes iiij kettells one chese racke vj botills one old bedstede one blancket one axe ij bylls one hachet & other Iorne ware		liij	[...]
Item all the trumperye in the mylke howse and			

		£	s	d
vj tubbes one barrill one fatte one bowlting tubbe & certen trumpery in the backhowse				[...]
Item the ledde & vj hoges of Rised backen				[...]
Item Rye barlye & mawlte				[...]
Item one boshell one skuttell seves Rackes forkes iiij sakes ij wennowinge clothes and plow tymber				[...]
In the stabull				
Item ij horse			xx	[...]
Item owld horse harnes				[*value illegible*]
Item one Ambre one bedstede & the clothes				[*value illegible*]
Item ij cartes			xxx	[...]
Item the wood in the yarde			xiij	[...]
Item iiij bare keyne & xij bolakes		vj	xiij	iiij
Item xl shipe		vj	xiij	iiij
Item v shotes & one sowe			xiij	iiij
Item xj hennes & one coke			iij	iiij
	[*Total*]	lj	xviij	ij

[*Exhibited at Bedford on 27 April 1569*]

Notes: Reginald Newold's burial has not been found.

52 Thomas Raneshawlle of Old Warden made 20 September 1570

Lincolnshire Archives, INV/51/28

The document is badly stained on the right side and some words are missing.

An Inventory of all [...] catelles & money as were [...] Thomas Raneshawlle of the [...] Warden within the countye of Bedf praysed by Jhon Marbery and Sir George Diche clerke the xx[th] daye of September a [*sic*] 1570

		£	s	d
Inprimis a Mare pris			xx	
Item weryinge Apparell pris			xl	
Item one tennyment pris		vj	xiij	iiij
In money		lx		
	Summa totalis	lxix	[*xiij*]	[*illeg.*]
	[*Corrected total*	*£69*	*13s*	*4d*]

[*Exhibited in 1571 on 16th of a month that is illegible*]

Notes: Thomas Raneshawlle's burial has not been found. The appraiser John Marbury held Warden Rectory by lease with his parents from the Crown (VCH *Bedford*, vol. 3, p. 255). George Diche was curate or vicar of Old Warden 1585–1604 (CCEd).

53 Robert Hanger of Souldrop made 10 April 1571

Lincolnshire Archives, INV/56/208

This inventory is in the same difficult handwriting as William Hoge, 1574 (no. 67). Much of it is set out as continuous text with values often in the middle of lines. For ease of reading, the normal layout with the value on the right has been adopted.

Thys Inventore of Roberdes Hangers mad the x day of aprelle In the yere of owr lorde god A thousan v hondrethe iij skore & xj

	£	s	d
Imprimis In the Halle a tabele a furme ij gyned stolys ij cheyeres		iiij	
Item a cobberd a hallyn		viij	
Item v kettellys pryse		x	
Item ij potes pryse		vj	
Item a grete pane the pryse		xiij	iiij
Item a chefyn dyshe a skymmer pryse			xvj
Item iij kosshyns the pryse			xij
Item a spete a peyer of cobbarnes a payer of pote hangyng a payer of pote hokes a rydyn Iron the pryse		ij	vj
Item In the Chamber ij Chestes the pryse		v	
Item iij bedes steds the pryse		iij	
Item ij keveryns ij blankat		x	
Item Iii [*3*] payer of flexsyn shetys		xij	
Item ix payer of hardyn shetes		xxvj	viij
Item a borde Clothe ij touwells the pryse		iij	iiij
Item j kauffer ij pyllos ij pylloberes		v	
Item the peynted Clothes the pryse		ij	
Item for hys apparell the pryse		x	
Item all the stufe In the mylke howse		xiij	
Item In puter a xj pesys the pryse		xj	
Item iij skanstexkes		ij	
Item ij horse & ij [*?*]borsbtys[15] the pryse	iiij		
Item iij bese & aboloxke the pryse	iij		
Item x shepe the pryse		xxvj	viij
Item akarte & karte gere the pryse		x	
Item a plow & plow gere the pryse		v	
Item In barle x akers & In pese x akers the pryse	vj	xiij	iiij
Item In [*?*]hode			x
Item iij hoges the pryse		iiij	
Item a coke iij henes the prayse			xij
Sum	xxv	xvj	
[*Corrected total*	*£23*	*10s*	*0d*]

wytnes Thomas Recherd, John Ed[*illeg.*]tys, Wylliam Ray, with other moe

[*No exhibition clause*]

Notes: Robert Hanger's burial has not been found. The attribution to Souldrop is supported by the presence of Hangers in Souldrop recorded in Bedfordshire Archives' catalogue and in later Souldrop parish registers (*BPR*, vol. 7).

15 This word is very difficult to read. It could be a mangled attempt at *horsebits*, referring to harness.

54 John Wynche of Luton, maltman made 28 May 1571

Lincolnshire Archives, INV/51/53

Some staining and fading at the right edge and down the centre fold of the paper, with some loss of words and values.

An Inventorie of the goodes of ~~late~~ Johne Wynche of Luton in the cowntie of Bedf malltman, lately deceasyd, praysed by Wylliam Crawleye of Bramingham, Thomas Crawleye, Thomas Watts, Wylliam Bayleye, Thomas Wynche of Luton the xxviij[th] day of Maye AD 1571

	£	s	d
In the hall, Inprimis two framyd tables			
a foorme & a footestole		xiij	
Item xvij ioynid stooles		xxij	
Item j baynede a fyer shovell, a fyer forke, & iron hangells		iij	iiij
In the parlour. The table		iiij	
Item the standing bed and a trundell bed		xxxiij	iiij
Item on the same bed a mattres, a fetherbed, ij blancks on coverlet ij boolsters		xl	
Item vj pillowes		xj	
Item on the trundellbed, a coverlet, a blanckyt, a mattrys, a boolster		viij	
Item vj payre of flaxen sheetes	iij		
Item iij payre of coorser sheetes		xx	
Item ix payre and a sheete & iij halfe sheetes of the coursest shetes	iiij		
Item other naperie ware of hys wyves and hyr hatte		x	
Item ij coffers and a fosser		x	
Item twoe billes		ij	
Item iij shirtes		iij	iiij
Item napkyns halfe a dosen		iij	
[...] a chayre			xij
[...] An old cubbard		vj	viij
[...] v cubbard clothes		x	
[...] ij bowes and a sheafe of arrowes		vj	viij
Item of pewter iij platers, xij disshes, iiij sawcers, a cup [...] salt sellers, and a potte		xvj	
Item iiij candellsticks a morter and a pestyll		iij	iiij
Item ij treas			viij
Item an old table and ij foormes		ij	viij
Item vj yards of black russett		xvj	
Item vj yards of whyte russet		ix	
Item xj yards and an halfe of whyte careseye		xxvij	vj
Item ij old bottells		ij	
Item iij table clothes		v	
Item a wollen whele, a cradell clothe & vij pownd of yarne		v	
Item waytes of led & a payr of skooles		iij	
[...] grete lofft: A standing bedstead and a trundell bedsteade		xl	
Item a mattrys, an old blancket, an old coverlet & a boolster & a pece of a fetherbed		xiij	iiij
Item a framyd table		x	
Item iij clokes		xl	
Item ij cootes, iiij ierkyns, an old sleveles friese cote, & an old gowne		xlvj	viij
[*In*] the litle chamber A bedsteade		xx	

Item a fetherbed, ij blancketts, a mattrys, a coverlet, & a boolster		liij	iiij
Item a payre of bayards, a fyre shovell & tonngues		v	
Item an old chayre			viij
Item a cheste		v	
[...] chamber. A standing bedstead		xiij	iiij
Item ij mattooks an hatchet & other iron stuffe		iij	iiij
Item ij new rydge wythes			iiij
Item iiij^{li} of black woll, iiij pesehookes an old bedstead & other trashe		iiij	
[...] butterey. Two lynnen wheles, rocks & tow, a pare of cards, earthe potts disshers & trenchers, loves & other stuffe		iij	iiij
[...] kytchin Three potts of brasse		xiij	iiij
Item vj kettells & a dripping panne		xx	
Item two posenetts, j skyllett, iiij pannes, j old latten basen a frying panne, a skymmer, and a payle		x	
Item a payr of cobbyornes, ij spyttes, pot hangells, a gridierne a cleaver, a tosting iron, a shredding knyfe, & other stuff in the kytchin		vj	viij
Item bacon iij hogges a flytch of a gammon		xx	
[...] yard Item a sowe & iiij pyges		x	
Item wood in the yarde		xx	
Item a gose, a gannder, v goslyngs, ij hennes, iiij ducks & a drake		iiij	vj

In the seller

A fatt, a kymmell, ij tubbs, ij fyrkyns, ij barrells, a tubb		x	
Item stone cruses, drincking cuppes, a tynne bottell, a standish & other stuffe			xx
Item two tubbs			xij
In the cubbords [*illeg.*] An hatt, a capp, and a woosted nightcapp		iiij	
Item an apron and capp of hys wyves			xvj
Item bookes		ij	vj
Item a ryding clothe			xvj
Item reedie money in a purse		xx	
Item a purse, dagger and gyrdle			xx
Item other stuff abowt the howse praysed at		xxvj	iiij
Item the mucke in the fealde & at home		xvj	
Item certeine apparell which was Roger Wynch hys apparell & hys stuffe		[*value illegible*]	
Summa	xliiij	xviij	ij
Debts owing to Johne Wynch not gevyn to hys soonne in hys life tyme, but still owing to hym and at thys present knowe to be hys	v		
Summa totalis	l	xj	x
The Debts that the seyd Johne Wynch dyd ow at hys deathe			
Inprimis He owid to Wylliam Crawley of Bramingham	xxxiij		
Item he owed to Johne Hamond of Purton	x		
Item to Wylliam Bayley of Luton	ix		
Item to Peter Greene		xliij	[*?*]iij
Item to Bunne of S Albans		xv	
Item to Richard Spicer alias Helder		vj	viij
Item to Cranch of Barton		xxij	iiij

~~Item rent due to~~			
Item to Anne Fyllon hys mayde		x	
Item Loodie claymith [*claimeth*]		vj	viij
Item for Roger Wynch hys brother he owid as folowithe			
Inprimis to Thomas Peter & Robart Barbar	iij		
Item Huggens claymithe		vj	
Item Bisshop claymithe		viij	vj
Item Robart Blacked claymithe		viij	
Item Storie claymithe		x	viij
Item Edward Wynch claymithe	xiij	vj	[*?*]viij
Summa totalis of the Debt is	lxxv	iij	[*illeg.*]

[*No exhibition clause*]

Notes: John Wynche's burial has not been found. There is a note on the inventory that administration was granted to Agnes Wynche, relict, and that she and Thomas Wynche of Luton, yeoman, were bound to administer the estate.

55 George Ellys of Sandy

made 30 May 1571

Lincolnshire Archives, INV/51/50

Some fading on the right side and some values are difficult to read.

This ys a true Inventorye of all the goodes cattalles and debtes which were George Ellys at the daye of hys death beinge the xvij[th] of Maye the yere of our Lorde god 1571 Pryced & valued the 30 of Maye by William Edroppe, Edwarde Bryttaine & John Springe

	£	s	d
In the hall			
In primis one table 2 fourmes & a bencheborde		ij	
Item an olde cubborde		iij	iiij
Item 2 olde chayres			xiij
Item 2 payneted clothes		ij	
Item 3 Brasse pottes		vj	viij
Item 2 pannes & 6 Kettelles		xviij	
Item 15 pewter platters & 5 sawcers		xiij	iiij
Item 4 pewter saltsellers olde			viij
Item one frying panne a scomer 2 lytle kettelles and posnet		ij	
Item 7 candlestickes & one chaffin dishe		iij	iiij
In the chambers			
Fyrst 2 old mattresses		iiij	
Item 3 coverlettes		vj	[*?*]viij
Item 9 payre & one shete		xxvj	viij
Item 6 bolsters 5 pyllowes & 5 pyllowbeeres		vij	
Item payneted clothes		v	
Item 5 coffers & one fosser		x	
Item 3 table clothes & 2 towelles		v	
Item 3 olde troughes & an arke		iij	iiij
Item one quarter of Rye & half a quarter of barley		xij	
Item 6 busshelles of malt		vj	
Item Rye sowne in the feilde	iij		
Item 34 acres of barleye in the felde	xij		

Item 13 acres & an halfe of ~~Rye~~ peese	iij	vj	viij
Item 4 horses & one colt	iiij		
Item 2 oxen 2 steares & 4 milche beastes	vj	vj	viij
Item calves weaners		x	
Item 28 shepe & tenne Lambes	iij	x	
Item One old bare carte		vj	viij
Item 2 yockes 2 teames & 2 plouges		viij	
Item cartgeares & plowghe geares			xij
Item 5 Bakon flitches		vj	viij
Item 7 stoare hogges		xiij	viij
Item 4 tubbes 2 old payles 2 bowles with other trashe		x	
Item 2 spittes a payre of cobyrons 2 payre of pott hangles two payre of pott hookes & one lytle tredd		v	
Item wodd in the yarde		iij	iiij
Item all hys wearing apparell		xiij	iiij
Item 2 Rackes Rakes of Iron a bushell a fanne One Ryddell & suche Lyke thynges		v	
Item one old axe a hatchett 3 pickforkes		ij	
Item other small triffles about the house		vj	viij
Item fyve slippes of yarne			xx
Item an hempe Lande		v	
[*Total*	*£43*	*19s*	*5d*]
He did owe		xxxvij	viij
Item he had oweinge		vj	viij
Summa totalis	xliij	xix	vj
[*Corrected total of assets minus debts*	*£42*	*8s*	*5d*]

[*Exhibited at Bedford on 16 June 1571*]

Notes: George Ellys was buried at Sandy on 19 May 1571.

56 Robert Capon of Bedford St Paul made 9 June 1571

Lincolnshire Archives, INV/51/26

The document is stained on the right hand top corner and creased. Some text has faded badly and is illegible. Words have been supplied in italics where the reading is obvious.

Bedd paul. The Inventorye of all the goodes of Robert Capon lately deceassed

	£	s	d
Fyrst in the halle on cubbord	[*value illegible*]		
Item x platters vj pewter potyngers v saucers ij saltes iij candlestykes ij pewter pottes on pewter goblet viij pewter trenchers		xx	
Item on fold table on Joyned forme		v	
Item ij chears v olde stoyles			xx
Item pented [*cloths*]		ij	vj
iij old quisshins & a bencher	[*value illegible*]		
Item iiij flower pottes			[*?*]xij
Item v stone cruces			v
Item ij old bylles			xij

In the kechyn

Fyrste in the kechyn on Iren barre ij hangles on payer of cobirens ij spyttes on payre of tonges one payer of pott [*illeg.*]	ij	vj
Item ij old frying panns		[*?*]xij
Item ij great pans		[*value illegible*]
Item ij litle ketles & on pott		[*value illegible*]
Item on posnet & a treade		viij
Item ij old platters & iij sawcers	ij	
In the parlowre within the hall		
Fyrste on bedstede on fetherbed on bolster ij pillows with all that belongethe to the bede	xx	
Item viij payer of shets better and worse	xx	
Item iij table cloythes	iiij	
Item ij towels		xij
Item vj napkins	ij	
Item ij chyrts [*?shirts* or *sheets*]	ij	vj
Item ij coffers		xx
Item pented colythes		xx
In the lofte over the hall		
Fyrste ij bedsteds	v	
Item on trundle bedstede		xx
Item on fether bedd on bolster on blankete on covering	x	
Item pented cloythes	ij	
In an other chamber		
Fyrste on bedstede & a mattres	iij	
Item ij pented cloythes		xx
in the parloure to the streyt		
Fyrste on standing bedstede on fether bedd on bolster on pyllowe on blanket on coveringe on tester with iij curtayns	xxxiij	4
Item on table on forme on carpeat iij quishins	x	
Item pented cloythes	ij	vj
Item on prese	v	
Item on litle forme & ij flower pottes		xiiij
in a chamber in the yarde		
Fyrste on old bedstede with a mattris	iij	4
Som tot ix	viij	vj

Praysed the ix daye of June in the yeare above sayd bye Peter Harve, Antonye Feld, [*illeg.*] William Clappam

[*No exhibition clause*]

Notes: Robert Capon's burial has not been found.

57 Agnes Hurst of Henlow made 15 June 1571

Lincolnshire Archives, INV/51/30

The top and right side of the document are stained. A few letters and words are almost illegible. Where they are obvious, they have been added in italics in square brackets.

An Inventorye of the goodes of A[*gnes*] Hurst leate of Henlow decessed [*made*] and prysed the xv daye of June in the xiij[th] yeare of the Raigne of our soverayne Lady Qwene Elizabethe by Thomas Retcheford, Thomas Underwoode and Edmund Caper

	£	s	d
Firste in money	xx		
Item a Fetherbedd a materes & a Bedsted		xiij	iiij
Item a Covering of d[*o*]rniskes a Redd blanket a bolester ij pillowes		x	
Item ~~two~~ three Cofers and ij fosers		vj	viij
Item painted clothes		iij	
Item foure paire of shetys		x	
Item twoo Table clothes			xx
Item vj pecis of pewter and ij porringers		iij	iiij
Item one brasse pott one brasse panne and one brasse kettle		iiij	
Item one short table and ij ioyned stoles		ij	iiij
Item ij Coysshins			xij
Item ij Tubbes			viij
Item ij silver spoones iiij silver Ringes and one littill gold Ring and one paire of silver hookes		vj	viij
Item the wollen apparell		xl	
Item her Lynen apparell		xx	
Item ij Pillowberes			xx
Item vj Table napkins and a worstedd Apron		ij	iiij
[*Total*	*£26*	*6s*	*8d*]

[*No exhibition clause*]

Notes: Agnes Hurst was buried at Henlow on 17 November 1569.

58 Henry Wolhed of Marston Moretaine undated; c. 1571

Lincolnshire Archives, INV/51/43

The Invetory of all the goodes & cattels movable & unm[*ov*]eble late Henry Wolhedes of Marson Morteyn made by the vewe and presentment of John Worsle, John Hunt, Roger Bosworthe & Edmund Jud & Thomas Shelle

	£	s	d
In prmys In the over chamber an old fether bed wythe all the Rest of the beddyng & lynnen withe iiij olde			

		£	s	d
cofers iij old paynted clothes ij bedstedes				
A pres & ij old formes			xx	
Item In the halle an old [*co*]berd A table a forme				
A benche bord and a chare wyth a hallyng			x	
Item the brasse and the pewter wyth iij canstkes			x	
Item yn the mylke howse and old coberd a saltyng				
trowgh wythe iij bordes			iij	iiij
Item In the buttry A knedyng trowghe a boultyng tubbe				
and to drynke tubbes			iij	iiij
Item In the kychyn a old arke a pen				
a smale spyt & a payr of cobyrons			v	
Item the tymber yn the yard & fyre wod			xxxiij	iiij
Item In the hay barne plowe tymber				
carte tymber & boardes prise			xxvj	viij
Item long carte a mukke carte & A payr of wheles			xx	
Item the corne and peese		iij	vj	viij
Item to horsses			xl	
Item iiij bese		v		
Item all the hogges			xx	
Item a parsell of shepe		iij	vj	viij
Item to plowghs plowe gere & carte gere				
wythe iij drawte rakes prise			x	
	The sum ys	xxj	xv	

[*Exhibited at Bedford on 15 June 1571*]

Notes: Henry Wolhed's burial has not been found.

59 John Gyllat of Staploe, Eaton Socon date illegible; made before mid-June 1571

Lincolnshire Archives, INV/51/34

Staining along the top and down the right side has made some words and most values illegible.

Octavo [*illeg.*] domini [*illeg.*]

A true Inventorye of all suche [*illeg.*] Jhon Gyllat hade at the daye of hys death made by [*illeg.*] Kyppes senior, Robart Graye Junior, Mathewe Alyn, Wy[*illeg.*] Barcocke, Jeames Alyn with other moe

	£	s	d
Inprimis iij kene & a hecforth praysed at	iiij		
Item vij ewes & seven lames praysed at		xx	
Item x other gesse shyppe praysed at		xx	
Item v hodges praysed at		viij	
Item a bare cart & carte geares & plowe &			
plowe geares praysed at	[*value illegible*]		
Item ix Acres of barley & wheate praysed at	[*?*]iij		[*illeg.*]
Item vj Acres of pease & fetches praysed at	[*value illegible*]		
Item all the brase & pewter praysed at	[*value illegible*]		
Item a cubborde & iij coffers praysed at	[*value illegible*]		
Item ij bedsteades with the paynted clothes & blankett	[*value illegible*]		
Item iij payre of shetes & ij candelstyckes			
ij table clothes & a towell praysed at	[*value illegible*]		

	£	s	d
Item a table & ij formes & a bench borde & a penne & pott hangells & pott hookes & a spete & iij toubes & on payle a cheare & stoles praysed at		[*value illegible*]	
Item v hennes & a cocke praysed at			xx
Item iij horse praysed at	iij		
Summa totalis	xvj	vij	viij

[*Exhibited at Bedford on 16 June 1571*]

Notes: John Gyllat's burial has not been found.

60 Richard Hawkins of Thorne, Houghton Regis — made 7 July 1571

Lincolnshire Archives, INV/51/182

An Invetory of all & sing[u]l[e]r goodes that were Ric[hard] Hawkins of Thorne in the parishe of Houghton Regis in the countye of Bedd made the vij day of July in the yeare of our Lord [*illeg.*] preased by William Hawkins, William Strange, Robert Hawkins & Ric[hard] Dyne

	£	s	d
In primis two mattresses price		x	
Item iij payre of flaxen sheetes		xx	
Item vj payre of harden shetes & iij table clothes		xx	
Item one coverlid & iij blanketes		xviij	
Item ij bolsters & ij pillowes		x	
Item iij coffers		vj	
Item paynted clothes		vj	viij
Item one potte ij ketles & eight peces of pewter		xxvj	viij
Item a speere cloth		vj	
Item a table & thinges belonginge to it		v	
Item Bordes & cleates		xx	
Item iij tod & di wooll		xlvj	viij
Item iiij toobbes vj bowles vj disshes iij dosen of trenchers & a dosen of spones		xiij	iiij
Item a Linnen wheele			x
Item pott hanginges & coblrons		v	
Item v horses ij coltes	xiij	vj	viij
Item ij cartes with one payre of wheles & cart geares		xlvj	viij
Item fyre wood Rackes & hurdles		xx	
Item four score sheepe	x		
Item v kyne iij calfes	vij	xiij	iiij
Item ix hogges & viij pigges		xl	
Item the croppe of corne & tilth	l		
[...] [*quar*]ter of mault & ij quarter of wheate		xlvj	viij
Summa totalis	lxxxxix	vij	vj

[*On the verso is a scribbled and highly abbreviated note. The page is damaged and some of the text is missing. It appears to be a grant of administration, possibly to Agnes Roberts at Houghton Regis, a bond by her and two husbandmen in the sum of £200 and an order to the rector of Throcking in Hertfordshire.*]

Notes: Richard Hawkins was buried at Houghton Regis on 12 July 1571. His widow Annis Hawkins married Richard Webb on 23 September 1571.

61 Henry Wyngar of Cardington, servant undated; 1573

Lincolnshire Archives, INV/56/214

A I[n]mitory made of the goodes of Henry Wyngar of Cardyngtone in the cu[n]te of Bedforde sarvant unto Wylliam Koxe of the same to[w]ne & cou[n]tie & prasyd at the dessressyone [*discretion*] of Jhone Fiesant, Wylliam Wellford & Gorge Hokkull

	£	s	d
In primus iij quarters of barly & v busshyles		xxjx	
Item iij havf [*half*] akeres of whette		xxx	
Item a rod of whette & a rodes end of whette		vj	viij
Item one shepe		iij	
Item a shette a tabulclothe & a kettell		vj	
Item	iij	xjx	viij
[*Corrected total*	*£3*	*14s*	*8d*]

[*No exhibition clause*]

Notes: Henry Wyngar's burial has not been found.

62 Margery Kynge of Pulloxhill, widow made 20 May 1573

Lincolnshire Archives, INV/56/229

This Invitorye ~~made~~ of all & sing[u]ler the goodes cattalles & debtes of Ma[r]gerie Kynge late of Pulloxhill widdow ~~late~~ deceased praysed[16] the xx^{ti} daye of Maye Anno domini 1573 ~~made~~ by Willyam Beamande & Richard Lake & Willyam Empye

	£	s	d
In primis fowre horse		liij	iiij
Item fowre Beastes	iiij		
Item xiij sheepe		xxvj	
Item fowre hogges		x	
Item sixe ackers of barly & beanes	iij		
Item three quarter of Barlye		xx	
Item for brasse and pewter		xx	
Item for a cubberde & all the treene ware		xiij	iiij
Item plowes & cartes		xiij	iiij
Item vj pare of sheetes		xx	
Item for the beddinge		x	
Item for two coffers		v	
The whole Sum is	xvj	xj	

by me Wyllm Bemunde, by me Rychard Lake

[*No exhibition clause*]

Notes: Margery Kynge's burial has not been found.

16 The words from *of all and singuler* to *praysed* have been inserted in a different hand from the remainder of the document.

63 Thomas Darlyng of Bletsoe made 16 December 1573

Lincolnshire Archives, INV/56/212

The inventory appears to be incomplete.

This Invetorie taken the xvj daye of Desember in the yeere of our Lorde god 1573 of the goodes of Thomas Darlyng late of Bletso deceased

	£	s	d
The croppe			
First the wheat Rie peese barley otes & heoy	xx		
Item the hole tylthe of lande of xiiij acars		xx	
Item ij acars j of [*wh*]eat & j of Rie price		vj	vij
Item fyfe horses price	v		
Item ij cartes with the geares belonging to them with the ploues & the geares belonging to them alsoo		xl	
Item v Kye and ij hefors price	vj	vj	viij
Item for xxviij shepe price		xlvij	viij
Item the wodd		xiij	iiij
Item vj hogges		x	
Item xiiij hennes & vj dockes & a drake		vj	viij
In the howse			
Item the brasse and the pwtar		xiij	iiij
Item j table j forme j chere and j cobard		v	
In the chaumber			
Item in the chaumber the pryce of thinges		xl	
Item in the other chaumbar the price of thinges there		xx	
In the backhowse			
Item in the backhouse the stooffe there		ij	vj
[*Total*	*£42*	*11s*	*10d*]

[*No exhibition clause*]

Notes: Thomas Darlyng's burial has not been found.

64 John Colbeck the elder of Tempsford, gentleman made 17 December 1573

Lincolnshire Archives, MISC WILLS J77

Slight damage and creasing at the right side of the page.

Thys ys the Inventory Indentyd made the xvij[th] day of December the sixtene yere of the Reign of Elizabeth by the grace of god of England ~~Fraunce & Ireland~~ Fraunce & Ireland quene defendor of the fayth etc of all the goodes Cattelles & dettes of John Colbeck of Temy[*sford*] in the County of Bed thelder gent dicessyd praysed by Thomas Hale Gent, Thomas Fyscher, Thomas Barcocke, Thomas Cowper and Rychard Henson husbondmen

	£	s	d
In the Hall			
In primis one Table & joyned Frame one Rownde Table one Fowlte Table ij Formes j Chare j yoyned stole & the hangynges in the Hall j payer of Cobyrons j candyllstycke of plate iij Cusshyns price		xx	[*illeg.*]

In the entry by the hall			
Item one Cubbord & Cubbord Clothe price		vj	viij
In the parlor			
Item one Table & Joyned Frame j Carpytt sixe Cusshyns j Rownde Table j Short Table j Chayr thre Formes ij Joyned stoles & one pece of Inboed waynscote & one payer of Cobyrons price		xiij	iiij
Item one Hearst of velvet with Imbroderyd worke price		xxvj	viij
Item two desckes & all hys Bookes price		xiij	iiij
Item iiij Chestes price		xiij	iiij
Item the paynted Clothes price		v	
Item hys apparyell price	v		
In the kytchyn			
Item seven brasse pottes vij pannes ix kettelles one posenett ij Chaffers j Skyllett j Chaffyndyshe one brasen morter with a pestell price	iiij		
Item one Gospan iiij spyttes j scomer ij payer of Rackes j Fyre shovell ij payer of Tonges j payer of bellowes a gredyron j Cole Rake ij payer of potthokes ij pott hangers ij ekes j payer of Cobyrons j Fyre panne j Chopyng knyffe & a Clever price		viij	
Item xvj peaweter platters iij Basons one Charye xviij peaweter dysshes xvj peawter poryngers ix sauceres viij Candyll styckes iij peawter Chamberpottes ij peawter saltselleres & iij peawter pottes price		xlvj	
Item one Casse or pen j dressyng bourde certayn shelves iij Chayres & other old Chayrs & stoles price		ij	viij
Item iij bowles vj payles & all other trene ware price		ij	
In the mylke howse & larder howse			
Item a Chese presse vij Chese Fattes j suter & one Charne		ij	iiij
Item a saltyng troffe a busshyll of salte & iiij Bacon Fletches		xij	
Item a musterd quarne & other old shelves & Implementes price		viij	viij
In the yellyng howse & buttery			
Item one yellyng Fatt j kymnell sixe Tubbes & other old tubbes j hogges hed & shelves & j old Cubburd price		vij	
Item seven drynkyng pottes ij glasses ix lether bottelles & one wycker bottell & Fower dosyn of trenshers price		v	
the napery ware			
Item xxxj payer of shettes wherof seven payer of theym ar[e] Flaxson price		lvj	viij
Item two long dyeper table Clothes & two other shorte dyeper table Clothes price		xv	
Item Fyve Towelles price		iiij	
Item sixe pyllowebers price		iiij	
Item xxij table Napkyns price		xiij	iiij
Item iiij longe table Clothes & iiij shorte ones price		xij	
Item Fyve Fetherbedes sixe pyllowes viij bowlsters & Five matryses price	v		
Item iiij Coverlydes price		xx	
Item iij other Coverlydes price		vj	viij
Item xviij blankettes price		xxvj	~~viij~~

Item eight bedstedes price		xiij	iiij
Item the hangynges for thre beddes price		xiij	iiij
Item Fyve Coffers ij Chestes & one lyttell Cubburd price		xvj	
Item one Chayr price			vj
Item xxx Cheses price		xiij	iiij
Item ij wallettes price			xij
Item a brusshe price			iiij
Item Fower slyppes & other Towe price		iiij	
Item seven yardes of whyte wollen Clothe & sixe yardes of Russett Clothe price		xvj	
Item one table callyd a Cownter & ij Close stoles price		iiij	
Item all the paynted Clothes in the Chamberes price		iij	iiij

Thynges pertaynyng unto husbanry

In the stable Item iij horses harnes for Cartyng & plowyng price	iiij		
Item ij long Cartes ij mucke Cartes & ij a [*sic*] payer of Shudde wheles price		liij	iiij
Item ij plowes ij plowe teames ij oxe yokes ij Cowleteres iij shares & thre trees belongyng to the plowes Rowles harrowes & plowe Tymber price		xiij	iiij
Item one Crowe of yron j mattocke Forkes Rakes peasen hokes j Cartrop spades shovelles ~~hov~~ hoves sykelles j sythe & other old yron price		vj	viij
Item iiij oxen ij steres xj beas ij bulles ij yeryng Calves price	xxiiij		
Item ij Geldynges ij saddelles & ij brydelles price		liij	iiij
Item seven shottes ij sowes & the hogges Troves price		xx	
Item xl hennes Capons Cockes Chyckyns duckes & gese price		viij	
Item Forty shepe price	vij		
Item hurdelles & Rackes price		ij	
Item ahovell price		xxvj	viij

In the bruyng howse & bake howse

Item one masshyng Fatte one bowletyng arke ij kymnelles j mowledyng bourd j drye Troffe & a Tryffatt ij payer of bowletylles iij syfes & one bruyng led or Fornas & other Implementes price		xvj	viij

In the garner & Barnes

Item one quarter of malte price		xvj	
Item ten quarters of pease beanes & Fetches price ten markes	[*6*	*13*	*4*]
Item one quarter of wheate price		xxvj	viij
Item iij quarters of Rye price iiij markes	[*2*	*13*	*4*]
Item thyrty quarters of Barly price xxx markes	[*20*	*0*	*0*]
Item a busshell & a stryke ij peckes & a halffe pecke ij skeppes ij skuttelles ij Fannes a sedcod & iiij baskettes price		iij	

In the malte howse

Item a hare for the kyll & sackes ij dry troffes & iiij busshelles of lyme & one quarne price		[*?*]xj	
Item j pumpe & yron ij buckettes & one yron Ioke price		v	
Item all the wood Tymber & bourdes price		xxvj	viij

Item all the haye price	iij	vj	viij
Item all hys armo[r] price		xxx	
Item one wollen whele & other thynges belongyng to huswyfrye price			xvj
Item led & leden wayttes & ~~Crtay~~ Certayn salt Fysshes price		vj	viij
Item iij ladders price			xvj
Item The plowe Tymber price		v	
Item ij acres of Rye sowen price		xxvj	viij
Item two acres of wheate sowen price		xxvj	viij
Item the tylthe of xviij acres of land price	iij		
Item xviij^{li} sylver spones price	iij	vj	viij
Item one sylver salte wayeng xvj ownces price	iij	iiij	
Item a lyttle sylver salte price		xiij	iiij
Item a sylver Nutte price	iij	xij	
Sum	Cxxxvj	viij	vj
[*Corrected total*	*£136*	*10s*	*2d*]

[*No exhibition clause*]

Notes: John Colbeck's burial has not been found. He made his will on 7 January 1573, leaving land in Tempsford and elsewhere to his wife Rose for life then amongst his five sons. On the same day he made a separate testament, making charitable bequests, giving small sums to his godchildren, 20 marks to each daughter and making his wife his residual legatee, but he excluded the portals and glass windows which were to remain in the house. His wife and son were appointed executors (Lincs Archives, MISC WILLS J77). Possibly this John Colbeck was one of the Commissioners of the Peace of that name under Edward VI and Philip and Mary (*CPR Edward VI*, vol. 1, p. 81 and *CPR Philip and Mary*, vol 1, p. 16).

65 Thomas Franckelyn of Marston Moretaine — undated; 1574

Lincolnshire Archives, INV/56/230

The inivitory [*sic*] of the goodes & cattelles of Thomas Franckelyn of Marston Mortayn late desesed praysed by Edward Wyghtstones gyntell & Rychard Baskarfelld & John Mowse yemen

	£	s	d
In prymus in the feld 31 accars of wheat rye & barly	xvj		
Item xxj acars of benes & pesse	viij		
Item xiij mylch kyne & a bull	xx		
Item [*illeg.*] bullockes of ij yeares old & iij gyst bease	xiij		
Item vj wenyng cavlles		xxiiij	
Item iiij horse a cobb & a nage	xij		
Item x bullockes of on year olld	iiij		
Item iiij skore & xviij shepe	xvj		
with in the yard			
Item old pease unthreshed	iij		
Item grayn threshed wheat rye & barly	iij	vj	viij
Item ij long carttes with showde whelles		liij	iiij
Item ij dung carttes		xiij	iiij
Item xj yung hoges		xxij	
Item carte harnes & plow harnes		xx	
Item ij plowes & plow tymbar		xx	

Item harowes & cart tymbar		xx	
Item for wode for the fyer		xl	
Item [*?*]clettes & bordes		v	
Item powlltre		v	
Item bease		iij	iiij
with yn the howes			
Item pewtter & brasse	iij		
Item hys aparell		xl	
Item shetes	iij		
Item iiij fether bedes & iij mattryes		xl	
Item coverynges blanckets bolsteres & pellowes		liij	iiij
Item tabelles formes bedstedes cofares paynted clothes & stolles fates & tubes		xl	
Item spetes cobyorns pothangares with other such stofe		iiij	
Item for horse halltares sythes pychforkes panelles with other trach & tryfelles unreconed		xxx	
Sume totall is	123		

[*No exhibition clause*]

Notes: Thomas Franckelyn's burial has not been found. The inventory is dated to 1572–75 in Lincolnshire Archives online catalogue and has been assigned to 1574.

66 Thomas Gillion of Riseley undated; 1574

Lincolnshire Archives, INV/56/213

The Invitorye of all the goods of Cattels & chattels of Thomas Gillion of Ryseleye late decessed

	£	s	d
Inprimis in the haule iij brasse pootes vj pan[n]s ij kettels xij peces of p[*ew*]t[e]r j pen[n]e j table & other implementes of household		liij	iiij
Item in the chamber iij beddes and bedsteds iij chestes painted cloths & x payre sheetes		liij	iiij
Item in the bolting house j bed j cheste ij twells with other implementes appertayning to the same		vj	viij
Item his apparrill & monye		xiij	iiij
Item vj beastes 5 boullocks	vij	iij	iiij
Item ij horsses v shootes & poltrye		liij	iiij
Item x acres wheat barley & rye	iiij		
Item ix acres pese & beanes		xl	
Item x sheepe		xl	
Item plowe & plowgeres carte and carte geres		xl	
Item woode & hoveles		xx	
Somma Totallis	xxvij	iij	
[*Corrected total*	*£27*	*3s*	*4d*]

Praysed by Willya[m] Kyrwood clarke, Rychard Smythe & John Bull

[*No exhibition clause*]

Notes: Thomas Gillion's burial has not been found. The inventory has been dated to 1574 on Lincolnshire Archives online catalogue. The handwriting is similar to no. 68 Simon Bulmer of Riseley and both may have been written by the same person, possibly William Kyrwood, vicar of Riseley.

67 William Hoge of Souldrop made 16 February 1574

Lincolnshire Archives, INV/56/209

The inventory is in the same difficult handwriting as Robert Hanger 1571 (no. 50). Some lines are set out as continuous text with values often in the middle of lines. For ease of reading, the normal layout with the value on the right has been adopted.

In the yer of oure lorde god a m ccccc & lxxiij the Inventore of Wylliam Hoge the xvj day of ~~Januare~~ Februare

	£	s	d
In the halle			
In prymys a tabylle a ~~frame~~ a Chayer pryse		v	
Item a pen a syde tabylle		iij	iiij
Item a Cheyer & v stolys			xij
Item a bras pote a leste pote vj ketylys pryse		viij	
Item ij paynted clothes the pryse			xx
Item In peuter vij pesys the pryse		iij	
Item a [*?*]kanstyc			ij
Item the gredarne the pote hokes the pote hangyn			viij
Item In bollys dyshes trenches [*?*]Ceffates the pryse			x
In the chamber			
Item a clake a cote a gyrkyn dublas a pare of hose		x	
Item a mattres a keverryn a blanket a bolster ij pylows		vj	
Item alle the lynnyng In the house the pryse		viij	
Item iij kofers a nold arke the pryse		iiij	
Item ij bedsteds ij kymnyllys the pryse		iij	
Item a barelle a cherne a [*?*]maune a payer of balans			[*?*]ix
In the barne			
Item In barle the pryce		xlvj	viij
Item In pese the pryse		xx	
Item a mare ij geldyns a stonded horse a kolte	iiij		
Item a kave iiij bulloxkes the pryse		liij	iiij
Item a neu a sharog & a lam hog		xij	
Item a shode [*?*]karte a payer of [*?*]bare welys		xx	
Item for ode [*wood?*] In the yerde the pryse		viij	
Item for v shotys the pryse		vj	viij
Item for a ploe the plloe gere		iij	
Item a naker of wote the pryse		vj	viij
Item In tylleg In the tylfylde vij akerres		xvj	iiij
Item In pese ij akers the pryse		vj	viij
Item iij laders iij bordys the pryse			xij
[*Total*	*£16*	*15s*	*9d*]

the praysers of thys Inventore Wylliam Raye, Thomas Recherdes & Recherd Hanger
[*No exhibition clause*]

Notes: William Hoge's burial has not been found. The attribution of William Hoge to Souldrop is supported by the prevalence of the surnames of two of the appraisers, Richards and Hanger, in Souldrop parish registers when they commence in 1602 (*BPR*, vol. 7).

68 Simon Bulmer of Riseley

made 11 April 1574

Lincolnshire Archives, INV/56/207

The Invetorye of all the goods & cattells moveables and unmoveables of Symont Bulmer of Rysleye dissessed the xj^th^ daye of Aprill the yere of our lord 1574

	£	s	d
Fyrste in the hale a cubbord A table A forme a pene			
Paynted Clothes with other implmentes of			
houshold as brasse and pewter		xxiij	iiij
In the Chamber And Loffte			
Beding and bedsteds syxe payre of sheetes	iij		
Item In the mylkehouse		vj	viij
Item ij acres whete and barleyghe		xxiij	iiij
Item ij acres of pese		xiij	iiij
Item v bestes	vij	vj	iiij
Item xxx sheepe	vj		
Item j shood carte j drag racke		xvj	
Item ij hovels & certayne wood in the yard		xvj	
In redye monye		v	
In the Chitchen one flycke bancon and other			
implementes of houshold and polterye		xiij	iiij
Item his aparrell		xiij	iiij
Debtes owing to Symont Bulmer			
Inprimis of Robart Fyshe of Ryseleye		xx	
Of Robart Bentleyghe of Rysleye		x	
Of the same Robart Bentleyghe j quarter			
of barleyge prise		xv	
of Willyam Swanne of Rysleyge		iij	iiij
Summa totalis	xxv	v	

Praysed By Wyllya[m] Kyrwood clarke, John Benyt of Swinshed, Jon Benyt of Rysleye Etc [*Exhibited at Bedford on 16 June 1574*]

Notes: Simon Bulmer's burial has not been found. See the note to no. 66 Thomas Gillion of Riseley about the possible writer of the inventory.

69 John Cowper of Willington

made 11 April 1574

Lincolnshire Archives, INV/56/215

An Inventory of all the goodes Cattells And Implementes of howshould of John Cowper deceass[*ed*] taken the xj Daye of Aprill in the xvj^th^ yeare of the quenes ma[jes]tie that nowe is prysed by Henrye [*?*]Boston [*?*]fester, Roberte Osborne with others [*illeg.*] with others mo[re] [*sic*]

	£	s	d
Imprimis in the Halle one Cubberd a table & certeyne formes and certeyne stoles Chare and Cusshens valued at		xxx	
Item certeyne Pewter in the halle valued at		xx	
Item one Basen and Candelstickes valued at		iij	iiij
Item all the Brasse valued at		xl	
Item the painted clothes valued at		vj	viij
Item in the Chambre ij Chestes & certeyne Coffers		xx	
Item ij fether beddes & ij Coveringes valewed at		xxx	
Item fyve matresses & two Coveringes valued at		xxvj	viij
Item vj bolsters & viij pillowes valewed at		xiij	iiij
Item the [...] [*p*]aynted Clothes in the Chamber		x	
Item certeyne sheetes & Pillowberes		xl	
Item certeyne table napkyns towells & other trifells		xiiij	
Item all the plowgh timber & bordes		xiij	iiij
Item the hovells & woodd		vj	viij
Item the Cartes		xlvj	viij
Summa	[*blank*]		
[*Sub-total*	*£16*	*0s*	*8d*]
Item the horses	v	vj	viij
Item plowes, plowgeres & Carte geres		xiij	iiij
Item for bease & two Steres	vj	xij	
Item two Bullockes & two calves		xxxiij	iiij
Item certeyne store hogges & two Sowes		xxvj	viij
Item thre shepe valued at		xxij	
Item all the wheat & Rye valewed at	v	iij	iiij
Item the Barlie that is nowe sowne	ix		
Item peece & otes nowe sowen	iij		
Item the lease valewed at	iiij		
Summa	[*blank*]		
[*Sub-total*	*£37*	*17s*	*4d*]
Summa totalis	[*blank*]		
[*Total*	*£53*	*18s*	*0d*]

[*No exhibition clause*]

Notes: John Cowper's burial has not been found. The attribution of John Cowper to Willington is taken from Lincolnshire Archives online catalogue.

70 John Spenser, senior, of Bedford, tanner undated; after 19 April 1574
Lincolnshire Archives, INV/56/227

The Inventarye of all the goodes and cattell of Jhon Spensers thelders tannor late of the towne of Bedford deceassed praysed by Robert Hitch & Robert Pettye thelder as foloweth

	£	s	d
first in the hall j foulden table j benche borde j coolorde iij cheares j forme iiij stooles ij Irone bares iiij Irone hookes j aundiorne j payer of tonges j fire sholve j painted clothe at		xxiiij	iiij

	£	s	d
in the chamber			
iij bedstedes and iiij coffers at		xiij	
j presse and v paynted clothes at		vij	
vij payre of shetes & j whitefrindged shet		xl	
vj table clothes iij shertes ij pillow beares		xx	viij
ij cearchowes and j towell at		ij	viij
in the lofte over the hall			
j fetherbed ij boulsters iiij pillowes j quilt j mattris ij coverledes iij blancketes j ship chist j bedsted and ij fossers at	iij	v	
in the butterye & the lofte over it			
j calderne and iij pannes		xxix	iiij
ix olde cettles at		xxvj	viij
vj brasse pottes and j posnet		xxxv	
iiij tubes j boulting arcke iij cimneles j trofe and a busshell j payre of rackes iij spittes ij gosse pannes ij payre of pothookes & other ~~implementes~~ olde implementes at		xxiiij	
for peweter and lattine			
viij platteres xij disshes vj sawsers ij sawltes ij chafine disshes vj candelstickes j basone and an ewer of lattin j morter of brasse j payre of bellowes j cubbord clothe at		xl	
in the milke howse			
j table j forme bordes and shelves		iij	iiij
in the stable olde trashe		iij	
in the milhowse the stone and the ringe		vj	
in the yeard woode fates olde bordes and a hovell and one hogstye	iij		
for lether barke ij hoges iiij hennes iiij duckes and other trifeles to the some of	x		
Somme is	xxx	x	iiij
[*Corrected total*	*£30*	*10s*	*0d*]

[*No exhibition clause*]

Notes: John Spenser was buried at Bedford, St Mary on 19 April 1574.

71 William Doe of Cranfield — made 9 May 1574

Lincolnshire Archives, INV/56/224

An Invitory of the goodes of William Doe late of Cranfyld deceased taken and prised the nynth day of May Anno 1574 by William Purryar, Jhon Sugar, Thomas Odell, Nic[o]las Girton, Jhon Allen, Jhon Odell & other inhabitantes of Cranfyld aforesayd

	£	s	d
Imprimis a Geldinge		xxxiij	iiij
Item a colt		viij	
Item four kyne	v		
Item one bullock		xix	viij
Item vj shepe		xxvj	viij

Item fyve wethers newe shorn		xxv	iiij
Item a calfe		vj	viij
Item a sowe too hoges		xv	
Item iij hens			xij
Item fyve cobordes		xl	
Item thirty thre peaces of pewter		xxx	
Item xiij candelstickes ij chafingdishes		ix	
Item ij basons		ij	
Item iij saltes & ij pewter pottes			xiiij
Item four panns fyve kettelles one skellet		liij	iiij
Item xij pottes on posnet too old ketteles	iij	vj	viij
Item iiij fetherbedes with their bolsters	iiij		
Item fyve pillows ~~w their~~ too bolsters		x	
Item iij mattresses		xv	
Item fyve coverlides, four blanketes		xxvj	viij
Item fyve cushens, on carpett		vj	viij
Item twenty & nyne pair of shetes	iiij		
Item seaven table clothes		vij	
Item four pillobers		iij	viij
Item eight Bedstedes		xij	
Item on[e] pa[i]r of sylver hokes too silver pines for ringes		v	
Item nyn[e] cofers		xx	
Item the paynted clothes		x	
Item iij tables ij moulding boordes & too formes		x	
Item iiij chayres & thre stoles		iij	iiij
Item tubes kinelles & boles		x	
Item his apparell & his wyves		xl	
Item a salting trofe & a fatt		iiij	
Item iiij spittes iij p[ai]r of cobyrons & too gospanns		xiij	iiij
Item on[e] andyron ij p[ai]r of pot hangers & all other trashe		xxvj	viij
Summa Totalis	xl		xiij
[*Corrected total*	*£41*	*1s*	*2d*]

[*No exhibition clause*]

Notes: William Doe's burial has not been found. He made his will in 1573, leaving £3 6s 8d and household goods to his daughter Elizabeth; his house and land in Cranfield, bedding, brewing equipment, two coats and a cloak to his son Edward; a heifer, bearing sheet, a pair of silver hooks, two silver pins and a silver ring to his daughter Ann; a silver ring each to Alice and Rachel. Two men received a colt and a gelding. Residual legatees were his daughters, Alice, Rachel, Joan [*sic*] and Ann. His daughter Alice and Harry Odell were appointed executors. A note on the back of the will recorded a letter to Dr Belley for a licence for John Odell and Alice Doe to marry without banns (Beds Archives, ABP/W1573/126).

72 Edmund Hare of Houghton Conquest made 31 May 1574
Lincolnshire Archives, INV/56/89

The trewe Invetorye of all the goods & cattell of on Edmond Hare, Latlye deceassed in Houghton Conqueste, praysed by Thomas Collins, Jhon Woodward & Wylliam Savage the xxxj[th] daye of Maye, Anno domini 1574[o]

	£	s	d
Inprimis iiij[or] horsses	v		
Item ij beasse, & a bollocke	iij		
Item ij hoggs & a shoit		x	
Item an old shud cart		xx	
Item five Acres of barleye	iij	vj	viij
Item sixe acrs of ~~pessone~~ peassone	iij		
Item an old fether bed & a bolster		xiij	iiij
Item ij keverlets		x	
Item A long cheiste		v	
Item ij old coffers		iij	iiij
Item An folded table		iij	iiij
Item viij payre of sheats		xx	
Item ij table clothes		iij	
Item A pyllowe with the beare			xx
Item iij brasse pannes		xv	
Item ij brasse potts		x	
Item ij posnetts		iij	iiij
Item A lytle posnet			xij
Item ij tubbs			xx
Item viij[th] peces of pewter		v	iiij
Item candelstickes & a chaffingdyche		ij	
Item A lattyn basone			xvj
Item vj sheape		xiij	viij
Summa totall	xxj	ix	iiij
[*Corrected total*	*£21*	*9s*	*8d*]

[*No exhibition clause*]

Notes: Edmund Hare was buried at Houghton Conquest on 15 March 1574.

73 Elizabeth Newman of Colmworth, widow made 7 June 1574
Lincolnshire Archives, INV/56/91
The handwriting is difficult to read.

This inventorie made the vij[th] daye of June in the yeare of our Lord 1574 of all the goodes of Elisabeth Newman late of Colmorth within the contie of Bedford wydow, beyng prysed & valued by Jeffrey Moore, Thomas Judd the yonger, Wylliam Moore, Nycolas Dicons, George Boston, John Blith with others as foloweth

	£	s	d
fyr[*s*]t seven peer of flaxen sheetes		lvj	
Item xj peer of harden sheetes		lv	
Item iiij table clothes		x	
Item ij smockes v towels & a walet		ix	

Item xiiij Karchers		xviij	
Item v aprons & iij table napkyns		iiij	
Item iiij bolsters & iiij pyllowes		xvj	
Item ij coverynges iiij blankettes		xvj	
Item 3 coofers with a litle hetch		xiij	iiij
Item ij bedstydyes & a old matras		iiij	
Item iiij quyshons one banker and also the paynted clothes		x	
Item in the Lytle chamber one bedstydle a blanckd a hetche & a litle undressd flaxe		viij	
Item all the tubbes payles chesefattes bolles & such lyke		xxxiij	iiij
Item the bras & peuter	iij		
Item in the hall one cupbord one penne a table a benchbord ij chearse with the paynted clothes		xxvj	viij
Item ij tredes ij spyttes one peer of tonges one grydyron one peere of pott hangynges		x	
Item one cheese racke a ches bord with a litle hempe		ij	
Item one hechyll			xij
Item the bacon in the rowf		xx	
Item one wynnowyng cloth, a heor for a Kylne & iij seckes		x	
Item v quarters of malt		iiij	x
Item ix bushels of ootes		x	
Item one half quarter of wheat		x	
Item iiij quarters & a hale [*sic*] of barlye	iij	viij	vj
Item ij quarters of beanes		xxiiij	
Item a hovell with peese	v		
Item one shod cart		xl	
Item one old tyre with a cart bodie & a dong cart		xxx	
Item plough geeres cart geers with coleurs halters & such lyke		xiij	iiij
Item tymber for a cart bodie		ij	
Item iij ploughes with fyrwood also		viij	
Item xvij sheepe & vj lambes	iij		
Item iiij kyne	[*?*]vj		
Item ij yearlyng calves		x	
Item iij calfes wayners		[*?*]xij	
Item one horse & ij coltes	vj		
Item x store hogges & one soywe		xxx	
Item ix goslynges		iij	
Item vij dockes			xxj
Item xiij hennes		iiij	
Item one grydyll ston ij drak rakcs		iij	iiij
Item iij sythes & iij ladders		iij	viij
Item iiij harrowes		iiij	

Item a plough teeme with the slyngers			xx
Item one load of wood in wylbyes[17]			xx
Item one hay cock ther also		xx	
Item of wheat & barlie xxiij acars & one half	xvj		
Item xviij acars of peese	vj		
Summa	lxxvj	vij	viij
[*Corrected total*	*£76*	*8s*	*1d*]

[*No exhibition clause*]

Notes: Elizabeth Newman's burial has not been found.

74 Thomas Smallwood of Willington, carpenter made 14 June 1574

Lincolnshire Archives, INV/56/210

The handwriting and spelling are particularly difficult.

Thys invytory made the xiiij day off June in the yere off our lord god 1574 off the ~~stuffe late~~ goodes & catells off Tomas Smallwodes off the towne of Wyllington carpynter & prayssyd by Tomas Shodbolt, John Cleyton, Edmund Cleyton & Robert Osmon

	£	s	d
Item in the hall a nolld cobert a fowldyd tabyll a benche bo[*rd*] a forme a turnyd chayer ij stolles iij payntyd clothes		xxvj	viij
Item in the chamber a lytyll fetherbed a bolster a coverlett a june bedsted a tester & iij lytyll payntyd clothes		xxiiij	
Item ix payer of harden shettes ij tabyll clothes & j towell		xxxiij	iiij
Item vj coffers a nolld cheste & a forme		xx	
Item ij bedstedes j coverlet a blanket iij lytyll pyllowes		vj	viij
Item in the buttry a noold trouth with other trashe		iij	
Item iij brass panes iij Kyttylles ij brass pottes	iij		
Item the pewter & the lattyn		xiij	iiij
Item in the bowllty howsshe a trowthe with dysshyes & spones & other trashe		iiij	
Item all the boerdes & the tymber		xxvj	viij
Item iij mylche beesse & a lytyll store bulloke	v		
Item ij hoges & a store		x	
Item the wud in the yard		xxvj	viij
Item a nacar off whett & Ry		xx	
Item iij acares & a halfe of barly & peesse		xl	
Item iij acares off falow		vj	viij
Item the leass off the howsshe for viij yeres		xxvj	viij

17 Wylbyes may be the name of a person or a place; it has not been identified.

		£	s	d
Item all hys toulles			x	
Item a payer of cobyarns a lytyll spytt a grydyarne a tred & pott hangges			iiij	
	sum	xxiij		xx

[*No exhibition clause*]

Notes: Thomas Smallwood's burial has not been found.

75 John Odell of Cranfield made 14 June 1574

Lincolnshire Archives, INV/56/222

The inventory of all John Odelles movables taken the xiiij daye [*of*] June and in the xvj yere of the quenes Ragne valued and praysed by Lenard Stevenson, John Shelly, Thomas Barnes

		£	s	d
Item in primis in the yarde: iij horsse praysed at		iiij	xiij	iiij
Item iij kynne praysed at		iiij		
Item vj ewes and vj la[*mb*]es, xxx^{s}, iiij other dry ship xij^{s}			[*42*]	
Item one sowe and vj stores pyges			xij	
Item one owld shude cartte			xxx	
Item one owld mucke cartte			vj	viij
Item one plowe and harnis for iij horsse			x	
Item ij Loodes of wood			v	
Item all the croppe and haye		xj		
Item all the fornitudde in the halle having no kichinge		iiij	v	
Item all the fornitudde in the bowlting howsse			x	
Item all the holle fornitude in the chambers		vj	xiij	iiij
	[*Total*	*£36*	*7s*	*4d*]

[*Exhibited at Bedford on 15 June 1574*]

Notes: John Odell's burial has not been found.

76 Edward Hawton of Bedford, tailor made 29 July 1574

Lincolnshire Archives, INV/56/88

xxix die Julij 1574. Thynventorye of the goodes of Edward Hawton of the towne of Bedford within the com' of Bed taylor deceased prysed by William Garland and Thomas Kyrke and Jhon Beacham

	£	s	d
In primis in the halle a framyd table		ij	vj
Item iij Joyned stoles & a chaire			xx
Item a lyttle old square table			vj
Item iiij Quyssyns of lystes			xij
Item one Cubbord		v	
Item ij lytle paynted clothe			xvj
Item xxij pewter platters & dyshes		xiij	iiij
Item xij porryngers & sawsers		iiij	

Item ij pewter pottes iiij lyttle pewter cuppes	ij	
Item viij latten Canstykis	ij	viij
Item ij chamber pottes of sayd mettle		xij
In the kechyn		
Item one forme a lyttle chayre		xij
Item a brewyng kettle	x	
Item vj other lytle kettels	v	
Item ij old pottes of brasse	v	
Item ij lytle posnettes		xvj
Item one skymer		ij
Item one old Tubbe with other trene dyshes a bowle a payle		xij
Item one fryinge panne		vj
Item iij lyttle wheles	ij	
Item one paynted clothe		iiij
Item a payre cobyorns a trevett one payre lytle cobyorns ij payre pott hoks a fyre shovell a gredyorn a payre tonges and a pott hangyng	iij	4
The Chamber over the Kechyn		
Item ij old bedstedes one mattres a [?]couge [*?coveringe*] of lystes a bowlster	v	
Item ij stoles and old ~~C~~ presse of ij boordes iij peces of paynted clothes		xij
The chamber over the hale		
Item one standynge bedd	x	
Item one fetherbed a mattres a bowlster one Coverynge	xx	
Item one Counter table vj old Coffers	x	
Item iij old forcer		xij
Item ij paynted clothes and other peace	ij	
Item one shelffe		ij
The Chamber over the shoppe		
Item ij bedstydes	x	
Item one old fether bed a mattres a bowlster a coverynge of lystes a blankett	xiij	4
Item a mattres a bowlster a lyst coveryng	v	
Item iij Coffers	vj	8
Item iij paynted clothes ~~of~~ upon parchement ij old parchement testors	ij	
The Shoppe		
Item one Shop boord a coffer a forcer one old cubburt of ij bordes ij shelves a watchyng byll	v	
Item ij payre taylors sheeres ij presse Irons		xij
The sellor		
Item serten old tubbes and kymmels ij erthen stenes with other old trashe	iij	iiij
naprye ware		
Item vj payre flaxen shetes vj payre ~~mylde~~ mydle herden viij payre of		

cowrser herden		L	
Item one dosen table napkyns of flaxen and herden		iiij	
Item iiij old flaxen table Clothes 3 harden		x	
Item vj pillow beres		iiij	
Item iiij pyllows		iiij	
Item ij Coverlettes one dornyx & thother carpet		x	
Item one Clothe gowne		xiij	iiij
Item one old [*?*]hovell and serten wood		x	
Summa totalis	xj	xiiij	iiij
[*Corrected total*	*£13*	*15s*	*6d*]

Copia concordat
[*No exhibition clause*]

Notes: Edward Hawton's burial has not been found.

77 Edward Benet of Riseley, yeoman made 26 September [*no year, c. 1572–75*]
Lincolnshire Archives, INV/56/211

The inventory of alle the goodes of Edward Benet of the [*sic*] Rysley in the Cownt[*ie*] of Bedf yeman Latlye Decessed praysed the xxvj Day of September by [*missing*]

	£	s	d
Fyrst hys hors & colttes	xiij		
Item Kyne & Boolookes	xvj	xiij	iiij
Item hys sheppe	ix		
Item hooges		xlvj	viij
Item the cropp in the yard	xx		
Item the heye	iij	xiij	iiij
Item Cartt & cart geyres ploo & ploo geyres	vij		
Item hovelles & wood in the yard	iiij	xiij	iiij
Item an fatte in the malt hows		x	
Item pullen in the yard		x	
Item Woolle		xiij	viij
Item implementtes in the halle		~~xxxiij~~ liij	iiij
Item beddes & bedstyedes with al other ymplementes belongyng to the sam beyinge in the chambers	xv		
Item brasse & pewttar with other ymplementtes in the kyechen	v		
Item in the boltyng hows the pryce		vj	iiij
Item hys aparelle		xiij	iiij
Summa totalis	C	xxxvj	iiij
[*Corrected total*	*£101*	*13s*	*4d*]

[*No exhibition clause*]

Notes: Edward Benet's burial has not been found. The inventory is dated to 1572–75 in Lincolnshire Archives online catalogue and, for want of other evidence, placed in 1574 by the editor.

78 Peter Larkyn of Sandy 9 December 1574
Lincolnshire Archives, INV/56/307

A true invetorye of all the singuler goodes of that was Peter Larkines at the daye of his departing

	£	s	d
Item for eight payer of sheetes		xiij	iiij
Item for to boulsteres		iij	iiij
Item for to other boulsteres		ij	
Item for foure pilowes			iiij
Item for five pilowebeares		iij	iiij
Item for to coveringes		viij	
Item for an other coveringes			xij
Item for to ould mattreses		v	
Item for thre bedstides			xviij
Item for foure cofores		viij	
Item for hanges of the bede			xx
Item for to chayeres			viij
Item for the table and the forme			xij
Item for the haling			xij
Item for anolde cofor			iiij
Item for to pottes of bras		v	
Item for thre ketteles		v	
Item for a pan		iij	
Item for the trene vesseles		iij	
Item for the spite and the cobirons			xvj
Item for five peses of pewter		iij	iiij
Item for five platteres of pewter		iij	iiij
Item for fouer canstikes			xvj
Item for to bease	iiij markes [*53s 4d*]		
Item for to hoogges and fouer stores		xiij	iiij
Item for the haye		vj	viij
the sum is	vij	viiij	ij

praysed by Thomas Underwood, Jhon Underwood and Roger Rawlie
ix die Junij apud Hutchen

Notes: Peter Larkyn was buried at Sandy on 9 December 1574 and the inventory has been attributed to that date. The last line of the inventory (ix die Junij apud Hutchen) is probably a note of exhibition at Hitchin on 9 June 1575.

79 Thomas Cater of Sandy made 28 December 1574
Lincolnshire Archives, INV/56/234

These Inventorye of all the goods & Cattells th[*at*] ~~whe~~ weare Thomas Caters of Sonndeye ~~at the daye of his deathe~~ made the xxviij[th] daye of December in the xvj yeare of oure Soveraygne ladye Quene Elyzabethe made & praysed by those men whose names insuethe vid[*elic*]et by Johne Taylore, Thomas Underwood, sir Roberte Mayes & others

	£	s	d
Inprymis in the Haule			
A foult table a bench bourde & A forme		xj	viij
A Rounde Table			xij
iiij Chayres		ij	
vj Cusshines		iij	
A Cubberd		v	
ij basones of pewter with an ewer & one of laten		iiij	
vj latyn Candelstykes		iiij	
ij latyn Chafyndyshes		v	
iij pewter ~~Sawsersers~~ Saltsellers			xij
iij Stoles			vj
peynted Clothes in the Haule with the Cumberd clothe		iiij	
In the parler			
A bedestede with a fetherbed a mattrys ij koverleds ij blankets ij bolsters One pyllowes		xl	
a Counter table		vj	viij
v Chese[18] & a fosser		xx	
ij Chayres iiij stoles & a forme		v	
One Cubberd		x	
peynted Clothes in the same parler		vj	viij
vj peyre of flecson shets		xl	
xiiij peyre of harden shets		l	
xij table Clothes		xx	
xij table Napkynes		vj	
iiij pyllowe beares		ij	
iij Sakes		iiij	vj
xij ells of newe Clothe		x	
ij Cottes one dublet & one payre of shouse		xx	
xij pewter platters vj pewter dysshes xij porringers viij Sawsers one pewter candelstyke ij pewter potts		xx	
One spyce morter & a pestell a tyne bottell and a breade grate		ij	vj
In the lyttell Chamber			
ij bedsteds & a houche		iiij	
a fetherbed ij mattresses ij kyverleds		xiij	iiij
In the Soller over the parler			
One Standynge bede & a trundell bede		v	
ij fether bedes		xl	
ij koverledes		xl	
iij blanketes		iij	
tester & Curtens abought the bede		vj	viij
peynted Clothes in the same Chamber		iij	
ij Tables iiij stoles ij Schares		x	
vj Corse Cusshens		ij	
ij velvet Cusshines & one imbroydered Cusshine		xiij	iiij
xij yards of rede & greane see		xx	

[18] From the context, this word is more likely to be chests than cheese.

ij Chese & a Cannope for a bede		xx	
One anndyon & a payre of tounges & a tressell for a bason of water			xij
In the Soller over the Haule			
ij bedstedes		ij	
ij fetherbeds ij mattresses ij keverleds ij bolsters ij pillowes		xxxiij	iiij
a table a forme ij ~~St~~ Chayres & a huche			viij
ij bedsteds with a driinge rake for chese & other smale Chese		vj	
In the kytchine			
vj brasse potes		xxx	
iiij brasepayes & v kettells		xxx	
ij Spytes ij Cobbirones & other trayse		vj	viij
a Chese prese ~~in the boultinge house~~ & a boultinge arke ~~& other treane vessells~~		xx	
iiij lether bottells			xij
In the Stable			
v Carte horse	xiij	xiij	iiij
xl quarters barley in the barne	xxx		
Rey x quarters	x		
One come of whete		x	
a pese reke of xvj quarters	x		
Certen Tymber in the Shude		xvj	
plowe tymber in the same Shude		xx	
Oulde fyerwoode & rakes in the yarde		xx	
iij Cartes & Carte geares plowe & plowe geares	vj	xiij	iiij
iiij ladders & ij drawinge rakes		viij	
ij draught Oxon	iiij		
vij mylche beasse	x		
ix gest bullokes	vij		
ij Calves		x	
v^xx Shepe	x		
xvij hogges & Shotes		xl	
heye in the barne & other places	iiij		
ij dossen hardells		iij	iiij
pollen & foules in the yarde		x	
A moult quarne a fatte a fan & a barlype		xvj	
vj quarters of drye & rawe moulte	iiij		
An oulde kyll hare		ij	
In the felde			
x acares of rye	viij		
halfe an acare of Wheate		x	
xxvij acares of telthe	vij		
xxxvj acares of brache londe		xl	
Summa totalis	viij^xx vj		
[*Corrected total*	*£165*	*7s*	*6d*]

[*No exhibition clause*]

Notes: Thomas Cater was buried at Sandy on 1 December 1574.

80 Thomas Androw of Luton, maltman undated; c. 1577
Lincolnshire Archives, INV/61/152

An Invetorie of the goodes of Thomas Androw of Luton the countie of Bedford maulteman Late deceased

	£	s	d
In the hall			
In primis One Cubbord one table eight stooles fower olde Cussions with the paynted clothes in the hall		xx	
Item sixe small kettles one brasse pott twoo posnetes Fyve Candlestickes thre pothangers an yron bayard & one spitt		xviij	
Item Tenn pewter disshes, one platter, syxe sawsers, twoo saltes, twoo flower pottes [...] stone pot & a stone Crewse		x	
In the chamber			
Item one standing bedd one plaine bedd twoo mattresses one pare of blancketes twoo bolsters twoo Coverlettes & fower pillowes		xxiij	iiij
Item Fower Cofers, Fower pare of flexen shetes seaven pare of towen shetes & one shete tenn pillowberes twoo table clothes Fower table nappkins twoo towelles three half shetes one curten & certaine painted clothes	vij		
Item one Dublet a lether Jerkin a Coate a cloke a hatt a Capp a pare of bootes, & Fower shertes		xxx	
Item fower drinck vessells a tubb a doossen of trenchers half a doossen of spoones fower disshes & a ladle		vj	viij
In the lofte			
Item One trundlebedd a mattresse twoo Coverletes a shorte table a longe table a forme & twoo old paynted clothes		xvj	
In the malt house			
Item twentie quarters of maulte	xiiij	vj	viij
Item twoo boosshells a skryne a Fann twoo baskettes a kyll-hare and nyntene sackes		xlviij	
In the stable			
Item twoo horses		liij	iiij
In the yard			
Item One Cowe one sow & twoo stores		xlvj	vii[*j*]
Item the woodd	x		
Item in dettes owyng within the countie of Hertford and Middlesex	ix	iij	
Some	liiij	j	viij

The praysers Thomas Wattes, John Tymes, Edward Peter the writer
[*No exhibition clause*]

Notes: Thomas Androw's burial has not been found. Edward Peter, the writer of the inventory, witnessed deeds in the 1570s and 1580s in Luton and was described in one as a scrivener (Beds Archives, DW240).

81 George Knight of Wilden made 28 April 1576
Lincolnshire Archives, INV/61/183

The Invetory of all thc goodes and Cattayle of George Knight of Wilden lately deceassed prased by Henry Wagstaffe, Henrye Smyth, William La[*v*]endore the xxviij day of Aprill Anno domini 1576

	£	s	d
Inprimis iij kyne & ij bullockes	v	xiij	iiij
Item ij hogges		vj	viij
Item the Brasse		xxx	
Item the peuter		x	
Item A fetherbed with ij pillows		xvj	
Item iij coverlettes & ij blanckettes		x	
Item viij paire of sheetes ij table clothes ij table napkins & a cubbord clothe		xx	
Item iij coffers ij tables A forme & a bench borde		xv	
Item ij chaires iij bedsteedes		iiij	
Item A bolting arke A Salting troofe A bushell iij tubes iij booles vj trenchers a cherme v dishes		x	
Item the paynted clothes		vj	viij
Item iij chussins			xij
Item A spit A paire of cobirons a tred the pot hangles		iij	
Item an Ax & A hatchet			xij
Item vj hennes & a cocke		ij	iiij
Summa totalis	xij	ix	

[*Exhibited at Bedford on 11 June 1577*]

Notes: George Knight's burial has not been found. A note on the verso of the inventory states that administration was granted to Anne Knight, relict. This is probably Amy Knight, widow, who was buried at Wilden on 15 June 1579.

82 William Lambert of Stagsden undated; 1577
Lincolnshire Archives, INV/61/168

The true Inventory of the goodes & cattell of William Lambert of Stagedon, take[n] & prised by Thomas Baswell, Jhon Lambart, Rychard Same, Ryc[hard] Swetstone & others

	£	s	d
Imprimis xxij acres of grayn	x		
Item vj kyne	vj		
Item iij calves		xx	
Item iij horsse	iiij		
Item a sowe & viij stores		xx	
Item iiij^or^ sheepe		x	
Item xvij pullin		iiij	
Item iij stockes of bees		v	
Item a shodd cart & an old muckcart		xl	
Item wood boordes, troghes & other implementes		xl	
Item iij lodes of hay		xv	

	£	s	d
Item a coburd, a table, a form with pewter, brasse, & other implementes	iij	vj	viij
Item a[n] other coburd, iiij^{or} cofers, iij bedstedes, iij boulsters, iiij^{or} pillous a fetherbed & mattresse iiij^{or} cover liddes, iij blankettes, xj p[ai]r of shetes paynted clothes & other implementes	v		
Item xv of wooll & yarn		vj	
Item tubbes, boles, & all coopery		x	
Item spittes, cobyrons & old Iron		iij	iiij
Summa	xxxvij		

[*No exhibition clause*]

Notes: William Lambert's burial has not been found. The inventory is dated to 1577 in Lincolnshire Archives online catalogue.

83 Jone Bedcote of Lidlington, widow — undated; 1577

Lincolnshire Archives, INV/61/166

An Inventorie of the goodes and cattell of Jone Bedcote late of Litlington in the countie of Bedford wyddow preysed and valued bye Thomas Anglesey, Fraunces Taylor with others

	£	s	d
Inprimis three coverlettes			
Item three payre of shetes			
Item two blanketes			
Item a boulster			
Item one pillowe			
Item three underclothes			
Item twoo bedsteedes		xx	
Item a cupporde			
Item a cofer & one foser		vj	viij
Item one arke & a cheeseracke			
Item two tubbes			
Item vj pownde of hemp & flax			
Item a baskett with one flaskett syxe boles with one small wyker hamper		vj	viij
Item half a quarter of barlye and a bushell of peson		vj	
Item three kettels, twoo skelletes one brasse potte a frying pan		x	
Item one Joggell of hey		iij	iiij
Item three ~~be~~ kyne and a bullocke valued at	v	xj	viij
Summa totalis	viij	iiij	iiij

be me Thomas Anglesey, be me frances tayler

[*No exhibition clause*]

Notes: Jone Bedcote was buried at Lidlington on 19 March 1577.

84 John Wolhed of Wilshamstead made 28 March 1577
Lincolnshire Archives, INV/61/155

This Inventory Indented bearinge Date the xxviij day of March in the xixth yeare of the Raigne of our soveraigne Ladie Elizabethe etc of all the goodes and Cattels of John Wolhed Late of Wylshamsted in the Counte of Bedforde Deceassed Praysed by us John Tanner, Thomas Smythe, Rycharde Dear[er], Thomas Wolhed withe others as followethe

	£	s	d
In primis a Coberde		ij	
Item viij platters ij pewter Disshes ij saltes and iij Candlestickes		vj	viij
Item ij lyttle brase potts ij kettles a brase panne iij lyttle kettles and a posnet		xvij	
Item a table a forme and ij bordes		ij	
Item the paynted clothes in the haule		iij	
Item a fetherbed ij boulsters ij matterisses ij Coveringes a blancket and bedsted		xxiij	
Item vij payre of sheetes ij pyllowbears ij table clothes and ij towells		xxiiij	
Item ij Coffers		v	
Item the hangins in the Chamber		iij	iiij
Item ij tubes, v barrels a troughe a busshell ij boolles a saltinge troughe an old ambre ij bottles a fryjnge panne, and an old bedsteed		xiij	iiij
Item a payre of Cobyrons a spyt a trevet and pothangers		iij	
Item ij cheese Rakes and a chearme			xij
Item vj flytches of bacon		xv	
Item an axe, a hatchet a byll and a howe			xij
Item a clothe basket and a maund			vj
Item iij horse and a coulte	iiij		
Item iiij steers	v		
Item iiij bease iij heckforthes and a yearlinge calfe	vij	vj	8
Item a Sowe and ij stoors		viij	
Item a shood carte and a dunge carte		xl	
Item a cart rope			xviij
Item Carte harnes and ploughe geer		x	
Item ij ploughe cheyns, a yoke, ij payre of fetters and a horse loke		v	
Item a Rame pugges		iij	
Item iiij plough beames iij harrowes ij dozen of ploughtymber redy hewed		v	vj
Item a hundrethe of borde		iiij	
Item a Role a ploughe and yrons		vj	
Item a hovell and wood		xiij	iiij
Item a fewe pease on a hovell		x	
Item wheat bearly and Rye		xx	
Item haye		x	
Item six hennes and a Coke		ij	iiij
Item x Dukes and drakes		ij	
Item a gowse and a gander			xvj

	£	s	d
Item a gryndston and an yron spyndle			xij
Item a draught rake and a forke			xx
Item vij acres of barely sowen	iij	x	
Item an acre of wheat and Rye sowen		xij	
Item viij acres of beanes and fetches sowen		liij	iiij
Summa totalis	xxxvj	vj	vj

[*Exhibited at Bedford on 11 June 1577*]

Notes: John Wolhed's burial has not been found.

85 John Skelliter of Girtford, Sandy made 15 April 1577

Lincolnshire Archives, INV/61/154

Slight damage on the top right side.

This ys the Trew Invetory of all the goodes and Catteles of Jhon Skelliter of Girtford in the parishe of Sandy dysceased the xiiij daie of Aprill in the yere of our Lord god 1577 praysed by John Symont and Roger Rawlyngs the xv[th] of Aprill as said

	£	s	d
Inprimis in the hawle ij tables		ij	viij
Item on litle Side bord			viij
Item ij buffet stowles and aforme			xvj
Item on old cheire			xij
Item a painted clothe in the hawle			xx
Item on Cupbord		x	
Item all the painted clothes aboute the howse		vij	
Item viij cusshinges			vj
Item [*remainder of line is blank*]			
Item in the Chamber iij old Cofers		vij	
Item iij bedstedes		iiij	
Item ij coverynges on blanket		vj	
Item on boulster tyke and ij pillowes		ij	
Item ij old mattresses		iij	
Item ij pannes and iiij ketteles		xviij	
Item iiij brasse pottes and on possnet		xv	
Item ij platters and x pewter dysshes		vij	
Item ij Lattin basins and iiij Candelstickes		iij	iiij
Item ij boulsteres		v	
Item on coverlet		vj	
Item on table cloth fyve flexen & ij of harden		v	viij
Item xj paier & on od sheite [*one odd sheet*] iij of them flexen		xl	
Item iiij kercheifes		viij	
Item ij flexon pillow beares and other ij of harden		iiij	
Item on forcer			xij
Item fyve slipes yarne		ij	vj
Item all her [*sic*] waringe wollen		xx	
Item on old copbord theire		iij	iiij
Item in the Lofte iij bussheles Barle		v	
Item ij shepe skynnes			viij
Item the hempe there		v	viij

Item ij oken bordes and aframe			xij
Item on Spit the pot hokes and hangins agredyrne		iij	iiij
Item ij tobbes apaiell apaire of bellous		ij	viij
Item in the yard all the fire wood and tymbre		xxvj	viij
Item v troughes		v	
Item certaine Rye in the house & peas		xxx	xx
Item iij geeis and on gander certaine pollin		iiij	viij
Item iij beas and on bullocke and on flitche bacon	v		
Item [*illeg.*] tares peaes on acare barle		xxix	
Item a cherne a cheis fat and all the haie in the howse			xviij
Somm	20	13	2
[*Corrected total*	*£20*	*2s*	*6d*]

[*No exhibition clause*]

Notes: John Skelliter's burial has not been found.

86 Joan Mayes of Everton, widow of William Mayes, yeoman made 24 May 1577
Lincolnshire Archives, INV/61/265

The Inventorye Indentyd made the xxiiij[th] daye of Maye in the xix[th] yere of the Reigne of our Sovereign ladye Elizabeth by the grace of God of England Fraunce & Ireland Quene defender of the feyth etc of all the goodes Cattelles & debtes of Johan[na] Mayes wydowe late of Everton in the Countye of Hunt decessyd late the wyff of Wyllyam Mayes late of Sutton in the Countye of Bedd yoman before decessyd and before, the wyff of Wyllyam Hale late of Everton aforseyd Gent Fyrst decessyd praysed by Rycherd Barrett & Symon Strynger yomen and Wyllyam Parker & Edward Carnebrooke alles Swetyng of the parrysshe of Everton aforseyd husbondmen

	£	s	d
In the hall			
Inprimis the paynted Clothes ther praysed att		v	iiij
Item the Cobborde Tables Fo[r]me Stooles & Casse praysed att		xx	
Item a lyttle Sylver Salte and Sixe sylver spones praysed att		l	
In the Chamber			
Item the paynted Clothes ther praysed att		iiij	viij
Item the best fetherbed Bolster & pyllowe praysed att		xxvj	viij
Item the other fetherbed Bolster and pyllowe praysed att		xiij	iiij
Item Fyve blankettes one mattrys & a quylte praysed att		xxiij	iiij
Item a Gyrte Bedstede with the hangynges and one other old Bedstede praysed att		xiij	
Item thre Flaxen sheetes and thre payer of harden sheetes praysed att		xxvij	
Item a Table Cloth of Dyaper worke & a Towell of the same and one Table Clothe of Flaxen & seaven Table napkyns with other smale harden lynnen prased att		xv	
Item thre Smockes thre pyllowebears thre neckerchewes			

with Fore Sleves Fyve kerchewes two Rayles & a wolstede aperne praysed att		xvj	
Item all hyr wearyng apparell praysed att		xlvj	viij
Item Fower Coffers with eight Slypps of lynnen yerne praysed att		xiiij	
Item all the Brasse praysed att		xxxiij	iiij
Item all the pewter and one Chaffyngdysshe & two Candelstyckes praysed att		xv	
In the kytchyn			
Item the Cobyerns Spyttes & Fryeng panne praysed att		vj	viij
Item the Flytches of Baken praysed att		vj	
Item all the Treene vesselles with payles Tubbes Buckett & boltyng arke praysed att		x	
In the yarde			
Item thre bease & a yong Calf praysed att	iiij	xvj	
Item Sixe shepe & a laine praysed att		xxiiij	
Item all the hogges praysed att		xx	
Item all the pullen praysed att			xvj
Item all the wood in the yarde praysed att		iij	iiij
Sum totalis	xxiiij	x	viij
[*Corrected total*	*£24*	*0s*	*4d*]

[*Exhibited by Thomas Hale*]

Notes: Joan Mayes's burial has not been found. She married first William Hale of Everton, gentleman, and secondly William Mayes of Sutton, who was dead by 1577 (see Beds Archives, PM1167). Her son Thomas Hale, gentleman, was appointed administrator.

87 Thomas Hill of Chicksands

undated; between 4 and 12 June 1577

Lincolnshire Archives, INV/61/171

The trew Inventorie of all the goodes & cattells of Thomas Hill deceased praysed by Nicholas Foster & Radylf Goward

	£	s	d
Item in primis xx[ti] acres of Rie & Barley	xv		
Item xx[ti] acres of pease	vij		
Item xiiij kyne	xvij		
Item iij bullockes		xl	
Item vj bollockes	iij		
Item iiij calves		xx	
Item v carte horsses	xvj	vj	viij
Item ij longe cartes		liij	iiij
Item carte & carte geres & plowe & plowe geres		xx	
Item xx[ti] sheppe	iiij	xiij	iiij
Item viij hogges & viij pigges		xx	
Item all implementes of howshold & wood in the yard	x		
Debtes owinge to the said Hill			
Item Elizabeth Wythe widdowe	v		
Item George Hill	iij		
Item George Louthorpe		xvj	

	£	s	d
Item Thomas Thodye		viij	
Item Thomas Lepere		vj	
Item Henry Robinson		vj	viij
Item Thomas Lynford		ij	
Item John Small		viij	
Sum totalis	lxxxxj		

[*Exhibited at Bedford on 12 June 1577*]

Thomas Hill was buried at Campton on 4 June 1577.

88 Thomas Smith of Keysoe, labourer made 10 June 1577
Lincolnshire Archives, INV/61/177

The inmatorye of the goodes of Thomas Smith late of Caysho deceased in the countye of Bedforde laborer made the x day of June Anno Domini 1577

	£	s	d
Item in the chamber a boulster a cover-lett a mattresse & a pyllow		x	
Item v payre of shetes		xiij	iiij
Item a Bedsteade iij cofers & a forme iij paynted clothes		vj	viij
Item in the haule ij pannes a potte & a lytell kettle		x	
Item a table & a forme & a chaire		iij	
Item iij candelstyckes ix peces of pewter		vj	viij
Item a spitte potte hangels dishes & spones with al other implementes with in the house		ij	
Item a Cowe & a bulloke		xl	
Item a lytell Sow		ij	
Item ij hoffels & x boardes		xiiij	
Item the resydewe of the tymber & the woode in the yarde		vj	
Item xxs in monye		[*xx*]	
The summe is	vj	xiij	viij

Praysers of these goodes Richarde Talbote, Edmunt Piccoke, Jhon Richardes with other mor
[*No exhibition clause*]

Notes: Thomas Smith's burial has not been found.

89 Gilbert Lapidge of Southill made 12 May 1579
Lincolnshire Archives, INV/64/118

An Inventory Indented taken the xij[th] day of May 1579 Et Anno regni regine E[lizabeth] 2jd[19] of all suche goodes and Cattalles as late were Gilbert Lapidge late of Southell decessed as followethe

19 The 21st year of the reign of Queen Elizabeth.

	£	s	d
Imprimis one Sorrelled geldinge		xx	
Item iiij Bease and Bullockes	iij	xiij	iiij
Item one Shepe		ij	
Item ij Brasse pottes		vj	viij
Item one Brasse panne		iij	iiij
Item iij kettelles		ij	
Item ij latten basons one chayfingdishe and a Skymer			xvj
Item ij tubbes ij Stoppes, iij pales and v Bolles		iij	viij
Item A newe meale Syve			iij
Item a Table with tresselles and twoo formes			xvj
Item A xj peces of pewther		iiij	
Item ij Candlestykes			viij
Item a kneding tubbe			iij
Item A Cherne and ij chesefattes			xiiij
Item A pewther potte			iiij
Item A fetherbed A Bolster iiij pyllowes, ij Coveringes & ij Bedsteides		xix	
Item one Salteseller			ij
Item v painted Clothes			xxij
Item A lyttell table & a benchebord			vj
Item an axe, A hatchett, A Bill a paire of Tonges & a paire of pott hookes			xviij
Item vij paire of shettes, A wallett iiij shertes & A handtowell		xviij	iiij
Item one fare chest and ij Cofferes		iij	
Item A paire of Andirons, A quyshen an Irone showing horne A Spitt and A chopping knyffe		ij	
Item A handsawe, A Brest wimble A hammer A paire of pinsons, iij other wymbles, An enterrer & A drawingknyfe			xvj
Item sertaine boordes, ij lyttell bord-Clothes, A shod shovell, A spade A hawe, ij picheforkes & A paire of fetteres		viij	vj
Item certaine apparell		vj	viij
Item his Office	v		
Som	xiiij	iij	ij

[*No exhibition clause*]

Notes: Gilbert Lapidge was buried at Southill on 11 May 1579. He was the bailiff of several manors within the lordship of Old Warden in the 1530s and 40s (Yvonne Nichols, ed. *The Court of Augmentation Accounts for Bedfordshire* (Bedfordshire Historical Record Society, 1984 and 1985), 2 vols, BHRS 63 and 64. Vol. 1 p. 95, vol. 2 p. 146). His tenement and lands were the subject of a case brought after his death by his son William in the Court of Chancery (TNA, C2/Eliz/L6/51).

90 Thomas Nyxe of Bletsoe, rector made 30 July 1579
Lincolnshire Archives, INV/64/117

An Inventory of all the goodes Cattailles plate, Jewelles & p[arce]lles which late were belonging to Thomas Nyxe parson of Bletyshoe dysceased praysed & valued by Rowland Mylner, Thomas Bevys, Robert Merytowne & John Churche the xxx[th] day of July Anno Domini 1579

	£	s	d
Inprimis viij beastes, ij bullockes, iiij Calves and j bull	x		
Item iiij horsses	iiij		
Item j shodde Cart & A dung cart		xx	
Item xviij hogges yong & old		xxv	
Item xxij Acr' of grayne where of x Acres of Barley j Acr' of Rye j Acr' of wheat & x Acr' of pease	vij		
Item in the yard xx pullen		v	
Item the fyre wood in the yard		v	
Item ij framed hovelles ij plowes plowe tymber, & other old implementes pertayning to husbandrye		xx	
Item old plowe geares & Cart geares lockes, fetters & other odd trashe		x	
Somma	xxv	v	
In the parlor			
Item j bedsteed, A fetherbed, j blancket j Coverlict & A bolster		x	
Item a Cubbord		vj	viij
Item a lyttle ioyned table, ij stooles & ij Chaires		iij	iiij
Item iij Coffers		iij	iiij
Item A forme			vj
Item ij painted Clothes		ij	
Item x paire of sheetes v bord clothes & j dousaine of napkins		xxvj	viij
Somma		Lij	vj
In the Chymney Chamber			
Item j Bedsteed, j fetherbed, j blancket ij Coverlictes & A bolster		vj	viij
Item A little square table & A chaire			xx
Somma		viij	iiij
In the chese loft			
Item xl Cheeses		vj	viij
Somma		vj	viij
In the Buttery Chamber			
Item A bedsteed, j fetherbed, j blancket j Coverlict & A bolster		x	
Item j old chest			xij
Somma		xj	
In the Bruehousse chamber			
Item j Bedsteed, j fetherbed, ij blanckettes j Bolster & one old trundle bedde		x	

	£	s	d
Item j old Chest & j old folding table		ij	
Somma		xij	

In the Kytchyn

	£	s	d
Item xiij old tubbes		v	
Item iiij spittes & ij paire of CobIrons		v	
Item iij flytches of Bacon		v	
Somma		xv	

In the milke housse

	£	s	d
Item j mault querne, j musterd querne, j old bolting tubbe, j old kneading bord, j Chese presse j Cherne, j whele & A grynding stone all valued at		vj	viij
Somma		vj	viij
Somma totall page	xxx	xvij	ij

[*side 2*]

In the servantes loft

	£	s	d
Item ij matteresses, j bedsteed, j blancket with other old trashe		vj	
Item in Rye & barlye ij quarters		x	
Somma		xvj	

In the hall

	£	s	d
Item painted Clothes			xx
Item ij framed tables & A square bord ij formes, viij stoles j chaire & A benche bord		xiij	iiij
Item A Cubberd & A penne		vj	viij
Item Brasse & pewter, dyshes, spones & trenchers		xl	
Item vj pillowes & vj Cushions		vj	viij
Somma	iij	viij	iiij
Somma pag’	iiij	iiij	iiij
Somma totalles of both pages is	xxxv		xviij

[*No exhibition clause*]

Notes: Thomas Nyxe’s burial has not been found. He was vicar of Keysoe 1543–54; rector of Bletsoe until his death in 1579; and possibly also at Thurleigh in 1540 (CCEd; Beds Archives, Fasti/1/Key and Fasti/1/Blet). Probate was granted on 31 May 1580 (Lincs Archives, Act Book A/iii/51).

91 Henry Comes of Stagsden — undated; c. 1579–80

Lincolnshire Archives, INV/64/116

The Inventorye of goodes and cattelles of Henry Comes of Stagedon late deceased praysed by William Burwaye vic[ar] of Stagedon & Thomas Wheler & William Mowse with others, as Followythe

	£	s	d
Imprimis all the grayne aswell wheat barly ottes ~~xl Acres~~ as pease & haye	xx		

Item iiij^{or} horse & ij coltes prysed	vj		
Item viij kyne price	viij		
Item vj bullockes & ij calves	vj	x	
Item fyftye sheepe	x		
Item viij stores hogges		xvj	
Item ij shodde cartes		xl	
Item all the poultery			xij
Item ij fetherbedes & all that belongythe to them		xl	
Item ij trusse bedes		xij	
Item a cubborde & a presse		xx	
Item xij peses of pewter		vj	
Item a tabell vj buffit stooles a forme a rownde tabell a chayer		xiij	iiij
Item iij brasse pottes a panne iij kettelles withe all the resydew		xx	
Item ij spyttes a gosepanne & cobyornes		ij	
Item a cheaste & viij payer of sheetes and iij towelles & iij borde clothes and vj pillowe beres & vj napkins		xxx	
Item plowes & plowe tymber & the carte geares & plowe geres		xx	
Item a querene		vj	
The ~~howse~~ Tubbes and disshes & all implementes abowtes the howse		x	
Summa totalis	lvij	vj	iiij
[*Corrected total*	*£62*	*6s*	*4d*]

[*No exhibition clause*]

Notes: Henry Comes' burial has not been found. The inventory is dated to 1579–80 in Lincolnshire Archives online catalogue.

92 William Read of Turvey undated; c. 1579–80

Lincolnshire Archives, INV/64/120

The Inventory of the goodes & Cattelles of Wylliam Reade late of Turvey in the county of Bed in the dyoces of Lyncoln praised immediatly after hys decesse by John Balle, John Stevynson, Wylliam Sonie & Bartilmewe Babyngton

	£	s	d
Fyrste a Table, a forme & tow Lowe Stooles		v	
one Cubberde & a deseborde		viij	
Syxe peces of pewter & tow Sawcers		v	
The Coffers & a foser		v	
The beddes with the furnyture		xx	
Syxe paire of Shetes		xij	
Item one Chreesete & a pothanger			xvj
Item one pott & a panne & two kettelles		xv	
Item two Tubbes a boltynge arke one payle & a mele		iiij	
Item fyve horses	vij		

	£	s	d
Item vij beesse, two steeres & two Calfes	x		
Item fyve Stoores		xij	
Item viij Shepe		xx	
Item two Shodde Cartes a longe carte & a donge carte two ploughes and foure pare of Geares	iiij		
Item one hovell & the wood in the yarde		xx	
Item xxxj acres of pease & barley	xij	xvj	viij
Item two quarters of malte		xvj	
Item foure quarters of Barley		xxxij	
Summa totalis	xlij	xij	

[*No exhibition clause*]

Notes: William Read's burial has not been found. The inventory is dated to 1579–80 in Lincolnshire Archives online catalogue.

93 John Robinson of Pavenham made 4 April 1580

Lincolnshire Archives, INV/64/112

Slight damage, affecting the right side with consequent loss of some pence values.

An Inventorie of the goodes and cattelles etc of John Robinsonne of Pavenham made the iiij[th] of Aprill 1580

	£	s	d
The haule			
Inprimis in the haule a cubborde with pewter uppon yt		xx	
Item the lattin uppon the same		iij	iiij
Item a table a benche borde, a forme, a chaire, and vj buffet stooles		x	
Item twoe olde painted clothes			xij
The Chamber			
Inprimis in the chamber iij coverlettes, iij mattresses a fetherbed, v boulsters, xij paire of sheetes whe[re]of iij sheetes are flexen		xxxiij	[...]
Item vij pillowes		v	
Item vij coffers, a buffet forme, and an olde chayre		xiij	iiij
Item vj olde bedsteedes		iij	iiij
The lafte over the entrie			
Inprimis in the lafte over the entrie a square table			xij
Item certeine bordes ther		x	
The kytchin			
Inprimis in the kitchin vij brasse pottes		xviij	
Item iiij brasse pannes		xiij	iiij
Item vj kettles iij skyllettes, & a posnett		x	
Item ij chafingdishes & ij skymmers		ij	
Item iij spittes a paire of cobirons, ij paire of pothookes ij pot hangers a grediron, & a tredde		v	
The boultinge house			
In the boultinge house an olde cubborde iiij olde tubbes iij olde barrelles a kimnell & a boultinge arke		x	
Item an olde troffe certeine tymber & olde hurdles		iij	iiij

	£	s	d
The qerne house			
In the qerne house a querne with other olde trashe		x	
The barne			
In the barne a cantche of corne unthreshte & some threshte		xiij	iiij
The yarde			
In the yarde an olde hovell and olde shood carte plowe timber cart tymber with other fyer woodde		xl	
Item iiij stockes of bees		vj	viij
Item iiij bestes and iiij bullockes	iiij		
The Feilde			
In the Feilde thre acres of barleye		xx	
Item thre acres of peas		xiij	iiij
Summa totalis	xvij	v	iiij

The prisers names John Heywarde Roberte Morris & Thomas Spirrie
[*No exhibition clause*]

Notes: John Robinson's burial has not been found.

94 Oliver Smyth of Milton Ernest, tanner made 4 April 1580
Lincolnshire Archives, INV/64/114

A true Invitorye of all the goodes & chattells of one Oliver Smith ~~in the countie~~ of Milton Ernes in the countie of Bedford Tanner latelye deceased taken the fourth day of April in the xxij yeare of the Reigne of oure sovereigne Ladye Elizabeth by the grace of god Quene of England Fraunce & Ireland defendoure of the faith etc by me Robert Sutton vicar there, Master Turnor, Frauncys Lindford, John Smith, Thomas Jackson and John Church as followeth

	£	s	d
In primis one Cubbord pryced at		x	
Item a Table a cheare a forme & a stole		iij	iiij
Item iiij puter platters pryced at		v	
Item vij puter dishes pryced at		v	iiij
Item fyve sawcers pryced at			xv
Item iij candlestickes iij saltsellers & vj puter sponnes		iij	
Item a latten bason pryced at			xx
Item ij brass pottes pryced at		vij	
Item iij kettells pryced at		viij	
Item one brass panne a posnet & a skimmer		vj	viij
Item a fryingpanne a paire of pothockes & a spitt and a gridyrone & a paire of pothangers		ij	vj
Item a painted cloth & iij cushins		iij	iiij
Item iij coffers & ij bedstedes		v	
Item iij coverledes and ij blancketes pryced at		xiij	iiij
Item one matteris ij bolsters & iij pillowes		xiij	iiij
Item x paire of shetes pryced at		xl	
Item iiij pillowbeers and iiij table napkins		xiij	iiij
Item a Towell and iij Table clothes		viij	
Item iiij painted clothes about the beddes		v	
Item x slipps of yarne pryced at		vj	viij

Item ij Tubs a stopp and a paile at		ij	vj
Item halfe a dosen dishes and a dosen of trenchers			iiij
Item iij milkeboles price		iij	iiij
Item foure kyne pryce	iiij		
Item one horse pryce		xx	
Item fyve shepe pryced at		xx	
Item iij dicker of leather pryced at	viij		
Item a dicker of fypes pryced at		xx	
Item iij lodes of barcke pryced at		xl	
Item vij dryefattes pryced at		xx	
Item ij Acres of barley		xx	
Item certen wood pryced at		iij	iiij
Item an olde hovell pryced at			xx
Summe Totall is	xxvij	xij	xj

[*No exhibition clause*]

Notes: Oliver Smyth was buried at Milton Ernest on 31 March 1580.

95 Richard Blythe the elder of Begwary, Eaton Socon, yeoman made 3 May 1580
Lincolnshire Archives, INV/64/119

A true Inventorye Indented of all the goodes & chattelles of Rychard Blythe the elder late of Beggarye in the parysshe of Eaton & Countye of Beddes yoma[n] made taken & praysed by Thomas Kyppest, William Barcock & John Luffe the thirde daye of Maye in the xxij[th] yere of the raygne of our Soveraigne ladye Elizabeth by the grace of god Quene of England Fraunce & Ireland defendor of the Fayth etc as followeth

	£	s	d
Inprimis viij mylche kene vj bullockes fyve calfes praysed at	xiij		
Item iiij[or] horse & coltes praysed at	x		
Item the barlye wheat malt & pease praysed at	ix	x	
Item xxviij Acres of wheat & barlye praysed at	xiiij		
Item xxij Acres of pease & otes praysed at	vij		
Item the hogges & the pygges praysed at		xvj	
Item squared tymber & woode praysed at		xiij	iiij
Item ij shud Cartes praysed at	iij		
Item iiij weanyng Caulfes praysed at		xiij	iiij
In the parlor chamber			
Item a bedsted & a Cubbord there praysed at		xx	
Item the pewter platters sawcere & pottes praysed at		x	
Item ij chayres praysed at		ij	
Item iiij[or] Coverleddes for beddes praysed at		xx	
Item a Fetherbed bolster & iij pyllowes praysed at		xxvj	viij
Item the hangenges & paynted clothes praysed at		iij	iiij
In the parlor			
Item the table forme & cusshens praysed at		vj	viij
Item one chest ij coffers & ij bofett stoles		xij	
Item the paynted clothes praysed at		ij	

In the halle

	£	s	d
Item the table the benche borde the forme & settle & a cubord praysed at		x	
Item ij basons vj peaces of pewter ij saltes & iiij Candelstickes an Ewer & a chaffyng dyshe		x	
Item thre brasse pottes ij postnettes praysed at		xxvj	viij
Item ij pannes viij kettelles praysed at		xx	
Item the hawlyng & spere towell		ij	
In the halle chamber & lafte over			
Item ij bedstedes a chest & a coffer the hangenges about the beddes		x	
Item ij bedstedes in the lafte over the halle		iiij	
Item x payre of shetes praysed at		xxv	
Item iij table clothes ij napkyns praysed att		iij	
Item one Coverled & vj blankettes ij bolsters & a pyllowe praysed at		vj	viij
Item a malt quarne & a ledde to brue in praysed att		xxxiij	iiij
Item a masshyng fatt & the bruyng vesselles		ix	
Item iiij barrelles praysed at		v	
Item ij Spyttes cobyrons gospannes & fryeng pannes praysed at		viij	
Item the musterd quarne & all the vesselles in the mylck howse praysed at		xj	
Item ij plowes & teames & all that long to them praysed at		vj	viij
Item the Cart geares & plowe geares		vj	viij
Item a meale tubbe a fanne a busshell a shrene & a barlyppe praysed at		x	
Item v bottelles praysed at		vj	viij
Item a Crowe of Iron Iron hammer the mattock the oxe teames & other tryffles praysed at		x	
Item a payre of Tonges fyer showell pothangelles & other tryfles praysed at		iiij	
Sum totalis	lxxv	iij	

[*No exhibition clause*]

Notes: Richard Blythe was buried at Eaton Socon on 23 March 1580.

96 Richard Plommer of Eversholt made 12 May 1580

Lincolnshire Archives, INV/64/127

The initial capital letters L *and* B *are identical. They have been transcribed as appropriate.*

A Juste & trew Invnetor [*sic*] of all suche goodes as Rychard Plomer Latte of Eversholt had at the tym of his deathe taken & prisid the the [*sic*] xij day of Maye in the yeare our lord 1580 prisyed by Robarte Rowbord, John Wyttemore, [*illeg.*] Longe with other mo[re]

	£	s	d
in the hall			
In primis on Coubart & xij pesses of peutter		x	

	£	s	d
Item on table a Forme with a Benche borde		iij	
Item on chayer ij olstoules			viij
in the chamber			
Item ij old Bedstedes			xij
Item on matrys oone [*sic*] old Fether bed		x	
Item vij payer of shettes		xiij	iiij
Item ij Coverlettes ij blanckytes tow bolsters ij pelows		xx^{ti}	
Item iiij old Couffers		iiij	
Item a payer of Cobyerons ij spyetes on and ndyeron [*andiron*] a payer of pothouckes and the hangers		iij	iiij
Item ij brase pottes iij kettls		xiij	iiij
Item iij old toubes & other tren ware		ij	
In the yeard			
Item iij kyene & iij Boulockes	vj		
Item ij horsys		xl	
Item al the wood in the yeard		ij	
Item tow old carte boddyes & other tymber a plowe & ij old Ladders		xx	
Item a sowe & iiij pygges		iiij	
In the Feld			
Item v akers of barlye on aker of Rye tow aakers of outtes on aker of benes	iiij		
Summa totalis	xvij	vj	viij

[*Exhibited at Dunstable on 2 June 1580*]

Notes: Richard Plommer's burial has not been found.

97 William Kerbey of Bedford, butcher made 20 May 1580

Lincolnshire Archives, LCC ADMONS 1580/88

Slight creasing. Several words and letters are partly obscured; where obvious, they have been inserted in italics within square brackets.

An Inventorye of the goodes and Chattelles of William Kerbey late of Bedford in the Countie of Bedf butcher deceassed vewede and praysed by Robert Hitche and Thomas Pettit the xxth day of May in the xxijth yeare of the raigne of our Soveraigne Lady Elizabeth by the grace of god Quene of England Fraunce & Ireland defendor of the faithe etc

	£	s	d
Inprimis in the hall [*one fraymed*] Table one Rownd Table, one Cubberd, one Forme, two buffet stoles one Chaire with the paintede clothes and other ymplementes ther valued at		xx	
In the kitchyne two kettelles, two pottes, one speit & other ymplementes ther		v	
In the back howse one panne, one table one Forme and other ymplementes ther		x	
In thother back howse an old cubberd, certeyn old wood & other ymplementes ther		v	

	£	s	d
In the Chamber over the hall a bedd with the furnyture, three Chestes, one Cubberd and other ymplementes ther		xx	
In the next Chamber two beddes with the furnyt[ure], one old bedstedd, two coffers one old chaire & other ymplementes their		x	
Twentye paire of sheetes and other Lynnen		xl	
An old coffer at the staire hedd			iiij
In the buttry three barreles three tubbes & other ymplementes ther		v	
In the Entry, a wollen wheall & a bord			xij
In an other Chamber a bedd, a matrisse three old bordes			xx
In the Chamber over the s[*t*]able a bedstedd [*two boldsters*] fowr pillowes two paire of blankets a Coverlet two chestes two pottes two kettelles foure old tubbes thre candlstickes, a [*chaffinge dishe*] a borde two tresselles and other ymplementes ther		[*xx*]	
Three dozen of pewter three saltes & other small peeces of brasse & pewter		xv	
In the yard two old hovelles a ladder & wood		x	
A leasse of the howse for certeyn yeares yet induringe	vj	xiij	iiij
An axe two clevers & other toelles in his shopp		iij	viij
Sum	xv		

[*No exhibition clause*]

Notes: William Kerbey was buried at Bedford, St Mary on 15 May 1579. Administration was granted to his widow Mary on 31 May 1580 and a bond was taken (Lincs Archives, Act Book A/iii/10 and LCC ADMONS 1580/88).

98 John Horsleye of Shefford, Campton

made 28 May 1580

Lincolnshire Archives, LCC ADMONS 1580/67

An Inventorye taken the xxviij[th] daye of Maye 1580 in the xxij[th] yere of the Reigne of our Sovereigne Ladye Elizabeth Quene of Englande etc of all the goodes and Cattell of John Horsleye late of Shefford in the Countie of Bedd deceased and praysed the same daye by Nicholas Thorgoode, William Cotton, Richarde Lodye, Richarde Lambe and in the p[rese]nce of Robert Fitzherrey parson of Camelton in Shefford aforesaid vidz

	£	s	d
In the Halle			
Inprimis one Table planckes and a Benche borde			xx
Item one olde Fourme and ij little stooles			vj
Item one paynted Clothe at			xvj
Item ij Sackes		ij	
Item one payer of Cobirons, ij payer of pott hangres and one fyre forke		v	
Item in the little Buttry			
Item all the Brasse and Pewter and all other the implementes in the same Buttrye		xx	

In the Drynck Buttrye			
Item all the Implementes together and			
stuff in the same Buttrye		xxvj	viij
In the parlor			
Item twoo Cubbordes at		xx	
Item uppon the same Cobbordes xv^{o}			
~~pl~~ pewter Platters and dishes			
one pewter Clandlestick twoo			
pewter pottes, ij^{o} latten Candlestickes			
and foure salt sellers		xxv	
Item more in the same parlor one			
Table with a frame, ij formes			
one Courte table, one Joyned			
stoole, one chayre, one payer			
of Tables and one Byble		xx	
In the Chamber over the Halle			
Item one Bedstede, one Trundle			
bedd ij fetherbedes and all other			
the furnyture to the same beddes			
belonginge, as theye be nowe			
standinge	iiij		
Item one Courte Cupborde one fourme			
Three Joyned stooles, one chayer			
and one Chiste and all his owne			
apparell in the same		l	
In the Chamber over the Shoppe			
Item three playne Bedstedes iij			
Cofers ij^{o} Brasse pottes one			
olde Table, and all the paynted			
Clothes in the same Chamber		xl	
In the Chamber over the Buttrye			
Item Tenne busshelles of wheate			
and one quarter of Barlye		xxvj	viij
In the greate Chamber			
Item twoo Bedstedes, ij fetherbedes			
with all the Furnyture to			
the same Beddes belonginge		liij	iiij
Item more one Counter Table			
one square Table with A			
frame one fourme and one			
other Table borde, and the			
paynted Clothes in the same			
Chamber		x	
In the Chamber over the storehowse			
Item one standinge Beddsted		xx	
Item all the Mawlte at		liij	iiij
Item all the woode and Tymber	v		
In the Kitchen			
Item all the Stuffe in the			
Kitchen togither at		xx	
Item Two Sowes at		xx	

	£	s	d
Item fyve kyne and two bullockes	ix		
Item Tenne Sheepe at		xxxiij	iiij
Item one Nagg		xl	
Item ij Acres of Barlye and three Roodes of Peaze		xxx	
Item vij^{o} payer of Sheetes fyne and Course, Thre borde Clothes and xij Napkyns	iij		
Item iiij pillowberes and twoo Hand towelles		viij	
Item the Lease of the Inne called the Dragon for Tenne yeres yett to come valued at	v		
Summa	lij	vj	x

Debtes owinge unto hym at the day of his deathe

Imprimis [*the remainder of the page is blank*]
[*No exhibition clause*]

Notes: John Horsleye was buried at Campton on 10 May 1580. Administration was granted to his widow Katherine on 31 May 1580 and a bond was taken (Lincs Archives, Act Book A/iii/10 and LCC ADMONS 1580/67). The appraiser Robert Fitzhenry was rector of Campton 1566–86 (CCEd; Beds Archives, Fasti/1/Camp). Possibly the Dragon was the Green Dragon in Shefford High Street described in a deed in 1631 (Beds Archives, X465/1).

99 Thomas Maynerd of Wootton made 30 May 1580
Lincolnshire Archives, INV/64/113

The Inventoryes of all suche goodes & catelles of Thomas Maynerd late of Wotton in the countye of Beddf & prised by Stephe[*n*] Estwycke & Thomas Harvey of the same towne & countye the xxxth of Maye Anno domini 1580

	£	s	d
In primis vj akers of barley & x akers of pease	vj		
Item iij horsses & on colt	vij		
Item vj keyne	vij		
Item iiij ~~Stowe~~ Store hogges		viij	
Item on long cart & cart geers		l	
Item ploughe & ploughe geers		v	
Item ij brasse pottes ij kettelles & on posnyt		xx	
Item x peces of pewter		x	
Item on Cubbord a Table a Forme on benche bord and other trashe in the haull		xx	
Item on matterys ij coverlyttes ij blanckyttes ij bolsters & ij pellows		xx	

Item vj peare of shettes and other lynnyn			xl
	Somm	xxviij	xiij

[*No exhibition clause*]

Notes: Thomas Maynerd was buried at Wootton on 9 April 1580.

100 John Francklyn of Thurleigh made 20 November 1581

Bedfordshire Archives, FN1248, p. 788

This is not an original inventory but a transcription from a document in Luke Francklin's Transcripts made 1740–74.

A true Inventorie Indented of all the Goods and Debts of John Francklyn of Thurleighe Deceased praysed by Alexander Hammond and Nicholas Overbury Gent. the 20th day of November in the 24th yeare of the Reigne of our Sovereigne Lady Elizabethe by the grace of God of England, Fraunce & Ireland Quene Defender of the Faithe etc [1581]

	£	s	d
Imprimis One Lease for certain yeares yet to come of the Fearme called the Burysteade in Thurleyghe in the county of Bedford over and above the yearlie Rent to the Lord and one Rent Charge yearly goinge out of the same	6	14	4
Debts due unto the said John Francklyn			
Item the L[or]d Compton	30	0	0
Item Lewis Dyve Esqr	5	0	0
Item Thomas Snag Esqr	10	0	0
Item John Stocker of London	2	0	0
Item John Cronte	5	0	0
Item Nicolas Stubb of Grenehouse	10	0	0
Item John Ventrys	12	0	0
Item Thomas Francklyn	6	0	0
[*Total*	*£86*	*14s*	*4d*]

Nicholas Overbury, Alex. Hammonde

[*No exhibition clause*]

Notes: John Francklyn's burial has not been found. He made his will on 16 January 1579, making provision for his wife and children through income from leases of several properties in Bedfordshire. He left the Burystead to his son George, who was his sole executor and who proved the will in London on 7 November 1581 (TNA, PROB11/63). The appraisers of the inventory were not local Bedfordshire men. Both were gentlemen and may have been colleagues of George Francklyn at the Middle Temple.

101 Richard Yerill of Chalton, Blunham made after 12 October 1582
Lincolnshire Archives, INV/69A/120

An Inventorye of the goodes and Cattell of Richarde Yerill of Chalton in the parishe of Blunh[*am*] in the Countie of Bedford who decessede the xij[th] of October in the yere of our lord god 1582

	£	s	d
Inprimis in the Chamber a bedstede a matris one bolster ij pilowes a coverlide a pare of shetes		x	
Item iiij Coffers standinge in the chamber with certeyne paynted Clothes		viij	viij
Item ij olde bedstedes with certeyne furniture and vj yardes of wollone clothe		xij	viij
Item ij bedes one olde cofere one olde arke with certeyne other clothes painted		x	
Item certeyne yerne withe other olde stuf		iij	iiij
Item ij Cubbardes a table a benche borde a forme with paynted clothes		xx	
Item pewter and brasse with a latteyne basone and Chaffingdishe		xxxiij	iiij
Item viij pare of shetes ij table clothes with a spere clothe		xxx	
Item in the kichine a spit a pare of Cobirons a gridirone with other stufe		vj	viij
Item in the buttrye a saultingtrofe with bolles botteles and other stufe		viij	
Item ij Quarters of pesse with certeyne olde bordes		xvij	iiij
Item in the barne by estimatione xiiij quarters with certeyne seches	vij	iij	iiij
Item v besse vj small bullockes one weyninge calfe	ix		
Item one sowe vij store piges		xvj	
Item ij pare of shude wheles with ij olde cartes		liij	iiij
Item a hovill with certeyne fire wode and ij rolles		xiij	iiij
Item xij shepe		xxvj	viij
Item vj horsse plought harnis and carte harnis	vij	vj	8
Item certeyne haye to the valure of		x	
Item v acars of whete and rye	iij	vj	8
Item xij acares of tilthe	iij		
Item hiche lande xx acares		xxxiij	iiij
Summa totalis	38	ix	iiij
[*Corrected total*	*£45*	*9s*	*4d*]

praysed by Robat Osborne, Thomas Grenlefe, Henry Busshipe and Johne Pecke

dettes of the saide Richard Yerrill

	£	s	d
Item to Edmunt Redman	x		
Item to Thomas Underwode of Girford		xx	
Item to Mayes of Besone – vj quarters of barley	iij	xij	
Item to Richarde Franke of Sandye for iij quarters of barleye		[*?*]30	
Item to Richard Thorpe for a quarter of pesse		x	
Item to the whell wright of Hiching		xv	iiij
Item to William Cole smithe		xiij	iiij

	£	s	d
Item to Richard Sturgis teyler		v	
Debitorum summa	xviij	xj	iiij
[Corrected total of debts	*£18*	*5s*	*8d*]

[*No exhibition clause*]

Notes: Richard Yerill was buried at Blunham on 13 October 1582.

102 Thomas Wennam of Wrestlingworth undated; c. 1583

Lincolnshire Archives, INV/69A/131

A iust and trew Inventary of the goodes and cattels of Thomas Wennam of Wraselingworth in the parishe of Hatley deceased

	£	s	d
Inprimis in the hall a table and frame a cupbord with other houshold stufe		xiij	iiij
Item in the chamber one bedsted a coverled a blankett ij cofers viij paire of shetes & other househould		xxxiij	iiij
Item in the kitchin pewter brase & other stuffe		x	
Item fower quarters wheat & Rye		liij	iiij
Item xl quarters of barly and pease	xx		
Item ij steres & sixe bease & bullockes	viij		
Item xx shepe	iij		
Item v horses	viij		
Item cartes & geares plowe & geares	iij		
Item viij store hogges		xiij	iiij
Item vj acres of wheat & Rye	iiij		
Item xxx acres of tilth	viij		
Summa	lx poundes	iij	iiij

praysers Edward Clarke, Thomas Sheppard, Nicholas Kayford, John Savage

[*No exhibition clause*]

Notes: Thomas Wennam's burial has not been found. Probate was granted on 17 June 1583 (Lincs Archives, Act Book A/iii/52).

103 Thomas Horne of Kempston made between January and June 1583

Lincolnshire Archives, INV/69A/117

This is the Invetorye off the gooddes and cattell off Thomas Horne off Kempstone lattly dyssesed

	£	s	d
In primys ij kenn		xl	
Item in wette and Rye ij quartars		xxvj	viij
Item in barlye syxe quartars	iij		
Item in smalle pesse ij quartars		xvj	
Item the heycoke in the yarde		xx	
Item the woode in the yarde		vij	
Item the brasse in the howsse		xvj	
Item in pewtar sixe pesses		iiij	
Item in the chamber ij coffars		iij	iiij
Item in shettes fyffe payer and towe pellows and ij pelowbers ij tabullnappkyns and ij boulstars		xvij	
Item one bede and a mattrys and one keverynge		vij	
Item in the mylke housse ij arkes ij troffes and towe mylke boulls ij toubes		viij	
Item one spytt and a payer off cobbyorns		ij	vj
Item ij tabull clothes iij towells		iiij	
Item in paynted clothes		iij	iiij
Item one ollde borde			vj
Sume totales is	xj	xv	iiij

[*No exhibition clause*]

Notes: Thomas Horne was buried at Kempston on 21 January 1583. Probate was granted on 17 June 1583 (Lincs Archives, Act Book A/iii/51).

104 Richard Stanbridge of Wootton, husbandman made between March and June 1583
Lincolnshire Archives INV/69A/132

An Inventorie of the goods and cattel of Richard Stanbridge of Wootton husbandman late deceased

	£	s	d
~~Inprimis the bedding coffers x peayres of sheetes with other furniture of a chamber~~			
Inprimis in one chamber the bedding, coffers, tenne payre of harden sheetes	iiij		
Item in the haulle a cupborde a frame table, the pewter & brasse with the painted cloathes	iij	vj	viij
Item xij busshels of graine		xiij	iiij
Item three kyne and a bullock	v		
Item ix sheepe hoggrels & ewes		xxx	
Item three shoates with a sowe and pigges		x	
Summa totalis	xv		

The witnesses of the prising of the premisses Richard Leverock Minister, Thomas Stanbridge, Thomas Harveye, Harrie Savage, Thomas Kent
[*No exhibition clause*]

Notes: Richard Stanbridge was buried at Wootton on 20 March 1583. The witness, Richard Leverock, was vicar of Wootton 1581–99 (CCEd; Beds Archives, Fasti/1/Woo). Probate was granted on 17 June 1583 (Lincs Archives, Act Book A/iii/52).

105 William Ethrope of Sandy made 2 April 1583
Lincolnshire Archives, INV/69A/119

A true Inventarie of all the goodes and cattles of William Ethrope of Sandye decessed praysed by Thomas Underwood and Henrie Dauson the second day of Aprill in the yeare 1583

	£	s	d
Inprimis in the hall a table aforme a cobbord an old ambrye a casse achaire a binche bord & a buffet stoole		xx	
Item all the paynted clothes		vj	viij
Item a paire of shetes a towell iij table clothe & vj napkines		xxviij	
Item iij coveringes j blancket ij bolsters ij pillowes ij bedsteds & j mattrice		xx	
Item iiij coffers		vj	viij
Item v kettles ij panes one skellet and ij pottes		xxvj	viij
Item xvj peces of peuter ij basons iiij candlestickes & ij saltes		x	
Item all the trene ware		v	
Item v bease and a bullocke	vj		
Item lx shepe	x		
Item all the barlie wheate and Rye		xl	
Item all the wood in the yeard		xx	
The somme ys	xxv	iij	

[*No exhibition clause*]

Notes: William Ethrope was buried at Sandy on 19 March 1584 as Eydroppe. Probate was granted on 17 June 1583 (Lincs Archives, Act Book A/iii/51).

106 Richard Stanton of Pertenhall made 6 April 1583
Lincolnshire Archives, INV/69A/130

The Inventorye of the goodes and cattelles movable and unmooveable of Rychard Stanton of Pertenhall in the Countye of Bedforde late Dysceased made & taken and prayced by these men, Jhon Graye, William Marcham, Jhon Rendalle, Thomas Shepparde, Robert Stanton & Thomas Levenge. the vjth day of Aprill 1583

	£	s	d
Stuffe in the hall			
Inprimis one table, a benche, a forme, ij stooles on chayre and the hangynges		xiij	iiij
Stuffe in the parler			
One table, ij ioyned formes, a benche, iiij stooles one Cuborde, one Cofer, one bed with the furnyture hangynges and quyshynges	iij	x	
Stuffe in the kytching			
One table, a forme, a benche, a chayre, a cubborde, a malt arke, a penne, vj stooles iij speates bellowes a fyre pan pothangyns, a treadde, a chafindyshe			

an Iron barre, poothockes, grydIron, CobbeIrons iiij brasse potes, vij ketteles, one pan, iij payles xij platters, vj pottingers, iiij saucers, iiij saltes iiij candelstyckes, a fryenge pan	iij	xvij	viij
In the camber over the parler			
One bedsteade, iij cofers, a fetherbead, on Coverled xij payre flexen and harden sheates vj pyllowbeers xij table napkings iij table clothes, ij pyllowes & hangynes	v	xvj	viij
In the other camber			
Twoo beddes furnyshed, on cofer and certaine yearne		xvj	iiij
Stuffe in the butterye			
Twoo stoppes, v tubbes, a yealyng fatte a laten morter & pestell		v	
Stuffe in the kyllehouse			
Item x bacon flytches		xxv	
An arke, a kymnell, a trodde & tubbe		v	
Item the woodde in the yearde		xl	
The stuffe in Mylke howse		iij	iiij
Item malte in the garnere		xxx	
Item the servantes camber a bedd & a barlepp		ij	vj
Item the haye		iij	iiij
Item an hundreth bordes		v	
Item twoo shod cartes	iij		
Item corne in barne	iij		
Item the pease ~~in~~ upon the hovell		xl	
Item the hovell of barly wheat & rye	vj	xiij	iiij
Item twoo shepe rackes & ij ladders		v	
Item ploughe & plough geares & cart geares with plought tymber		xl	
Item beehyves		xxx	
Item vj horses and coltes	xij		
Item viij mylche kyne	viij		
Item v steares & heyghforthe ij yeares olde	iij		
Item yearinge calves		xxv	
Item sucking calves		xv	
Item on sowe & vj stores		xxvj	
Item threschore and tenne sheepe	xij		
Item xij acres of barly	vij	x	
Item one acre and a halfe of wheate		xx	
Item xxiiij acres of pease	x		
Item hennes and geese		v	
Item his apparell		xx	
Item v stone of woule	iij		
Sum	C	iij	ij
[*Corrected total*	*£100*	*2s*	*6d*]

[*No exhibition clause*]

Notes: Richard Stanton was buried at Pertenhall on 8 February 1583. Probate was granted on 17 June 1583 (Lincs Archives, Act Book A/iii/52).

107 Richard Crawley of Otebridge, Luton, yeoman made 7 May 1583
Lincolnshire Archives, INV/224/187
The inventory is creased in a few places; words are cramped but legible.

Thinventarye of all and sing[u]ler the goodes and Chattells late of Richard Crawley late of Otebridge within the paroche of Luton in the Countie of Bedf yoman deceassed prized by Thomas Hoo gent, Thomas Crawley, William Trubbe, William Howe, John Northe & John Peacock the seaventh daye of Maye Anno domini 1583 as followeth

	£	s	d
Inprimis the wheate in the barne at Oatebridge and in the maltehowse at Newemyllende prized at	xviij		
Item the donge in the yarde at Newemyllende		xxvj	viij
Item the donge on thisside George Norrys his howse		v	
Item the donge a boute the howse at Otebridge		xl	
Item the otes and Bullymonge in the Chapple the peaze in the peaze howse and the haye in the hayehowse	xiiij	x	
Item the wood in the yarde	iiij		
Item one Longe Carte & one donge Carte bothe upon the wheeles geven to the Chylde		xlvj	viij
Item one olde dongeCarte bodye one olde Longecarte bodye olde hyrdles Coweracks & swynetroffes		x	
Item vij kyne	x	x	
Item xxxvj shepe wherof ix of them be Cooples	vj		
Item x hogges		l	
Item v horses with their harnesse	ix		
Item a ploughe with the furniture and twoe payre of harrowes		xxvj	viij
Item ij fannes a bus and a stryke		ij	
Item xvj flytches of bacon	iij		
Summa	Lxxv	vij	
In the haull			
A Table a payre of tressells a forme three bechen bourdes stoles a Cutbord a wheele a Chayre iiij drinckinge pottes iiij olde Quisshions pottehangers a grydiron a payre of bellowes & an olde paynted clothe		xiij	iiij
Summa prized		xiij	iiij
In the lofte over the Chamber			
Inprimis one bedstedd one fetherbedd one boulster one pillowe a payre of flexen sheetes ij blanckettes a Coverlett and a pillowebere geven to the Childe	iij	iij	iiij
Item one Cheste twoe Cofers a greate brasse pott a cawdron and a kettle geven to the chylde		xxx	
Item v peazehookes a bearinge byll a foreste byll a table a payre of trestles a hanginge shelfe certein woll three Sythes & a bowe		viij	
Item x olde syckles a Cheseracke twoe shelfes a cofer with olde iron and three augars		xv	
Item ij bedsteddes vj blanckettes twoe boulsters one pillowe twoe Coveringes & twoe mattresses		xxx	iiij
Summa	vij	vj	viij

In the Chamber

Inprimis twoe bedsteddes one mattresse twoe chestes one Cofer one Cutbord three blanckettes one Coveringe one boulster one shelf & certein paynted clothes		xxxj	viij
Item xij payre of towen sheetes & twoe table clothes		xl	
Item one Curtayne one flexen shete one towell & viij napkins		xiij	
Item his apparell		xx	
Summa	v	iiij	viij

In the kytchin

Inprimis a boultinge hutche twoe troffes with Covers a Cheese presse ij payles ij tubbes one ferkyn a Cherme one payre of Andirons a trevett a spytt a payre of Cobbeyrons a ladder a peele of iron a litle fatte and certein other lumber there		xx	
Item vij hennes ij Cockes vij duckes & a drake		vij	ij
Item one gryndstone		v	
Summa		xxxij	ij

In the Buttery

Inprimis v pewter platters v pewter disshes iiij[or] sawcers twoe porringers one salte seller vj pewter spoones twoe lattyn Candlestickes and one pewter pott		xvj	
Item iiij[or] kettles ij brasse pottes ij postnettes a fryeng pann ij skymmers & an olde brasse pann		xvj	
Item iij tubbes ij fattes five booles a fyrkyn three leather bottells five shelfes & other ymplementes there		xx	
Item ij bylles one axe ij shovells a mattocke one payre of Carte traces foure payre of ploughe traces		v	
Item twoe sackes & ij ropes		iij	iiij
Summa	iij		iiij

In The feyldes

Inprimis in a certein close called Preistecrofte v acre of peaze and v acres of Bullymonge prized at	v	vj	viij
Item x acres of wheate in Byrchefelde prized at	xiij	vj	viij
Item foure acres di of wheate in Crodlefelde	vij	x	
Item v acres of Bullymonge in Ashefordfeld	iiij	vj	viij
Item one close of wheate called Chappleclose cont by estimacon twoe acres and an halfe	iiij	iij	iiij
Item in Oatebridgefelde xj acres of Bullymonge	ix	x	
Item in Hidefelde iij acres of wheate	iij		
Item one close of wheate conteyninge by estimacon vij acres called Bandelande Close	xvj	vj	viij
Item three acres of wheate in Sowerd felde	iiij		
Item three acres and an half of peaze in otebridgefelde		xlvj	viij
Item half an acre of wheate in Staplefordfeld		xv	
Item one acre of Bullymonge in Blackwaterfelde		xiij	iiij
Item one lease of a messuage & land in Newemyllende geven to the childe which is valued to be yerely worthe over & above the rent which is reserved out of the same		xxvj	viij

		£	s	d
Item one lease of otebridgehowse enduringe for three yeres		vj		
	Summa	Lxxvij	v	
	[*Corrected sub-total*	*£78*	*11s*	*8d*]
	Summa Totalis	viij[xx]x	ix	ij
	[*Corrected total*	*£171*	*15s*	*10d*]

[*No exhibition clause*]

Notes: Richard Crawley's burial has not been found. Administration was granted to Thomas Crawley and William Hatch of Luton on 15 June 1583 (Lincs Archives, Act Book A/iii/51).

108 William Greene of Langford

made 21 May 1583

Lincolnshire Archives, LCC ADMONS 1583/508

The Inventorie of the goods of William Greene deceased praised by Edmund Underwood, John Wallis, William Hemmyng the xxj[th] day of May Anno Domini 1583

	£	s	d
Item in the halle one cubbord		xij	
one table upon tressells two formes one chayer & one stoole		v	
Item the inner chamneber one bedsteed two mattrises one blanket one coverlet two bolsters two pilloes & painted clothes		xxviij	
one chest & three cofers		x	
Three payer of sheets three pillobers one spere cloth one cubbord cloth [*space*] one table cloth two table napkins		xx	
Item his apparell		xxxvj	viij
Item for barle in the loft		lvj	
Item for otes		ij	vj
Item the brasse & one candelsticke and the pewter		xxv	
Item thre tubbs two barells with other trashe		viij	
Item thre bease	iiij	vj	
Item one sowe & vj stores		xviij	
Item all the woud in the yeard & dounge		xx	
More wood in the woode		xviij	
Item two akers of barle		xxxij	
Item vij akers of peas & otes	iij	x	
Item lxxxvj sheepe	xij	x	
Item woule in the howse		xx	
Item all the pulling in the yeard		v	
Summe	xxxvj	ij	ij

Detts William Greene owed

	£	s	d
Item unto Gariet Searle		xiij	iiij
Item unto James Cooper		vj	viii
Item unto Henry Thrassell		xxxij	
Item unto Edmund Randell		xxviij	ij

to be payd unto him upon St James day so that he require no more of Elyzabeth Greene wydowe or yf he go a bout to molest her then this is voyde

Wylliam Stringer oweth unto William Greene		xij	viij
[*Corrected total including 12s 8d owed to him*	*£36*	*14s*	*10d*]

[*No exhibition clause*]

Notes: William Greene's burial has not been found. Administration was granted to his widow Elizabeth on 18 June 1583 and a bond was taken; the inventory value noted as £36 2s (Lincs Archives, Act Book A/iii/52 and LCC ADMONS 1583/508).

109 Joan Williamson of Bedford, widow made June 1583

Lincolnshire Archives, INV/69A/118

An Inventory taken & made of all the goodes & Cattailles late belonging to Johan Williamson of Bedford in the Countye of Bedford wydowe deceased togythere with all houshould stuff & elles whatsoever praysed & viewed by Thomas Abbeys, John Pavenham & others in June Anno domini 1583 as follow[th]

	£	s	d
Inprimis in the hall			
Item ij Cubbordes viz: one great & one small with xij pieces of pewter upon the same j table with a frame & a forme to yt ij Chaires iiij Cuyssions, j paire of bellowes ij Chanlffing dyshes, j spyning whele & iij lyttle stoles, all prayesed at		xxvj	viij
In the long parlor within the hall			
Item a standing bedsteed, j fetherbeed one Coverlicte & a bolster, ij tables, iij formes & other small thinges		xx	
In the lyttle parlor beneth thaforesaid parlor			
Item j Bedsteed, j Fetherbed, a bolster & a coverlict, a square table, & a Carpet of dornixe, & ij formes with the painted Clothes about the same parlor		xvj	
In the Chamber over the streat			
Item ij standing bedsteedes & a trundle bedsteed ij fetherbedes iij Coverlyctes, j mattryce iij Bolsters iij pillowes, iiij Coffers & the painted Clothes withe Courtaines am[*ounte*]th all for the some of		xl	
In the Kytchyn & Bruehousse			
Item a panne ij kettles, ij pottes & a poscenet j tryvet, j dripping panne, j frying panne j spyt, with oth[*er*] small implementes am[*ounte*]th all to the Some of		xiij	iiij
In the yeard			
Item in woode, hurdelles, hovelles & bordes & poles for stalles all is		xl	

	£	s	d
In the Buttery & in the shop			
Item in Brasse, pewter, pottes, Barrelles Tubbes, Tresselles & other implementes in the same am[*ounte*]th all to		xxxvj	
In the Seller			
Item in Barrelles, Tubbes, pottes & glasses with other tryfles & implementes all is		v	
All the naperye			
Item in sheetes, table Clothes, towelles napkins & elles am[*ounte*]th to		xxvj	viij
Summa totallis	xj	iij	viij

Signum praedi[ctis] Thomas Abbarye, Signum praedi[ctis] Johanis Pavenham, per me Johanem Metheringham scriptor
[*No exhibition clause*]

Notes: Joan Williamson's burial has not been found. John Metheringham, who wrote the inventory, was a scrivener living in Bedford. Probate was granted on 17 June 1583 (Lincs Archives, Act Book A/iii/51).

110 John Kyppis the younger of Duloe, Eaton Socon made 13 February 1585
Lincolnshire Archives, LCC ADMONS 1585/1066

An Inventorye of the goodes and Cattells of John Kyppis of Dulowe in the Countie of Bedd the younger deceassed the xiij[th] daye of Februarye in the xxvij[th] yere of her Ma[jes]ties reigne praysed by John Kyppys senior, Mychaell Goodsonne, Thomas Kyppis Junior and John Castell as followethe

	£	s	d
In the Haull			
Inprimis one framed Table, one folden Table, two formes, iiij stooles, one bence bord, one painte Clothe, one paire of tongues, one fier shovell with pott hangers		xxvj	viij
In the Chamber			
Item one Coubourd, one trusse bedd with a tester, one trundell bedd, one Chest, one cheere		xlvj	viij
Item one fetherbedd, ij mattresses ij Coveringes, ij blanckettes, ij boulsters iij pyllowes, iij chusshinges	iij		
Item hanginges of the Chamber		x	
Item iiij paire of flexen sheetes v paire of harden sheetes, iij table clothes, one coubord clothe iij pyllowe beeres, one dosen of table napkynes	iiij	xiiij	
In an other Chamber			
Item ij Coffers, one bedd, one boulster,			

	£	s	d
one blancket iij spyninge wheeles, ij peeces of wollen clothe		xx	
In the kytchyne			
Item xxj[tie] peeces of pewter		xxvj	viij
Item one brasse panne, iij kettells, ij pottes, ij posnetes, one chafinge dishe one skymmer, one spytte, one paire of Anndyrons, with tubbes, barrells and other ymplementes	iij		
Cattell			
Item one horse		xxvj	viij
Item vj kyne ij bullockes	x		
Item xviij sheepe	iij	vj	viij
Item hogges younge and olde [*illeg.*]		xxiij	iiij
Grayne			
Item vij Acres of pease		liij	viij
Item one Acre of wheate		xvj	
Item iiij quarters of barley		xl	
Item viij Acres & di of Tylthe	iij		
Item Pullen xxj[tie]		vj	viij
Sum totalis	xlj	xvij	

Debtes which the within named John Kyppis did owe at the tyme of his deathe Amountyth to the some of	vij	v	iiij

[*No exhibition clause*]

Notes: John Kyppis was buried at Eaton Socon on 15 February 1585. Administration was granted to his widow Elizabeth on 26 July 1585 and a bond was taken; the inventory value was noted as £41 15s 2d (Lincs Archives, Act Book A/iii/77 and LCC ADMONS 1585/1066).

111 Robert Cartere of Northill — made between April and September 1585

Lincolnshire Archives, MISC WILLS J/85

The top left corner is damaged and text on the left of the first eight lines is missing.

[...] A true Imventorie of all [*damaged*] of Robert Cartere late of Northill [...] [*prai*]sed by Thomas Cartere, Robert Carter

	£	s	d
[...] one Cowe, one Bredere, & on calf	iiij		
[...] lambs		xxiij	ij
[...] forme, & Benches		xiij	iiij
[...] Basone, one Candlsticke, on Chafingdishe			
[...] [*?c*]ertaine peutre		x	viij
[*I*]tem certaine Brasse		xxvj	vj
Item to Bills			xvj
Item on fetherbed, on Boulstere, on coverled to Blanckets		xxx	
Item viij paire of shets, on Table clothe on kerchere		xxiij	vj
Item on Curtaine & certaine painted clothes		iij	iiij
Item to Coffers		vj	viij

	£	s	d
Item his Aparrell		xx	
Item on old Coberte, to old arks & all othere Implements		xiij	iiij
Sum	12	11	10

per me Anthon[y] Hogett [*signature*], Robarte Carter [*signature*], Thomas Carters marke
[*Exhibited before Master John Belley on 22 September 1585*]

Notes: Robert Cartere was buried at Northill on 17 April 1585. One of the appraisers, Anthony Hogett, was curate of Northill 1585–1604 (CCEd; Beds Archives, Fasti/1/Nor).

112 Thomas Benet of Bolnhurst undated; c. 1587–88
Lincolnshire Archives, INV/76/226

of Bolnehurst. A note of the goods & cattals of Thomas Benet that now is dessessed

	£	s	d
Imprimis one havill with all that is in it		xxx	
Item Another halvill & all that is in that		xliij	iiij
Item v peces timber with other certaine smal pecis		vj	iiij
Item vj quarters of barlye		xl	
Item vj busshils of barlye		v	
Item xiiij busshils wheate		xvj	iiij
Item vij Acars of weat & barlye	iiij	xiij	iiij
Item in pertnall feld xx arcres barrlye & weat	xiij	xiij	iiij
Item xxiiij acars pese	ix	xij	
Item vj horses	xij		
Item xxvj shepe & vij lambs		l	
Item xj besse	xij	xvj	viij
Item viij bullockes & caufes	iij	vj	viij
Item ij hoviles price		xx	
Item iiij quarters malt		xxxij	
Item cartes & cart geres	iiij	x	
Item plouthes & plow geres		vj	viij
Item the fyre wode		xv	
Item fyve table bords		xij	vj
Item the brasse		xlvj	viij
Item the pawter		xiij	iiij
Item viij bedstedes		viij	
Item beding shetes matteres pillows bolsters price	vj	xiij	iiij
Item cubbards & cowfars		xxxiij	iiij
Item xj hodges & vij pigks		lviij	
Item ix hens & ij cokes		ij	ix
Item xxvij acars folow grond		xl	
Item one yeare in a farme Lying at Pertnall		xx	
Item vij years in a cotage Lying at Bolnhurst		xxvj	viij
Some is	93	11	3

[*No exhibition clause*]

Notes: Thomas Benet's burial has not been found. The inventory is dated to 1587–88 in Lincolnshire Archives online catalogue.

113 Robert Russell of Yelden, tailor made 6 October 1587
Lincolnshire Archives, INV/76/236

The Inventorie of the goodes & chattelles of Robart Russell lait of Yelden taylor deceased, valuad & pryced by Wylliam Weylde, Hughe Maxey & Thomas Barcock the vj of October anno domini ~~1588~~ 1587

	£	s	d
The haull			
In primis a coupbourd, a framed table, a benchebourd a pen, a Forme & iiijth stooles		xiiij	
Item a brasse pott two kettells a gredyron a fryenge pan, pott hooks & pott hanginges wyth a tryvett		vj	viij
Item vth pewter platers two sawcers on candlestyck a salt seller & olde paynted hanginges		iij	iiij
Item two tubbes, a stoope, two payles a kymnell a coffer an old almery, an olde pen, two lyning wheles a woolling whele & an olde ark		viij	
the chamber			
Item a mattresse, two bolsters, iiijth ~~pillobeares~~ pylloes two coverlettes & two bedd steades		xiiij	
Item iijth coffers one payr of flaxen sheetes vth payre of harden sheetes iijth pillobears two napkins & a table cloyth		xxiiij	4
the yarde			
Item barley & pease		xxx	
Item iijth Kyne & a bullock	iiij	x	
Item vj ewes & vth lambe hooges		xxxvj	8
Item woode		x	
Somme is	xj	xvij	

[*No exhibition clause*]

Notes: Robert Russell's burial has not been found. The inventory is in the same handwriting and spelling as Joan Parker 1588 (*119*).

114 William Grey of Eaton [Socon], husbandman made 29 December 1587
Bedfordshire Archives, T 48/9
The inventory is stained in places and is incomplete. It was originally printed in Bedfordshire Notes and Queries, *vol. 3, pp. 252–4 as the inventory of William Gutch and is printed here with amendments.*

An Inventory of the goods and Chattalls of William Grey late of Eaton in the dioces of Lyncoln husbandman decessed taken the xxixth daye of December in Anno Domini 1587 praysed by

Henrye Marlebro gentillman, Thomas Marcham, Roberte Wrighte, John Kinge and Thomas Androwe etc

	£	s	d
In the hall			
Item A table ij° trestells a forme and a bench bord praysed at		iiij	
Item a chaire at			x
Item a spyninge whele at			x
Item iij stooles at			iiij
Item a brusshe at			iij
Item viij peces of pewter at		vj	viij
Item all the paynted clothes there at		iiij	vj
In the Chamber			
Item iij° bedsteddes at		iij	
Item iij Coffers at		xj	
Item a coverlet at		vj	viij
Item v paire of Sheetes at		xx	
Item a Table clothe at		ij	vj
Item the paynted clothes in the ch[*a*]mber		ij	vj
Item all his wearinge apparell		xx	
Item his wieves apparrell also		xiij	iiij
Item ij° shirtes		ij	
Item all his wieves Lynnen at		iiij	
In the upper chamber			
Item all the fruyte in the Chamber		ix	iiij
Item a chese at			vj
vj loves of bredd & iiij^{or} aple pasties			xvj
Item certain bordes there at			xij
Item iij^{li} of butter at			ix
A dyshe and grease cherm			iiij
In another chamber			
Item iij lynnen wheeles & a paire of cardes		ij	
Item all the woolle there at		iij	iiij
Item all the hempe with the slipp of yarne		vj	
Item a bedsteed a blankett & ij° pyllowes			xx
Item a ladder at			xij
In the kitchen			
Item iiij^{or} flytches of bakon a ballrybb and a chyne		xij	
Item all the brasse the Iron with a laver and a Candell sticke		viij	
In the boultinge howse			
Item ij° syves a maunde a skepp and a cloath baskett at			xvj
Item a masshinge fatte a fryinge panne a boultinge pype a wasshe tubb a stopp and ij° sickles at		v	
Item vj bolles a clensinge dysshe ij° Chessfattes and a tankard at		iij	
Item xj dyshes at			vj

In the buttry			
Item vj trenchers iiij^{or} spoones			iij
Item an Alestall with ij° bordes and a tubb at		[*value illegible*]	
Item ij° bottells & old Iron at		iiij	
In another chamber			
Item a sacke at			vij
Item an Iron dragge & a wood dragge			
~~Item~~ a bedstedd flees with other emplementes		vj	viij
Item ij° sackes at			xij
In the Stable			
Item vij horse at	iiij	xiij	iiij
Item all the Carte geares ploughe geares and ij° pannelles at		viij	
Item geares aboute the hovell			xij
In the Yarde			
Item a paire of wheeles a carte bodye a brake a whele barrowe and other woode under the hovell with a ploughe		xiij	iiij
Item a ploughe at		v	
Item a shodd Carte at		xx	
Item a Teame and other ploughe geares with an old wheele at		v	
Item x hurdells & other old tymber			xx
Item an old Carte at		vj	viij
Item a shode carte at		xl	
Item xxx^{tie} lamhogges at ij^{s} viij^{d} a peece	iiij		
Item there are ij° more wanting if thes be founde to be of that value			
Item the Mucke carte bodye and an hurdell gate		iij	
Item x bullockes at	viij	vj	viij
Item all the hens in the yarde		vj	
Item iij hogges		xxj	
Item xiiij^{en} s[*t*]ore piges at iij^{s} a pece		xlij	
Item the Strawe & hey in the barne		xxx	
Item a cocke of haye & another of Strawe		xij	
[*The page has been cut across and the inventory ends here*]			
[*Total to this point*	*£36*	*6s*	*9d*]

[*No exhibition clause*]

Notes: William Grey's burial has not been found.

115 John Warner of Caddington made 1 December 1587
Lincolnshire Archives, INV/76/215

Anno Dm 1587 7mo die Decembris. This ys the inventarye of all & singular the goodes and cattelles of John Warner late of the parishe of Caddington deceassed; and priced by Thomas Basill alias Flower, Thomas Braye, John Evans and Edward Spencer Anno & die praedict'

	£	s	d
Inprimis 3 tubbes 4 firkins one troughe & 2 leetle kettles priced at		x	
Item one mattrisse bedde with all furnetures, one coveringe a paier of sheetes a boulster 2 formes and 2 bourdes with a sorye painted clothe priced at		xiij	iiij
Item one strawen bedde with the furnitures & 2 cheastes		vj	viij
Item an oulde coubburde, a table a bentche, 5 pewter dishes an Irone potte a salter, 2 quart pottes and a spitte, and an other oulde painted clothe priced at		x	
Item 3 shotte hoggys priced at		x	
Item the wheate and peace in the barne priced at		xlvj	viij
Sum	iiij	xvj	viij

[*No exhibition clause*]

Notes: John Warner's burial has not been found.

116 Walter Maye of Potton undated; 1587–1588
Lincolnshire Archives, INV/76/229

A true Inventorie of all such goodes as were latelie the goodes of Walter Maye of Potton deceassed and priced by William Horlie, Mychaell Thorpe, John Bluet & John Thomas alias Moodie

	£	s	d
His goodes in the hall			
Imprimis a Cubbard & ij folding tables & ij formes		xx	
Item xiiij pieces of pewter		x	
Item iiij ~~pewter~~ Candlestickes ij saltsellers & a chafingdishe		iij	
Item iiij Chaires a ioynt stoole		ij	vj
Item the hanginges in the hall three quisshions a lettice one gostpan		iiij	
Item iiij bed steedes		iiij	
Item j fetherbed & iij matrices iiij boulsters iiij pillowes		xl	
Item iiij Couerlets		vj	viij
Item ij Cofers		v	
Item xvj paire of sheetes		xxxij	
Item ij pottes & iij kettles		xx	
Item ij barrelles & ij tubbes & his apparrell		x	
Item ij acres of Ry in the howse		xl	
Item ij acres of pease & an halfe acre of barlie		xx	
Item his hay		xiij	iiij
Item ij horses a cow & a bullock	iij	vj	viij
Item a cart & cartgeres a plough & plough geres		x	
Item bordes in the yeard		xxxiij	iiij

	£	s	d
Item tymber in the yeard	iij		
Item other wood in the yeard		xxx	
Item ij acres of Ry in the field		xl	
Item iiij hennes one cock & the bucket		iij	iiij
Sertaine trashe		x	
Summa totalis	xxiiij	iij	x

[*No exhibition clause*]

Notes: Walter Maye's burial has not been found. The inventory is dated to 1587–88 in Lincolnshire Archives.

117 Joan Pettet of Podington, widow — made 3 March 1588

Lincolnshire Archives, INV/76/230

Puddington in the Cont' of Bedd. A True Invitory of all the goodes[20] & Cattelles & chattell moveable & unmovable of Joan Pettet vid[*ua*] mad iij day of March ~~Ando~~ Anno domini 1587 as foloweth

	£	s	d
The chamber			
Item ij bedsteedes with furnutur therto belongyng vallowed at		xl	
Item ij Coffers prased at		iij	iiij
The hawle			
Item ij old Tables ij formes one trought & pated chothes [*painted cloths*]		v	
The Chytchen			
Item iij Brase potes iij Brase pans j kettell A payre of pot hangles And A Spete valued		xl	
Item iiij platters ij lattyn cand dilstykes one Salseller presed		iij	iiij
The yard & the barne			
Item iij beastes & A bulloke & x shepe valued at	v	v	
Item ij lodes of Barle valued		x	
Summa totalis	x	vj	viij

[*No exhibition clause*]

Notes: Joan Pettet's burial has not been found.

20 The terminal letter of *goodes* and *cattelles* in the heading have been written as ȝ (yogh) rather than the normal terminal *es* used elsewhere in the inventory. They have been transcribed here as *es* because that is clearly what was intended.

118 Reynald Radwell of Kempston made 4 March 1588
Lincolnshire Archives, INV/76/234

Anno Domini 1588 Mar iiij. The inventorye of Reynold Radwell his moveables

	£	s	d
Imprimis a standing bed a mattresse a fetherbed a boulster a blanket a coverlet ij pillowes		xl	
Item iij coverlets a boulster a pillowe		xiij	iiij
Item his pewter and ij candelstickes		xij	
Item vij peare of sheetes		xx	
Item ij table clothes viij table napkins a coobbert clothe a speyre clothe iij pillowe beares		xiij	iiij
a coobbert		xij	
iij coffers		x	
a chear			viij
a table		vj	viij
ij pannes ij kettels a brasse pott a postnet		xxv	
a foorme			xij
a freing pan a gridion a trevet		ij	
ij steeres and a bullocke		xlvj	viij
ij kine		liij	iiij
ij old horses and ther geares		xx	
Summa totalis	xiij	xvj	

pricers Thomas Harvye, William Hills, Richard White
[*No exhibition clause*]

Notes: Reynald Radwell was buried at Kempston on 5 March 1588. Although the inventory is dated 4 March 1588 (1589 New Style), the parish register is clear that he was buried on 5 March 1587 (1588 New Style) (*BPR*, vol. 39, p. 69). The parish register dating has been adopted.

119 Joan Parker of Yelden, widow made 28 March 1588
Lincolnshire Archives, INV/76/235

The Inventorye of the goodes of Joan Parker ~~of~~ lait of Yelden wyddowe deceased, valued & pryced by Hughe Maxey, Wylliam Wylde & Gualter Austen the xxviij[th] daye of Marche anno domini 1588

	£	s	d
Haull			
In primis a table a forme, with stooles, a chayre, iiij[th] olde quyshones, a bench bourd wyth old paynted hanginges		viij	
Item a pen, a lyninnge wheele a gredyron pott hangynges a kettell, iij small skeletes, a paile, a tubbe, a stoope & a kemnell		vij	
Item iij peuter chardgers iij peuter dyshes, a salt seller, & a peuter pott wyth ij sawcers		vij	

The chamber

Item a chest, a settell & a coffer		vj	viij
Item an olde worne fetherbedd ij coverlettes, a reede blankett a bolster, a pyllo, a flaxen sheete iij payre of harden sheetes, & ij beddsteades		xxxj	iiij
Item the lease of the housse		xl	
Item ij shepe		v	
Item a cowe		xxx	
Item wood		ij	
Some totall	vj	xvij	

[*No exhibition clause*]

Notes: Joan Parker's burial has not been found. The inventory is in the same handwriting and spelling as Robert Russell's in 1587 (*113*).

120 William Wheeler of Great Barford, husbandman made 12 May 1588

Lincolnshire Archives, INV/76/233

This inventory has been carefully and stylishly written. The sheet of paper has been used landscape rather than the normal portrait direction. Many items have been priced as they occur, without a value at the end of the line. For ease of reading, the normal layout with the value of each Item *on the right has been adopted.*

A true Invent: of alle the Goods and Chattles of what kynd or sort soever of Wiliame Wheeler of Barphord husbond manne larte discessed Anno Domini 1588 Die Mens Maii 12°

	£	s	d
Alle things in the Halle			
Inprimis one Coobord; one Table toow Forms, a Backbord twooe Shelvs, 5 Stools paynted Cloths 7 Quooshions		xx	
Alle thi[n]gs in Parlor			
Item 4er Bedsteeds 8s 8d 3 Bowlsters; 4er Pyllows, 7 Pyllowbears 8s 4d an ould Chest, 4er Coffers 9s 4d		[*26*	*4*]
Item alle the paynted Clothes in the Parlor 3s 4d three Coverlets, twooe Blanckettes an old Flockbed an undercloth 10s 8d		[*14*]	
Item eleevne Pair of Sheetes 29s 4d three Bordcloths one dyoper Towelle, one Dyoper Table Napkyn, eighte oother Napkins of hempteare 9s 8d Hys shyetes together with alle the rest of his Apparille 40s		[*79*	*0*]
All the thi[n]gs in the Kytchenne			
Alle things conteined in the Kytchenne valued or pryzed at		55	4
Item certaine Backon flytchees and cheeze 7s the Leashe of his Farme 4li 4er Horses 2 Coults 11li 6s 8d	[*15*	*13*	*8*]
Item 7 Beasts 10li 10s. Syx Stears, tenne Calfs vjli xiijs iiijd 4er Hogs and Pigs valued 45[21]	[*17*	*3*	*4*]

21 There is no currency value following *45*. The value of the hogs and pigs has not been included in the sum inserted at the end of the line.

Item 40[tie] Sheep prized at	8		
Item Powltreey Ware 2s 6d. 7 Quarter of graine 46s 8d. 40[tie] Acr[e] of Wheate Rye, & Barley 26[li] 13[s] 4[d]	*[29*	*2*	*6]*
Item 10 Acr[e] of Peaze 3[li] 6[s] 8[d]. Cart and cart Gears, Plowe and Plowgeare, Harrows Plowtymber and Axeltrees prized atte 4[er li] Tow ould Hovyls togeither withe alle the Wood in the yard valued at 26[s] 8[d]	*[8*	*13*	*4]*
Summa Total	89	14	2
[*Corrected total but lacking the incomplete value for hogs and pigs*[22]	*£88*	*7s*	*6d*]

The Valuers John Clerk vicar, Roger Favylle, Wiliame Jones, Robert Adams
[*No exhibition clause*]

Notes: William Wheeler's burial has not been found. The appraiser, John Clarke, was vicar of Great Barford 1579–85 and of Potton 1574–92 (CCEd).

121 John Watkins of Caddington made 13 May 1588
Lincolnshire Archives, LCC ADMONS 1588/674

13° die Maij Anno Domini 1588. A true Inventary of all the goodes cattelles of John Watkins of Caddington late deceassed priced by Thomas Braye, Alen Ansteed, Thomas Bashill and John Evans

	£	s	d
Inprimis one Cowe and a calfe priced at		xl	
Item ij geese a gander & a xj golins		v	
Item a table with a frame an ould coubbord a chayer & a hen penne		v	
Item an oulde potte with 4 ould Cettles 2 candelstikes one pewter dishe a salter & a spitte		x	
Item a fringe panne a payle iij mylke boules vj wodden dishes & vj trunsures		ij	iiij
Item a pott hookes a payer of hangers a hedginge bill & a [*?*]chaier and a hatchet			xij
Item 3 ould painted clothes			xvj
Item 2 sory beddsteedes & bedd clothes as 4 oulde blanketes an ould coverlet, & 2 boulsters		vj	viij
Item 2 payer of sheetes with other simple linen		vj	viij
Item a blewe coat & a frice coat		vj	viij
Item 2 oulde casokes priced at		viij	
Item 3 oulde cofferes		iiij	
Item a fanne a sheddcod & a sheeve			xx
Item 3 oulde wheeles 4 shythes & ould yreon		vj	viij
Item ~~3~~ 2 ould barrelles a boulting hutche & a troughe		vj	viij
Item a grindstone			xvj

22 The difference between the inventory total and the corrected total is 26s 8d (2 marks).

Item [*?*]3:4 ackers & a Roode of wheate growinge	iiij	vj	viij
Summa totalis	9	8	4
[*Corrected total*	*£9*	*19s*	*8d*]

[*No exhibition clause*]

Notes: John Watkins was buried at Caddington on 1 April 1588. Margaret Watkins, possibly his wife, was buried a few days earlier on 27 March 1588. Administration was granted to George Watkins at Dunstable on 20 June 1588 and a bond was taken; the inventory value was noted as £9 8s 4d (Lincs Archives, Act Book A/iii/98 and LCC ADMONS 1588/674).

122 Agnes Smithe of Wilden, widow made 25 May 1588
Lincolnshire Archives, INV/76/228

A true Inventorie of all the goodes & Cattels of Agnes Smithe widowe late of Wilden desessed the xxv[th] day of Maye Anno domini 1588 by Steven Smithe, Edmond Crow and Abraham Smithe

	£	s	d
Imprimis xvij Shippe	iij		
Item iij Coverlettes & iiij blanketes		xxxvj	viij
Item one fetherbed twoe mattresses ij bolsters & iij pillowes		l	
Item one quilte & v yardes of russet cloth		xiiij	
Item two gownes iij red peticoates a halfe kirtle & three other old coates		liij	iiij
Item eight pevter platters ij Candlestickes on morter a salt seller a chaffin dyshe & one latin plate for a candle		xvij	
Item one brasse potte one kettle & a Skillet		xv	
Item one litle cubbard iij coffers one forme & two chaires		xxvj	viij
Item ix pare of flexen sheetes	iij		
Item ix pare of harden sheetes & one table cloth		xxviij	
Item v flexen smockes v flexen apernes & one harden sheete vj harden smockes x harden apernes		xxij	
Item iij pillowe beares on towell ij keerchers & on table napkin		x	
Item iiij kerchers & two neckerchers		viij	
Item vj silver spoones		xx	
Sum totale	xxj		viij
A note of debtes owinge to the said Agnes Smithe			
Imprimis Richard Smithe oweth to the said Agnes	lij		
[*Corrected total*	*£73*	*0s*	*8d*]

[*No exhibition clause*]

Notes: Agnes Smith was buried at Wilden on 15 May 1588.

123 William Swan of Nether Dean, Dean, husbandman made 19 June 1588
Lincolnshire Archives, INV/76/232

The Inventary of all and singulare the goodes and cattalles of William Swan husbandman of Netherdean in the county of Bedforde decessed the xix of June In the yere of our Lord God 1588

	£	s	d
Imprimis the crape	viij		
Item beastes and bullockes tene	x		
Item Two horsses	iij		
Item sheepe xviij	iij		
Item hogges		x	
Item cart, plow, and other thinges to them belonginge		xl	
Item the woode in the yarde		xx	
Item the framed hoveles		xx	
Item six behyves		xij	
Item all maner of howshold stuffe	xvj		
Summa	xlv	ij	

Seen and valued by William Eston yeoman, Henry Boone and Johne Boule
[*No exhibition clause*]

Notes: William Swan was buried at Dean on 13 April 1588.

124 Alice Peacocke of Kempston, widow undated; after 21 June 1588
Lincolnshire Archives, INV/76/231

A true Inventorie of all the goodes & Cattalles of Alice Peacocke widowe late of Kempston in the Countie of Bedf decessed

	£	s	d
The hall			
Inprimis a cubberd a litle table with a frame ij formes foure buffet stoles two chaires a square table a cubbord clothe thre painted clothes		xvj	
The chambirs			
Thre Coffers xvj paire of shetes thre table clothes two towelles vj table napkins one ioynte bed one fetherbed ij mattrisses foure boulsters thre pillowes ij coveringes iij blanckettes ij bedstedes iij pillowberes vj painted clothes	v		
vj kettles one pane ij brase pottes one posnit one dozen of puter ij saucers thre candelstickes one salte seller		xl	
Thre tubbes iij barrelles iij kymmels one boltinge ark a saltinge trough five boules two dozen of trenchers			

one dozen of dyshes one dozen of spones			xij
for plowe timber and fire wood		iiij	
A Cowe			xxx
Two pigges iij hennes			ij
	Sum	xiiij	

[*No exhibition clause*]

Notes: Alice Peacocke was buried at Kempston on 21 June 1588.

125 Thomas Baie of Tempsford, yeoman made 27 November 1590

Lincolnshire Archives, INV/80/159

This is a fair copy, beautifully written.

An Inventorie of all the Goodes Chattells Moveables & housholde Stuff which were Thomas Baies late of Temesforde in the Countie of Bedfs yoman deceassed made & praised the xxvij[th] daie of November in the xxxiij[th] yere of the Reigne of our Sovereigne Ladie Elizabeth by the grace of god Queene of Englande Fraunce & Irelande defender of the Faithe etc By Thomas Cowper, Richard Parkin, Henrie Rayner and Thomas Huckle Praisers indifferently chosen with [*?*]profescacion of addinge or deminishinge as occasion and right shall require 1590

		£	s	d
In the Hall				
Imprimis a Table, a Casse, & a Cupbourde			xiij	iiij
Item two Chaires, Foure Buffet Stooles, a litle chaire & a back Stoole			v	
Item Pothookes & hangers, a Fire shovell, Tonges and suche like ymplementes			vj	viij
Item Foure Pottes, ix kettles, Foure pannes one Morter one Chaffingdishe one posnet one warminge pan, a chaffer, vj candlestickes & a spice morter		iij		
Item xxj platters, eighte pewter dishes, sixe saucers sixe porringers two saltcellers two chamber pottes Seventene tinne spoones & a pewter Potte			xxx	
	Summe	v	xv	
In the Parlour				
Item a Table, a Carpet, iiij turned settles one Forme one Liverie table a chaire & a buffet stoole			xv	
Item painted clothes Cushions & a mustard querne			x	
	Summe		xxv	
In the Buttrye				
Item one Cupborde three Barrelles one tub iiij linnen wheeles iij hetchelles with other implementes			xx	
In the ynner Parlour				
Item two Standing Beddes two Coffers & a Rounde Table			xl	
Item two Fetherbeddes two mattresses two Coverlettes two Bolsters & two pillowes		iij		
Item Painted Clothes & wearinge apparels			xl	
Item two blankettes & vj yardes of wollen clothe			xx	

Item three paire of flaxen sheetes two paire of hempe teare and Seven paire of harden	iij		
Item Seven table Clothes twelve table napkins two towelles and Sixe pillowbeeres		xl	
Summe	xiij		
In the Chamber over the hall			
Item Foure Bedstedes & two Coffers		xx	
Item one Fetherbed iij mattresses vij bolsters iiij Coverlettes one pillowe & three Blankettes		xl	
Item Painted clothes		vj	viij
Item eight Silver Spoones		xl	
Summe	v	vj	viij
In the cheese Chamber			
Item three cheses, chese Rackes & other implementes		xiij	iiij
In the chamber over the Buttrie			
Item three Bottles a Seedcod a wollen wheele butter & honie with other ymplementes		vj	viij
In the kitchen			
Item iiij milkebolles iiij Chesefattes a butter cherme a salte troff a clever with other ymplementes		vj	viij
Item foure Spittes, a drippinge pan, a fryinge pan a paire of Cobyrons a paire of tonges two Pothangers & a hetchele		xiij	iiij
Item a Boultinge vessel a mouldinge boorde & a Barrel with suche other ymplementes		v	
Item two hogges in Salte		x	
Item two yeelinge Fattes a Barrel a paile and two Tubbes		v	
Summe		xl	
In the henne house			
Item a Penne and certeine Ropes			xx
In the longe house			
Item a Fatte, a tub, a barrel & a carte bodye		vj	viij
In the Stable			
Item Plowe geeres		vj	viij
In the yarde			
Item a Hovell two Cartes a carte bodie, iiij plowes a paire of harrowes & certen timber & boordes	vj		
Item Firewoode		vj	viij
Summe	vj	vj	viij
Cattell			
Item Nine Hogges		xl	
Item Five kyne two Steeres Foure calves two heiffers two Bullockes & a Bulchin	xiij	vj	viij
Item foure Horses	iij	vj	viij
Item Sixe Stockes of Bees		x	
Summe	xix	iij	iiij
In the Fielde			
Item Seaven Acres of wheate & Rie sowen	iiij	xiij	iiij
Item of Tilthe Fourtene Acres	iiij	xiij	iiij

Item of Brache twelve Acres		xxiiij	
Summe	x	x	viij
Corne & Haye			
Item in the Barne, Barlie wheate & Rie	xxvj	xiij	iiij
Item a Hovele of Pease	iij	vj	viij
Item Haye		xl	
Item Sackes, a winnowe Sheete & olde yron		vj	viij
Summe	xxxij	vj	viij
Summe Totalis huius Inventarij	lxxxxviij	ix	

[*No exhibition clause*]

Notes: Thomas Baie's burial has not been found.

126 Henry Gale of Knotting and Southoe, Hunts, labourer made 17 April 1591
Lincolnshire Archives, MISC WILLS K/6

1591. Inventorey of all suche goodes and catell as was Harey Gale of Sowtho praysed by Jhon Tayler, Jhon Byllyngham, Nycholas Grene as folowethe the xvij day of Apryll

	£	s	d
Item iij besse	iiij		
Item ij shepe and a lame		xij	
Item ij peare of shettes and a table clothe		vij	
Item ij pellowes and a pello bere			xij
Item one cofer			xij
Item one coverlet		ij	
Item one coet ij gerkens one peare of hosse one cloke		xiij	iiij
Item one bedsted and ij bords			xx
Item one chettell			xviij
Item in money		x	
Sum is	vj	ix	vj

Signum William Gale executor, Nycholas Grene [*signature*]
[*Exhibited by William Gale, executor, before John Belley at Buckden on 13 May 1591. The sign of the executor William Gale is a carefully drawn cross with all four arms of the same length, each ending with a serif.*]

Notes: Henry Gale was buried at Southoe, Hunts, on 31 March 1591. He made his will on 27 December 1588, describing himself as a labourer of Knotting. He left household goods and crops to Jane Hale, and crops to two other people. The residual legatee was his brother William Gale to whom probate was granted at Buckden on 13 May 1591 (Lincs Archives, MISC WILLS K/6). Below the exhibition clause and in the same handwriting are three sums: pro probatione 3s 6d; pro consignatio 8d; and pro sigillo 6d. These are the sums paid for probate, sealing and signing, amounting to 4s 8d.

127 John Smythe of Everton, husbandman made 3 April 1591
Lincolnshire Archives, MISC WILLS K/8

A trewe Inventorye of the goodes & Cattells of Jhon Smythe husband[man] in the paryshe of Everton in the Countie of Bedf departed the thirde day of Aprill in the yere of our lorde god 1591

	£	s	d
in the howse			
A forme iij stoles ij Coffers iij Bedsteedes a Caske		viij	x
ij table Clothes ij pillowe beres & xij payre of sheetes		xxxviij	
iij Coverleddes iiij bolsters ij pillowes		xij	viij
ij matteres & paynted Clothes		x	
x[ll] of yerne		v	
a panne a brasse potte iiij ketles a posenette		xv	vj
x peeces of pewter a Chayffyngdysshe a grediorne		v	x
ij Cheres			x
a Cloke ij Jerkynses a trusse a paire of hose		viij	
iij tubbes ij sackes a grinston & other trasshe		vj	
x busshells Barlye & Rye		xxiiij	
a long Carte a donge Carte ij payre of wheles		xxviij	
a plowgh plowghgeres Carte geres & other trasshe		vij	
a hovell & woode in the yerde		xvj	viij
iij steres iij beasse & ij Calves	vij		
iiij horse		xl	
vj shepe iiij shotes		xxxvij	iiij
xviij acres of grayne in the feildes	xij		
A Judgemente a gaynste Chrystopher Fanscrafte	iij	vj	viij
Summa totalis	xxxv	x	iiij

The praysers hereof William Winche, Jhon Cartewright & Jhon Gibson
[*No exhibition clause*]

Notes: John Smythe's burial has not been found.

128 Nicholas Bucher alias Sibthorpe of Felmersham, labourer made 6 April 1591
Lincolnshire Archives INV/80/160

The true Inventorie of all the goodes and Chatelles of Nicholas Bucher alias Sibthorpe late of Felmersham in the Countie of Bedforde Laborer deceassed priced by William Coffin, Johne Harbarde & Roberte Burley neighboures ther: and written downe in the sixthe day of Aprill 1591

	£	s	d
Firste one brasse pott and an olde kettle		v	
Item two lattinge candlesticke			xij
Item sixe pewter dishes		iiij	
Item one litle pewter pott			iij
Item three olde sheetes		iij	
Item one olde coverledde		ij	

		£	s	d
Item one olde featherbedd & one olde boulster			vj	
Item one coffer				xvj
Item one verie olde broken coffer				vj
Item one cowe			xxiij	iiij
The debtes due to Nich[ol]as Bucher alias Sibthorpe				
George Smithe of Felmersham oweth that I lent hime			xx	
Item Johne Bury of Felmersham			v	
Item Johne Dune of Pavenham			vij	
Item Edwarde Still of Felmersham Clerque			xiij	iiij
	Summa	iiij	xj	ix

[*No exhibition clause*]

Notes: the burial of Nicholas Bucher alias Sibthorpe has not been found. Nearly half his inventory value was money owed to him. One of those owing him money was Edward Still, who was vicar of Felmersham 1579–91 (CCEd; Beds Archives, Fasti/1/Fel).

129 Elsabeth Woollet of Wilshamstead, widow made 10 April 1591

Lincolnshire Archives, MISC WILLS K/7

There is slight damage at the foot of the inventory.

Anno Domini 1591. An Inventorie of the goods & Cattle of Elsabeth Woollet widowe lately disceased: Taken the tent day of Aprile

	£	s	d
Inprimis Fower beasts & a yeareling Calfe	v		
Two Stores; one Ewe & a Lambe		x	
Fower payer of Shets and on single Sheet		xiij	4
Two Pillobeares		ij	vj
Two Cooverlets		vj	
Three Bolsters ~~and~~ one Fether Beed and a Mattrise		xx	
Two Coffers one Chest, & three Bedsteads		x	
Five Painted Clothes		vj	viij
A Penn and a Chese racke		ij	viij
A Pan and five Cettles		xvj	
Two Potes and a Posnet		x	
Twele [*sic*] peces of Peuter, three Candlesticks, and two Salts		xiij	
A Table, a Forme, Two Cooberts A Pen and Two Chares		x	
A Table Cloth and a speare Cloth		iij	iiij
Tubes Barrels and all treing Ware		xvj	

	£	s	d
Three Steanes two Pitchers and drinking Pote & a milke pan			vj
Two Lodde of Woode		x	
Two racks & a hogges troughe			xij
Eight hennes and a Cocke		iij	
Two Geese			xij
Three Duckes and a dracke			xvj
Five Cotes and a Cloke		xx	
A Spite a Frying Pan a grediron a Treed a payer of pote Hanings a payer of Hookes and a payer of Bellowes		ij	
One halfe Acre of Pease and one Roode of Barley		vj	viij
Seaven Bords		iij	iiij
An horse Racke and manger			xvj
Ten Bushells of Barley		xx	
Two Bushells of Pease		v	
Summa totalis	xv	xv	viij
[*Corrected total*	*£15*	*14s*	*8d*]

By us Georg Edwards, Rychard Deare, Symon Stratton, Hugh [...], He[...]
[*No exhibition clause*]

Notes: Elsabeth Woollet's burial has not been found.

130 John Bull of Riseley, ploughwright made 13 April 1591
Lincolnshire Archives INV/80/162

A trewe Inventory of all the goodes & Chattels of John Bull lait of Ryseley in the Countie of Bedd Plowright deceassed seen & prized the 13 daie of Aprill in the 33 yeare of the reigne of oure sov[erei]gn Ladie Elizabeth by the grace of god etc Anno domini 1591 by Thomas Fishe the yonger, William Musgrave, Richard Smithe and Thomas Pennel of Ryseley afore said in the said Countie of Bedd husband[*men*]

	£	s	d
Imprimis iij Cart horse pr[*ice*]	iij		
Item ix milche beast iiij bullockes iij yearing [*sic*] Calves	ix		
Item xxix Cupples of ewes and lambes and x gest sheeppe pr[*ice*]	xiiij		
Item Tymber fierwood & bordes the price	v		
Item Tilth sown with wheat and barly iij acres p[*rice*]		xl	
Item pease land sown ij acres & a half price		xx	
Item xij busshells of Barly pr[*ice*]		xxiiij	
Item xij busshells of malt price		xxviij	
Item ij hogges pr[*ice*]		viij	

	£	s	d
Item one shodd Cart plowe and plowe gears Cart and Carte gears pr[*ice*]		xxx	
Item wheat hay & pease pr[*ice*]		xx	
Howshould stuf pr[*ice*]	xj		
Summa Invent	fiftie poundes xs		

[*No exhibition clause*]

Notes: John Bull's burial has not been found.

131 Alice Cooke of Eaton Bray, widow made 27 May 1591

Lincolnshire Archives, INV/80/163

An Invytorye a mayd the xxvij[th] daye of Maye in the yeare of ouer lord god 1591 of all the goodes and cattyll of Alyes Cooke wedowe late dessed wyth in the parishe of Eyton and wyth in the cuntye of Bedford by the prasers heare of as foloweyth John Goage the Elder, John Buckemaster the youngger & Thomas Burr, Thomas Cutlat the Elder wyth other more

	£	s	d
Item ij bussylls of wheate		v	iiij
Item balrlye [*sic*] & malte vij bussyles		xv	
Item For ij ackers & Rode of bracly whyeat in the feld		xxxij	vj
Item for on acker of barlye & on of pecess		xxviij	
Item for ij beyste & a bullocke	iij		
Item for ij shype and lame		xiiij	
Item for j smal stor ~~hog~~ pygge		iij	
Item for pult[r]ye		ij	
Item for vij shetes and atabylclothe & ij pelloberes		xvj	
Item for viij peces of small lynan		iij	
Item for all hour [*her*] waryng aparyll		xxiij	
~~Item for ij~~ Item on flece of wooll			xviij
Item for heardyn [*?*]linan yearn ix[l]		iij	
Item j cofer & on old [*?*]arck		iij	
Item iiij peces of brase & a smal lattyn pote and a puter platter		vj	viij
Item on wooland wyyll on [*?*]tobe on spette and a axe and hanggares over the fyer and a farges baryll		iij	
Item for atabyll and abacke bord			xij
Item abole and ij pales & all the Rest of the trene fassyll small & gret & agredyer wyth iiij Rybes & fane & a [*?*]crene pote		ij	viij
the sum	xj		viij
[*Corrected total*	*£11*	*2s*	*8d*]

[*No exhibition clause*]

Notes: Alice Cooke was buried at Eaton Bray on 18 May 1591.

132 Joane Hewett of Melchbourne, widow undated; before June 1591
Lincolnshire Archives, INV/80/157
The document is stained on the top right side.

An Inventorie of all the goodes and kattell of Joane Hewett widdowe of Melchborne with in the Countie of Bedforde latlie disceased prised by Thomas Turner, Gregorie Hipwell with others

	£	s	d
Imprimis Apparell prised at		xx	
Two beddes and all that belonge to them 7 paire of sheettes a cobborde a [*?*]penne			
2 cofferres with other implementes in the Chamber prised at	v		
A table and a forme and 2 buffett stooles a cheare and the painted clothes			
with other implementes in the hall prised at		xx	
The brasse and peuter a spitt and cobirons the pot hanginges		xx	
A Saltinge troffe a litell fatt and 2 tubbes with other implementes		x	
The cheese and a bacon flicke prised at		x	
Two olde hovelles prised at		xxxv	
All the woode prised at		x	
The Pullen prised		iij	
one hogge prised		iiij	
4 beastes and 2 bullockes prised	vij		
26 sheepe prised	vj	x	
The barleye and the wheatte prised at	v		
The pees and the heay prised at		xxxv	
Summa totalis	xxxj	xvij	

[*Exhibited at Bedford on* [*?*]*7 June 1591*]

Notes: Joane Hewett's burial has not been found.

133 Francis Godfreye of Girtford, Sandy made 13 August 1592
Lincolnshire Archives, MISC WILLS K/37

1592 This is the true Inventorye of all the goodes & Chattells of Frauncis Godfreye of Girtforde in the paryshe of Sandey & in the Countie of Bedforde desseased Indented And made the xiij[th] daye of Auguste in the xxxiiij[th] yeare of the Raigne of our Soveraigne Lady Elizabeth by the grace of god Quene of Englande Fraunce & Ireland defendor of the fayethe etc prased by William Bromesall, Josue Cator, Robert Maies & Edwarde Sutton As followethe

	£	s	d
Imprimis one Cubborde one table ij formes & j buffett stoole		xxiij	iiij
Item All the Brasse And pewter And other Implementes ther		xx	
Item ij bedsteedes & iiij Coffers		xviij	vj
Item j fetherbedde iij mattrices iij Coverlettes iij bolsters & iij pillowes		xxx	
Item ix paier of sheeites iij table Clothes with table nappkins & other lynnen		xxv	vj

Item tubbes Barrells And All other treene ware		xiij	iiij
Item vj horsses	xiij	vj	viij
Item xiij beesse & bullockes	xx		
Item iij scoore sheepe	xiij	x	
Item all the Barlie wheate Rie otes And peesse	xxix	x	
Item A leasse of A farme	xij	vj	viij
Item All the tylthe	iiij		
Item All his wearinge Apparrell		x	
Item j Carte And all the woode		xl	
Somme totalis	101	14	

[*No exhibition clause*]

Notes: Francis Godfreye was buried at Sandy on 10 August 1593, according to the burial register transcription (*BPR*, vol. 6, p. A87). This is likely to be a mistake for 10 August 1592.

134 Alce Negouse of Shelton, widow made 3 January 1593

Lincolnshire Archives, MISC WILLS K/33

The document is creased on the right side, obscuring some values, and damaged at the foot.

The Inventorye of all suche goodes & chattayles as Alce Negouse widdowe late of Shelton dyed scised [*died seised*] of made the 3 of Januarij Anno 1592 and praysed by Master Mallorye, Richard Dillingham, Henrye Negouse, Gilbart Negouse, George Negouse with others

	£	s	d
In the Halle			
In primis 2 tables 2 formes & a chayre		15	
In the Parlor			
Item A table, 5 stooles, a cheire & a benche settle		14	
Item A Cupbord, a Cheaste & 5 chushyns		27	4
Item 3 basons, a ure, 4 candlesticks a litle salt A cupbord clothe with other implementes		6	8
Item A warmingpan, a fyre Shovell a fire forke, a payre of tongues & bellowes		5	
Item 3 lynnen Curtaynes with other implementes		5	
Item A glasse Casse with glasses		4	
Item A Standing bed with fetherbed matteris 2 blanketes 2 coverlydes with Curtayns & ij vallens with a trundle bed	iiij		
Item 6 Silver spones		18	
In the lofte			
Item on Standing bed with a fetherbed, 2 bolsteres a mattris 3 blankettes, a coverled, with 4 Curtaynes	iij		
Item An other Standingbed with fetherbed, 2 bolsters 2 blankettes, 2 coverlides, a Quilt, with curtayns & tester		50	
Item on Cheiste with 3 Coverlides, A Quilt 6 pillowes on payre of Sheetes & a chushyn	5		
Item a Round table a fetherbed & a towell		23	4
Item A nother Cheist with 6 payre of Sheetes, a dussen table napkyns, 2 table clothes & a towell	iiij		

	£	s	d
Item a trunke Covered with leather		10	
Item 16 peeces of peaudre & a cheire with other implementes		16	
Item 2 brasse pans, an old kettle with on other kettle		20	
Item on brasse pott		10	
Item A garner with Iron beame & waytes		30	
Item in plate		40	
Item the leasse holde of Master Mallerye		20	
Summa totalis	31	14	4

Comittend: Gilberto Negouse de Shelton [*words faded and torn*] yeoman [...] Negouse de [*illeg.*]
[*No exhibition clause*]

Notes: Alice Negouse's burial has not been found.

135 Christopher Morryce of Pavenham, blacksmith made after June 1593

Lincolnshire Archives, INV/85/261

A trew & iust Inventorie of all the goodes & cattells of Christopher Morryce of Pavenham blacksmythe indyfferentlie valewed & praysed by Robert Frisbey, Wylliam Lambert, & Robert Ynglishe, etc in anno domini 1594

	£	s	d
In prymes			
iij milch beastes and on yearling bullouck praysed at	iiij		
viij sheep praysed at		xxxij	
An Anfilde A bellows and a vyse and iij payre of tonnges All beinge veary old preased		xiij	iiij
ij Candelstickes and xij pewter dishes being veary smalle with a salt praysed at		v	
1 bras pan ij bras pates iiij cetles 1 Cherffendish and a skimmer a frying pan and payre of Cobiorns with a spit praysed at		xx	
A little fyer wode		v	
A old Cubard a pen mad lyck [*made like*] a cubard iiij tubes 1 Boulting vessell a saulting troufe and a chearme ij pealles 1 hachat praysed at		xx	iiij
A cobard A table A forme a benchbord A Cheare A buffit stole at		xx	x
1 payre of pot hangers at			viij
1 peayre of flaxen sheetes ij payre of teare of hemten sheetes vij payre of harden shetes		xx	

1 materris A Blanket ij Coverlites			
ij pillows ij Boalsturs		x	
iij shelfbordes A Cheese wrack			
1 linnin wheell a wollon wheell			
a mault barell		iij	iiij
iij table Clothes ij Cubard Clothes			
iiij Cushens with All his a paring		xiij	iiij
iiij Coffers and ij bedes		xij	
All the paynted Close		iij	iiij
A quarter of Barlie in the house		xij	
A acer of tillige		x	
1 acer of pease land		xxj	
a hamer for a smyth with all			
other toles		ij	
A gridiorne and a tread			viij
Ashot [*a shott*]		iij	iiij
ij flyches of bacan		v	
A spit morter & apestell		ij	
xij spones vj pewter spones xij trenchers xij dishes		[*value lacking*]	
The Full Som of this Inventor is Just	xv	xvj	ij

[*No exhibition clause*]

Notes: Christopher Morryce was buried at Pavenham on 29 June 1593.

136 Thomas Arrowsmith of Elstow made 13 October 1593

Lincolnshire Archives, LCC ADMONS 1594/6

An Inventorie of the goodes & Cattelles of Thomas Arrowsmith of Elsto diseased taken this xiij[th] day of October Anno Domini 1593

	£	s	d
Item one table & ij tresselles with iij			
formes praised at		ij	
Item Certen painted Clothes priced at			xij
Item ij kettelles praised at		iiij	
Item a red sowe and vj pigges priced at		viij	
Item Certen faggottes & wood priced at		v	
Item an old Cofer priced at			iiij
Item ij bedsteddes priced at		iij	
Item an old matterice & ij old			
Coverlettes priced at			xij
Item Certen haye priced at			viij
The some is		xxiiij	viij
[*Corrected total*		*25s*	*0d*]

praised the day & yere abovesaid by Thomas Porny, Robert Wolmer, John Sharpe and Wm Dimocke

[*No exhibition clause*]

Notes: Thomas Arrowsmith's burial has not been found. Administration was granted to his daughter Alice on 27 May 1594 and a bond was taken (Lincs Archives, Act Book A/iii/156 and LCC ADMONS 1594/6).

137 Edward Goodwyn of Clifton made 20 November 1593
Lincolnshire Archives, LCC ADMONS 1594/170

An Inventorie indented of all the goodes & Cattells of Edward Goodwyn late of Clyffton decessyd made & preysed the xx[th] day of November 1593 by John Goodwyn & John Chyld preysers as followethe

	£	s	d
Inprimis the table Benchbord cubbord & other ymplementes in the hawle		xx	
Item ij Beddsteedes with the Beddinge & other furniture about them	iij	vj	viij
Item certen lynnen & the hanginges in the chamber		xxvj	viij
Item the Brasse Pewter & other thinges in the kitchyn		xl	
Item the kymnells boles & other wodden ware in the Mylkhowse		vj	viij
Item iiij[or] horses	x		
Item iij Bease & iiij[or] bullockes	vij		
Item x Sheepe		xl	
Item iij hogges & ij stores		xx	
Item certen heaye & the ymplementes about the Stable		xxx	
Item the grayne in the Barne	v		
Item the Cart & Cart geers plough & plough geers	iij	vj	viij
Item the Poultry in the yard		iij	iiij
Summa	xxxviij		

[*No exhibition clause*]

Notes: Edward Goodwyn was buried at Clifton on 23 October 1593. Administration was granted on 27 May 1594, the inventory being noted as £38 and a bond being taken (Lincs Archives, Act Book A/iii/156 and LCC ADMONS 1594/170). He was a churchwarden in 1589–90 (*BPR*, vol. 62, p. 110).

138 Henry Dillingham of Shelton made 24 November 1593
Lincolnshire Archives, INV/85/277

The Inventorye of all suche goodes and chattells as Henry Dillingham of Shelton dyed seassed of the 24 daye of Novembre Anno domini 1593 And praysed by these men William Dillingham, Richard Dillingham, Henry Negouse Christoffor Foxe, Harry Dillingham, Gilbart Negause with others etc – Humffraye Dillingham

	£	s	d
In the halle			
In primis A great table and a syde table		20	
Item A Cuppbord		23	4
Item A Round table, 10 stooles, 3 cheares 2 formes, a cupbord clothe withe the hangings in the halle		36	

In the gest chamber

Item A Joyned standing bed, a fetherbed a mattris, 2 bolsters, & a coverlyd	3	6	8
Item Another standingbed with a colored tester, a mattris & a coverlyd		33	4
Item A great chest, a quilt, a gray blankett and 2 whyte blanketts		22	4
Item 2 other chestes, 10 paire of flaxen sheetes & an ode sheete, 3 flaxen table clothes, & a diapre table clothe	7	10	
Item 24 elnes of lynnen clothe in two partes & 5 elne of course harden		22	
Item A nother litle chest, a cheire & a syde saddle		8	
Item a 11 peices of pewdre in the litle table 2 peces of pewdre on the cupborde 2 candlesticks & a salt with a stone Jugge		21	

In the Inner Parler

Item 3 bedsteds, on fetherbed, 3 mattresses 4 bolsters, & on pillowe, 2 other bolsters 4 blanketts & the paynted clothes	3	6	8
Item on chest, 4 paire of harden sheetes 12 table napkyns & 2 pillowbeers and on other chest		36	

In the Loft over

Item An old bedsted, a hareclothe, 72 pounds of flaxe, 13 pounds of wollen yarne 5 yards of Russett at fullers, & 12 pounds of hopps		58	

In the Buttry & Kitchine

Item 5 barrells 3 salts, 4 peces of pewdre 50 pounds of buttre & 30 cheisses		35	
Item on greate pan, 5 pottes, a postnet 5 kettells and a chaffingdishe		56	
Item 2 candlesticks, a frying pan, a colendre 8 peces of pewdre & 3 Juggs		6	
Item A Salting troughe 12 dishes 12 trenchers 2 chappingknyffs, 3 pailes, a morter & pestle a litle table, a forme & a bread gratte		7	
Item 3 spitts a paire of lanndIrons & a paire of cobIrons, 2 paire of pott hokes, the beame and hanging hokes over the fyre		10	
Item A musterd querne, 2 wollen wheeles 3 lynnen wheels, 4 lether bottles, 2 hogsheds 4 wymbles, a handsawe, A pitchpan, a brand		12	
Item 2 stones weight of lead, 3 baskettes, 2 paire of wollen cards, 2 paire of boltings and a standing candlesticke		3	4

In the kylne

Item A Steping fatt, a bushell, 2 greatt kymnells, a bolting arke, 5 tubbes, 3 Round kymnells & a meele		27	

Item A mashingfatt, a lead, a brandIron, a mowlding bord, a fyreforke, a ladder for the kylne a paire of [*illeg.*] & 2 old salt barrells		11	
In the milk house			
Item A cheisse presse, a cherme, A washetubb 2 booles, 3 kans, 6 earthen pans, a litle kymnell a boole, a hare syffe, 9 shelffes		11	
In the yarde			
Item 10 bakon hogges, 6 stoares & a sowe and 5 pyggs	6		
Item 10 ducks & 3 geesse		5	
The Stable			
Item in the Stable 9 horsses & 2 coltes	20		
Item 5 paire of cartgeers, 2 cart saddles 2 paire of thillstrapps, 2 belly bands, 2 cart roppes, 8 paire of plowegeeres, 2 followe plowes 2 seeding plowes & teeme & toggwithe		15	
Item Rackes, mangers & planks in the stable and 7 halters		8	
Item iij longe shod carts, & 2 dungcart bodyes	5	10	
Item 8 sacks & A windowclothe		13	4
Item 3 hovells		50	
Item 3 quarters of malt on the floore			
Item 3 quarters of ootes & a halffe			
Item in the greate barne 2 bays of barly & 6 loades			
Item A hovell of barlye	37		
Item A mowe of wheate	10		
Item A Ricke of peasse	8		
Item 30 loades of haye	13		
Item plowtymbre, 4 laddres & racks & other wood with fyre woode	5	6	8
Item 12 milcke beastes, 10 bullockes, 7 calffs	34	10	
Item the pullyn		10	
Item in the Feild a 11 [*sic*] Acres of wheat	11		
Item 8 Score Sheppe & 13	47		
Item the tylthe 49 Acres	24		
Item the peisse Lande		20	
Summa totalis	cclxiiij	ix	viij

[*Exhibited at Bedford on 27 May 1594*]

Notes: Henry Dillingham's burial has not been found. The Parsons deposit at Bedfordshire Archives contains an account of the Dillingham family (Beds Archives, PA).

139 Henry Lattimer of Riseley, possibly a carpenter made 16 [...] 1594
Lincolnshire Archives, LCC ADMONS 1594/81
The inventory has been written on a narrow sheet of paper. The left side is torn and some letters or words at the beginning of most lines are missing. They have been supplied where obvious.

[*A tr*]ewe Inventorie of all the [*goo*]des Chattelles of Henrie [*Latt*]imer lait of Ryseley in [*the*] Countie of Bed ~~deceassed~~ [*car*]pendor deceassed seene [...] the xvjth daie of [...] the yeare of oure [*lord*] god 1594 By John [...] And Anthonie [...] of Ryseley in the [*c*]ountie of Bedf aforesaid [...]

	£	s	d
[*Inpri*]mis in the Hall one foulded [*ta*]ble and ij formes, one cheare [...] buffet stoole price		v	
[*Item*] one ould Cubberde one ould [...]nne the paintted Clothes [*p*]rice		iiij	
[*Item*] vj peeces of pewther [...] Braspanne ij latten [*Ca*]ndlestickes one pewther salt one Litle Braspott ij skellettes one skymmer pr[*ice*]		x	
In the parlor			
Item ij Borden Bedsteades iiij^{or} Copfers pr[*ice*]		viij	
Item ij Blanckettes, ij pillowes ij coveringes ij pillow bears iij paire flexen sheettes, one paire teare of hempe ij paire of harden iiij^{or} table napkins, ij hand towelles [*p*]rice		xxx	
[*Item*] his Apparrell		viij	
[*Item*] in the Lofte Certein bordes [...] trashe pr[*ice*]		iij	iiij
In the Kitching			
[*Item*] [*o*]ne litle Arcke one [...] ij tubbes and other [...] pr[*ice*]		iiij	
[...] & a Calf iiij^{or} [...] hennes & A cocke [...]		xliij	iiij
[*In*] the Barne Certeine [...] & tymbre & fyer wood [...]		xiij	iiij
Summa totalis	vj	ix	

[*No exhibition clause*]

Notes: Henry Lattimer's burial has not been found. Administration was granted to his widow Alice on 27 May 1594 and a bond was taken (Lincs Archives, Act Book A/iii/156 and LCC ADMONS 1594/81).

140 Henry Rayner of Keysoe, carpenter made 14 February 1594
Lincolnshire Archives, INV/85/260

An Inventorye of the moveable goodes of Henrye Rayner late deceassed carpinter of Kaysho in the Countye of Bedford made the fouretenth daye of Februarye Anno domini 1593 praysed by John Richardes thelder and John Gore with others

	£	s	d
Inprimis two Dublets two pare of britches one Jearkyne two pare of stockinges two hates two shertes two neck bandes and one pare of showes		xxvj	viij
Item two pare of shetes one boulster a coveringe and a blancket an under cloth with a bedstede one table cloth & two pillowe beares		xvj	
Item foure peces of pewter		ij	
Item one coffer two bordes one theale thre paynted clothes two formes a litle dore and pare of framed tresseles		vij	
Item one Kymnel and two tubes		iij	iiij
Item two pare of cart geares		ij	
Item a plough teame with certayne olde Iron		ij	viij
Item two sithes redye geared		iij	
Item one brase pot and a brasse pan		vij	
Item two lattin candelstickes			xij
Item an axe			xij
Item certayne plough timber		vj	viij
Debtes due unto the Testator			
Inprimis William Rayner my eldest brother oweth me		xl	
John Richardes Junior oweth me		xx	
Walter Burlye oweth me		xl	
Item Thomas Rolte oweth me		lvij	x
Item Richard Rayner oweth me		xvj	
Item Master Gleson oweth me		xvj	
Item William Folbeck oweth		x	viij
Summa totalis	xiij	xviij	x

[*No exhibition clause*]

Notes: Henry Rayner's burial has not been found.

141 Thomas Wright of Wootton made 22 April 1594

Lincolnshire Archives, INV/85/257

The writing is clear but faint and difficult to read.

The Inventorie of All the goods and Chatells & debtes of Thomas Wright late of Wotton in the County of Bedf deceassed made & prised the xxij[th] daie of Aprill Anno domini 1594 by Gilberte Stoughton, Thomas Boswarde, William Wolhed as followethe: viz

	£	s	d
Hall			
Fyrste in the hall of his late dwellinge howse a table with a frame; ix Joyned stooles, twoe chaires, vj grene quishions, a fier shovell, tonges, bellowes, iiij potte hangers & a grene benche Clothe		xxv	
Parlor			
Item a square table with a frame, a grene Carpette, a Cubborde, ij cofers, a bedstede a fetherbed bolster iiij pillowes iiij Coverlettes, v blanquettes	v	xiij	iiij
Parlor Chamber			
Item a bedstede a Coverlette, a Cofer, iij blanquettes, & iiij pillowes		xlviij	
Chamber ouer the same parllor			
Item a bedstede a square table & a Cofer		xiij	iiij
Chamber ouer thother parllor			
Item a bedstede, ij fetherbeddes, v Coverlettes, a grene carpette, v blanquettes, ij Cofers, ij bolsters, a pillowe & a Chaire	vij	x	
Chamber over the hall			
Item a bedstede a fetherbedde ij mattrices a bolster, a blanquette, ij cofers & a deske		xl	
Item xxv paire of sheetes x table clothes iij dosen of table napkins xij pillowbeers viij hande towells	ix	xvj	
Buttrey			
Item pewter in all		xliij	iiij
Item barrells, tubbes, a safe & a powdringe troffe		xx	
Kytchine			
Item v brasse pottes, ij brasse pannes, iiij kyttells, vj candestickes, a chafing dishe a morter & pestell		lv	
Item ij spyttes ij trefittes, a fire forke, ij paire of Andirons, iiij paire of pott hookes & a frieng panne		x	
Item iiij tubbs, a kymnell shelves & other olde thinges there		v	
Item an arke for meale & to bolte in & viij flytches of bacon		xxxvij	
Mylkehowse			
Item a yelinge fatt & a Cowler, a cheese presse, iij cheese Rackes, a tubbe, a charme			

mylbooles, ij olde pannes, lether bottell shelves & other olde lumber there		[?]xx	
In the yarde			
Item a hovell		xiij	iiij
Item fier woode		vij	
Item boardes [?]cleates & tymber	iiij	x	
Item [?]half a hovell		[?]xx	
Item ij Sythes		iij	iiij
Item olde Iron		v	
Item a busshell			xij
Item ploughe tymber & axtres		x	
Item a Longe carte & donge carte		xlv	
Item harrowes		vj	viij
Item a Rolle & olde woode		iiij	
Item ploughes & other necessaries of husbandrie		lj	viij
Item horsse harnes for carte & ploughe		xiij	iiij
Item olde Lumber		v	
Grayne			
Item a quarter di of wheate		xxiiij	
Item a quarter of pease		x	
Item iiij quarters of malte		xl	
Item ix quarters of barley	iiij	x	
Item xiij acres of pease	viij	xiij	iiij
Item an acre di of wheat		xxx	
Cattell			
Item iiij horsse & geldinges	x		
Item xxxij coples & [*illeg.*][23] xxiij other sheepe	xxxij		
Item v kyne & calves	ix		
Item iij kyne without calves	iiij		
Item one bulluck		xxxv	[*illeg.*]
Item iiij bulluckes of 3 yeres olde	v	vj	viij
Item vj bullackes of 2 yeres olde	vj		
Item vij yereling bullackes	iij	x	
Item vij hogges		xxxv	
Item vj pigges		vj	viij
Summa totalis huius Invent[arii]	Cxlij	xvij	
[*Corrected total*	*£144*	*12s*	*0d*]

[*No exhibition clause*]

Notes: Thomas Wright was buried at Wootton on 19 March 1594.

23 Characters that might be a number (such as *xl*) have been blotted as if they have been deleted and *xxiij* substituted.

142 Henry Wattes rector of Potsgrove, clerk made 23 April 1594
Lincolnshire Archives, INV/85/258

An Inventory of the goodes of Henry Wattes Clarke & parson of Potesgrave in the County of Bedff late deceased beinge praysed the 23 of Aprill Anno domini 1594 by Thomas Robinson, Singleton Godfree, ~~William~~ John Spufforde of Potesgrave aforesaid as followeth

	£	s	d
In primis one Cow		xxvj	
Item pease unthreshed		xiij	iiij
Item ~~Corne or~~ barly		xiij	iiij
Item barly straw			x
Item certayne fagattes		x	
Item hay		iiij	vj
Item in the Hall j table & a frame			
j stole and j Chayre		iij	iiij
Item j Cubbord, a long forme a payre			
of yron Dogges		iij	
Item j spitt, j payre of Cobyrons			
j Hatchet, j gridyron			xvj
Item pothookes j Candlestick, j Curry-			
Combe, j a saltseller			x
Item j table Cloth, j five bushell			
sack, j wallet			xxij
Item in the bruehouse iij tubbes,			
j bushell, ij bushell bag		iiij	x
Item iiij ketteles, j skillet & j posnet		vij	vj
Item iij firkins, ij Chesfattes, j tunnell		ij	
Item v booles, j payle, j linen wheele		ij	vj
Item j bedsteed, j bridel & saddel &			
a payre of bootes		xj	
Item in the lofte certayne maulte		xlv	
Item tyles, & old Cart & wheles			
and Certayne wood		iij	vj
Item certayne tymber & a ladder			xij
Item a cole pan, ij Chestes j buffet			
stoole		x	
Item a brasse pott		vj	
Item a pewter bottle, j sawser			
iij pewter dishes			xvj
Item vj new pewter dishes & a sawser		iij	
Item a square table, & a close Chayre		iij	iiij
Item a dry fatt, j Cart Roope & bed cord			xvj
Item a peck & half pecke shelf			
boordes and Cordes			iiij
Item in his Camber a standing bedsteed		xj	
Item ij bigger Chestes		vj	iiij
Item ij fetherbeddes j bolster & ij			
pillowes		xxxiij	iiij
Item ij Coverliddes, on mattresse		vj	viij
Item a cloke Cloth ~~cloth~~		xxvj	viij
Item shelves & paynted clothes			viij

	£	s	d
Item his bookes	v		
Item a blanket & a half one a flock bed		iij	viij
Item v sheetes ij table Clothes & iij pillowbeeres		xiiij	
Item a surplisse		iiij	
Item his Apparel		xl	
Item a payer of Course sheetes		ij	vj
Item a Chamberpott, ij candlestickes a Cushen Capcasse etc		ij	iiij
Item olde yron & lead		ij	iij
Item [*blank*]	xiij		
Dettes owinge unto hym	12		
Sum totalis	46	14	5
Charges of the buriall		33	4

[*No exhibition clause*]

Notes: Henry Wattes' burial has not been found. He was vicar of Felmersham cum Pavenham 1561; vicar of Streatley 1561–71; rector of Potsgrove 1571–94; and licensed as a preacher in 1585 (CCEd; Beds Archives, Fasti/1/Fel, Fasti/1/Str, Fasti/1/Pots). The 1607 glebe terrier, taken during the time of his successor, describes the parsonage as having three bays covered partly with tile and partly with thatch, with chambers over. There were five rooms: the hall, buttery, kitchen and chambers over the hall and buttery; and also a thatched barn of four bays (Beds Archives, ABE 1).

143 Raynold Ireland of Wilshamstead, labourer — made 29 April 1594

Lincolnshire Archives, MISC WILLS K/94

The Inventorie of the goodes and Cattels of Raynold Ireland of Wylshamsted in the Counte of Bedforde Laborer late deceased taken the xxix[th] daye of Aprill in the xxxvj yeare of the raigne of our Soveraigne Ladie Elizabethe by the grace of god of England Fraunce and Ireland Queene defendris of the faythe etcetr as followethe

	£	s	d
In primis in the haule a Table a forme a Cubborde ij chaires and iiij stooles		xx	
Item xvij peces of pewter		x	
Item vj porringers iiij sawcers ij saltes iiij pewter pootes j Candlesticke		iij	iiij
Item the paynted Clothes in the haule and ij Cusshinges		iij	iiij
Item vj brase pootes ij kettles ij pannes ij possenetes vj Candlestickes and a skymmer		xxvj	viij
Item in the Chamber iij bedsteedes vj Cofers		xvj	
Item iij mattresses a fetherbed iij boulsters and iiij pyllowes		xxx	
Item ij Coverletes iij blanketes		vj	viij
Item the paynted Clothes in the Chamber			xx
Item iij payre of flexen sheetes iiij payre of harten and vj payre of tare of hempe		xlvj	viij

Item iiij Table clothes xij napkines a towell xiij pyllowberes and ij cobberd clothes			xx	
Item vj handtowells				xvj
Item all his waringe geare			xvj	
Item a preesse			ij	
Item xxiij slypes of yarne			viij	
Item vj tubbes ij barrells a saltingetroughe iij payles and certaine other lumber			vj	viij
Item xxviij busshilles of grayne			xxxv	
Item iij quarters of barley more			xxx	
Item certaine wheate to threshe by estimation			xij	
Item viij acres of wheate pease and barley		iiij		
Item certaine woode			x	
Item certaine elme borde and halfe yntche borde and quarters			viij	viij
Item vj myltche beesse and on hecforthe with calve		ix	vj	viij
Item a steare bullocke ij hecforthes ij yerlinges and a vened calfe		iij	vj	viij
Item xx^{ti} coples of shepe		v		
Item xxxij drye shepe		vj	viij	
Item iij stoores and a sowe			xiij	iiij
Item ij bacon hogges			xvj	
Item certane [*?*]spinge wheles, bylles hatchetes and other implementes			v	
	Summa	xlv	ix	viij

Debtes owinge hime

In primis Wylliam Taylor oweth him		x		
Item ther remaynethe in the handes of one Conquest of [*?*]Westinge in the Counte of Huntington		x		
In the handes of John Cawnell Jun of Wylshamsted		vj		
	Summa totalis	lxxj	ix	viij

Praysed by Thomas Decons gent George Edwardes [...] [*Wil*]liam Tomson, George Coucke John Aubone [...] with others
[*No exhibition clause*]

Notes: Raynold Ireland was buried at Wilshamstead on 13 March 1594. His wife and sons were beneficiaries under the will of the appraiser, William Tomson, in 1596 (Beds Archives, P22/25/3/1).

144 Robert Wattes of Wymington, husbandman made 9 May 1594
Lincolnshire Archives, LCC ADMONS 1594/157

The Inventerie of all the goodes of Roberte Wattes late of Wemyngten in the countye of Bedforde husbandman deceased praysed the ixth daye of Maye 1594 by Thomas Greye, Rychard Jones, Frauncys Jones and Robert Purney

	£	s	d
Inprimis in the halle A framed table two framed formes, A benche, A benche			

borde, two other tables, A forme & in paynted clothes, cheares, & other smale implementes of house		xxx	
Item in the parlar one standinge bedde A cubborde, two chestes two coffers, two buffete stoles one fetherbede, one bolster, two pyllowes A lytle table, foure quysshens two coveringes, two blanketes, A carpete clothe & other smale thinges	iiij	x	
Item in sheetes pyllowbeares, table napkyns, toweles and table clothes	iij		
Item in the chamber over the parlar two bedsteades, A matrise, A bolster, tow pyllowes, two coverletes, A blanket, A lytle coffer, A cradle & paynted clothes		xl	
Item in brasse and pewter with An yron pote, A friinge panne one yron barre pote hanginges, A paire of Andyrones, and A spyte		xl	
Item in the boltynge house A Knedynge troughe, A boltinge barrell, tubbes payles, mylke bolles, shelves & other smale implementes of house		vj	viij
Item in lynnen yarne		vj	viij
Item in malte, barlye, wheate & Rie		xxvj	viij
Item the croppe upon the grounde	xx		
Item foure olde horses	vj	xiij	iiij
Item in kyne and bullockes	xiij	vj	viij
Item in ewes lambes & other sheepe	vij	x	
Item in hogges		xx	
Item in cartes, plowes, harrowes, plowe tymber, carte tymber, plowe geares and carte geares	iij		
Item in hovelles and other woode		xxx	
Summa	lxviij		

[*No exhibition clause*]

Notes: Robert Wattes' burial has not been found. Administration was granted to his widow Margaret on 27 May 1594 and a bond was taken (Lincs Archives, Act Book A/iii/156 and LCC ADMONS 1595/157).

145 Oliver Lynforde of Bromham made on 10 May 1594

Lincolnshire Archives, INV/85/259

The right edge near the foot of the document is damaged and several values are missing.

The Inventorie of the goodes and Cattells moveable and unmovable of Oliver Lynforde late of Bromham in the Countie of Bedf deceased, taken the x[th] day of Maie, in the yeare of the Raigne of our Soveraigne ladie Elizabeth the Queenes ma[jes]itie that nowe is, the xxxvj[th] preysed by William Dyxe, William Morgan, Thomas Digbie and Lewis Sympson, preysors theof

	£	s	d
Inprimis five horses	viij		
Item foure kyne	iiij		
Item fyve toe yeare old bullocks	iij	vj	viij
Item three Calves		xvj	
Item three weyned Calves		xij	
Item tenn sheepe		ls	
Item sixe hogges and a bore		xxxv	
Item syxe hennes and a Cock		ij	iiij
Item syxe ducks and a drake		ij	iiij
Item on gander and a goose			xvj
In the hall			
Item xvj peeces of pewter and toe sawcers		x	
Item a pewter pott iij pewter saltes & four little Candlestycks			xvj
Item a Cubbert & a table a forme and a penn		x	
Item a Chaire & iiij old stooles			xij
Item iiij kettles and a brasse pott		vj	viij
Item ix fletches of bacon		xxij	vj
Item vj Cheeses			xij
Item ij painted Clothes & ij sheelfs		iij	iiij
In the Chamber above the halle			
Item on fetherbed & a boulster a paire of blanquettes iij Coverlettes iiij pyllowes		xx	
Item a Chest and iij quoffers		vj	viij
Item old hangings & toe formes		iij	iiij
Item v flaxen sheetes & toe pillow beers		xiiij	
Item v paire of sheetes and a sheet of hardene		xxij	
In the lofte over the same Chamber			
Item an old bedsteed & a boulster a old blanquett & a mattres and toe paynted Clothes		iij	iiij
Item a pann & a pitch panne the brand and a byll		ij	vj
Item ix slypps of harden		iiij	vj
Item an old share and old Iron		iij	vj
Item a bottell a Cheece racke and Certen old trasshe		v	
In the nether house			
Item a spitt a paire of Cobirons a tred, a grydiron, potthoks & the hanging		v	
Item an old ark & a kymnell		vj	viij
Item an old Chest ij salting trowes and a Cover		vj	
Item viij[t] tubbs		viij	

Item a Churne a bushell a stop ij payles Certen Cheese fatts a suter & vj dyshes		ij	vj
Item a lether bottell & a frieng pann			xij
In the lofte over the same house			
Item a fatt an old Cheste a riddle and a rieing syve		iiij	
Item iij rakes & shacke forkes			vj
Item ij quarters ij bushells of Rie		xxx	
Item barlie iij bushells		iiij	
Item malte iij bushells		iiij	vj
In the entry			
Item toe sythes iiij pickforkes a Carte rope and a pyche		iiij	iiij
Item three wheeles		ij	vj
In the barne			
Item hey		iij	iiij
Item vj pigges		iij	
Item ij old sackes			xij
Item a hoggs trowgh			xij
Item a paire of harrows, an old plowe, a harrow sleed		ij	viij
In the yarde			
Item a Carte and shood wheels		xxvj	viij
Item a muck Carte with a paire of newe shood wheells		xl	
Item ij hovells		xxvj	viij
Item an other hovell at the barne end		iij	iiij
In the stables			
Item axtrees and plowe tymber		xx	[...]
Item iiij leather Collers & the harnes		vj	viij
Item iij paire of fetters and iij Lookes		iij	iiij
Item a rack and a manger			xx
Item a byll a hatched a paire of pyncers, and an axe		ij	vj
the fyelde			
Item v acres of wheet	v		
Item vij Acres of Rie	v		
Item viij Acres of barlie in the tylth	v	vj	[...]
Item xiij Acres of brach barlie	vij		[...]
Item [...] Acres of & [*sic*] a half of peece	iiij		[...]
Item an Acres & a half of Otes		viij	
Item toe plowes with the furniture		xx	
Item x old hurdles			[*?*]xx
Summa	lxx		x

William Dyxe marke, William Morgan marke, Thomas Digbies marke, Lewis Simpsons marke
[*No exhibition clause*]

Notes: Oliver Lynforde was buried at Bromham on 20 April 1594.

146 Ambrose Gregorye of Eversholt, yeoman made 13 May 1594
Lincolnshire Archives, LCC ADMONS 1594/173

A true Inventorye of all the goodes & Chattelles of Ambrose Gregorye of Eversholte in the Countye of Bedforde deceased, prysed by John Whytebreade, Nicholas Style, Symone Collines & Ambrose Burte of the same parishe the xiij[th] daye of Maye in the yere of oure Lord God 1594

	£	s	d
The Hall			
Inprimis A Byble		x	
Item A Cubborde		xx	
Item A table, A forme, & iij ioyned stooles		xiij	iiij
Item A payre of Cobbournes, A fyre shovell, potte hangers, A payre of tongues, one cusshine, & A blacke Cruse		iij	iiij
Item one platter, v pewlter disshes iiij sawcers, & halfe A doozen spoones		vj	viij
Item ij pewlter Candlestickes, A pewlter Cuppe, A pewlter chamber potte, & ij salte sellares		iiij	
The kitchen			
Item A payre of Andyorns, ij Spyttes, A gryddyorne, & A drippinge panne		iiij	
Item A lattine Strayner			xviij
Item ij kettles, & A brasse potte		xx	
Item A payre of bellowes			xij
Item A Tubbe & ij payles		iij	
Item A payre of pinsores, A hammer, A Choppinge knife, An Irone shooinge horne, & A Sheepe brande			xvj
Item iiij earthen pottes, & ij milke pannes			viij
The Chamber			
Item ij ioyned bedsteades And an other olde plaine bedsteade		xl	
Item A greate ioyned Cheste		vj	viij
Item A Coffer & A forcer		v	
Item ij bowlsters, & A flocke bowlster ij pillowes, And ij old blankettes		xiij	iiij
Item A flaskett, ij Skaines of lynnen yarne, & vj bedstaves			xviij
Item ij mattresses, A Coverlette, & A blankett		xxvj	viij
Item All the lynnen new & olde		xxxiij	iiij
Item All the apparell of the sayde Ambrose Gregorye		xl	
Item A dagger		iij	
The yarde			
Item A bill & A hatchett			xij
Item ij Coltes & An olde nagge		liij	iiij
Item iij kyne & A bullocke	vij	vj	viij
Item An olde Mare		x	
Item A stoare		iij	iiij

	£	s	d
Item An Ewe, & A lambe, & A tegge		vij	
Item A Shovell An olde sythe & ij small Spyres with other trashe		ij	vj
Item all the donge, & A Racke in [?]Grannounds[24] yarde boughte of Ambrose Butte		xx	
Item [*deletions*; *illeg.*] all thinges in the sayde yarde boughte of the sayde Ambrose Butte	xij		
Item x Acres or there aboutes of Rye & wheate iiij Acres of tilthe & iiij Acres of oates	xv		
Item in the handes of Master Asteye	vj		
And in the handes of Master Bredymane	vj		
payde by the sayde Ambrose in parte of paymente for his tyme when the leases of all that which he helde of the Queene, shoulde be taken of eyther of them againe with the reste of the tenementes			
Summa totalis	lxv	ij	ij
[*Corrected total*	*£64*	*2s*	*2d*]

[*Exhibited by the administrator at Toddington*]

Notes: Ambrose Gregorye's burial has not been found. Administration was granted on 29 May 1594 and a bond was taken (Lincs Archives, Act Book A/iii/157 and LLC ADMONS 1594/173).

147 John Rushe of Wilden, labourer made 24 May 1594

Lincolnshire Archives, INV/85/276

A true & perfecte Inventorye of all the goodes & chattelles of John Rushe of Wilden Laborer deassed made & valewed the xxiiij[th] day of Maye Anno domini 1594, by us William Wagstaffe & Abraham Smithe

	£	s	d
Imprimis six kyne valewed at	vj		
Item two yearinge bullockes three weaners valewed at		xx	
Item one horse & one colte		xiij	iiij
Item the grasse in the closes where the Cattle doe goe in Eaton Soocon		xxvj	viij
Item xxxiij[th] sheepe wherof soome be couples	iiij		
Item two sowes & tenne pigges		x	
Item the halfe parte of xij or xiij landes of otes & fecthes which Richard Rushe & he sue [*sowed*] together		viij	
Item two acres of pease otes & fecthe		xiij	iiij
Item two acres of wheate & barlye wherof one halfe acre is of Rich Rushes lande		xxvj	viij
Item two pare of harden sheetes		viij	
Item three flaxen sheetes		ix	
Item two pare of hempe harden sheetes		vj	
Item two harden table clothes		ij	vj
Item two pillowe beares & two table napkins		ij	iiij

24 Grannounds may be Granams or Granams House (Beds Archives, AD2584).

Item one Coverlet two blankettes two bolsters two pillowes a Mattresse & all his apparrell		xxvij	vj
Item two Cofers one boulting Arke one kneadinge trofe two bedsteedes & all other implementes in the chamber		viij	
Item one Cubbarde one table one forme one chare three stooles one penne one cradle two tubbes one charme one kimnell two wheeles & one barrell		xvj	iiij
Item all the paynted clothes in the house		ij	vj
Item eighte peeces of pewter three saltes one Candlesticke two kettles & two skilletes		xj	
Item one fryinge panne a speete a pare of Cobyrons a grediron a pare of potte hanginges with other emplementes		ij	
Item three bacon flicthes		iiij	
Item one axe one hoe one sawe & certayne small tooles		ij	
Item three hennes & thirteene chickens		ij	j
Item one hovell & all wood in the yarde		x	
Item one sythe & all the compasse in the yarde with all other small implementes in the house & in the yarde unnamed		ij	
Summ total	xxj	xiij	iij

[*Exhibited at Bedford on 27 May 1594*]

Notes: John Rushe was buried at Wilden on 12 May 1594.

148 Elizabeth Robinson of Ravensden, widow made 18 June 1595

Lincolnshire Archives, INV/86/328

The sheet is torn with loss of text and values in a few places.

The Inventory of the goodes & cattells of Elizabethe Robinson of Ravensden in the com' of Bedd widdow late deceased praised by Gerrard Fitzgeofferye gent, John Rawlins, Thomas Ryslelye of the same parishe & com' afore said & Gerrerd Rootam of Goldington in the com' aforsaid the xviijth daye of June 1595 Anno R[eg]ne Elizabeth xxxvijth etc

	£	s	d
In primis two akers wheate at xxxiij^{s} iiij^{d} the Aker a mountyth to	vj	vj	8
Item ix akers barlye at xxx^{s} the aker	xiij	x	
Item xij Akers peze & otes at xvj^{s}	ix	xij	
Item lx lodes of compasst		xx	
Item iij horses price	viij	[*?*]~~xiij~~	[*?*]~~viij~~
Item ij coltes price		Liij	iiij
Item ix copples at ix^{s} the copple	iiij	xix	
Item xv drie sheepe	v		
Item the halfe of iij sheepe		~~viij~~ ix	
Item iiij^{or} mylche kyne	viij		
Item ij oxen price	v		
Item ij steeres price		Liij	iiij
Item one hecfore price		xxx	
Item iiij^{or} yerelinges & the vantage		xliiij	
Item iij wenelinge calves price		xx	
Item the halffe of a ~~j~~ j swyne		xxxiij	iiij

Item the halffe of v suckinge pigges		iij	iiij
Item the halfe of xxv pullen		iiij	
Item ix stockes of bees price		xl	
Item the halfe of barly unthresshed on a hovell		xxij	vj
Item ij Quarters peze		xxxij	
Item wheate xx bushells	v		
Item ix bushells & halfe malte dimd pecke		xxxj	j
Item ix bushells barlye		xxij	vj
Item one standinge bedd in the loft with the fetherbedd mattresse boulster & ij pyllowes a thrum tester and a coverlett		xlvj	viij
Item one thrundell bedd in the same chamber a mattresse one bolster ij pillowes a blanckett & a coverlett		xx	
Item one other bedsted in the same chamber with a matrice ij bolsters & a coverlett		vj	viij
Item iij coffers in the same chamber		x	
Item one little fetherbed apperteininge to the trundell bedd		xiij	iiij
Item one Cubbert or presse in the nether chamber one standinge bedstidd a boordyd bedstid a litle coffer & one olde straw chaire		xxvj	viij
Item in the halle a table with a frame one cubbert ij litle foormes on chaire ij buffet stooles one olde cheste the hangynges by the walles with the shelves in the halle		xx	
Item ij bedstedes in the lofte over the [*b*]utrye		ij	vj
Item in the Back howse a leade a Brewinge vessell a hangyng for kettels one washe tubbe an old penne		xx	
Item in the brew howse iiijor barrells one tunnynge vessell ij coolers iij litle kymnells a mustard quarne a boultinge fatte a kymnell a mouldinge boord a cheese presse ij drincke stalles & other Implementes there		xl	
Item in the buttrye j tubbe ij little barrells j saltinge troughe a Tunninge tubbe with shelves & other Imple mentes & a drincke stalle		xiij	iiij
Item in the milckehowse one table one Coffer ij powdringevessells			

iiij^or^ cheeseboordes one Chearme			
one milcke bowle		xij	
Item in the chamber above the			
milcke howse an olde chearme			
a linnen wheele and a chese Racke		ij	
Item iij flitches & halfe of bacon		xv	
Item ij spittes brasse pott			
kettle a panne with ij Eares			
a payre of cobyrons a fryinge			
panne ij old pannes		xxvj	[?]viij
Item one bason & yewre fyve			
grate pewter dyshes ij litle			
pewter dyshes three sawsers			
[...] spoo[...]			
[...] a goblet			
[...] a pewter [...] [*c*]hamber			
[...] [*m*]orter & a pestell			
a warmyng panne ij can			
styckes a chafyng dyshe & a			
hetchell		xvj	[...]
Item one hovell next the			
barne		xx	
Item the halfe of one newe barne at the			
greate barnes ende & a			
shudd at the ende of it	~~iij~~	xxx	
Item wheate strawe and chaffe			xv
Item j shud carte with the bodye		xx	
Item ij muckcart bodies wyth			
a payre of lugg wheeles & an			
old carte body		vj	viij
Item all the wood in the yard			
& the hogges troughes		iiij	
Item halfe of the hovell next			
the ~~barne~~ lane		vj	viij
Item the Rackes in the stable			
the Rafters the boordes there			
& other Implementes there		xx	
Item ij plowes iiij^or^ shares ij			
cultors with teames ther			
unto belongynge plowes and			
plow geares & carte geares		xx	
Item a payre of Iron draughes			
for a carte		ij	vj
Item viij plowe Beames and some			
other plowe tymber		iij	iiij
Item a malte quarne		iij	iiij
Item one dragge Rake with all other			
smalle Rakes & pychforkes with sythes			
iij ladders ij Rackes ij bushelles			
j carte Rope ij hooves ij hattchelles			
j spade j skoppett j Shovell there			

	£	s	d
sackes & a wynowe clothe		x	
Item vj payre & halfe of sheetes one table clothe ij payre pillow beeres ij towells		xl	
Item one teare hempe bowlster one clothe baskett & ~~ij~~ a hand baskett			xviij
Item iij payles			xij
Somma totalis amounth	Cx	viij	ij
[*Corrected total*	*£110*	*7s*	*2d*]

[*No exhibition clause*]

Notes: Elizabeth Robinson was buried at Ravensden on 2 June 1595.

149 Raphe Briten of Sutton, yeoman and servant made 22 August 1595

Lincolnshire Archives, MISC WILLS L/4

Damaged at the right lower edge and some figures are missing.

A trow and perfecte Inventorye Indented of all such goodes & chattells as were Raphe Britens Late of Sutton in the countie of Bedf yeoman deceassed & Servante unto the right Wor[shipfu]ll John Burgoyne of Sutton aforesaid esquire made the xxijth day of Auguste in the xxxvijth yere of the Reigne of our sovereigne Ladye Elizabeth the Quenes Ma[jes]tie that now ys etc and praysed by Bartholomew Chisshull gent, John [*?*]Carr gent, John Symcottes gent & James Bramfeld yeoman as followeth

	£	s	d
Imprimis two old lyvery clokes		xxvj	viij
Item iiij paire of old venecyans		vj	viij
Item a doblett & a Jerkyn		v	
Item vij pai[*re*] of old stockinges		iij	iiij
Item iiij shirte bands		ij	
Item iiij shirtes		vj	viij
Item ij old hattes			xij
Item an aquavite bottle & a paire of knyves			viij
Item an old paire of bootes			[*?*]xvj
Item vj paire of old shoes		ij	
Item a pece of sole lether			viij
Item a cheste		iij	
Item ij other doblettes		viij	
Item an other paire of venecyans			xx
Item v old shirte bands more			xij
Item iiij shirtes more		iij	iiij
Item iij handkerchers			xij
Item a cypres hatt bande			vj
Item a sworde & a dagger		vj	[...]
Item a saddle & a snaffle		[*value illegible*]	
Summa totalis	iiij	vij	x

John [*?*]Carr [*signature*], B Chysshull [*signature*], John Symcottes [*signature*], James Bra[*m*]feld [*signature*]

[*No exhibition clause*]

Notes: Raphe Briten was buried at Sutton on 12 August 1595. He was a servant of John Burgoyne (c.1538–1605), MP for Bedford in 1563 (https://www.historyofparliamentonline.org/volume/1558-1603/member/burgoyne-john-1538-1605). Two of the appraisers, Chysshull and Symcottes, were also Burgoyne's servants and later entrusted with carrying out several provisions in Burgoyne's will (TNA, PROB 11/105/589).

150 Richard Kyrcke of Potton, labourer made 9 February 1596

Lincolnshire Archives, MISC WILLS L/6

An Inventorie of all the goods & cattell of Richard Kyrcke late of Potton in the countie of Bedford laborer deceased praised ixth day of Februarie 1595

	£	s	d
In the Hall			
Imprimis j little square table ij Longe formes iij shorter formes		ij	
Item a Joine stole & iij other with a chaire			xij
Item ij kettles of brasse & ij little kettels		iij	
Item i tubb a bowle & a paile & a spitt			xvj
Item a paire of pott hangers & pott hookes			xij
Item a painted cloth a bill an axe			xviij
Item a brass pott			xx
In the chamber			
Item a borded bedstede an owld quilte a coverlett of darnacles a bowlster & ij pillowes		iiij	
Item iij paire of shettes & ij other bowlsteres & a pillowe		ix	
Item iiij chestes ij tubbes & a powdring troughe		vj	viij
Item ij pewter dishes & a brasenn candlestick			x
Item a grete case a lether bottle & a linnen wheele		iiij	iiij
Item a scomer a friing pann a charme & other owld trash			xij
Item ij painted clothes a hatchet a sithe a forme & an owld cradle		iij	
Item a cow & a calfe & ij shetes [*sic*]		xxx	
Item an acer of rie		xiij	iiij
Summa	iiij	iij	viij

prized by Thomas Crabtree vic:, Thomas Coley, Thomas Harper, Jeames Bramfeld
[*No exhibition clause*]

Notes: Richard Kyrcke's burial has not been found. Thomas Crabtree, one of the appraisers, was vicar of Potton 1592–1618 (CCEd, Beds Archives, Fasti/1/Pott). See *301* for his inventory.

151 John Place of Eaton Socon, yeoman made 29 March 1596
Lincolnshire Archives, MISC WILLS K/115

A True Inventorye indented of all the goods & chattels of John Place of Eaton Soocon in the county of Bedford deceased made & proved by John Stocker gent, John Sparroo, John Goodwyn, Walter Wake & Richard Barcoke the xxix[th] daie of Marche in the xxxviij[th] yeare of the raigne of our soveraigne Ladye Elizabethe by the grace of god Quene of England France & Ireland defendor of the faith etc

	£	s	d
Imprimis in apparrell	vij		
The Hale			
Item in the Hale on Long table & forme a round table a bench bord a paynted clothe ij chares ij Iron barrs & pott hangings a fire shovell a paire of Toungs & fire forke		xxvj	viij
The Parler			
Item in the parler a court cubbard a square Table a littell table certaine hangings vj buffet stoles vj cuhshins on paire of Anndirons a lyttell chare		l	
The newe chamber			
Item in the newe chamber ij gyrthe beds with testers a bolster matrice ij pyllows a coverled & other things belonginge to the beds	v		
Item on great chest a trunke a coffer a wiker chare a lyttell chare		xx	
Item iij payre of flexen shetes iij paire of hempe tare iiij paire of harden	iij		
Item xx table napkins iij pillow beares ij cubbard clothes & handtowels & other Lynyn		vj	viij
The outward chamber			
Item in the outward chamber a standinge bedd a trundle bed ij fether beds ij coverleds ij blanketes ij bolster on chest & ij coffers	iiij	x	
Item a bedsted a flocke bed a bolster a coveringe a cradell		viij	
Item xl slypps of yearne		xx	
the servantes chamber			
Item iij bedsteds iij matrices iij bolsters iij coverings		xxxiij	iiij
The Buttery			
Item on yellinge Fatt & barrels a saffe vj shelves & other implementes		l	
Item ij basons & ewer & pewter platters iiij porringers iij sawcers		xiij	iiij
Item xij sylver spones	iij	vj	viij

Item ij brass potts ij kettels a posnet a frying panne a scummer a chaffinge dishe iij candelsticks		xxxv	
The kichen			
Item on copper a mashing fatt certaine tubs iij spetes a paire of Rackes iij drippinge pannes a tred a gridiron & other implementes	iiij		
Item iij iron wedges a mattocke piche forks a paire of scooles & waightes a drage rake & other rakes & shovels		xx	
Item a moulding table a kneding troffe a boulting tunne a mustard quarne with tubs & other implementes		xx	
The boltinge house & milke house			
Item on chese presse a charme iij mylke boles v chesfats iij shelves		x	
Item fyve yards of graye russet iij yards of white casy clothe		xx	
The Stable			
Item ij Geldings with sadles & bridels	vj		
Item fyve cart horses	xiiij		
Item ij Longe carts & ij paire of wheles shode & ij tumbrils	iiij	x	
Item carte gares & plowe geares & carte ropes		xxvj	viij
The yarde			
Item plowes & plowe Timber & carte Timber		l	
Item a Jynn & ropes		x	
Item building timber & firewoode	vj	xiij	iiij
Item ij hovels a role bordes Ladders rakes & other smale timber & hemp	x		
Item the cumpas or mucke		xx	
The barne			
Item in pease & chaffe		xxx	
Item Six quarters of barlye	vj		
Item certaine fullers earthe		xx	
Item vij sackes & wynno clothe		x	
The mill house			
Item ij crowes of iron xij mill bills a sawe a grindstone a hachat foure arckes iij old myll stones wymbles & timber & other implementes	iij		
Item a boat		xx	
The close			
Item xij mylche bease	xxviij		
Item viij bullocks	viij		
Item fyve bullocks being Smale	iij		
Item certaine hey	iij		
Item ix cooples & Ten other shipe	vj	vj	viij

	£	s	d
Item x hogges	iiij		
Item x henns & ij cockes		iij	iiij
Item ij geese & a gander		iij	
The feilde			
Item iij acres & a rode of wheat	iiij	x	
Item xiiij acres of tylth corne	xviij	xiij	iiij
Item x acres tylth unsowen	vj		
Item xviij[th] acres of pease & otes	xvj		
Item Six acres of breach Land unsowen		xl	
Item a Lease of the manor & Lordshipp of Eaton in possession	lx		
Item a Lease in reversion of the said manor	Cxl		
certaine goods geven to his wife as followeth			
Item a Longe table a cubbard a buffet forme ij carpets vj stoles iij cushins a cubbard clothe	iij		
Item ij fether beds with a matrice on paire of blankets ij bolsters iiij pillows ij coverleds fyve curtaynes a trundle bed a chest ij coffers & ij cushins	ix		
Item xj paire of flexen shetes fyve paire of hempe tare fyve paire of harden sheetes	vj	xiij	iiij
Item iiij pillowe beares iiij table clothes ij dosen & half of table napkins	iij		
Item iiij cubbard clothes		vj	viij
Item on great brasse pann iij brasse pots iiij kettels a chaffer ij Laten candelsticks a Latten Ladle a scummer a chaffing diche a lyttell kettell a Laver	iij	x	
Item x pewter platters xv pewter dishes vj porringers vj sawcers ij pewter potts ij pewter candlesticks ij salts a Latten basen		xl	
Item a gilded masser with a cover ij sylver Spones		xl	
Item a pynnyan clothe & pynnyan		v	
Summa totalis	CCCCxxxiij		xij
[Corrected total	*£432*	*1s*	*0d]*

[*Exhibited by Frances Place, administratrix on 23 April 1596. She made her mark beneath the exhibition clause.*]

Notes: John Place was buried at Eaton Socon on 29 March 1596. He made his will on 22 March 1596, describing himself as a yeoman and requesting burial in the church. He left his property to the child his wife Izabell was carrying if it was male, after her death. If it was female, she was to receive £20. He gave his wife the goods she brought on marriage, the goods in the best chamber (probably listed in the inventory as 'certaine goods geven to his wife as followeth'), £52 and his property for her lifetime. There were detailed provisions for his leases and other goods to go to his brothers and for paying the legacies from his father's will that he was administering. (His father, Ralph Place, was buried at Eaton Socon on 13 November 1594.) He appointed his brother Raffe as his executor and his mother Frances as administratrix to act until Raffe was 24 (he was baptised in 1576 and died in 1611). See *217* for his inventory. Probate of John Place's will was granted to his mother Frances on 23 April 1596 (Lincs Archives, MISC WILLS K/115).

152 John Colbecke of Tempsford, gentleman made 1 December 1596

Lincolnshire Archives, MISC WILLS K/130

The document is badly damaged, especially at the top, also faded and creased. Some words are illegible.

A Trewe Inventory indentyid of all [*?*]such goods Chattells debts [*?*]plate & [*?*]Mony as late were Jhon Colbeckes of Tempsford in the Countie of Bedf[or]d [*illeg.*] deceased valued & prysed by Dyve Downes, Wylliam Hale gent, & Thomas Staple yeoman [...] fyrst Daye of December in [...] xxxix[th] yeare of the Ray[*gne*] [...] of our Soveraigne Ladye Eliza[*beth*] by the grace of god of Englond Fraunce & Ireland Queene Defendrice of the fayth etc as here after doth Ensue that ys to saye

		£	s	d
In the Hale				
Inprimis one [*cup*]board A bench A forme				
Joy[*ne*]d towe hye st[*oo*]les vj lowe stooles price			xviij	
Item A Joyned Chayer price			ij	vj
Item a Carved Chest p[rice]			x	
Item A bard Chest pr[ice]			xiij	iiij
Item towe Carpits viij Cushyns stufte				
& thre unstufte pr[ice]			xx	
Item A payer of CobIrons pr[ice]			iij	iiij
Item A Candell plate pr[ice]				viij
	Summa	[*£3*][25]	vij	x
In the great parlor				
Item A great Chest of sypers pr[ice]			xxvj	viij
	Summa		xxvj	viij
In the lytle parlor				
Item A table A forme & a court Cubbord			vj	
Item a Rapier pr[ice]			iij	iiij
Item a Candell plate pr[ice]				viij
	Summa		x	
In the towe butteries				
Item viij kylderkyns towe barrells &				
other od trashe			xiij	iiij
	Summa		xiij	iiij
In the Mylke howse				
Item a powderinge Trofe & Cover A				
powderinge tubb A kymnell A Salt				
boxe A Syvinge Dishe & tongs with other				
trash			viij	
	Summa		viij	
In the kytchyn				
Item towe tables towe formes A Cubbord				
& A payer of tables pr[ice]			xiij	
Item a payer of CobIrons A fyer fork A payer				
of tongs A payr of Racks, thre pot hang				
-ings A barr of Iron to hang them on A				
fyer pan & A payer of bellowes			xij	
	Summa		xxv	

25 The pound value is missing on the document through damage and has been supplied here.

In the larder howse

Item An old Cubbord A Settill towe shelves, towe payles, A Stopp A bread grate A stone Morter & pestill with other trashe		iij	iiij
Summa		iij	iiij

In the Chamber over the larder

Item A bedsted A fetherbed A matteris A Tester payned with Damaske & velvit fyve Curtaynes therto belonginge, towe bowlsters one of Downe thother of featheres towe Downe pyllowes A Coverlet of Orase & towe white blankyts	iiij		
Item A levery Cubbord A waynskott Chayer towe Cushyns one of Needel worke thother of Turkey & A Carpit pr[ice]		v	
Summa	iiij	v	

In the Chamber over the kytchyn

Item A bedsted A feather bed a boulster A Coverlet & towe blankyts A Tester of saye & thre Curtaynes An old payntyd [*painted*] hanginge, & a Matteris of Jack stufe		xxvj	viij
Summa		xxvj	viij

In the parlor Chamber

Item a Coverlet A boulster towe pyllowes, towe blankyts thre Curtaynes of saye & the Chamber hangd with saye		xviij	
Item towe great Chests, one bard with Iron towe lytle spruse Coffers		xx	
Item A Cubbord the Cloth & Cushyn to yt with an other lytle Cushyn		vj	viij
Item thre payer of fyne sheets		xx	
Item ix payer & an od one of Course		xxx	
Item A Table Cloath thre towels & fower napkyns of Diaper Damaske		xv	
Item fyve pyllowebears tenn Napkyns of flaxen thre flaxen Table Cloathes & fower Course table Cloathes		xv	vj
Summa	vj	v	ij

In the Clossit

Item one presse one Coffer & A table		vj	viij
Summa		vj	viij

In the Chamber next the parlor Chamber

Item A bedsted A fetherbed A boulster A Coverlet A blankyt A Tester A Matteris		xviij	
Summa		xviij	

In the Mayds Chaymner

Item A fetherbed A boulster A pyllowe & towe blankyts		x	
Summa		x	

In the Chamber over the buttery

Item A presse A fetherbed A boulster A pyllowe towe blankits & A byll			xviij	
	Summa		xviij	

In the Aple Chamber

Item A Coffer				xviij
Item thre Dublets A fryse Jerkyn A spanishe leather Jerkyn thre payer of britches towe hatts fower payre of stockings & towe Clookes			xxx	
Item towe shirts			iiij	
Item A Clooke bag				xviij
	Summa		xxxvij	

In the stoore Chamber

Item Lead & wayts			xij	
Item towe smale potts of brasse & a skyllet			viij	
Item thre other old broken brasse pots			v	
Item one other great brase pott			vj	
Item fyve spytts			iiij	
Item iiij^or old kettels			iiij	
Item A brason pot with one eare or Chafer				xviij
Item A brason Morter & pestill			ij	vj
Item thre old Warmeinge panns one without A Cover			iij	iiij
Item one Drippinge pann & towe frieng pans			iij	
Item towe great & thre smale Candelsticks of Lattyn			ij	
Item towe old Chafindishes towe skymers, towe payer of old AndIorns & a Crowe of Iron			iiij	
Item towe bags of hops			iij	iiij
Item A Tennon sawe towe Iron Wedges old hynges fower lether bottels & fower of stone, Musturd seed, A bag of Nayles, one old peece, Onyons An Iron peele A planke towe payer of Skoles & beames An Earthern platter tynd thre peas -howks A plowe Cheane old Iron & other od trashe			xiij	iiij
	Summa	iij	xij	
Item towe great Chardgers xx^ti platters of A lesser sort, ten Dishes of A lesser agayne, thre frute Dishes thre porringeres ix Sawsers A Cullander thre pye plates A bason & Ewer A great pewter pott thre salt selleres & thre Chamber potts			xlij	
	Summa	v	xiiij	

		£	s	d
In the brewe howse				
Item thre great brasse pans fower lesser towe basons of brasse & an old kettill			xlij	
Item thre trevits			iij	
Item A Mashe tub A yealdinge tub A kymnell A Tunnell A hearsyve A knedinge trofe A boultinge Ark A Drie trofe thre old buck tubs & other trashe			xiij	iiij
Item thre old sacks & a bagg				xij
	Summa		lix	iiij
In the Graynerie				
Item fower bushells of peas			viij	
	Summa		viij	
In the hen howse				
Item towe old peens towe tubs & other trashe				xij
Item over agaynst the Dore in the yard A querne or Milstone				vj
	Summa			xviij
In the kyll howse				
Item A Cheese presse A mustard querne A wollen wheele with other trashe			iiij	
	Summa		iiij	
In the Malt howse				
Item A payer of unshod wheles			x	
Item fower Ladders			ij	vj
Item towe Cart ladders				viij
Item An Axe				vj
Item all the Tymber squard & unsquard with all the boords wood & other trashe		iij	vj	x
	Summa	iiij		vj
In the Hovell in the Clos				
Item towe Cart bodies & all the tymber within yt & on bothe syds yt		iij		
	Summa	iij		
In the Hovill in the home yard & yard & in the Dovehowse Close				
Item towe Racks & all the tymber & other wood therin & in the same yard & in the Dovehowse Close			xxvj	viij
	Summa		xxvj	viij
In the Oxe howse				
Item A payer of wooden harrowes A well whele with all the wood planks boords hurdles & Tymber therin			xl	
	Summa		xl	
In the Haye howse				
Item Haye ther			xl	
	Summa		xl	
In the further stable				
Item a Mattoke, a spade, an old well buket, A Rowle A Ratt trappe A				

bynge [*?bin*] A pyckforke A blacke byll with all the wood & Tymber In & over the same & over the lytle Chamber by yt			xx	
	Summa		xx	

In the store howse or worke howse

Item towe old Chests an old Drag Raak head			xij	
Item Lyme ~~Summa xx~~s			ij	
Item plowe Tymber & Cart Tymber lath & other wood & Tymber		iij	vj	
	Summa	iiij		

In thother stable & Chafe howse

Item A syve A seed Cod A trofe & A shovell				xij
Item A browne baye geldinge		iij	vj	viij
	Summa	iij	vij	viij

In the Corne barne

Item A skreene A bushell thre pyckforks A Rydle A fann A shovell towe lytle ladderes			vj	viij
Item Rye unthrasht			xxxiij	iiij
Item Barly unthrasht		vj	xiij	iiij
Item pease unthrasht		ix		
Item haye ther			xx	
	Summa	xviij	xiij	iiij

In the Ortchyard

Item A grynston hangyd				xij
	Summa			xij

In the yard

Item thre bease & A Calf		vij		
Item ij Sowes ij shoots & viij wening pigs			xxvj	viij
Item xij hynes A Cocke v Ducks & a gander			vj	viij
Item the Cumpase			x	
	Summa	ix	iij	iiij

The plate & Mony

Item A Goblet & A salte of Silver & gilt & xij Silver Spones		vij		
Item in Mony		x		
	Summa	xvij		

Detts sperat

Of Thomas Cowper of Harradon in the ~~Countie~~ parishe of Carrington in the Countie of bedf[or]d yeoman as Appearith by A statute & the Defeasaunce		lxxv		
	Summa totalis	Clxxiiij		xx
	[*Corrected total at least*	*£177*	*12s*	*4d*]

Debts oweinge

Inprimis to the said Thomas Cooper as ys Manyfestid by witnes			xxv	viij
Item to widdowe Baker of Tempsford			xx	
Item to Edward Armes of the same			vj	viij
Item to Jhon Tansley of Potten			xij	

	£	s	d
Item to the Cunstables for the subsidie & fiftene & A levie for soldiers[26]		v	x
Item the Chardgis of his buriall as Appereth by the bills of Accompt	vij	x	ij
Summa	xj		iiij
Summa totalis			[*blank*]

Dyve Downes [*signature*], William Hale [*signature*], Thomas Staple [*signature*]
[*Exhibited by Dive Downes, administrator before Dr John Belley on 9 December 1596. The exhibition clause was signed by William Lowe, deputy registrar and notary public.*]

Notes: John Colbecke's burial has not been found. He was described as a gentleman in a deed of 1599 (Beds Archives, BS1293).

153 William Barcock of Little Staughton, husbandman made 17 May 1597
Lincolnshire Archives, MISC WILLS K/104

The Inventorye of all the goods and Chattells of William Barcock late of Little Stoughton disceased prised and valued the xvij[th] day of May Anno Domini 1597 by us John Scott, John Newcome, John Castoll, Richard Prior

	£	s	d
Inprimis in the hall one table one Cubbord stooles and other Implements		xxx	
Item in the parlour on Featherbed and the furniture one table one Cheste with other Implements	v		
Item in the servants Chamber one bedsted and furniture with other Implements		xl	
Item in the Buttry barells tubs and other Implements		x	
Item the brasse pewter speets and other Implements	iij[27]	~~lx~~	
Item foure and thirty payre of flexen sheets and harden, sixe table Clothes, ij Cubbord Clothes with other parcells of linen	viij		
Item Grane thresshed and other provison for housekepinge		xl	
Item his apparell		xxx	

26 The subsidy, fifteenth and levy were taxes granted by Parliament in 1593. The subsidy was a tax on goods and land spread over four annual payments. The fifteenth was to be paid in four unequal instalments annually from November 1593. The levy was a tax for the relief of soldiers maimed in the service of the Queen and state. It was a weekly charge imposed on parishes and payable at county quarter sessions. The payments recorded here may have been those currently due or arrears (M. Jurkowski, C. L. Smith and D. Crook, *Lay Taxes in England and Wales 1188–1688*, PRO Publications, 1998. Public Record Office Handbook no. 31, p. 165–7).

27 The value has been corrected and is in the same colour ink as the exhibition clause. The correction is in two stages. To the original value of 10s has been added fifty, then the new value of 60s has been crossed out and £3 substituted.

Item vi horses and Coltes	xij		
Item viij bease	xij		
Item ix bullockes	vi		
Item xij sheepe	iij		
Item ix store piggs		xx	
Item the Pullane		iij	
Item Cartes and Cartgeares plows and plowgears	v		
Item hovells and wood in the yard		xxx	
Item the lease of the Farme		xx	
Item in the field xxvi acres of barley and wheat	xxvi		
Item xxvi acres of pease and oates	xvij	iij	iiij
Item parte of another Cropp of grayne at Dovolhoe uppon the ground with some other household stuffe and ~~some~~ other Implements	v		
Summa Totalis	Cxiij	xvi	iiij
[*Corrected total*	*£113*	*6s*	*4d*]

[*Exhibited by Elenor Barcock, executrix, on 20 May 1597*]

Notes: William Barcock's burial has not been found.

154 William Hobeme of Sutton, labourer made 23 June 1597

Lincolnshire Archives, MISC WILLS K/101

A trew and perfecte Inventorye Indented of all the goodes & Cattelles which were late William Hobemes of Sutton in the countye of Bedf Laborer deceassed made the xxiij[th] day of June in the xxxix[th] yere of the Reigne of our sovereigne Ladye Elizabethe the Quenes Ma[jes]ty that now ys etc And praysed by Nicholas Evered gent:, John Symcottes gent, and Bartholomew Gyllman husbandman as followeth etc

	£	s	d
Imprimis Lij shepe pryce	x		
Item ij bease pryce	iij		
Item wolle pryce		v	
Item ij olde chestes pryce		ij	
Item a bedstede & a plancke pryce		ij	
Item all his apparell pryce		vj	viij
Item certaine cloth for shirtes [*written in a different ink and hand*]			[*blank*]
Som	xiij	xv	viij

Nicholas Everrarde [*signature*], John Symcott [*signature*], Bartylmew Gylman [*signature*]
[*Exhibited by the executor, George Robinson, on 27 June 1597*]

Notes: William Hobeme was buried at Sutton on 18 June 1597. He made his will on 17 June 1597. He gave £10 and his two beast to his master, who is unnamed; 16 sheep to four named people; a horseskin and clothes to two others; and forgave another his debts. He appointed George Robinson his executor (Lincs Archives, MISC WILLS/K/101).

155 Edward Turner of Milton Ernest, gentleman made 30 September 1597
Lincolnshire Archives, INV/90/134
The end of the inventory is creased and some words and figures are obscured.

An Inventorie of all the goodes & Chattells of Edward Turnor of Milton Ernes in the countie of Bedford gent Deceased taken the 30 of September Anno 1597 by Robert Sutton Clarke Francys Lynforde George Gale and Anthonye [*?*]Chyfelde

	£	s	d
In primis his wearing Apparel	iij		
In the hall			
Item a long table, a square table ij Joyned formes, one cheare viij Joyned stooles, one Liverey table, iij carpet clothes		xl	
Item vj Cushins		v	
In the butterie			
Item a Barrell, a fatt, a Stopp a paire of scoales, a paire of Andyrons & other Implementes		xx	
In the Chamber over the hall			
Item a truss Bedd, ij fether bedes ij bolsters, ij pillowes, a cover lidd, a blancket, a straw bedd curtaynes vallances and a trund le bedd	vij		
Item a square table, a bedforme ij cheares, a liverey cubborde & a warming pan		xl	
Item ix Todd of wooll	ix		
In the upper Chamber			
a Bedsteade & other thinges there		xxvj	viij
Item & other fether bed, a bolster a quylt & a paire of sheetes		xx	
Item ij dosen Cart cloutes & other Iron		viij	
Over the kytchin			
first one truss bedd & an other bedd a press & iij chestes		xxxiij	4
Item halfe a Quarter maulte ij chese Rackes, a barrell and other Implementes		xx	
Item xx paire of harden sheetes ij paire flaxen sheetes ij Dosen of table napkyns, iiij pillow beares & v table clothes	v	x	
In the kytchin			
Item a cubboard, a pen, a table a forme with other Implcmentes		xl	
Item iiij platters, vj puter dishes viij porringers, ij fruit dishes			

ij saltes iiij Tuns, v chamber pottes, ij basons		xx	
Item iiij brass pottes		l	
Item vj kettles		xxx	
Item pothangers, Racks ij spittes iiij candlestickes, spyce morter iij paire of Andyrons & the chym ney barr		xvj	viij
Item ij boolting arkes iij tubbes a kymnell, a chearme, a kne ading trough a table, a dragg nett with other Implementes		xl	
Item ij dragg Rackes		vj	
Item a chese press mylke booles		~~vj~~ viij	~~viij~~
In the Iner butterie			
Item iiij barrells a salting trough with other Implementes		xxv	viij
Item one gelding	iiij		
Item v horses & coltes	xvij		
Item vij^{xx} & xviij shepe	xl		
Item xij melch beastes	xxiiij		
Item ij oxen	v		
Item ix Bullockes	xij		
Item vij calves	iij	x	
Item x hogges	v		
Item iij shodd cartes	v		
Item cart geares & plowe geares plowes & plowe geares [*sic*] plowe tymber and cart tymber		xl	
Item Tymber & other wood about the yarde	iiij		
Item a framed hovell with pale about it		xl	
Item hay	x		
Item the Cropp	lxx		
Item the tylth lande & pease Lande	xiiij		
Item all the poultry		x	
Somme is ij hundred iij score & fyve poundes & x^{s} iiij^{d}	265	10	4
[*Corrected total*	*£264*	*19s*	*4d*]

[*Exhibited at Bedford on 27 May 1598*]

Notes: Edward Turner was buried in Milton Ernest on 27 September 1597 as Edmund Turner, gentleman. The appraiser, Robert Sutton, was vicar of Milton Ernest, 1576–1611 (CCEd, Beds Archives, Fasti/1/MiltonE).

156 Robert Stanton of Pertenhall, yeoman made 20 October 1597
Lincolnshire Archives, MISC WILLS K/102

A treue and perfect Inventarye of all and singuler suche goodes & Cattell Chattells & debtes as did belong unto Robert Stanton late of Pertinhall in the Countie of Bedford yeoman At the tyme of his death

		£	s	d
Inprimis in the Hall A table with the frame, ij formes, a Rownd table certayne Chaires stooles Cushins paynted cloathes & other smale thinges to the value of			xxxiij	iiij
Item in the Parlor & Chambers iij Joyned Beadsteades, iij bourden beadsteades, iij Fetherbeades, ij mattresses certayne Coverlettes blankittes & other cloathes & furniture for beadding		xxvij		
Item certayne sheetes, pillowbeares, Tableclothes napkyns & other smale peces of Lynin		xiiij		
Item A long table in the parlor A long table A Cubbard certayne stooles Coffers paynted Cloathes & other smale thinges		vij		
Item in the seller over the hall a litl Cubbard ij Chestes & a Chaire			xxx	
Item the other chambers certayne Coffers paynted cloathes & other smale thinges			xiij	iiij
Item certayne wooll		v		
Item towe teare & new lynin & woollyn cloath		vij	vj	viij
Item in the Butterye An Alestall a Safe certayne Barrells shelfeboardes & other smale thinges			xxvj	viij
Item in the kitchin certayne Brasse Pewter speetes Cobyrons, potthangles & other smale implementes of yron		x		
Item a table a greate Arke a Cubard under the stayres An Ambrye & other smale thinges in the kytchin			xl	
Item certayne Butter, Cheese, Bacon & Apples		x	x	
Item certayne shelves mylkboales tubbes and other implementes in the mylkhowse, garner and Backhowse			l	
	Summa	xC	x	
Item in the yard & abroad, viij myltch kyne, one [?]fall Cowe, iij steres, ij heyfordes iij bulls, iiij weanlyng Calves		xxxij		
Item v horses ij geldinges, ij Coultes		xxxvj		
Item xlix sheepe		xiiij		
Item v hogges, A boare, A Sowe and vj pigges		iiij		
Item certayne geese duckes & other pullyn			xx	
Item viij Beehyves			xl	

	£	s	d
Item certayne haye & Corne	xC		
Item certayne hovells Ladders, Tymber & fyrewood	vij		
Item certayne Cartes & Cartgeares Plowghes and Ploughgeares	vj	x	
Item A lease for ij yeares yett to come of A Closse called Stockin & xxij^{t} Acr of Land	xij		
Item A lease for vj yeares to come of on Acr di of Land called [*?*]Wilgills		x	
Item All his Apparell	~~vj~~ v		
Summa	CCx		
Summa totalis	CCC	x	

Seene & praysed the xxth daye of October 1597 by Henry Walker, Anthony Gore, William Mancy [*signature*] & others
[*No exhibition clause*]

Notes: Robert Stanton was buried at Pertenhall on 30 September 1597. He made his will (which is severely damaged) in September 1597. He gave his wife Joan his house and land until his son John reached the age of 20; the lease of 22 acres and the lease of Wilgills from Corpus Christi College, Oxford to the use of his son John; and all his animals and grain to his wife. He gave 20s to two of his uncles and directed his wife to pay £26 which he owed to his brother for his portion. He directed his wife to bring up their son and when he reached 20, she was to deliver all the agricultural equipment, that year's crops, and some of the furniture. He gave the residue to his wife and appointed her executrix. She was granted probate at Godmanchester on 21 October 1597 (Lincs Archives, MISC WILLS/K/102).

157 Thomas Grenheffe of Blunham — made 16 December 1597

Lincolnshire Archives, MISC WILLS K/95

This inventory is faded and badly damaged. A large portion on the right side is missing. Some text and many values have been lost.

An Inventory of the goodes and Catell of Thomas Grenheffe of Blunham in the Countie [*of*] Bedf who d[*ecea*]sed the xvjth of Decembrr 15[*97*]

	£	s	d
Imprimis in the hall one table ij formes one bench one Cobarde iiij Chares vj stoles			[...]
Item xj Cusshines abenche coveringe with paynted [...]			[...]
Item in the Chamber abedsted amatris ij fetheb[*eds*] apare of blanket acoverlyd one bolster ij pillowes with [*?*]seaye [...] [*?cur*]tynes to the same beade belonginge	iij		
Item one Cowbard one great Chest one table aforme ij Chares ij buffet stoles		30	
Item another Chambre abedsted amatris aflocbed atrundelbed ~~one~~ 4 cofers with hanginges in the same		xl	
Item another loft abedsted amatris acoverlid iij Chestes		xlvj	8
Item an olde bedsted sadell brydel with other stuffe		x	

Item in the kichinge aboulting arke with other trene vesselles with aturned casse		xiij	4
Item in brasse pewter and lattine vessell	v		
Item j pouderinge trofe and another with certyne barryles and other bruinge vesseles		33	iiij
Item one framed hovill with the fire wode tymbr squared and ruffe with tymbr sawne and and [*sic*] unsawen and certyne bord			[...]
Item spites cobirons Jackes fyer shovles [...]			[...]
pot hokes pothangeles grydirone ii [...]			[...]
Item xviijth pare of shetes iiij [...]			[...]
viij pilowberes with xij napk[...]			[...]
Item the carte and carte g[...]			[...]
ploughe geres with all mann[...]			[...]
Item plough-tymbre and [...]			[...]
at another howse beinge			[...]
Item barleye unthrosshed by estim[...]			[...]
Item in whet and rye			[...]
Item in haye valued at			[...]
Item by estimation in whete & rye sowne & [...]			[...]
Item in tylthe and brache lande			[...]
Item vj horse & ij Coltes			[...]
Item vj mylche besse ~~v stores and heffers &~~ [...]			[...]
Item one sowe ij hoges vj stores			[...]
Item vj stockes of beese			[...]
Item vj sylvere spones			[...]
Item xx lambes v olde shepe	vij		
Item in pulline to the value of		iiij	
Item iiij fliches of bakon		xx	
Item the dead mans apparrill	iij		
Item ij bylles ore boundes for the deate of	ix	vj	
Summa totalis one hundrethe	lxxiij	xiij	8

prysed by Larranc Hill baylife, George Cowper, Robart Garner, Thomas Samuell
[*No exhibition clause*]

Notes: Thomas Grenheffe was buried at Blunham on 16 December 1597, as Thomas Greenleaf and described as 'senex'. Agnes Greenleaf, widow was buried on 20 December 1597.

158 William Ridge of Southill, vicar — made 3 January 1598

Lincolnshire Archives, LCC 1598/154

The trewe Inventorye of the good and cattles of William Ridge late minister of Southill in the Countie of Bedd deceased taken the thirde daye of Januarye Anno Domini 1598 regnique Domine nostre Elizabethe die gra[tie] Anglie Franc' et Hibernie regine fidei defensor etc quadragesimo and praysed by William Cumberland, Richard Carrington, Thomas Barbar and others

	£	s	d
In primis xxij bookes in folio with forty six of an other sort with certaine paper bookes and			

other ~~smale~~ old bookes of smale valure	v		
Item five brasse pottes and a chafer eight kettles greate and little twoe skillettes with a warminge panne and twoe candlestickes		lij	
Item one charger, six platters one bason, six old pewter dishes, five porringers, eight sawcers, one pewter candlesticke and three saltes, three drippinge pannes, and a lattin morter, twoe chamber pottes, and twoe dozen of spones with three drinkinge cuppes		xxiij	iiij
Item twoe spittes, twoe greate rackes, twoe paire of Andirones, on iron plate to laye before the Fier, twoe gridirons, three paire of pott-hangers, a Fryinge panne, a drippinge panne, a tostinge plate and twoe trivettes		xvj	
Item certaine glasse for windowes with a casement		x	
Item twoe Fattinge hogges and twoe stores		l	
Item seaven milch kien and twoe bullockes	xvij		
Item nyne sheepe	iij		
Item certaine woode valued at		xxvj	viij
Item one horse valued at		xxx	
Item a parcell of haye		xxx	
Item twelve bushelles of wheate	iij		
Item twoe standinge Beddes with twoe trundle beddes unto them, ~~fowre pillowes~~ three canopie bedsteades and three other plaine bedes		l	
Item twoe Featherbedes, twoe bolsters unto them fowre pillowes, two coverlettes, five paire of blankettes, one mattresse, and a flockbed & twoe flocke bolsters	iiij	iij	iiij
Item twelve paire of sheetes vz iiijor of flax and the rest[28] of tare of hempe and ~~tw~~ towe	iiij		
Item twelve tableclothes, seaven dozen of tablenapkinnes, three towelles, iiijor paire of holland pillowbeares and eight paire of flaxen and lockeram	iij	xiij	iiij
Item a cubbard and fowre chestes a deske with fowre boxes		xxx	
Item Five chaires		xiij	iiij
Item all his waringe apparrell as gownes dublettes, cotes, hose etc	iij		
Item certaine painted clothes with tenne cushinnes		xij	
Item six framed tables with a livery cubbard		xxxiij	iiij
Item three Formes, xij Joyned stoles, seaven dores, xxjtie bordes, certaine quarters and trestles		xl	

28 *the rest* has been changed from *three* in a different ink.

	£	s	d
Item a bruinge panne, iiij^{or} hogsheades a chese presse, milke boules, tubbes, mealekimnelles with other implementes		xl	
Item eleven hundred lath and half, eight plowe beames, vj extries, and twoe dozen of smale peces vz copsies, neckes and shares		xxvj	viij
Summa totalis	lxvij		

[*Exhibited at Bedford on 27 May 1598*]

Notes: William Ridge was buried at Southill on 28 December 1597. He was curate of Linslade, Bucks, in 1585 and vicar of Southill from 1586 until his death (CCEd, Beds Archives, Fasti/1/South).

159 Edward Slowe of Studham, husbandman

made 3 February 1598

Lincolnshire Archives, INV/90/146

An Inventory of the goodes & chattells of Edwarde Slowe late of Stodham in the countie of Bedd husbandman deceased, prised & valued the thirde day of February 1597 by George Slowe, Thomas Portres, William Pace

	£	s	d
Imprimis all his apparrell & the mony in his purse	iiij		
Item one cubborde, one table, ij chaires iij ioyne stooles, brasse pewter, & other implements in the hall	v		
Item five bedstedds with their furniture	v	xiij	iiij
Item sixe chests and all his ~~a~~ Apry ware	iij	vj	viij
Item iiij^{or} todds of wooll	iiij		
Item one quarne, a powdringe trowghe, five tubbes, mattockes, shovells & other implements there	iij		
Item all his bacon		xl	
Item five horses and a colte with their furniture	xxv		
Item plowghes, carts wheeles & harrowes	viij		
Item five bease & a bullocke	[*?*]v		
Item one fatte bullocke & two fattinge hoggs	v		
Item viij store hogges		lviij	iiij
Item his powltry		x	
Item his woodde		xl	
Item his wheate in the barne	xl		
Item barly, pease, oats tilles & teares	xxiiij		
Item wheate on the grownde	xliiij		
Item lxx sheepe	xxxvj	vj	viij
Summa	214	10	
[*Corrected total*	*£219*	*15s*	*0d*]

[*Exhibited at Dunstable on 30 May 1598*]

Notes: Edward Slowe was buried at Studham on 7 January 1598.

160 Thomas Charge of Toddington, labourer made February 1598
Lincolnshire Archives, INV/90/148

An Inventory indented ~~made~~ of all the good & Chattells of Thomas Charge of Tuddington in the County of Bedf laborer late disceased; as they were vewed & prised by Thomas Rainolde sen, Thomas Hill, Richard Bowstred & Thomas Raynoldes Jun made the [*blank*] daie of February in the yeare of our Lord god 1597

	£	s	d
In primis all the goods in the chamnber [*sic*]: as bedding & such like is prised at		xx	
Item one brasse pot		ij	
Item one kettle		ij	
Item one panne		v	
Item two little kettles			xviij
Item five peawghter dishes			xx
Item ij sawcers, one salte, & two candlestickes			vj
Item an old aumbrey			viij
Item a table, a forme & a benche bourde			xvj
Item a old whele			vj
Item a frying panne			iiij
Item ij [*?*]bolles & a bushell			xij
Item a paier of pothookes and hangers, a gredeyron, a paire of cobyrons & a spit			xvj
Item ij chaiers & a skimmer			ix
Item painted cloathes			iiij
Item a chesfat, a spade, a bill, & a axe			xiij
Item for fier wood		ij	
Item a treen platter & peaughter platter			iiij
Item an heifer & a calfe		xl	
Item an old cowe		xxx	
Item a yeareling bullock		x	
Item an acre of beanes & theches		x	
Item a leace		xx	
Summa totalis	vij	xij	iiij
Allocant[ur] d[i]c[t]a deb[i]ta Joannes [*?*]Belley[29]			
Item the debtes that he lefte to paye were	iij	vj	viij

[*Exhibited by the administratrix at Dunstable on 30 May 1598*]

Notes: Thomas Charge was buried at Toddington on 7 February 1598.

29 This line and the note of exhibition have been written in the same hand.

161 William Storer of Eaton Socon, husbandman made 30 March 1598
Lincolnshire Archives, MISC WILLS K/109

The Inventarie of all & singuler the goodes Cattells and debtes of William Storer husbandman deceased within the Towne of Eaton in the Countye of Bedford prased the xxx[th] daye of March in the Fourtieth yere of the Raygne of our soveraygne Ladie Elizabeth by the grace of god Quene of England France & Irelande defender of the fayth etc by John Goodwine, John Stocker & Thomas Thodie as hereafter followeth

	£	s	d
In the Hall			
Fyrst one Cubbard		vj	viij
Item A Table & a Forme		iiij	
Item iij[red] Cheeres			xx
Item Paynted Cloathes		iij	
In the Kytchine			
Item iiij[or] brasse pannes		x	
Item a brasse Pott & a little Kittle		ij	
Item ij Spittes and a ~~brass~~ Fryeng panne			xx
Item An old Cubbard & A Table		iiij	
Item iiij[or] Tubbes		ij	vj
Item A Kymnell A bolting Arke & A Bushell		iij	
In the Chamber over the Kytchine			
Item A Bedsted & A Coverlet		ij	
In the Chamber next the Hall			
Item ij Bedstedes & ij Flockbeddes		x	
Item ij Bolsters & ij Pyllowes		v	
Item ij Blancketes & ij Keverlletes		xiij	iiij
Item ij Coffers		iij	iiij
Item A Beere barrell			xviij
Item paynted Cloathes		vj	viij
Lynnen			
Item A payer off Flexon sheettes A payer of hemp Tayer ij payer of hurden		xx	
Item A Table Cloath A Towell, ij Pyllowbeeres iiij[or] Napkines		vj	viij
Pewter			
Item vj pewter platters iij old dishes ij Sawsers iij Candelstickes, ij Pewter Saltes		viij	
Apparell			
his Apparrell		xx	
Cattell			
Item a Cowe & a Calf		xlvj	
Debtes			
Debtes owing to hym	lxxxix		
Summe is	lxxxxix	xj	
[*Corrected total*	*£98*	*1s*	*0d*]

[*Exhibited by John Storer, one of the executors, before Dr John Belley on 22 April 1598. John Storer made his mark below the exhibition clause.*]

Notes: William Storer was buried at Eaton Socon on 23 March 1598. He made his will on 3 March 1598. He forgave his eldest son John £21 which he owed to the testator. He gave 10s each to John's four children at age 21; and cheese-making equipment and a woollen wheel to

John's wife, Elizabeth, and the gallon brass kettle to their daughter, none of which were listed in the inventory. He gave £30 to son William, £23 of which he owed the testator. He gave £24 and a red cow and her calf to son Phillip (both listed); and £3 10s, a linen wheel and a brass pot (neither of which are listed) to his daughter and 10s each to her three children. He gave the rest of his household stuff to the two younger sons and appointed the eldest son, John and his son-in-law as residual legatees and executors. Probate was granted to John Storer by Dr John Belley on 22 April 1598 (Lincs Archives, MISC WILLS/K/109).

162 Gerrard Fittes Geffreie of Ravensden, gentleman made 8 April 1598
Lincolnshire Archives, INV/90/133

The inventorie of all the goodes and cattelles of Gearard Fittes Geffreie of Ravensden in the countie of Bedd gen' deceased praised by John Rawlen yoman, John Bigge yoman & Christopher Atkinson husbandman the viij[th] daie of Aprill 1598

	£	s	d
In primis ix kine price	xx		
Item three yerlinge calves price	iij		
Item fowre wenyd calves price		xl	
Item xlviij sheepe of the which x of them be yewis & lambes price	xxj	xij	
Item a horse & a coulte price	vj		
Item vij shotes price		xl	
Item geese & all other pullen price		x	
Item one Aker wheate & ix Akers barlie	xiij	vj	8
Item x Akers peese price	vj	xiij	iiij
Item xj bushelles wheete price		lij	
Item xiiij bushelles barlei price		xl	
Item xx[ti] bushelles peaze price		xl	
Item one shuyd carte and one bare carte	iij		
Item plowe & plowe geres & carte geres & other plowe geres with a muckecarte		xx	
Item one hovell price	iij		
Item seaven boorde price		vj	viij
Item all other fyre wood & tymber price	iij		
Item in the chamber above the halle iiij[or] bedstedes with the furniture	iiij		
Item the painted clothes with other furniture in the same chamber and iiij[or] chestes		xxvj	viij
Item vij paire sheetes iij table clothes one of dyaper ij towelles vij pillowe beeres xij napkyns price	iiij	6	8
Item iiij[or] blankettes & a coverlett		xx	
Item ij dubblettes ij paire hosen & ij paire stockinges price		xl	
Item in the parlore one Fetherbedd a standinge Beddes with pillowes boulsters coveringes iij chestes ij blanketes & the hanginges there price	v		

Item in the nether chamber on bedd stedd a mattres & all other furniture		xx	
Item in halle xxvj peces pewter vj canstyckes a salte a brasse morter & pestell		xl	
Item ij cubbertes a longe table over a frame		xxxiij	iiij
Item a benche boorde a forme cheyres & stooles with the payntyd clothes		xxvj	8
Item in the keachyn all the treene ware spyttes cobbyornes & all other implementes there		xl	
Item v flyches bacon price		xxv	
Item the The [*sic*] Lease Remaynynge	lx		
Item haye pryce	iij		
Summa totales on hundred	Lxxxiij		
[*Corrected total*	*£181*	*19s*	*0d*]

[*Exhibited by the executrix at Bedford on 27 May 1598*]

Notes: Gerrard Fittes Geffreie's burial has not been found, neither at Ravensden nor elsewhere. He made his will on 30 January 1598, requesting burial at Thurleigh. He left the remainder of the lease of his land in Ravensden and half his sheep and beasts to his son Thomas, provided that he paid an annual sum to the testator's wife and the legacies to his children. He left his wife Anne the house and its contents. She was the residual legatee and executrix and proved the will before Dr Belley at Bedford on 27 May 1598 (Lincs Archives, LCC WILLS 1597–8/212).

163 Timothy Warde of Wilden, husbandman made 12 April 1598
Lincolnshire Archives, INV/90/130

An Inventarie made by Thomas Peete, Abraham Smith, Stephan Smithe and Edmunde Croe of all the moveable goodes that Timothye Warde husbandman of Wilden in the countye of Bedd late deceassed had the xij[th] day of Aprill & in the yeare of our Lorde god a thousand fyve hundred nyntye eighte as followeth

	£	s	d
Imprimis seventeene acres of wheate priced at	xxij	xiij	iiij
Item thirtie acres of barlye priced at	xxx		
Item fyftye acres of pease & oates priced at	xxv		
Item the barlye in the barne priced at	vij		
Item a canshe of pease at		xxvj	viij
Item a litle haye at		xx	
Item tenne mylche bease at	xix		
Item sixe bullockes priced at	viij		
Item fyve yearlinges at	iij	vj	viij
Item three weaninge calves at		xx	
Item fourtye seven sheepe at	x		
Item seven horses at	xviij		
Item eighte hogges at		l	
Item three longe cartes & two tumbrels priced at	vij		

Item three plowes there furniture plowtimber plowe geares carte geares carte ropes harrowes & dragrakes priced at		xxx	
Item hovell laders tymber fyrewoode one role hurdels cribbes & hoggestroves at	iiij		
Item one croe of iron one axe one hacthet one bylle sythes fetters & leastaves		vj	viij
Item all the pullen at		iiij	
In the halle & chambers			
Imprimis the glasse & waynescotte excepted as standers to the howse			
Item one Cubbarde two tables two formes two Chayres & stooles at		xxx	
Item one Cubbard clothe curtaynes & cushens at		x	
Item two beddes two Chestes one Lyverye cubbarde one fetherbedde one bolster two pyllowes one coverlet three blankettes and two matrisses priced at	vj		
Item one chayre & fyve curtaynes at		xx	
Item twentie pare of sheetes tenne pillowebeares syxe boardeclothes two dozen of table napkines and hand towels priced at	vj	xiij	viij
In the litle chamber			
Imprimis all the woollen clothes at		xxvj	viij
Item two beddes with theire furniture & two Chestes at	iij		
Item the bruinge vessell & other thinges in the butterye at		xxvj	viij
Item a Maulte quearne with other thinges at		x	
Item in the kytchen a table a cubbarde penne with other tryfles at		vj	viij
Item in the Mylkehouse the mylkevessell priced at		iij	iiij
Item the brasse pewter spittes andyrenes pothookes & pothangles at		l	
Item paynted clothes		x	
Item his apparrell priced at		l	
Summa totale	Clxxxix	xiiij	iiij

Thomas Peete, Abraham Smithe, Edmunde Croe, Stephan Smithe
[*Exhibited at Bedford on 27 May 1598*]

Notes: Timothy Warde was buried at Wilden on 4 April 1598, described as a yeoman.

164 Margerie Swanne of Nether Dean, Dean, widow — made 22 April 1598

Lincolnshire Archives, INV/90/132

The true Inventorie of the goodes and Chattelles of Margerie Swanne of Netherdeane in the Countie of Bedford widowe deceassed made & proved by William Boone & William Marshall the xxij[th] day of Aprill in the xl[eth] yeare of the Raigne of our soveraigne Ladie Queene Elizabeth etc

	£	s	d
In the Chamber			
Imprimis a Cofer, & certen small parcelles of Lynnen		v	

Item ij paire of sheetes & a towell		vj	
Item one Cubbord, one bedsteede with the bedding ij old cofers, an old chaire a charne a Tubb, & other small Implementes		iiij	
In a lofte over the chamber			
Certen old Iron ij bordes ij theales a bed sted, one sheete a wollen wheele & Certen other trashe		x	
In the hall			
Imprimis vij peeces of brasse six peces of pewter & an old frienge pan		xxij	
Item the painted Clothes, a tubb a stopp a paile a paire of Cobirons, & spitt ij bordes & a matt		viij	
Item the Bacon		viij	
In the Stable			
Imprimis a horse		liij	iiij
Item a teame of Iron & tugg withes, a dragg, a troughe a rake & manger & other trashe		vj	viij
In the Barne			
Imprimis wheate & Corne		xx	
Item hay & pease a quearn a Carte bodie readie [*?*]sawen		xiij	iiij
Cattell			
Imprimis one Cowe fowre sheepe foure hogges five hens & a Cocke	v	ij	
The yard			
A hovell, a dunghill a harrow two gates & wood		xxvj	viij
In the feild			
Inprimis one half acre of wheate, ij acres & a half of Barley fower acres & a half of pease	vij		
Sum totalis	xx		
[*Corrected total*	*£21*	*5s*	*0d*]

[*No exhibition clause*]

Notes: Margerie Swanne was buried as 'Mother Swane widowe' at Dean on 20 April 1598.

165 John Gibbes of Eversholt, yeoman

made 27 May 1598

Lincolnshire Archives, INV/90/147

The right side is badly damaged. Many values have been lost or are illegible.

A true Inventorye of all the goodes & Chattles of Jhon Gibbes of Eversholte in the County of Bedd yeomann deceased prysed by Jhon Gregory, Thomas Symonte, Ambrose Ryddell, Steven Roobarde & Nicholas Style the xxvij[th] daye of Maye in the yeare of the Raigne of the Queenes ma[jes]tie that nowe is the fortethe Anno domini 1598

	£	s	d
In the halle			
In primis A Cubborde			xvj
Item a table frame; benche & forme		x	
Item an olde Arke; a Chayre; Stooles kushinns & a Cradle		vj	viij
Item A fyre shovell a bayarde two payre of pott hangers, & A gridierone		ij	
Item a payre of Bellowse			vj
Item the paynted Clothes		v	
In the Chamber			
In primis two bedsteades, & a trundle bedd		xx	
Item a little table & haulfe a doosen of Joyned stooles		x	
Item fowre Coffers & A chayre			xviij
Item fowre flocke beddes		xx	
Item two Coverliddes & six blanckettes		l	
Item three boulsters & fowre pillowes		xxviij	
Item xvj payre of sheetes & an odd sheet	v	xiij	iiij
Item six table Cothes [*sic*]		xiij	iiij
Item xvj table nappkinnes		viij	
Item six elles and a haulfe of new clothe		viij	
Item ix pillowbeares		xiij	iiij
Item xvj yardes of redd Clothe		xl	
Item his weareing apparell		xl	
Item the Curteynes & paynted Clothes		vj	viij
Item a sworde and dagger		v	
In an olde Chamber			
In primis certeyne maulte	v		
Item certeyne corne threshed		xiij	iiij
Item two olde bedd steades & two old Coffers		iij	iiij
Item certeyne woole		viij	
In the Buttery			
In primis the peulter, as platters spoones Candlestickes & a sault seller		x	[...]
Item two brasse pottes		xij	[...]
Item three pannes		xiij	iiij
Item three spittes, a posnitt, A frying pann a payre of Andeierons, & a skimer, fowre kettles and two trevettes		xxx	
Item fowre bottles		ij	vj
Item Toobes, Barrelles boules a Chearme and other necessaryes		xxiij	
Item two doosen of trenchers			viij
In the boulting howse			
In primis A boultinge huche, A kneading troughe two bushelles, A wheele, A payre of stocke cardes & other implementes		xx	
In the cheese lofte			
In primis the Cheese shelves & two Cheese rackes		v	
Item xx[ti] skeynes		x	

In the kill howse

In primis two fattes		xiij	iiij
Item xx[ti] poundes of hempe		v	
Item an olde heire Clothe		v	
Item a peachell & a searchell		j	viij

In the barne

In primis A percell of Rye		[?]xxvj	
Item a parcell of Oates		xx	
Item two fannes and a seedcodd		ij	viij

In the stable

In primis fowre horsses	xj		
Item the harnesse & the Ropes		xiij	iiij
Item a payre of draughtes, two ploughe Chaynes two payre of fetters, two lockes, two yokes & hookes		[*value illegible*]	
A saddle and other implementes		[*value illegible*]	

In the yarde

In primis two longe Cartes, two dounge Cartes & two payre of wheeles		iij	[...]
Item A stacke of pease		xl	
Item a hovell		xxx	
Item squared timber Rackes troughes pales and fyrewood		lvj	
Item the Composte		xxx[s] *or* xxv[s]	
Item A ploughe & olde harrowes		x	
Item A sowe; tenne hogges, & fowre pigges		iiij	
Item A mattocke, picheforkes a draughte Rake wedges, an Axe, a hachatt, a spade, a shovell & the olde ierone		vj	[?]vj
Item sackes			[...]
Item A Cocke, hennes & Chickens			[...]
Item x shipp & fowre lambes			[...]
Item ix bease			[...]
Item seaven bullockes			[...]
Item three steares		xj	[...]
Item viij fatting keene		[?]x	[...]
Item three weaned Calves		xxxvj	[...]
Item three bullockes of two yeares olde	v		
Item fowre drawing steares	xij		

The cropp one the gronnde

In primis A Close of Rye conteyning by estimacione three ackers & a haulfe	iiij	[...]	[...]
Item five akers & a haulfe of Rye, wheate and Barley in a feilde called Weste Feilde	vj	[...]	[...]
Item a Close of Rye and wheate called P[...] Stockinges conteyneing by estimacione viij [...]	[...]		
Item a parcell of barley in Little feilde, on [...] by estimacione three ackers			[...]
Item a parcell of pease in the same feild by estimacione fowre ackers			[...]
Item pease & beanes in a feilde called Coc [...] feilde & a feilde called beane meade feil[*d*] [...]			

teyning by estimacione six ackers			[...]
Item xij ackers and a haulfe of Oat [...]			
same feildes			[...]
Item in mony			[...]
Summa totalis			[...]
[*inventory value noted on the grant of probate*	*£198*	*16s*	*0d*]

[*No exhibition clause*]

Notes: John Gibbes' burial has not been found. He made his will on 18 May 1598. He gave half the sum of 19s, which the parish owed him from his time as churchwarden, to the church. He noted that the fine for the 21-year lease of his tenement for the use of his son John had been agreed and desired his executors to pay it, complete the transaction and have the use of the first nine years of the lease. He gave 40 marks, bedding and household linen to his wife, who was to live in the house with his executors and receive food, drink and clothing while she remained unmarried. If she remarried or left the house taking their son with her, she was to have £4 a year for nine years to bring up their son. There were other bequests to family and servants. The residue was given to his brother Edward Gybbes and his uncle John Symmes who were appointed executors and to whom probate was granted at Dunstable on 30 May 1598 (Beds Archives, ABP/W 1598/178).

166 [*blank*] Ward of Chawston, Roxton, single woman made in 1598

Lincolnshire Archives, MISC WILLS K/135

The document is damaged in the top, right corner and words are missing.

Aninventorye taken the [...] in the xl yere of the Raign [...] Soveraigne Ladye Elizabethe by the g[*race of god*] of England Fraunce & Irelande Qu[...] of the faythe etc of all such goodes [...] Ward Late of Chalsterne Alias Chalsto[...] parishe of Roxton & in the Countye of B[...] Singell woman with which she dyed sceased of a[...] foloweth

	£	s	d
Imprimis ij gownes the on of Clothe the other of lithe grograyne prysed		xxvj	viij
Item ij petycotes ~~prysed~~ the on of red buffyn the other of Red grogen prised		xv	
Item a payre of whaled bone bodyes of sick in prised		ij	
Item ij ould Curtells a hatte pri[*ced*]		iij	iiij
Item in dyveres parcells of wearinge linnin prised at		xxvj	viij
Item a payre of brawe stockins a blacke aperne of danaske an other of blacke durance a pece of blewe clothe a lokeinge glasse & a runnde boxe & a square boxe to put Linnin in		x	
Sum Totalis	iiij	ij	viij

The prayseres Roger Hunt [*signature*], James Shotbolt [*signature*], Signum Ricard Emery

[*Exhibited by Thomas Warde and Geoffrey Barcocke, administrators, at Buckden on 1 November 1598. The mark of Thomas Ward follows the exhibition clause.*]

Notes: Her burial has not been found.

167 Edward Bull of Riseley, ploughwright made 25 March 1601
Lincolnshire Archives, INV/95/89

A true and perfect Inventory of all the goods and Chattells of Edward Bull late of Riesly Plowright decessed valued & prise[*d*] [*th*]e xxv[th] day of March in the xliij[th] yeare of the reigne of our soveraigne Lady Elizabeth etc by Robert Sampson yeoman, John [*?*]Abone & William Parkar husbandman as Followeth

	£	s	d
Imprimis one Cubbord		xvj	
Item ij bedsteds iij Coffers		xxx	
Item iij Candlestickes ij saltes j mortar		iiij	
Item xij peices of pewter		xij	
Item vij payre of flexen sheetes		lvj	
Item viij pillow beares		xvj	
Item iij payre of sheetes of hemp teare		xvj	
Item iiij payre of harden sheetes		xvj	
Item iiij table Clothes		x	
Item xv table napkins with other small lynnen		vj	viij
Item iiij harden pillow beares		ij	
Item j fetherbed j Covering & ij blankettes		xlv	
Item j matteris j bolster iij pillowes j Covering		xxv	
Item xiiij harden slipps & ten teare hempe slipps & all other implementes in the great loft		xiij	iiij
Item his apparell		xl	
Item iij quarters of barley j quarter of malt half a quarter of pease & other implementes in the inner loft	v		
Item j pott iij kettles dishes spoones & other implementes		xiij	iiij
Item xx[ti] ells of new wollen Cloth	iij		
Item v barrells & other implementes in the buttry		xiij	iiij
Item ij tubbes j kneading trough j cherne with other implementes in the milke house		vj	
Item plough tymber & rough tymber & cart tymber with all the wod in the yard	xx		
Item x quarter of grayne to thresh	x		
Item hay	iij	vj	viij
Item iiij horses	xiiij		
Item ij Cartes & Cart geares plough & plough geares	iiij		
Item xij bease & bullockes	xv		
Item 92 sheepe	xxvij		
Item x acars of pease sowed	vj	13	4
Item v acars of wheate & barly sowed	v		
Item vij acars of tilth to sow	iij		
Item viij flitches of bacon		xl	
Item j sheepe hovell with fagottes theron		x	
Item vij hoggs		xx	
Item hennes & duckes		v	
Item workeing tooles		x	iiij

	£	s	d
Item stockes of bees		xxxiij	
Item xj peices of pewter ij pottes ij pannes v kettles ij posnettes j table j Cubbord j Chest & iij Coffers viij payre of sheetes j flock bed j fetherbed iij bolsters ij pillowes j Covering iij blankettes ij bedstidds j yeal: ding Fatt with other implementtes not named	xj		
Summa totall	149	19	

[*No exhibition clause*]

Notes: Edward Bull's burial has not been found.

168 Thomas Staple of Tempsford, yeoman — made 15 April 1601

Lincolnshire Archives, INV/95/91

The inventory is damaged at the bottom and items may be missing.

Temisford in Com' Bed' lincoln' dioces. Th[*e*] Inventorie of all the goodes & Cattelles of Thomas Staple of Temisford in the Countie of Bedd and dioc[*ese*] of Lincoln yeoman decessed prised by William Barcock, John Dallington & Thomas Tingay of Bareford aforeseyd husbandmen and Roberte Adams of Bareford yeoman the fiftenth day of Aprill Anno domini 1601

	£	s	d
In the Haulle			
In primis, a Table & Frame, a folte Table a joined forme & an other forme a Rounde table the benche bourdes the hanginges in the haulle a Cupborde & a Clothe to yt, two Chayres & two ~~Item~~ Cushins a barre of Iron bering a spitt & an Iron pote price		xl	
In the parlor			
Item a framed Folte Table, a Forme, two Joyned stooles, a wicker Chayre, a Chest, and a spruse Chest and the painted Clothes price		xiij	iiij
Item a standing bedsteede, a feather-bedde, a bolster two pillowes, two blanckettes a Coverlett & the Tester & valence price		l	
Item darnix for sixe Cuschins price		iiij	
Item woollen Clothe & linnen Clothe price		xxx	
Item linnen yarne, the blades to winde them on, and a baskett price		xiij	iiij
In the Chamber next the parlour			
Item a standing bedstede, a Troundell bed, a mattrice, iij blanckettes, ij bolsters, a Coverlett, a Cheste, an arke, and painted Clothes price		xxx	

In the Chamber at the haulle dore			
Item a standing bedstede, and an other bedd, a Fetherbed a bolste & ij pellowes ij blanckettes a Coverlett, a mattresse, a bolster, iiij more blanckettes an other pillowe iij Coffers, the painted Clothes there & a warming panne price	iij		
Item his apparell, and a black bill		xl	
In the Chese Chamber			
Item a bedstede, an arke, a forme, a Chese Rack two shelves & bordes a Coffer a Trounke a Clothe baskett thre maundes, a skeppe, hempe, woll Cardes linnen Wheles, a hetchell, Reeles & a Riddell price		x	
Item wheate price		xl	
Item old Iron Tyres for wheles, a Crowe of Iron & other old Iron, an old sawe Chese & honny price		xiij	iiij
Summa	xvij	iiij	
In the maydes Chamber			
Item a bedstede, ij blanckettes, an under Clothe, a Cheste, and an arke price		vj	viij
In the buttry			
Item a poudring troughe, a mustard quarne Foure shelves & bourdes and other old thinges and thre barrelles		x	
In the kittchin			
Item a Table, a Forme, thre shelves a wicker-Chayre, an other Chayre, ij Joyned stooles & a Coffer		iij	iiij
Item a payre of Rackes a payre of Iron dogges two pott hangers, one hooke and two payre of pott hookes price		xiij	iiij
Item a payre of bellowes, a fyer shovell, a payre of Tounges & a lanterne price		ij	
Item thre brasse pottes, iiij kettelles, ij pannes, one possenett, ij Chaffers, a fryeng panne, a gredeyron, a scomer price		xxxiij	iiij
Item iiij payles, iij dozen Trenschers, trene plattes & dishes price			xx
Item thre spittes		iiij	
Item pewter platters, disches, porringers, sawsers & a basen & ewer price		xvj	
Item a Chaffing dishe, pestell & morter iiij laten Candelstickes price		x	
Item bottelles, behyves & other Trasche price		v	
Item glasses & drinking Cupps & an hower glasse		ij	
Item ij littell silver spones		iiij	
Item xliij payre of sheetes	iij		
Item x table Clothes one dozen & one table napkins iiij payre of pillow beres, with other linnen price		xxx	
Item a Tredde		ij	

	£	s	d
Item booles, Chesefattes, Cowlers, Charmes earthen pottes ij olde arkes, a Cupbord & a ~~kned~~ kneading Tubbe price		xj	
Item Tubbes, Rakes, Forkes, shelves & other [...]		5	
Item hammers, pincers, hatchettes, ij sawes, ij buschelles, a peck, a fanne, a Skrene Cives, Riddelles scottelles & sackes price		xiij	iiij
Summa	xj	xij	viij
[*Total*	*£28*	*16s*	*8d*]

[*No exhibition clause*]

Notes: Thomas Staple's burial has not been found.

169 Thomas Harper of Bedford St Peter Merton, servant made 20 May 1601
Lincolnshire Archives, INV/95/122A
Slight creasing.

Villa Bedff S[anc]t[i] Petri Martini. An Inventorie of the goodes [...] & Chattells which were Thomas Harpers decessyd, made & praised the xx[th] daye of Maye 1601

	£	s	d
Inprimis iij Sheepe		xij	
A Cubbord & iij Coffers		xij	
Wearing Apparell & other trashe		xx	
in reddye monye		xxxvj	v
Debtes spirate	xxvj	13	4
Debtes despirate	vj	13	4
Summa	xxxvij	vij	j

[*Exhibited at Bedford on 2 July 1601*]

Notes: Thomas Harper was buried at St Peter Merton, Bedford on 4 December 1600 as Thomas Grene alias Harper. He made his will on 1 December 1600 as Thomas Harper alias Green. He gave clothes, a coffer, a cupboard, two sheep and varying sums of money to his four sisters, their families and a fellow servant. The money was almost £55, more than the amount he was owed and his ready money. Some of it was in the hands of named people including his employer, Mistress Yarrow (probably Margaret Yarrow, widow of John Yarrow, gentleman of Bedford). His executors, Edward Simes and Robert Ridge, were granted probate by Dr John Belley at Bedford on 2 July 1601 (Lincs Archives, LCC WILLS/1601/ii/114).

170 Nicholas Bryde of Tempsford made 29 June 1601
Lincolnshire Archives, INV/95/90

A trewe Inventorye of all the goodes Chatles and Householdestuffe of the late Nicholas Bryde of Tempesford within the Countye of Bedforde deceassed vewed and praysed the xxix[th] daye of June Anno domini 1601. Praysed by theese whose names are heareunder written

	£	s	d
Inprimis in the Halle one Cubborde and a turned pen		xx	

Item two chayres one table one forme and two coffers		viij	
Item the paynted clothes aboute the halle two cushons a benche[30] matte two candlestickes two glasses and a reele		ij	vj
In the parlor			
Item one bedsted with a paynted testerne Oone curtayne		ij	vj
Item a Fetherbed one bolster two pillowes one coverled and one blancket and a leyttle trundlebed		xvj	
Item lyttle table one forme two Joyned stooles one chayre two coffers one truncke a boxe and a payre of tables		xij	
Item one payre of Flexen sheetes and foure payre of teare hempe sheetes thre pillowe beares thre bordeclothes and eyghte table napkins and a lookeinge glasse		xviij	
Item the hangeinges aboute the sayde parlor		ij	vj
In the Kytchin			
Item one bed of boordes with a paynted testerne one Fetherbed one bolster one coverlede one blancket		xij	
Item one lytle chayre and foure stooles one forme one rounde table a moldeinge boarde and one coffer		iij	iiij
Item a boltinge arke two kneadinge troves one olde arke two shelves one wollen wheele and a leinen wheele		iij	
Item a cherme fyve booles two payles and foure dyshes			xx
Item two brasse potes two payre of pot hookes thre payre of pot hanginges one payre of andyrons one payre of tonges a fyre shovell a greyron a trevit and a payre of bellowes		x	
Item fyve tubbes and a clothe flasket two seckes and two bages thre slypes of Lynnen yarne with other trashe		vj	viij
Item a lytle furnase		ij	vj
In the butterye			
Item fyve barrelles an olde saltinge troughe a yeeldinge fat a saffe thre bottles thre lytles shelves with other trashe		vj	viij
In the myke house			
Item thre mylke booles fyve smale shelves with other Implementes		ij	
Item thre platters foure sacers one porenger one salte seller syxe spones		iij	
In the yarde			
Item one howell two rackes two formes certayne woode [*word rubbed out*] two ladders with certayne trashe		xiij	iiij
Item two bease		xl	
Item a kocke and a hen			viij
Item his aparrell		xiij	
Somma totalis	ix	xix	iiij

Willyam Balls, John Pepper, John Cowper and William Rushe
[*No exhibition clause*]

Notes: Nicholas Bryde's burial has not been found.

30 *benche* was originally written and *s* has been written over *c*.

171 Thomas Ryseleye of Ravensden, yeoman made 17 May 1602

Lincolnshire Archives, MISC WILLS L/44

Three copies survive. The transcription has been made from the undamaged copy, which seems to be the formal version. It is indented and has a formally written heading and a full exhibition clause. It has been compared with the other two copies. There are only minor differences of spelling, except as noted below.

The Inventorye of all the goodes and Chattells of Thomas Ryseleye of Ravensden in the Countie of Bedd and dioces of Lincoln deceased praysed by William Rushe, William Wyon & William Kinge senior the xvij[th] daie of Maie 1602

	£	s	d
Inprimis three Cartehowses [carte horses *in the other copies*] price	vij		
Item xxiij sheepe and six Lambes price	vij		
Item iij kine and Calves price	vij		
Item ij geste kine & iij bullockes price	v		
Item vij hogges price		xxxv	
Item ij acres wheate price	iij		
Item xv acres barley price	xv		
Item xv acres Pease price	ix		
Item iij quarters wheate price		xl	
Item vj bushels barley price		vij	
Item ij longe Cartes a mucke Carte & ij paire Wheeles	iij		
Item ij plowghes furnished ploughe geares Carte geares and other furniture belongeinge therto with one Rowle Harrowes & all other thinges belongeinge to yt		xl	
Item one hovel unroufed & a hovel roufed & j ladder price	iij		
Item all the woode in the yarde nexte the hall & ij hogges troughes		xl	
Item plowghe timber and paile about the yarde price		xxx	
Item all the woode the beene house a grindestone & the bees [beene *in one of the copies*] in the greene yarde price	iij		
Item vj halfe inche bordes a malte querne a leade to brue in a bowlteinge Arke & all other bordes price		xl	
Item the paile about the Orcharde price	vj		
Item xiiij pewter platters iiij sawcers iiij porrengers iiij saltes five Candlestickes		xx	
Item ij greate brasse pottes a greate brasse kettle & a great brasse pane	iij		
Item iiij myddleinge brasse kettles a little brasse potte ij little kettles a gosse panne a gredyron a Fryeinge panne pottehangeinges pott hookes fire shovel fire tonges ij spittes a barre of Iron in the Chimney		xxvj	viij
Item one hogge bacon price		x	
Item one Cheste in the lofte iiij paire flaxen sheetes one holland sheete		xxxiiij	
Item vij Coveringes vij blankettes & ij mattresses price	iij	vj	viij
Item in the parlor j standeinge bedde a strawe bedde ij Feather beddes vij bolsters vj pillowes vj pillowebeires	iiij	xiij	iiij
Item j newe standeinge bedde steade price		xiij	iiij
Item iiij other beddesteades price		v	iiij

	£	s	d
Item iij paire hempe teare sheetes vj paire harden sheetes vj borde clothes xij Table napkens flaxen & teare hempe ij longe towels of Flaxen price	iij	ij	
Item his apparrell and weareinge clothes price		xiij	iiij
Item a Cubberd & vij coffers price		xxiiij	
Item a Table on a frame Form[*es*] stooles chaires price		xiij	iiij
Item iij barrells iiij Tubbes ij pailes with all other treene thinges		x	
Item Billes hatchetes & all other necessarie tooles price		iij	iiij
Item ij theles the painted clothes in Chambers & hall and all other thinges		iij	iiij
Item xij hennes & a Cocke price		iiij	iiij
Item a skreene a busshell a Fanne & a chasteinge [castinge *in the other copies*] shovel		ij	vj
Item a salteinge troughe & all other troughes price		ij	
[*The other two copies have another item listed, crossed out and illegible*]			
Summa totalis	iiij^{xx}xviij	ij	ij
[*Corrected total*	*£102*	*19s*	*6d*]

[*Exhibited by John Ryseleye, administrator, at Buckden on 21 June 1602*]

Notes: Thomas Ryseleye was buried at Ravensden on 19 April 1602. The other two copies of the inventory have a total of six score and £14 and 3d crossed out and four score £18 2s 2d written in its place in a different hand. He made his nuncupative will on 18 April 1602, describing himself as a yeoman. He left all his goods equally to his wife Elizabeth and brother John. Probate was granted by Robert Hasell at Buckden on 20 April 1602 (Lincs Archives, MISC WILLS/L/44).

172 Thomas Coxe of Eaton Socon, labourer made 3 January 1603

Lincolnshire Archives, MISC WILLS L/41

An Inventorye of the goodes & Cattells of Thomas Coxe late of Eaton Soocon in the countye of Bedford, labourer, deceased, made & pryzed the iijth day of Januarye Anno Domini 1602. By John Stocker gent., Richard Blyth, Valentyne Smith, Thomas Mirrell & others.

	£	s	d
In the Chamber			
Imprimis one gyrt bed with a Tester		xvj	
Item A Trundell bed		iij	
Item one fetherbed		xx	
Item j coverlett & ij blankettes		x	
Item ij bolsters j pillow & A thrumbd coverlett		x	
Item ij payre of flexon sheetes		xiij	iiij
Item ix payre of harden sheetes		xx	
Item A liverye Cubbord		vj	viij
Item j Chest & iij coffors		xiij	iiij
Item iij Boxes		iij	iiij
Item A wicker Chaire & a barrell		iij	
Item the painted Clothes		v	
In the laft over the Chamber			
Item ij borded bed stides		ij	

Item A mattris, A coverlett, A bolster, & ij pillows		v	
Item A cheese presse & A crowe of Iron		iiij	
Item ij linnen wheeles		ij	
Item ij painted clothes			xij
In the hall			
Item A Cubbord		xiij	iiij
Item A pen		v	
Item A framed Table & A forme		xij	
Item ij chaires			xvj
Item A cradle			xx
Item iij brasse pottes		xij	
Item iiij kettells		xij	
Item ij posnetes a chafin dish & A frieing pan		ij	
Item vj latten candlestickes & A littell morter		iiij	
Item A fire shovell, A payre of tonges, pot hangells A spit, A grediron & A payre of Bellowes		iiij	
Item xviij peeces of pewter		vj	viij
Item iij bord clothes & iiij table napkins		xij	
Item the painted clothes		iij	iiij
Item in the laft over the hall			
Item A salting troffe & ij kimnells		iij	iiij
Item a bolting Arke, A Chirme A tenor sawe A mottocke, A woollen wheele & other trash		vj	iiij
in the yard & abroad			
Item iij half acres of Tylth		xv	
Item barlye		xxx	
Item pease		xv	
Item hea	iij		
Item iij beastes	iiij		
Item xx[tie] sheepe	iiij		
Item ij hogges		xij	iiij
Item iij stockes of bees		x	
Item v hennes & A cocke		iij	
Item plowe timber		v	
Item the wood		xx	
Item A grindston, ij ladders A drag Rake iij forkes iij Tubbs & ij payles		x	viij
Item the monye oweing by specialtye & otherwise a mounteth unto	81	5	6
Summa totalis	Cix	iiij	vj
[*Corrected total*	*£110*	*3s*	*2d*]

[*Exhibited before John Belley by Rose Coxe, executrix, on 13 January 1603*]

Notes: Thomas Coxe was buried at Eaton Socon on 18 December 1602. His widow Rose married George Wright at Eaton Socon on 6 June 1603.

173 John Dillingham of Dean, yeoman made 3 January 1604
Bedfordshire Archives, PA180

An Inventorie of the goodes of John Dillingham in the parish of Deane in the countie of Bedford yoman late decessed taken by Henry Dillingham of Deane Henrie Dillingham of Cottesbatch [*Leicestershire*] Henry Pecocke of [*?*]Keshoe William Dillingham of Clipson the third daye of Januarye in the yeares of the raigne of our soveraigne Lord James by the grace of god of Englande Scotland Fraunce & Irelande kinge defender of the faithe etc that is to saie of England Fraunce and Ireland the firste & of Scotland the seaven & thirtith

	£	s	d
In primis his apparrell	v		
Item his wives apparrell		xl	
Item in money	iij		
Item thirteene yardes of newe woollen Cloth prised att		xliij	iiij
Item an apron of riche taffata prised at		x	
Item foure cushions prised att		xx	
Item one Presse three Cofers foure boxes ~~prised att~~ a heckle ij bedstedes	iij	iij	iiij
Item Eight paire of Flaxon sheetes ten paire of hurden sheetes twoo dozen of table napkins two bordeclothes 7 pillowberes foure towells & a face cloth prised att	xix		
Item foure other smale linnens prised att		xxx	
Item in the Chamber twoo fetherbedes two matterisses, two paire of sheetes two blankettes three hillinges two bolsters & six pillowes prised att	ix		
Item in the inner parlor five Towells three paire of hurden sheetes six bordclothes three table napkins two wallettes two pillowberes		xl	
Item there also two bedstedes one cofer & three Chaires prised att		xx	
Item theire also two fetherbedes twoo matteresses twoo bolsters one pillow three blankettes one hillinge & curtaines prised att	v	x	
Item in the nether parlor one bedstede one matterisse a thromcloth one hillinge & a little Chaire prised att		xxiij	iiij
Item in the Butterie two fattes three hogsheades twoo barrells three bottles and other implementes prised att	iiij		
Item over the butterie a presse meeles and other implementes with flaxe		xl	
Item in the hall foure tables, nine stooles, foure Chaires, one Cubborde three benches with other implementes prised att	viij		
Item in the kitchin one table three and twentie peices of brasse with pewter & other implementes prised att	v		
Item in the daye house a Chirne a Cheesepresse a powderinge trough with bowles and other implementes prised att		xl	
Item over the dayehouse one bedstede one matterisse three hillinges a blanket a thromcloth with other implementes prised att		xxiij	iiij
Item nine sackes and a skreene prised att		xx	

Item in the olde daye house a powderinge trough salt		xx	
Item in the brewhowse a lead a furnace a hairecloth a kneadinge troughe a boulting arke & a moulding table prised att	iiij		
Item a grindeston and trowgh prised att		v	
Item in the Cheese Chamber cheeses with shelves prised att	iiij		
Item in the Rickeyard three Cartes with Sheepe Cribbs lugges and ladders prised att	x		
Item in the sheepe coate a Rowle with plowe timber prised att		xx	
Item twoo hovells prised att	iiij		
Item the woode there and beast Cribbs prised att		xx	
Item the Gardner and plowetimber there prised att	iij		
Item the hey in the nether Barne prised att	iij		
Item in the stable five horses prised att	xxiiij		
Item the geares halters & collers prised att		xl	
Item Eleven kyne and three Calves prised att	xxiiij		
Item the Cropp of graine att home Eight Acres of Wheate sowen the tilth and pease earth prised att	xliij	ij	viij
Item foure score and foure sheepe prised att	xxviij		
Item the woode & pales about the horse ponde prised att	v		
Item six bacon hogges prised att	v		
Item a Sowe and ten stores with the pullin prised att	ijj		
Item the cow standardes & wood over them in the Cowhouse prised att		xx	
Item Thomas Cowper of Ravensden oweth him	xvj		
Item Henrie Hodgekins oweth him	v	x	
Item Thomas Boone oweth him	ix		
Item Thomas Raffe of Shelton oweth him	iiij	iij	iiij
Item a side saddle a Cloke and savegard and an olde saddle prised at		xxx	
Sum is	288	15	
[*Corrected total*	*£281*	*14s*	*4d*]

[*Exhibited on 7 March 1604*]

Notes: John Dillingham was buried at Dean on 10 December 1603, described as the elder. The appraiser Henry Pecocke of Keysoe was Dillingham's brother-in-law, having married Elizabeth Dillingham at Dean on 20 June 1594. John Dillingham made his will on 1 December 1603 describing himself as the son and heir of William Dillingham of Dean and asking to be buried next to his wife, Agnes, who had been buried there on 30 June 1602. He had two very young sons and left £100 to the younger, Oliver, and the residue from his goods to the elder, John, and made provision for their upbringing and education. He made bequests of money to family and servants. The grant of probate was made by William Smith on 7 March 1604 to the executors, his brothers George Dillingham, who appeared in person, and Gilbert Dillingham who was represented by Arthur Claver, notary public (Beds Archives R1603–4: 26/25d). John Dillingham was related, but not closely, to Francis Dillingham, see *349.*

174 Richard Martin of Caddington, blacksmith made 30 March 1604
Lincolnshire Archives, INV/99/46

30: die Marcij: Anno domini 1604.
This ys the true and right Inventarye of all, & singular the goodes & chattelles of Richard Martin of the parishe of Caddington in the Countie of Bedff & dioc[ese] of Lincolne late deceassed and priced: by Thomas Flowre alias Basill, Thomas Neele, & John Buckm[aste]r

	£	s	d
Inprimis in the upper chamber a symple bedsteede with suche furniture therunto, belonginge priced at		xiij	iiij
Item ix paier of seetes, iiij pillow iiij peelowe beares, v table napkins, ij table clothes priced at		49	6
Item 3 Cofferes		6	8
Item in the neither Chamber: 2: beddsteedes, with such furniture thereunto belonginge, & 2: cofferrs		xx	
Item in the hawle a table with a frame, 6 ioyne stoole a cobborde, 4 cozons 2: cheres		xxij	
Item 2 symple fleeches of bakon		5	
Item 5 litle keetles 2: oulde, brasse pottes, 9 peeces of pewter, 2 kandellsteekes, a salt, & other smale deale of pewter		xxx	
Item his wearinge apparell		x	
Item 2 arndeyreons, one spitte: 2 potte hangers, a fire shovell: a payer of tonges, & other lumbery		xiij	iiij
Item 2 Geese a gander, 4°: hennes & a coke		v	
Item a payer of belowes, an Anvile, a peckhorne with other tooles, in the shoppe	iij	vj	viij
Summa totalis	xij		xviij

[*Exhibited by the executrix before Otthowell Hill*]

Notes: Richard Martin was buried at Caddington on 12 March 1604. He made his will on 6 March 1604, describing himself as a blacksmith. He gave his house and land to his wife Agnes for life, then to his son Edward on condition that he pay £40 to the youngest son John. He gave £20 each to his daughters Bridgett and Agnes at the age of 21. He appointed his wife residual legatee and executrix and she was granted probate by Dr Otthowell Hill at Dunstable on 8 August 1604 (Lincs Archives, LCC WILLS/1604/i/25).

175 Elizabeth Child of Roxton, widow made 25 July 1604
Lincolnshire Archives, INV/99/42

A true Inventorie of all the goods and cattell of the late deceased Elzabeth Childe of Roxton in the countie of Bedf wedowe made the xxv[th] day of Julie Anno Domini1604 by Thomas Child yeoman, William Morrell yeoman, Thomas Swifte weaver, and Richard Scarret butcher

	£	s	d
Inprimis viij bease	xiiij		
Item two bullockes		xl	
Item iij weaned calves		xx	
Item xiiij sheepe and lambes		xlvi	viij
Item iij horses	ix		
Item ij hogges, ij sowes, vj shotes and v pigges		xxxv	

Item viij hennes		ij	viij
Item xxxiiij Akers and iij Roodes of wheate, Rie, Barley and Pease	xxx		
Item iiij Akers and halfe a Roode of medowes		xxvj	viij
Item iij loades of hay		xxx	
Item ij paire of shod wheeles, and tire for an other paire, a tumbrell, iij longe carte bodies and their necessaries	iij		
Item plowes and plowe geares, and harrowes, and their necessaries		xx	
Item iij rowles		x	
Item a bridle, halters, and horse harnesse		vj	viij
Item in the stable, the racke, the maunger, the chaffe house, the plowe timber and whatsoever else there before unnamed		x	
Item exe trees and other timber, a pen, ij brakes, a forme, tubbes, pot irons, and all other thinges in and belonginge to the backe house		xiij	iiij
Item vj hovels and rafters, and sparrees, and fagottes, and their necessaries	iiij		
Item hempe		iij	iiij
Item iiij ladders		iij	iiij
Item cowe cribbes, troughes, and the compasse about the yarde		x	
Item all her fire woode, and iij fallinge yates		xl	
Item a grindle stone and the necessaries to it		ij	
Item xv Akers of tilth	v		
Item bordes		v	
Item a sithe, shovels, forkes, a croe of yran rakes and such like		ij	
Item in the hall a longe table, and frame for it, iij formes, bench and bench bord, painted clothes, a pen, iiij chaires, and other necessaries there		xiij	iiij
Item x kettels, iij pannes, iij brasse pots ij posnets, a chafin dish, a warminge pan iij candlestickes and a morter	iij		
Item xix pieces of pewter, iiij saltes, spoones and a pewter potte		x	
Item in the parlour, ij borded bedsteeds vj coverlets, ij mattresses, a feather bed, ij bolsters, iij pillowes, a cupbord, iij chestes and a coffer	iij		
Item xvj paire of sheetes, vj pillowe beares, iiij table napkins, and iij bord clothes	iiij		
Item painted clothes in the parlour		iij	iiij
Item in the buttrie v barrels, vj tubbes a kimnell, and a shelfe		xij	
Item in the parlour chamber, a borded bedsteed, a cheste, ij coffers, certaine cheese, a cheese racke, and olde yron		xvj	

	£	s	d
Item xij bushels of wheate		xxiiij	
Item ij quarters of barley		xxiiij	
Item ij bushels of Rie		iij	iiij
Item a scrine		iij	iiij
Item in an upper chamber, a cheese racke, cheese bordes, and tresles		xiij	iiij
Item a cheese presse, draught rakes, ij fattes, a boltinge arke, a kimnell iiij sackes, a winnowinge cloth with other necessaries in the boltinge house		x	
Item in the milke house, bowls, a saltinge troughe, a churme, a pen, shelfes, and other necessaries with the butter and cheese there		xij	
Item in the servantes chamber ij borded bedsteeds with their furniture		vj	viij
Item a drinke stall, ij shelfes, a lanthorne, old yron, fetters, a cloth basket, and such like necessaries		v	
Item of bacon iij fletches and a peice		x	
Item pot hangles, pot hookes bellowes and such like necessaries			xx
Item ix pound of wooll		vj	
Item her apparell		xx	
Item in gould	iij	x	
Item the lease of her Farme	xxx		
Item windowes, lattices, stooles and whatsover before unnamed		ij	
[Total	*£134*	*12s*	*8d]*

	£	s	d
The Debtes which she the said Elizabeth Child did owe at her death			
Inprimis to Thomas Childe her sonne in Lawe	vj	xiij	iiij
Item to William Childe	v		
Item to Thomas Child the sonne of the foresaid Thomas		xx	
Item to Jane Childe		xx	
Item to the Executors of Richard Child of Knapwell		x	
Item to William Bundie of Wilden		v	
Item to Thomas Bundie of Wilden	x		
Item to Mistres Shadbolt of Chilverston	v	x	
Item to James Bundie her Executour	iij		
Item to John Bundie her servante	iiij		
[Total of debts	*£39*	*6s*	*4d]*

Signum Thomae Childe [*mark*], Thomas Swifte [*signature*], Signum Gulielmi Merrell [*mark*], Richard Skarret [*signature*]
[*Exhibited before Ottwell Hill at Bedford on 6 August 1604*]

Notes: Elizabeth Child was buried at Roxton on 5 July 1604. She made her will on 17 May 1600, leaving many of the animals and goods listed in her inventory to Thomas Child her 'son-in-law' (maybe her stepson), his children and others from the Bundie and Covington families. She left 20s each to Thomas and Jane Child, the children of Thomas Child, and this may be the sum listed among her debts. Her brother James Bundie was residual legatee and executor and was granted probate by Dr Otthowell Hill at Bedford on 6 August 1604 (Lincs Archives, LCC WILLS/1604/i/113).

176 James Duckington of Dunstable, innholder made 5 June 1604
Lincolnshire Archives, INV/99/45

Anno Domini 1604º Junij quinto. The true Eventorie of all the goods and Chattels of James Duckington late of Dunstaple in the county of Bedford Inneholder

	£	s	d
Inprimis in the great Chamber one standing bedsteed with a trundle bedd	2	10	
Item one downe bed and one featherbed and two boultsters	9		
Item two coverlets, three blancketes	4		
Item one Rugg, one quylt, and two pillowes	2		
Item five Curtaines one Vallance	1	10	
Item two Carpetes six cushens	2		
Item one Chayer & six stoles		13	
Item one long table, one square table and a Court cubbard	1	4	
Item one close stole and a pan		4	
Item the Painted clothes windscot & a forme	1	10	
The Totall somme	24	7	
[*Corrected total*	*£24*	*11s*	*0d*]
The low Parlour			
Inprimis one standing bed with a trundle bedd courtaine and vallance	3	6	8
Item two featherbeds two boulsters	5		
Item two Ruges one coverlettes, two blanckets		50	
Item two Pillowes		5	
Item a chare and six stooles		12	
Item a long table a frame & Court cubbard		13	
Item five cutshens and a window curtaine		4	
Item the Painted clothes and windscott		16	
summa totalis	13	6	8
The Hall Parlour			
Item a bedsted with a trundle bedd	4	10	
Item two featherbedds and two boulsters	6		
Item two coverlettes one blanket	1	10	
Item one paire of courtains one frendge		33	4
Item one long table a square table and two fourmes	1		
Item one wicker Chaire and foure stoles		6	6
Item thre cushens two window courtaines with the Rods			18
Item the Painted clothes & windscott	1	5	
summa totalis	16	6	4
The Seller Parlour			
Item two standing bedds & a trundle bed	1		

Item three feather beds two boulsters	3	10	
Item one Coverlett, one Rugg, two blanketes	2	15	
Item one mattrice five courtaines one vallance one frendge		10	
Item one square table and a paire of tables and an old chaire		vj	
Item the Painted clothes and windscott		13	4
summa totalis	8	4	4
[*Corrected total*	*£8*	*14s*	*4d*]

[*The exhibition clause was added here at the foot of the page in a different hand. It is not transcribed here but summarised at the end of the inventory.*]

[*second page*]

The Gratious Parlour

Item one standing bedsteed with a trundle bed	1	10	
Item two featherbeds two boulsters	3	6	8
Item one flocke bed one canvase bolster and one Pillow		15	
Item two coverletts, one quilt, one blanket		18	
Item five courtaines and vallance		13	4
Item one chaire five stoles		9	
Item a court cubbard windscot & painted clothes		6	8
summa totalis	8	3	8
[*Corrected total*	*£7*	*18s*	*8d*]

The Tabatt chamber

Item one standing feild bed with a trundle bedd with courtains and vallance	3	10	
Item one downe bed one featherbed and two boultsters	6		
Item one greene Rugge, one coverlett and three blancketts	2		
Item one carpet one cubbard cloth one window courtaine and five cushens	1		
Item one table, one frame, vij stooles one court cubbard & one chaire	1		
Item the windscott and painted clothes		13	4
summa totalis	14	3	4

The kitchen chamber

Item two bedsteds, two feather beds
and two boultsters
Item two coveringes, two Rugges
five Pillowes, two curtaines one carpett
one table, two stooles, with a bench board

summa totalis	6	2	4

The Gate houschamber

Item two bedsteds	2		
Item two feather beds two boulsters	4	10	
Item one covering, one Rugg, one blankett	1	10	
Item iij Curtaines and one Frendg		13	4
Item one table with a frame one fourme, iij cushens, the windscot		12	
summa totalis	9	5	4

The Butlers chamber

Item one standing bed, one trundle bed		16	
Item ij featherbeds, two boultsters	3		
Item one coverlett one Rug, two blanketes and one Pillow		32	
Item foure courtaines and vallance		10	
Item one carpett and iiij cushens		15	
Item one table and a frame one court cubbard, one chaire iij stoles		20	
Item the windscott and painted clothes		13	4
summa totalis	8	6	4

The crowne chamber

Item one feild bed with courtains and vallance	3		
Item another bedsted		10	
Item two featherbeds and two boultsters	3	6	8
Item two coveringes one rugg one blanket and two Pillowes	2	12	
Item two carpetes and five cushens		6	8
Item two little tables one fourme two stooles, windscot, and painted clothes		30	
summa totalis	xj	v	iiij

[*page three*]

The New chamber

Item one feild bed with curtaines & vallance	3	6	8
Item another bedsted with a trundlebed with iij curtaines and a frendge		20	
Item iij featherbeds thre boulsters	5		
Item one coverlet, two Rugges foure blanketes and two Pillowes	3	15	
Item one carpett & iiij cushens		15	
Item two little tables one court cubbard one chaire & foure stooles		20	
Item the windscot and painted cloathes		13	4
summa totalis	15	14	
[*Corrected total*	*£15*	*10s*	*0d*]

The Paradise chamber

Item two bedsteds and one little table		10	
Item ij featherbedds and ij boulsters	3		
Item iiij Rugges, one covering, one Pillow		46	8
summa totalis	5	13	4
[*Corrected total*	*£5*	*16s*	*8d*]

The kitchen Parlour

Item for the beds and bedding		50	
Item for the well bucket the horse trophe and other Tubbes		20	
Item for the Dunge		31	

The Stable

the Stables and Pigion house with Plankes, Rackes and maingers	7		

The Hostlery			
Item for many trifles or lumber		10	
Item for the wodd	20		
Item for the Hay	3		
The Wine seller			
Item for the wine and vessells	5		
Item the wine Potts		24	
Item sheilfes settels, bottels and other trifles		5	
The kitchen			
Item in the kitchen for all manner of brasse, Pewter, latten & iron work with a cubbard, formes, and shelfes	13		
Item for al the Plate	26		
Item vj paire of hallon sheetes	4		
Item in other flexon and tow shetes	12		
Item for Pillow beares of alsortes		36	
Item for board clothes of all sortes	4		
Item in table napkins, x dozen		50	
Item in towels and cubbard cloaths	16		
Item two cloakes, iij dubletes with the rest	5		
Item the Gelding, saddle, and bridle	5		
Item in money	30		
Summa totalis	CCCvij	xix	vj
[*Corrected total*	*£302*	*12s*	*4d*]

[*Exhibited by the executrix before Dr Ottowell Hill at Dunstable (Missenden was first written then deleted) on 8 August 1604*]

Notes: James Duckington was buried at Dunstable on 1 July 1604. He made his will on 27 June 1604, requesting burial in Dunstable churchyard near his brothers and sisters. He gave his mother Anne £10 and use of the Gratious Parlour for the duration of his lease of the Crown inn. He charged his executrix with paying £100 which he was bound to pay to his brother Giles at the end of his apprenticeship. His wife was residual legatee and executrix and was granted probate on 8 August 1604 (Lincs Archives LCC WILLS 1604/i/51). In April and May 1602, he consulted Dr Napier, who prescribed for 'Pleurisy a high coloured water cleere hath a cough & stitche' and noted that he was 26 and lately married (to Elizabeth Swinfenn in Dunstable on 19 January 1602) (Forman and Napier, case nos 16886, 16922 and 16980). After his death, Elizabeth Duckington married John Broughe in Dunstable on 24 January 1605.

177 Christopher Bennet of Cotton End, Cardington, yeoman made 16 January 1605
Lincolnshire Archives, INV/99/113
The inventory has a few holes and damage to the right side at the end of the document. Missing letters have been added in italics in brackets where they are obvious.

An Inventorie [*in*]dented ~~made~~ of all the goodes and Chattelles of [*Chr*]istopher Bennet of Cotton Ende in the parri[*sh*] of Cardington in the Countie of Bedf yeoman decessed made the xvj[th] daye of Januarie in the seconde yere of the Raigne of our soveraigne lorde James by the grace of god kinge of Englande Fraunce & Irelande defender of the faithe and of Scotlande the xxxviij[th]

	£	s	d
Goodes in the hale			
Inprimis one Table one Forme and one Cubborde		xx	
Item ij Chaires one buffett stole and ij other stooles		v	
Item one penn & ij shelves		ij	vj
Item ij pootes iiij brasse kettles ij possnettes & a skimmer		xxx	
Item ij drippinge pannes & one friynge panne		ij	vj
Item one paire of andirons a paire of tonges one fire shovell one gridiron one trevet a paire of bellowes ij paire of hangines a paire of pott hookes & one Iron barr		x	
Item xijj pewter dysshes iiij frwite dysshes iiij poringers j & sawcers ij saltes one Chamber pott and iiij other pewter pottes		xx	
Item iiij latin Candlesticekes and one skimmer		x	
Goodes in the chamber			
Item ~~one~~ iij Bedsteedes iij Cheestes		xl	
Item one fetherbed iiij coverletes iiij ~~coverle~~ blankettes ij flocke bedes and five pillowes	v		
Item on Looking glasse			xviij
Item iij spinninge wheeles of lynnin & one of woolle		iij	iiij
Item iij Coffers & iiij shelves		vj	viij
Item Certaine painted cloathes		v	
Item a paire of stocke Cardes and ij [*word deleted*] barrilles		ij	vj
Item certaine woll		vj	viij
Item halfe a quarter of peasse		vj	
Item one hettchett ij Iron Lookes			xviij
Item iij paire of flexen sheetes and ix paire of others	iiij		
Item vj table cloathes five towelles ij dozan of napkines and fowre pillobers		xlvj	
Item one Cubborde cloathe		x	
Item vij quartes of honie		x	
Item one morter and certaine drinkinge pottes & glasses		ij	vj
Item certaine treene dysshes and trenchers			xij

	£	s	d
Item one axe ij hattchetes ij Iron wedges a paire of pinsers & one hammer		iij	
Goodes in the day howse			
Item all the Cheese	iij	x	
Item one truncke ij Coffers certaine bordes & other trashe		xxxiij	iiij
Item ij sackes and five busshelles of barlye		xij	
Item iiij potes of potted butter		xiij	iiij
Item iij barrelles one settle one Cherme milke boles & mylke pannes ij tubbes & certaine other thinges in the milke howsse		l	
Item vij stockes of bees		xxxv	
Item one saltinge troffe one busshell certaine boardes and other thinges		xl	
Item Certaine tymber & fyre wood	vj		
Item one lyttle howsse Rowffed		vij	
Item Certaine barlye pease and Rye beinge six acres	viij		
Item a newe howsse called the dayrie howsse	v		
Item one Barne and the haye within it	x		
Item the Compasse in the yearde		v	
Item one lyttle corne barne	iij		
Item iiij shotes & one Sowe		xx	
Item viij Geese		v	iiij
Item xv hen[*nes*] & a cock		vij	
Item iij score & tenn woll sheepe	xv		
Item viij beasse & iij bullockes	xxj	[...]	
Item his weareinge raparrell		xxx	
Item debtes which are owinge	xiij		
Item vj acres of tylth & brache		l	
The prayssers names John Pecke John Tye			
Summa Totalis	Cxx	xiij	viij
[*Corrected total*	*£121*	*3s*	*8d*]

[*Exhibited at Lincoln on 23 January 1605*]

Notes: Christopher Bennet was buried at Cardington on 30 July 1604.

178 John Brewtye of Sutton, yeoman made 27 May 1605
Bedfordshire Archives, ABP W1605/126

An Inventorye Taken the 27th day of Maye Anno Domini 1605 of all the goodes Cattell Chattelles & moveables of John Brewtyes of Sutton in the Countye of Beddf deceased the 13th day of Maye as followth

	£	s	d
Inprimis in the Hale one Table with a frame the bench bord ij formes with stoole & Chayres		xx	
Item j side Table			xx
Item j Cubbord with xxti peices of Pewter ij pewter pottes j salte ij Candlestickes j Spice morter & vj [?]spoones		xx	
Item the payted Clothes & iij Cushiones		v	
In the Chamber next the hale			
Item ij standing Beddstedes with one fetherbedd iij bolstres j mattrisse ij Blanckettes & ij Coveringes		xxxiij	iiij
Item iij Cofferes		v	
Item the hanginges in the same Chamber			xx
In the nether Chamber			
Item j Joyned Bedsteed with a fetherbedd ij bolstres & iij pillowes ij Blanckettes & one Coverlitt		xl	
Item j standing Beddstede with one flocke bedd ij bolsteres j Blanckett & j Coverlitt		xiij	
Item iiij Chestes		x	
Item the payted Clothes		ij	
Lynnen			
Item vij payer of Sheetes		xxx	
Item ij Longe Table Clothes iiijor sheates		x	
Item ij dozen of Table napkines		x	
Item vj pillowberes		vj	viij
Brasse			
Item iij kettelles ij pottes ij possnettes j warming pann j Chafing dishe ij Chamber potts j friinge Pann & ij scimmeres & j drippinge Pann		xx	
In the kitchen			
Item j Casse with a chesse prese & Chesse fattes with other stufe		x	
In the Buttry			
Item j pouldring Troffe j boltinge Arke & iij Barrelles		v	
Item vj Tubbes & ij kimnelles		x	
Item xij milke boles j Cherme & ij shelves		v	
Item the Coblernes j spitt & ij pott hangers		ij	
Item the wode in the yarde & the hovell		xxx	
Item vij Acres of Tilthe grayne & ij Acres j Rode of Peesse	vij	vj	viij

	£	s	d
Item ix shepe		xlv	
Item iij hogges		xij	
Item iiij Beasse & ij Bullockes	x		
Item his wearinge Apparrelles		xl	
Summa totalis	xxxvj	xiiij	

Praysers Bartholomew Gilman, Thomas Smithe, Nicolas Plummer
[*No exhibition clause*]

Notes: John Brewtye died on 13 May 1605 and was buried on 14 May. He made his will on 11 May 1605, leaving his household goods first to his wife then, after her death, to his daughters Dorothy Tomlyne and Ann Barber who also received £5 each from £40 left to him by his master John Burgoyne in his will (TNA, PROB 11/105/589). He left a cloak to each of his sons-in-law; £5 from the £40 and a heifer to one granddaughter; and small bequests to other family and servants. His wife Joan and son-in-law Thomas Tomlyne were residual legatees and executors, with his wife having the use of his goods for life. Probate was granted to them on 27 June 1605 (Beds Archives, ABP/W1605/126).

179 Anthony Ballarde of Elstow, yeoman — made 9 March 1607

Bedfordshire Archives, ABP/W1606–07/86
The document is torn along the fold and a few words are missing.

An Inventory of all the goodes & Catelles of Anthony Ballarde of Elstowe in the County of Beddford yeoman decesed taken this ix[th] day of March in the yeare of our lord Everlastinge on thowsand Six hundreth & sixe & praised by us whose names ar hearunder writen vidlet: William Dimocke, Jeffry Adington, Thomas Cranffeld, John Baliard, William Hoddle & Humffry Newole

	£	s	d
Item in the halle a tabell with a fram with stoules to it And other goodes standinge ther all together to the value of	iiij		
Item in the butry iiij barilles A safe with A drinkstall & other thinges		xxvj	viij
Item ij silver spownes		vj	viij
Item in the Chamber on Joyned bed with a trondle bed		x	
Item A fether bed A matris & iij bolstres ij pillowes		xl	
Item A bordn bed & other bedinge		xx	
Item A littell Cobrd		ij	vj
Item tenn pair of sheetes		lv	
Item vj pillow beares & xij table napkins iij towles vj bordclothes		xxiiij	
Item painted Clothes in the Chamber		vj	iiij
Item v Coferes & some other linen		viij	
Item in the [...] A skreen & ij arkes a castingshovell a fane & tow sackes		xv	
Item [...]		vj	viij
Item in the boltinge howse or kichen sartain brase & peutr & other thinges ther together standinge	iiij		
Item iiij fliches of bakon And sertain Chees		xxij	
Item ij milche beas	iiij		
Item iij Caves newly weant		xxvj	viij
Item ij hodges		xvj	
Item ij littell mowes of barly	viij		

	£	s	d
Item sertain wheate & peas sown	viij		
Item the tilth	iij		
Item sertain timber redy squared	xx	iij	iiij
Item his waring reparill		xlvj	viij
Item sertain fyrwood in the yard & bordes & other goodes not named in the house & yard		xx	
[*Total*	*£68*	*15s*	*6d*]

William Dimocke [*signature*], J Jeffry Addington [*signature*], John Ballard [*signature*], Humffry Newould [*signature*], signum Thomi Cranffeld, signum Williami Hoddle
[*No exhibition clause*]

Notes: Anthony Ballarde was buried at Elstow on 22 January 1607. He made his will on 18 January 1607 leaving an acre called Gates acre to grandson Anthony Baliard [*sic*]; the messuage in which the testator and his son lived and his land to son John, on condition that his wife Joan had them for her life, son John doing all the work; and 20s to his daughter. His wife Joan was the residual legatee and executrix and was granted probate on 26 March 1607 (Beds Archives, ABP/W1606–07/86).

180 John Hopham of Radwell End, Felmersham, husbandman made 1 June 1607
Lincolnshire Archives, INV/104/77

A true Inventory of all suche goodes & Chattls as John Hophm late of Felmersham died possessed of beinge priced the fyrst of June Anno Domini 1607 by George Joyes, Henry Negoose

	£	s	d
Inprimis his apparell		xx	
Item in the custody of Gyles Perry one chest twelve payre of sheetes thre bord clothes one towell thre table napkinges		xlij	
Item two brasse pannes ~~for~~ foure litle kettles one brasse potte four [*letter deleted*] candlestickes		xx	
Item ten pewter dishes thre sawseres		v	
Item one bedstead with paynted clothes		iij	4
Item a Bench bord & a bench with a Joyned forme		ij	
Item two ould fether bedes		xiij	4
Item one heckforth with a calfe		xl	
Item debtes owinge unto him	xxiiij		
Sum tot[*al*]	xxxj	vij	viij
[*Corrected total*	*£31*	*5s*	*8d*]

George Jeyes, Henrie Negus prezes of theis goodes
[*Exhibited by the executrix before Otthowell Hill at Bedford on 17 July 1607*]

Notes: John Hopham was buried at Felmersham on 27 April 1607. He made his will on 27 April 1607, as Hoffham and describing himself as a husbandman. He gave his cottage and barn (which were occupied by tenants) to his daughter Marie and after her death to his daughter Rose Berrie, directing Rose and another daughter, Sibbell Wooddam, to use the cottage to ensure that Marie was adequately looked after. He gave the featherbeds to Rose and Sibbell and £5 which was held by Robert Berrie to Rose's five sons and a kettle and brass pot held by Giles Perry to Rose's daughter. The remainder of his goods were to be used for the maintenance of his daughter Marie by Rose and Sibbell, who were appointed executrices. Probate was granted to them by Dr Otthowell Hill at Bedford on 17 July 1607 (Lincs Archives, LCC WILLS/1607/i/80).

181 Oliver Luke of Begwary, Eaton Socon, gentleman made 22 June 1607
Bedfordshire Archives, ABP/W1607/98

A trewe and perfytt Inventorye of all the goodes Chattelles and moveables of Olyver Luke of Beggwarye in the parryshe of Eaton Soken in the Countye of Bedd gent deceassed made the xxij[th] daye of June in the yeare of our Lorde god 1607 prysed and valued by Gylbert Rowse gent Richarde Blythe, Richarde Crowe, & Richard Barkock as Followethe. viz

	£	s	d
Imprimis his Apparrell	vj	xiij	iiij
Item in the Hall Armorr and other Furnyture	iij		
Item in the Parlor the Furnyture there	iij	vj	viij
Item in the Chamber over the Parlor one Joyned Bedd two feather beddes with lynnen and furnyture there	xiij	vj	viij
In the two Chambers over the buttrey the furnyture there	xij		
Item in the two Chambers over the Kytchen ij beddes with furnyture & other goodes in the same	xij		
Item in the Kytchen brwinghowse the boultinge howse and milkhouse goodes in the same	vj		
Item in the Cheaseloafte Chease & other ymplementes		xxvj	viij
Item in the mens Chamber ij beddes with furnyture		l	
Item in the Larder howse and the two buttreys the Furnyture in the said howses	v		
Item Eightene Akars of Barley	xxiiij		
Item Three Akers of Wheate	iiij	x	
Item Eightene Akers of Peasse and Otes	xij		
Item the meadowe grownde	v	iij	iiij
Item Wheate, Barley, and hey in the Barne	viij		
Item Syxtene milche Beasse and a Bull	xl		
Item Store Bullockes Shepe and a geldinge	xiiij	x	
Item in the Garner plowe tymber with other ymplementes		xlvj	viij
Item furnyture in the Stable, Ladders & Compasse		xxvj	viij
Item Fyer woode tymber and old hovells	vij		
Item Swyne and Powltrey	v	x	
Item in the mawlthouse one quarter of pease & other ymplementes		xlvj	viij
Item Brasse, Pewter, Spyttes & Cobyrons	vj		
Item Plate viz A Salt Eight Sylver spones Two sylver Cuppes the one gylte	vj	xiij	iiij
Item debtes dewe uppon seven severall Bondes	CClxxx		
And withowt specyaltye other	x		
Summa	CCCClxxxxv	iij	iiij
[*Corrected total*	*£494*	*10s*	*0d*]

Gilbert Rous [*signature*], Richard Crowe [*signature*], The marke of Richard Blyeth, Richard Barcoke [*signature*]
[*No exhibition clause*]

Notes: Oliver Luke was buried at Eaton Socon on 18 June 1607. He made his will on 14 June 1607, leaving fifteen acres 'for her own use' and the residue to his wife Frances, who was his executrix. His father, Walter Luke, was one of the supervisors. The will was proved on 6 July 1607 (Beds Archives, ABP/W1607/98).

182 John Smith of Milton Ernest, yeoman

made 26 June 1607

Lincolnshire Archives, INV/104/80

An Inventorie of all the goodes & Chatteles of John Smith late of Milton Ernis in the Count[*y*] of Bedfordd yeoman deceased, prised by us Edwarde Harrison, Thomas Perie the xxvj[th] day of June 1607

	£	s	d
Imprimis ij Acr and one Rode of wheate		xl	
Item x acr of Barley	vij		
Item ix acr of pease	v		
Item xiiij acr of tylth lande		xxx	
Item ij acr j Rodd di of meddow		xiiij	
Item iij horse	iij	vj	
Item iiij Cowes	v		
Item ij sowes & v pigges		xiij	
Item xij duckes iij geese viij henes & ij Cockes		iiij	
Item one Calf ij sheepe		x	
Item one pen j planke ij bordes one Cubbarde one table j forme j Chaire with other bordes		xj	viij
Item iij Bedes ij Coverledes ij bolsters ij pillowes ij paire of sheetes j pillow beare j bordcloth ij napkins		xx	
Item in the Buttry ij barrels ij shelves a drinckestall		iij	4
Item a bedsteadd a wollen whele a Cartrope with other trash in the Chamber		ij	
Item in the pott loft a malt arke a pitchforke a syth with plow tymber & other Implementes		x	
In the kitchin			
Item one paire of pothangers ij ketles a skillet a paire of tonges a tub iij peces of pewter a spit a moldinge table a hen pen with other trash		x	
In the parlour			
Item all his apparrell		xx	
Item a bedsteade a coffer a flasket ij fleses of woll with other trash		iij	iiij
Item in the great loft a busshill a fan a skep a Chese racke		ij	vj
Item in the aple lofte xiij Cheses ij bordes & bakon		iiij	
Item in the stable plow geres & Cart geres		vj	viij
Item in the barne iij Cartes j Carte bodie a gig with other tymber		l	
Item in the stable olde rafters		iij	
Item wode in the yarde		x	
Item plow tymber [*?*]one sticke a role a harrow		xx	
Item wode in one house in the yarde		xl	

	£	s	d
Item in the milke house a chese presse & a chirme			
Item Certaine milke boles		v	
Item in mony by a Bonde	xv		
Item Certaine bordes & Joysts		x	
Item one lease of Lande		xx	
Som tot is	53	viij	ij
[*Corrected total*	*£53*	*8s*	*6d*]

Edvard Harrison his marke, Thomas Perie his marke
[*No exhibition clause*]

Notes: John Smith was buried at Milton Ernest on 22 June 1607.

183 William Knight of Colmworth

made 29 June 1607

Lincolnshire Archives, INV/104/78

The writing is cramped, with deletions and insertions in several places. Many values are squashed at the edge of the page and are difficult to read.

The Inventorie of all goodes Catteles chattels & [*word deleted*] howshould stuffe of William Knight late of Colmorth deceased praysed by John Goodman Junior George More William [*word deleted*] Jease and John [*?*]Lane the Twenty and Ninth day of June Anno Domini 1607

	£	s	d
In the close			
Imprimis fowre beast	xj		
Item three calfe		xxx	
Item foure sheepe and a lame		xx	
Item one sowe		x	
Item one Table ~~with~~ in the hale with the fra[me]			
Item on bench borde one forme and sqware			
Table One Cubburd		13	4
Item one glasse case		ij	
Item one brasse pane			
Three brasse pottes on posnet one Chaffinnge dish		04	
Item eight pewter platters six pewter dishes			
Item six savsers two salts		26	8
Item three latine Candelsticke two pewter candlestick		v	
Item two pewter tunes, the painted clothes one brushe, three buffet stoole and one cheyer		x	
Item foure peecice of wolle		ij	6
Item In the parloure one Table with the frame		vj	[*?*]viij
Item two chesse		xvj	
Item Joyned bedd, one fether bedd, one bowlster, four pillows on blancked one Coverled one strave bede iij^{li} vj^{s} viij^{d}	3	6	8
Item painted clothes and glas windoes		x	
Item one Coverled two Cuisheins feefftene yardes of cloth	3		
Item his apparell		x	
Item one presse, on buffet stoole, one boxe		v	

Item one pare of flaxen sheetes		xij	
Item one pare of Tare hempe five pare of harden sheetes		38	
Item five pillowbees three harden boord clothes six Table napkins on ~~pare~~ tare of hempe pillowbeers		23	4
Item fowre pillowbees ~~two shillinges~~		ij	6
Item the loft over the halle two borden bedd stetes one gyrt bedd steed		x	
Item foure blancketes, two bowlsters, fowre pillows two mattrasis three sheets two Coffer one cradle two formes		xl	
Item Nine sheet of flexen on flexen bord cloth One pillowebeere ~~one clothe~~ and on Towell	iij	iiij	
Item one Chaire, on Chamber pott & a Cloake [*this line has been inserted*]		xix	viij
Item in the loft over the parlore on borden bedd steede painted clothes and on bord		v	
Item in the milke house two tubbs		iij	
Item foure kettels		xx	
Item six boules fowre Cheese fattes		vj	
Item one charm, and on pewter bason		ij	
Item two formes, two stooles, two shelves and other bordes on Trunke		iij	4
Item in the boultinge howse on boultinge tunne one troffe on bushell one barell on forme One pecke one bushell of Rie on sacke on bage and glas		x	
Item in the ~~Backe howse~~ Sincke howse three Barels Twoe Tubes on wolen wheele one pen two pare of wolen cardes one pare of Stock cardes one [*?*]washe barell on hemblocke one drinke stale and other trashe		26	8
Item in the kitchin one foulden Table foure stooles pott hanginges on pare of hand giorns one speet one greid-eiorne		xiij	iiij
Item one ould cubburd three pales one fryinge pane fowre pewter dishis spoones and other implments		xiij	4
Item in the loft over the milke howse and bowltinge house two bottels on kimmill on boultinge hutch one Rake two shelves		xiij	iiij
Item hempetowe woole butter gresse Two linen wheeles, fowre Tressels on Cart rope and other implimentes		xxx	
Item in the entrie on lanterne one [*?*]~~fork~~ swinele			xij
Item in the feild wheate groweinge		8	
Item in the cheese howse and cheese loft two and thirty cheeses bordes hempe tresels one cheese pres one hemp~~blocke~~ brake		xxvj	viij
~~Item hembrake~~			

Item two flettches of baken		xiij	4
Item two hogges		xx	
Item six hives of Bees		xxx	
Item six hens on cock chicke		vj	
Item thirtee gees		8	
Item one hempe land		xiij	
Item ould wode	iiij	x	
Item Two laders		vj	8
Haye and strawe		xx	
All thinges unprised and forgotten		xiij	4
Summa huius			
57^{li} 18^{s} 4^{d}			
Summa totalis	Lvij	xviij	iiij
[*Corrected total*	*£56*	*9s*	*4d*]

[*Exhibited by the executrix at Bedford on 17 July 1607*]

Notes: William Knight was buried at Colmworth on 16 June 1607. He made his will on 10 May 1607. He gave his house and land to his wife Margery for life, then to his son Jeffry. He gave £10 to his daughter Joan, £20 to his daughter Margaret and £10 to his son Jeffry. His wife was residual legatee and executrix and was granted probate by Dr Otthowell Hill at Bedford on 17 July 1607 (Lincs Archives, LCC WILLS/1607/i/94).

184 Katherine Phillipe of Stotfold, widow — made 6 July 1607

Lincolnshire Archives, INV/104/79

Poor handwriting. Some figures have been crossed out and new figures substituted; they are difficult to read.

A true Inventorie of all the goodes & Chatteles of Katherine Phillippe widd[*ow*] late wyfe of Jeames Phillipe of Statfould afore saide ~~wid~~ yeoman deceassed made by us whose names are here underwritten the sixthe day of July in the fyfth ~~& forteth~~ yeare of the Raigne of our most gracious soveraigne lorde Jeames by the grace of god kinge of England France & Irelande & of Scotlande the forteth

	£	s	d
Imprimis wheate braley pease Oates & other grayne to the vallue of fortie acres growing in the Common feldes of Statfould at fyftie two pouldes	lij		
Item thre horses at	iiij		
Item a halfe parte of one other horse		xx	
Item fyve bease in the yarde	viij		
Item hodes & a sowe & piges at		xx ~~vij~~	
Item hennes Cockes duckes & drackes at		x	
Item plowc & plowe geares Carte & carte geares plowe tymber & carte tymber at	v		
Item ~~Corne~~ wheate rye barlie bease [*pease*] mault in the house threshed at		v	
Item in the yarde wood Cowe racks & other implementes about the yarde	iij	vj	viij

	£	s	d
Item dunge in the yearde at		xx	
Item in the hall ij Cubberdes ~~a table~~ a bencheborde a frame a forme one oulde table two Chares with the paynted Clothes & other implementes aboute the house at		xxvj	viij
Item brasse peuter with two Candelstickes at		xxx	
Item shetes tablecloth & other lynnen at		xl	
Item two beddes a fetherbed with a boulster a pillowe two Cuverletes with other things to the bedes		xxx	
Item vj cofers a chest at		xiij	iiij
Item sackes fannes a busshell at		x	
Item bease and bacones in the ruffe		x	
Item other implementes about the house & yarde at		v	
~~Item her wearing apparrell at~~		~~xxx~~	
Item barreles tubes wheles a bottell pease hookes forkes mattockes Shoveles & Chese rackes at		xxvj	viij
Item her wearing apparrell at		xxx	
	lxxxvij	iij	iiij

By us John Fytzakerley gent, Gerrard Spencer yeoman, Thomas Lylleye yeoman
[*Exhibited at Bedford*]

Notes: Katherine Phillipe's burial has not been found. Her husband James Philip was buried at Stotfold on 10 March 1599. She made her will on 6 October 1603 giving money, household goods or animals to her sons, daughters and others. She gave her tilth and breach equally to her three sons; made financial arrangements about loans with two sons; gave one son half the unbequeathed goods; and gave the residue to son Thomas who was also appointed executor. He was granted probate by Dr Otthowell Hill at Bedford on 17 July 1607 (Lincs Archives, LCC WILLS/1607/i/170).

185 Richard Burdsey of Dunstable, turner

made 4 August 1607

Lincolnshire Archives, INV/104/162
Slight damage to the document.

An Inventary of all the goodes & chattells of Richard Burdsey of Dunstable deceased taken the fourthe daye of August 1607 praysed by Henry Waine and Henry Chapman of the same Towne as [*follo*]withe

	£	s	d
Imprimis 2 Cubberdes a table & a forme		vj	
Item 2 Cheyers & 4 Stooles		iij	iiij
Item 2 Andiorns 2 payer of tonges apayer of ~~pott hockes~~ pot haninges apayer of Bellowes & pot huckes			xviij
Item the Brase about the house		vj	viij
Item the pewter in the house		vij	
Item 2 spittes			viij
Item a fryinge pane			vj
Item the Copper ware and other lomber		ij	vj
Item 6 dishes a ladell achoping knyfe a skymer			viij
Item 6 trenchers			j
Item a dripinge panne			iij

	£	s	d
Item 4 quishens			iiij
Item a table & aforme		ij	vj
Item [*character deleted*] 3 bedsteedes		vj	viij
Item bedinge in the house		vj	viij
Item a littell Cheyr			iij
Item 4 payer of Sheetes		x	
Item a Curtayne 2 pillobeeres 2 napkynes		iij	iiij
Item the paynted Clothes in the house		ij	
Item his weringe apparrell		v	
Item 2 table Clothes		ij	
Item his workinge tooles		xiij	iiij
Item a grinstone			vj
Item 2 owld milstones		iij	iiij
Item a littell hand mill to grind maulte		xx	
Item a littell huche to put maulte in			xij
Item a pigg			xviij
Item the wood about the house		xx	
Item 5 Chestes		viij	
The some is	vij		vij
[*Corrected total*	*£6*	*15s*	*7d*]

[*Exhibited by the executrix in person before Master Otthowell Hill, surrogate for Master John Belley, at Ampthill on 20 October 1607. The exhibition clause was signed by William* [*?*]*Francis.*]

Notes: Richard Burdsey was buried at Dunstable on 7 June 1607. He made his will on 6 June 1607, describing himself as a turner. He left everything to his wife, Joan, whom he appointed executrix. She was granted probate by Dr Otthowell Hill at Ampthill on 30 October 1607 (Lincs Archives, LCC WILLS/1607/i/191). Note the discrepancy in dates of exhibition and probate; one may be a mistake.

186 Henry Halsey alias Chamber the elder of Cantlow, Caddington, yeoman — made 19 January 1608

Bedfordshire Archives, DW 301

The inventory has several holes and a few words are missing. Missing letters have been supplied where obvious.

The true Inventorye of all the Goodes cattle and moveables of Henrye Halsey alias Chamber late of Cantlow in the parishe of Caddington in the Cou[*nty*]e of Bedd thelder deceased made the xix[th] day of Januarye Anno D[*omine*] [*1*]607 And in the Fyfte yeare of the Raigne of our soveraigne Lorde James by [*the*] grace of God Kinge of Englande Fraunce & Irelande defender of the Fa[*ith*] etc & of Scotlande the xlj[th]

	£	s	d
In the Chamber over the Ha[*l*]le			
In primis One great Chest with two Lockes		x	
Item One standinge Bedd a Feather Bedd a bolster a mattris a paier of blanckettes a coverlett one pilowe and two paier of towen sheetes		xlvj	viij
In the Chamber over the parloure			
Item one Bedstede a mattris a bolster a paier of blanckettes & a Coverlett		x	

In the Buttrie

Item two spittes one maulte querne two powdringe troffes all the Wooden Vessell and drincke Barrelles		xxv	

In the Hawle

Item vj pewter platters two pewter dishes one flower pott three lattin candlestickes and one lattin basen		x	
Item two olde Formes			xij

In the kitchin

Item One brasse pan with two eares two greate ket[*tles*] two brasse pottes a drippinge pan a fryinge pan a knedinge troffe a hare cu[...]de [*?cuborde*] ij little spittes & ij pot hangles	iij		
Item one Warminge pan		iij	iiij
Item one paier of Andiornes a fire forke a fire shovell a paier of cobiornes & a gridiorne		iij	iiij
Item one Chaier two stooles one little table & a little chest		vj	viij
Item one olde Cofare in the parloure			xij
Item Five Todd of Wooll at xx^{s} the tod	v		
Item xxx^{ti} shepe	ix		
Item one Cowe and a Calfe		xlvj	viij
Item Of wheate in the Barne by estimacion [*?*]sixe quarters	viij	xvj	
Item of pease and Tilles Foure quarters and [*a*] halfe	iij		
Item of Oates Five quarters		xlv	
Item twelve Acres of wheate one the ground [*?at*] xxx^{s} an Acre	xviij		
Item three paier & a sheete of towen & a ta[*ble c*]lothe		xij	
Item all his wayringe Apparrell		xl	
Item in Rawe maulte two quarters and two busshell at ij^{s} the busshell		xxxvj	
Somma totalis	lxj	xij	viij

praysed by William Parrott, Edwarde Dermer, William H[*ay*]warde, Thomas Parratt and Roberte Steppinge

Debtes owinge to the said Henrie Halsey alias Chambr

John Humfrey of Hudnoll	xj		
Edwarde Hayes alias Brotherton of Great Gaddisdin	xj		
William Doggett	v		
Edwarde Dermer of Onyons	iiij		
	31		
~~Somma totalis~~	~~lxxxviij~~	~~xij~~	~~viij~~

More Goodes which cam to knowledge afterwardes

Item two olde Bedstedes 4^{s} vij old blanckettes 7^{s} a spice morter & a pestell 2^{s} 6^{d} an old laver 18^{d} a paier of skales & smale waightes 4^{s} iiij leather bottels 5^{s} two mattockes 2^{s} an old axe & two old hatchettes 12^{d} two old spynnyng wheles 3^{s} an old busshell and a sead cod 2^{s} and an old chest [*2^{s}*]		xxxiiij	
Somma totalis	lxxxxiiij	vj	viij

[*Exhibited on 10 March 1608*]

Notes: Henry Halsey alias Chamber was buried at Caddington on 5 January 1608. He made his will on 3 March 1607 leaving 10s to each of his daughters; £12 to son Henry; furniture including the bed and bedding in the chamber over the parlour that he used to son Thomas;

and his crops and the residue equally to his two sons who were also executors. Probate was granted to son Henry on 10 March 1608 (Beds Archives ABP/W1607–8/157).

187 Robert Fish of Riseley, husbandman made 23 April 1608

Lincolnshire Archives, LCC ADMONS 1608/43

The ink has bled through the paper.

A trewe Inventorie of all the goodes and chattells of Robert Fish Lait of Ryseley in the Countie of Bedd husbandman deceassed priced by Thomas Lord and Beniamen Stookes the 23 daie of Aprill in the year of our Lord god 1608

	£	s	d
In the Hall			
Inprimis one framed table iij buffett stooles one Joyned form iij Chears one Cubbord one penne one benchebord one other bord & one copfer		xvj	
Item ij brasin Ketles ij brasin pottes one chaffing dishe one Skymmer ij latten Candelstickes		x	
Item ix ~~viij~~ pewter dishes ij saltes		v	
In the parlor			
Item iij ould copfers ij fossers one ould Cubberd ij standing Bedds one borden bed stead and the paintted Clothes		xv	
Item one fether bed iij boulsters ij pillowes iij koverges one mattris ij blanckettes		xx	
Item iij ould Arkes one Copfer one bedstead one ould wheele		viij	
Item ij yron spites one paire Cobyrons with other smale Implementtes		ij	
Item iij paire of flexen sheettes iiij paire of harden one flexen table Cloth ~~one~~ vij table napkins ij pillowebears		xxvj	viij
Item iij ~~horse~~ Cart horse	vij		
Item vj quarters of barlye iij quarters of pease	vij	x	
Item iij ~~be~~ milche beast and one bullock & one yong calf	vj		
Item Cart and Cart gears plowe and plowe gears & harrowes		xiij	iiij
Item one Sowe & fyve pigges		x	
~~Item redie monie~~	~~[?]j~~		
Item the wheat and telthe land	iiij		
Suma total	30	17	
[*Corrected total*	*£30*	*16s*	*0d*]
debtes deducted the whole rem[*aining*] is		xxxviij	x
[*Corrected total after deduction of debts*	*£1*	*17s*	*10d*]

The Debtes of the within named Robert Fishe which he did owe at the tyme of his death

Item to Master Olyver Harvie	xj	xj	
Item to Thomas Daie	v		
Item to Thomas Darlyn	iij	vj	
Item to John Gell of Yeelding	iij		xx
Item to Beniame Stookes		xl	
Item to John Burdsey	iij		
Item to Gidding		xiiij	vj
Item Henrie Hodgeskin of Deane		v	
Item the sum of the debtes that he oweth	28	18	2

[*Exhibited by the executor in person at Bedford on 20 August 1608*]

Notes: Robert Fish was buried at Riseley on 13 February 1608.

188 Joan Beamond of Pulloxhill, widow made 7 June 1608

Lincolnshire Archives, INV/107A/68

A true Inventorie of all such goods and chattells as were lately the goods and chattells of Johane Beamond widowe of William Beamond late of Pulloxhill deceased ~~made~~ praised and made by us Thomas Atwell, Robert Beamond, Roger Neele and George Atwell made the seventh day of June Anno domini 1608

	£	s	d
Inprimis the best bedsteede in the loufte		13	4
Item the second bedsteede in the same lofte		xij	
Item an other bedsteede		6	8
Item a cofer in the lofte		x	
Item a presse a chaire a stoole		iij	iiij
Item a salting trough		6	8
Item ij barrells		v	
Item a brasse pott		v	
Item a warming pann		iij	iiij
Item a kettle		iiij	iiij
Item ij platters		iij	iiij
Item a chafingdish & a kandlestick		ij	vj
Item a bottle			xx
Item a spitt and a bayard		ij	vj
Item a boulting hutch		ij	vj
Item a wheele & a hetchell		ij	viij
Item a painted cloth		ij	
Item a fetherbed 2 boulsters 2 fustian pillowes		50	
Item a mattrice		12	
Item a coverlet & iiij blankets		26	8
Item 3 paire of fine sheetes		45	
Item 4 paire of courser sheetes		40	
Item 2 tableclothes		12	
Item 4 pillowbeares		12	
Item one sheete of hempteare		v	
Item one course sheete		ij	vj
Item ~~one~~ ij cushins		v	

Item all her wearing apparrell	v		
Item in redy mony	13	16	
Item 3 sheetes		9	
Summa	34	2	

Thomas Atwell [*mark*], Robart Beamount [*signature*], Roger Neele [*mark*], George Atwell [*signature*]
[*Exhibited by the executor at Dunstable on 18 August 1608*]

Notes: The Bishop's transcript of the Pulloxhill burial register records Joan *wife* of William Bement being buried on 24 *July* 1608 (*BPR*, vol. 22, p. B23). Possibly, this is a mistake for *widow* and an earlier date in the year. She made her will on 26 February 1608 describing herself as a widow and her deceased husband as a husbandman (Lincs Archives, LCC WILLS/1608/i/57).

189 George Fossey of Bidwell, Houghton Regis, husbandman undated; between June and August 1608
Lincolnshire Archives, INV/107A/70

A true Inventorie of all the goodes that were Latly George Fosseys of Bydwell in the parishe of Houghton Regis decessed

	£	s	d
Imprimis his dublett & hose		v	
Item other apparell			xvj
Item iij shirtes		iiij	
Item iiij bandes			xvj
Item his hatt			xij
Item a sheete		iij	iiij
Item his stockings			xvj
Item a chest		ij	
Item owing in one place	vj		
Item owinge	v		
Item owing	xxij		
Item owinge		L	
Item owing		vj	
	35	15	9
[*Corrected total*	*£36*	*15s*	*4d*]

Praised by us Thomas Howse, Richard Blankensopp, Thomas Tompkins script'
[*Exhibited by the executor at Dunstable on 18 August 1608*]

Notes: George Fossey's burial has not been found. He made his will on 20 June 1608, describing himself as a husbandman. He gave varying sums of money amounting to £36 12s to his brothers, sisters, nieces and others. He appointed his brother Thomas as residual legatee and executor, to whom probate was granted by Dr Otthowell Hill at Dunstable on 18 August 1608 (Lincs Archives, LCC WILLS/1608/i/56).

190 Lucy Feild of Shefford, widow made 4 August 1608
Lincolnshire Archives, INV/107A/79

An Inventorie of all the goodes and Chattells of Lucie Feild of Shefford in the Countie of Bedf widow late deceased made the fourth day of August 1608 and prized by Oliver Thody, Thomas Stevens and William Goldsmith

	£	s	d
Inprimis in the hall one Cupbord five peeces of pewter a pott shelf a Candlestecke a table a forme and a Chare		xxiiij	ij
Item in the kitchin one malte querne ij kettells ij kettles [*sic*] and a fryinge panne		xij	vj
Item in the great Chamber one borded bed one Couerlett one blankett one mattresse one bolster one pillow and a Cofer		xj	vj
In the buttery one barrell one tubbe and a kneadinge trough		v	
Item in the parlour a bedsted and one Cofer and the furniture to the bedsead		xxx	
Item in the larder one saltinge trough a lynnen wheele and a wollen wheele		vij	iiij
Item in the litle butterie a litle brasse pott a posnet and an old kettle		vj	viij
Item in the mens Chamber one borded bedsted and the furniture		v	
Item in the Chamber next the gatehouse woll and hempe		vj	viij
Item in the milkehouse a cheese presse shelves and other thinges		v	
Item the lynnen one paire of flaxen sheetes one paire of hempen sheetes and other lynnen		xx	
Item her apparrell		xxx	
Item iij horses	ix		
Item five beastes iij weanelinges five hogges xxij sheepe and lambes	xiij	vj	viij
Item one Carte one dunge Carte ij hovells cartes plankes plough geares and Carte geares and wood	vj	xiij	iiij
Item v acres of wheat ij acres and a half of Rie xix acres of barly vj acres and a half of pease and beanes iij acres and a half of oates and v loades of hay	lij	x	
Summa	lxxx	xiij	x
[*Corrected total*	*£89*	*13s*	*10d*]

[*Exhibited by the executor at Bedford on 20 August 1608*]

Notes: Lucy Feild was buried at Shefford on 23 July 1608. She made her will on 20 July 1608, referring to her husband as Edward Feild (who died in 1604). After small bequests to friends and children, she left half the lease of the farm to her son John and the grain and cattle to her two sons John and Nicholas Feild. The will was proved before Master Otthowell Hill by the executor, her son John, at Bedford on 20 August 1608 (Lincs Archives, LCC WILLS/1608/i/17).

191 John Ellis of Souldrop, tailor made 8 August 1608

Lincolnshire Archives, INV/107A/81

Slight damage down the right side. No values appear to be missing.

A true Inventorie of the goodes of John Ellis of Souldropp on the Counti of Bedd taylor deceassed priced the eight day of August in the yeare of our Lord god on thousand six hundred & eight as Folloeth

	£	s	d
In primis debtes owing to the sayd John Ellis	five		
off Shorllings skynes five & twenty		seven	
on tode of woll		xvj	
on Blankett for a bed		ij	
two brasse kettelles		ij	
All themplementes within the house		viij	
the wood in the yeard		ij	
Sum is	vj	xvij	

The priceres William Byth-Rey, the marke of William Byth Rey, John Barber, The marke of John Barber, Henry Joyes [*signature*]

[*No exhibition clause*]

Notes: John Ellis was buried at Souldrop on 21 July 1608. He made his will on 16 June 1608, leaving his house and grounds called Bareswigg to Elizabeth Elliott, who was also his residual legatee and executrix. She was granted probate by Edward Clerke at Bedford on 20 August 1608 (Lincs Archives, LCC WILLS/1608/i/16).

192 Grace Clarke of Potton, widow made 16 August 1608

Lincolnshire Archives, INV/107A/78

A true & perfect Inventorie of all the goods & chattells of Grace Clarke[31] widowe layt of Pottonn deceased prized by Master William Horley, Tho Harper, John Harper & others the xvj[th] of August 1608 as followeth

	£	s	d
Inprimis in the hall a cubbard a table tow fourmes three ioyned stools, a settle tow wickar chears a speare cloth whith paynted cloths		xl	
Item tow panns one brass pott, a possnett a laver & also			

31 The name Clarke has been inserted.

	£	s	d
tow brazen candlestickes foure platters a pewder pott a cupp tow pewder candlestickes & tow saltes		xxxi	viij
Item eight peices of pewder litle & great els where & half a duzen kettells tow brass pottes & a possnett		xxxi	
Item three spittes a trevett tow frying panns a cass a kneading trough with tow bowls & a tubb & other trash		xx	
Item a press in the parlor a bedstead tow fether-beddes tow blankettes tow coverlettes tow bowlsters tow pillows twelve yeardes of cloth & a warming pann & other triffls ther	iij	x	
Item in the loft over the hall three bedsteades one fetherbedd tow matrices tow boulsters tow blanketes tow pyllowes & foure coffers	iij		
Item a pouldring trough tow shelvs eight payre of sheetes five pillowbears tow boardcloths		lv	
Item in money & all hir apparell & tenne quarters of malte	xvj		
Item thre flitches of Backen foure young shoates one sowe & three sheip		lviij	
Item a cowe & a calfe		xl	
Item tow acres of Rie	vj		
Item tymber tow ladders fire wood & also certayn pullen about the yeard & other trash		xxxi	
Item one horse		l	
Item a few boardes with certayn brakes upon them		xv	
Item tow fanns one bushell a stricke the shovells a skreyne & a cheise press		xx	
Item tow acres of peaze		xxvj	viij
Item certayne hemp tow wheils an old cart body & other trash & triffles about the house forgotten in all		xxiiij	
Suma totalis	~~xl~~ 49	iij	iiij
[*Corrected total*	*£50*	*12s*	*4d*]

[*Exhibited by the executor at Bedford on 20 August 1608*]

Notes: Grace Clarke was buried at Potton on 29 June 1608. She made her will on 28 June 1608, giving half her brassware, one third of her pewterware and half an acre of rye to each of her two daughters, Joan Warde and Marrian Swanne. Marrian also received 40s, household goods and one hive of bees, which are not listed in the inventory. Joan Warde's children were given a sheep or weanling and 20s each. The last third of the pewterware and residue were given to her son John Clarke who was appointed executor. Probate was granted to him by Dr Otthowell Hill at Bedford on 20 August 1608 (Lincs Archives, LCC WILLS/1608/i/77).

193 William Ordwaye of Dunstable, yeoman made 28 November 1608
Bedfordshire Archives, ABP/W1609/148

An Inventorie Indented of all the goods and cattelles Impelmentes [*sic*] and howsold stuffe which weare of William Ordwayes of Dunstables in the Countie of Bedford yeoman deceassed

At the tyme of his death taken and praysed by William Ashwell, John Chapman and William Chapman the xxviijth day of November in the sixte yeare of the raigne of our soveraigne Lord Kinge James Anno Domini 1608. As followeth viz

	£	s	d
In the hall of his dwellinge howse			
A table with a frame with vj stoles a round table			
a Cuberte a cheare with glasse and waynscot		xxx	
Item a setle a pare of And Iorne an Iorne bare			
a pare of tonges a pare of belowes twoe salt			
selers iiij kandelstickes & a slice		viij	
Item vj Cusians a brushe a botell		iiij	
In the Parler			
Item on standinge bed with the furniter with			
a truckell bed and the furniter	iiij		
Item iij Chestes and a litell Cofer			
with a close stole with a paynted cloth		xx	
Item [*?*]xix pare of Shetes iij dosen of			
napkines vjj pare of pillow beres ij twoels	viij		
In the Buttery			
Item iij brase potes iij ketels afrying pane			
ij dripinge panes ij spites a shreding knife			
a skymer with other trashe		xxx	
In the Chamber over the halle			
Item twoe standinge bedes with ther furniter	vj		
Item one table iij chests twoe formes			
ij paynted Clothes with acheare		xx	
Item on coverlet	iij		
Item vjjj tabell clothes		xvj	
In the kichine			
Item one furnis twoe ketels one pane			
a trowfe and a tube		xl	
In the seller			
Item one fate ij tubes iij kimnyles			
iij litell barelles		ix	
Item xl peces of pewter a quart pote			
a bason		xl	
Item xiij bushll of wheate and a scacke			
of Corne by estemacon iij quarter	vij	x	
Item vij silver spones ij dosen of pewter			
spones a wollen whell and a lynnen			
whell		l	
Item in debtes owinge which be good	lxvij		
Item the wood in the yeard and house		xxx	
Item his wearinge apparell		xxx	
~~Summa totalis~~	~~xliiij~~	~~vij~~	
Somma ~~dettes lxvij~~li totalis	Cxj	vij	
[*Corrected total*	*£111*	*17s*	*0d*]

Willi Ashwell [*signature*], William Chapman [*signature*], John Chapmans marke

[*No exhibition clause*]

Notes: William Ordwaye was buried at Dunstable on 21 November 1608. He made his will on 27 October 1606, leaving small bequests to several people including his wife's family (the Chapmans); his and his son William's servants; and 20s 'toward the taking owte of Dunstable Pryviledge late renewed'. He gave his wife Elizabeth a house in South Street called the Volte for life, which was let, and two acres for life, then to his grandson Joseph Ordway; and his house and other houses and twenty-four acres to his wife, then to his grandson William Ordway. The table and cupboard in the hall and the glass and wainscot in the house, the standing bed in the parlour and three pairs of sheets were to remain in the house. After his wife's death, £80 was to be divided equally among the eight children of his son William. His wife was residual legatee and executrix. The will was witnessed by the writer, Robert Bostock clerk and notary public, and proved by the executrix on 16 May 1609 (Beds Archives, ABP/W1609/148). The oath was administered to her by John Richardson, curate of Dunstable (CCEd).

194 Thomas Goldsmith of Eaton Socon, shepherd made 12 October 1609
Lincolnshire Archives, INV/108/61

An Invitorie of all the goods Houshold stuffe and other thinges which late were Thomas Goldsmithes Late of Eaton deseased valued and priced by George Covengton and William [*?*]Worley the xij[th] daie of October 1609

	£	s	d
Item ij Cofers		vj	viij
Item v fleses of woll		iij	iiij
Item one hatchet			iij
Item one pitchfork			iiij
Item a Russet Cloke		iij	iiij
Item a frese cote		iij	iiij
Item ij lether dubletes		iiij	
Item a lether Jacket			viij
Item a paire of bretches		ij	
Item an old hat			iiij
Item iij wethers		xij	
Item iij ewes		x	
Item iij Lambes and iiij[or] Lambhoges		xvij	
Item v ewes ij Lambes partable		xvj	viij
Item money in his purs			iiij
Summa Totalis	iij	v	iij
[*Corrected total*	*£4*	*0s*	*3d*]

[*Exhibited by the executor on 23 September 1611. The exhibition clause was signed by George Pormorth, notary public.*]

Notes: There is no record of the burial of Thomas Goldsmith in Bedfordshire in 1609, however two men called Thomas Goldston were buried in Eaton Socon on 20 May and 11 August 1609. Possibly one of these names was a mistake for Goldsmith. He made his will on 22 March 1608, giving his occupation as shepherd and place of residence as Eaton Socon. He left goods and money to his brothers and sisters and listed nearly £34 owing to him, mainly by family members. He left his cottage to his brother William, who was his residual legatee and executor, to whom probate was granted by Christopher Wivell on 23 September 1611 (Lincs Archives,

MISC WILLS/F/162). Note that the money owing according to the will was not mentioned in the inventory.

195 Alexander Hopkin of Wrestlingworth undated; between 28 October and 16 November 1609

Lincolnshire Archives, LCC ADMONS 1609/69

A true Inventarie of all the goodes debtes and Chattels of Alexander Hopkin of Wrestlingworth in the county of Bedd deceased as followeth

	£	s	d
Inprimis his apparell		xiij	iiij
Item twoo little pillowes & one Blanket		xiiij	
Item three shirtes[32] and a table cloth		vj	
Item three old Pewter platteres a Candlesticke & a [*blank*]			xx
Item an olde Chaire			xij
Item an olde Stoole			vj
Item a Pillowebere 2 Capps one kerchiefe, 2 shirtes, 4 bandes		vj	
Item in money oweinge unto him	xxj	xiiij	
Item a little bourded bedsteade, mattrice with furniture		xiiij	
Summa	xxiiij	x	vj

Rich: Cullicke, Myles Sill
[*Exhibited at Potton on 16 November 1609*]

Notes: Alexander Hopkin was buried at Wrestlingworth on 28 October 1609. Administration was granted to Thomas Lodge on 16 September 1609 and a bond was taken (Lincs Archives, Act Book A/ix/1 and LCC ADMONS 1609/69). Note: the date of administration on 16 September must be a mistake for November, as he was not buried until 28 October.

196 Richard Thompson of Langford, labourer made 22 December 1609

Lincolnshire Archives, INV/108/26

An Inventorie of the goodes & chattels of Richard Thompson of Langford in the County of Bedf. latelie disceased taken the 22 day of December Anno ~~[...]sup[er]~~ domini 1609

	£	s	d
Imprimis a table & a forme in the hall		v	
Item three kettles a posnet & a frying pan		x	
Item six peeces of peuter two saltes & two candlestickes		vj	viij
Item two tubbes a pashall & an hetchell		ij	vj
Item two shelves a payre of pothangers & other trash			xviij

32 This word is clearly *shirtes*, but given the occurrence of two shirts later in the inventory and no sheets, it may be a mistake for sheets.

In the chamber

Item two bedsteedes two coveringes two matrices on blanketes		xiij	4
Item two boulsters & two pillowes		iij	4
Item three shirtes and four bandes		vj	viij
Item three chestes and a ioyned stoole		iiij	
Item four payres of sheetes and a towell		xi	
Item three old paynted cloathes and a basket			xij
Item an old cloake and his wearing apperrell		vj	viij

In the yard

Item a Cowe		xxx	
Item wood		xiij	4
Item hey and haume		vj	viij
Item hemp		two	
Item on curry of corne		x	
Item three hens			xx
Item mony abroad owing three & thirtie pounds viz			
upon bond[33]			
Jo: Trickhey of Langford	vj		
Rob: Hemming	v		
Rob: Wallis	v		
Steven Hinton	v		
Master Jo Frauncis vicar	v		
William Ashford		xl	
Ric Heming	v		
Jo: Date		x	
Summa totalis ~~xxxix[li] xv[s] iiij[d]~~	xl	v	iiij

praysed by us John Trickhey, Stephan Hinton, Robert Ashford

[*Exhibited by Agnes Tompson, relict and executrix, on 18 January 1610. The exhibition clause was signed by William Styrroppe, notary public.*]

Notes: Richard Thompson was buried at Langford on 7 December 1609, described as a labourer. He made his will on 6 December 1609. He gave £5 to his brother if he came to collect it; £5 10s to his wife's daughter; and the 10s that John Dale (Date in inventory) owed him to the poor of Langford. The residual legatee and executrix was his wife Agnes, to whom probate was granted by Christopher Wyvell at Potton on 18 January 1610 (Lincs Archives, MISC WILLS/F/16).

197 William Brace of Millbrook, yeoman

undated; c. 1611 or later

Bedfordshire Archives, ABP4/182

This is a note about the administration of the estate, not an inventory. It is undated and was probably made a year or more after his death in October 1610.

A note of such somme and sommes of money as have bene paid upon specialties or sufficient proofe and knowledge of the same for William Brace late of Milbrooke in the Countie of Bedf deceased and beinge the severall debtes of the said William Brace, and paid by Roberte Stapleton etc

33 The words *upon bond* are at the side of the list of people who owed him money. It is not clear if the words refer to all of the people.

	£	s	d
Imprimis paid to Alice Brace wief of the said William Brace	Cxij	x	
Item paid to William Savage of Ampthill		xiiij	ix
Item paid to Thomas Hillersdon gent	xxj		
Item paid to Francis Stanton gent	x	ij	
Item to Richard Saunders esquier	xix		
Item to Edward Pennyfather	iij		
Item to Henry Waters	ix	viij	iij
Item to William Wood	xlij		
Item paid to Richard Harvey Clerke	v		
Item paid more to the said Richard Harvey	xj		
Item paid to Thomas Kent	xx		
Item paid to Richard Smyth	v	iij	
Item paid to the Churchwardens of Milbrooke		xx	
Item paid to George Birdesey	vj		
Item to John Webbe of Malden		iij	viij
Item paid to William Heddy		ij	iiij
Item paid to Peter Sutton and William Say		vj	vj
Item paid to Richard Whitebread		xj	viij
Item paid to Elizabeth Brace		v	
Item paid to William Brace his servaunt		xj	ob
Item to Gabriell Greene Clerk		xl	
Item paid to the Joyner		xxx	v
Item paid as appeareth by an accompt of diverse disbursementes and layinges out	xxx	v	ij
Summa totalis	CCCj	xiij	ix ob
[*Corrected total*	*£301*	*15s*	*0½d*]
Item delivered by the consent of Master Saunders to Elizabeth Brace			
one paire of sheetes and a blankett geven by her uncle William Brace and prized at		xviij	

A note of so much money as is yett to pay upon specialties			
Inprimis to Launder of Ridgemonnt	xj		
Item to Tuckey of Aspley Guise	xj		
Item to John Bellinge	ix		
Item to John Ford	xj		
Item to Parker of Steppingeley	v	x	
Item to Margarett Brace	iij		
Item to Robert Stapleton	xxiij	vj	viij
Summa totalis	lxxiij	xvj	viij
Over and besides all the legacies viz			
Imprimis to Alice Brace widowe yerely duringe her naturall lief	viij		
Item to her more yerely upon agreement		xl	
Item to Gartrude Stafford for xvj[tene] yeares every yeare	v		
Item to Johane Whitebread	C		
Item to Elizabeth Brace	x		
Item to Richard Brace	v		
Item to the Overseers	vj	xiij	iiij

Item to Master Greene			xx	
	Sum	Cxxij	xiij	iiij
	[*Corrected total*	*£137*	*13s*	*4d*]

besides the yerely annuities of viij[li]
xl[s] and v[li] above recited

Notes: William Brace was buried at Millbrook on 12 October 1610. He made his will, describing himself as a yeoman, on 30 July 1610, leaving an annuity of £8 to his wife Alice; an annuity of £5 for sixteen years to Gartheritt (Gartrude in the account) Stafford, mother of his 'reputed' son; £100 to Joan Whitbread his maidservant for her wages and the money he held for her; £10 and £5 respectively to his niece Elizabeth Brace and nephew Richard Brace. The residual legatee and executor was his 'reputed son William Stafford late Brace'. He appointed Richard S (the surname is lost through damage, presumably Stapleton) gentleman of Marston and John Stokes vicar of Bromham as overseers. Probate was granted to Robert Stapleton during the minority of the executor William Stafford on 11 December 1610 (Beds Archives, ABP4/1610/142). The document transcribed here is a record of the administration of the estate, although not presented as a probate account. Of the people to whom the testator owed money, Richard Harvey was vicar of Husborne Crawley 1579–1614 and Gabriel Greene was rector of Millbrook 1598–1614 (CCEd). The overseer John Stokes was appointed vicar of Bromham in 1608 (CCEd).

198 Thomas Young of Thurleigh, labourer made 1 February 1610
Lincolnshire Archives, LCC ADMONS 1610/266

A true & perfect Invitorye of all the goodes & cattels whiche Thomas Yonge of Thurlyghe In the countye of Bedforde Laborer had & was In possession of at the time of his deathe Taken the furst of Februarie as folloethe 169 [*i.e. 1609*]

	£	s	d
Imprimis all the bease preaised at	vj		
Item all the sheepe praysed at	iiij		
Item owne sowe & pidges praysed at		x	
Item all hovells & woode pr[aised] at	iij		
Item all the barly & pese pr[aised] at		xl	
Item all the haye pr[aised] at		x	
Item all the tilthe & peseland pr[aised] at		xx	
Item all the bedes with ther furniture & the coffers & chestes with the naprie & linen pr[aised] at		xxx	
Item owne cubbard a pene a table formes stooles coushens painted clothes pr[aised] at		xx	
Item all the brase & peuter dishes spones spites cobbiarnes pocte hangginges pr[aised] at		x	
Item all the bordes garners twobes wheles shovles sithes exses hachats grinstone pr[aised] at		x	
Item all his werringe aparrell pr[aised] at		x	
Some is[34]	xxj		

34 This line has been inserted in a different hand.

Item his detes to be payde out of this sume wiche comes to		xl	

The names of the prayesers as folloethe Robart Jones [*signature*], George Galle [*signature*]
[*Exhibited by Martha Young, administratrix, on 23 May 1610*]

Notes: Thomas Young was buried at Thurleigh on 7 January 1610. Administration was granted to his widow Martha on 23 May 1610 and a bond was taken (Lincs Archives, Act Book A/ix/2 and LCC ADMONS 1610/266).

199 Robert Mayes of Sandy, husbandman made 2 February 1610
Lincolnshire Archives, INV/108/6

A true and perfect Inventary of all and singuler the goodes chattells and debtes of Robert Mayes late of Sandey in the Countye of Bedford deceased valued and praysed by Thomas Underwood and Robert Britten of Girtford in the parishe of Sandey aforeaid yeomen the second day of February in the yeare of our Lord God one thousand six hundred and nyne as followeth

	£	s	d
In the Halle			
Inprimis one long table with a Frame and forme to it		xj	
Item one ioyned Cupbord and the settle and the cloth uppon it		xij	
Item three ioyned Chayres			xx
Item three buffet stooles			xvj
Item one wicker Chayre			viij
Item fyve Cushions		ij	
Item one payre of Andirons and pot hangers one payre of bellowes a glasse casse the paynted cloth and all other implements in the hall		viij	
Summa		xxxvj	viij
In the Parlour			
Item one standing bedsteed corded and a foote pace to it		xx	
Item one feather bed one boulster three pillowes the Curtayns & roddes		xxxiij	iiij
Item one Coverlet and two blancketes		x	
Item one trundle bed corded		ij	
Item one Court Cupbord		x	
Item one glasse Cupbord and one ~~litle~~ needle worke Cushion and A litle ioyned Chayre		x	
Item two turned Chayres six ioyned stooles a great wicker Chayre and A glasse casse		ix	
Item one payre of Creeps one payre of tonges and a fire shovell		iiij	
Item a ioyned box with a locke			xx

Item one truncke with lockes and			
a key		v	
Item the bench bord the wainscot six			
Cushions and the paynted clothes		xxiiij	
Item one great holland Christening			
sheet		xxvj	viij
Item fyve payre and one sheet of			
flaxen sheetes		xliiij	
Item one diaper tablecloth		v	
Item one diaper towell			xij
Item fyve payre of hemp sheetes		xxvj	viij
Item one linnen Cupbord cloth			xx
Item nyne mildewd flaxen napkins		vj	
Item one diaper Cupbord cloth		ij	
Item two flaxen pillow beers with seamis		iij	iiij
Item fyve payres and one sheet			
of course hardon sheetes		xiiij	
Item two payre of hardon sheetes more		vj	
Item fyve pillow beers more		v	
Item fyve table Clothes and one other sheet		ix	
Summa	xiiij	xix	iiij
[*Corrected sub-total*	*£13*	*19s*	*4d*]

In the Milkhouse

Item one powdring tubb foure			
bowles two Chirms and all other			
implementes ther		xij	
Summa patet			

In the Chamber

Item one standing bed corded			
with a testerne of cloth over it		vj	viij
Item one featherbed three bolster			
two blancketes one Coverlet and			
two other course coverlettes			
and one other coverlet and a boulster		xxiij	iiij
Item one boorded bedsteed one			
kneading kimmell and a cloth			
basket and a flasket		v	
Item three Coffers and a box		xx	
Item the paynted cloth and a			
window cloth			xij
Summa		lvj	

In the lofte over the Halle

Item six quarters and six bushells			
of barley	iiij		
Item foure bushells of pease and			
certayne implements there		xx	
Item old lomber in an other			
litle rome		iij	iiij
Summa	v	iij	iiij

In the lofte over the Chamber			
Item two mattresses two Coverlettes two andirons a blancket and a flock bolster		x	
Summa patet			
In the buttery			
Item two hogsheddes three barrells two bowles two trayes foure bottles and shelves and certayne other trashe		xx	
Summa patet			
In the Kitchin			
Item eight tubbes two barrells and a kimnell		xvj	
Item two Casses		iiij	
Item foure payles two boules the shelves dishes and other trashe		v	
Summa		xxv	
In the boulting house			
Item one boulting arke one troughe one Cheese presse and certayne other trashe		x	
Summa patet			
In the Chamber over the Parlour			
Item one Coffer one ioyned Chayre one side table one Forme one featherbed one boulster one Cushion a castnett and a Carpet		xxxiij	iiij
Item one ioyned box		ij	vj
Item six kettles		xx	
Item two brasse pottes and a posnet		x	
Item lxx pownd of pewter for vj[d] per [li]		xxxv	
Item one lattyn chafeingdishe			xij
Item two Chamber pottes		ij	
Item one morter		ij	vj
Item in the kitchen one brewing copper one payre of Cobirons three spites one drippeing pann two fryeing pannes one trevet one gridiron and potthangers		xx	
Item one old warmeing pan			vj
Item all the testators apparrell		xl	
Item foure flitches of bacon		xxiiij	
Item one silver cupp and xj silver spoones	v		
Item ready money in the house	iiij	x	viij
Item one bible and other bookes		vj	viij
Summa	xix	viij	ij
In the yarde			
Item seaven steares	ix	x	
Item two Calves		xxvj	viij

Item one litle redd Cowe bullocke		xxvj	viij
Item one other redd Cowbullocke		xx	
Item three bease	ix		
Item in the barne one skreene one riddle one fanne one scuttle and a bushell		x	
Item in the same barne ten quarters of barley at xij^{s} a qrt	vj		
Item one quarter of wheat		xx	
Item upon a hovell a quarter of pease		xviij	
Item one mare		xx	
Item one hovell with rafters & bordes		xx	
Item two sheddes with the timber and boords over them		xl	
Item in the malthouse ij bushells of Rye		v	
Item one drye tubb one payre of stockcardes one hen penn and six sheepskynns		vj	
Item [*word deleted and illegible*] another hovell one stocke of boardes		xvj	
Item two Cart boddyes		vj	viij
Item the tymber lieing in the street		xl	
Item one sowe and nyne piggs		xxv	
Item six [*?*]shoats	iij		
Item one blacke horse	v	x	
Item one black colte		xx	
Item fyve henns and a cocke		ij	
Item three hoggs troughes			xvj
Item the fire wood in and about the yard		x	
Summa	xlix	xiij	iiij

In the barne at Richardsons

Item xxxiiij^{or} quaters of barley	xx	viij	
Item in the Rye house three quarters and a half of Rye	iij	iij	
Item one [*?*]boate		x	
Summa	xxiiij	j	

In the feild

Item eight score and two sheep and lambhogges prised at	xxxiij		
Item three acres of Rye	iiij		
Item two acres of wheat		xl	
Item foure acres of tilth at xxx^{s} an acre	vj		
Item three acres of brach land		xxiiij	
Item debtes due unto the said Roberte Mayes more then he owed	xliiij	xj	iiij
Item the lease of berrey breach	xviij		
Item three ladders		ij	vj

	£	s	d
Item certayne pease in a leanto and certayne oates besides		vij	
Item certayne hurdles Cowe cribbs with a Rowle and all other lumber		x	
Summa	Cix	xiiij	x
Summa totalis huius Inven[tor]ij	CCxxviij	ix	viij
[Corrected total	*£230*	*9s*	*8d]*

A note of all such of the howshold st[*u*]ff of the fore said Roberte Mayes as Susan his wife did choose accordeing to the will of him the said Robert being parte of that housholdstuff which she did bringe unto the said Robert at her marriage with him Valued and praised indifferently by John Underwood and Thomas Ayre of the parishe of Sandey afore said yeomen the First day of February Anno Domini 1609 as followeth vizt:

	£	s	d
Inprimis one greene turkey coverlet		xv	
Item one wainscot cupbord with the foot pace and cloth upon it		xv	
Item xviij platters and dishes two sawcers and foure porringers		xxiiij	vj
Item ij lattyn Candlestickes two pewter Candlestickes and three salt sellers		v	
Item eleaven shipp trenchers			v
Item one great kettle		xij	
Item fyve other kettles a scunder and a posnett		ix	
Item one drippeing pann		iij	
Item one great brasse pott		ix	
Item one brazen morter and a pestle		ij	
Item one warmeing pann		ij	vj
Item one wainscot bedsteed corded with a fringed vallance and a trundle bed under it corded and a foote pace to it		xxx	
Item a feather bed a mattrice and a straw bed		xl	
Item three bolsters and three pillowes		xxx	
Item two coverlettes ij blanckettes and a mattrice		xx	
Item one wainscot Chest		vj	
Item nyne middle harden sheetes		xxij	
Item fyve table clothes		viij	
Item fyve flaxen sheetes on flaxen table cloth and two pillowbeers		xxvj	viij
Item one box with a locke		ij	
Item one ioyned table with the Frame and two Formes		xv	
Item twelve table napkyns one [*?*]spirecloth one Cupbord cloth and one sheet		iiij	
Item fower payre of hardon sheetes		xx	

Summa totalis huius parcelle	xvj		j
[*Corrected total*	*£16*	*1s*	*1d*]
[*Total of his goods and the goods taken by his wife*	*£246*	*10s*	*9d*]

[*Exhibited by William Bromsaile, notary public, representing James Taylor, the executor named in the will, on 20 June 1610. The exhibition clause was signed by John Jackson, notary public.*]

Notes: Robert Mayes was buried at Sandy on 1 February 1610.

200 Alice Austin of Potton, widow made 5 February [1610]
Lincolnshire Archives, INV/108/2

A true and perfect inventory of all the goods and chattels of Alice Austin of Pottonn latly deceased praysed the fift day of February by Robert Austin and Mathew Austin and Henry Chambers

	£	s	d
Inprimis in the chamber two bedsteads a fetherbed a materis two boulsters two kiverlets with other stufe	iij		
Item five coffers five payer of sheets with other linen		xxx	
Item in the hall a round table a forme and a bench bord with other painted cloths in the hall and chamber		viij	
Item brasse and pewelter with other stuffe		50	
Item in the kitchin a kneadingtrough a poulderingtrough with other barrels and tubs		x	
Item a cow three sheepe and the fowles in the yeard		liij	iiij
Item the wood in the yeard		iij	iiij
Item the Rie in the barne		xxx	
Item two ackers and a half of rie		50	
Summa Totalitur	14	14	viij

[*Exhibited at Potton on 15 February 1610. The exhibition clause was signed by William Styrruppe.*]

Notes: Alice Austin was buried as widow Astin at Potton on 3 February 1610.

201 Thomas Tappe of Morend, Felmersham made 16 February 1610
Lincolnshire Archives, INV/108/3

An Inventarye taken the xvj[th] daye of Februarye 1609[35] by William Barber, Robert Smythe and Robert Tappe of all the goodes and Cattle of on[*e*] Thomas Tappe of Morend in the parishe of Felmersham and Countie of Bed late deceased

35 *1609* and the words *of Morend in the parishe of Felmersham and Countie of Bed* are in a different hand.

	£	s	d
Imprimis ij qt of barlye		xxij	
Item halffe a qt of wheat		ix	
Item peasse and otes		xxxiij	iiij
Item for plowe timber and extrees		xxx	
Item for iiij hogges a sowe & pigges		xxxij	
Item for woode		viij	
Item on fetherbed withe all thinges theire unto belonging		xxx	
Item for sheetes and other Lynan		xxx	
Item too Coffers		vj	viij
Item brasse & pewter		xxiij	iiij
Item forkes Rakes and shovels		ij	vj
Item in the halle on Cubbert a table stooles and other thinges		xxvj	viij
Item on bedstead and a Coffer		v	
Item for Coverled		x	
Item bees		x	
Item Cartes and plowes wyth harnis theire unto belonginge		xxvj	viij
Item apples and hempe		iij	iiij
Item ij flitchis of bacon a bar of Iron and hanggers for apot		xiiij	
Item a coke hens and duckes		iij	iiij
A boote and netes		xiij	iiij
Item tubes & barrils acharme and payles		viij	

praysers William Barbar [*signature*], Robert Smythe [*signature*], Robart Tapp [*signature*]

	£	s	d
Summa	14	5	2
[*Corrected total*	*£17*	*7s*	*2d*]

[*Exhibited by the executor on 1 February 1609, i.e. 1610*]

Notes: Thomas Tappe was buried in Felmersham on 20 December 1609. The dates of making and exhibiting the inventory (16 and 1 February respectively) have been correctly transcribed. There has clearly been a mistake, probably in the date of exhibition.

202 Elizabeth Field of Luton, widow undated; between February and November 1610
Lincolnshire Archives, INV/108/20

There are two documents. One is a complete inventory in draft, which is the text here transcribed. The other is the beginning of a fair copy, ending after 'a warming pan' at the end of the first item.

The Inventory of all the goodes and chattles late Elizabeth Fields Widow of Luton ~~deceased with~~ in the County of Bedford while shee lived prised by Robert Pruddon [*Bruddon in the fair copy*] and Robert Craweley

	£	s	d
Inprimis twoo brasse pannes a porredge pott and twoe possenets a dripping pan and a warmine pan		xvj	
Item twoo spitts		iij	

Item xix peeces of pewter and a spice morter		xviij	
Item twoo candlesticks and a saltseller		ij	
Item one fether bedd one bolster 3 pillowes one fetherbed ticke three blanketts and a mattres	iij	xiij	iiij
Item 3 cusshins			xvj
Item 10 paire of sheets and twoo table cloths	iiij		
Item 9 pillowbeers and twelve napkins		xv	
Item 6 silver spoones		xl	
Item hir apparell	v		
Item fower cofers and a boxe		xxij	
Summa totalis	xviij	x	viij

Signum Ro. [*mark*] Crawley, Ro. [*mark*] Pruddon

Detes desperate

Item oweng by Willm Hawkyns of Aston upon a bill	xxx		
Item by [*word deleted and illegible*] John Clarke of Welwyn	v		
Summa totalis	liij	x	viij

[*Exhibited by the executor George Field on 8 November 1610*]

Notes: Elizabeth Field was buried as Mother Feild at Luton on 22 February 1610. She made her will on 17 February 1610, requesting burial in Luton church. She made bequests of varying sums of money amounting to £70 to grandchildren and one daughter and sheets to her son. She gave her daughter Joan Winch all the household goods in her chamber and elsewhere in Joan's house. She appointed her son George Feild residual legatee and executor and Joan's husband as supervisor. Probate was granted by Christopher Wyvell at Hitchin on 8 November 1610 (Lincs Archives, MISC WILLS/F/45).

203 Richard Ebbes of Sandy made 12 March 1610

Lincolnshire Archives, INV/108/4

Bedford. A true & perfect Inventorie of all such goods and Chattels of Richard Ebbes: lately deseassed at Sandie prized the xij[th] daie of March Anno Domini 1609 in the presence of these whose names are under written

	£	s	d
Inprimis in the hall the table, the stooles the Cheeres the Cussines the yron things about the fire & the painted Cloathes and the Bookes		xx	viij
Item in the Chamber the Bed, the Running Bede the warmyng pann, three Coffers the sheetes the Bord Cloathes, the table napkines the pillow beares, Cubbord the pewter	vj	xv	
Item in the loft over the Chamber the bed and other thinges		xviij	
Item in the Chichin the Brasse		xx	
Item in the Milkhouse things tendinge to that use		xx	
Item in the yord [*sic*] one horse, the milch Cattell two yong bullockes, three yong Caules, one sheepe, two hogges, and the hovels	xxiij	xvij	
Item his apparell		xiij	iiij

	£	s	d
Item desperate detes & goodes unremembred		v	
Somma totalis	xxxv	ix	

Thomas Thomason his marke, Willyam Freeman, Henrie Ebbes
[*Exhibited by Mildred Ebbes, relict and executrix, named in the will, at Potton on 14 March 1610. The exhibition clause was signed by John Jackson, notary public.*]

Notes: Richard Ebbes was buried at Sandy on 10 March 1610.

204 John Dalington of Tempsford, husbandman

made 12 March 1610

Lincolnshire Archives, INV/108/31

A true and perfecte Inventorie of all the goodes and Chatles ~~late~~ of John Dalington late of Tempsford within the Countie of Bedford ~~husbandman~~ deceased vewed and praysed the twelfe daye of Marche in the yeare of our Lorde god one thousand syxe hundrethe and nyne and in the yeares of the Raygne of our Soveraygne Lorde Jeames by the grace of god Kinge of Englande Scotlande Fraunce and Irelande defendor of the faythe etc That is to saye of England Fraunce and Irelande the seventhe and of Scotlande the three and Fortythe ~~and three~~ By these whose names are heare under set downe That is to say William Barkock, Mathew Baynes, Thomas Newman and Jefferye Rogers, Inhabitantes within the sayde Towne of Tempsford

	£	s	d
Imprimis In the Halle one Table and a Frame one forme two benche boardes two chayres fyve stooles foure cushions one litle table two cubbordes two paynted clothes with other Implementes there		xxviij	ij
In his Lodginge Chamber			
Item one Joyned bedsted one boarded bedsted two coverledes fyve blanketes one materice one flockbed one bolster one pillowe with all the hanginges aboute the Chamber		xl	
Item thre coffers two formes one cubborde and a standinge stoole		xvj	
In the servantes Chamber			
Item one Joyned bedsted one olde coverled one olde blankete one Mattrice two pillowes two olde underclothes two olde paynted clothes one coffer one Hetchell and a bill with other Implementes		xiij	iiij
In the Chamber above it			
Item one Joyned bedsted one trundlebed one covereled one Fether bed one Materice one bolster two tables two tressells two formes ~~and~~ one chayre one barrell with all other Implementes there beinge		xl	
In the cheese chamber			
Item one olde cofer foure shellves one chese racke two olde paynted clothes one earthen pote one payre of stockardes one trap to catche rates syxe sickles two peces of newe lynen clothe nyne slipps of yarne with certayne hempe and tooe and all other Implementes there		xx	

In the garner			
Item the barlye there twelve bottles fyve			
Rakes thre ryeinge seves one peece of whitlether			
two payre of caddes for wolle apayre of scales			
apayre of olde bootes with all other Implementes	vj		
In another chamber			
Item one boarded bedsted one olde coverled two olde			
~~cover~~ pillowes certayne carte ropes with other			
horse and oxe ropes certayne spynninge wheeles			
certayne bee hyves certayne olde yron two			
barrells with all other trashe there beinge		xvj	
In the butterye			
Item some barrells one saltingetrofe one			
boultinge arke two kneadinge kymnells			
one olde fat two tubbes foure shelves one			
charme one drinkstall one lyttle forme			
with all other thinges there beinge		xx	
In the milke house			
Item eyghte milke booles one creame pot			
one cleansinge dyshe syxe cheese fates			
foure lyttle shelves and other Implementes		x	
In the kytchin			
Item twentye and two peces of pewlter			
bothe smalle and greate thre salte sellers			
seven pewlter spones		xiij	iiij
Item two greate brasse pans thre brasse potes seven			
kettles one skyllet one warminge pan fyve candle			
stickes one bason one spyce morter two little			
pewlter potes	iij		
Item one pen one cheese presse one mouldinge board			
thre tubbes one stope one washe barrell one			
olde cubbarde two shelves one clothe baskete			
thre spytes one payre of andyrons two payre			
of pot hanginges one payre of tonges one fyre			
shovell one fyre forke two trevites one gredyron			
one yron peele with all other Implementes ~~there~~		xx	
Item syxtene dyshes and nyne spones one			
lanthorne			xx
more that was forgotton in his loginge chamber			
Item two coverledes foure pillowes one peece			
of newe wollen clothe and one peece			
new lynsye woollsy		xx	
Item all his wearing aparrell namelye			
two cloakes foure dubletes two payre of			
breches with the Resydue of it		xxx	
the lynnyn			
Item thirtene payre of sheetes and one			
sheete syxe pillowe beares five boarde			
clothes with certayne hand towells		xl	
Item nyne sackes and thre winnowe clothes		xx	

The cartes and ploughes			
Item foure payre of shoed wheeles thre longe cartes with there furniture two donge cartes with all maner of ploughes and harrowes oxe yoakes and teames with all other Implementes belonginge unto them	viij		
Item two dosen of hurdles and one hurdle		v	
Item one sowe and eyghte stoores		xl	
Item syxe horses	xiiij		
Item seven cowes foure steares thre bullockes and thre yeare olde calves	xxv		
Item fourescore and thre sheepe	xx		
Item nynetene kockes and hennes and capons		viij	
Item thre hovells with the rafters uppon them		xl	
Item cowe cribes and hodge troves withall other woode aboute the yard		xx	
another sheet of paper sewn on			
In the worke house			
Item one maulte quarne one grend stone thre drage Rakes syxe exteryes withall maner of ploughe tymber and all manner of tooles and necessarye Implementes within the sayde workehouse with certayne sythes and snathes		xl	
In the maulte chamber			
Item thre bushell of maulte one net thre tressells with other trashe		x	
In the maulte house			
Item certayne plankes and Rafters		iij	iiij
Item a hayre for the kylln		v	
Item certayne ladders		iij	iiij
Item all manner of shovells spades mukforkes and pickforkes		iiij	
Item two Rooles		v	
Item wheate and Rye to thrashe in the rye house	iij	x	
Item all the barlye in the barn tharshed and unthrashed with certayne pease standinge uppon a hovell	xx		
Item one bushell one fanne two Riddles two syves and one peck		iiij	
Item certayne haye in the hayehouse and one weaned calfe there		xl	
Item carte geares and ploughe geares lockes and Fetters pannells and gyrthes & halters		xiij	iiij
Item composte in the yarde		vij	
In the tylthe feelde			
Item syxe acres and a halfe of wheate and Rye	vj		
Item tylthe lande unsowne twentye fyve acres	xij	x	

In the brache feeld

Item twentie fyve acres of peason oates and wheate sowen there	xv		
Item ten acres theyre unsowne		liij	iiij
Item foure stockes of bees		xij	
Item twelve flitches of bakon		xl	
Somma totalis	viij^xx	viij	iiij
[*Corrected total*	*£168*	*1s*	*10d*]

The praysers handes William [*mark*] Barkocke, Mathew [*mark*] Baynes, Thomas Neuman [*signature*], Jeferye [*mark*] Rogers
[*Exhibited by John Dalington, executor, at Ampthill on 29 March 1610*]

Notes: John Dalington was buried at Tempsford on 8 March 1610. He made his will on 26 February 1609, describing himself as a husbandman. He divided his household goods between his son John and his wife Elizabeth, to whom he also gave 4 cows, 12 sheep, 2 stocks of bees and £14. He gave a sheep to each of her four children, his son John's children and a godson and made other small bequests. His son John was the residual legatee and executor and he obtained probate at Ampthill on 29 March 1610 (Lincs Archives, MISC WILLS/F/138).

205 William Searle of Dunton made 19 May 1610

Lincolnshire Archives, INV/108/12
The document is damaged down the right side. Some words and values are missing.

A true Inventorye of all the goods & Chattles of [...] Searle disceased Maye 19th 1610 priced by Rolan [...] & Thomas Norman, Maye 19th 1610

	£	s	d
In primis in the Chamber where he laye, and died a cofe[...] sixe payer of sheets		13	[...]
Item towe bullockes of 2 yeares old	3	[...]	[...]
Item one little Bullock		20	
Item on Ewe & a lambe		6	[...]
Item 9 acres of Barlye oats & peason	6	[...]	[...]
Item 5 horsses	15	[...]	[...]
Summa	27	13	4

[*Exhibited by John Searle, father and executor, on 2 June 1610. The exhibition clause was signed by John Jackson, notary public.*]

Notes: William Searle was buried at Dunton on 20 May 1610. His Christian name and place of residence, missing from the inventory, can be deduced from the name of his father and executor and the Searle burials recorded in Dunton's parish register in 1610 (*BPR*, vol. 64, pp. 76–7). One was for William Searle, who was baptised there in 1579 as the son of John Searle; another was Robert Searle who was William's brother (*207*). The missing name of the appraiser is probably Roland Woodward, who was one of the appraisers for Robert Searle (*207*).

206 Francis Coper of Potton made 26 May 1610
Lincolnshire Archives, INV/108/9

A true and perfect Inventory of the goods and chattels of Frauncis Coper layt of Pottonn deceased prized by us John Hall, Alexander Atkingsonn, Thomas Chichly, Richard Wilshire the sixe and twentie day of May Anno Domini1610 as followeth

	£	s	d
Inprimis in the hall a table a benchbord a forme with paynted cloaths and two spitts one andiron a fiershouel and other trash		xij	
Item in the parlor a boarded beadstead with a straw bedd two blanquets one bolster two pillowes and a couerlet with three chests a cupbard and paynted cloaths and other triffels		xx	
Item in the kitching pewder greator and lessor sixeteene peices two brass potts three kettels		xviij	
Item two tubbs three kemnells two barrells a boulting ark		vij	
Item sixe payer of sheits sixe napkings two boardcloaths three pillowbeares		xvj	
Item certeyn wood in the yeard a sow and sixe piggs with a bucket and a cheane and other trash		xxxiij	iiij
Item an acre of rie		xxiiij	
Item his apparrell		xxx	
Summa totaliter	8		4

[*Exhibited by Alice Cooper, executrix, on 2 June 1610. The exhibition clause was signed by John Jackson, notary public.*]

Notes: Francis Cooper [*sic*] was buried at Potton on 11 May 1610. Alice Coope [*sic*], widow, married Edward Coal at Potton on 22 January 1611. This is probably Alice Cooper.

207 Robert Searle of Milloe, Dunton made 29 May 1610
Lincolnshire Archives, INV/108/11

A true Inventory of all the goodes & cattles of Robertt Searle of Millohe disceased April 8th priced by Rowland Woodward & Thomas Norman Maye 29 1610

	£	s	d
Inprimis in the hall a table a cubbord, a forme cheares & stooles		20	
Item paynted cloths			20
Item 4 platters, 2 dishes 2 Candlesticks		6	8
Item in the chamber 2 bedsteeds		5	
Item a fetherbedd, 2 coverletts, a mattris, 2 boulsters & a blanckett		30	

Item 6 payer of sheets		28	
Item 2 pillowes & 6 pillowe beers		6	8
Item 2 Cofers		5	
Item paynted cloths		5	
Item in the little house a brasse pott a pan 3 kettls 2 little poosnetts		26	8
Item an old case		2	6
Item 2 Tubbs a charne, a barrell a boultinge arcke 2 shelfes, 6 boules		7	
Item a fryinge pan & pott hookes		1	6
Item fyre wood in the yard		1	4
Item a hogge		4	
Item a cowe		33	4
Item a calfe		13	4
Item 4 sheepe & 2 lambes		20	
Item 3 halfe acres of Barlye		30	
Item an acre of pease		13	4
Item a cocke & sixe hens		2	6
Summa	13	3	6

[*Exhibited by Mary Searle, relict and executrix, on 2 June 1610. The exhibition clause was signed by John Jacksonne, notary public.*]

Notes: Robert Searle was buried at Dunton on 9 April 1610. The inventory gives his date of death as 8 April. He was born in 1573, the son of John Searle and thus brother of William Searle (*205*).

208 Rodger Burden of Silsoe, Flitton, fletcher — made 2 June 1610

Bedfordshire Archives, ABP/W1610/106

A true Inventory of all the goods Cattells and Chattels of Rodger Burden of Silvesho in the parishe of Flitton in the County of Bed Fletcher deceased, taken the second day of June, Anno Regni Domini nostri Jacobi Regis Anglie etc Octavo et Scotiae xliij°. Praysers Robert Child, Richard Wood, Richard Milward, Edward Hill, Reynold Hill

	£	s	d
Imprimis two acres of wheat	iiij	xiij	iiij
Item one acre of Rye		xvj	
Item three acres of Barley	iiij	vj	viij
Item two acres of Beanes		xlvj	viij
Item three acres of Oates	iij	vj	viij
Item fyve beasts	xiiij	vj	viij
Item on bullocke		xxvj	viij
Item on horse		liij	iiij
Item six sheep		xl	
Item foure hoggs		xliij	
Item foure piggs		xvj	
Item tenn pullets		vj	viij
Item in ready money		xl	
Item his weareing apparrell		xx	
Item in the hall two cupbordes		xxiij	iiij

Item two tables in the hall, sixe ioyned stooles & on old forme		xx	
Item wenscote in the hall and two benche coffers		xx	
Item paynted clothes in the hall		ix	
Item bords & shelves in the hall		ij	vj
Item two flittches of bacon		xvj	
Item in the hall on spytt, two payre andeyrons, hookes tongues gridyron and five shoveles		vj	
Item in the bedchamber on standing bed, on fether bed, two boulster two pillowes, on matteresse, ~~three~~ two blankets, on bed covering		l	
Item on coffer in the Chamber		v	
Item new wollen clothe being seven yardes		xviij	
Item twelve payre of sheets	iij		
Item three table cloathes, foure pillow beeres, and other smale linen		xx	
Item in the other chamber on standing bed, two old quilts, on blanket on bowlester		xv	
Item on other bedsteed, on [*b*]lanket, on new matteresse, on bowlester on bedcoveringe		xvj	viij
Item on coffer		iiij	
Item on presse in the chamber		ij	
Item paynted clothes in the chambers		viij	
Item sixe bushells of mault		xij	
Item three bushells of wheat and Rye		vj	
Item twenty and foure cheeses		x	
Item old bords in the loftes			xij
Item in yarne		viij	
Item in brasse, fyve kytles, on pott, on morter, on skellet		xxvj	viij
Item all treen warre, tubbes etc		vj	
Item boards in the kytchin			xviij
Item in the milke house, barrells, bowles, bordes & other trifles		xv	
Item in pewter eleven old dyshes, two candlestickes, on salte, on chaffing dyshe etc		viij	vj
Item in the shoppe bowes and bowe staves		xxxij	iiij
Item ~~for~~ arrowes, and arrowe stayles	iij	xiiij	
Item arrowe tymber	iij	vj	viij
Item arrowe heads		vj	viij
Item workeing tooles		xx	
Item three cupboards in the shopp		viij	iiij
Item the hovell next William Burdens		xxvj	viij
Item the hovell for the stable		xxvj	viij
Item the cowe house, hovell and hogges coats		xxx	
Item the hovell called the worke house		xxvj	viij
Item on brasse pott		viij	
Item apeltrees		v	
Item firewood		xx	
Item a Quearne and on cheese presse		x	

	£	s	d
Item the well buckett and chaine			xij
Item twentie loades of dounge		x	
Suma totalis	lxxix	xiiij	x
[Corrected total	*£80*	*3s*	*10d]*

[Exhibited by William Burden, who was described as one of the executors, on 3 July 1610. He was the overseer of the will.]

Notes: Rodger Burden was buried at Flitton on 18 May 1610. He made his will on 30 March 1610, describing himself as a fletcher. After bequests of money or goods to grandchildren and other children, he left the hay house next to his yard and his best cow to his son William; a hovell called the stable to Thomas Coles; and a hovell called the work house, the cow house and the hogs' cote to Nicolas Burden. His wife Joan was to have the use of all his goods during her lifetime, then they were to be divided amongst his family. His wife and son Nicolas were appointed executors and granted probate on 3 July 1610. His son William was overseer (Beds Archives, ABP/W1610/106). On the verso of the inventory is a note of the commission to Richard Wood, vicar of Flitton to administer an oath to Joan Burden, the relict.

209 Thomas Abraham alias Bolnest of Potton, maltster made 9 June 1610

Lincolnshire Archives, INV/108/13

The opening heading is in a different handwriting from the body of the inventory and on a separate slip of paper sewn on to the top of the inventory. The words underneath are not visible. The transcription here is taken from the slip and the words visible on the main sheet of paper.

A true and perfect Inventarie of all the moveables goodes and chattells of Thomas Abraham alias Bolnest of Potton within the Countie of Bad maltster deceased Prized by Frauncis Ponnfret, Henry Wallis, Thomas Allam [*blank*] the ix[th] of June Anno 1610 as followeth

	£	s	d
Inprimis in the Hall a long table one forme two chears a cubbard with twenty tow peices of pewder, great & smaller 6 quishinges a warming pann whith certayn paynted cloths & a bench board	iij		
Item in the parlor above the hall thre chestes tow bedsteedes one old fetherbedd one matterice two couerletes two blanketes two boulsters three pellows, fourteen payres of sheetes 4 pillowbears one boardcloth nyne table nabkyns ~~two peces of pewder~~ & other triffls	x		
Item in the Kitchen one brass pott, five panns & kettls a skillet, an other lesser brass pott a brazen candlesticke with a payre of pothangers, a fire shovell tonges & pellows[36] & an iron barr with other triffls		xl	
Item in the loft one old standing bedd with a matterce one bowlster one coverlet & other thinges of small worth a kneading trough a bowlting arke with a yeilding fatt two barrells a bowlting arke payls bowls dishes		xxiiij	

36 *Pellows* is likely to be bellows, not pillows.

Item the yeard certayn dung with certayne fire wood, timber one bucket & a cheyne	v	x	
Item certayne rie in an old house unthrashed one fanne one bushell one ridle rackes pitchforkes & other trash	v	x	
Item malt hay boardes straw in the barn a skreyne certayn wheels a cloth basket with other trash	xlij		
Item one blynd horse, four shoates certeyne pullen		xl	
Item three acres of rie in the heath	vj		
Item forty shillinges in money		xl	
Item his apparell one cloak two dubletes two payre of britches, with hattes shirtes bandes etc		xl	
Summa totalis	81	iiij	

Frances Pomfrett [*signature*], Henry Wallis [*signature*], The mark of Thomas Allam
[*Exhibited by Joan Bolnest alias Abraham, relict and executrix, named in the will, on 9 June 1610. The exhibition clause was signed by John Jackson, notary public.*]

Notes: Thomas Abraham alias Bolnest was buried at Potton on 11 June 1610.

210 Edward Freeman, junior, of Stotfold, gentleman made 16 July 1610
Lincolnshire Archives, INV/108/16
Only this fragment survives.

A true Inventarie of all the goodes and chattels of Edward Freeman the younger late of Stotfold in the County of Bedd gent deceased made & valued by Gerrard Spencer, William Allen, William Cooper and Thomas Freeman the xvj[th] daie of Julie in the yeare of the raigne of our most gracious soveraigne Lord James by the grace of god king of England France & Ireland defender of the faith etc the eight and of Scotland the xliij[th]

	£	s	d
Imprimis in the Parlor one Cupboard with a Cupboard cloth of Lynnen one feather bedde, a bolster a blanket twoo boxes three Formes one ioynde stoole at		lvj	
[*Total of the whole inventory taken from the Act Book*	*£411*	*2s*	*6d*]

[*No exhibition clause*]

Notes: Edward Freeman was buried at Stotfold on 8 July 1610 as Master Edward Freeman junior. Administration was granted to Edward Freeman on 26 July 1610 and a bond was taken (Lincs Archives, Act Book A/ix/2 and LCC ADMONS 1610/28). For the inventory of his father Edward Freeman of Stotfold in 1618 see *300*.

211 John Horne of Whipsnade, husbandman or yeoman made 21 September 1610
Lincolnshire Archives, INV/108/17

An Inventorie of all the goods and Chattles of John Horne late of Whipsnayde within the countie of Bedd husbandmanne deceased pryzed & vallued this 21 of September 1610 by Nic Twysell minister, John Beamond, Myles Horne & Tho: Heywood

	£	s	d
Inprimis his apparrell & monie in his purse	iiij		
In the hall			
Item one table with a fraime & a rounde table with iiij° stooles		xiij	iiij
In the Parlor			
Item one bedsteed one chest & a chayre with other implementes		xxvj	viij
In the Chamber over the kitchin			
Item one standing bedde with a featherbedde & thother furniture Item one trundlebedde with the furniture one Cooberde one Counter one Arke & other implements	vj	xiij	iiij
In the chamber over the hall			
Item woll apples & hoppes		xl	
In the Buttrie			
Item one Salttrowe & a little coobberd		x	
In the kitchin			
Item brasse and pewter one querne spites and other things	iiij	x	
Bacon at the Roosse [*sic*]		xx	
In the Malt lofte			
Item malte and other things		xx	
Item Bees 2 stokes		x	
Grayne in the barnes with the hay ~~towe horse~~	xlj		
In the Stable			
~~with the furniture~~ Two horse with the furniture	vj[37]	x	
Item twoo milch kyne 2 bullocks & 2 Calves	vij		
Item 30 shepe	vij	x	
Item hogges & stoares	4	10[38]	
Item pullen		xx	
Item Lynnen and other Naperie	vj	xiij	iiij
Item Cartes plowes & harrowes	vj		
Fynallly [*sic*] other thinges fogottenne		xxx	
Summa totalis	Ciij	xvj	viij

[*Exhibited by Agnes Horne and John Horne, executors named in the will, at Hitchin on 27 September 1610. The exhibition clause was signed by John Jackson, notary public and deputy registrar.*]

Notes: Only the Bishop's Transcripts of Whipsnade parish registers have survived for the early seventeenth century and they look incomplete. They record the burial of John Horne on 5 October 1610, which was eight days after the inventory was exhibited (*BPR*, vol. 25, p. B9). One date must be a mistake. John Horne made his will on 20 December 1609, describing himself as a yeoman. He left his house and 27½ acres to his wife Agnes for life and then to his son John to whom he left his other freehold land on condition that he gave his brother William £20 when he reached 21. William was also given £10 by the testator. His wife and son John were residual legatees and executors. They were granted probate by Christopher Wyvell at Hitchin on 27 September 1610 (Lincs Archives, MISC WILLS/F/41). The appraiser, Nicholas Twysell was rector of Whipsnade, 1593–1622 (CCEd).

37 Originally *vj vlj* and deleted.

38 Originally *xx*^{s} then deleted.

212 Thomas Sexton of Wyboston, Eaton Socon, labourer made 9 November 1610
Bedfordshire Archives, ABP4/181

An Inventory of all the goods of Thomas Sexton late of Wyboston within the parish of Eaton in the Countie of Bedford labourer deceased, made & prised the xj[th] day of November 1610: By Richard Tingey and Jonas Thodie

	£	s	d
Imprimis in monye bonds and debts owing	xvj	xviij	
Item his apparrell		xx	
Item a Coffer		ij	
Item twelve bushells of barly		xviij	
Summe is	xviij	xviij	

Richard Tingeys marke, Jonas Thodie [*signature*]
[*No exhibition clause*]

Notes: Thomas Sexton was buried at Eaton Socon on 21 July 1601. He made his will on 19 July 1601, itemising money owed to him by eight people, almost amounting to the £16 18s listed in the inventory. He gave most of it and 12 bushels of barley to his brother-in-law Richard Tyngy and some to James Tyngy when he completed his apprenticeship. The residual legatee and executrix was his sister Anne Tingy, to whom probate was granted on 29 October 1610 (Beds Archives, ABP/1610–1611/90). The will was made and he died nine years before his will was proved. His inventory was made after his will was proved.

213 Nicholas Chappell of Wrest, Flitton, yeoman made December 1610
Bedfordshire Archives, ABP/W1610/83

An Inventary of the goodes and chattelles of Nicholas Chappell late of Wrest deceased

	£	s	d
Imprimis 2 paire of sheetes		vj	viij
Item one coverlet		iij	iiij
Item one bolster			xij
Item two pillowes		ij	
Item one pillowbere			xij
Item a great chest		ij	
Item a frieing pan			vj
Item a kettle			xij
Item 2 boxes			iiij
Item all his apparell		xl	
Item a Sadle			iiij
Item in readie money	ix		
Item owing by Law: Coleman of Shitlington	ix		
Item owing by John Carter & John Purret of Luton	xxxiij	vij	
Item owing by William Hewet		L	
Item owing by Henry Richardson		x	
Item owing by William Chappell	iij		
Summa	Lx	v	viij
[*Corrected total*	*£60*	*5s*	*2d*]

[*Exhibited by Thomas Halfpene, one of the executors, on 11 December 1610*]

Notes: Nicholas Chappell was buried at Flitton on 1 December 1610. He made his will on 9 November 1610, describing himself as a yeoman. He left £25 and household goods to his daughter Martha; £30 to his daughter Mary; 5s each to his sister, brother, nephews, nieces and others. He left items of clothing to several people (his working 'sute of apparrell', a fur-lined jerkin, his best suit and a saddle, a gown and two pairs of shoes). His daughters (both under 21) were residual legatees. Benjamin Hale and Thomas Halpenny were appointed executors. Probate was granted to Thomas Halfpenie on 11 December 1610, power being reserved to the other executor (Beds Archives, ABP/W/1610/83).

214 William Chambers of Potton, yeoman and tanner made 20 December 1610

Lincolnshire Archives INV/108/27

The inventory is faded at the top right-hand side. Missing words and letters have been inserted where obvious.

A true Invetarie of all the goodes and chattells late of William Chamberes of Pott[*on*] in the Countie of Beddf deceased ma[*de*] the twenteth daie of December Anno D[*omini*] 1610 by George Robinson the elder, Thomas Harper, John Harper, William Chamberes and Frances Hearne [*as*] followeth

	£	s	d
In the Hall			
Inprimis one Table with the frame a forme the bench and other therunto belongeinge with chayres and stooles & potthangers		xx	
In the Parlor			
Item one Cupboard a chaire with stooles & boxes		xx	
In the greate Parlor			
Item a longe table with a forme a square table with the fraimes & certaine stooles with a chest a chaire a court cupboard & the benches		liij	iiij
In the chamber ouer the greate parlor			
Item 2 ioynd beddes with the furniture therunto belongeinge a Chest, a Coffer a Liverie table & the cloth a bason & Ewer	x		
In a little Chamber over the greate parlor			
Item a ioynd bedde with the furniture, a liverie table ij chaires a little stoole	vj	xiij	iiij
more in the Chamber over the greate parlor			
Item certaine sheetes and table clothes and other Lynnen	vj	xiij	iiij
Item in the seller five hoggesheades & other Implementes		xiij	iiij
Item in the butterie adioyneinge to the hall 50tie peeces little and greate of pewter and brass	iiij		
Item in the lofte ouer the hall one standeinge bedsteede with ij featherbeddes & other furniture ij Cofferes	iiij		

Item in a lofte adioyneinge twoo servantes beddes with the furniture		xl	
Item in the kitchin certaine implementes		xxx	
Item in the brewehouse the leade and the querne & other breweinge vesseles	iiij		
Item in the milkehouse certaine milke booles and other thinges ther unto perteineinge		xxx	
Item in the yard iij beastes ij horses & vij shoates, a hogge and one sowe	xj		
Item in the stables twoo teames & cart geares with rackes & Mangeres		xiij	iiij
Item in the yard the rafters of a hovell with the strawe upon yt & an old Cart body and other trashe & rackes and hoggesetroughes		xx	
Item the pullen		xx	
Item xlij sheepe	x		
Item the ledder tand [*tanned*] and untand & all all [*sic*] other implementes belongeinge to the tanneres trade	xCviij		
Item an olde ploughe 2 iron dragge raikes and a ladder		iiij	iiij
Item in the malthouse pease 3 quarteres and a halfe		xlvj	viij
Item in the malt lofte barlie 10 busheles		xvj	viij
Item malt a quarter		xiij	iiij
Item pease seaven busheles		xj	viij
Item woole & other thinges		iij	iiij
Item trashe and thinges unsene		x	
Item iij acres and a halfe of Rie in the heath field & iij acres wheate & Rie in the old field	viij	xiij	iiij
Item the whole some of barlie in both the barnes 35 quarteres at xvj^{s} the quarter	xxviij		
Item the Haie a ladder a skrene & other thinges		xxxiij	iiij
Item his apparrell	v		
Item oweinge him by bondes	CxCj	viij	
Item in desparate debtes		xxx	
Item all his strawe and chaffe	iiij	xvj	
Item all his rie accordeinge to 18^{s} the quarter	xij	xvij	iij
Somme is	CCCCxxvj	x	vij

[*Exhibited by Joan Chambers, relict and executrix, named in the will on 9 March 1611. The exhibition clause was signed by John Jacksonne, notary public.*]

Notes: William Chambers was buried at Potton on 9 December 1610. He made his will on 3 December 1610, describing himself as a yeoman. Goods in his inventory identify him as a tanner as well as farming. He gave his wife Joan an annuity of £8 being the interest from a sum of £80 and after her death the sum was to be divided equally among his children. She also received two beasts and the use of his household goods for life after which she could dispose of them among their children. He left sums varying from £20 to £80 to his four daughters and one son; the value of his grain was to be divided equally among three of his daughters and three sons. His grandchildren were given two sheep each. The residue was given to his son Thomas. His wife and son Thomas were executors. Probate was granted by Christopher Wyvill to Joan Chambers who appeared in person at Potton on 18 January 1611, with power reserved to Thomas (Lincs Archives, MISC WILLS/F/17).

215 Richard Tiplady of Dunstable made 5 February 1611
Lincolnshire Archives, LCC ADMONS 1610/77

Quinto die mensis Februarij Anno Domini 1610 Anno que regni domini nostri Jacobi nu[*n*]c regis etc octavo et Scot xliiijº.[39] An Inventory of all the goodes of Richard Tiplady deceased late of Dunstable in the county of Bedf Taken the day and yeare above saide preysed by Roger Fynch, Nycholas Sage and others v3

	£	s	d
Imprimis his wearing apparell		x	
Item one Fetherbedd being an ould one		x	
Item one ould Boulster		v	
Item a paire of owld sheetes and a happharlett			xx
Item one ould bedd stead		iiij	
Item one owld Cheste			xviij
Item all the owld Lumber		ij	ij
The sume is		xxxiiij	iiij

Roger Fynche [*signature*], Nicholas Sage [*signature*], [*illeg.*] Marshe [*signature*]
[*Exhibited by John Tiplady, administrator and brother, on 28 February 1611. The exhibition clause was signed by John Jackson, notary public.*]

Notes: Richard Tiplady was buried at Dunstable on 2 February 1611. Administration was granted to John Tiplady on 28 February 1611 and a bond was taken (Lincs Archives, Act Book A/ix/40 and LCC ADMONS 1610/77).

216 Walter Forest of Sutton made 14 February 1611
Lincolnshire Archives, LCC ADMONS 1610/29
The handwriting is difficult.

Feb 14 anno domini 1610. An Inventory of the goodes and dettes of Gualter Forest late of Sutton in the county of Bedforde deceased as they were praysed by those whose names are heereunder Written.

	£	s	d
Inprimis in the hall 1 chaire, 4 stooles 2 spittes, 2 drippeing pannes a paire of Jacks, 1 pair of pot hangers, a Grediron, a Trevet			

39 Translation: 5 February AD 1610 and in the eighth year of the reign of our lord James, now king etc and the forty-fourth year [of his reign] in Scotland.

6 woodden dishes, 1 doozen of trenchers, 1 linnen wheele, 1 wollen wheele with som other necessaries		13	4
Item 1 great kettle, 3 lesser kettles, 3 brasse pottes 1 skciller 2 scummers a chaffendish		xv	
Item 2 doozen of Peuter		xviij	
Item 10 candlestickes		x	
Item 4 saltes, 1 quarte pot, 1 pinte pot, 2 drinckeing cuppes 1 warmeing pan and a chamber pot		x	
Item 1 table, 1 cupborde, 1 forme		xxiij	
Item 3 cheastes 1 wicker chaire, a boxe, 3 Cushions and paynted clothes with other implements		35	
Item xj paire of sheets	iij		
Item 2 table clothes, 5 pillowbeers 3 hand towells 11 napkins		30	
Item 5 boulsteres 6 pillowes		33	4
Item a fetherbed with a bedsteed 1 boulster 1 covering 1 blancket		46	8
Item A trundle bed and a forme		vj	viij
Item a bedsteede a flocke bed 2 blancketts		13	4
Item a coffer and 2 bordes with 2 painted clothes & other stuffe		vj	8
Item a Quilt 2 pillows 3 curtaynes with rodes		23	4
Item a Tod of woll		xvj	
Item 3 tubbes, 2 barrlls [*or bawlls*], 1 kneedeing troffe, a boulteing ark 3 shelves		viij	
Item 2 pannells 2 Ropes, 2 clevers, a [*?*]rideing thrum 2 beames with other small things		vj	
Item wood, studds and Rootes		xviij	
Item for 7 hogges 4 pigges	iij	10	
Item for a horse		xl	
[*end of page; total at the foot*]	25	2	4
Item iij sheepe		10	
Item 2 cowes and 1 hide	iij	xij	viij
Item for Compase		xj	
Item cheeses & butter		x	
Item his apparell		26	8
Item for halfe a kiln [*sic*], 1 stone and a halfe of tallow 1 pond of suet		xiiij	
Item received for a stall		xx	
Item left in mony in the [*?*]perse	iij	xiiij	
Item received of Master Bagen		xj	
Item due from Cadwell		viij	
from William [*?*]Key		x	
from Francis Pumfret		iij	
from Mayes of Gurforde		v	
Item a calfe		13	4
Item for a bullocke from one of Gransden		25	
Item 4 hennes and a cock		ij	vj
Sum is	40	~~16~~ 18	vj

Jarrard Balls [*signature*], Thomas Heward his merk, Davy Brotherton his make, Nicholas Plummer his marke

A note of dettes oweing by Water Forest

Item to Jhon Hall of Potton	viij		
Item for the childes nurseing		10	
Item to Master Holton		x	4
Item for the pasturing of a calfe		13	4
Item for the herdmans wages		ij	4
Item ~~for~~ to the hogherd			18
Summa is	9	17	vj

Certayne dettes claimed but not knowen as yet

by Henry Crooke	4		
Goodman Wade of Potton		30	
Jhon Austen		30	
Sum is	vij		

[*Exhibited by Sara Forrest, relict and administratrix, on 15 February 1611. The exhibition clause was signed by John Jacksonne, notary public.*]

Notes: Walter Forest was buried at Sutton on 2 August 1610. Administration was granted to his widow Sara on 17 January 1611 and a bond was taken (Lincs Archives, Act Book A/ix/3 and LCC ADMONS 1610/29). Sara Forrest married John Gilman at Sutton on 1 July 1611.

217 Raphe Place of Eaton Socon, gentleman made 30 March 1611

Lincolnshire Archives, INV/108/150

The Inventorie of the Goodes Chattells Cattells and movables of Raphe Place of Eaton in the Countie of Bedd gent deceased made the xxx[th] day of March Anno Domini 1611 by William Yarwaye, Thomas Kippest, Frauncyes Coxe and George Coventon as Followeth

	£	s	d
Imprimis his Apparrell		liij	iiij
In the Hawle			
Item a long Table with a Frame a round table a benche a great Cheire ij other Chaires painted Clothes Iron barres pott hangers fire shovell fire forke tongs an Iron beame with Scales & waightes and other implementes		xl	
In the Parlor			
Item a Court Cubbord a square Table with a frame a paire of Andirons certaine Bookes vj Cushins v Joyned stooles the hanginges or painted Clothes three benche boardes and other Implementes	iij	vj	viij
In the best Chamber over the Parlor			
Item two beddstedds standing with the Testors over them a flocke bedd a Fether beadd a boulster twoe blankets and one Coveringe	iiij	vj	8
Item a wicker Chaire & one Andiron		ij	viij
In the Chamber over the Entrye			
Item a standing bedstead ij Flock bedds one Fether bead ij blankettes a Coverledd			

a Covering iij Coffers and a Chaire		xl	
In the Chamber over the Haule			
Item two great Chestes a Coffer a Fetherbed a mattrice a boulster & other thinges		33	4
Item a Covering iiij paire of flexen Sheetes iiij paire of hemp taire Sheets vii paire of harden Sheetes v bord Clothes v pilloe beeres iij dozen Nappkins vj hand towells and other small Lynnen	v	xv	
In the Chamber over the kytchine			
Item twoe trundell bedsteads certaine hempe and other Implementes		xx	
In the Chamber over the Buttrye			
Item iij litle Fyrkines iij bords a Cheese Racke a Drie Fatt aples & other Implements		vj	8
In the Butterye			
Item x Barrells a hogeshedd a saffe a yeeling Fatt drinke stales a round Table certaine shelves and bords & other Implementes		xl	
Item a spice Morter and Pestell		vj	
Item a bason and ewer a great Charger a litle bason iiij pewter Platters iij pewter dyshes vj porringers vj sawcers ij Saults and a pewter pott		xviij	
Item a Chaffinge Dyshe and twoe latten Candelstickes		vj	
Item xij Silver Spoones		vj	
In the kytchine			
Item a Copper with Furnice ij kettles ij brasse Pottes a Possenett iij Spittes iij dripping pannes A paire of Racks a Tread a Scummer A mouldinge board a Coffer A syfting Troffe a boulting tonne A mustard Quarne a Mashing Fatt and one Tubbe	4	13	4
In the Larder House			
Item iij powdring Tubbes a saulting Troaffe and annother Tubbe		xij	
Item xij Flitches of Bacon	iij		
In the Servantes Chamber			
Item iij Bedsteads with the bedding and Furniture one Sawe one Axe Iron wedges And certaine other Tooles		xxvj	viij
In the Milke House			
Item a Cheese Presse a Charme certaine Shelves and other Implementes		x	
In the Stables			
Item viij Horses	xviij		
Item ij Geldynges	ix		
Item Ploughes plough geares Cartes Carte geares Harroes Roles a			

Jine and other Implementes		xl	
Item a Sadle and bridle		vj	viij
In the Barne			
Item iiij Quarters of Barley	iij		
Item v Quarters of Rye	iiij		
In the Yarde			
Item certaine Ladders Timber Fire Woodd Cowe Cribbes and other thinges	3	vj	8
Item ij Hovells with their Rooffes	vj	13	4
Item iiij long Cartes iiij paire of Wheeles ij Tumbrells or Mucke Cartes	viij		
Item Tenne Bease and a Bull	xxij		
Item xj Bullocks	xiiij		
Item vj Calves		xl	
Item Nyne litle Bulloks	vj	xiij	4
Item v Schore and iiij Sheep	xxx		
Item xiij Hogges	4	6	8
Item Nyne Pigges		xxij	vj
Item iij Score Acres of barley and wheate in the Tylth Field and lv Acres in the breach Field of Pease Corne and Ootes Seaven Schore and Fower teene Pownds	[*154*]		
Item a Screene		v	
Item certaine Mucke and Compasse		xl	
Item a Lease of certaine Lande of the Heires of Master Tailor	viij		
Item a lease of the manor of Eaton cum Soca	200		
Item Owing to the Testator by Master Luke		xxxij	
Sum Totall	672	9	2
[*Corrected total*	*£537*	*8s*	*6d*]

The Prizers Wm Yarwaye [*signature*], Thomas Kyppest [*signature*], Signum Francis Coxe, The marke of Geo Coventon
[*No exhibition clause*]

Notes: Raphe Place was buried at Eaton Socon on 29 March 1611. He made his will on 20 March 1611, requesting burial in the parish church. He appointed his sister Eden Place executrix, directing her to sell his lease of the manor of Eaton Socon and pay the debts and legacies he owed to his sisters Agnes and Judith under their father and his brother, John Place's wills; and to sell his freeholds in Eaton Socon and pay the legacies in his will. He gave about £200 in legacies to family and servants and an annuity of £3 to his mother. His sister Eden renounced executorship and probate was granted to the testator's brother Francis Place by Christopher Wyvell at Hitchin on 6 June 1611 (Lincs Archives, MISC WILLS/F/23). His brother John Place's inventory is *151*.

218 William Haynes of Sutton made 1 April 1611

Lincolnshire Archives, LCC ADMONS 1611/271

The document begins with the line Item a coburd in the hale *and ends with the heading beginning* A true and perfect Inventary. *For ease of reading, the normal sequence of the heading followed by the list of goods has been adopted. Two people have written the inventory. One, with a very poor hand, has listed the goods; the other, a more practised writer, has written the heading and made an addition to the list.*

A true and perfect Inventary of all and singuler the goodes chattells and debtes of William Haynes late of Sutton in the Countie of Bedd deceased Taken and prised the first day of Aprill in the yeare of our Lord God 1611 By Richard Searle, Robert Fickis and Thomas Smith of Sutton aforesaid as followeth vizt

	£	s	d
Item a coburd in the hale praisd at		x	
Item a long table and a frame to it and [...] and a forme		x	
a bench borde toe Cheres			xx
a haling			xij
eyg [*eight*] pecis of peuter at		v	
on bras pot iiij ceteles praiest at		viij	
toe lenin wheles and a peare of pot hangeres praist at			xx
a old Chest and a halling praisd at		ij	
in the Camber agine a standing bed toe coverledes foure peare of shetes and pented Clothes ~~praies att~~ and a materis ij boulsters ij pillowes [*this line has been inserted in a different hand*]		xxxx	
Item fower Chestes prayesd at		x	
Item a coate a dublet and a peare of hose prais		v	
Item wode praised at		vj	viij
Item thre tubes and on paile praysd at		ij	vj
Item haye in the barne		iij	
Item compas in the yeard		ij	
Item toe lomes and geares be longing to them		xxxx	
Item on cowe on bolack and a ckafe prayesd at three poundes	[*3*]		
Item on pedge prayesd at		iij	iiij
[*word deleted*] prayeseres Thomas Smyth, Robert Vkis, Rycherd Searle			
Summa	x	xj	x

[*Exhibited by the administratrix at Potton on 2 April 1611*]

Notes: William Haynes was buried at Sutton on 18 March 1611. Administration was granted to his widow Mary on 6 April 1611 and a bond was taken (Lincs Archives, Act Book A/ix/5 and LCC ADMONS 1611/271).

219 Richard Dyer of Stopsley, Luton, labourer made c.April 1611

Lincolnshire Archives, INV/108/50

The beginning of the first two lines are faded and just legible.

An [*Inven*]tory of all the cattell & goods of Rychard Dyer of Stopsley [*who dyed*] the iiij[th] day of Aprill in the yeare fo [*sic*] our lord god: 1611

	£	s	d
Inprimis			
Item i cowe		xlvj	viij
Item vj shepe		xl	
Item ij storse		x	
Item for bees		vj	viij
Item for pullayne		iij	iiij
Item for all his grayne		liij	iiij
Item for all his housholde	iij		
Item for wood		x	
Item for theyr apparell	iij		
sum is	xiiij	x	

The praysers weare Thomas [*mark*] Pygott & Wyllyam Wattes [*signature*]

[*Exhibited in person by the son, one of the executors named in the will, on 4 July 1611. The exhibition clause was signed by George Pormoth, public notary.*]

Notes: 'Father' Dyar died on 4 April 1611 and was buried at Luton on 5 April. 'Mother' Diar was buried at Luton on 9 April. The inventory includes the value of *their* clothes, indicating that it was made after Mother Diar's death. Richard Dyer made his will on 24 March 1611, giving money or furniture and a swarm of bees to each of his three daughters after his wife's death; 10s to one grandson and a lamb to the other; and leaving the remainder to his wife and son Richard who were joint executors. Probate was granted on 6 May 1611 (Beds Archives, ABP/1611/160).

220 William Shreeve of Toddington made 19 April 1611

Lincolnshire Archives, INV/108/32

A true Inventorie conteineinge all such goodes chattells and chattell [*sic*] as were of William Shreeve late of Todington in the Countie of Bedford deceased at the time of his death taken and praysed the xix[th] of Aprill Anno Domini 1611 by Richard Johnson, Thomas Spufford, Thomas Cowden and John Brinkelowe In the presence of Francis Rollenson the writer thereof

	£	s	d
Inprimis the stuffe in the parlour beinge a Court Cupbord a Cupbord a table and frame a ioyned chaire & a forme		xxxiij	iiij
Item in the hall a Table and a frame 3 ioyned stooles & a Matted chaire		xiij	iiij
Item one Chest		ij	
Item one Coffer			x
Item one Trunke		v	
Item one standeinge bedstede		xxvj	viij
Item one Court Cupbord in the chamber		vj	viij
Item 2 Feather beddes	iij		

Item three bolsters		x	
Item three pillowes		ij	
Item three Coverlettes		xx	
Item three paire of blankettes		xv	
Item one Liverie bedde		iij	iiij
Item one warmeinge panne		ij	vj
Item Curtaines of the windowe			vj
Item one Cupbord clothe & a carpet		xvj	
Item tenne paires of Sheetes	iij		
Item fowre pillowebeires		iiij	
Item 2 dozen and a halfe of table napkins		xij	
Item fowre table clothes		xij	
Item in the kitchin all the brasse		xl	
Item the pewter candlestickes spoones salt selleres & basen		xiij	iiij
Item one paire of rackes one paire of Andyrons, the potthangers two spittes, one Fryenge panne one paire of bellowes & 1 gredyron		xij	
Item one wollen wheele			xij
Item in the chamber over the kitchin wheate malt oates & barley		xlij	
Item one bedsteade of boardes with the furniture upon yt		x	
Item Charcoole		v	
Item bacon		xiij	iiij
Item woolle		viij	
Item one cheese racke & a shelfe & the cheeses & tallowe, 2 sives, one bushell one halfe pecke, 2 kymnelles one haire sive one serse and certaine hoppes		xv	
Item all the Lumber & stuffe in the dairie		xv	
Item 2 loade of woode in the yard		xiij	iiij
Item lath plankes boardes in the barne and twoo old Tubbes		vj	viij
Item 2 pigges and a sowe		xx	
Item one calfe		x	
Item the donge in the yard			xij
Item one Cocke and Henns		ij	
Item three shirtes[40]		x	
Item one barne standeinge in Langley	iiij		
Item haie in the barne		xl	
Item railes and one Ladder		vj	viij
Item twoo kine	v		
Item one Cowe 2 heiferes and Five steares	xv		

40 *Shirts* are out of context here. Possibly *shotes* were meant.

Item one barne of twoo baies at his house in Todington	iij		
Item one peece of Timber		x	
Item twentie nyne couples of sheepe	x	iij	
Item fiftie twoo drie sheepe	xv	xij	
Item one mare and a mare colt of 2 yeares old	v		
Item in readie money	xvj	xviij	viij
Item his apparell lefte ungiven before his death	iij		
Item one Cupbord and a chest and other implementes in his chamber at the mannor		v	
Item one bond of an hundreth pownde to be paid the 2 of October anno domini 1611	C		
Item one assignement of a lease called the lease of Todington warren made unto Wm Shreeve and his executors for the payement of one hundreth pownd upon the 2 daie of October A° domini 1612	C		
Item his parte of the lease of Langlie[41] dureinge the tearme valued at	xxx		
Item his Lease of Ipsawe hill[42] valued at		x	
Item the Lease of his house in the towne of Todington valued at	xl		
Item his debtes upon specialties	xxxiij		
Item his other debtes	xxxiij		
Some is	CCCCxxxiiij	viij	ij
[*Corrected total*	*£444*	*8s*	*2d*]

[*Exhibited by the executors, William Newman and Henry Smyth, on 23 May 1611. The exhibition clause was signed by John Jacksonne.*]

Notes: William Shreeve was buried at Toddington on 17 April 1611. Francis Rollenson (Rawlinson), the writer of the inventory, was vicar of Middle Rasen, Lincs, 1589–1603, rector of South Kelsey St Nicholas, Lincs, 1603–30 and rector of Toddington 1613–30 (Venn ACAD, CCEd).

41 Langley was one of the common fields of Toddington.

42 Ipslow hill in Toddington.

221 Mathew Cartar of Shillington, yeoman made 25 April 1611

Lincolnshire Archives, INV/108/47

The left side of the document is creased and torn.

The Invetorye of the goodes of Mathew Cartar late of [*S*]hitlington desseassed made & prised by John Hanscombe, Thomas Ensam & Richard Iverye the xxv[th] of Aprill Anno domini as foloweth

	£	s	d
In the hall			
first a Cupbord atable & a frame with the longe forme [*a*] little table a chaire iiij Joined stooles & other stooles with the bench boarde prise		xxiij	iiij
Item twelve peeces of pewter a morter twoo Candelstickes & twoo saltes prise		xiij	iiij
Item the pott hookes & hangers a paire of Andirons a paire of tonges a paire of bellowes a spitt a tredd & a grediron prise		vj	viij
Item thre Flitches of bacon prise		x	
Item the painted clothes in the hall & iiij cushins		iiij	
I[*n*] the buttrye & milke house			
Item twoo brasse pottes Five kettels a frienge pan & a scimmer prise		xxvj	viij
Item twoo tubbes twoo barrells & twoo pailes prise		vj	viij
Item the shelves & setles milk vessells with the cheeses & cheese Rack prise		xij	
In the chambers			
Item thre bedsteedes & iiij coffers prise		x	
Item a Fetherbed twoo pillowes twoo boulsters a mattres twoo coverletes & ij blanketes prise		xlvj	viij
Item one paire of fleccen sheetes twoo paire of hemp tare thre paire of hemptoo thre table clothes the pillow bears iiij table napkins certaine skaines & rough hempe prise		xxxiij	iiij
Item a wollen wheele a linnin wheele a cloth basket & a hand baskett prise		ij	vj
Item the wooll in the house prise		x	
Item his apparell		xiij	iiij
in the lofte in the yard			
Item Six bushels of malt twoo bushells of wheate with a bushell a fann & a tubb prise		xxiij	
Item iij pikforkes mattock spad shovell & twoo wedges prise		iij	vj
Item the wood in the yard the ladders rackes & troughes prise		xxviij	iiij
Item twoo beasse & a heiffer prise	vj		
Item vj Cowples & xij drye sheepe prise	iij		
Item the pullin in the yard		iij	iiij
Item one aker of beanes on half aker of wheat & one half aker of barlye prise		liij	iiij

	£	s	d
Item the donge in the yard		iij	iiij
The whole somme is	xxv	ix	viij
[*Corrected total*	*£25*	*13s*	*4d*]
The Charges of his funerall		xxxiij	iiij

[*Two exhibition clauses are on the verso, written in different hands. The first, dated 6 May 1611, did not name the person who exhibited it and included the power to add more goods if they come to light. The second was exhibited by the executrix at Hitchin on 2 July 1611, with the same power.*]

Notes: Mathew Carter was buried at Shillington on 15 April 1611. He made his will on 23 February 1611, describing himself as a yeoman. He made small bequests to married daughters and grandchildren and appointed his wife Joan as residual legatee and executrix. She obtained probate on 6 May 1611 (Beds Archives, ABP/W1611/9).

222 William Johnson of Bornend, Cranfield, husbandman made 13 May 1611

Lincolnshire Archives, INV/108/152

The true and perfitt Inventarie of all and sing[u]ler the goodes debtes & Chattells of William Jhnson Late while he Lyved of Cranfeilde in the Countye of Bedford husbandman deceased, made and prised the xiij[th] daye of Maye Anno domini 1610 By Richard Cooke the elder, George Baker and Robert Byngham

	£	s	d
Imprimis the Apparell of the said deceased		xl	
Item Foure Horses	viij		
Item nyne drye Sheepe at v[s] vj[d] a peece		xlix	vj
Item Fyve Cooples at vij[s] a coople		xxxv	
Item three Cooples more		xxix	
Item three Storers		xiij	
Item twoe dunge Cartes & a longe Carte		xlvj	viij
Item one longe Carte	iij	vj	viij
Item Seaven Beastes	xiiij		
Item three yearelinge Bullockes		xlv	
Item Foure weaninge Calves		xx	
Item one hovell		xx	
Item one other hovell		x	
Item Eighte ploughe Beames		v	iiij
Item Neckes and Sheathes twoe dosen and Foure		vj	
Item eighte broade Reshes		ij	viij
Item one ploughe and a paire of harrowes		iiij	
Item all the other wood in the yarde		vj	viij
Item a dunge Carte bodye and Foure Ploughe handells		ij	
Item an olde Ladder			iiij
Item a parcell of Barley		x	
Item a parcell of hey		vij	

	£	s	d
Item a Carte bodye		iij	
Item a Sowe and Pygges		xx	
Item one paire of Fill stroppes all the geares and halters and a Carte rope		v	
Item Foure Storrs		xxiiij	
Item xvij Acres and iij Roodes of white grayne and xiiij Acres and a Roode of Pease	xxxviij		
Summa Totalis huius Inven[ta]rij	lxxxiij	x	x

[*Exhibited by Richard East, notary public, for Anne Johnson, relict and administratrix, at Hitchin on 6 June 1611. The exhibition clause was signed by John Jacson, notary public.*]

Notes: William Johnson was buried at Cranfield on 23 April 1611, described as being of Bornend. Administration was granted to his widow Anne on 27 May 1611 and a bond was taken (Lincs Archives, Act Book A/ix/6 and LCC ADMONS 1611/280).

223 John Gale of Oakley, husbandman made 28 May 1611

Lincolnshire Archives, LCC ADMONS 1611/266

The Inventory of all such goodes as were of John Gale late of Okeley in the countie of Bedf husban[dm]an (and in the Dioces of Lincolne) deceased vaulued and prised the xxviij day of May 1611 by William Barcocke and Edmond Gale husban[dm]en of the same towne & countie

	£	s	d
Imprimis the cobert		viij	
Item i bench borde & ii formes		iiij	
Item the painted clooes in the halle		v	
Item iiij kettels & on posinghe		xx	
Item v platers & on candellstik		vii	
Item i spisce morter & pestell		ii	
Item on standinge bed stead on fetherbed and other ~~bed~~ things beloinge		xl	
Item i littell bedsteade i mattris & a bolster		vi	viii
Item vi paire of sheetes & on tablecloth		xx	
Item ii cofers in the chamber		iii	
Item in the milch house i cofer ii barels one tob ii formes & other impellmentes		x	
Item on cow & a bolock	iii		
Item ii stores		x	
Item for vii akers of wheat rye & barley and pese	vii		
summa totalis	xvi	xv	viij

The marke of William Barcoke [*no mark*], The marke of Edmond Gale, The ma[*rk of*] William Barcock

[*Exhibited by Katherine Gale, relict and administratrix, at Bedford on 23 September 1611. She was bound in the sum of £30 to administer his estate properly.*]

Notes: John Gale was buried at Oakley as John Gale senior on 9 May 1611. Administration was granted to his widow Katherine on 23 September 1611 and a bond was taken (Lincs Archives, Act Book A/ix/8 and, LCC ADMONS 1611/266).

224 Robert Spufforde of Stopsley, Luton, yeoman made 31 May 1611
Lincolnshire Archives, INV/108/45
The inventory is faded.

Thinventary Indented of all & singler the goodes Cattalls Chattells debtes rightes and Credittes of Roberte Spufforde late of Stopesley in the parishe of Luton in the Countye of Bedd yoman deceassed taken valued & praised by William Howe, Thomas Piggott, William Brittaine & John Atwood yomen the last daye of Maye Anno Domini 1611 and in the yeares of the Raigne of our sovereigne Lorde James by the grace of god of England Scotland Fraunce & Ireland kinge defender of the faithe etc of Englande Fraunce and Ireland the Nyneth & of Scotland the foure and fortith as followeth videlt

	£	s	d
In the Haull			
Inprimis a Cupbord & a Cupbord shelfe valued at		xx	
Item twoe Joyned tables with the frames		xx	
Item a longe forme sixe greate ioyned stooles & three lesser ioyned stooles		xij	
Item three Chayres one litle playne stoole an olde salte barrell a hanging shelfe a Reele & foure quisshions		vj	viij
Item twoe Andirons, twoe potte hangers a fire shovell a paire of tonges a gridiron a paire of bellowes a pott shelfe a waighte to use aboute lynneon three steeles & the paynted clothes		x	
Summa	iij	viij	viij
In the Chamber over the Haull			
Inprimis a Joyned Bedsteed		xx	
Item a mattresse a featherbedd three blanckettes a Coverlett twoe boulsters three fustian pillowes all lyenge on the same Bedsteed	iiij		
Item twoe playne bedsteedes upon theme lyenge five blanckettes a [*?cover*]lett a paire of sheetes and twoe boulsters and upon thother [*?ly*]enge a mattresse Five blanckettes a Coverlett a boulster and three pillowes		xl	
Item Foure Cofers		xx	
Item his apparell		xl	
Item in one Cofer tenn paire of sheetes touwen valued at		l	
Item one holland blacke seamed sheete and seaven pillowebeeres in the same Cofer		xxx	
Item in one other Cofer three paire of toowen sheetes Seaven tableclothes of toowen and three Pillowe beeres		xl	
Item in one other Cofer One paire of flexen sheetes seaven paire of hempe tayre sheetes		liij	iiij
Item foure toowen tableclothes & three of hempetaire five halfe sheetes & twelve table napkins		xl	
Summa	xx	xiij	iiij
In the lofte over the Entrey			
Inprimis a Trundle bedd a mattresse three blanckettes twoe boulsters twoe pillowes a paire of sheetes and a Coverlett		xxv	
Item a butter Charme & foure pitchforkes		v	
Item foure paire of toowen sheetes one white seamed flexen sheete foure handtowells three wallettes seaven pillowebeeres toowen			

and one lynneon Cloth called a foldinge Cloth and a short tablecloth		xxvj	viij
Summa		lvj	viij

In The kytchin

Inprimis twoe brasse pottes a payre of pottehookes sixe kettles and one posnett		xxx	
Item one dozen of pewter platters one pewter fruyte dishe foure porringers sixe sawcers three saltesellers a candlesticke and a chafinge dishe		xx	
Item a kneding troughe with a Cover twoe formes certein henn Casses a mustard Quarne a peele three payles a hoggetubbe a lanterne foure bottles and a cheese presse		xx	
Item a paire of Andirons a spitt and iron drippinge pann an axe a mattocke twoe hatchettes a longe bill a morter a pestle foure wedges a fryeng pann a slyce twoe hammers a paire of pynsers twoe longe raakes a garden raake a sythe reddy hanged a shorte ladder & twoe awgers		xxvj	viij
Item a spade a shood shovell a sheepe hooke a boultinge hutche a hobbing iron three pitchforkes a troughe & other ymplementes there		iij	iiij
Summa	v		

In the Buttry

Item three drincke barrells a vergis barrell a Charme Seaven Cheese fattes five treen platters a tanckerd divers disshes spoones trenchers boles a paire of scales a pounde waighte a halfe pounde a paire of stocke cardes three paire of woll cardes one wollen wheele a lynnoen wheele drincke stalls sixe shelves three earthen pytchers twoe wodden ladles a breadgrate twoe mousetrapps a ratte trappe a drincke Tunnell a clensinge dishe a skymmer a pottelidde & other ymplementes there		xx	
Summa patet		xx	

In The maltehowse

Inprimis a parcell of wheate in the strawe		x	
Item a longe carte with all furniture		xxvj	viij
Item a plowe with all furniture		vj	viij
Item twoe drincke fattes foure drincke tubbes a buckinge tubbe a greate bole a longe ladder a shorte ladder a yotinge troughe and a scuppott a greate henn penn thirtene ploughe beames & other ploughe tymber a playne bedsteed & certein fyrewood		xl	
Item a kylne hayre		vj	viij
Item a malte Quarne		xiij	iiij
Summa	v	iij	iiij

In the garner

Inprimis a scryen a busshell a stryke a pecke a halfe pecke twoe Fannes three malte shovells a Castinge shovell a hanginge shelfe an olde tubbe twoe poundes of woll foure baskettes with Covers a cloth baskett & a flaskett		xx	
Item Five sackes & foure baggs		xiij	iiij
Summa		xxxiij	iiij

	£	s	d
In the Gardner lofte			
Inprimis the malte there	x		
Item a powdringe troughe with a Cover a Cheese racke a tennan Sawe a Cake Peele Five sickles eighteene pounde of too spunn and unspunn three Pease hookes three shackforkes a course sacken clothe a foorme a paire of scales twoe extry pynnes a hetchell a riddle three iron hookes with certein olde iron & other lumber		xxv	
Summa	xj	v	
In the Barne			
Inprimis Twoe paire of Harrowes		x	
Item a Ladder a racke a hay hooke a seedcod a paire of Fetters a horselock a Cuttinge knife and a hand barrowe		v	
Item a parcell of haye		ij	vj
Summa		xvij	vj
In the Stable			
Inprimis a halter pannell girte and pylche a donge forke and a donge raake		iij	iiij
Item a weanlinge Calfe		viij	
Summa		xj	iiij
In the yarde and feildes			
Inprimis twoe bease & a yeerling bullocke	v	xij	
Item twoe hogges		xvj	
Item the Pullen		vj	vj
Item the wood		xxx	
Item eighteene Elme bourdes		xiij	iiij
Item the donge twoe Coweracke foure hoggestroves a sheperack foure hurdles and a grindstone		xiij	iiij
Item twelve Cooples	v		
Item Nyneteene other sheepe	vj	vj	viij
Item wheate & Barley	vj	xiij	iiij
Summa	xxvij	xj	ij
Debtes due to the Testator			
Inprimis due by George Gregory of Eversholte	vj	xij	
Item due by the same George		xviij	
Item by the same George and by William Gregory his brother	xxiiij	iiij	
Item due by John Spufford brother of the Testator	xj		
Item due by Thomas Starnell of Luton Maltester	x	iiij	
Item due by John Crawley thelder		vij	x
Item in reddy monney	iiij	xiiij	vij
Summa	lviij		v
[*Total*	*£138*	*0s*	*9d*]
Item due by the Testator to Elizabeth his daughter	iij	xiij	
Summa totalis allocatis allocand[43]	Cxxxiiij	vij	ix

Signum de Margarete, Signum de Anne, Executrices
[*Exhibited by Ann Spufford, executrix, at Hitchin, Herts, on 20 June 1611*]

Notes: Robert Spufforde was buried at Luton on 29 May 1611, as Father Spufford. He made his will on 8 June 1610, requesting burial near his wife. He gave £20, a bed and bedding and

43 This total excludes the amount due to his daughter.

household goods to his daughter Elizabeth; an annuity of 4 marks to her from the income from his property and after her death to her first child; and eight sheep. He gave £17 to his daughter Helen Dix; and 20s to each of her children. He gave his messuage and tenement in Stopsley to his daughters Margaret and Ann, who were also residual legatees and executrices and were granted probate by Christopher Wyvell at Hitchin on 20 June 1610 (surely a mistake for 1611) (Lincs Archives, MISC WILLS/F/11).

225 John Woodwarde of Barton in the Clay, innholder made 13 June 1611
Lincolnshire Archives, INV/108/51

The true and perfitt Inventarye of all and sing[u]ler the goodes debtes and Chattells of John Woodwarde late while he Lyved of Barton in the Claye in the Countye of Bedford deceased made and prised the Thirteneth daye of June Anno Domini 1611 By Christofer Goldsmythe, Thomas Allen and Richard Hodges

	£	s	d
Imprimis Twoe Store hogges		xij	
Item Six hennes and a Cooke		iij	iiij
Item in the new Lofte one standinge Bedd, a Featherbedd twoe pillowes a boulster a blanckett & a Coverlett		liij	iiij
Item more in the same Chamber one Co[ur]te Cupborde, a rownde Table with a frame, twoe ioyned fourmes, one Stoole a paynted clothe with other smale necessaryes		xx	
Item in the newe parler one standinge Bedd with the Curteyns & hanginges one Featherbedd twoe boolsters one blanckett one Coverlett a pallatte and one Trundle Bedd	iij		
Item in the same roome one Table with the frame, twoe ioyned Foormes one ioyned stoole and a Carpett, twoe Chairs, Eighte olde ~~Ch~~ Cusshions and some wainscott aboute the Benches		xxx	
Item in the olde parlor one standinge Bedd one trundle bedd with the furniture one olde Table with tressells, twoe ioyned Foarmes with other smale necessaryes		xl	
Item in the olde Loftes, Foure olde Bedstedes with the Furniture, foure Cofers one Boxe, Twentye Cheeses with all the other ymplementes and necessaryes	iij		
Item a d[*o*]sen paire of sheetes, Fyve table Clothes with ij apryns and all the other Lynnen	iiij		

Item in the Halle one Cupborde a Table with the Frame, one other Table, foure ioyned stooles, one fourme one chaire some wainscott aboute the Benches with some other necessaryes and all the paynted Clothes aboute the howse		xl	
Item all the Brasse and Pewter the Laton ware with the warminge panne	iij		
Item Spittes and Gospannes, Cobirons and Rackes, hatchettes and bills with all other yron ware and olde Iron		xx	
Item Brewenge vessells and drincke vessells and necessaryes for bakeinge Chese presse fullenge troughe and all other necessary ymplementes aboute any of the howses and one mault myll and a mustarde myll		xl	
Item twoe olde Cupbordes and a paire of Tables		vj	viij
Item one Carte bodye Carte Tymber and ploughe Tymber and buildinge Tymber with planckes and Boordes and Fire wood in the yarde, Ladders a greate Iron Racke and other Lumber in the yarde one kyll haire and one ploughe with the yrons	iij		
Item one Hovell, and mangers and Rackes in the Stable		x	
Item all the grayne in the howses and groweinge in the Feildes	vj	vj	viij
Item his wearinge Apparell		xiij	iiij
Item xij skeynes of Flaxen yarne		xij	
Item Twoe stockes of Bees		vj	viij
Summa Totalis huius Inventorij	xxxvij	xiiij	

Debtes oweinge by the sayde deceased at the tyme of his deathe

Imprimis to Thomas Man	iij	iij	iiij
Item to Master Luke Norton		xxxvj	viij
Summa	v		

[*Exhibited by Mary Woodwarde, relict and executrix, at Hitchin on 4 July 1611*]

Notes: John Woodwarde was buried at Barton on 12 June 1611, described as householder. He made his will on 21 June 1609, describing himself as an innholder. He gave his mill, a cart, and a cupboard in the kitchen to his son Francis as standards in the house; furniture and bedding to daughter Mary. He divided the residue into two parts and gave one to his wife Mary and the other to his daughters Margaret and Joan. He appointed his wife as executrix and she was granted probate by Christopher Wyvell at Hitchin on 4 July 1611 (Lincs Archives, MISC WILLS/F/12).

226 Annis Wine of Eyeworth, widow made 13 June 1611
Lincolnshire Archives, INV/108/52

An Inventorie of all the goods of Annis Wine Widdowe late of Eyworth in the Countye of Bedford late disceased prized the 13th day of June 1611

	£	s	d
Inprimis in the loft over the chamber			
one bedstead & other smale thinges		xiij	iiij
In the chamber two bedsteads and			
the beddinge vj payre of sheets			
other smale lynninge & 2 ould coffers		xxviij	iiij
Item on young heiforde		xviij	
In the milke house a chese presse &			
x milke boules & a charme		xiij	iiij
In the halle halfe on cubbord		ij	vj
Item vj platters a morter a saucer			
& iij candlestickes		iij	vj
Item 2 brasse potts achauendish			
2 litle kettles & a litle possnett		vj	viij
Item 2 planck tables an ould coffer			
2 chayres iij stooles 2 tubbs and			
an ould painted cloth		v	
Item hir cloths & monye in hir purse		x	
The whole some is	~~3~~		~~8~~
	5		8

~~prized the 13th day of June~~ by James Atterton [*signature*], John Cullicke [*signature*]
[*Exhibited by William Wine, one of the executors, on 4 July 1611. The exhibition clause was signed by George Pormorth, notary public.*]

Notes: Annis Wine was buried at Eyeworth on 11 May 1611, as Widow Wine.

227 George Bucke of Leagrave, Luton, glover made 15 June 1611
Lincolnshire Archives, INV/108/43

The true Inventorie of All the Goodes cattell and moveables of George Bucke late of Ligrave in the parrishe of Luton in the Countie of Bedd glover deceased made the xv[th] day of June Anno Domini 1611 as followeth viz

	£	s	d
In primis all his wayringe Apparrell		x	
Item in brasse and pewter		xxx	
Item a table a cubberd & stooles		x	
Item certeine barrils boles & dishes		v	
Item one Allome Kymnell tubbes & tooles		iij	iiij
Item two bayardes beddinge and Cofarres		xl	
Item wooll yarne and leather		xx	
Item certeine stockes of Beene [*sic, bees*]		xx	
Item two bullockes		xl	
Item certeine bordes and woode		v	
Item two Acres of edge graine		xx	

Item halfe a dosen of hennes		ij	vj
Somma totallis	x	v	x

Praysed by Richard Hydd and Robard Brigges and William Brigges

Debtes owinge by the said George Bucke			
unto George [*blank*] of Lidlington	iiij		
to William Bigge		xxiiij	
to Robert Steppinge		ij	iiij
Som	v	vij	iiij

[*Exhibited by Joan, daughter of the deceased and administratrix, at Hitchin, Herts, on 20 June 1611*]

Notes: George Bucke was buried at Luton on 22 May 1611. In his nuncupative will he left half his goods to his daughter Joan and the other half to his wife Marian for her life then to Joan. Probate was granted to Joan Bucke by Christopher Wyvell at Hitchin on 20 June 1611 and a bond was taken (Lincs Archives, MISC WILLS/F/8 and Act Book A/ix/7).

228 Thomas Burtholl of Stopsley, Luton

made 18 June 1611

Lincolnshire Archives, INV/108/42

The true Inventorye of All the Goodes cattell chattels debtes and moveables of Thomas Burtholl late of Stoppesley in the parishe of Luton in the Countie of Bedd deceased made the xviijth daie of June anno Domini 1611

	£	s	d
In the Hawle			
In primis a Cubberde with a shelfe & a cubberd cloth		viij	
Item a table a forme & a paire of tresselles		iij	iiij
Item an olde chaire v stooles one ioyned stoole a boultinge hutche ij pailes iij boles trenchers spoines and a paier of bellies		x	
Item a woollen wheele a lynnen wheele two pott hangers a gridiorne a brushe and two olde cusshins		v	
Item v kettles a posnet iij saulte sellers iij sawcers one candlesticke x pewter dishes a ladle iiij peces of old pewter & a kymmell		xxvj	viij
Item two flytches of bacon		x	
Item a hen casse ij barrils a seve a paier of wooll cardes a paier of tow cardes a grind stone a Reele a paier of skaeles ij^{li} of leade iij shelves an old barrill two pottes & a pecke		v	
In the Chamber over the Hawle			
Item two bedstedes on flocke bed ij blanckettes iij sheetes ij coverlettes ij bolsters & ij pillowes		xxxv	
Item iiij cheses iiij heeves & a presse of bordes		xiij	iiij
Item a bagge of feathers & certeine wooll a wool basket certeine lynnen alreadie spon in skeines & bottams and some unspon		xv	

	£	s	d
Item two cloeth baskettes a chese racke and olde painted clothes		ij	
Item the testators workinge tooles		xxx	
Item the testators apparrell		xx	
Item two paier of flexen sheetes iij pillowe beeres xj table napkins ij paier of towen shetes ij table clothes a halfe sheete & a wallett		xxxv	
In the Gardeine			
Item two heeves of Bees		x	
In the yarde			
Item a Cowe		xlvj	viij
Item one hogge 5s and the compost 6s 8d		xj	viij
Item a stocke of elme bordes with some planckes		xiij	iiij
Item woode and tymber 40s and two ladders 2s		xlij	
In the Feilde			
Item one Acre of thetches and oetes		x	
Item vij shepe and fowre Lambes		xlv	
Item olde Iorne			xx
Item one wainlinge Calfe		x	
Item Pulleine and geese		xvj	
Debtes owinge to the testator			
John Heath of Lilley		viij	
William Bigge of Stoppesley		iij	iiij
Summa totalis	xxj	xvj	

Praysed by Willimi How, John Crawly [*signature*]
[*Exhibited by the executrix at Hitchin, Herts, on 20 June 1611*]

Notes: Thomas Burtholl was buried at Luton on 29 May 1611. He made his will on 28 May 1611, leaving £20 to his daughter Agnes at age 20, and sheep, a cow and household goods immediately. He asked his wife to take Agnes in if she was out of service at any time before that age. He left his house to his wife Joan until his son William reached 21. He appointed his wife Joan executrix, to whom probate was granted by Christopher Wyvell at Hitchin on 20 June 1611 (Lincs Archives, MISC WILLS/F/6).

229 Thomas Miller of Potton, carpenter — made 24 June 1611

Lincolnshire Archives, INV/108/49

A true & perfect Inventory of all the goodes & chattls of Thomas Miller carpenter layt of Pottonn within the countie of Bedford deceased prized the 24th of June Anno Domini 1611

	£	s	d
Inprimis in the hall hous one cubard a table, a forme & certayn old stools with a paynted cloth tenn peices of pewter a payre of pothangers whith two bgards, a brass pott, two kettls whith ~~matters~~ trash of small value		xxx	

Item in a chamber thre bedsteads two matterices two coffers whith paynted cloths & other small thinges		xiij	
Item five payre of sheetes & one odd sheet with old table cloths & towels & certeyn sorry lynnen		xviij	
Item in the loft a fann & one wollen wheel a payre of stock kardes & other trash		vj	
Item certayn wood in the yeard a grind stone a litle sheip rack with a litle straw upon the hovell		xvj	
Item a hogscoat & a hogstrough two shoates 13s		xiij	~~iiij~~
Item in the shopp certayn towls a whippsaw a tennre saw with one axe chizells & other towls		ix	
Item one acre of Rie in the feild		xvj	
Item his apparell & other goodes not remembred		vij	viij
Sum totaliter	vj	xiij	viij
[*Corrected total*	*£6*	*8s*	*8d*]

[*Exhibited by Elizabeth Miller, relict and administratrix, on 29 June 1611*]

Notes: Thomas Miller was buried at Potton on 17 June 1611.

230 Edward Lockkey of Bedford St John made 26 June 1611

Lincolnshire Archives, INV/108/65

An Inventorie of all the goodes and Cattells of Edward Lockkey diseased of the parrish of Snt John Baptist in in [*sic*] Bedford taken the 26 of June 1611 and praysed by these whose names are here under written

	£	s	d
Imprimis one Table with a Frame 3 stooles 2 Cheres and one square Table	0	i5	0
Item one Cubbert 2 glas shelves one Falinge Table and fortie peeseyes of peauter	4	6	8
Item one Lattese with pottes and glasseyes	0	i	4
Item 6 Cushens and 5 Candlestickes	0	8	0
Item 4 spittes a pare of Andirons with pott hangers Tonges and bellouse	0	8	0
In the little parler			
Item one bedsteed one Fetherbed one boulster one Coverlid one blankett with Curtines	3	6	8
Item one Table one levarie Cubbart one Chest one Chere and one Forme	0	i3	4

In the great Parler

Item one bedsteade one Fetherbed one boulster one Coverled blanket 2 pillous Curtins and Trundle bed	5	0	0
Item one Cubbert with a pres a square Table one Chest 3 boxseyes & a fourme	i	i3	4
Item a pare of AndIrons a Candle plate with a looking glas	0	2	0
In the bras house			
Item 3 bras pottes 5 kettles a bras pann a scummer a brason Ladle 2 frying panns and a gridiron	3	0	0
In the butterie			
Item 4 barrels 3 Toubs 2 stops and a kymnelle	0	i3	4
In the Chambers			
Item 3 bedsteedes 2 mattriseyes one Coverlid 2 boulsteres one blanket and 2 Coffers one Chere with harden and Flaxsen yurne	2	0	0
Lynen			
Item i9 pare of sheets one dussen of napkins 4 bourd Clothes 3 pare of pillou beres 4 Touels	8	0	0
In the backhouse			
Item a boulting Arcke moulding bourdes ~~Trough~~ kneding Trough with peeles [*?*]boultils and waightes	i	0	0
Wood in the yard			
Item all the Fagottes and hard wood	2i	6	8
Item a hovell with serten hurdles and other ould things	2	0	0
Item a Rack and manger with 4 spining wheles	0	6	8
Item 8 Coople of owes and Lames	3	0	0
Item the parties wering apparrele diseasled [*sic, deceased*]	1	6	8
Sum is	59	7	8

[*Exhibited by the executrix on 23 September 1611. The exhibition clause was signed by George Pormouth, notary public.*]

Notes: Edward Lockkey was buried at Bedford St John on 13 June 1611.

231 George Negusse of Shelton, yeoman

made 27 June 1611

Lincolnshire Archives, INV/108/117

A true Inventory of all the Goods and Chattells of George Negusse of Shelton in the County of Bedfford yeoman late deceassed prized the 27th day of June Anno domini 1611 by these vz William Beridge minister, William Negusse, Thomas Negusse, John Negusse Henry Negusse, Richard Abarn, Richard Lay & others

	£	s	d
In primis In the Hall			
A Cupboord a table, 2 formes, 5 stooles, 3 chayres a glasscase, a frame for glasses with other implements there		40	
In the Parlor			
On old Cupboord, 3 old coffers, a shelfe, a forme, and paynted clothes		18	8
In the Buttery			
Two hogsheads 6 barrells, 10 bottells, a leatherne iack 3 shelves, 2 beerestalls, a tunnell, a piggen, an old stoole with other odd implements		56	4
In the chamber over the buttery, old iron wimbles, 2 axes, a 2 handsaw, a handsaw & other implements		23	4
In the kitchin			
Bacon a salting trough 4 brasse potts 7 kettles 2 possnetts, 2 driping pans, 5 spitts 2 frying pans a chaver, 2 payre of Cob-irons, a payre of tonges a fire-shovell, a payre of pott hooks & 3 other hookes	8	6	6
Item a framed table, 3 formes, 3 chayres, a bench, 4 shelves, 2 salt barrells, a mustard querne, 2 latten chaving dishes, 2 skymmers, a grediron and 2 chopping knives		14	
Item 3 stooles, a lanthorne, a tankard, woodden dishes & spoones, trenchers with other implements		6	
In the Chamber over the Parlor			
A square table, a trundle-bedd, 3 chests, a box 2 chayres and a stoole		41	
Item a feather-bedd, a bolster, 3 pillowes 4 coveringes and a blankett	8	5	
Item [*?*]10 Cushens		18	
Item in pewter, 2 chargers, 30 great platters, one cullender, 2 basons, a plate, 6 butter dishes 10 porrengers, 11 sausers, a quart pott, 5 salts, 2 candlesticks & 2 chamber potts	3	9	3
Item 2 latten morteres & 2 pestills, 2 latten candlesticks, a latten ladle & a warming pan		10	6
Item in new linnen cloth, 14 elnes of teere of hempe, 11 elnes of hempe hards, 14 elnes of flax harden, & 5 elnes of flaxen cloth		45	
Item in new woollen cloth, 8 yards of fyne russett, 4 yards of gray, 2 yards of white & a bearing blankett		48	4
Item his Apparell	7		
Item 2 silver spoones		10	
In the great chest 26 payre of harden sheetes	5	4	
Item 14 payre of flaxen sheetes	14		
Item 6 flaxen boord clothes, 4 harden boordclothes, 6 payre of flaxen pillowbeers, 14 flaxen table napkins, 10 harden napkins, 6 curtaines, and vallances, glasse bottells, litle boxes with other odd implements	5	2	8

In the Chamber over the Hall			
An Apple closett, a long trough, a great chest, 5 coffers, 2 cradles a forme & a cloth flaskett		42	
Item 2 bedstedds, 2 feather bedds, 3 bolsters, 2 pillowes, 2 mattresses, 4 blanketts, 4 coverlidds paynted clothes with other odd implements	9	10	
In the chamber over the kitchin			
Two oate meale skyps, certaine oate meale and gritts, 2 forkes, a club & a bill, 2 forke steales with other odd implements		9	4
In the milk house			
Two brasse pans, 3 tubbs, 2 powdering trunks, a chyrme, 5 boules, 4 payles a stop, 8 cheese fatts 5 shelves, 2 formes and a buffett stoole		59	
Item certaine old boordes, a cheese presse, butter skales, wooll skales, Leaden waightes, creame potts & butter potts, 2 barrells with Liquor		27	8
Item in cheese	3	6	8
Item 5 shelves, a cheese rack, 3 Linnen wheeles, a payre of stock cards, 2 heckles, a tub, yarne, 11 pounds of coloured wooll with other implements		37	2
Cortaine hookes & the glasse in the windowes		15	
In the malt house			
Three fatts, 3 kymnells, 5 tubbs, a trunke, a woollen wheele, a stone of feathers, 3 sives 2 scuttles, henpens with other odd implements	3	5	8
In the malt chamber 3 quarters & a halfe of barley, wheate, pease, a skreene a haire cloth, a winnowing cloth, 5 sacks & a boord	6	13	4
In the boulting house, a boulting arke, a kneading troughe, a moldingboord, 2 kymnells with other implements		14	
In the backhouse, a mashing stall, a brandlett, an old kettle, 3 peales, a hen pen, & a swilling trough		5	
In the neates house, [...] neate stall, a ladder, a harrow, and two litle troughes		5	
In the Stable			
Eight horses in the stable	36		
In the Servantes chamber a bedsted with beding a side saddle, a pillion and pillion cloth, a saddle 3 pannells, a sideleape & barleape, forkes and rakes, 2 barrs of [*ir*]on, a bushell, a mattock, a molestaffe, sythes, a drag, 2 stable forkes, two shovells, with other implements there		52	
Item in an other chamber, bedsteds, a malt quernc with other implements there	6		
In the yarde			
Item 26 milch kine bullocks and calves	55		
Plowes and plowtimber, 16 boords, Carts and cart-timber with furniture belonging to the carts, harrowes, roles, sheepe racks			

cart-geares & plow geares, cart ropes halters, locks & fetters, tyes & teathers	19		12
Item 3 hives of bees		20	
A grindlestone, the pales in the yard, the gates, the timber, & all the fire wood in the yarde	4	5	
The swine	7	10	
The pullen in the yarde		20	
Item 7 score woolled sheepe	60		
The sheepe coate at Warrens with a litle hovell	4		
The Grayne in the feild, vz wheate, barley, pease and oates	120		
The remaynder of the lease of Warrens	50		
Summa totalis	467	16	5

[*Exhibited by the relict and executrix at Buckden on 2 October 1611. The exhibition clause was signed by Edward Liveley, notary public.*]

Notes: George Negusse was buried at Shelton on 26 June 1611. His will is badly damaged. It was proved by his wife before Robert Hasell, surrogate for Christopher Wivell, at Buckden on 2 October 1611 (Lincs Archives, MISC WILLS/F/139).

232 Robert Sharp of Clifton undated; July 1611

Lincolnshire Archives, INV/108/48

The Inventory of all the moveable goodes of Robert Sharp of Clyfton lat of [*sic*] deceased

	£	s	d
In the parlers			
First a ioyned bed with a tester a feather bed a bolster a pillow and a coveringe	iij		
Item a ioyned table with thre formes		xx	
Item a cubbord and fyve chestes		xxx	
Item in the cheste at the beds feete tenne pare of ordinary sheetes fower pillow bears two table clothes and halfe a dozen napkyns	iij		
Item on the cubbord twelve peces of pewter thre candlestiks and a salt		x	
Item two bolsters two pillowes and a covering with other lyninge		xiij	iiij
In the Chamber			
First two beds with thre sheets and other thinges belonging to them		xx	
Item two coffers, paynted clothes with other things		vj	viij
In the hall			
First a table a forme fower chears fower stooles the bench with the bench plancke		xx	
Item a cubbard with other things		xiij	iiij

In the kyching			
First on pott two porsnets seaven kettles with other thinges		xxx	
In the buttrye			
First fower tubs thre barrels two charmes fyve boyls with other things		xx	
Things abroade			
First fyve horses	xj		
Item syx beastes & two bullockes	xj		
Item syx hoggs		xl	
Item seaven sheepe and one lambe		xxxiij	iiij
Item eleave[*n*] pullyne		iiij	
Item syx forcks two rakes with other implementes		viij	
Item carts and cartes geares plowes and plowe geares	vij		
Item two hovels with fire woode	iij		
Item two acrs of wheate and rye	iiij		
Item eyghte acrs of barly	xxvij		
Item forttene acrs of peece and oates	viij		
Item fyftenne acrs of tylth yet to make	v		
the fower acrs of meaddowe		xl	
Item his apparrell		xl	
Som total	99	8	8

W: Irlande [*signature*], George Berrie [*mark*], John Greene [*mark*]
[*Exhibited by the executor on 2 July 1611. The exhibition clause was signed by George Pormorth, notary public.*]

Notes: Robert Sharp was buried at Clifton on 20 July 1611. He was a churchwarden 1602–03 (*BPR*, vol. 62, pp. 70, 99). Note the discrepancy between the date of burial and exhibiting the inventory; presumably an error in one or other document.

233 Augustine Topclyffe, vicar of Willington made 12 July 1611
Lincolnshire Archives, INV/108/62

An Inventory of the goodes & Chattells of Augustine Topclyffe of Willington in the Countie of Bedfforde, Clarke made and taken by William Greenough vicar of Cople, Humffray Cartwrighte, Thomas Shatbolte, Thomas Hills & George Fadlutt with others the xij[th] day of July 1611 as followethe

	£	s	d
Inprimis, One Acre & a halffe of wheate & Rye and Three Acres of Breach Barlye	viij		
Item Two kine, one Bullocke, & a weaninge Calffe	vij	vj	v[*iij*]
Item Twelve sheepe, and sixe lambes	iiij	iiij	
Item Three stoare Hogges		xxx	
Item Fower wayninge Pigges		x	

	£	s	d
Item All the Roughe Timber in the yearde squared & unsquared, two ladders, one Hovell, certaine boardes & theales under the sayd Hovell with a parcell of boardes, & other timber in the Barne	xiiij		
Item in the Barne one screene, one Fanne, one Bushell fower pitchforkes		x	
Item in Brasse, & Pewter		xxx	
Item in wooll sixe Toddes	iiij	xvj	
Item one little hanginge Cupboarde		x	
Item For the Barne, Hoggscoate, one leantoe two loftes, & one [*?*]Quern twentie Marckes or as Sir William Gostwicke shall ~~appointe~~ gette f of the nexte Incumbente	xiij	xiij	iiij
Item Two bed-steedes with the furniture		L	
Item All the Linnen with the Chists containinge it		xl	
Item One Chiste of woollen		xl	
Item Certaine Tubbs, with Barells & other thinges		xx	
Summa totalis	lxiiij	0	0

[*Exhibited by the executrix on 23 September 1611. The exhibition clause was signed by George Pormorth, notary public.*]

Notes: Augustine Topclyffe's burial has not been found. He made his will on 12 July 1611, leaving £10 to each of his two children at age 21; and the residue and provision for the children's upbringing to his wife Alice whom he appointed his executrix. He directed that half the value of his books (which were not included in the inventory) were to be used for part of his son's support. Probate was granted to his widow by Christopher Wyvell on 23 September 1611 (Lincs Archives, MISC WILLS/F/156 and Act Book A/ix/8). In the 1607 glebe terrier taken during his tenure, the vicarage was described as 'a poore litle vicarage house thacht beinge one storie unchambered' and a 'pretie' thatched barn of three bays, erected in 1594 at Augustine Topcliffe's expense. Augustine Topcliffe matriculated at Trinity College, Cambridge in 1581 and was vicar of Willington 1588–1611 (Venn ACAD; CCEd; Beds Archives, Fasti/1/Will). According to Venn ACAD, he was rector of Shelton but this is not recorded in CCEd or Beds Archives, Fasti/1/Shel.

234 Anne Style of Woburn, widow

made 16 July 1611

Lincolnshire Archives, INV/108/83

A true Inventorie Indented of all the goodes & Chattells which Anne Style of Wooburne in the County of Bedd widowe late deceassed had at the tyme of her death: made and prized by Thomas Style gent, John Coaleman & John Kinge: the 16 day of July Anno domini 1611

	£	s	d
Imprimis in the Hall one Long table a forme & a settle		xiij	iiij
Item one Little table with a Cupboord in it		iiij	
Item one standing bedsteed a fether bed a mattris two boulsters two blanckettes one Covelett and a little forme standing by the bedside		xl	

Item One standing Cupboord & a cheere there			x	
Item one barre of iron in the Chimney there			iij	iiij
Item the painted clothes there			iij	iiij
Item two basons two Ewers one pynte pott two flower pottes of pewter			vj	
	Sum is	iiij		
Item in the little parlor one table with a frame two Carpettes & fower Cussions			xv	iiij
Item one standing bedstead one feather bed one mattris two boulsters fower pillowes one paire of woollen blanckettes two Coverlettes & other furniture to the same bed belonginge		iij	vj	viij
Item one forme one ioyned stoole and two little stooles and a little cheare			iij	iiij
Item one Cupboord			vj	viij
Item two smale Cofers and one little fosser			ij	vj
Item eight pewter platters			xiij	iiij
Item nyne lesser peeces of pewter			v	
Item two pewter candlestickes and one little pewter pott			ij	
Item sixe table clothes & a drincking clothe			xv	
Item eight table napkins & one longe towell			vj	
Item six paire of sheetes			xxxiij	iiij
Item five pillowe beares			iij	iiij
Item wearing lynnen & one stuffe Apron			xx	
Item one little paire of Andirons & other implementes in the Chimney for the Fier			ij	
Item one silver & gilt salt seller			xl	
Item fower silver spoones			xxiiij	
Item two gold rings			xx	
Item the painted clothes			iij	iiij
	Sum is	xiiij	j	x
Item in the further parlor one old bedsteed three chest			x	
Item Seaven paire of sheetes			xxvj	viij
Item one paire of blanckettes & a bench cloth			ij	
Item ~~three~~ fower gownes				

fower petticoates a cloake & other wearing clothes	v		
Item the painted clothes			xij
Sum is	vj	xix	viij
Item in the Lower house where the brasse standeth one brasse pann & a little brasse bason		vj	viij
Item one brasse pott		vij	
Item two old brasse kettles		vj	viij
Item a little gosse pan			xij
Item two little brasse pottes one posnett two old brasse kettles a spice morter & a little spitt a little pan		viij	
Item iiij^or^ peeces of pewter & ij porringers & ij sawcers		ij	vj
Item shelves & other old Lumber there			xij
Sum is		xxxij	x
Item in the Studdy over the hall two Cofers & other small thinges		v	
Sum is		v	
Item five small peeces of timber old wodd & other implementes in the yard		xiij	iiij
Sum is		xiij	iiij
Item xij pound of woll		vij	
Item eight sheepe & iiij^or^ lambes		xxx	
Item one old cowe		xxxiij	iiij
Sum is	iij	x	iiij
Sum totalis	xxxj	iij	

Thom: Style [*signature*], John Collman [*signature*], John Kinge [*signature*]
[*Exhibited by the executor on 26 September 1611. The exhibition clause was signed by George Pormorth, notary public.*]

Notes: Anne Style was buried at Woburn on 10 July 1611. She may have been the widow of Robert Style who was buried at Woburn on 1 December 1567 and thus widowed for many decades. In 1582 a messuage in Woburn with orchard, garden and close of meadow or pasture was occupied by Anne Style, widow, and owned by John Style of Little Missenden, Bucks, gentleman (Beds Archives, R6/63/1/4) and in 1584 she was referred to as the widow of Robert Style when she was a deponent in a case before Flitwick manorial court (Beds Archives, LL1/67). In 1627 Thomas Style of Little Missenden, Bucks, gentleman sold the messuage formerly occupied by his grandmother Anne Style for £195 (Beds Archives, R6/63/1/4 and R6/63/1/8). She made her will on 1 October 1608. Almost every item in the inventory was listed among the gifts to children and grandchildren, e.g. the two gold rings went to her daughter and daughter-in-law, the silver spoons to grandchildren and the wine pint pot can be identifed with the pint pot in the hall. She gave copyhold land in Steppingley to her son John, who was residual legatee and executor and was granted probate by Christopher Wivell at Missenden on 26 September 1611 (Lincs Archives, LCC WILLS/1611/ii/275).

235 George Adams, senior, of Luton, yeoman made 19 July 1611
Lincolnshire Archives, INV/108/60
A beautifully written inventory in two columns. Presented here as continuous text.

The true Inventorie of all the Goodes cattell chattels money plate and moveables of George Adams the elder late of Luton in the Countie of Bedforde yeoman deceased made the xix[th] day of July Anno domini 1611 and in the yeares of the Raigne of our soveraigne Lorde James by the grace God Kynge of Englande Fraunce & Irelande defender of the Faithe etc and of Scotlande the Fower and Fortieth as followeth viz

	£	s	d
In the hawle			
In primis a little Joined Table		ij	vj
Item vj Joyned stooles a litle ioyned forme & a litle forme		vj	
Item a longe Table		x	
Item two Chaires and a little Chaire		ij	vj
In the parloure			
Item a longe Table with a Frame		v	
Item v Joyned stooles & two little stooles		iiij	
Item two Cubbordes with two painted cubborde cloathes		xxx	
Item a standinge bedd a truckle bed a coverlet a feather bed a mattris two bolsters curteines and a strawe bed		l	
Item two Chestes sixe cushins a chaire a warmynge pan and a little boxe		xij	
Item xvj[tene] pewter platters five pewter dishes two basons three pewter pottes one earthen pott two saulte sellers a lattle [*?laten* or *little*] candlesticke & a pewter one		xxvj	
Item two paire of sheetes		ij	
Item an olde table clothe five shert bandes a fallinge band xij necachers iij kirchiffes two crosse clothes one waste coate one aperne a fuschane wast cote with other lynnen		iiij	
Item a mole staffe and two paier of shoyes		iij	
In the Loft over the parloure			
Item sixe busshelles of wheate		xviij	
Item fortie poundes of wooll		xxiij	iiij
Item nyne boordes two planckes quarters & other Implementes		xiij	iiij
Item sixe pease hookes iiij shelves a butter cherme a hetchill a mustarde querne a chese racke six siules [*sic*] five pitchforkes with other Lumber		x	
In the highe Lofte			
Item a standinge Bedd a Feather Bed a mattris a strawe bed one bolster one pillow a coverlett & a blanckett	iij		
Item a little table & a frame ij ioyned formes and fowre stooles		v	
Item sixe Chestes		x	
Item three bylles		ij	
Item two Rackes a spitt & a curteine Rod		iiij	
Item the painted cloathes there		ij	
Item two tennannt sawes iij awgers an Addes with other Lumber		iij	

Item Eighte paier of sheetes three table napkins three table clothes one of Diaper one of flexen and one towen	xxvj	
Item one pillowe beere		viij
Item nyne yardes of woollen Clothe	xviij	
Item xx[ti] poundes of three pennie towen yarne	x	
In the Lofte over the buttrie		
Item a standinge bed	xiij	iiij
Item a Feather bed a bolster a mattris a strawe bed five pillowes & two Coverlettes and a blankett	xliiij	
Item five chestes two wainscot & iij plaine ones and one little chest	xv	
Item seaven table clothes sixe table napkins fowre paire of pillowe beeres sixe paier of sheetes one od sheete a towell three shertes iij smockes and a velvet gerdle	lij	
Item a blacke Cloke and a tayney Cloke	xxvj	
Item two dubletes two paier of hose two Jerkins a blacke cote ij paier of stockinges & a wast cote	xxxvj	
Item five bowes a shefe of arrowes two swordes a ioyned stoole and a forme	iiij	
Item all the painted Clothes in the same chamber a curteine and a paier of sheares	vj	viij
In the maides chamber over the kitchin		
Item a Bedstede a mattris a bolster and blancket a coverlett & a strawe bed	x	
Item a ioyned forme and the painted clothes there	ij	
In the servantes chamber		
Item three Bedsteddes three coverlettes three mattrices one strawe bed three blanckettes on paire of sheetes three bolsters on pillowe & a feather bed	xx	
Item a Chest an old chest a pillion & a saddle	ij	
Item all the painted clothes there		xij
Item two olde Clokes		xvj
Item fower Awgers two shelves a brest wimbell and a chissell	ij	
In the litle buttrie		
Item seaven shelves two bottles & other Lumber	v	
In the kitchin		
Item one olde table an old cubberde & a little forme	v	iiij
Item a lattin candlesticke & a chafinge dishe		xx
Item a fire forke two Andiornes a paier of tonges a fire shovell fowre pot hangers an Iorne bar a gridiorne a paier of cobiornes and a paier of bellies	x	
Item one lattin basen seaven pewter platters three sawcers a smale morter with a pestell and one saulte celler	x	
Item a brushe two shelves a lanthorne ij chaires		

one of them of wicker painted clothes and other Lumber there		iij	
[*total for the first column*]	£31	12s	8d

In the greate Buttrie

Item Fower brasse pottes sixe brasse kettles two brasse posnettes two brasen ladles & a skimmer		xxxv	
Item one Iorne drippinge pan a fryinge pan a trevet and a spitt		ij	
Item certeine troffes tubbes boles a Cherme and other Lumber there		xij	

In the Seller

Item Eleaven barrilles the settles and other Lumber there		x	

In the maulthouse & Lofte

Item Ten busshells of maulte		xxiiij	
Item the woode in the maulthowse		lvj	

In the yarde

Item all the woode in and aboute the yarde	iiij		
Item the Spires with owt the dore		x	
Item two longe Cartes two dounge cartes and fowre paier of wheles	iiij		
Item Eighte hogges and Fower store hogges	iij	vj	
Item three bigge Flitches of bacon and two little Flitches		xxv	

In the Stable

Item Fowre Horses	viij		
Item horse collarres harneis & other furniture		xxx	
Item two buckettes with the chaines and Ropes		v	
Item two mattockes and a shovell			xviij
Item a maulte querne		xij	
Item a horse troffe			xvj
Item two busshelles a fan and certeine shovels		iiij	
Item two paier of harrowes fowre cowse rackes one horse racke three Ladders two greate Rakes and one gatheringe Rake		xxij	
Item two Lodes of haye		xl	

In the Feildes

Item Eightene Acres of wheate in a Close at Nokes hill	xxxvj		
Item five Acres of Barley in the Common Feilde	x		
Item Eighte Acres of graine in a Close in the Hawte	viij		
Item Ten Acres of aster croppe graine in Bridge Feilde	ix		
Item Three Acres of graine in stabbleford feilde	iij		
Item five Acres of pease in a Close at Readinge hill	iiij		
Item two Acres of Fetches		xxvj	viij
Item the grasse in Spittell Close	iiij		
Item the grasse in a close on the backside and in two Closes at black water bridge	iij		

Item all the dounge in the yarde and a doungehill at Spittell close gate		xx	
Item a woollen wheele a hat two stockes of bees with the wexe in the emptie heeves three bordes which cover them the Chese presse pottes and glasses and the cappes		xviij	
Item a plowe the sharre two cowlters plowe wheles two plowe chaines and other Implementes belonginge to a plowe one Rowle two dounge Rakes and two dounge forkes		x	
Item Sixe kyne	x		
Item Fortie and three olde shepe	x		
Item Fyfteene Lambes		xxxiij	
In the maulte shop			
Item a bedsted a querne a paier of stocke cardes a bowltinge hutch a knedinge troffe splentes and lathes and other Lumber there		xvj	
Item One Lease of two tenementes in Luton aforesaid		xl	
Item in readie money in the howse		viij	
Item two dosen of hurdles		viij	
[*total for the second column*]	£139	15s	6d
[*Corrected total for the second column*	*£138*	*10s*	*6d*]
Summa totalis	Clxxj	viij	ij
[*Corrected total*	*£170*	*3s*	*2d*]

praised by Edward Evered [*signature*], John Blackwall [*signature*], the marke of William Crawley

Desperat debt owinge to the saide George Adams			
Edward Chalkeley and Thomas Chalkeley	xxij		
[*Total including desperate debts*	*£192*	*3s*	*2d*]
Debtes which the saide George Adams did owe at the tyme of his deathe			
To Thomas Cheiney Esquire	xxj		
To John Lowin of Chesson	liiij		
To Robert Naper alias Sandie Esquire	xxxiij		
To one [*blank*] Payes of Roxforde	xx		
The Somm of his debt is	Cxxviij		

[*Exhibited by the executor on 19 September 1611. The exhibition clause was signed by George Pormorte, notary public.*]

Notes: George Adams was buried at Luton on 8 July 1611. He made his will on 4 July 1611, leaving money, a cow each and household goods to his two daughters; land and household goods to his two sons; and sheep and money to his grandchildren. His son George, who was residual legatee and executor, proved the will at Hitchin on 19 September 1611 (Lincs Archives, MISC WILLS/F/157).

236 Edward Jones of Luton, dyer made 25 July 1611

Lincolnshire Archives, INV/108/59

Thinventary Indented of all & singler the goodes Cattells & Chattells of Edward Jones late of Luton in the Countye of Bedd dyar deceassed taken valued & praised by Thomas Paratt gent,

John Camfeild thelder and John Atwood the Five and Twentith daye of July Anno Domini 1611 and in the yeares of the Raigne of our Sovereigne Lorde James by the grace of god of England Scotland Fraunce & Irelande kinge Defender of the faythe etc of England Fraunce & Ireland the Nyneth and of Scotland the Foure & Fortith as Followeth viz

	£	s	d
In the haull			
Inprimis a Joyned table with a frame foure greate ioyned stooles & twoe litle Joyned stooles valued at		x	
Item a Cupbord and a Cupbord cloth a lyvery Cupbord & a potteshelfe a Chaire Sixe Quisshions & the paynted clothes there		xxviij	iiij
Summa		xxxviij	iiij
In the Chamber over the haull			
Inprimis a Joyned Bedsteed a featherbedd a mattresse a boulster twoe blanckettes a Coverlett with the Curtaynes and vallances		Liij	iiij
Item a Joyned table with a frame a Joyned Forme & sixe Joyned stooles		xiij	iiij
Item a litle square table with a Cupbord in yt a wycker Chaire & twoe Quisshions		vj	viij
Item a litle paire of Copirons a fire shovell & the paynted clothes		iij	iiij
Summa	iij	xvj	viij
In the Chamber over the shoppe			
Inprimis a Joyned Bedsteed a featherbedd twoe boulsters a pillowe a blanckett & a Coverlett		xxx	
Item a plaine halfehedded Bedsteed & a trondle Bedd twoe boulsters a pillowe twoe mattresses & twoe blanckettes		xiij	iiij
Item Five Cofers and twoe pillowes		xxx	
Item an olde Joyned stoole & a litle ioyned stoole without a hedd a litle broken chaire a windowe Curtaine & the paynted clothes		iij	iiij
Item three paire of Flexen sheetes, twelve paire of Towen sheetes foure table clothes a dozen & an halfe of flexen table napkins & a dozen of Towen and one blacke seamed sheete twoe paire of hollande pillowebeeres and twoe paire of flexen pillowebeeres & sixe hande Towells	iij	vj	viij
Item his apparell		xl	
Item a wollen wheele a Clothbaskett a paire of Tressells with two bordes a paire of stocke cardes twoe paire of woll cardes and other Lumber in the Chamber over the kytchin		ij	vj
Summa	ix	v	x
In the kytchin			
Inprimis a square table with a frame a dresser a lowe shorte foorme with certen shelves		iij	iiij

Item a morter a pestle a brusshe and twoe litle Joyned stooles		iij	iiij
Item twoe brasse pottes Five brasse kettles foure postnettes a chafinge dishe Five spyttes Twoe Andirons a paire of tonges twoe pottehookes twoe paire of pottehangers a paire of bellowes a fyre shovell a slyce & a breade grate		L	
Item Twoe dryppinge pannes a fryenge pann a gridiron a kymnell a bole a skymmer a basting ladle one lattin Candlestick foure pewter Candlestickes twoe saltesellers Five platters eighte pewter disshes foure peuter porringers eight sawcers Five fruyte dishes a pewter bason a pewter drincke pott a dozen of pewter spoones a pewter cupp & two pewter Chamber pottes		xxx	
Item twoe kylderkins Foure Firkins three kymnells a greate bole twoe litle boles a yeldinge Fatt & twoe hanging shelves in the sellar		x	
Summa	iiij	xvj	viij
In the Buttery			
Item a powdringe troughe an olde hayre Cupborde twoe lynneon wheeles a boultinge hutche and three shelves		vj	viij
Item a plaine Trondlebedd a mattresse a boulster a blanckett & a Coverlett in the lofte over the Buttery		xiij	iiij
Item a horse in the Stable		xl	
Summa	iij		
In the Longe howse			
Item a masshinge Tubbe an iron beame with a paire of scales & certen leaden waightes an iron morter an olde troughe foure shooters a water Carte & three ladders		x	
Summa patet		x	
In the woadehowse & dyehowse			
Inprimis a woade fatte a kytte & a Jacke a plaine bedsteed with the furniture & a shelfe		xiij	iiij
Item twoe Liccour Fattes twoe furnaces thone of brasse thother of leade three olde tubbes three shootes & a pearche & a wynche	viij		
Item wood in the yarde		xx	
Summa	ix	xiij	iiij
Summa totalis	xxxiij		x
Debtes due by the Testator			
Inprimis due to Thomas Crawley gent	iiij		
Item due to R[*i*]chard Easte gent	xvj		
Item due to George Slowe	v		
Item due to Roberte Hilles	v		
Item due to Edward Crawley of Barton		xl	

Item due to Edward Catherall		iij
	Summa	xxxv

[*Exhibited by the executrix at Hitchin, Herts, on 30 July 1611. The exhibition clause was signed by George Pormorth, notary public.*]

Notes: Goodman Joones was buried at Luton on 12 July 1611. He made his will on 8 July 1611. He gave all his dyeing vessels to his son-in-law Joseph Laurence after his wife Jane's death. He appointed Jane his residual legatee and executrix, to whom probate was granted by Christopher Wyvell at Hitchin on 30 July 1611 (Lincs Archives, MISC WILLS/F/10).

237 John Gardener of Barford, singleman

made 29 July 1611

Lincolnshire Archives, LCC ADMONS 1611/269

Slight damage along the right edge.

A true Inventorie of all such goods & chattells as were of late one John Gardeners of Barefoot in the county of Bedf singleman deceased priced & valued by Thomas Springe & Rogere Favell the 29 day of Julij in the ningthe yere of the Reigne of our most graciouse sovereigne Lord kinge James etc in the yere off our lord god 16[...]

	£	s	d
Inprimis upon bond	3		
Item for a cowe		46	8
Item 9 sheepe & 4 lambes		40	
Item all his wearinge apparell		26	8
Item one litle coffer & 3 shertes		3	4
Item for woole sold to Hindes wife		6	
Sum	9	2	8

[*Exhibited by Thomas Gardener, brother and administrator, on 23 September 1611. The exhibition clause has an abbreviated and illegible signature of a notary public.*]

Notes: John Gardener's burial has not been found. Administration was granted to Thomas Gardener of Chickley [*Chicheley*], Bucks, on 23 September 1611 and a bond was taken (Lincs Archives, Act Book A/ix/8 and LCC ADMONS 1611/269).

238 Thomas Smyth of Husborne Crawley, tanner

made 5 August 1611

Lincolnshire Archives, LCC ADMONS 1611/190

Staining and fading in places.

[*illeg.*] Invitory of all the goodes and Cattles of Thomas Smyth of Hushborn Crawley decessed supprissed [*appraised*] and valyed by Henry Kettle, Robart Blee, William Auddely and Frances Smyth the v day of August 1611

	£	s	d
Imprimis the First is sume barley growing in the back sid to the vallie of iij^{l}	iij		
Item some heay which did growe in the backsid to the valy of		iiij	
Item tow mylche kenne to the valy of iij^{l}	iij		
Item on sowe and four pigges to the valie of		viij	
Item on shorne shipe to the valy of		iiij	

Item the woodde in the yeard to the valie of		iiij	
Item the doggne in the yeard to the valie of			xij
Item on table on Forme on bench bord to the valie		v	
Item on Cobbord to the valie of		iij	iiij
Item tow Chares to stolles to the valie of			xviij
Item iiij formes one stolle to the valie of			xvj
Item iij kettles on pane on skemer on poott to the valey of		xij	
Item iiij platters on salte on Candlestacke to the valie		iij	iiij
Item on spitte on Cobbiron on Fringpane to the valie of			xvj
Item on standing pen to the walle to valie of			xviij
Item on salting trouffe one barrill on tobee on old Chest and on kneadinge trouffe three old bordes to the valie of		iiij	
Item old dyshies spones Chisfates trencheres pottes picheres panes to the valied of			xij
Item on beadstid with [*blank*] a tester over yt to the valie of		vj	viij
Item three old beadstides to the valie of		ij	vj
Item tow [*word deleted and illegible*] craddles to the valie of			xij
Item three whiles to the valie of		iij	
Item tow Cheastes to the valie of		ij	
Item an old barrill towe old bordes to the valie of			viij
Item tow old Coverleites to the valie of		iij	iiij
Item three pare of old sheetes and on old Flexen sheete to the vale		vij	
Item on bolster tow pillowbeares on pillowe and on old Flockbead to the valie of		iij	
Item to old table Clothes to the valie of			xvj
Item tow old pented Clothes to the valie of			xij
Item on flease of wolle to the valie of			xvj
Item tow old peeles to the valie of			viij
Item tow old bottles to the valie of			viij
Item all his warring apparrile to the valie of		xiij	iiij
Item his old shooes to the valie of			xij
Item owing to him uppon a bond due at Michaelmas [*this line and the value are in a different hand*]	viij		
The some is	xviij	xiij	ij
[*Corrected total*	*£19*	*3s*	*10d*]

The mark of Robert Blee, By me Henry Kettle [*signature*], The marke of Williame Auddely
[*Exhibited by the administrator on 23 September 1611. The exhibition clause was signed by George Pormorth, notary public.*]

Notes: Thomas Smyth was buried at Husborne Crawley on 30 July 1611 and described as a tanner. His wife was buried three days earlier. Administration was granted to his son Thomas Smith on 23 September 1611 and a bond was taken (Lincs Archives, Act Book A/ix/8 and LCC ADMONS 1611/190). The possible writer of the inventory, Henry Kettle, was a yeoman living in Husborne Crawley.

239 John Stalford of Sundon, husbandman made 15 August 1611

Lincolnshire Archives, INV/108/86

An inventorie of all the goodes of Jhon Stalforde of Sondon in the Countie of Bedforde husbandman late deceased beinge praysed the Fiftene daye of Auguste Anno domini 1611 by Thomas Pepiate and Richard Sames, Jhon Morton and Edmunde Keinge of Sondon

	£	s	d
Firste on Cobarde		xiij	iiij
Item a presse a table and a forme with Certayne Joyned stoles		xij	
Item three Chares with other stoles and a potshelfe		vj	viij
Item fourten peces of peuter three sausers ij saltes and three Candellstick es and a peuter Cup with aspice morter		xx	
Item on brase pote vj kettelles and a panne		xxx	
Item on spite a driping pan apare of pothookes and iij pare of potte hangers ij Chefingdishies and a gridiron a fire shoule and a pare of tonges and a pare of belowes		x	
Item in the butteri on salting trough a drinke stale iij tubbes v barelles v boles and a kimnill with Certayne disshes with a dozen of trenshers and a dozen of spomes [*sic*] with three payles		xxij	
Item the paynted Clothes in the hall and Chamber		ij	
Item his apparell		xl	
Item in the Chamber on standinge bede		xx	
Item vj Cofers with on bedsted		xx	
Item iiij Coveringes viij blanketes and xix pare of shetes	vj	vj	8
Item vj bolsters iij pillowes vj pillowe beares ij fether bedes iij matrices	iiij		
Item v tabell Clothes x table napkeins v toweles		xx	
Item vj Chushens		iij	
Item in an upper lofte iij bedstedes and Certayne shelves a linan whele and a wolen whele		x	
Item a malt quearne a Chese presse a kneadinge trough a fanne a bushell with Cer tayne other old lumber		xvj	8
Item vj pitch forkes iiij pease			

hookes with iij d[...]se rakes and ij sithes		xij	
Item ij longe Cartes ij dung Cartes and iij pare of wheles and ij olde plowes and a pare of harrowes with Certayne olde harnesse and Cartayne olde Carte ropes	vj		
Item Certayne bordes and plankes with Certayne plowe timber and other timber	iij	vj	8
Item all the woode in the yarde with with [*sic*] Certayne old Courackes a hogge trofe and Certayne ladders		xxx	
Item iiij beastes or keine with ij bullokes	viij		
Item iij hogges and iiij pigges		xl	
Item xx shepe	iiij		
Item the pullen in the yard		xiij	
Item xxj acres of barlye and wheate	xxxj		
Item of pease and otes xxij Acres	xj		
Item the haye		xvj	
Item xx acres of tilth	iiij		
Summa totalis	lxxxxv	x	

the marke of Thomas Pepiat, bi me Rychard Sam [*signature*], the marke of Jhon Morton [*Exhibited by the executor on 27 September 1611. The exhibition clause was signed by George Pormorth, notary public.*]

Notes: No burial is recorded for John Stalford (or Scalford) in Sundon but there is a burial for John Stalworth on 6 August 1611. John Stalworth had a customary messuage, three closes and 140 acres of land in Sundon in 1610. John Morton, one of the appraisers, witnessed the deed of enfranchisement (Beds Archives, T42/82). The writer of the inventory Richard Sam (or Same) was a husbandman from Sundon. John Scalford made his will on 2 August 1611. He gave £20 each to four of his five sons at age 24 and to his two daughters at age 21. He gave his wife Elizabeth and son William half his goods and half the land, which they were to farm jointly. The residual legatee and executor was son William, to whom probate was granted by Christopher Wivell on 27 September 1612 (Lincs Archives, LCC WILLS, 1611/ii/276).

240 William Bull of Dunstable, labourer made 22 August 1611

Lincolnshire Archives, LCC ADMONS 1611/255

An Inventorye Indented mad and taken the 22th daie of August in Anno Domini 1611 of the goodes and Chattells of William Bull Late of Dunstable in Com' Bedf Laborer disceased & praised by us whose names are hereunder written as followeth viz

	£	s	d
In primis all his waringe Apparrell		Liij	iiij
Item ij shirtts ij bandes ij paier of stockinges and apaier of shooes		v	
in the Hall			
Item a table a Frame on forme & iiij stooles		vj	
Item on olde Cobbard		ij	iiij
Item ij beanche boardes			viij
Item viij pewter disshes & on frutte dishe		iiij	iiij
Item ij pewter Candellstickes		iij	iiij
Item iij pewter saltes			xij
Item on pewter pinte pott iiij sawsers & vj sponnes			xviij
Item a brasse potte & iij kettells		xij	ij
Item on brasse panne on Chaffine dishe a Skymmer & on skyllet		vj	vj
Item a fryenge panne, a grdiorne, a paire of tonges a paier of dogge Iornes a hanginge hooke & a paier of potte hookes			xxij
Item on olde Chaire ij Cusshions & a paier of bellowes			x
Item on Sword and a dagger			xvj
in the Chamber			
Item on bedstead & a trondell bed		ij	vj
Item ij feather bowlsters ij pillowes ij olde Coverletts and ij blancketts		xvj	
Item on paier of flaxon sheetts		v	
Item iij paier of towen sheetts		vj	
Item on olde diaper table Clothe a towen table Clothe & vj table napkines		v	ij
Item vj pillowe Leares [*sic, Beares*]		vj	
Item iiij Coffers & ij boxes		viij	
Item woode boardes and other Lombar		xx	
Item on axe iij wedges & a beattell			xvj
Item all the painted Clothes abowt the howse		iij	iiij
Item ij horses price	iij	x	
Item iiij acres of wheate & ottes be the more or lesse	iiij	iij	iiij
Item xj sheeppe at iiij[s] vj[d] apec		xlix	vj
Item on Sowe & iij shootts		xx	
Item a littell Carte		viij	
Item on dunge hill		vj	viij
Item xx[li] of woole at viij[d] a li		xiij	iiij
Some ys	xxj	iiij	iiij
[*Corrected total*	*£21*	*5s*	*4d*]

Roger Fynche [*signature*], John Norton [*signature*], Thomas Cole [*signature*]
[*Exhibited by Jane Bull, administratrix and relict, on 27 September 1611. A note records that a bond was taken from her and John Norton. The exhibition clause was signed by George Pormorth, notary public.*]

Notes: William Bull was buried at Dunstable on 24 July 1611. The grant of administration and bond are recorded formally at Lincs Archives, Act Book A/ix/10 and LCC ADMONS 1611/255.

241 Richard Spenly alias Newald of Bedford St Paul, miller made 26 August 1611
Lincolnshire Archives, INV/108/64

Bedford St Paul. An Inventory Indented, of all the goods Chattells & howseholde stuffe of Richard Spenly alias Newald late of the towne of Bedford in the County of Bedford Miller deceased taken and prised by Thomas Croote, John Richardson & Simon Dockerill the six & twentieth daie of August 1611 in the nynth yeare of the raigne of our soveraigne Lord King James of England etc

	£	s	d
In the hall			
On Cupborde		xij	
A long table with a frame, a settle with a bench borde & ij formes		xiij	iiij
A little square table & thre stooles		iij	
Two oulde chaires		j	iiij
One paire of playing tables & a pott shelfe		ij	vj
An Iron barr in the Chimnye a pott hanginge crepers bellowes & tongs		iiij	
The painted cloaths		iij	iiij
In the Parlor			
One feather bedd		xxx	
A Coverlett & blanckett		x	
A paire of hardon sheets		v	
A boulster & straw bedd		v	
A standing bed truckle bed & foote pace		xx	
One greate Chest & two lyttle chests		xvj	
Three payre of sheets		xv	
In the Buttrye			
Thre pewter dishes		ij	
A fryeng pan a dripping pan & a gridiron		ij	iiij
A pot shelfe fyve boards & other implements		ij	vj
In the Chamber over the parlor			
Two ould Bedsteeds		ix	
An old Cubbord and old Coffer & an old counter		iiij	
A Coverlett a mattris a blanckett a Boulster ij pillowes one strawbed and a pillow beare		xvj	iij
One woollen wheele & other lomber		iiij	
The painted cloaths		iiij	
In the buttry			
A barrell a candlestick a drinckstall a long shelfe a wheele a lanthorne & other ymplements		iiij	
In the Kitchen			
A brasse pott a greate old kettle two small kettells an old pan		xv	
A paire of Cobirons & ij spytts		iiij	
Two henns & a cock			xiij
Fower old ladders & the wood		x	
Two Iron wedges & a hatchett & v millbills		iij	iiij
Two old mill horses		xvj	

A lease of a pightell of land		x	
A boulting trough		ij	
wearing Apperell		v	
Somm	xij	xiiij	vij
[*Corrected total*	*£12*	*15s*	*0d*]

[*Exhibited by the executrix on 23 September 1611. The exhibition clause was signed by George Pormorth, notary public.*]

Notes: Richard Newhould was buried at Bedford St Paul's on 11 August 1611. He made his will on 7 August 1611, calling himself Richard Newold. He left everything to his wife Joan to be used to bring up his daughter Margaret. Although no debts were listed in the inventory, he made detailed arrangements for a kinsman to obtain 40s owed to the testator, probably what would be called a desperate debt. He appointed his wife Joan as executrix, to whom probate was granted by Christopher Wivell at Bedford on 23 September 1611 (Lincs Archives, MISC WILLS/F/159).

242 Thomas Elmar of Shillington, yeoman — undated; September 1611

Lincolnshire Archives, INV/108/66

A true Inventorie indented of all the goods and chattells as well moveabell as immoveabell of Thomas Elmar late of Shitlington in the Countie of Bedf: being valued and prised by Master John Paratt, John Hanscombe, Martin Borrowe, Thomas Couch and Thomas Fowler

	£	s	d
Imprimis in the chamber over the parlour tow standing beds on on [*sic*] flock bed a matteris 2 blanckets on coverlid towe boulsters		30	
on cofer and one fourme		2	
In the parlour			
one ioyned bed a featherbed on matteris 2 boulsters 3 pillows one coverlid and tow blanckets		46	8
Item 3 chests 2 boxes a square tabell one stoole one fourme with the painted clothes		20	
Item five flexen sheetes and sixe paire of hemp tare and foure paire of toowen sheetes		54	
Item sixe tabell cloths foure pillowbears eleaven tabell napkins and other peeces of linnen		15	
In the Halle			
A cubborde a tabell and a frame seaven ioyned stooles foure chaires 2 boorded stooles one benchboorde and the painted clothes		25	
Item five cusshions one potshelves and potts 2 potthangers on iron barre a payre of cobirons a barrell with salt in it		5	
In the chambers over the Hall & Kitchin			
Item tow boorded beds with their furniture 2 coverlids one cofer a linnen wheele and a woollen		40	
In the cheese loft			
Item cheese and other implements		6	8

In the Kitchin

	£	s	d
Item on brasse pott 4 kettells on brasse pan on bason a bedpan 2 brasse posnets 3 spitts 2 paire of Andirons a fryinge panne on treavitt and other smalle implements		30	
Item sixe and twentie peeces of peuter sixe porringers tow saucers tow saltseller 6 spoones 4 candellsticks		30	
Item the bruing vessells barrells tubs pailes bowls disshes trenchers salting trough a boolting arke shelves and other implements		20	
Item his apparrell	3		
Item 3 bease on bullock and 3 hogs	7		
Item the graine in the barnes	10		
Item the tilth in the feild		20	
Item the woode in the yarde on hovill and the utensills		20	
Item the foules in the yarde		3	4
Summa totalis	38	7	8

[*Exhibited by the executor on 23 September 1611. The exhibition clause was signed by George Pormorth, notary public.*]

Thomas Elmar and his wife were buried at Shillington on 6 September 1611. He made his will on 28 August 1611, describing himself as a yeoman. He left half his household goods and £7 a year to his wife Joan during her life, the annuity to be paid by his son William from the profits of William's house. He gave varying sums of money to his son-in-law, three married daughters and three grandchildren and the residue to his son William who was appointed executor and to whom probate was granted by Christopher Wivell at Bedford on 23 September 1611 (Lincs Archives, MISC WILLS/F/160).

243 Ellen Cawne of Wilshamstead, widow — made 11 September 1611

Lincolnshire Archives, INV/108/63

A true Inventorye of the goods of Ellyne Cawne of Willshamsted widowe, made the xj daye of September Anno Domini 1611

	£	s	d
Imprimis one bedsted		ij	
Item a matterice two boalsters, two pillowes, two coveringes, three blankets		xl	
Item two payre of flaxen sheets		xiij	iiij
Item seven payre of tarehempe sheetes		xxxv	
Item three pillowebears		iiij	
Item thre peeces of newe tarehempe cloath		x	
Item one peece of newe harden cloath		vij	
Item a newe peece of woollen cloath of five yeards		x	
Item xiij apernes		viij	viij
Item x smocks		xv	
Item wearing kercheifes		v	
Item wearing neckercheifes		v	
Item one longe towell			xvj

	£	s	d
Item five peeces of pewter platters, thre pewter spoons, one sawcer and a salte		vj	
Item one brasen candlesticke			xij
Item sixe woodden dishes and viij trenchers			viij
Item five petticoates		xvj	viij
Item fower wastcoates		ij	
Item one brasse pot and a brasse pan		x	
Item one kettle			xviij
Item one brasen posnet			xviij
Item towe boarde cloathes		iiij	
Item two coffers		iij	
Item one hat		ij	
Owinge to her by her sonne John Cawne	xxvj		
Summa totalis	xxxvj	iiij	viij

The praisers were these William Palmer, Nicholas Cawne, John Cawne
[*Exhibited by the executor at Bedford on 23 September 1611. The exhibition clause was signed by George Pormorth, notary public.*]

Notes: Ellen Cawne was buried at Wilshamstead on 26 August 1611. She may have been the widow of John Cawne, senior, buried in Wilshamstead 8 October 1607.

244 Nathan Scarrett of Haynes made 18 September 1611
Lincolnshire Archives, INV/108/85

An Inventory of the goods and Chattells stocke and Cattell of Nathan Scarrett late of Hawnes in the County of Bedford deceassed had made and taken the xviij[th] day of September anno domini 1611 by the Inhabitantes of Maudene whose names are subscribed: as followeth

	£	s	d
Inprimis his lyverie Cloake		xiij	iiij
Item another olde cloake		iiij	
Item a paire of hose and a dublet		viij	vj
Item another payer of hose and a dublet		vj	viij
Item his old cloathes: his shirtes bandes bootes shooes and a hatte		xj	
Item for his truncke			xx
Item a nagge and a mare colte	iiij	x	
Item in money	xv	viij	
Summa is	xxij	iij	ij

Thomas Mercer [*signature*], Segesmund Byrd [*signature*]
[*Exhibited by the executor on 27 September 1611. The exhibition clause was signed by George Pormorth, notary public.*]

Notes: Nathan Scarrett was buried at Haynes on 16 August 1611.

245 Leonard Harwood of Little Staughton, bachelor and servant made 20 September 1611

Lincolnshire Archives, LCC ADMONS 1611/348

Slight damage and staining.

An Inventory Indented of the goods & Chattels of Leonard Harwood a batchelor servant late of Little Stoughton in the Countie of Bedd taken and praised by Walter Catterell and Edmond Dennys the xx[th] daie of September 1611

		£	s	d
Inprimis his wearing apparell vizt two doubletts one paire of hose two coats one paire of Stockings two shirts a forke & a paire of hedging mittens			xxiij	
Item in mony and bonds		vj	xiij	iiij
	Som	vij	xvj	iiij

Wallter Cheatwell [*signature*], signum Ed[mon]di Dennys, praisers of the s[ai]d goods

[*Exhibited by the administrator on 23 September 1611. The exhibition clause was signed by George Pormorth, notary public.*]

Notes: Leonard Harwood's burial has not been found. Administration was granted to his brother Fulco Harwood on 23 September 1611 and a bond was taken (Lincs Archives, Act Book A/ix/8 and LCC ADMONS 1611/348).

246 Richard Hancocke of Blunham made 23 September 1611

Lincolnshire Archives, LCC ADMONS 1611/277

A true and perfect Inventarie of all and singular the goodes debts rights and chattells of Richard Hancocke late of the parishe of Blunham in the Countie of Bedford deceased prized and valued the xxiij[th] dai of September Anno domini 1611

	£	s	d
In the Hall			
Inprimis a framed table and a forme		x	
Item a penne		ij	vj
Item a Cupbord		x	
Item a salteing troffe & a Coffer		x	
Item ~~the~~ three brasse kettells and a posnett		x	
Item v pewter platters a salt seller a bason and a candlesticke		vj	viij
Item twoo stooles a spitte a tredde a paire of pothangers a side table a Cheare and a Forme		v	
Item all the painted ~~clothet~~ clothes		v	
Item the bord and Joyces over the hall		xiij	iiij
Item three booles a Cheesfat and a boulting arke		ij	
In a loft over the Hall			
Item a beddsteade a Coffer & thre boardes		v	
In the Chamber next the Hall			
Inprimis a ioyned bedde & iij Chestes		xxxiij	iiij
Item in the second Chamber a beadsteade and a barrell		ij	

Item the painted clothes in both the chambers		ij	vj
Item a feather bedde and a flocke bedde twoo ticke bolsters twoo pillowes a harden bolster and a little pillowe		l	
Item ij coverlettes and iij blanketes		x	
Item a bedforme a stoole & a flasket			xij
Item in the Chamber above trash at		iiij	iiij
Item a paire of holland shetes and a halfe shete a diaper tablecloth & a napkin		xxvj	viij
Item twoo paires of teare hemp shetes		xiij	iiij
Item twoo paires of hardne shetes		v	iiij
Item a board cloth & a speare cloth		v	
Item 2 paires of teare pillowebeires & halfe a dozin of Napkins		vij	
Item twoo Hovelles and the wood		xliiij	iiij
Some is	xiiij	iiij	iiij

[*Exhibited by Thomas Hancocke, son and administrator of his nuncupative will, on 26 October 1611. The exhibition clause was signed by John Jacksonne, notary public.*]

Notes: Richard Hancocke's burial has not been found. Administration was granted to Thomas Hancock of Southill on 26 October 1611 and a bond was taken (Lincs Archives, Act Book A/ix/12 and LCC ADMONS 1611/277). The next inventory is that of his widow, Agnes (*247*).

247 Agnes Hancocke of Moggerhanger, Blunham, widow made 23 September 1611
Lincolnshire Archives, LCC ADMONS 1611/275

A true and perfect Inventorie of all and singular the goodes debtes rights and chattells of Agnes Hancocke widowe late of Maugeranger in the parish of Blunham and countie of Bedford deceased made and taken the 23 daie of September Anno domini 1611

	£	s	d
Inprimis her wearing apparell and all her wearing Lynnen		xx	
Item debts owing unto her	iij	vj	
Item a Cowe and a bullocke		liij	iiij
Some is	vj	xix	iiij

[*Exhibited by Thomas Hancocke, son and administrator, on 26 October 1611*]

Notes: Agnes widow of Richard Hancock was buried at Blunham on 21 September 1611. Her will was undated. She gave most of the items listed in her husband's inventory (including the wood, hovel and boards and joists over the hall) and the cow and bullock listed in hers to sons, daughters, grandchildren and others. Probate was granted to her son Thomas by Thomas Crabtree surrogate for Henry Hickman on 26 October 1611 (Lincs Archives, MISC WILLS/F/163). There is also a note of this administration and a bond at Lincs Archives, Act Book A/ix/12 and LCC ADMONS 1611/275. The previous inventory is her husband's (*246*).

248 Agnes Rawlins of Bolnhurst, widow made 25 September 1611

Lincolnshire Archives, INV/108/104

The places of residence of people owing her money have been added in a different hand.

A true Inventory of all the goods and chatels dettes and credites houshouldstufe and Implementes of houshold of Agnes Rawlins widoe late of Bolnehurst in the Countie of Bed[for]ds decesed takene and prayesed the xxvth daye of September in the ninth yeare of the Rayne of our Soverayne Lord King James of England etc by by [*sic*] John Fitzhue gent and John Blith and Henrie Slowe yemen

	£	s	d
Imprimis in the hale one cobard and six platers one pewter pot and a candelstike and a morter and other Implementes		xx	
Item in the parlar a bedsted and a fether bed two pilloes and a tabell and other thinges ther		xlv	
Item in the milke house two brase panes one brase pot one ketell and a postnet with a littell ketell and other thinges ther	iij		
Item in the kishin two stooles and two spites and a bason and other thinges		x	
Item in the buttery two barils two toubes and a cimnell		vij	
Item in the uper chamber a chest at vij^{s} foure pare of flexen shetes xl^{s} thre pare of tare of hempe shetes xxiiij^{s} and eleven tabell napkins xj^{s} and [*?*]foure borde clothes xiij^{s} thre pare of harden shetes x^{s} and two other clothes ij^{s} an other thing	vj	xiij	
Item a quilte and a bolster at		x	
Item one smale chest and a chere and other Implementes		vj	
Item cortaynes and a matris		x	
Item a chest more vj^{s} and a keverlid xxxiij^{s} and seven peces of golde iij^{li} x^{s} and in silver xij and halfe a dosen of silver spones xxxviij^{s}	vij	xviij	
Item waring Reparill and other lenan	vj		
Dettes owing to the sayed Agnes Rawlins upon spetialltie			
Imprimis Thomas Robinson of Bolnhurst with others	xj		
Item William Sanders of Pertnale with others	x	v	
Item Thomas Bow of Riseley	iiij	viij	
Item ~~Thomas~~ Richard Easton late of Deane with others	xj		
Some of this beforenamed is	lxv	xij	
Dettes owing more to the sayed Agnes Rawlins upon spetialti and without but doutful to ~~bed~~ be desprat			
Item John More late of Ravensden	x	x	
Item Robart Faldo of Northmyms	xxij		
Item William Keling late of Ravensden	x		
Item Steven Smith of Bromham	iiij		
Item Thomas Geari of Ravensden with owt sptialtie		xxx	
Item John Tishmus of Norrill	iij	vjj	
~~Item William Wodward late of Houghton~~	~~xxx~~		
Some of this is[44]	lxxxi	vjj	
Some totalis is[45]	~~Cxlvj~~ Cxvj	xix	

44 The total of money owing to her includes William Wodward's debt of £30.

45 The deleted figure of £146 is the total of her goods plus the money owing to her *including* William Wodward's debt. The figure of £116 *excludes* William Wodward's debt.

Dettes oing by the sayed Agnes Rawlins

	£	s	d
Item to Stevan Rolte	xviij		
Item to Frances Lawe hir Sarvante for wages		xiij	vj

John Fitzhughe [*signature*], the marke of John Blith, the marke of Henry Slowe
[?]xj October 1611 per executor [*in a different hand*]
[*Exhibited by the executor on 19 October 1611. The exhibition clause was signed by George Pormorth, notary public.*]

Notes: Agnes Rawlins was buried at Bolnhurst on 30 August 1611. She made her will on 26 August 1611. She gave £15 each to two grandchildren; 3s 4d each to her other grandchildren; and the gown she last made to Agnes Salloway. She appointed her grandson Stephen Rolte residual legatee and executor, to whom probate was granted by Christopher Wivell on 3 October 1611 (Lincs Archives, MISC WILLS/F/158).

249 John Aynsworth of Potton made 1 October 1611
Lincolnshire Archives, LCC ADMONS 1611/250

A true & perfect Inventorie of all the goodes & chattells of John Aynsworth layt of Potton deceased prized by thes whos names be under written the first of October Anno Domini 1611

	£	s	d
Imprimis in the dwelling house A table upon a frame one cubbard & a cass paynted clothes, 2 peices of pewder a frying pann, 2 chears and other triffls about the fire		xx	
Item in the lodging chamber one borded bedstead, 3 sheetes two coffers, & one other bad bedstead one boulster a blanket with other trash		x	
Item in the shopp one Andfeild 2 payre of bellows, a beakhorne a vice thre payr of tonges 4 hammers with fils & other trash		xl	
Item in the yeard wood & straw 2 litl pigges & other trash		x	
Summa totaliter	iiij		

Wyllyam Horly [*signature*], signum Tho Haukyn, Mathew Thorne [*signature*], signum Jarret Butcher
[*Exhibited by Elizabeth Ainsworth, relict and administratrix, on 5 October 1611. The exhibition clause was signed by John Jacksonne, notary public.*]

Notes: John Aynsworth's burial has not been found. Administration was granted to his widow Elizabeth on 5 October 1611 and a bond taken (Lincs, Act Book A/ix/11 and LCC ADMONS 1611/250).

250 Francis Marshe of Eaton Bray, gentleman made 10 October 1611

Lincolnshire Archives, INV/108/133

The inventory is creased. Most letters and words in creases are decipherable and have been inserted in italics.

An Inventory of all the goodes & Chattells and Implementes of houshold of Frauncis Marshe late of Eyton in the County of Bedf gent deceased, prysed by William Mackreth, Edward Crawly, I [*sic*] William Crawly the Tenth day of October in the ix[th] yeare of the raigne of our Soveraigne Lord Kinge James by the grace of god kinge of England Fraunce & Ireland & of Scotland the Fyve & Fortyeth defender of the Fayth Annoq[ue] Domini 1611

	£	s	d
Inprimis silver spones xj		lv	
Item one silver bell salt parcell guilt		xlviij	
one parcell guilt bole of silver		xl	
one silver beaker		xxx	
one standinge bedstead [*with*] valance of redd & grene silke wrought with gold with a frenge of silke & v silke Curtaynes to yt with a fetherbed ij bolsters, ij pillowes ij blankettes & a tapestry Coveringe	viij		
one Co[ur]t Cupbord a square table, a settle & 2 Chayres		xviij	
a trockle bedstead with a fetherbed a boulster ij pillowes & j Coverlett		liij	4
one payre of an Irons, a fyre shovell & a par of tonges		v	
In another Chamber a standinge bedstead with a fetherbedd ij boulsters, ij pillowes ij blankettes & a Coverlett, with a settle	iiij		
one Chest & a square table		xiij	4
one dosen of Tapestry Cushions		xxiiij	
iij grene Cushions		vj	
ij table Carpettes & ij Co[ur]t Cupbord carpettes		L	
In another Chamber ij lyvery bedsteades with a fetherbed & a flockbedd, iij bolsters iij pillowes, a tapestry Coveringe & ij blankettes & an old tapestry Coverlett & 2 blankettes	iiij	x	
one walnutt tre Chest		xiij	4
one black Chest with Iron barrs		x	
ij Chestes of Ferr		vj	8
ij oken Chestes & a box & a deske		viij	
a great weynscott Chest		v	
paynted Clothes		xx	
xj payre of Fyne sheettes	vj	xiij	4
viij payre of Fyne pillowbiers		xxxij	
ix payre of course sheetes		L	
A longe diaper table Clothe		xx	
v other Fyne table clothes		xxxiij	4
viij square table clothes		xx	
a diaper towell		vj	8
iiij Co[ur]t Cupbord Clothes		xiij	4

j fyne damaske napkine	ij	vj
viij fyne holland napkins	viij	
xix fyne flexen napkyns	xvj	
ij Cupboard Clothes	ij	
ij towells	ij	
A bason & an ewer of Pewter	v	
viij brode Pewter platters	xvj	
vj deep broth dishes of Pewter	vj	
vj lesser platters	~~vj~~ ix	
xvj midlinge platters	xvj	
iij midlinge brothe dishes	iij	
viij Co[ur]t dishes	v	4
iiij sallett dishes	ij	viij
xxj sawcers	vij	
ij pye plates	ij	
vj porrengers	ij	
iij dishes of Pewter more	iij	
a Cullander		xij
fruyte dishes		xij
v basons	v	
3 peeces of Pewter		xviij
3 Chamberpottes	iij	
a pewter Flagon	ij	vj
ij litle Flagons	vj	
vj Pewter pottes	viij	
ij Flower pottes		viij
4 brasen Candlestickes	x	
vj lesser Brasen Candlestickes	vj	
ij Chaffine dishes	viij	
ij Skymmers		xviij
4 saltes		xx
a brasen Morter with a pestle	vj	viij
vij brasse pottes	xl	
a great panne with 2 eares to boyle Fyshe	v	
iiij brasse possnettes	x	
vij brasse & Copper kettles	xxx	
a warminge panne	ij	vj
a steele with a brasse Cover to warme a bedd	v	
a brasse Chaffer	iij	4
a payre of great Rackes	xx	
a payre of litle rackes & ij Iron barrs	x	
two payre of an Irons	vij	
two payres of tonges, a fyer forke an Iron rake, a fyer stick & a tosting Iron	v	
4 hookes to hange pottes on & 3 pott hookes	viij	vj
a fryinge panne & a brasse panne	iij	
a mill quearne[46]	xiij	4

46 *mill quearne* is possibly an error for malt quern or milk churn.

vij spittes		xx	
a musterd mill		ij	
a styll		ij	
a fyer shovell			xij
a Cleaver a shredding kniff & chopping kniff		iij	
ij grydirons & 2 peeles		ij	
ij drippinge pannes & a bastinge ladle		iiij	
A longe table with a frame & a weynscott back, ij Joynt formes, a Chayre & 4 highe Joynte stooles, 3 lytle Joynt stoles a Court Cupbord & a lytle turned chayre		xxxvj	8
iij stoles & a payre of bellowes			xij
a bible & a booke of the Institucion of xpian [*Christian*] religion[47]		x	
ij tables & iij playne formes		vj	viij
a glasse shelf		ij	
a bushell, a skryne, a peck & a Fanne		vij	
vj barrells 2 beare stales a par of slynges & a beare tubb		xvj	
a veriuce barrell			xij
a powdringe trowghe with a Cover		iiij	
a dresser bord, a grease Cupbord a hayre Cupbord, a glasse Cupbord & a shelf		vj	
a yeldinge Fatt		x	
a meyshinge tubb		iij	4
A meyshinge Fatt		v	
a Cooler		ij	
two Kymnells			xx
a boultinge hutche			xx
ij meale tubbs		ij	
iij boles			xviij
a grynde stone			xij
a tenante Sawe & a hand sawe		ij	
hammer & pincers			viij
two wheeles for wollen & lynnen		iij	
a weynscott presse		vj	8
a drawght Rake			xij
a mattock & a payringe Iron			xvj
a payre of Scales			xij
two tubbs & 2 [*?*]tuns		ij	vj
two ewes		x	
Item his Apparell	iiij		
Summa totalis	lxxxj	xiiij	viij
[*Corrected total*	*£81*	*17s*	*8d*]

~~W Mark~~ the marke of Edward Crawley

47 An English translation of the last, 1559, edition of John Calvin's *Institutio Christianae Religionis* was made by Thomas Norton and published in several editions from 1561 onwards under the title *The Institution of Christian Religion*. Francis Marshe (who was a near neigbour of Norton and his family at Sharpenhoe) might have had any of these editions.

debtes due by specialtyes			
First due by William Mackreth	C		
by Thomas Beeche upon a bond	xx		
by William Sandes esq upon a byll	xxx		
by Tho Saell upon a bond	x		
by William Pryor upon a bond	x		
by William Crawley upon a bond	x		
by John Rogers upon a bond	xij		
Summa	Clxxxxij		
Summa totalis	CClxxxiij	xiiij	viij
[*Corrected total*	*£273*	*17s*	*8d*]

William Mackreth, the marke of William Crawley, the marke of Edward Crawley
[*No exhibition clause*]

Notes: Francis Marshe was buried at Eaton Bray on 3 August 1611.

251 Henry Ingram of Blunham, labourer made 28 November 1611
Lincolnshire Archives, LCC ADMONS 1611/279

November the 28 daye 1611. An Inventorye made of all the goodes & mooveables that was Henry Ingrames of Blonham in the Count of Bedd laborrare lat dicessed being seene praysed and pryssed by Thomas Hill & Thomas Cranfeild Inhabitantes of Blonham the daye & yeare firste above written Thomas Graye[48]

	£	s	d
Inprimis in the Hall A cubbord a table a forme a bench board with other Implementes		xxx	
Item Brass and Pewlter		xxviij	
Item in the Chamber a bedsteed a mattris a coverlite one bolster & v pillowes		x	
Item in Lynine vj payre of sheetes ij pillow bears & a borde Clothe		xl	
Item iij Chestes one Coffer an old Amberye		xiij	iiij
Item in the Lofte a beadsteed a traye with other Implementes		v	
Some tottall is	vj	vj	iiij

Thomas Hill, Thomas Cranfeild, Thomas Graye[49]
[*Exhibited by Jelian Ingram, relict and administratrix, on 30 November 1611. The exhibition clause has been written twice in two different hands. One exhibition clause was signed by George Pormorth, notary public.*]

Notes: Henry Ingram was buried at Blunham on 4 March 1609, described as 'senex et impotence'. His widow Julian was buried on 13 January 1617 and described as 'an ould widow'. Administration fees were noted on the inventory: administration 2s 6d, sealing and signing the bond 1s 10d, total 4s 4d. Administration was granted to his widow Julian on 30 November 1611 and a bond taken (Lincs Archives, Act Book A/ix/14 and LCC ADMONS 1611/279). Note the delay between the dates of burial and the inventory being made.

48 *Thomas Graye* is written in a different hand.
49 This name is in the same writing and ink as *Thomas Graye* in the inventory's heading, and different from the writing of the inventory.

252 William Sherley of Bletsoe, yeoman undated; made before 24 March 1612
Bedfordshire Archives, ABP/W1611/144

A true Inventary of all such goodes & Chattells which was at the death of William Sherley of Blettsoo late deceased in his owne possession at that instant praised by Robert Parsansom of Rysley & Robert Jones of Thurleigh

	£	s	d
In the Parlor			
Imprimis a bedsteede a featherbed and a flockbed unto it, a Coveringe a blanckett, a boulster of feathers, and 2 of flocke, tow Pillowes, & vallens and Curtins unto the bedd	05	10	0
Item a Table, 3 Chaires, 5 low stooles, tow Coushings and a window Curtin	01	10	0
In the Hall			
Item 2 bibles with other bookes	01	10	0
Item a lounge [*long*] Table & a Square Table 6 ioyned Stooles, a livery Cubberd, a wenchcoate portale with a Cubberd in the same, and a lounge forme	02	10	0
Item a bench and a seat of wenchcoate a portale of the same, and on pare of Tables	01	13	4
In the Kitchinor			
Item 2 littell owld tables & tow Formes	00	04	0
Item a Cradle & tow wicker Chaires	00	10	0
Item a Saffe	00	08	0
Item tow spittes, a pare of Iron Rackes, a par of Cobirons a dripping pane, and 2 potthangers	01	05	0
Item 3 brasse panns, 2 kettell, 2 brasse pottes, 2 possenettes a Chaffer, a warminge pan, a pestell & morter & a brasse Candlestick	04	00	0
Item tow doosen of peauter dishes of too sortes, & 12 sawcers	02	10	0
Item 8 porrinngers, three dooble saltes, six ~~fritt~~ frut dishes, 2 par of peauter Candlestickes, 5 dooz[en] of peauter spoones a peauter boule, a quarte pott, a Cupp, & 3 Chamber potts	01	00	
Item 4 Bacon fliches	02	00	0
In the Parlor Chamber			
Item a standing beddsteed, a feather bedd, a flockbedd, a coveringe tow blanckettes and a boulster	05	00	0
Item three great Chestes, & 2 littell Coffers	01	06	8
Item 2 owld trunckes, a wicker chaire and a stoole	00	16	8
In the hale Chamber			
Item a trucklebedd, a flockbed, a boulster a pare of pillowes a blanckett, and a Covering	01	00	0
Item 3 Chestes, & 2 littell boxes, a wenchcoate presse	02	10	0
Item a spinninge wheele for wollen, & 2 lennen wheeles three hatchelles and windinge blades	00	15	0
Item a pare of holland Sheetes, 3 pare of flaxen sheetes	04	13	4
Item foure pare of hemptare sheetes	02	10	0
Item 7 pare of harden sheetes	02	00	0
Item 3 pare of holland pillowbears	01	00	0

Item 3 pare of flaxen pillowbears	00	10	0
Item 4 par of hemptare pillowbears	00	04	0
Item 4 flexen boord cloaths & 6 ordinary	01	10	0
Item 2 doozen of flaxen napkings	01	00	0
Item 2 lounge flexen towells	00	05	0
Item 6 shorte towelles	00	02	0
Item a lounge gowne	01	10	0
Item 2 sutes of apparell	04	10	0
Item 4 Cloackes	06	00	0
Item a Saddle & bridle	00	07	0
In the Kitching Chamber			
Item a standinge bed a flockbed, a white Rogge, tow boulsters and a pare of blanckettes	02	00	[...]
Item a Truckell bedd tow flockbedes, 3 blanckettes, 2 boulsteres and a Coveringe	02	10	0
Item a littell Table a deske & 3 boxes	00	13	4
Item in the Butery & Milkhouse			
Tow Hoghsedes & 4 barrelles	01	00	0
Item a powderinge Tobb, tow Kimnailes, 3 boules a Cherne	01	00	0
Item a Cheespresse, 12 Cheesfattes, 5 Tobbes, a Fatt, & Shelves	01	10	0
In the Mill			
Item a bedd of bord, a flockbedd, a boulster, 2 blanckettes and A Coveringe	01	00	0
Item 3 Coffers for Corne, a bushell, a peck, a halfpeck, and a boulting Arcke	01	10	0
Item 2 Iron barrs, a sleidg 12 milbilles, a loung hand sawe, and 2 shorte hand sawes, & 4 Augers	01	10	0
Item a Cast nett	00	10	0
In the Yarde			
Item Timber with other woode in the yard & in the parck	07	00	0
Item Theales & borde	01	10	0
Item tow howfeildes Rooffed over the toppes of six bayes	05	00	0
Item a baye nagge	04	10	0
Item 2 smale baies of Haye	03	00	0
Item five milch Cowes	15	00	0
Item a pale aboute the hoggyard & some pale in the Orchard	03	10	0
Item tow Bottes [*?boats*] v[li] Item a milston iiij[li]	09	00	0
Item a wheelbarrow, Forkes, & Rackes	00	05	0
Item a Sowe, a Hogge, 4 Shoutes, and tow Pigges	02	00	0
Item an Oxx	06	00	0
Item 3 Ladders	00	06	8
Item a leantoo of borde	00	10	0
Item a Sworde a dagger, and other thinges hear not menc[*i*]oned	01	10	0
Item the Lease of the Howse & Mill	066	13	4
Som total	201	16	4
[*Corrected total*	*£200*	*18s*	*4d*]
Item a Bridge of bord not mencioned before	005	00	0
Some total	206	16	4
[*Corrected total*	*£205*	*18s*	*4d*]

[*Exhibited on 24 March 1612*]

Notes: William Sherley was buried at Bletsoe on 8 December 1611. He made his will on 5 December 1611, describing himself as a yeoman. He left £10 to each of his four children at the age of 18 and his gold ring with a seal to the eldest. His wife Judith was charged with bringing them up and was his residual legatee and executrix. Probate was granted to her on 24 March 1612. A commission was issued to John Orme, rector of Bletsoe and William Tapp, curate, to administer the oath to her, which was done by the latter on 23 March 1612 (Beds Archives, ABP/W1611/144). Judith Sherley remarried in 1613.

253 John Swift of Nether Shelton, Marston Moretaine made 5 January 1612
Bedfordshire Archives, ABP/W1610–1611/4

A true Inventory of the goodes & chattle of John Swifte late of Marstone Morten deceased January the vth 1611 Thomas Smithe the parson, Thomas Bosworth the elder & John Reade beinge praysers

	£	s	d
In the hall			
Imprimis one ~~great~~ table with a frame ~~a~~ ij formes a benche board & a backe of latice		vj	
Item another table with ij tresselles & an old plancke forme ij cast[50] chayres			xviij
Item ij little cubbeardes		viij	
Item ij platters & x ~~more~~ peeces more of smale pewter		v	4
Item ij duzen of old trenchers & ix pewter spoones			viij
Item v bottles greate & smale with ij litle brasse pottes		x	
Item iiij smale brasse candlestickes with ij old salsellers			xx
Item ij old painted clothes		ij	
In the upper chamber			
A bedesteed ~~ij~~ an old mattrice a bolster ij blankettes & a covering with rugge painted clothes ~~& ij coffers~~		~~xx~~	
his wearing apparell & ij old coffers		xx	
Item viij^{l} of woll		iiij	
Item j ~~ij~~ hatchettes an ax ij old billes with old irone		ij	
Item an old shotchill & ij^{l} of yearne			vj
In the farther nether room			
A salting troughe ij barrells a kimnell with other lumber		vij	
In the nether roome			
A beddsteed ij old blankettes ij old chestes & ix sheetes & ij painted clothes		xxiiij	
In the ij [?]out nether roomes			
[*illeg.*] boards ij sythes ij banking Irons a molestapple 4 pickforkes a old woollen & linnen wheele		viij	
Item other trumpery		v	
Item wood		vj	viij

50 This word is faint and badly formed.

Item ij old bottles & other dishes			xviij
Summa	v	xiij	x

Thomas Smithe [*signature*], John Reades marke, Thomas Bosworthes marke
[*Exhibited on 21 January 1612*]

Notes: John Swift was buried at Marston Moretaine on 7 January 1612. His nuncupative will provided for his wife Alice to have two nether rooms at the north end of his house with an adjoining garden plot for her life and half his goods. His son William was to have the remainder of his house, orchard and garden and the other half of his goods. Probate was granted to his widow on 21 January 1612 (Beds Archives, ABP/W1610–1611/4).

254 Alice Hunt of Stanford, Southill, widow made 11 January 1612
Lincolnshire Archives, LCC ADMONS 1611/273

A true and perfecte Inventarie of all and singuler the goodes debtes rightes and chattells of Alce Hunt late of Stanford in the Countie of Bedf deceased made the eleaventh daie of Januarie 1611

	£	s	d
Inprimis which she gave to Alce the daughter of Nicholas Retchford one brasse pott one brasse panne a posnett halfe a dozen of Pewter platters 3 porringers, 2 candlestickes & a little pewter potte		xx	
Item six paires of sheetes one bedsteade with the beddeinge thereon one Pillowe one coffer, one little boxe, one table clothe, one gredyron one saltseller, one forme & a table		xxx	
Item old yron			xij
Item 2 paires of sheetes given to Thomas Retchefordes wife		viij	
Item one paire of sheetes given to Alce the daughter of Richard East		iij	iiij
[*change of handwriting*] Item 4 lambes given to Clement Eastes children		viij	
Item one ewe and a lambe to the daughter of John East		v	
Item two pewter dishes to Robert sonne of Nicholas Rechford			xij
Item one stock of bees and a swarme		ij	
Item in readie money which she gave as followeth vizt			

To Alice the daughter of Nich Rechford	viij		
Item to John and Robert sonnes of Robert Rechford	10		
Item to Nich. Rechford hes sonne	xx		
Item to three of his children 20s a peece	iij		
Item to Clement sonne of James East		x	
Item to Nicholas his brother		xx	
Item to the poore		vj	viij
Item to Robert sonne of Nich. Rechford	iij		
Item to Nicholas sonne of Thomas Rechford		xl	
Item her wearing apparell		xl	
Some is	Lix	ix	
[*Corrected total*	*£53*	*15s*	*0d*]

[*Exhibited by Robert Retchford, administrator, on 18 January 1612*]

Notes: Alice Hunt widow was buried at Southill on 1 January 1612. On 4 January 1608 she made an agreement with her son Robert Retchford for her maintenance during her life and disposed of her goods. If the arrangement was unsuccessful and Alice left her son, he would pay her £5 a year. The inventory records the disposition of her household goods in this document to family and others. Probate was granted to her son Robert Retchford by Thomas Crabtree surrogate for Christopher Wivell on 18 January 1612 and a bond was taken (Lincs Archives, MISC WILLS/F/134; Act Book A/ix/15; and LCC ADMONS 1611/273).

255 William Asmond of Turvey, husbandman made 29 January 1612

Lincolnshire Archives, INV/108/127

A true Inventorye of all the mooveable goodes and Chattells of Wm Asmond late of Turvye in the Countye of Bedf: husbandman deceased taken the xxix[th] of Januarye Anno Domini 1611 & by Hugh Clyfton, Lewes Norman & George Hoton

	£	s	d
Imprimis his Apparell		xx	
in the hawle			
Item one Cubberd one longe Table one other lytle Table one Chayre v stooles two Coffers & certen other Commodytyes		l	
in the Chamber			
Item ij Beddes with Furnyture to them ij Coffers vj pare of sheetes ij pillowberes j bord Cloth & other small Commodityes	iiij	x	

	£	s	d
in the lower howse			
Item j boltynge Arke one Fatt j barrell & certen other Trashe		x	
in the Stable			
Item j horse		xxx	
Item the Cartgeeres & plough geeres		x	
in the yard			
Item j Long Cart & a doung Cart		l	
Item the Hovells & wood & ploughes		xl	
Item j Cowe & a Bullocke		l	
Item iij sheepe		xv	
Item iij store hogges		xij	
Item the Corne pease & Haye	vj	x	
Item iiij Acres of Tylthe & halfe Acre of wheate & iij Acres of Peaseland	iij		
Item j fleaked howse		xl	
Item the Lease of the howse	iiij		
Summ	xxxiiij	vij	

Hughe Clyfton [*signature*], Lewes Norman [*signature*], signum Georgij Hoton
[*Exhibited by Simon Asmond, executor, on 30 January 1611/12. The exhibition clause was signed by George Pormorth, notary public.*]

Notes: William Asmond was buried as William Osmond at Turvey on 25 December 1611.

256 Thomas Whysson of Langford, husbandman made 9 March 1612
Lincolnshire Archives, INV/108/131

An Inventorye of all the goodes and Chattelles of Thomas Whysson late of Langford in the County of Bedf deceassed taken by Anthony Renolde, William ~~Renold~~ Hemminge and Roberte Hemminge the ~~ff~~ nynthe daye of Marche in Anno domini 1611

	£	s	d
In the Haule			
Inprimis in the Hall one table one forme and one benche boarde		viij	
Item one Cubberde		xiij	iiij
Item two Cushions one stoole A Chayre and two spinninge wheeles		iij	iiij
Item ~~platteres~~ eyghte platteres five Sawceres A pynte pott of pewter		x	
Item fower dishes & A wooden platter & A Salte box & the paynted clothes in the haule		ij	vj
Item one Kettell one pottage pott A posnett & A skillett & one chaffeinge dyshe		xij	
Item one Flyshe of Bacon		vj	

~~In the Chamber~~ one[51]

Fryinge pann one gyrdyron A spitt two Candelstickes & A payre of bellowes & A payre of pott hangeres & A payre of pott hookes	iij	iiij

In the Chamber

Imprimis one Feather bedd one blankett one Coverlett and the bedstead & one mattrice & two boulsteres	xl	
Item five Chestes and litle Cofferes	xxx	
Item ~~three~~ twoe payre of harden sheetes & two table Cloathes	xiij	iiij
Item ~~one one~~ two payre of hempe tare sheetes	xiiij	
Item three pillowe beares & halfe a dozen of table napkins	ix	
Item two pillowes a lite bedstead & cloathe baskett	v	
Item his wareinge apparell	x	
Item the paynted cloathes aboute the chamber	x	

In the Lofte over the haule

Item one bedsteade one mattryce & one boulster and A blankett	x	
Item two old sackes A shovell & one wheele & two pond of towe		xx
Item the paynted Cloathes aboute the lofte	v	

In the lofte over the Chamber

Item vij hempe sheaves	v	x
Item two or three old bee heaves two olde nettes and A Cheese racke		xij

In the Butterye

Item one Soltinge troughe on kimnell and one boultinge arke one tubb & twoo barelles	x	
Item one Charne two payles with other trashe in the butterye	v	

In the barne

Item A litle bullymonge in the Strawe	vj	viij
Item A litle Srawe [*sic*]	iij	iiij
Item one Shodd Carte one ploughe & A shorte ladder	xlvj	viij

51 The heading *In the chamber* seems to be a mistake in copying. It looks as if the scribe wrote *Item one* followed by *In the chamber one*; then realised his mistake; deleted *In the chamber*; wrote *Flyshe of bacon* and its value above *In the chamber*; and continued with *Fryinge pann* following on from *one*.

In the Stable

	£	s	d
Item Colleres and old harnesse & A pannell & A carte sedle		viij	
Item a fann A bushell & A payre of roopes		iiij	

In the yarde

	£	s	d
Item one Sowe & twoe pigges		viij	
Item one Cowe & A calfe & A bullocke	iij	vj	viij
Item one hovell with the wood and one payre of harrowes & two pith forkes & one draughte rake		xiij	iiij
Item five hennes and one Cocke		iij	iiij
Item the Compasse in the yard		xiij	iiij
Item two stockes of bees		vj	viij
Summa totalis	xx	viij	iiij

Anthony Renolde [*signature*], the marke of William Hemminge, the marke of Roberte Hemminge

[*Exhibited by the executrix on 22 March 1612. The exhibition clause was signed by George Pormouth, notary public.*]

Notes: Thomas Whysson was buried at Langford on 28 February 1612, described as a labourer. He made his will on 24 February 1612, as Thomas Wesson a husbandman. He gave 12d to each of his brothers and 6d to each of his godchildren. He gave the residue to his wife Elizabeth whom he also appointed his executrix. She was granted probate by Christopher Wivell on 12 March 1612 (Lincs Archives, MISC WILLS/F/31).

257 William Beyston of Bletsoe, yeoman — made 10 March 1612

Lincolnshire Archives, INV/108/153a and b

There are two copies, a and b. The transcription has been made from copy a. There are only minor spelling variations, except as noted. Neither have a total nor an exhibition clause.

An Inventarye of all the moveable goodes of William Beyston of Bletsoe late deceased Praysed by John Maxie and Roberte Churche the tenth day of Marche in the yeare of our Lord God one thowsand sixe hundreth & Eleven & John Merryton

	£	s	d
Inprimis one oulde girte bed & a litle trunchin coffer		xvj	
Item twoe deskes		iij	
Item one table, sixe stooles, the settle, one chayre & one cubbord		xxxiij	iiij
Item twoe trusse beddes and one trundle bed		xxiij	iiij
Item twoe litle[52] coffers & one blacke chaier		v	

52 *litle* in copy b only.

Item one cubbord twoe old tables one forme twoe tressles and one old chaire		x	
Item Eight barrells one saltinge trough		xiij	iiij
Item one old pen one cheese presse three tubbes		viij	
Item one paile twoe kimnels & a boultinge Arcke & ij litle kimnels		iij	iiij
Item one old[53] coffer withoute a Lydd			xij
Item fowre kettles twoe brasse pottes & the[54] litle posnettes		xxvj	8
Item one Todde weighte		ij	vj
Item three old wheeles		ij	vj
Item ten platters & twoe candlestickes twoe saltes twoe chamber pottes		x	
Item one spice morter & one latten candlesticke		ij	
Item twoe spyttes[55] one payre of Andyrons one fire shovell one payre of tonges one grediron the bellowes & brindlett one paier of cobbiron and the hangeinges		vj	8
Item twoe[56] featherbeddes one old flockebedd & fowre coveringes		xl	
Item twoe pillowes three boulsters twoe pillowe beeres & three blanckettes		xvj	viij
Item one payre of flaxen sheetes three payre of harden[57] one table clothe one dozen of harden napkins, & one cubbord clothe and twoe towells		xx	
Item one litle worcke howse[58] & one quarne with other ymplementes		xx	
Item sixe framed hovells	vj	iij	iiij
Item one shodd carte		xlvj	viij
Item plowes & plough tymbers		vj	viij
Item Carte geres & ploughe geares		xxiij	iiij
Item one arke & bordes & other ymplementes in the stable		xxij	
Item three horses	ix		

53 *old* in copy a only.
54 *three* in copy b.
55 *pittes* in copy b.
56 *one* in copy b.
57 *three payre of harden* have been omitted from copy b.
58 *gowse* in copy b.

Item five milch beas & nyne bullockes	xv		
Item seaven sheepe		xxij	
Item sixe hogges & seaven pigges		liij	iiij
Item xix acres of barly twoe acres of wheate & iij roodes of rye	xxiij		
Item eighteene acres of pease	xj	xiij	viij
Item eighte Loades of haye	iiij		
Item all the fire woode about the yard with one tymber tree		xxx	
Item for pitchforkes, rakes harrowes, bills hatchettes sackes & a wynowe clothe		ix	
Summa totalis huius Inven[to]rij			[*blank*]
[*Total*	*£92*	*6s*	*8d*]

[*No exhibition clause*]

Notes: William Beyston was buried at Bletsoe on 4 September 1611. He made his will on 14 February 1610, giving £15 to his youngest son at age 24 and directing his eldest son to buy him a heifer and to pay towards his apprenticeship; and £10 to his second son. His eldest son, Thomas, who was residual legatee and executor, obtained probate on 4 February 1612 (Lincs Archives, MISC WILLS/F/131).

258 William Coste of Pillinge, Marston Moretaine, labourer made April or May 1612
Bedfordshire Archives, ABP4/183

The inventory is damaged down the right side; some letters and figures are missing. Some sections of the inventory have been laid out as continuous text with values in the middle of a line. For ease in comparing this with other inventories, the inventory has been laid out in the standard format.

The true Inventory of the goodes and Cattell of William Coste Lately deceased

	£	s	d
First wee prayse in the Hall one table and a frame two little formes and a Cupboord apene under It at		[*?*]x	
Wee prayse three Little stooles and two bole dishes three deshes and two payles at		iij	
We prayse in the neither Chamber one standing bedd with a teaster and one Cubbard and a Chest a Coffer and a little table and a Cheare at fortye shill[*ings*]		40	
Wee prayse foure payre of sheetes one bankate [...] old Coverliddes and an old matrise & Bolster and one pillowe		xx	
Wee prayse two little kettles foure little platters at		x	
We prayse a Barrill and a tubb two treane platteres one Chestfoote		ij	

we praise one cowe five nobles		[*33*	*4*]
[*Total*	*£5*	*18s*	*4d*]

[*Exhibited by the executrix at Ampthill on 12 May 1612. The exhibition clause was signed by* [*?*]*William Bromsall, notary public.*]

Notes: William Coste was buried at Marston Moretaine on 4 April 1612. He made his will on 4 March 1612, describing himself as a labourer. He left a cow to his wife Agnes; and furniture, his tenement and land, which is described, to his daughters. The furniture was a cupboard in the nether chamber; the table, its frame and two forms in the hall; the 'bigger carved chest' and the joined chair; a joined standing bed with a tester; a coffer, a little square table and a cupboard with a pen. The residual legatee and executrix was his wife, who was granted probate on 12 May 1612 (Beds Archives, ABP4/183).

259 Henry Yarwell of Souldrop made July 1612

Bedfordshire Archives, ABP/W1612/226

An Inventorye of the moveable gooddes of Henrye Yarwell late deceased at Souldropp the [*blank*] daye of Julye Anno Domini 1612

	£	s	d
Inprimis His apparrell		xx	
Item in the Halle a table a frame & a forme		iij	iiij
Item a cobberd a penne iiij peces of brasse vj peces of pewter with other implementes		xx	
Item in the chamber ij bedstedes, ij coverlettes, ij blankettes ij boulsters one cofer v payre of shetes with other implementes		xl	
Item in the loft an old cofer a chesse racke with other implementes		x	
Item in the nether howse a malte querne a kimnell iij tubbes a boulting arke with other implementes		viij	
Item one Hovell with a roffe & the woode in the yarde		xl	
Item iij bease	iiij		
Item ij calves		x	
Item x gest shepe & iiij cooples		liij	iiij
Item ij roodes of wheate & xvij acres and an halfe of barlye otes & pease	xiiij	viij	
The whole summe is	xxviij	xij	viij

Praysers of these gooddes Willyam Bethraye, Henry Jeyes [*signature*], Jhon Bytherey [*signature*], William Palladey his mark

[*Exhibited on 4 August 1612*]

Notes: Henry Yarwell was buried at Souldrop on 14 July 1612.

260 Edward Catherall of Luton, brewer made 5 March 1613

Bedfordshire Archives, Z1268/2

This inventory was in private hands until 2021. It was seen by Rev. J. E. Brown, vicar of Studham, who published part of it in The Antiquary *(vol. 42, January-December 1906, pp. 27–9) and by Dr Joan Schneider who published the whole of it in the* Manshead Archaeological Society Journal *(vol. 19, pp. 30–41). It was given to the editor of this volume by Dick Pilkinton of Markyate in 2021 and donated to Bedfordshire Archives.*

The Inventary Indented of all & singler the goodes Cattalls Chattells Debtes rightes and credittes of Edward Catherall late of Luton in the Countie of Beds Brewer deceassed taken valued & praised by Michaell Daldorne, Roger Winton, John Atwood & John Pilgryme yomen the fifte Daye of Marche Anno Domini 1612 and in the yeares of the raigne of our soveraigne Lorde James by the grace of god of Englande Scotlande Fraunce & Irelande kinge Defender of the faithe etc of Englande Fraunce & Irelande the Tenthe and of Scotlande the sixe and Fortith as followeth videlt

	£	s	d
In the Haull			
Inprimis a table with the frame and a forme a Cupbord foure litle chaires a Cupbord cloth a bayard & an iron for Seacoles		xx	
Item a Benche & a Bencheborde & the paynted clothes valued at		iij	iiij
Summa		xxiij	iiij
In the parlour			
Inprimis a Table with a frame Twoe formes a benche & benche boordes		xiij	iiij
Item a graate Cupborde & the paynted clothes		vj	viij
Summa		xx	
In the Chamber over the Haull			
Inprimis a longe ioyned table with a frame sixe greate ioyned stooles and twoe litle ioyned stooles		xxx	
Item a Joyned Bedsteed a Trondle bedd twoe featherbedds a strawe bedd a boulster Twoe pillowes Twoe blanckettes a Coverlett & the Curtaynes	vj		
Item foure other Coverlettes	iij	vj	viij
Item a Cupborde & the shelfe		xxiij	iiij
Item a Box for Lynneon sixe newe Quisshions a paire of tables and an hamper		xx	
Item all the Pewter viz[t] Platters Disshes Sawcers, porringers, Salte Sellers, pottes, Candlestickes, spoones, a lattin morter & a pestle three lattin Candlestickes a greate Cheaste a litle Fosser & the paynted clothes	iij		
Item one Paire of hollande sheetes Nyne paire of flexen sheetes Thirtie paire of Tooen sheetes, Twelve hollande pillowebeers twelve flaxen pillowebeeres, eighteene Tableclothes sixe dozen of table napkins, thone			

halfe flexen & thother halfe Tooen, Twelve Towells & twoe cupbord clothes	xx		
Summa	xxxvj	x	
[corrected sub-total	*£36*	*0s*	*0d]*

In the Chamber over the parlour

Item a standinge Bedsteed a Trondle bedd a featherbedd a boulster twoe litle pillowes twoe blanckettes, Foure Cofers, Tenn poundes of lynneon yarne & a Todd of woll	iiij	x	
Summa p3	iiij	x	

In the Chamber over the kytchin

Inprimis a Joyned Bedsteed a plaine Bedsteed, a Trondlebedd twoe featherbeddes Twoe strawe beddes Three blanckettes twoe Coverlettes twoe boulsters & twoe pillowes	iij		
Item a Joyned square ~~table~~ drawenge table twoe ioyned stooles three square ioyned boxes for lynneon three Chaires, three Cheastes, a byble, Rastalls abridgemente of the Statutes, & the paynted clothes	iij		
Item certein iron & steele a sworde, a dagger, Twoe Trowells a shoed shovell and a shoed spade a litle playner and a tostinge plate		xiij	iiij
Item his apparell	vj	xiij	iiij
Summa	xiij	vj	viij

In the Kytchin

Inprimis sixe brasse pottes eighte kettles Foure postnettes three skommers a bastinge ladle foure spittes a paire of rackes twoe drippinge pannes twoe iron peeles a paire of Cobirons three pottehangers, a fire slyce twoe fire shovells, a paire of tonges twoe gridirons, twoe fryenge pannes foure paire of pottehookes one Chafinge dishe a breade graate a brasse morter, an iron pestle & a paire of bellowes	viij		
Item a mouldinge boorde a plaine litle table, certein shelves with boles woodden disshes & Trenchers a Cradle a Cloth baskett three playne stooles and other ymplementes there		xx	
Item eighte Flitches of Bacon		liij	iiij
Summa	xj	xiij	iiij

In the Larder

Inprimis Twoe powdringe Troves with Covers a powdringe Tubbe, twoe lesser tubbes a butter Charme three boles twoe Cheese fattes and a grease Ferkyn		xl	
Item eighte breastes of beife		xxxiij	iiij
Item the fleshe in Powder		xx	
Summa	iiij	xiij	iiij

Inprimis In the parlour over the way Twoe ioyned tables with frames tenn ioyned stooles and a Corte Cupborde		xxxiij	iiij
Item in the Chamber over that parlour a standinge bedsteed a trondlebedd a featherbedd a strawe bedd twoo boulsters a blanckett a Coverlett a litle square table too stooles and twoo foormes		xl	
Item in the Middle Chamber a standing bedsteed a trondlebedd a feather bedd, a mattresse Twoe boulsters twoe blanckettes a Coverlett and a litle longe table		xl	
Item in the Further Chamber a standinge bedsteed a Trondlebedd three featherbeddes, twoe boulsters, a pillowe Twoe blanckettes a ~~pillowe~~ Coverlett twoe ioyned stooles twoe square tables & one frame	iiij		
Summa	ix	xiij	iiij
Inprimis in the Storelofte Foure iron wedges eighte iron straakes an iron spindle & other olde iron & lumber there		xiij	iiij
Item in the stoorehowse under the Gallery Foure plowe wheeles and a wheelebarrowe wheele, three Awgars a donge raake a mattock and other lumber there		xiij	iiij
Item in the lofte nexte the gatehowse a Troughe, a Tubbe with asshes a boultinge hutche a Kymnell a Fanne a Tubbe with feathers & twoe sackes with feathers		xx	
Summa		xlvj	viij
Inprimis in the servantes Chamber a plaine bedsteed with the furniture		x	
Item in the Hoppe lofte the Hoppes there		xij	
Item sixe quarters of Barley	vij		
Item eighte warpes of Fisshe		viij	
Item Foure Pitchforkes seaven litle iron gatheringe raakes & three Peasehookes		vij	
Item Five busshells of wheate & Rie in the wheate lofte		xx	
Item foure quarters of oates	iij	xij	
Item Seaven sackes		ix	
Item a busshell a Fann & a Cheeserack		ij	
Item a Maltemyll with a rack & manger in the Millhowse		l	
Item three Troves twoe Tubbes and a grindinge stone in the welhowse nexte the Mill		viij	
Item a rack and a manger in the litle stable by the well		iij	
Item certein Seacoles & certein pavinge tyles in the malteshopp		xx	
Summa	xviij		xij

In the Maltelofte

Inprimis Tenn quarters of Malte	xij		
Item Twoe shovells and an olde sack			xx

Item a Beame a paire of scalles & a leaden waighte wayeng Nyneteene poundes in the kylne howse		x	
Item a kylne haire		vj	viij
Item a greate raake hedd		ij	
Item Five quarters of rawe malte in the Maltehowse	vj		
Item twoe olde Carte bodyes three greate raakes certein elme boordes and beechen boordes and other lumber there		xxx	
Summa	xx	x	iiij

In the Geastes Staple

Inprimis Twoe rackes and twoe mangers as they stande		x	
Item in the horse stable Foure horses & a gelding with their harnesse for plowe and Carte	xx		
Item a Racke a Manger & an olde Cartebodye		x	
Item in the Chaffe howse a greate drye fatt a barrell a scuttle a sive a fanne Five sackes & an olde Lanterne		xvij	
Item the Chaffe & other lumber there		xxvj	viij
Item wheate & Rie in the barne at home	viij		
Item a parcell of Bullymonge there	iij	vj	viij
Summa	xxxiiij	x	iiij

In the Brewehowse

Inprimis the Lyccour Tunn the Brewinge Copper the Masshinge Tunn the underback the sweete worte Tunn the yeeldinge Tunn Twoe Coolers and the Gutter	xxx		
Item the stalles the standinges Barrells kylderkins kymnells Twoe bearinge Tubbes, a worte Tubbe, other Tubbes Twoe paire of slynges & other ymplementes there	x		
Summa	xl		

In the Woodhowse & Hovell

Inprimis Wood & Tymber	xiij	vj	viij
Item in the yarde Five kyne & a steere	x		
Item tenn hogges & Tenn stores	xv		
Item Twoe donge Cartes one longe Carte a beere Carte with shoed wheeles	viij		
Item the Cowerackes hoggestroves & other lumber aboute the yarde		x	
Summa	xlvj	xvj	viij

In the Barnes at Lowes wick

Inprimis oates & Chaffe	xij		
Item a parcell of Haye		xxiij	iiij
Item three longe sheeperackes an olde Gynne Twoe longe Carte bodyes a beere Carte bodye Twoe ladders twoe Carte ladders false raves twoe			

rolles certein Tymber, boordes, Eveslath Chippes & other lumber there	xiij	vj	viij
Item Thirteene Drie sheepe & thirteene eawes & lammes	x	vj	viij
Item the plowes & harrowes with the furniture therto belonginge		xx	
Summa	xxxvij	xvj	viij

In the Feildes

Inprimis eighteene acres of wheate & twoe acres & an halfe of Rye	liij	vj	viij
Item the edgelande	l		
Item the Tilthe	l		
Item the wood & Tymber in Gregory shawe wood	l		
Summa	CCiij	vj	viij

Debtes Due to the Testator

Inprimis Due by James Raves of Holborne in the Countye of Midd	x		
Item by John Brangwin of Waltham Abbey		xl	
Item by Thomas Vyall of [*blank*] in the Countie of Essex		x	
Item by Edward Taylor	xiij		
Item by John Barber of Edmonton		xl	
By John Saunders		xxx	
By Josua Peter		x	
By Roger Turner		xxxiiij	iiij
By Roberte Oxenforde		v	
By Welles of Hockliffe		x	
By Gourney of Markeyate Streate		x	
By John Anstey of Markeyate	vij		
By Thomas Tipladye		iiij	
By Humfrey Glover		iiij	
By Richard Bardolffe esquire		xviij	viij
By Mistress Fraunces Cheyne widowe		xx	
By John Tappes		v	
By Master Andrewe Duffin		vj	viij
By Thomas Bent	v		
John Milles		vj	
by William Kylbey		v	
by Roberte Stoakes		xxx	
By Frauncis Pigott		viij	iiij
by John Moores		v	
by Thomas Hill		xxj	vj
by John Bigge of Lawrence Ende		ij	
by Thomas Feilde		xviij	
Summa	lj	vij	
[*Corrected sub-total*	*£52*	*3s*	*6d*]
[*Total*	*£537*	*11s*	*10d*]

Debtes Due by the Testator

Inprimis To William Preston of Childwick gent	lx		
Item to John Etheridge	lxxj	v	
Item to Thomas Daye	xxiij	xv	
Item to Roger Winton	xliiij		
Item to Roberte Halsey	xxxiij		

	£	s	d
Summa CCxxxij			
Summa Totalis allocatis allocand[59]	CCCv	v	iiij
[*Corrected total of goods and money minus debts*	*£305*	*11s*	*10d*]

[*Exhibited by Elizabeth his widow on 18 March 1613. The exhibition clause has been signed by Edmund Woodhall, who was registrar of the Prerogative Court of Canterbury in London.*]

Notes: Edward Catherall was buried at Luton on 16 February 1613 as Edward Katherall alias Hookes. He made his will on 25 April 1612, asking to be buried near his first wife. He left the house where he lived, one acre, another messuage in Castle Street, Luton, with a close of twenty acres of arable and pasture to son George at age 21 and also his malting and brewing equipment; a close of meadow and cottage in Luton and fifteen acres of arable to son Edward; two tenements in Luton to son Peter; a messuage in Luton and eleven acres to son Abraham; a close and three acres of land to son John; and £20 each to his sons. The property bequests were to take effect when each son reached the age of 21. Elizabeth his (second) wife was to have all these properties during the sons' minorities to bring them up. She was given two acres in West Hyde. His wife and sons were joint residual legatees and she was executrix. She proved the will on 17 March 1613 (TNA, PROB 11/121). According to the dating, the inventory was exhibited in London one day after the will was proved there.

261 Abraham Doggat of Bedford — made 8 March 1613

Bedfordshire Archives, ABP4/184

An Inventarie of the goods of Abraham Doggat deceased taken the viij[th] of Martch 1612 as followeth

	£	s	d
Item In the parler one coobbard		xviij	
Item one coort coobbard		vij	
Item a table		xiij	4
Item ij formes and vj stooles		viij	
Item a truckle bed iiij chears and iiij boxes		xi	
Item a glasse shelfe ij smale andirons		ij	
Item vj cushions ij coverleds one pare of curtains	iij		
Item one bason and ewer a morter and pestell		viij	
Item ij peauter candlesticks and iij lattin candlesticks		iij	vj
Item 4 salts xiij peauter platters ~~vj~~ 8 poringers		xvj	8
one litle basone and x smale peeces of peauter		iij	4
Item one chamber pot and vj other smale peauter pots and ix ~~peauter~~ spoons		iiij	
Item a warming pann and ij coobbard cloathes		iiij	
Item one dozen of flexen napkins a dozen of midle harden napkins and a litell table cloath ij dieper napkins		xiij	
Item a wodden platter and ij glasses			viij
[*sub-total*]	8	12	6
In the butterie			
Item iij boorels one poudering truncke a cherme		ix	
iiij kimnils iij booles and ij earthen pans & a pot		v	vj

[59] £305 5s 4d is the total of his goods less his debts.

	£	s	d
Item ij dripping pans ij brasse potts a skimmer		ix	
ij leather Jackes and one breadegrate		ij	vj
Item ij spittes ij dozen of trenshers v chesefats & a suter		3	vj
In the hale			
Item one coorte cubbard a hamper a cloth basket and ij sadels		x	
Item all his dressed leather	iij		
In the kitchin			
Item one brasse pan iij kettels one brasse pot		xlij	
ij skillets one pare of potthookes & a skimmer		ij	
Item one frieing pan a lattin ladle and gridiron		iij	
Item a wollen whele a pare of tonges a fierershovell iij pot hangers and an Iron barr		vj	
Item one tubb ij pailes and other ode lumber		vj	
In the boulting house			
Item i kimnill a trevet and other stuffe there		v	
In the milke house			
Item one cheesepresse 3 tubs and a yelding fat		vij	
In the chamber over the parlour			
Item ij Bedsteds a table j chest ij coafers & one cradle		xxx	
Item one fetherbed iij boulsters		l	
Item one flocke bed ij blanckets & a coverled		x	
Item j coverled ij blanckets a matris & a flockebed		vij	
Item a matteris 4 boulsters 2 pillowes & ij blanckets		viij	
Item ij pare of flexen sheets		xiij	4
Item ij board cloaths and a dieper towell		v	
Item xij pare of harden sheets		xxxvj	
Item 4 pillowebears v handtowels		v	
Item all his woll		xl	
Item scales and waightes		vj	
[*sub-total*]	19	0	10
In the workehowse			
Item ij fats a tub & a kimnell		xxx	
more there one horse hide ~~shee~~ pelts & lime		x	
Item i hogge		vj	8
Item that is due unto him by Enterdewse		xlviij	
more due as apeareth by bond and bill	vj	x	
more that John Fisher of Bedford oweth him as John Spenser of Kembstone will witnes		xx	
more that Cristofer Burrowe oweth		xxvj	8
John Phillip senior for ij sheepe		xiij	4
Item all his aparell		xx	
totalis	xlij	xviij	
Item for a horse which was passed over to Thomas Hawes the last of dece[*?mber*] as will be prooved by divers witneses		~~liij~~ 53	4
Summa totalis	xlv	xi	viij
[*Corrected total*	*£45*	*11s*	*4d*]

Tho Hawes Jn: [*signature*], William Faldo [*signature*], William Fitzhughe
[*No exhibition clause*]

Notes: the inventory does not give Abraham Doggat's place of residence, however an Abraham Doggat was buried at Bedford St Mary on 20 February 1613. The three witnesses are in the parish registers for St Mary and St Paul, Bedford (*BPR*, vol. 35, p. 61; *BPR*, vol. 58).

262 Agnes Prior of Barton in the Clay, widow made 6 October 1613
Bedfordshire Archives, ABP/W1613/210

A True Inventarye of all the goodes and Chattayles of Annys Prior late of Barton in Le Claye in the Countye of Bedforde wydowe deceassed, pryced by Thomas Brassher, and Thomas Prior of Barton the vj[th] of October 1613

	£	s	d
In primis A Table plancke with Trestles, Twoe Joyned stooles and Three Cushions		iiij	
Item all her brewinge vesselles, and other dayrye stuffe		xxj	viij
Item all the rackes and mawngers about the yardes			xij
Item A Gryndstone, and A Sythe, and other harvest Tooles		xiij	iiij
Item all the fyer woodde in the yardes		ij	vj
Item all her brasse and pewter in the howsse		xxv	
Item all her Lynnen and naperye in the howsse		xx	
Item all the beddes and beddinge in the howsse		xxiij	iiij
Item all her wearinge apparell		xxx	
Item all the kytchen stuffe and Canstyckes		x	
Item a stocke of Bees		iij	iiij
Item Three mylche bease, and a weanelinge	5		
Item Three stores and A Sowehogge		xx	
Item all the grayne in the barnes unthreshed	xx		
Item all the haye in the hayehowsses		xl	
Item all the cheeses, and all the fruyte and wooll in the howsse		x	
Item all the pullyne in the yardes		iiij	
Somme Totalis	xxxvj	viij	ij

[*Exhibited on 2 November 1613*]

Notes: Agnes Prior was buried at Barton on 12 September 1613. She declared her nuncupative will on 9 September 1613, leaving yarn, clothing, furniture, sheep and bullocks to her sons, their wives, her grandchildren and her maid. She appointed her son Thomas her residual legatee and executor. The witnesses were her son Mathew and her maid Joan Norton. The executor's brothers Henry, Michael and John Prior contested the will. The witnesses to the will, Mathew Prior (husbandman of Barton aged about 40) and Joan Norton (of Hawnes aged about 30), swore statements to the church court as to its accuracy and that she was of sound mind. Probate was granted to the executor by John Smith on 2 November 1613 (Beds Archives, ABP/W1613/210).

263 Hugh Harris the elder of Markyate Street, Studham, yeoman made 27 October 1613
Bedfordshire Archives, ABP/W1612–1613/185

A true Inventory of all the goodes of Hugh Harris thelder of Markiate within the parish of Studham in the County of Bedford yeoman diseased taken on Wednesday beinge the 27th day of October 1613 by Richard Fouke gentl[eman], Samuel Hopkins, Thomas Munne and John Bridon as followeth

	£	s	d
Imprimis his apparrell & monny in his purse	iij		
In the hall			
A cupborde, a small table, Cobyrons, & other small implements		xxvj	viij
In the buttery next the hall			
A table boarde, 4 kymnells, 2 payles bowles & other small thinges		xij	
In the kitchin			
A small rounde table & a side table 2 chaires 3 stooles and a fourme with other small implementes there		xx	
In the buttery next the kitchin			
One bras pott, one kyttle and a skymmer, a morter and posnett & xij spoones		xl	
Twenty peices of pewter		xv	
A fewe other small implements		ij	vj
In the chamber over the hall			
A Court Cupborde, ij fetherbeds, a boulsters, iij pillowes and one Coverlyd	iiij		
Six cushins, ij stooles, and other small implements		xij	
In the Chamber over the kitchin			
A bedsted, a fetherbed & strawbed, ij boulsters, ij pillowes ij payre of curtens, ij blankettes, & iij Coverlyds	viij		
A table, iij Chestes, a trunke, & iij Cushins		xxvj	viij
Two peices of wollen cloath x yardes		xl	
Sheetes flaxen & hempen xiiij payre	iiij		
Pillowbeeres x payre, iij table cloathes, one dozen & a halfe of napkyns, with other implements	iij	vj	viij
In the next Chamber			
A bedsted, a wollbed, ij boulsters, a blankett & a Coverlyd		xxvj	viij
Two Chests		v	
Armory for a horsman with other implements		xxxiij	iiij
Fruite and other small thinges		xv	
In the yarde			
A loade of woode		vj	viij
A well buckett with the appurtinances		x	
A ladder, iiij tubbs and other lumber		x	
Fowre pigges		xx	
In the garden			
Five hives of beeze		xx	
In the barne at home			
Hay and peason and chaffe & strawe	iiij		
In the barne at Chevarills greene			
Wheate unthrashed	v		
Pease and hay and chaffe	iij		
Other odd thinges not sett downe by name		xx	
Wheate upon the grounde iij acres & a halfe	iiij		
Summa totalis	lvj	viij	ij

[*Exhibited by the executor on 1 December 1613*]

Notes: Hugh Harris was buried at Studham on 26 October 1613. He made his will on 30 November 1612, requesting burial in the parish church and providing a kilderkin of beer, a dozen loaves and two cheeses for the poor of the parish at his burial and requested his son John to host a 'good drinkeinge' for his neighbours. He gave his daughter Elizabeth use of two upstairs chambers and two ground floor rooms in his house, called the Swanne, for life (or 40s per annum) while she was separated from her husband. He left household possessions (except the armory, sword and dagger) and beehives, growing wheat, and firewood for life to his wife Joan; and bequests to sons, daughters and grandchildren. His son John was the residual legatee and executor. The will was written by Samuel Hopkins, the vicar of Studham, who has a very elegant hand. Probate was granted on 1 December 1613 (Beds Archives, ABP/W1612–1613/185.) His widow Joan was buried on 15 December 1614.

264 Alice Day of Tilbrook, widow undated; between February and June 1614
Lincolnshire Archives, INV/114/135

A true Inventarie indented of all the moveable goodes of Alice Day of Tilbrock deceased, taken and prised by Robert Nicolles, John Mayes and Willam Holland

	£	s	d
Imprimis one yong heyfor		xx	
Item 3 sheepe		viij	
Item a table		v	
Item 3 cofers & a boxe		vj	
Item 6 stooles, a penne & a table		vj	
Item a bedd & bedding belonging to the same		xl	
Item a trundle bedd a mattresse & a quilt		xvj	
Item two sorrie bedsteddes		iiij	
Item a barrell, a tubb & other stuff		xx	
Item in brasse		xx	
Item in pewter		v	
Item a speet & landirons		v	
Item sheetes & other Lynnen		xx	
Item [?]aladder an ark & cheese presse and wood		vj	
Item a benchbord & a glasse boxe		vj	
Item a hovell, hay & a table		xxx	
Item her wearing apparell		xl	
Item one cowe & one heyfor	iij	xj	iiij
Item certaine Barlie unthreshed		xxx	
Summa	xviij	ij	iiij
[*Corrected total*	*£17*	*18s*	*4d*]

[*Exhibited by the executor on 6 June 1614*]

Notes: Alice Day was buried at Tilbrook on 25 January 1614. She made her will on 22 January 1614, giving 5s each to five grandchildren and a great pan to a sixth. She gave the hovel, hay and a table to her eldest son; and the beds and bedding to the other two sons, who were appointed residual legatees and executors. They were granted probate by Christopher Wyvell at Bedford on 6 June 1614 (Lincs Archives, Act Book A/xi/205 and LCC WILLS/1614/i/189).

265 Alice Warde of Marston Moretaine, widow undated; made February to July 1614
Lincolnshire Archives, INV/114/390

This ys a true Inventarye of the goods [*of*] Alice Warde of Marston wedwe lately deceased

	£	s	d
Imprimis one Table and a forme		vj	viij
Item one Cupbord		iiij	
Item Twoe Coverlettes		viij	
Item Three paire of Sheetes		viij	
Item three Boulstes		viij	
Item Foure ~~Cofes~~ Cofers		viij	
Item one Chayre and a Stole		iij	
Item vj peeces of pewter Three Candlestickes and one Saltseller		x	
Item Twoe olde kettles one Potte one chafinge disshe		viij	
Item Twoe bedsteedes		viij	
Item Twoe matryces		v	
Item for smalle trashe and broken stuffe		ij	
Item ij pillowes and pillowberes		iiij	
Summa Totalis	iiij	ij	viij

[*Exhibited by John Warde, executor, at Ampthill on 30 July 1614*]

Notes: Alice Warde was buried at Marston Moretaine on 24 February 1614. She made her will on 12 February 1613, leaving a bed, bedding, a cofer, platters and a candlestick to grandsons and a friend. She cancelled a bond made by her son William to pay 20s a year to her and her son John. She gave the residue to her son John, whom she appointed executor, directing that her son William should help him. Probate was granted to John by Christopher Wivell at Ampthill on 30 July 1614 (Lincs Archives, LCC WILLS/1614/i/40).

266 Humfrey Margate of Wrestlingworth, servant made 17 March 1614
Lincolnshire Archives, LCC ADMONS 1614/206

The goodes of Humfre Margate of Warslingworth in the County of Bedford sarvant desesed the 17th of March Anno domini 1613

	£	s	d
Inprimis one chest		vj	
Item one shert		ij	vj
Item 8 bandes			xvj
Item all his waringe apparill		xiij	iiij
Item in mone		ij	ij
Summa totalis		xxv	iiij

These goodes ware prasede by us whose names are under written Myles Sill [*signature*], William Warde [*signature*], John Thurgood [*signature*]
[*Exhibited by Joan Sharpe alias Margate, his sister, at Bedford on 6 June 1614*]

Notes: Humfrey Margate was buried at Wrestlingworth on 17 March 1614, described as bachelor. Administration was granted to Joane Sharpe alias Margetts before Christopher Wyvell at Bedford on 6 June 1614 and signed by William Stirrop, notary public and a bond was taken (Lincs Archives, Act Book A/xi/205 and LCC ADMONS 1614/206).

267 Humfrey Mee of Shelton, carpenter made 28 March 1614
Lincolnshire Archives, INV/114/136

A true Inventory of all the goods & Chattells of Humfery Mee of Shelton in the County of Bedford Carpenter late diceassed pryzed the 28th day of March 1614 by these vzt Master Raph Malory gent, William Boridge minister, John Ley yeoman, Clement Harrison & others

	£	s	d
In the Hall			
A long table, a short table, a Cupbard, stooles, a bench boord, a forme with other Lumberdes there belonging to the Hall		33	4
In the parlour			
One standing bedsted with a fetherbed a mattris, a boulster, a blankett & a coverlid		33	4
Item a livery Cupboord, a table, 3 chests with certaine cushens & other Lumberdy		26	8
His Apparrell			
Three Cloakes, 3 Jerkins, 2 dubletts 2 payre of breeches with shirts stockings and shoes	6		
In the mayds parlor			
Two Coffers, a boorden bed 3 blanketts a boulster, a mattris with other implements there		20	
In an other inward Roome			
A boorden bed, a mattris, a pillow a Coffer, a pillion & a pillion cloth with certaine fethers & other lumberdy		20	
In the best chamber			
Two trusse beds, 2 fether bedds, 2 Coverlidds two blanketts, 2 boulsters 4 pillowes, & two mattrisses	6		
Item within the same Chamber 2 Coverlidds 4 blanketts, 2 pillowes, curtaines for a bed, a table, 2 chests with other Lumberdy	3	3	4
In the cheese chamber			
Certaine cheese, a cheese rack, stock-cards cheese boords with other trash		40	
In the buttery			
Six barrells, a table, a fatt, a powdering trough with other trash		40	
In the milk house, boules and pannes, a Chirme with other implements		10	
In the kitchin			
A malt-querne, a cheese-presse, 4 tubbs, 4 kymnells with other implements		33	4
Item in the kitchin 3 potts, 2 pans, 2 kettles, 2 driping-pans, 2 spitts, a payre of Aundirons, a brandlett,			

2 payre of pott-hooks, 2 posnetts and a skymmer	4		
Item a 11 [*sic*] flitches of Bacon		55	
Item in pewter, 18 platters, 8 porrengers, 2 pewter candlesticks, 2 latten candlesticks, a latten chaffingdishe, 5 fruit dishes, six sawsers, 18 spoones, 4 salts		33	4
In Linnen			
Eight payre of flaxen sheetes, 16 payre of harden sheetes, 7 long boord clothes, 4 short boord-clothes, one hollon sheete, a damask sheete, a dyaper boord-cloth, 3 doozen and a halfe of table napkins, 9 pillowbeeres, with smaller wearing Linnen	17	10	
Wearing apparrell, 2 gownes 3 petticoates, a cloake and save-gard	4		
In the yard			
Wheate barley & pease to thresh	16		
Item the wood hovells & pales in the yard	35		
In the shop, plowtimber and Cart-timber, with all his tooles belonging to his trade	17		
In the stable			
five horses	25		
Three Carts & Cart geares, 2 plowes with all furniture therunto belonging	11		
All the Beasts in the yard	35		
The Hay		40	
foure hoggs, 2 gryndle stones and all the pullen in the yard		46	8
In the feild			
Ewes & lambes 23 couples with 39 other sheepe, weathers and lambehoggs	18		
The tylth in the feild Wheate, barley & pease	40		
Summa totalis	259	5	

[*Exhibited on 6 June 1614*]

Notes: Humfrey Mee was buried at Shelton on 22 March 1614. The appraiser Ralph Malory was the lord of the manor and the testator's landlord and William Berridge was curate of Shelton. He made his will on 20 March 1614. He gave 5s each to his daughter Margarett's children, living in Lincolnshire; a strike of barley to his daughter Elizabeth; and half his goods to his son John at marriage as long as he obeyed his mother. His unnamed wife was appointed executrix and was granted probate by Christopher Wivell at Bedford on 6 June 1614 (Lincs Archives, LCC WILLS/1614/i/164 and Act Book A/xi/205).

268 John Tompkins of Bidwell, Houghton Regis, husbandman made 27 April 1614
Lincolnshire Archives, INV/114/138

A true Inventorie indented & made the 27 day of Aprill Anno domini 1614 of all the goodes & chattells that were lat John Tompkins of Bidwell in the parish of Houghton Regis decessed:

	£	s	d
Inprimis all his warringe apparell		l	
His money in his purse		iij	
The grain in the field	v		
For wheate & mault in the house		l	
Item for woole		xxxv	
Item the cubbord & the presse		xx	
Item the pewter		xx	
Item the brasse		xl	
Item the table, formes & stols & cussens		xxvj	viij
Item the chests coffers & bedds		xxxiij	iiij
Item the bedding sheets with other linnen	v		
Item the coverlettes & blanketts		xl	
Item the barrells tubs & woodden vessell		xx	
Item the salting trough		v	
Item the bacon in the rough[60]	iiij		
Item the bease & the shepe & the hoggs	viij		
Item the wood & compasse	iij		
Item the haie & the strawe		xx	
Item the chaffe		ij	vj
Item the Poultery		x	
Item the gridiron & pothangings & all other Lumber		x	
Summa totalis	44	5	6

Praised by us William Prior, Thomas Purton, Thomas Wallyes & me Thomas Tompkins vic[*ar*]
[*Exhibited by the executrix at Luton on 7 June 1614*]

Notes: John Tompkins was buried at Houghton Regis on 1 April 1614. He made his will in 1614, describing himself as a husbandman. He gave his house and land to his wife Jane for life, then to Radulph Tompkins, the son of Thomas Tompkins, the vicar. He made small bequests to people called Tompkins, probably family members, although the relationships were not always set out. He appointed his wife as residual legatee and executrix. She was granted probate by Christopher Wyvell at Luton on 7 June 1614 (Lincs Archives, LCC WILLS/1614/i/228). Thomas Tompkins was vicar of Houghton Regis 1607–41, possibly longer (CCEd; Beds Archives, Fasti/1/HoughtonR; *BPR*, vol. 65, p. 174). The relationship, if any, between the vicar and the testator has not been found.

269 John Hall of Caddington, labourer undated; made between April and June 1614
Lincolnshire Archives, INV/114/139

This is the true and Righte Invitorye of the goodes and Chattells of John Hall late deceassed in the parishe of Caddington in the countye of Bedd in the diocesse of Linkehorne

60 possibly *roof*.

	£	s	d
Inprimis his table forme and stooles and one Chaire		iij	iiij
Brasse and pewter			
a spitte and two Irons		v	
One simple Cubbord and other woodden stuffe		iij	iiij
One Coffer		ij	
Bed and Bedding with one simple payre of sheetes		x	
paynted Clothes			x
wood			xij
Some totall		xxv	vj

Oliver Smithe the writer of same
The praysers are These William Sparkes [*mark*], Thomas Moores [*mark*]
[*Exhibited by the executrix at Luton on 7 June 1614*]

Notes: John Hall was buried at Caddington on 14 April 1614. Oliver Smith the writer of the inventory was the parish clerk of Caddington. John Hall made his will on 23 March 1610, describing himself as a labourer. He stated that his house and grounds used to be two tenements and left them to his wife Alice for her life, then to be divided again and given to two sons, on condition of payments to another son and daughter and George Rotheram. He made his wife residual legatee and executrix, and she was granted probate by Christopher Wivell at Luton on 7 June 1614 (Lincs Archives, LCC WILLS/1614/i/230).

270 George Dickerman of Marston Moretaine, cook made 7 May 1614
Lincolnshire Archives, INV/114/133

The Inventarie of the goodes & chattelles debtes and creddites of George Dickerman late of Marston Morton in the countie of Bed Cook deceased made the vij[th] daie of May Anno domini 1614 by those whose names are subscribed vizt

	£	s	d
Imprimis in readie money		xl	
Item all his wearing & Lynen apparell	iij	vj	viij
Item a standing bedd a feather bedd a mattrice, a boulster, 2 pillowe, 2 pillowbers, a coverlet, a blanket & one paire of sheetes	v		
Item a presse		vj	
Item an other bedsteed, 2 featherbedds, 3 boulsteres a pillowe, 2 coverlet, & 2 blankettes	iiij		
Item a feather bedd Tick		vj	
Item a chest, 3 cofers, & 2 litle boxes		x	vj
Item 2 paire of flaxen sheetes, 6 paire of harding, 2 bord cloths, & 4 table napkins		Lij	iiij
Item all his bookes		ij	
Item a cupbord & cupbord cloth, a table, 2 formes, & 3 stooles		xiiij	
Item 10 peeces of pewter, 4 saltes, 3 candle-stickes, a pewter pot, 3 tunnes, a spice morter & a basen		xiiij	vj

	£	s	d
Item a brasse pott, 4 kettles, 2 skillet and a skymmer		xx	
Item a round table, a forme, a dresser bord, & other implementes in the kitchin		v	
Item a malt querne, a pen, a salting trough a charme, an iron pott, a litle foulding table, a chaire & other implementes in the milkhowse		xxiij	
Item one ark ov hould iron		xiij	iiij
Item 3 flitches of bacon		x	
Item a fann, a draugh-rake, & 4 bords		vj	
Item 4 bushelles & a half of mault, 2 bushells of barlie, & 5 peck of pease		xxij	vj
Item 3 half acres of barlie, & 3 half acres of pease	v	vj	viij
Item hay		xiij	iiij
Item 7 plowe beames, 3 axeetres		viij	
Item tymber, fier wood, rackes, payles & other implementes of houshould & husbandry	iiij	x	
Item a cowe, 2 yearling calves, and a weaneng calf	v	vj	viij
Item 9 sheepe	iij	xij	
Item j sowe & 3 hogges		xxx	
Item all the strawe & Compost		vij	
Good debtes			
Item one debte receaved since his death	xiij		
Item owing by [*blank*] Cletherall of Newport	xx		
Item owing by Thomas Chevall of Hardmead	xxij		
Item owing by Stephen Odell of Marson	x		
Item owing by Richard Wellyn of Hardmead	xxxvj		
Summa totalis	Cxlvij	v	vj

Prisers Thomas Sugar, John Francklin
[*Exhibited by the executrix at Bedford on 6 June 1614*]

Notes: George Dickerman was buried at Marston Moretaine on 15 April 1614. He made a nuncupative will, appointing his wife Alice as his executrix and leaving her £40 and his household goods, except the best bed which he gave with another £40 to his daughter Alice. His sons Thomas and George were given £20 each and his sisters £2 each. Any money remaining above £125 was to be divided equally between the two sons. Probate was granted to his widow Alice before Christopher Wivell at Bedford on 6 June 1614 (Lincs Archives, LCC WILLS/1614/i/188 and Act Book A/xi/205). She died in 1624, leaving a nuncupative will which also mentioned the sons and daughter (Beds Archives ABP/W1624–25/107). George Dickerman consulted Dr Napier to have an astrological chart drawn up in 1604 when his age was noted as 43, giving him a date of birth of 1561 and age at death of 53 (Forman and Napier, case no. 21409).

271 Thomas Samuel of Blunham, husbandman made 19 May 1614
Lincolnshire Archives, INV/114/134
Document creased and some values are missing.

May the 19, Anno 1614
A trewe Inventorye of all sutche goodes Chattell and Cattell as was Thomas Samuels of Blonham in the Countie of Bedf Husbandman late diceased beinge seene praysed & prised by William Hanskome, Thomas Feassaunte & Thomas Wrighte Inhabitantes of Blonham 1614

	£	s	d
Inprimis In the Hall a Cobbord 17 peces of peulter ij Candell sticke a sault ij brase potes v kettles a frying pan ij boles iij sawsers a littell Cobbard a table & fourme and other Implementes	iiij		
Item in the Chamber iij borded beades with Furniture and iij Chestes prised at		liiij	
Item in linne iij payre of teare of hempe sheetes on sheet v payre of Hardone iij table napkines iij pillowes iij table Clothes & a speare Clothe	iij	v	
Item paynted Clothes		v	
Item in the Buttrie iiij barrelles iij tubes a stope a saulting trofe v boles & ij paylles pric[*e*]		xx	
Item in the kitchine a payer of Cobirons ij spites & Implementes in the kitchine price at		vj	viij
Item in the backhouse a kinmell a boultinge trofe with other Implementes pric[*e*] at		vj	viij
Item in the lofte wheat Rye & barlye pric[*e*]		xxxiij	
Item in the yard along Cart a Cart bodye & A muck Cart ij plowes with other Implementes	iiij		
Item in the stable iiij horsses with Furniture	xiij	vj	8
Item iiij beasse ij steres a bull aweaned Calfe	xiij	6	8
Item one sowe & piges & v stores		xl	
Item in the hayhouse bordes plankes & other Implementes	iij		
Item in the yarde ij hovels a shude with strawe one them[61]	iij		
Item in tymber & Fyre woode price at	xv		
Item iij halfe akers of wheat & iiij akers of Rye	vij		
Item xjx akers of tylthe & brache barlye	xxiiij		
Item xij acers of pease	xij		
Item one sheepe		v	
Item in Compas		xx	
Item viij hens & a Coke		iij	
Item his Reparrell		xl	
signum Willyam Hanskome, signum Thomas Feassante, signum Thomas Wrighte			
Some totall is	113	16	8
[*Corrected total*	[*£113*	*11s*	*8d*]

[*Exhibited by the executors at Bedford on 6 June 1614*]

Notes: Thomas Samuel was buried at Blunham on 14 May 1614, described as 'senex'. He made his will on 17 April 1614. He gave three acres, lying in half acres in various fields, some of it free land, to his wife Isabell for life and then to son Francis; and also beds, bedding,

61 i.e., two thatched hovells and a shed.

furniture, household goods, growing crops and animals. He gave his youngest sons ploughs, carts, horse harness, animals, wood and timber and appointed them his executors. They were granted probate by Christopher Wivell at Bedford on 6 June 1614 (Lincs Archives, LCC WILLS/1614/i/341 and Act Book A/xi/205 where the value of the inventory was noted as £118 16s 8d).

272 John Abbice of Bedford made 6 June 1614

Lincolnshire Archives, LCC ADMONS 1614/4

A true Inventorie of all suche goodes as were John Abbices deceased prased by Thomas Millerd and Georg Harrison the vj[th] of June 1614

	£	s	d
Imprimis one courte cobbarde vj buffett stooles and tow other stoles		xx	
Item one pare of Andirons a pare of tonges a pare of hookes a fiershovell a bare of Iron		v	
Item v kettles one brasse pote a posnett a pare of pote hookes		xxx	
Item one wicker cradell one wicker chaire			xvj
Item one spite one grediron one pare of bellowes		ij	
Item iiij platters iij basons one ure v candelsticks ij tasters		xv	
Item one truncke		iiij	
Item one bolting arcke one barrell ij tobbes		v	
Item v coffers and one boxe		xiij	4
Item one Worminge pann		ij	vj
Item v porrengers and iij sawsers		iij	
Item iiij pare of sheetes iij board cloathes iiij pillowbeares viij napkins		xx	
Item ij coverlettes ij blanckettes one matteris one bolster ij pilloberes v curtaynes		xxx	
Item wood		xx	
Item his reparrell	iij		
Item all other ode Implementes of houshould stuffe		x	
some totall is	xij	j	ij

The marke of Thomas Millerd, The marke of Georg Harison

[*Exhibited by the administratrix at Bedford on 6 June 1614. A note at the foot of the inventory reads: Fiat ad Marie rel[ic]ta et Will Abbice de Bedford yeo. The exhibition clause was signed by William Abbis.*]

Notes: John Abbice was buried at Bedford St Paul's on 13 May 1614. Administration was granted to his widow Mary by Christopher Wyvell at Bedford on 6 June 1614 and a bond was taken (Lincs Archives, Act Book A/xi/205 and LCC ADMONS 1614/4).

273 John Ventam of Eaton Bray, husbandman made 6 June 1614
Lincolnshire Archives, LCC ADMONS 1614/23

A true Inventorie of all the goodes cattels and chattels of John Ventam late of Eyton in the countie of Bedforde husbandman deceased, taken and prised the sixt day of June, Anno Domini 1614 Annoq[ue] regni Domini nostri Jacobi Dei gra[tie] Angliae Francie et Hiberniae Regis, fidei defensoris etc duodecimo, et Scotiae quadragesimo septimo, by John Jenkins yeoman, James Cooke husbandman and William Cooke weaver

	£	s	d
Imprimis all his wearinge apparell prised at		xl	
Item his money in his purse		vij	j
Item a cubbert a table with a frame, a forme, three ioyned stooles & a benche borde		xxj	
Item three bedsteddes and three cofers		xxij	
Item two coverlettes two blankettes a matterice one boulster & three pillowes		xxxiij	iiij
Item fyve paire of sheetes three pillowebeeres one table cloth, three table napkins, & a peice of linnin cloth		xxxviij	vj
Item wooll, a remnant of wollen cloth and foure cusshions		xv	iiij
Item paynted clothes		ij	vj
Item pewter		viij	vj
Item a lattin morter a lattin bason two lattin candelstickes & a chafin dish		vij	iiij
Item a brasse pot, a brasse pan, three kettelles & two skillettes		xxxiij	iiij
Item a fryenge pan, an iron spit, a paire of cobborns one iron hanger, a paire of pothookes a gridiorne, a paire of tonges, an iron peele, two iron wedges an axxe a hatchet a byll and certaine olde iron		x	
Item a cherme, two barrelles one tubbe a kymnell a stappe an other treene ware		xvj	
Item a saltinge trough, a woollen wheele a linnin wheele a drinke stall and shelves		xiiij	
Item barley and Rye within dores		xvj	vj
Item cheese and cheese rackes		v	
Item a flitch of bacon		viij	ij
Item a cheese presse		ij	
Item a longe cart a dounge cart an olde paire of wheeles a paire of harrowes a draught rake a mattooke a sholve a pease hooke a sythe three pitchforkes roapes and ladders		xxxv	
Item a racke and a maunger a paire of harnis & a cassaddell		ij	vj
Item a fanne a seedcood two leather bottelles, sackes, erthen vesselles and other implementes within doare		viij	
Item Tymber		xvj	iiij
Item fyre wood and boardes		xxvj	viij
Item haye		iiij	
Item three roodes of pease and fetches		xx	

Item three mylch beastes one bullocke two stoare pigges and one sheepe	viij	iij	iiij
Item poulterie		ij	vj
Item a wheele barrowe, a dounge forke & soyle in the yearde		vij	
Summa totalis	xxix	v	xj

The marke of John Jekins, James Cooke [*signature*], William Cooke [*signature*]
[*Exhibited by Agnes Ventam, executrix, on 7 June 1614. The exhibition clause was signed by George Pormorth, notary public.*]

Notes: John Ventam was buried at Eaton Bray on 5 June 1614 as John Bentam. He was a churchwarden in 1610/11 (*BPR*, vol. 73, p. 148). By his undated will, he gave his freehold land in Eaton Bray and Edlesborough (Bucks) and his horse and carts to Edward Scrivener and his wife Ursula (the testator's sister); small sums of money to nephews and nieces; and the remainder to his wife Agnes, who was appointed executrix. He appointed James Cook and Edward Scrivener as his overseers. Witnesses were William Mackreth, William Cook and James Cook. Probate was granted to his widow Agnes Fentam by Christopher Wyvell at Luton on 7 June 1614 and signed by George Pormorth, notary public (Lincs Archives, Act Book A/xi/206). The will was disputed by Edward and Ursula Scrivener and came before John Smyth, registrar, at the church court at Ampthill on 19 July 1614. The hearings and depositions made by the witnesses to the making of the will revealed that this may have been a dispute between the deceased's birth family and his second wife and stepson. A grant of probate was made to Ursula Scrivener on 21 April 1615, Agnes Ventam having renounced administration (Will and church court case at Beds Archives, ABP/W/1615/185).

274 William Davye of Dunstable, maltster made 9 July 1614

Lincolnshire Archives, INV/114/386

The top of the document is slightly creased. Missing letters have been supplied in square brackets.

An Inventory of all the goodes of William [*D*]avye late of Dunstable in the Countie of Bedd malster deceased taken the ix[th] day of Julie i614 and prysed by John Meadgate gen' and Robert Haddon baker of Dunstable aforsaid vz

	£	s	d
Inprimis his wearinge apparell		v	
Item five bushell of beanes & pease		x	
Item 3 quarters and ij bushelle of oates		xlviij	
Item 3 kettles and one brasse pott one pan Item 2 platters and one brasse candlestick and one quarte pot		vj	viij
Item 2 owld Chestes j owld chaire j ould counter		ij	vj
Item money in his purse		xiiij	iiij ob
Item one bushell ~~on~~ one pecke ~~& one half~~ one rack and a maunger certeine wood		ij	vj
Item the haie and Chaffe		vj	viij
Item one paire of AndeIrons & j hooke		ij	
Suma tot	iiij	xvij	viij ob

John Medgere [*signature*], Robert Haddon [*signature*]
[*Exhibited by the executor at Dunstable on 27 July 1614*]

Notes: William Davye was buried at Dunstable on 9 July 1614.

275 Edward Browne of Stotfold undated; made between 18 and 26 July 1614
Lincolnshire Archives, INV/114/385

A true Inventorie of the goodes & chattells of Edward Browne of Statfold in the countye of Bedford late deceased

	£	s	d
Inprimis in the hall one table one forme A benchbord a Joyne stoole & one litle round table		vj	viij
Item one Cubbord a case one other old cubbord		xiij	iiij
Item an old saltinge troffe A hanginge shelfe & A pot shelfe		iij	iiij
Item paynted clothes in the Hall			xij
Item x ketles three posnittes an old brasse pott	j	xiij	iiij
Item the Pewter		xx	
Item dishes spoones & wooden platters six bowles		iij	iiij
Item seaven lattyn candlestickes & A pewter candlestickes & two saltes		iiij	
Item in the litle lofte old troch & three barrells		v	
Item in the Chamber one bedstead A coveringe A bolster & three pillowes		vj	viij
Item in the same chamber two coffers		v	
Item in the chamber one cubbord A potshelfe foure coffers two chaires & A round table		xxj	8
Item one Bedstead two blanketts & A bolster		x	
Item three payre of sheettes A curtaine j pillowbeere		xiij	iiij
Item tenn payre of sheetes eight pillowbeares three short table clothes	ij	x	
Item one Bedstead three Mattes two bolsters foure pillowes two Coveringes two blanketts & A payre of sheetes	j	xiij	iiij
Item three Coffers & A fosser		x	
Item three wheeles & other old troch in the lofte		iij	iiij
Item the loumes in the shoppe with the furniture to them belonginge	iiij		
Item two beastes & A wendling Calfe	v		
Item fyve lambes & seaven sheepe	iij	xij	
Item A sowe & two pigges		xiij	iiij
Item wood in the yard with two ladders	ij		
Item one Acre of Corne	j	xiij	iiij
Item hay in the barne		vj	viij
Item dounge in the yard		vij	
Item hennes in the yard		iij	iiij
Item his wearinge Apparell	j	x	
Some total	xxxj	ix	

[*Exhibited by the executor on 26 July 1614*]

Notes: Edward Browne was buried at Stotfold on 18 July 1614, described as 'an old man'. He made his will on 2 July 1614. He gave his wife Marian all the goods she brought to the marriage and barley, fruit, wood and the chamber or leanto next to the hall to live in or sell. He made small bequests to friends, family and godchildren. His son Edward was residual legatee and executor and was granted probate by Christopher Wivell at Hitchin on 26 July 1614 (Lincs Archives, LCC WILLS/1614/i/148).

276 Katherine Clarke of Stotfold, widow made 22 July 1614
Lincolnshire Archives, INV/114/384

A true Inventory of all the moveable goodes & Chattelles that were in the possession of Katherine Clarke late of Stotfold deceased wyddowe as they were praised by William Ford & Robert Cooper this p[rese]nt xxij[th] of July in Anno domini 1614

	£	s	d
Imprimis in the hall a table & frame & fourme & bench board		iij	iiij
Item a Cupboard		vj	viij
Item an old Chasse a powldring tubb & hutch & two or three litle stooles & two old Churmes		vj	viij
Item old painted Cloths			xij
Item a stone & half of hempe		iiij	
Item a linen wheele & a litle barrell & half peck		ij	
Item in the Chamebr an old bedsted with a featherbed, two bolsters one pillowe two blankettes & a Coverlett		xij	
Item two Coffers & a forcer		vj	
Item the paintid Cloths		iij	iiij
Item fower yardes of new wollen cloth		xij	
Item a new bolster & pillowe		vj	viij
Item sixe paire of sheetes & one sheete a speare cloth a table cloth, three pillow beares, two napkins a kercher		xl	
Item eight pewter platters a candlestick a salt, a porrenger three spoones & an old pott		x	
Item three old platters, two sawcers a porrenger, & salt		ij	vj
Item one brasse pott, fower kettles, a panne a ladle, a Chaffinge dish & a Candlestick & two posnetes		xxxiij	iiij
Item in the yard woode & hempe		iiij	
Item a spitt a fying pan a gridiron 2 paire pott hookes & Cobirons		v	
Item in monie	v		
Item her Apparrell		xx	
Item an henne			viij
William Forde his marke			
Robert Godfrey alias Cooper his marke			
Sum	xiij	xix	ij

[*Exhibited by the executor at Ampthill on 26 July 1614*]

Notes: Katherine Clarke was buried at Stotfold on 18 July 1614. She made her will on 8 July 1614, making her mark as Katherine Clarke alias Retchford. She gave money to her son William Retchford and her eldest son Richard Retchford 'if he be living and come again.' William was given household goods and four yards of new russett cloth (listed in the inventory). Anne Morris was given household goods and 1½ stone of hemp (listed in the inventory) to buy a lamb. Her son-in-law Robert Morris was residual legatee and executor. He was granted probate by Christopher Wivell at Ampthill on 26 July 1614 (Lincs Archives, LCC WILLS/1614/i/450). The inventory is in the same handwriting as that of Thomas Petchett of Stotfold 1618 (*304*).

277 William Allyn the elder of Sandy, yeoman made 31 July 1614
Bedfordshire Archives, ABP 1614/172

An Inventorye of the goods Chatells of William of [*sic*] Allyn of Sandey disceased the [*word deleted and illegible*] last day of July

	£	s	d
[*line inserted*] a gune a head peese a sword		vj	
Imprimis in the parlor ij Tables ij Formes iij Chaires vij Coshines		xxvj	viij
Item a Bdsted [*sic*] ij Fetherbeds ij Coverings on blanket iiij pilowes v Curtaines	iij	vj	viij
Item on Cobbord xij platters iiij Saltes on Cupp on Candelstick vj Sausers viij Poringers a dosen of peuter spoones with other Implements		xxxxvj	viij
The Haule			
Imprimis a Table iiij Stooles on Cobbord on Bason x peeces of peuter on Iron barr ij pot hangers ij Annderirons a paire of Tonges a paire of Bellostes ij salts ij Candelsticks & the painted Clothes with a bible & other litle Bookes		xxxxx	
The kitchin			
Imprimis vij pans ~~iiij~~ iij Cettells ix Brasse potts iiij Spitts iij Tredds a Casse ij Troffes & other Implements	vj	xiij	iiij
The Seller & Buttery			
Imprimis the Bruing fatt with Barrells a Coppord & other Implements		xxxxxiij	iiij
The Loft over the parlour			
Imprimis ij Beddsteds ij fetherbeds a flockebed a Matteres ij Coverings ij Blankets & a coffer		xxxxxiij	iiij
The Loft over the seller & Buttery			
Imprimis a Bedd iiij Coffers a forme & other Implements		xx	
The loft over the Hale			
Imprimis the Implements in it		viij	
Item xvj paire of sheets iiji [*sic*] Table clothes viij Pilowbeers a drinking cloth xiiij Table napkins	x		
The Loft over Kitchin			
Imprimis ij Bedds & the Bedding two Coffers and the wenskott		xxxxxiij	iiij
Item his apparrell		xxxxvj	viij
Item vij horses & geldings	xxj		
Item iij Beaste	v		
Item ploughes & poughgeers Carts & Cartgeers with other furniture therto belonging	x		
Item a hovell & Rooles dragrakes with the wood in the yard		xxxx	
Item ploughbeames		vj	
The Cropp of Graine			
Imprimis the ~~whe~~ wheate vj acres & half	ix		
Item Rye xxiij acres & half	xxx		
Item Barley xxxxix acres	lx		
Item Pease xx acres with otes	xx		

	£	s	d
Item the Tymber of a Barne & other Timber	x		
~~Sume is two hundred & six pounds~~			
~~Sume is nyne score and xvj^{li}~~			
praised by Robert Britten [*signature*], Edward Sutton *signature*] & William Wynn [*signature*]			
Item the Implements in bothe Garners & the Loft above them		xxx	
Item the xx Lodes of haye	vj	xiij	iiij
Item the hemp		vj	viij
Item a Sow & piggs		xxx	
Item the Tylthe Land		x	
The whole Summe is two hundred and sixteentie pounds	[*216*	*0*	*0*]

[*Exhibited by the executrix on 8 August 1614*]

Notes: William Allyn was buried at Sandy on 30 July 1614. He made his will on 30 April 1614, describing himself as a yeoman. He gave small sums of money to his married son and daughter and grandchildren; £20 and the bed 'at the stare head in the chamber over the parlor' and bedding to his unmarried daughter Elizabeth; £20 and the new bedstead in the chamber over the kitchen, with its bedding to his unmarried daughter Ann; property in Sandy, Northill, Girtford and Stratford to his second to sixth sons; and £40 to his youngest son. His wife Margaret was given all his land for one crop before the bequests to the sons came into effect. She was his residual legatee, guardian to the children and executrix and was granted probate on 8 August 1614. The witnesses, Jasper Emery and Peter Knott, made statements confirming the contents of the will (Beds Archives, ABP 1614/172).

278 Robert Purney of Bedford St Peter undated; between January and June 1615

Bedfordshire Archives, ABP4/185

An Inventary of all such Goodes as was in the Custody of Robert Purney late desesed

	£	s	d
Imprimis in the Hale on Cuberd		xiii	
also Tenn pewtir platers 2 sawsers on porenger a saultseler 3 brasen Canstikes		ix	
2 formes 3 stooles and on chaire		v	
on brase pot 4 brase keateles		xvj	
on fring pane on spitt on gridiron a pare of Cab Irnes		ij	vj
the pented Clothes		jj	
fower Eles of new linen Cloth		jjj	
in the lodging chamber 7 pare of sheetes ~~and~~ 3 pilobears & a tabl Cloth on napkin		x	[...]
on fether bed 2 boulsters 4 pilowes 2 Covelates and on blanket		xxv	
on [*?*]bedstidell 4 Coffers		xx	
his wearing apparell		x	
in the woatmill house on bushell & a half of woatmill worth		v	
4 Coffers on bushell a ~~C~~ kimnell and a halfe pek a tunell 2 meswers		x	

	£	s	d
on a [*sic*] dosen of hurdeles		ij	
a Marter			vj
on pare of blades & a barell		j	
on bar of Irn & a chain		jj	
on bushell of whete 3 pekes of barly		v	
on linen wheele a fate a mealle sive		4	
2 laders		j	
2 tubes on barell		jj	
barley straw		jjj	
2 loades of wood & fagotes		xvj	
on ~~fleit~~ Flitch of Bakon		jjjj	
mony in the house		xxxix	vj
mony owing him	xxix		
Som is	41		6
[*Corrected total*	*£39*	*10s*	*6d*]

William Lavinder [*signature*], Thomas Jones [*mark*]
[*Exhibited on 20 June 1615*]

Notes: The heading on the inventory does not identify the place of residence or the date when the inventory was made. It is attributed to Bedford St Peter because Robert Purney was buried there on 15 January 1615 and families with the surnames of the appraisers were living there.

279 John Manton of Willington made 9 February 1615
Bedfordshire Archives, ABP/W1614–1615/208

A true Inventory of all the goods Cattell & chattells of John Manton of Willington deceased, as it was taken the ix[th] of February 1614

	£	s	d
Imprimis the beasse		xl	
Item the pewter		x	
Item a morter & candlestickes		iiij	
Item a Cupbord, a penne, table & forme, painted clothes & other implementes		xx	
Item a cupbord & a bed, & certen boords		viij	iiij
Item in the bowlting house, an arke, tubbes etc		x	
Item iij Tubbes, ij payles, & a cherme		viij	
Item a standing bed & other things belonging to it		xl	
Item sheets vj payre & a sheete		xxvj	viij
Item Five coffers		xx	
Item hempe teare & toe & other things		v	
Item the Corne & heye		xxxiij	iiij
Item the hovill		xiij	iiij
Item iij Cowes	vij		
Item the wood		vj	viij
Item the Tilth & brach		x	
Item a store pigge		vj	viij
Item the butter & cheese		vj	viij
Item bacon		x	
Item his wearing apparell		x	

Item debts of mony due to him	xij		
Item a sheepe		v	
Item certen other implemts		v	
[*in the margin*] 33li 13s 8d			
The totall Summe is	xxxiij	xviij	viij

Prized by us Tho: Adams [*signature*], Signum Humph Cartwright, Thomas Shortboulte [*signature*], Thomas Clayton [*signature*], Signum Thomas Osmond
[*Exhibited by the executrix on 27 March 1615*]

Notes: John Manton was buried at Willington on 7 February 1615. He made his will on 22 January 1615, making bequests to sons and daughters, most of which were to be paid after his wife's death or in her lifetime if she could spare them. Wife Ellen was residual legatee and executrix and she proved the will on 27 March 1615. The will was written by Thomas Adams the vicar of Willington, who signed both the will and inventory. He was issued with a commission by John Smith, procurator general of the Consistory Court of Bedford, on 3 March 1615 to administer the oath to Ellen Manton to swear that John Manton's will was his last will and that she would administer his goods according to its provisions (Beds Archives, ABP/W1614–1615/208).

280 Thomas Mason of Souldrop, rector

made 20 February 1615
Bedfordshire Archives, ABP/W1614–1615/234

An Inventary of the goods of Thomas Mason Parson of Souldropp deceased made the twentieth day of February 1614 and praysed as followeth

	£	s	d
The Hall chamber			
Inprimis one seeled bedsteed with Curtaynes and rodds		xxx	
Item another standing bedd a trundle bedd and two chests		xv	iiij
Item all the linnen	v	xiij	iiij
Item one coverlidd three blan ketts a flockbedd, and the painted cloathes a round table and a chayre		xxxiiij	
Item three boulsters & a pillowe		x	
The servants Chamber			
Item pease & other things		xx	
The new Chamber			
Item the kimnell bords and other trashe		xvj	
Item fower pownds of flaxe		iiij	
Item pewter		xxj	vj
The mill howse			
Item yron		iiij	vj
Item a mault mill with other things		x	
The buttrye			
Item barrells and other things therin		xvij	

The Parlor			
Item a cupboard & a chest		xxvj	viij
Item two coffers and a box		vj	viij
Item one feather bedd one boulster three pillowes one coverlidd a blankett and a borded bedd		xl	
Item boules and dishes spoones & trenchers			xvj
The hall			
Item two tables five chayres eight ioyned stooles two formes a glasse case		xxxij	vj
Item fower Cushions		iij	
Item a paire of Andyrons pott hangings an yron barr fyer shovell and tongs		vij	
Item six flitches of bacon a still	iij	xvj	
The kitchen			
The brasse and for all other things & for plowetimber	v	iij	iiij
Item five bease and one bullock a yeare old	xiij	vj	viij
Item two hoggs three horses plowe geares cart geares	xiiij	xvj	viij
Item two long carts with shodd wheeles and other furniture to them belonging, three harrowes and for wood & other things	vij	xv	iiij
The great Barne			
Item the barly wheat & pease the hay the screene and Gige with other things as sacks and bushell and what else in the barne	xx		
Item the pease the hay in the yard the frames of the hovells and other things belonging to them with the Compasse	xvj		
Item the sheepe the hennes		xxxvj	
Item three silver spoones a ring a guilte boule and his apparrell	vj	xvj	
Item a payre of fetters an yron tye a saddle and bridle		viij	viij
Item three Roodes of wheat growing in the feildes		xxiij	iiij
Item a cutting knife		ij	viij
Item the bookes with other things in the studdye		xl	
Debts owing to Master Mason			
Item oweing ~~by Tobias Mason~~ in specialty	xj		
Item owing by Tobias Mason		xv	viij
Item owing by Henry Angell		xij	vj

Item things lent to my sister[62]			xij
Summa	Cxxiiij	xj	
[*Corrected total*	*£126*	*6s*	*8d*]

Debts owing by Master Mason

Item owing to Thomas Mason		xxv	
Item owing to Will: Hanger Jun		lv	
Item spent at London & owing there	iij	vj	viij
Item owing more		iij	iiij
[*Debts*	*£7*	*10s*	*0d*]

This Inventary made by these men Henry Jeyes, William Hanger Junior, John Bitherey
[*Exhibited by Thomas Mason junior, administrator, on 8 April 1615*]

Notes: Thomas Mason, 'a minister from John Pembertons in Chancery Lane' was buried at St Dunstan in the West, London on 18 February 1615. Thomas Mason was vicar of Keysoe 1573–85, rector of Souldrop 29 October 1590 to his death and licensed preacher there from 3 November 1606 (CCEd). The 1607 glebe terrier described his house as a two storey timber and stone building of four bays and covered with straw. The upper storey covered three bays. It had seven rooms, including a hall and a kitchen; the other rooms were not named. There was a timber and stone barn of six large bays (Beds Archives, ABE 1).

281 Thomas Burton of Felmersham made May–June 1615

Bedfordshire Archives, ABP/W1615/199

The heading of the inventory appears beneath the total but has been reproduced here in the usual place at the beginning. Some of the values are unclear, having been written over.

A tru Imnitary made of all the goodes of Thomas Burten in the yeare of our Lord god 1615 by Roberd Tappe, John Coossin & William Hemington

	£	s	d
Imprimis first his aparrill		40	
Item sixe beace	13	6	8
Item for his hoges		40	
Item for his greene in the feelde	[*?*]30		
Item for hesi [*sic*] greene at his house	5		
Item for his haye		20	
Item for too Cartes & a hovell	4		
Item for his woode		[*?*]20	
Item for his linninie	10		
Item for his bedes & beddinge with all other thinges in that Roome	10		
Item for all thinges that is in the halle		40	
Item for brace & peyter		50	
Item for tubes & barrilles with all oter thinges	3		
Somma totalis	87	16	8
[*Corrected total*	*£85*	*16s*	*8d*]

[*Exhibited by the executrix on 3 June 1615*]

62 i.e., lent to the sister of Thomas Mason, the administrator.

Notes: Thomas Burton was buried at Felmersham on 19 May 1615. He made his will on 17 May 1615, leaving 40s and his house and land in Felmersham to his son William at age 21. His unnamed wife was the residual legatee and executrix, and was granted probate on 3 June 1615 (Beds Archives, ABP/W1615/199).

282 Edward Fletchar of Houghton Regis made 26 March 1616
Bedfordshire Archives, ABP/W1616/134

An Inventory of the said Will of Edward Fletchar decessed indented & made the 26 of March

	£	s	d
First his apparell		x	
Item the beddinge		xiij	iiij
Item the Cubbord		ij	
Item the pewter a candlestick a spice morter		x	
Item the brasse		xiij	iiij
Item the sheetes		xx	
Item two coffers & two boxes		iiij	
Item two barrels & a tubb		ij	
Item the wood		x	
Item the shevells dishes trenchers & other implementes		iiij	
Summa totalis	iiij	8	8

Praised by us Henrie Tutthill, Simon Freman, Edward Winter, Christopher White & Tho: Tompkins
[*Exhibited on 10 April 1616*]

Notes: Edward Fletchar was buried at Houghton Regis on 25 March 1616. His will, made on 25 March 1616 and possibly nuncupative, and his inventory were written on the same sheet of paper with the probate clause on the verso. He made bequests to son Thomas, daughter Margarett White, and Margaret Dewbury. The residual legatee and executrix was his wife Alice, who obtained probate on 10 April 1616 (Beds Archives, ABP/W1616/134).

283 Edward Kelke of Cople, tailor made 21 April 1616
Bedfordshire Archives, ABP/W/1616–1617/118

A True Inventory of all the goodes of Edward Kelke of Cople in the County of Bedford, Taylor: lately deceased: made the xxj day of Aprill in the yeare of our Lord 1616, by George Underwood, and Peter Morgan, & others, as followeth

	£	s	d
Inprimis In the Chamber one Bed-steed, & one Foarme		ij	
Item one old Cupboarde there		iij	iiij
Item five Coaffers there also		xiiij	
Item one old Bason, & three Candlestickes			xiiij
Item Two old Coveringes belonginge to the bedde		iij	iiij
Item Five sheetes one pillowe & one Boulstar		xiiij	
Item In the howse one old Casse a little Trough one ladder, and a fewe boardes		vj	viij

	£	s	d
Item one Brasse pott two kettles, one platter, & two sausers		vj	
Item one payre of Pothookes, & one payre of Bellowes		ij	
Item one stapp, a Bowle, two or three dishes, & one pott to drinke in			xviij
Item all the wood in and aboute the house, or yarde		vj	viij
Item the Hempe			~~xx~~ xij
Item the house it sellffe		xxx	
Item his wayringe Apparell		vj	viij
The somme is	iiij	xviij	iiij

[*Exhibited on 25 May 1616*]

Notes: Edward Kelke was buried at Cople on 10 April 1616, described as 'pauper et paterfamilias' (*BPR*, vol. 10, p. B36). He made a nuncupative will beginning 'I will not (sayd he) give any thinge from my wiffe' except a brass pot to his married daughter. The will was proved on 25 May 1616 and administration granted to the principal legatee, as the will did not appoint an executor (Beds Archives, ABP/W/1616–1617/118).

284 Nicholas Galligan of Cople made 29 June 1616

Bedfordshire Archives, ABP/W1616–1617/104

A true Inventorie of such goodes as were Nicholas Galligans lately deceased of Cople in the County of Bedfford: made by Roberte Warner & Richard Purser the xxix[th] of June 1616 as followethe

	£	s	d
Imprimis Two payre of Hardon sheetes, & one odde sheete		viij	iiij
Item Two Coueringes, & one Blanquette		iiij	vj
Item One Boulster, & one Pillowe		ij	
Item One Bedstead			xij
Item One old Coaffer			xij
Item Three poundes of Toah			viij
Item Two Boardes			vij
Item One kimnell, & an old Boultinge vessell			xij
Item Fower old paynted cloathes		ij	
Item two foarmes, one stoole, a shorte plancke, & a Cupborde		x	vj
Item A table, a foarme, & two stooles			xxij
Item A Penne, and an old Troughe		ij	vj
Item A Brasse potte, & two small kettles		viij	
Item Five peeces of Pewter		ij	vj
Item 7 dishes, & 2 cup-dishes			xij
Item Pot-hookes, pot-hangers, & a Grate-yron			xij
Item A Bill, a Hatchet, a Houe, & a Candle-sticke			xx
Item A stoppe, a payle, & other small thinges		ij	vj
Item Two old Sithes, & a fewe old boardes in the Leantoe		ij	iiij
Item Two Hives of Bees, & fower Ladders		xij	
Item A Hovell, and a Laintoe		xiiij	
Item All the wood with the inwarde hedges		x	
Item All the Hempe		iij	iiij
Item A stower Pigge		vj	viij
Item A small Bottle			ij

	£	s	d
Item His apparell		viij	
The somme of these particulers is	v	vij	vij
[*Corrected total*	*£5*	*10s*	*1d*]

[*Exhibited by Joan Galligan, administratrix, on 6 July 1616*]

Notes: Nicholas Galligan was buried at Cople on 26 June 1616, described as 'senior, pauper et paterfamilias' (*BPR*, vol. 10, p. B37). He made his nuncupative will on 25 June 1616 and gave a platter to each of his children and the residue to his wife. Administration with will annexed was granted to Jane Galligan, his relict on 6 July 1616 (Beds Archives, ABP/W1616–1617/104).

285 Oliver Bunker of Tingrith, husbandman or yeoman made 26 August 1616

Bedfordshire Archives, ABP/W1616/78

An Inventorie made by George Andrew, Richard Spicer, John Lawrence and John Holstocke prisers of all ~~such~~ goodes and chattells of Oliver Bunker husband[*man*] deceased made the xxvith of August 1616

	£	s	d
In the hall			
A table forme ~~two tressells~~ and other Implementes		xiij	iiij
In the kitchin			
Brasse and pewter		l	
two spittes a fyer shovell tonges pott hangers two pailes two tubbs three barells a cheese presse and other Implementes		xx	
In the milke howse			
A saltinge trowgh a cherme a busshell seaven milke boles six shelves twelve bordes and other Implementes		xxiij	iiij
In the boltinge howse			
A boltinge hutche and a kneadinge trowgh		ij	
In the chamber next the hall			
A boarded bedsteed a flockbedd and a matteris a coverlet ~~a matteris~~ two bolsters and a pillowe a blankett ~~and a coverlet~~		xxxiiij	
three old cofers and a box		vij	
Eight paire of sheetes and an odd sheete and all other linnen	iiij		
In the Inner chamber			
two boarded bedsteedes a woolbed a matteris two coverlettes three blankettes		xxvj	viij
a bolster and two pillowes		v	
an old cubberd and paynted clothes		iij	iiij
his waringe clothes		xxx	

	£	s	d
In the loft over the chamber			
An old Arke certen wooll old yron and other Implementes		xx	
In the chamber over the hall			
Certen cheeses half a quarter of malt two shelves and other Implementes		xlvj	viij
Fyve beaste and a bullock	xv		
Fower horses	ix		
Eight sheepe and three lambes	iij	vj	viij
Fower stores on hogge a sow and three pigges		l	
In the stable			
Cart harnes and plowghe harnys and other thinges		xx	
In the cow howse			
two Roles certen plowgh timber and cart timber and other Implementes		xx	
In the yard			
One ould hovell, 2 donge Carts one longe Cart, 2 paire of shodd wheeles, 3 Cowe Rackes, 2 paire of harrowes, 2 plowes, 2 timber loggs, one dosen of hurdles	iiij	vj	v[*iij*]
A, ~~the doongg in the yard and~~ xj Akers of tilth	vij		
Graine in the Barnes	liiij		
the hay	iij	vj	viij
Summa totalis	Cxviij	xj	iiij
[*In a different hand*] Item more certaine bordes turffe & other implementes		xxiij	iiij
[*Total*	*£119*	*14s*	*8d*]

Richard Spicer [*signature*], George Andrews [*signature*], the marke of John Lawrence, the marke of John Holstocke

[*Exhibited by J. Whitaker, notary public for Joan Bunker, the relict and executrix, on 9 October 1616. Commission to Humfrey Hill, rector of Tingrith, to administer the oath to Joan Bunker, which he did on 4 October 1616.*]

Notes: Oliver Bunker was buried at Tingrith on 25 August 1616. He made his will on 15 November 1611, describing himself as a yeoman and requesting burial in Tingrith church. He made pecuniary bequests amounting to £80 to his five sons and his grandchildren. They were to be paid after his and his wife's deaths by her executor from the bond to Oliver Bunker made by William Buncker of Hertingfordbury and George Bunker of Bengeo on 1 December 1593. The residual legatee and executrix was his wife Joan, to whom probate was granted on 9 October 1616 (Beds Archives, ABP/W1616/78). Joan died in 1625 and left a will (Beds Archives, ABP/1624–25/203).

286 John Rule of Tempsford, smith made 2 October 1616
Bedfordshire Archives, ABP/W1616–1617/248

An Inventory of the goods & Chattells of John Rule late of Tempsford in the County of Bedford Smith deceassed Indifferently prised by Henry Rayner, Robert Abbott, Thomas Staploe & Henry Finch This Second day of October Anno Domini 1616 as Followeth

	£	s	d
Inprimis All his Shopp Tooles		xxxiij	iiij
Item Certen Scores oweing to hime at the day of his death		xiij	iiij
Item his Apparrell		x	vj
Item a Coffer A Booke A potshelf An Aquavite bottle with other Implementes		xj	
Item a Cock & Henn			xij
Summa totalis	iij	ix	ij

[*Exhibited by the administratrix on 17 June 1617*]

Notes: John Rule was buried at Tempsford on 8 August 1616. He made a nuncupative will on 7 August 1616 giving all his goods to his mother 'to helpe to maintayne hir for she had bine a most loving & kinde mother unto hime' but not appointing an executor. Both Elizabeth Rule and Thomas Rule (whose relationship is unstated) sought administration of the will. The case was heard before John Smith at the church court at Ampthill on 17 December 1616. Jane Purret and Frances Rule (the deceased's sister), who witnessed the will, gave evidence to its contents. The court granted probate to Elizabeth Rule as the principal legatee on 17 June 1617 (Beds Archives, ABP/W1616–1617/248). Elizabeth Rule, widow, was buried in Tempsford on 25 November 1630.

287 William Kippest of Northill, gentleman made 5 December 1616
Bedfordshire Archives, ABP/W/1616–1617/54

A true Inventorye of the goods and chattell of William Kippest of Norrill in the countye of Bedff: gent late deceased made by Robart Kippest, Thomas Yarwaye and Edward Truxton the fyft daye of Decembr Anno Domini 1616

	£	s	d
Imprimis his apparrill and his gould ringe	xx		
Item on trunck and linnen within it	xiiij		
Item fetherbeds, coverlets blankets pillowes and other beddinge	xvj		
Item thre carpets	ij		
Item truncks chests and boxes	v		
Item wrought chayres and wrought stoles and cusshions	iij		
Item for a silver gylt salt and other plate	x		
Item for a bason and Eweres and other pewter	v		
Item for Andirons fyer shovell and tonges	j		
Item for spittes and drippinge panes and other Implements		xx	
Item for kettels pots and other brasse	iij	x	
Item a womans saddle a pillioorn [*smudged*] and other furniture	iiij		

Item for wardens and Apples	ij		
Item for fyshe millions and onyons		xx	
Item for chese	iij		
Item for bease	xx		
Item for hodges	v		
Item for land readye sowne with Rye	xij		
Item for corne in the tyth barne	xxxj		
Item for corne in the other barne	xj		
Item for haye in an other barne	iij	x	
Item for horses	v	x	
Item a charme and other thinge belonginge to the darye		xiij	iiij
Item for hennes and other powltrye		xx	
Item for hemp and flax		xx	
Item for the hangines tables and other Implements in the dyninge chambe[r]	x		
Item for a bed, hangines and cubbard and other Implements in the great chambe[r]	vij	xiij	iiij
Item in the starehed chamber a table and a court cubbard and other thinges		xxxvj	
Item six ordinarye bedsteds	j		
Item a baringe Clouth and Child beed lynninge	iiij		
Item in the chambe[r] within the dyninge Roome a chest, a cubbard and a court cubbard		xvj	viij
Item in the chamb[e]r over the pastrye on bedsted and a cubbard		ix	iiij
Item in the longe chambe[r] on bedsted and a tub		xxvij	
Item in the butterye a saffe and hodgsheads and other thinges		xxxvj	viij
Item in the kitchin the cubbard the table the Jack and other Implements	ij	j	vj
Item in the lardrye and pastrye a bacon troffe a powdringe tub and other thinges		xiiij	
Item in the boultinge house, knedinge troffes and boultinge arcks		xxviij	
Item in the bruehouse tubs and barrils and other implements		xxiij	vj
Item for wood for the fyer		xxxvj	
Item for the hampers and bookes in them	ij		
Item for baskets trenchers and other small Implements	ij		
Item mony owinge without bonde	xvij	iij	
Item mony owinge uppon bonde	322		
Item mony in the house	vj		
Item yron barrs & other ymplementes		xl	
Summa totalis	568	8	4

[*Exhibited by the executrix on 14 December 1616*]

Notes: Master William Kippest was buried at Northill on 16 November 1616. He made his will on 21 November 1616, requesting burial in Northill church. The date in the will includes the English and Scottish regnal years and is clearly 1616. Perhaps the date of burial in the parish register or the day of the month of making the will is wrong. He left £100 to daughter Edith at marriage or 21 (she was baptised in 1615) and his land in Eaton Socon to the child his wife was carrying, whether boy or girl, noting that his mother had a life interest in nine acres. There is no subsequent baptism nor burial for a Kippest child in Northill parish registers. He made pecuniary bequests to brothers and sisters, forgiving one brother £10 of the debt he owed the testator, probably part of the money due to him recorded in the inventory. His wife Edith was the residual legatee and executrix. The will was proved on 14 December 1616 (Beds Archives, ABP/W1616–1617/54).

288 Walter Merrill of Cople, carpenter made 12 December 1616
Bedfordshire Archives, ABP/W1616–1617/49

A True Inventory of all the Goodes & Chattelles of Walter Merrill of Copell in the Countie of Bedfforde, Carpenter, deceassed: made the xij[th] of December 1616: by Roberte Warner: Oliver Purser and Thomas Bearde: as followethe

	£	s	d
In the Chamber			
Imprimis Two sere Bedsteedes, two Coverlectes upon them, three Blanquetes, one flocke-bedde, one Matrice, two Boulsters, and three Pillowes		xx	
Item Five paire of Hempe-teere sheetes		xxv	
Item Fower Pillowbeers, one Napkine, & one Towell		v	
Item fower Coaffers		x	
Item Two shelves, one Boxe, one stoole with other thinges		v	
In the Hall			
One Table, a frame, and a fourme		iij	iiij
Item One Cheare, one stoole, with other small stooles there		iij	iiij
Item One Cupboarde in the same Hall		x	
Item One penne there		vj	viij
Item Two Brasse potes, three kettles, one skellet and one Possnette		xx	
Item Eighte peeces of Pewter, three Saucers, two Candle-stickes, one Salte, and a little Potte		v	
Item One payre of Bellowes, one Pothanger, Pott-hookes and a Gryd-yron, with other trashe there			xij
In the Lofte over the Hall			
Imprimis: The Lofte it selffe, and a seare Bedsteed		v	
Item: The Hempe there		v	
Item: Two whipp Sawes, one Crow of yron, and all his Carpenters tooles		x	
In the Boultinge house			
One Boultinge Arke, three Tubbs, one stoppe one Chearme, two Barrelles, one fryinge panne two Cheese-fattes, with other trifles there		viij	
In the Barne			
Imprimis: The Barne it selffe		xl	
Item: a parcell of Hay, three Bushelles of Barly with certaine fodder of Strawe		xvj	

In the yaorde

	£	s	d
Inprimis: One Cow-house, two Leane-toos, two ladders one Cow-racke, and all the wood there		xx	
Item: the Grind-stone		j	
Item: All the Pulleine		ij	
Item: Two kine, and one Bullocke	v		
Item: His wayringe Apparell		x	
Summa totalis	xvj	xj	iiij

the marke of Roberte Warner, the marke of Oliver Purser, the marke of Thomas Bearde
[*Exhibited on 14 December 1616*]

Notes: Walter Merrill was buried at Cople on 3 November 1616, described as 'paterfamilias'. His nuncupative will was made on 26 October. 'I have not so much wealthe: But what I have I doe give to my wiffe for the bringinge upp of my children and the payinge of my debtes'. The will was signed by William Greenough, vicar of Cople. It was proved on 14 December 1616 and, there being no executor named, administration was granted to Millicent Merrill, the principal legatee and his widow (Beds Archives, ABP/W1616–1617/49).

289 Margaret Gayton of Cople, widow

made 14 December 1616

Bedfordshire Archives, ABP/W1616–1617/18

A True Inventory of all the Goodes & Chatteles of Margarette Gayton widdowe late of Cople in the Countie of Bedfforde, deceassed: made the 14th day of December in the yeare of our Lord God 1616: by George Underwood, & George Clayton both of Cople aforesayd: as followeth

	£	s	d
Inprimis The dwellinge house		xiij	iiij
Item Three Coaffers in the same Roume		viij	
Item A Rounde Table, a Chaire and fower joyned stooles		vij	
Item An old boarded Bedsteed, a Matrice, a Boulster, a pillowe, & an old Coverlecte		x	
Item five sheetes, and a table-cloath, two table-Napkins, and a Pillow-beere		xv	
Item An olde Platter, one Saucer, one Candle-sticke, & a little Pewter Pott			xvj
Item A fryinge Panne a little kettle and Pott: posnette, and a Scommer		vj	
Item A payre of Pot-hangers, one fyer shovell an old Gredyron, and a payre of Bellowes		ij	
Item Three Earthen pottes, & 3 drinkinge pottes 3 dishes, 3 spoones, a shreadinge kniffe, & a wooden Candle-sticke			xv
Item in the Hay-House			
Inprimis The Hay house it selffe		xx	
Item A penne, & two kemnells		x	
Item Three Bushells of Barly, & one bushell of Rye		ix	
Item A fanne, & other small thinges there		vj	
In the feild & yarde			
Inprimis One Roode of Rye		viij	

	£	s	d
Item A parcell of wood in the yarde			xvj
All her wayringe apparell, her Linnen and her Hatte		xvj	
Summa totalis	vj	xiij	iij

George Underwood [*signature*], George Clayton [*signature*]
[*Exhibited by Margaret Gayton on 1 February 1617*]

Notes: Margaret Gayton was buried at Cople on 24 November 1616. An undated nuncupative will made 'in the time of her sicknesse' made a bequest to daughter Lucy; and the residue to daughter Margaret because 'she hath ever lived with us, and hath by her worke and paines takeinge helped to maintaine me & my husband deceassed' provided that she pays her husband's legacy of 5s to their grandson. The will records what she had said 'almost a yeare before her death'. Administration was granted to her daughter Margaret Gayton as principal legatee on 1 February 1617 (Beds Archives, ABP/W1616–1617/18). Thomas Gayton, 'paterfamilias', possibly her husband was buried at Cople on 20 March 1614.

290 William Passell of Cople

made 17 January 1617

Bedfordshire Archives, ABP/W1616–1617/23

A true Inventory of all the goodes & Chattelles of William Passell late of Cople deceassed: made by Mathew Wates & George Clayton Inhabitantes of the sayd Parish the 17th day of January Anno 1616 as followethe

	£	s	d
In the Hall			
Inprimis. One Table, one Foarme, one Penne, one Cupboarde, and one Bench-Boarde		v	
Item One shelffe, one greate Bole, six bole-dishes, fower Cheese-fattes, three treen Platters, fower wooden dishes, spoones, & trenchers		iiij	
Item Two Payles, two Staynes, two pitchers, two pipkins, and a Creame-potte		ij	vj
Item One woolen wheele, & a Linnen wheele		ij	
Item Two Cheese shelves			viij
Item One fryinge-panne, & 3 bottles			xiiij
Item a Grate-yron, and a pothangers			xij
Item One Brasse pott, & pothookes: two greater kettles, & two smaller kettles		xiij	iiij
Item Eight Pewter platters, two Sausers, one peuter Cuppe, two Candle-sticks, three Saltes, & two pewter spoones		xij	
Item A kneadinge trough, one Arke, & two payre of sheares		vj	
In the Chamber			
Inprimis. Two Chistes, two Coaffers, & one Boxe		xiiij	
Item Two payre of flaxen sheetes, two payre of Hempe Teare sheetes, and fower payre of Hardon sheetes		xl	
Item One Table-clothe & three payre of Pillowbeers		xx	
Item One Bed-steed with certai[*n*]e bedinge, viz, one Boulster, two Pillowes, & one Coverlette		x	

	£	s	d
Item All the painted Clothes there		iij	iiij
In the Lofte over the Chamber			
One seare Bedsteed, 1 Boulstar, one Coverlette one Cheese-Racke, & other Trash there		x	
In the Yaorde			
Imprimis. A percell of Legge-wood, & of Loppe		xv	
Item A Lenetooe att the Southend of his house a Ladder, & a parcell of Hay therein also		xv	
Item Seaven poundes of Teere, & Towe		ij	vj
Item A small Leanetoe att the other end of the house		ij	vj
Item A Cowe		liij	iiij
All his wayringe Apparell		xiij	iiij
Summa totalis	xij	vj	viij

Math: Wattes [*signature*], George Clayton [*signature*]
[*Exhibited by Anne Passell on 1 February 1617*]

Notes: William Passell was buried at Cople on 13 January 1617, described as 'paterfamilias'. His nuncupative will was 'uttered' on 7 January 1617 before William Greenough, vicar of Cople and Richard Purser. He gave the bedstead in the loft, a coffer and bedlinen to his son Walter; and all his remaining goods to his daughter Anne including a cow, from which she was to wean a calf and give it to Walter. No executor was named. Probate was granted to the main legatee Anne on 1 February 1617 (Beds Archives, ABP/W1616–1617/23).

291 John Harden of Dunton made 10 April 1617
Bedfordshire Archives, ABP/W1616–1617/259

A true Inventory of all the goods and cattles of John Harden disceased priced Aprill the tenth daye by William Barbor and Robert Negoose 1617

	£	s	d
In primis in the Hall a table a forme a casse cheares, and stooles		xvj	8
Item a little table and paynted clothe		5	
Item a potshelfe with other shelfes			18
Item pothangings, fyre shovell, tongs, a range for to hold up the coles, a payer of bellowes		8	
Item a brasse pott, a pan, with other brasse		53	4
In the buttrye			
Item sixe barrels with their frames		13	4
Item fower tubbs, 2 kimnels & 2 little barrils		16	
Item a Saltingtrough		3	4
In the shoppe			
Item a payer of lommes		40	
Item a bedsteed		8	
In the Chamber			
Item a bedd with all the furniture belonginge to it		50	
Item a Cubbord		13	4
Item pewter upon the cubbord head		10	
Item 4 Cofers		20	
Item x payer of sheets, table cloths & other lynnen		55	
Item paynted cloths		5	

		£	s	d
Item old iron in the lofte			3	4
Item bacon in the same lofte			30	
In the barne				
Item 2 quarters of barlye			40	
Item 2 quarters of peyson			32	
Item a hovell in the yeard			20	
Item fyerwood & strawe			20	
Item 2 piggs			8	
Item dunge in the yeard			6	8
Item bords & other smale Tymber			8	
Item a cock & five hens			5	
Item 3 roods of peason			13	4
Item the lease of ther house		6	13	4
Item his Apparell			20	
	Summa totalis	32	18	2

[*Exhibited by the executrix on 22 May 1617*]

Notes: John Harden was buried at Dunton on 2 April 1617. He made his will on 21 March 1617 and gave his looms and other items to his son Thomas; and the residue to wife Mary who was appointed executrix. She was granted probate on 22 May 1617 (Beds Archives, ABP/W1616–1617/259).

292 Robert Clapham, rector of Tilbrook, clerk made 16 May 1617

Huntingdonshire Archives, AH18/3/26

The document is damaged with loss of text along the folds and loss of some values down the right side.

A true Inventorie of all the goodes and Chattelles of Robert Clapham of Tilbrocke in the Countie of Bedford Clarke deceased praysed and valued by Robert Hawkyns and Edward Allen the Sixtenth day of Maye In the yeare of our Lord God 1617 as followeth

	£	s	d
In the parler			
Imprimis one standing bed and a trundelebed		xxv	
Item tow Coverletes	iij		
Item three boulsters two fetherbedes	iij		
Item Curtaines with Ringges frindges and Roodes		[*?*]xxiij	
Item three blanketes		xiij	
Item one longe table fower stoles and A forme		xxiij	
Item two short tables		vj	viij
Item a bench bord		v	
Item one Cubburd		xx	
Item one Chest		x	
Item a wycker chare a warming panne and fower littell [*?*]stole		viij	
Item viij Cus[*hions*]		x	
[*two lines missing*]			
Imprimis a [...] [*t*]able and A benchbord 2 formes 2 [...] tables and a Cubord	[*?*]x		
Item one Chai[*r*] three stoles		x	

In the Chamber

	£	s	d
Imprimis 2 standing beddes one trundle bed		xvj	
Item fower Chest 3 Coffers and a forcer		xl	
Item a fetherbedd bolsteres and matrices	iij		
Item fyve Coverlettes		xx	

In the buttre

	£	s	d
Imprimis x platters		xviij	
Item seven pewter dishes		vj	
Item poringers and Sassars		iiij	
Item 2 pewter Candelstickes and three lattin		iij	
Item 4 saltes and a dossen of sponnes		iiij	
Item one hogges head and fyve barreles		xiij	
Item fower flower pottes		ij	

In an other Chamber

	£	s	d
Item one trusbed and two Coffers		xvj	
Item xij pare of flexen sheetes	[*?*]vj		
Item x pare of [*h*]arden sheetes	iij		
Item a dossen of pillow beares		xx	
Item 2 flexen table clothes and fyve harden		xl	
Item two dossen of table napkins		xl	
[*?*]Item six pellowes		xx	

In the kytchin

	£	s	d
[*I*]mprimis one gre[*a*]t pan and three brasse pottes		xl	
[...] [*k*]ettelles panes and possnetes		xx	
Item AndIrons and speets		v	
Item [*?*]pennes a molding bord and brewing vessell		xv	
Item bellowes fire pan and gred Iren		iij	

In the the bolting house

	£	s	d
Item tubbes and payles a salting trof~~gh~~ a bolting arke and kneding troughe and Cheese preese a winno[*wi*]ng cloth and sackes with other Implementes		xxx	
Item Linning whelles and a woulling		iij	iiij

In the y[*ar*]d

	£	s	d
[*Damaged; lines missing. Only four words of these two or three lines have survived*] Imprimis fower [...] and two	[*value missing*]		

In the [...] Chamber

	£	s	d
Item Chest and [...] Racke and other Implements in the same Chamber		xx	
Item the Rent of the personage	lxxx		
Item his bookes and his apparell	vj	xiij	iiij
signum Robert [*mark*] Hawkynes, Edward Allen [*signature*]			
The sum totales is	142	16	4

[*Exhibited by William Langley on 26 November 1617 before R. Furley, deputy registrar*]

Notes: Robert Clapham was buried at Tilbrook on 19 December 1616. He made his will on 20 July 1616 and it was proved on 19 July 1617 (Hunts Archives, AH20/20/192; BHRS, vol. 2, p. 57). He was ordained in 1569, curate of Eynesbury 1572–73, and rector of Tilbrook from May 1573 until his death (CCEd; Beds Archives, Fasti/1/Tilb); he was not a graduate.

293 Bridgete Francklin of Potton, widow — made 30 May 1617

Bedfordshire Archives, APB4/186

Potton. A True Inventarie of the goodes and Chattelles of Bridgete Francklin widdowe prised by Thomas Warde and William Bennett the 30th day of May Anno domini 1617

	£	s	d
Imprimis in the hall iij Coffers a Cuppbord a litle table woollen wheele two Sythes		xij	
Item five sheetes j Coverlet j bolster two pillowes one ould Bedd		xxxij	
Item one kettle two peces of pewter a small fring pann with other trashe		v	
Item eight pound of wooll colered		viij	
Item a paire of Bellewes			xij
Item one ould bedsteed and certayne hempe		iij	
Item her apparrell		xl	
Item ij penns with certayne chickins		iij	
Summa	v	iiij	

Tho: Warde [*signature*], William Bennett [*signature*]

Debtes owing by the sayd deceased

	£	s	d
Item for Rent		xiij	iiij
Item to divers others		xv	vij

[*Exhibited by Agnes Lymer, administratrix, on 2 June 1617*]

Notes: Bridgete Francklin was buried in Potton on 29 April 1617 as 'wife' of Master Franckline. She made a nuncupative will on 24 May 1617, giving a cupboard and a red petticoat to Edith Lymer and the residue to Annis Lymer and her children, as her next of kin. There being no executor named in the will, administration was granted to Annis Lymer on 2 June 1617 (Beds Archives, ABP/W1617/182).

294 Mathew Montague of Everton — made before June 1617

Huntingdonshire Archives, AH18/13/16

The document is torn across the centre and one or more lines are missing. It is also faded and stained. The heading, amendments and total have been written in a different hand from the list of goods.

An Inventary of the goodes of Mathew Mounta[*gue*] of Everton

	£	s	d
Imprimis 2 beestes one Cowe[63]	4[64]	xl	

[63] *One Cowe* has been inserted in a different hand.

[64] *£4* has been deleted and *40s* substituted.

Item 4 shaerge		16	
Item one pigg		5	
Item in the hall table with other things		7	
Item things in the the [*sic*] chamber		6	
Item things in an other chamber		7	
Item his aparrell		[*value missing*]	
Tear; one or more lines missing			
Item his hay & strawe & wood		[*value missing*]	
Item his linenn, sheets & other linen		20	
Sum	~~ix~~	~~viij~~	
	vij		viij

[*Exhibited by Agnes Mountague, widow and administratix on 6 June 1617. The exhibition clause was signed by R. Furley, deputy registrar.*]

Notes: Mathew Montague's burial has not been found.

295 John Ydoll of Swineshead made 10 June 1617

Huntingdonshire Archives, AH18/24/2

A true invitorie of the goodes of Jhon Ydoll late of Swynshed deceased prysed by Jhon Partesoyle & Peter Musgrave the tenth daye of June 1617

	£	s	d
Imprimis his wearing apparell	1	10	0
Item his redie monie & debtes upon specialtie	22	8	0
Item one table, 4 stooles, one coffer, a cheese pres a payre of andirons with other thinges in the hall	1	5	0
The chamber			
Item one bedstead & one cubboard, 2 coffers 2 Boxs, on chayre	2	10	0
Item 3 coverlettes, 3 blankettes, 2 bolsters, 4 pillowes, two matterisses	4	10	0
Item 15 payre of sheetes, 4 boardclothes, 10 pillowebeers, ~~6~~ 12 tablenapkins with other small lynnen	7	0	0
Item 13 peeces of pewter 2 candlestickes a water pott with other small pewter	1	0	0
In the loft			
Item on old bedsteed, a matteris 2 blankettes on sacke 2 bushels barlie, a wheele and other implementes	1	2	0
Another chamber			
Item on brasse pan 3 kettles 2 brasse pottes A morter, a chafandish with other small brasse	2	15	0
Item a pen a troffe, 3 barrells 2 tubs with other implementes	1	0	0
[*T*]he kytchin			
Item a bolting tub with other implementes	0	10	0
Item 2 mylch kyne, 2 calves, 2 pigges	6	8	0

Item 5 cowples & 3 lamhogges	3	10	0
Item 12 spars, fyerwood, a grinston, haye and certeine compas	1	0	0
[*Total*]	56	18	0
[*Corrected total*	*£56*	*8s*	*0d*]

[*Exhibited by Elizabeth Ydoll, relict and administratrix, on 13 June 1617. The exhibition clause was signed by R. Furley, deputy registrar.*]

Notes: John Ydell was buried at Swineshead on 7 June 1617.

296 Henry Marshe made 27 June 1617

Bedfordshire Archives, ABP4/187

~~1617~~ A True Inventarie of the goods of Heanry Marshe leate desessed the xxvij of June

	£	s	d
Inprimis in the heall			
A Tabell with A frame and tow forms, and benchbord and tow Cusshins		xx	
Item A pott shealf		ij	vj
Item tow Cettells, A posnit, A Cheafinge dishe, A dripping pane a fringe pane, and A skomer, and on peall, A spet A griddirne, on peare of tonngs, and A peare of beallows, with sartin other things		xx	
Item three Chears			xij
Item a peantid Cloth			vj
In the Chamber			
Item A yinde bedsted, A Flock bed, tow bolsters, ~~an~~ 3 pillows, tow Coverleds	iij		
Item A Cubbeard		xx	
Item tenne platters, and tow salts and tow Candillstickes on dosson of spones, tow drinkin copes, and sartin othre small pealtes [*pewter?*]		xx	
Item three Cheachests and A bucks		xx	
Item A letell tabel and A old Cheare, and three peantid Clowes, and A lockine glase		iij	iiij
Item ix peare of sheats, and A dossone of narpkins, tow bord Clowes, v pillow beares with sartine othr linnine	v		
Item his waring A pearrill		xxvj	viij

in the Butetry [*sic*]

Item tow lettell barills, A Cammil and A tobe, and sartine other trashe		x
The Sume Totall is	xv	iiij

John Underwoode [*signature*], Nickls Wards marke
[*Exhibited on 30 June 1617*]

Notes: Henry Marshe's burial has not been found nor his place of residence.

297 Robert Juggins the elder of Cranfield

undated; made between 18 October and December 1617

Bedfordshire Archives, ABP/W1616–1617/224

An Invetorie of the goods and cattells of Robert Juggins Late ~~deseased~~ of Cranfeeld in the County of Bedd deceased praised & made by those whose names are underwritten

	£	s	d
Inprimis his apparrell	3		
Item one Joyned bedd & two other beds	1	6	8
Item tow Coverlids & seven blanquets	3	6	8
Item nine peare of sheetes foure pillowbeares one table cloth one towell and a brushe	3	11	
Item one fetherbed and two bolsters and two pillowes	2		
Item two Chestes and one box		16	
Item two Cobards & three tables & Corte table and one pot shilfe	1	13	4
Item two cheares two Joyned stooles with other smaule stooles		3	4
Item thirteene platters fower litle pew ter dishes two sault sillers & thre porringers		13	4
Item four brase potts two kettels one spi semorter one basen three candle stickes a Chafeinge dish and one posnett	1	6	8
Item nine milke vesseles foure tubs three barriles two payles and a churne	1	3	4
Item one boltinge vessell one kneadinge kimb nill with other things in the bake house	1		
Item two potthangers two pare of pothookes one pare of handdiernes one fringpan one gredierne two spits aladle dishes and spoones		8	
Item two sett of hookes two carts and mayles beelonginge to there trade		6	8
Item threescore & five sheepe and lambs	16		
Item thre geldinges a mare and a colte	8		
Item eight beasts	20		
Item foure yearelinges & three weane lings	8		

Item old hay and new hay	13		
Item three hogges	3		
Item three framed hovilles with all his other wood	5	10	
Item two longecarts two doncarts tw[*o*] pare of shood wheeles plow and geares	6		
Item wheate barley pease and the bushell	20		
Item foure acres of wheate soen	6		
Item one dosen and a halfe of hurdles		4	
Item geese henes and duckes		5	
Suma	126	14	

Thomas Wheler [*signature*], Robert Morton [*signature*], George Baker [*signature*], William Parkins [*mark*]
[*Exhibited by Agnes Juggens, executrix, on 2 December 1617*]

Notes: Robert Juggins was buried at Cranfield on 18 October 1617. His nuncupative will was made on 10 or 11 April 1617, giving everything, except his bed, to his wife Agnes to discharge his debts and provide his children's portions. Probate was granted to his widow on 2 December 1617. The two witnesses to the will corroborated its terms and stated that Robert Juggins had surrendered his copyhold to George Baker, headborough (Beds Archives, ABP/W1616–1617/224).

298 Henry Large of Everton made 19 November 1617
Huntingdonshire Archives, AH18/12/48
Damage to the top left corner and along the horizontal fold in the middle of the inventory, resulting in loss of words.

[*A*]n Inventory taken the xix[th] day of [*Nove*]mber Anno Domini 1617 of All the goods Cattell Chatthell & movables of Henry Lardge of Everton in the Countye of Beddf As Followeth

	£	s	d
Inprimis in the Hale j Cubbord j Casse j Table j Chayer with other Trumperye		xx	
Item in the Chamber ij Boarded Beddsteedes ij olde fethrbeddes iij olde bolstres ij pillowes ij Blanckettes ij olde coverlettes & the hanging		xl	
Item ij olde coffers j Chayre & A pott shelfe		v	
Item iiij[or] payer of sheettes j ode sheete iij pillowbeers of hemptare ij napkines		xxvj	viij
Item ix peaces of pewter ij sawcers j salte & j olde friinge pann		x	
Item ij kettell j little pott		ix	
Item the Rie in the yard vj bȝ		xx	
Item the hay in the yard		xl	
Item j hovell ~~with~~ with harne uppon it		xx	
Item j olde [*?*]Cowhouse [...]		xiij	[...]
Item [...] j sithe & [...]		vj	
Item iiij Bease & ij [*?*]wenell cavles	ix		
Item two Acrs dm of Tilth		xxxiij	iiij

Item the hempe in the yard		v	
Item j Cocke & j henn			xvj
Item his waringe Aparrell		xx	
Summa	xxij	v	iiij
[*Corrected total*	*£22*	*9s*	*4d*]

Praysers Thomas [*?*]Tomlyn, John Larke his mark, Wm [*?*]Baines [*?Barnes*] his mark
[*Exhibited by Margaret Large, relict and executrix, on 15 December 1617. The exhibition clause was signed by R. Furley, deputy registrar.*]

Notes: Henry Large was buried at Everton on 15 November 1617.

299 Robert Savidge of Bromham, fuller made 20 February 1618

Bedfordshire Archives, ABP4/85, 86

There are two copies of the inventory, identical except for minor spelling variations and as noted below. The transcription has been made from ABP4/86.

The true Inventary of all the goodes & chattells of Robert Savidge fuller late of Bromeham in the County of Bedd deceased taken & prised the xx[th] daye of February in the year of our Lord god 1617: by John Godfrey and John Purney.

	£	s	d
Inprimis his Apparell		v	
In the hall			
Item j Table with a frame, a forme, j pen, j Chayre, j bench & bench bord, iij bordes iiij little stooles, & certayne paynted cloathes		xiiij	
In the chamber			
Item iij ioyned bedsteedes, iij Coffers, one Cubbord, iij drinke barrells, & ij bottells		xxxiij	iiij
Item iij payre of flexen sheetes, iij sheetes of tare hemp, ij payre of harden sheetes & one sheete, one bord cloth, ij napkins, & one Towell		xxxvij	x
Item ij flocke beddes, iiij coverlettes, j blankett, iij bolsters, ij pillowes, iiij pillowbeares		xxxviij	iiij
Item j parcell of wooll with a sacke		xx	
Item the Tenters & all implem[*en*]tes belonging to his trade		xliij	
Item iiij kettles, a posnett, j dripping pan & ij spittes		xv	
Item j old bourden bedsteed & certayne bordes		vij	
Item a payre of cobirons, & old Iron, j spade j mattocke, j bill, j axe, j hatchett		iiij	
Item iij Tubbs, & a kneading troffe		iij	
Item xj pewter platters, iiij sawcers, j candlesticke, a qu[*art*] pott, iij saltes		xiij	iiij
Item dishes, spoones, boules, j payre of bellowes, pott hangers, hookes, & other lumber		v	

In the yarde

	£	s	d
Item ij Cowes & j bullock	vij		
Item a parcell of haye		x	
Item ij fleakes, & iiij hurdles			xviij
Item ij tymber stickes		ij	
Item a parcell of fire woodd		vj	viij
Item a hogscoate & ij gates		ij	
Item a parcell of compasse		ij	vj
Item j hogge, & a store pigge		xx	
Item ij hogstroffes			vj
Item a parcell of Tenter Tymber		ij	vj
Item iij bayes of housing, & a hovell	v		
Item one parcell of cheese		viij	
Item[65] j cocke & iiij hens		ij	vj
Item other trash & trumpery		ij	
Summa totalis	xxvj	xvj	vj
[*Corrected total*	*£26*	*19s*	*0d*]

Prizers: John Godfrey his marke, John Purney his marke
[*Exhibited by Dorothea Savadge, administratrix, on 22 May 1618*]

Notes: Robert Savidge was buried at Bromham on 16 November 1617. Dorothy Savage, widow, was buried at Bromham on 3 December 1638.

300 Edward Fremane of Stotfold, gentleman made 20 March 1618
Bedfordshire Archives, ABP4/188
Slight damage.

A true Inventory of all & singuler the goodes & Cattells of Edward Fremane of Stotfold gen[*t*] deceased taken the 20th daye of March 1617 by us whose names ar he under written

	£	s	d
Imprimis in the hall a table wyth a Frame ij Cobordes a cheare & other movables in the same rome	iij		
Item in the parlor a Table with a Frame iij Cheares ij Cobardes vj stolls wyth all other thinges in the same parler	v		
Item in the Lettell Chamber a standing Beed wyth the furnytur on yt a Cobard a wycker chear & some other thinges in the same rome	vj		
Item in the chamber over the Lyttell parler a standing beed with the furnytur ij Chestes wyth other goodes in the same Roome	v	x	
Item in the Chamber over the hall on standinge beed ij other beedes with the furnytur on theme a Table on cheste with other thinges in the same Roome	vj		
Item in the chamber over the parlor a standinge beed wyth the furnytur on yt a fayre preese a great Cheste a Table			

65 This whole line is only in this copy.

ij trunkes x Joyned stooles a wycker cheayre wyth other thinges in the same Rome	xiij	vj	viij
Item on Carpitt iij Coverleedes a peese of new woollen Cloth a boulster and ij pewlowes with all other thinges in the sam Roome	x		
Item Fortie payr of Seetes	xvj		
Item xiij Table Clothes	iiij		
Item xiij Towells		xLvj	viij
Item iiij dosone & v Table napkins		L	
Item xx pelow bears	iij	vj	viij
Item in the Butterry v hoggsheades a Troffe ij boultenge arkes wyth other thinges in the sayd Roome		xl	
Item in the Lettell Butterry ij barrills a Saffe & other thinges		xiij	iiij
Item in the mylke house a soulting troffe a Saffe a powderinge Tubb with other thinges		L	
Item in the kitchin vij spittes ij Longe Cobyarnes ij goose pannes ij Iron bares & other thinges in the sayd Roome	iij		
Item in the bruhouse a moult quarne a Copper bruinge vessell a troffe with other thinges in the same rome	iij	x	
Item in the servantes Chamber ij borded beedes with furnytur & other thinges in the same Room		xx	
Item in the Loofte over the kitchin yarne beheses a playn beed with other thinges in the sayd rome	iij		
Item dyvers peess of Brase a warmynge panne a chafinge dyshe	vj	xiij	iiij
Item basone & ure pewter pootes soultes poringers platters & other pewter	iij	vj	viij
Item viij hogges of Bacone	vj		
Item iiij sylver spones		xxvj	viij
Item the Barly in the Barne	xL		
Item ij hovills of pease	x		
Item on hovill of wootes	vj		
Item on cantch of wheat & Rye	x		
Item ij hovills	iij		
Item grayne in the garner & other thinges	v		
Item v bease v bolockes	xxvj		
Item some iij^xx [*60*] shepp	xx		
Item the hogges in yard	v		
Item the haye that is to spend	x		
Item ix horses	Lviij		
Item v payre of Showd wheles ij Longe Cartes iij dounge Cartes harows plows Cartgears plow gears & plow tymber	xx		
Item the wood in the yard	xiij		
Item vij acers of Tylth	x		
Item the Brach Lond Sown	xv		
Item his waringe apparrill	v		
Item xx henns xx duckes iij Turkes		xxx	
Item vj acers wheat & Rye	xij		
Item in Redy mony		L	
Item debtes due to the testator	xx		
~~and~~	~~x~~	~~iij~~	~~iiij~~

	£	s	d
Item on Lease of iiij[xx] v acers of Land which the testator held of Stephen Butler and a Lease of certayn other Landes which he held of Beckingham Butlere	CCC		
Some is	vijCv	iij	viij
[*Corrected total*	*£706*	*3s*	*4d*]

Tho: Patornoster [*signature*], William Allyn [*signature*]
[*No exhibition clause*]

Notes: Edward Fremane was buried at Stotfold on 14 March 1618. He made his will on 3 March 1617, disposing of several houses and at least 95 acres. He left £400 to his grandson Edward Freeman (son of Edward Freeman (*210*) who died in 1610); money or goods to his four daughters; other small bequests; an annuity of £13 6s 8d to his wife Susan (on condition that she gave up her dower lands), the use of a house called Frenches and his household goods for life; and another house, the reversion of Frenches and other land to his son Abraham who was residual legatee and executor and was granted probate on 25 April 1618 (Beds Archives, ABP/W1618–1619/168). Susanna Freeman was buried on 11 March 1631 and left a will (Beds Archives, ABP/W/1631/146).

301 Thomas Crabtree, vicar of Potton

made 3 April 1618

Bedfordshire Archives, ABP/W/1618–1619/134

A true and perfect Inventary of all and singuler the goodes debtes rightes and chattelles of Thomas Crabtree late vicar of Potton in the County of Bedf deceased made the thirde daie of Aprill Anno domini 1618 by us whose names are underwritten

	£	s	d
In the Hall			
Inprimis one draweinge Table one forme three ioyned stooles a Lyvery Cupboard a presse cupboard two little tables three Chaires and a glasse Case & a foote presse	iij	xiij	iiij
Item Fire shovell tongges Andyrons and other yron worke & fowre Cushions		x	
In the Parlour			
Item one standeinge bedstead & a trundell bedde one greate chest a lyvery Cupboard a Table a Trunke twoo chaires a forme a stoole & twoo boxes		lij	
Item one Featherbedd three pillowes one bolster an old coverlett one blankett 4 curtens with yron roddes a Carpet three Cushions a paire of bellowes; Tonges & Fireshovell and other yron worke & the painted clothes	vj		
Item his weareing Apparell	v		
Item ~~he~~ bookes & shelves & deskes in the studie	v		
Item a silver saltseller & syx silver spones	iij	x	

In the Chamber over the Hall			
Item a standeing bedstedde & a trundell bedde one forme one stoole ~~thre~~ fouer chaires a foote presse a chest & a wicker chaire & a Lyvery Cupboard	iij	xvij	
Item twoo Featherbeddes three bolsteres 2 coverlettes ~~three bolsteres~~ a mattresse three blankettes three Cushions vallances & ~~curtens~~ painted clothes with other smale thinges	vj		
In the Chamber over the Parlour			
Item two standeing bedstedes and a trndell bedde three chestes a chaire a stoole & certaine shelves		xxxiij	iiij
Item twoo Featherbeddes foure bolsteres three pillowes two mattresses three blankettes twoo coverlettes twoo curtens, certaine woolle ~~and~~ painted clothes & a warmeinge panne	viij		
Item nyne & twenty paires of sheetes & five dozen & eight Napkins five tableclothes six pillowebeires & eightene towelles	x	x	
Item one blankett a pillow & a mattresse		vj	viij
Item a Calleter a headepiece a sword a little trundell bede & other odde implementes in the little Lofte		xiij	iiij
In the Kitchen			
Item twoo brasse pottes fowre spittes three kettelles a stille a dryppeing panne a bakeing panne a brasen Ewre morter & pestell three skomeres potthookes & all other thinges there		l	
Item all the Pewter		liij	iiij
Item Bacon		xxxiij	iiij
In the Milke house			
Item a powthering troffe a table milke vesselles shelves & other thinges		ix	
In the Breuehouse			
Item the breweing vesselles a Casse a Leade formes a buckett & a rope to the well with other stuffe		xlvj	viij
In the Apple Lofte			
Item certaine Rye & wheate a cheeserack & other thinges there		xlvj	viij
In the Seller			
Item a safe fowre hoggesheades three kymnelles & other smalle thinges there		xxx	
In the lofte over the Seller			
Item foure wheeles a cradle an old safe & other trashe		xvj	
In the Garner			
Item Rye & barley a bushell & other thinges		xxvj	viij

In the Barne

Item Haie strawe, old Timber a Fanne Forkes & other trashe there	iiij		

In the Furse house the foreyard & Garden

Item a hand sawe a hammer a hatchett certaine wynmelles & other toules		v	
Item certaine Firewoode & strawe & a dragge Rake		vj	
Item Five stockes of Bees		xxv	

In the Dunge yard

Item a hovell with strawe upon yt twoo Ladders a hoggestroffe certaine Tyles & Timber & the dunge	iij		
Item three Cowes & twoo shootes	x		
Item the graine in the field & closes & the Tylthe	xviij		

In the Lofte over the north Church porch

Item certaine hemp Firewoode and other trashe there		xx	
Item debtes oweinge to the deceased	Cl		
Summa Totalis	CClx	xiij	iiij

Pricers John Durrant [*signature*], John Jacksonne [*signature*], John Harpar senier [*signature*], John Harper iunior [*signature*], Willyam Robinson [*signature*]
[*No exhibition clause*]

Notes: Thomas Crabtree's burial has not been found. He was vicar of Potton from 1592 until his death and appointed a licensed preacher in Potton and throughout the diocese of Lincoln in 1604 (CCEd; Beds Archives, Fasti/1/Pott). When he consulted Dr Napier in 1615, his age was noted as 50 (Forman and Napier, case no. 41969). He made his will on 4 May 1616, requesting burial in the chancel of Potton church. He left money, furniture and books to his children, including the cupboard in the hall with the foot press and a linen wheel to one daughter; a bed in the loft over the parlour to another daughter; and the remainder of his books and a desk to his eldest son. He also left houses in Hitchin and land in Potton. His wife Alice was residual legatee and executrix, and was granted probate on 8 May 1618 (Beds Archives, ABP/W1618–1619/134). Alice died in 1618 and was buried in Potton on 24 December and left a will appointing her son-in-law John Durrant as executor (*381*) (Beds Archives, ABP/W1618–19/25). The signature of John Jacksonne, one of the appraisers, looks like that of the notary public who has signed exhibition clauses on other inventories. See also the inventory of John Durrant (*381*).

302 Hugh Albrite of Dunstable, tailor — made 15 July 1618

Lincolnshire Archives, INV/122/117
The inventory is fragile and damaged.

An Inventorey all the goodes & chatteles late of Hugh Albrite late of Dunstable In the county of Bedds tailer Deceased, & prised by George Okeland, Robert Hadden, Tho Albrit and Wm Marsh the 15 Day of Julie Anno Domini 1618

	£	s	d
Inprimis all his weareinge Apparell	6	[?]	0

In the hall a greate table cheste One little table one forme One Chaire one cubbord & certeine shelves hookes & Ierons in the chimney with other small thinges & 3 stooles	1	6	0
Item in the shopp vzt A shopp bord One old presse certeine shelves & little bordes	0	13	4
Item 2 old stooles sheares yard and pressing Ierons & certeine old beddinge	1	0	0
Item in the chamber over the shopp One ioyned Bedstead one fetherbed One Boulster 3 pillowes One Coverlett 3 blanckettes	4	6	8
Item one table with a Frame 3 chestes one court cubbord 2 boxes one whicker cheare one cradle & certeine shelves & Bordes	1	0	0
Item malte by estynitecion 26 quarters	27	0	0
Item in the chamber over the hall One bedstead one blanckett One wooll bedd one boulster One bushell 2 old chestes one forme 2 tubbs certeine old shelves certeine honie pottes one bushell of wheat a little wooll & 4 small scuttles	1	0	0
Item all the lynnen	2	10	0
Item all the Brasse & pewter	2	0	0
Item a small parcell of skins a little parcell of silke & a small parcell of fustyan ~~sewinge silke~~	0	13	4
Item all the wood in the yard at	2	3	4
Item [*?*]v hives of bees ~~at~~ & certeine bee hives	1	13	4
Item one pigg at	0	6	8
Item One black geldinge	3	6	8
Item 2 severall obligacions one of 7li & the other of 4li 10s 8d	11	4 [*sic*]	8
Item certeine cowpery ware & other small thinges	0	5	0
Item the intereste in the Baylywicke from this day untill the 2j day of December next ensewinge	15	0	0

Tho Albright his mark [T A], Robert Haddon [*signature*], the marke of George Okeland et mei William Marshe [*signature*]

Summa totalis	81	9	[...]

[*Exhibited by the executrix at Dunstable on 17 September 1618*]

Notes: Hugh Albrite was buried at Dunstable on 3 July 1618 as Hugh Aberet. He made his will on 23 June 1617, leaving £10 and four stocks of bees to each of his two daughters at the age of 21. His wife, who was unnamed, was residual legatee and executrix. She was granted probate at Dunstable on 17 September 1618 (Lincs Archives, LINCS WILLS 1618/i/14). The appraiser, William Marsh, was the schoolmaster in Dunstable from at least 1604.

303 Lawrence Underwoode of Arlesey, stringer made 2 August 1618

Lincolnshire Archives, INV/122/115

Some damage at the top right edge and a hole on the left side. Where obvious, missing letters have been supplied.

An Inventory of all the goodes Cattelles Chattelles and utense[*ls*] of Howshoulde of Lawrence Underwoodes latte of Arlesey in the County of Bedd deceased praysed the second daye of August Anno 1618 by William Coper and John Sprign[...] [*?Sprignell*] praysors

	£	s	d
Imprimis five bease	x		
Item a bullocke		xx	
Item a Calfe		x	
Item two horse	iiij		
Item certayn hempe an a house ~~and~~ [*illeg.*]	iiij		
Item a lease of his house	vj	xiij	iiij
Item certayn wood and payles		xxxx	
Item certayn hoges		xx	
Item certayne haye and pease	iiij		
Item owinge me by one Wallow alias Warin		xlij	
I[*tem*] owinge me by one John West		xx	vj
Item in redy money more		xxj	
Item certayn Hempe and other ware		xxvj	viij
Item certayn boardes and Cheeses		xx	
Item in the lofte 3 beades and the thinges belonginge to them two Cofers and certayn Lynan		xl	
Item in the Chaple at roffe [*sic*] and othe trashe		iiij	
Item in the hale a Cobard a table and othre stooles and a forme		x	
Item certayn brasse and pewter and other trash in the darye		xxx	
Item his waringe aparrill		x	
Item certeyne compasse his working toles and other trash in the stable and a sheep		l	
Suma	xlvj	viij	vj
[*Corrected total*	*£46*	*17s*	*6d*]

[*Exhibited by the executrix at Hitchin, Herts, on 18 September 1618*]

Notes: Lawrence Underwoode was buried at Arlesey on 31 July 1618. He made his nuncupative will on 29 July 1618, being described as a stringer. He gave his horses and cows to his two sons and daughters. He appointed his wife Anne residual legatee and executrix and she was granted probate by James Rolfe at Hitchin on 18 September 1618 (Lincs Archives, LCC WILLS/1618/i/142).

304 Thomas Petchet of Stotfold made 16 September 1618

Lincolnshire Archives, INV/121/386

A true Inventory of all the moveable goodes & Chattelles that were in possession of Thomas Petchet late of Stotfold deceased as they were praised by William Freeman & Edward Gray this p[rese]nt xvj^th^ of September in Anno domini 1618

	£	s	d
Imprimis in the hall a table a fourme & a bench board		ij	
Item a Cubboard & a Chasse		xij	
Item two chaires a wheele a Churme a potshelfe		ij	vj
Item a saltingtrough 2 barrelles one tubb fower wooden bowles		iiij	
Item 2 brasse pottes, three kettels, a frying pan a gridiron		xij	
Item sixe pewtr dishes, 2 candlestickes, a salt, a morter		iiij	
Item a spitt, a pothangr a paire of bellowes			xvj
Item painted clothes		ij	
Item in the Chambr two bedsteddes, 3 blanckettes, 2 coverlettes 2 bolsters & three pillowes		xx	
Item 7 paire of sheetes, 5 napkins, 4 pillowbeares & one table cloth		xx	
Item sixe Coffers & painted Clothes		xvij	
Item Carpentrs tooles		iiij	
Item his Apparrell		viij	
Item fower acres of barly	viij		
Item one acre of wheate & mislin		xl	
Item half an acree of peese, half an acre of fitches, & half acre of lintels		xx	
Item Haye		xij	
Item Hempe		vj	
Item Apples		vj	viij
Item woode		xiij	iiij
Item two cowes, two yong bullockes & a calf	vj		
Item fower pigges		vj	
Item 3 sheepe		x	
Item 4 hens & a cocke		iij	
Item an acre of tilth		vj	viij
Item 3 ladders, a fan, an hogges trough		ij	vj
Summa	xxv	xv	

William Freeman, Edward Graye

[*Exhibited by the administratrix at Bedford on 19 September 1618*]

Notes: Thomas Petchet was buried at Stotfold on 18 July 1618. Administration was granted to his widow Jane on 18 September 1618 (Lincs Archives, Act Book A/x/42). The inventory is in the same handwriting as that of Katherine Clarke of Stotfold 1614 (*276*).

305 Simonde Massane of Everton made 19 September 1618

Huntingdonshire Archives, AH18/13/22

The document is very badly damaged. The top right section and a large patch in the centre are missing. The remaining text is stained in places.

1618 A true Inventorie [...] Simonde Massane of [...] the Countie of Hun[...] upon the xixth of S[...] names are underwrigh[*ten*] [...] folethe etc

	£	s	d
Imprimis i Couberte acase and a table in the [...]		[*value missing*]	
Item ij Cheyers and 3 stoules		[*value missing*]	
Item ij brase potes & the Ceatles		[*value missing*]	
Item for the peuter		[*value missing*]	
Item ij laten Candlstiekes			[*?*]xij
Item iiij Toubes ij Є kemneles and other treene ware		[*?*]xx	
Item iij bedstedes and the bedinge [*?*]therunto [*be*]longing		liij	4
Item 3 Cofers a table and a ould Couberd		xiij	iij
Item a par of holonte shetes and xjth par of other shetes		xliij	[...]
Item iiij pellowbers vj napkinges ij table Clothes & oth		[*value missing*]	
Item for woule and Cheses and other [...] shuch like thinges		xx	[...]
Item ij beast [...] Cowe [...]	iiij		
Item a yearling [...] heyf[...]		xxx	
Item ij hadges [*?hogs*]		xxx	
Item for the greane in the ba[*rn*]	iiij		
Item the hey in the hey house		xxx	
Item the Beese		xx	
Item for xxth sheepe and lammes	v	x	
Item for the woode		x	
Item for 3 hodgtroufe and a grenstone		vj	viij
Item for the Freute in the orchatt		x	
Item for his apparill		xxx	
Item the Hempe[66]		[*vj*	*viij*]
Sume is	[*?*]xxxiij	v	iiij

Richard Cowper [*signature*], Richard Barrett [*signature*], Jhon Caucottes [*signature*]

~~Item the hempe~~ ~~vj~~ ~~viij~~

[*Exhibited by Isabell Mason, widow, in 1618 on the 13th of the month; the name of the month is missing. The exhibition clause was signed by R. Furley, deputy registrar.*]

Notes: Simonde Massane's burial has not been found.

66 This line is written in a different hand.

306 George Francklin of Bolnhurst, esquire made 17 November 1618

Bedfordshire Archives, FN 1094

The document is damaged on the right hand side. Missing words and figures have been inserted in square brackets where obvious.

An Inventorie [*of*] all and singuler the goods chatle[*s*] and debtes of George Franckl[*in*] late while he lived of Bolnehu[*rst*] in the Countie of Bedd Es[*q*] deceased valued & prized [*the*] seaventeenth daie of Novem[*ber*] in the yeare of our lord g[*od*] one thowsand sixe hundred eighteene By Thomas Anglesey [...] and Hugh [...] vizt

	£	s	d
Inprimis in readie money in gould & silver	Cvij	[...]	vj
Item a chaine of gould and other Jewells	lxxxiiij	x	
Item in Plate	lxxxx		
Item his Apparell	lviij	xiij	ii[*ij*]
Item lynnen	Cxxij	xiiij	
Item Bedsteedes	xviij	vj	vi[*ij*]
Item featherbedds coverlettes and other furniture	lxxxv		[...]
Item vallances curt[*ains*] [...]	[*value missing*]		
Item Carpettes Cushions windowe curtaines etc	xxvj	ij	
Item tables formes stooles chaires and such like	xxiiij	vj	8
Item Pewter and brasse	xxxix	viij	viij
Item andirons tonges fire-shovells bellowes & such like	iiij	iiij	
Item Chestes and Trunckes	viij		
Item the milkehouse at	[*value missing*]		
Item the bakehouse brewhouse and boultinge howse at	xviij	ix	vj
Item Armour & furniture for service at	xxij	vj	8
Item the Butteries at	x		
Item bookes and mapps at	xvj	iij	4
Item Woolle hopps and necessaries in a garret at	xxxvij		
Item lead coale and iron at	xv	xiij	[*iiij*]
Item a Coache and Coach geers & Clocke and a Jacke at	xxxviij		
Item stills Cesternes quernes fishinge nettes and divers other thinges at	xxj	xv	8
Item oxen milche beastes gueldinges and other Catell	Clxxxxj	vj	viij
Item Grayne in the			

garner & barne at	Cliiij	x	
Item haye and strawe at	Lij		
Item plowes, cartes and furniture belonginge to husbandrie at	xxv		
Item hovells at	v		
Item Ladders and other necessaries at	ij	vj	8
Item Tymber and board at	x		
Item Wood in the Woodyard at	xv		
Item utensills in the Storehouse at	iij		
Item a Lease of certaine Land in the parishe of Thurley	xvj		
Item debtes owinge to him	MMviijCviij	v	iij
Item other debtes forgiven by him in his will	CCC		
Summa totalis huius Inventarij	MMMMCCCClxxj	xv	iij

[*Exhibited by Master Robert Rawleng, notary public, on 19 December 1618. The exhibition clause was signed by Edmund Woodhall, registrar of the Prerogative Court of Canterbury.*]

Notes: George Francklin was buried at Bolnhurst on 7 September 1618. He was admitted to the Middle Temple in 1567 and built a new chamber there in 1577 (*Minutes of Parliament of the Middle Temple*, ed. by Charles Trice Martin, London, 1904, vol. 1, p. 162, 218). He came from an upwardly mobile yeoman family and attained the office of High Sheriff of Bedfordshire in 1602–3.[67] He made his will on 24 August 1618, describing himself as an esquire. He made provision for his six children, including paying the debts of £500 of his eldest son Edmund, and gave bequests and gold rings to many family members. He referred to his house Mavourn, other land in Bolnhurst and land in twelve other Bedfordshire parishes and in Buckinghamshire. He left his chambers in the Middle Temple to his son Edmund who was his residual legatee. The will referred to many household and farming items that occur in the inventory. His sons Edmund and John were appointed executors and proved the will on 27 November 1618 (TNA, PROB 11/132/625).

307 Thomas Wood of Milton Bryan, labourer made 30 September 1619
Bedfordshire Archives, ABP4/90

September the xxx[th] Anno domini 1619
A true Imnitorye of the goodes of Thomas Wood lat of Myllton Bryant in the County of Beddfsh Labourer deceased, Taken and preased by Master Nicloas Johnsonn and John Lucye bothe of Myllton aforesaide

67 See the *Visitations of Bedfordshire*, p. 120 and Beds Archives, FN and FN999 for an account of the Francklin family; the papers contain many documents relating to George Francklin's property dealings in Bedfordshire. His house, Mavourrn Farm, is described in David H. Kennett, Angela Simco and Terence Paul Smith, 'The Moated Site and Timber-framed Building at Mavourn Farm, Bolnhurst', *Bedfordshire Archaeology* (1986), pp. 77–85 and 'Mavourn Farm Bolnhurst' in Bedfordshire Archives, Community Histories – Bolnhurst.

	£	s	d
Item his weareing Appryll		xx	
Item the Tabell form and benche bordes		iiij	
Item A Cobberd and A pott shelf		x	
Item on other square Tablle			xij
Item A dyshe pene iij shilves and tow Joynd stolles		ij	
Item on wollen whell and on lynen whell		ij	
Item tow brasse pottes		viij	
Item on pott hanger tonges and fyer showell on fryeinge pane and on pare of hand Ieornes		iiij	
Item iiij lettel brasse Kittelles ij possnottes and A skymer		x	
Item all the pewtter		v	
Item on Cheare and towe old Cushenes			xij
Item for A Lanthorne			vj
Item towe borded beddes with the furnytuer belonginge unto them		xxx	
Item iij Chestes and on windscott boxe		viij	
Item v pare of sheettes with other Lynen		xxiij	iiij
Item ij drinke barrelles j tubb ij bordes and other small Impellmentes		iij	iiij
Item all the palles aboute the yarde		xl	
Item j ladder a grenstone and A sythe		v	
Item the fyerwood		ij	
Summa Totalles is	ix		2
[*Corrected total*	*£8*	*19s*	*2d*]

Nicholas Johnson [*signature*], John Lucy [*signature*]
[*Exhibited on 11 October 1619*]

Notes: Thomas Wood was buried at Milton Bryan on 5 September 1619.

308 Oliver Aspland of Bletsoe, miller made 5 January 1620

Bedfordshire Archives, ABP4/190

The document is very faint, especially the figures.

A Invtary taken of all the goods and ~~Catt~~ Chattell of Olyver Aspland latly deseased miler on the fift day of Jenivarie Ano Dom 1619

	£	s	d
Imprimis for a cloake and all his wearing aparill		l	
Item in the hall two ~~Cab~~ Cubbards two tables sixe stoules with other old trash		l	
Item in the Cambar over the Buttre one bed with the Furnitur be longing to it and all things therin besides		liij	iiij
Item in the Cambar over the hall on bede with Furnitur to it and all things ~~and all th~~ therin besids		xlvj	v[*ii*]j
In the Camber over the kiching two beds on chest with all other things therein besides		xxxiij	iiij

Item one chest of linene	iij		
Item in the kiching on pen iij tubes on table with the brasse and peuter and other old trash therin		xl	
Item in the Buttre on salting trowfe iiij barrills and other old trashe		xiij	iiij
Item the wheat mill with the stones and the going geares with sertayn bordes and all other trashe therin with the boat	iij	vj	viij
Item two Hovells seartayne palse and all the wood in the yard		xl	
Item for the lease of the milles	x		
Sum	~~xxx~~	~~viij~~	~~iiij~~
	32	13	4
Anoat of all the Debts of Oliver Aspeland late deseased miller			
Imprimis Master [*?*]~~Cerre~~ Keir	xxv		
Item Jacob Gylse	v		
Item William Bull	iij	x	
Item Master Eston		xxx	
Item to Roman Bolton		xx	
Item to John Smyth		xx	
Item to Master Drayton		xx	
Item to Jerome Crofts		x	
Item to Trusteron Parker		x	
Item to Tho Berry		viij	
Item to Roger White		ix	
Item to Tho Barnes		vj	
Item for Rent that is now to be payd		xlv	
Item for provision for two burialls		xl	
Sum	xliiij	viij	

[*No exhibition clause*]

Notes: Oliver Aspland was buried at Bletsoe on 28 November 1619. The names of his creditors (Keir, Gyles, Eston, Crofts, Drayton, Bull and Trustrum Parker) occur in Bletsoe parish registers at this period.

309 Thomas Alen of Bedford St Mary undated; possibly January 1620

Bedfordshire Archives, ABP4/198

The document has faded and some of the figures are unclear.

An Inventarie of the goodes of Thomas Alen of Bedford St Marie

	£	s	d
Ine prymose [*Inprimis*] in the halle wone coborde		iii	iiii
wone round Tabell		i	
wone olde cofere			vi
wone cofere more		i	vi
wone cheare		i	
tooe olde borded bedes		iii	
wone barelle			x
wone pare of sheates		iii	iiii

thri pounde of tooe		ii	viii
tooe olde wheales			xviii
wone olde bede			iii
tooe olde stoles			vi
wone olde tobe		i	
wone brase bole		iii	iiii
tooe letelle cateles		ii	viii
tooe partere dyches		i	
vi dyches and toe spones			viii
wone payle			iiii
wone chafinge dyche			vi
wone fyreshovle grydirne pothockes and hangeres		i	iiii
wone hachete			iiii
iiii pyges		vi	viii
wode		i	iiii
wone blankete and bolstere		ii	
wone bushelle			viii
tooe forkes and a shovle		i	
olde pented close		i	
wone hare syfe			iiii
I owe to Master Joye		vii	
to Gooddee Gaskyne		ii	
	Summa	57	2
	[*Corrected total*	*52s*	*7d*]
hee hathe lefte me in to Beamemanes mane [*sic*]		xxiii	
and ls to his systere		[*50*]	
and mastere Palye		ix	

[*No exhibition clause.*]

Notes: This is possibly Thomas Allen who was buried at Bedford St Mary's on 15 January 1620. Master Joye could have been Richard Joye of Staple Inn, London and appraiser of Thomas Grene's inventory in 1625 (*357*). People called Gaskin, Beamond and Paley feature in St Mary's parish registers in this period.

310 Thomas Younge of Langford, labourer made 16 January 1620

Bedfordshire Archives, ABP/W1618–1619/190

This document is a copy of his will and inventory written sequentially on one sheet of paper.

An Inmitory of Thomas Younges goods & Chattells lately deceased praysed by John Trickhey: Tho: Colmer: Jo. Dutton: and Henry Younge the xvjth of January Anno Domini 1619

	£	s	d
Inprimis: j Cowe and j bullocke		xl	
Item fower flitches		xvj	
Item j Cocke & vj hennes		iij	iiij
Item in the Hale j Table j Cubborde A dishborde the stooles & all the woodden ware in the Halle		xx	
Item brasse & pewter		xx	
Item ij beddsteedes & furniture to them		[*?*]xvij	viij

Item j salting troughe ij Cofers j barrell & the painted Clothes		x	
Item sheetes & pillowbear[*e*]s		xx	
Item xij hempsheaves		viij	
Item his wareing apparrell		iiij	
[*Total*	*£7*	*19s*	*0d*]

[*No exhibition clause*]

Notes: Thomas Younge was buried at Langford on 27 November 1618. He made his will on 13 October 1618, describing himself as a labourer. He left his house and land to his wife Agnes for 20 years to bring up their children; then to his son John, paying £4 to son Thomas. He left all his goods to his wife, who was executrix. Sons John and Thomas were baptised in 1611 and 1615. The grant of probate to his widow Agnes on 20 April 1620 was recorded on the back of the sheet containing the will and inventory. Agnes Young married Ralph Rutlie in October 1620.

311 John Simpson of Blunham, labourer made 10 May 1620

Bedfordshire Archives, ABP/W1620–1621/219

An Inventory of the goods & Chattells of John Simpson of Blunham in the Countie of Bedford Laborer deceased seene and valued by John Wright, John Huckle, John Tompson and Thomas Cranfild all of Blunham upon the tenthe day of Maye in the yeare of our lord god 1620.

	£	s	d
Item in the Hall one table with a frame & a forme belonging to yt withe one old Casse		viij	
Item syxe stooles		ij	
Item in the Chamber one boarded bed sted one litle table and two Coffers		x	
Item one boalster one pillow one Coverlid & two paire of sheetes with painted Cloathes		xiiij	
Item two tubs, two Barrells, two sides for a bed, one kimnell & other small Implmentes		viij	
Item one peece of Lynnen Cloath with yarne & toe		xx	
Item for hemp sheaves, and a Mattocke		vij	
Item for brasse & pewter, one frying pan one gredIron dyshes & boales with a lynnen wheele and other small Implmentes		xiij	iiij
Item for wood and Compasse two sythes one shovell & a foarke		vj	viij
Item two bease	iij	vj	viij
Item three sheepe & a pig		xviij	
Item one flitche of baken		vj	viij
Item for Rye		v	
Item for mony due uppon bonds	xxj		
Item for his apparrell		xx	
The full somme ys	xxxj	v	iiij

the marke of John Wright, the marke of John Huckle, Thomas Cranfilde [*signature*], John Tompson his marke

[*Exhibited by Jane Simpson, the executrix, on 6 July 1620*]

Notes: John Simpson was buried at Blunham on 18 April 1620. His nuncupative will was dated 18 April 1620. He gave £6 each to his two sons at age 21 and the residue to his wife Jane, whom he appointed executrix and who was granted probate on 6 July 1620. The probate clause was signed by John Smythe who held the commission to grant probate (Beds Archives, ABP/W1620–1621/219).

312 Widow Seare of Caddington made 19 May 1620
Bedfordshire Archives, ABP4/192

An Imvitarie mad of the goods of the widdow Seare baring dat xix day of May 1620

	£	s	d
one table with the frame and a forme		iiij	
one coubard		viij	
the iron a bout the fier		iij	vj
the brase and puater		viij	
one iron pot and a fring pan		iiij	
one mattocke and a showel			viij
in the Chamber next the hoale tow bedsteds		ij	
one blanked tow coverleds		iij	
one boulster one pillow fand [*sic, and*] a flock bed		xij	
five pare of sheets tow taboll clothes		xv	
six table napkens and one pillobere		iij	
tow chestes		viij	
in the loft over the hoale tow bedsteds		x	
one fether bed and a bulster		xvj	
one flocke bed and a flock boulster		viij	
three coverleds and a blanket		x	
one chest a worne table a oyne stowle		x	
tow tubs tow barrells tow cemnles and the wodden ware		v	
the fire wodd about the house		iij	iiij
the sume of this parcell is	vj	xiij	vj

Thomas Skinner [*signature*], John Baydon [*signature*], Thomas Seare [*signature*] praisers
[*No exhibition clause*]

Notes: Widow Seare's burial has not been found.

313 Helen Drawsworth of Bedford St Mary, widow undated; after December 1620
Bedfordshire Archives, ABP/W/1620–21/1A
This list of goods has been written on one section of a folded sheet of paper. There are two short statements on other sections of the sheet. All look to be rough notes rather than finished documents.

Widdowe Drawsworth hir d[*ee*]de of gift

	£	s	d
A Cloake		17	
a chest		xij	
3 kettels		xvj	

	£	s	d
a possenet		ij	
a materis & ij kiverleds		xx	
j pare of harden sheets		4	
xij duckes		iij	
bandes ~~plaine~~ & ruffes			xij
[*Total*	*£3*	*15s*	*0d*]

[*No exhibition clause*]

Notes: Helen Drawsworth was buried at Bedford St Mary's on 5 December 1620. By deed drawn up on 19 March 1620, she gave all her goods after her death to Brudenell Martin of Buckden, Northants brickmaker, in return for which he was to care for her during her life. The church court took statements from several people. One deponent said that Helen Drawsworth had claimed that she did not get anything from Brudenell Martin and wished she had not executed the deed. Other deponents said that she was content with the arrangement. George and Millicent Wiggins asked for repayment from Brudenell Martin for the money they spent on the funeral of John Drawesworth, her husband, on 3 January 1620. One of the notes on this document states that Master Hawes of Bedford recorded a quarter of a year later that the Wigginses 'knew what she wanted'. Another note records that the Wiggins had taken on administration.

314 John Storer of Eaton Socon, shearman or husbandman made 11 March 1621

Lincolnshire Archives, INV/124/57

The Inventarie of the goods & chattells of John Storer late of Eaton Socon in the county of Bedd sheareman deceased made & prised the xj[th] daie of Marche Anno domini 1620 By George Smythe, Jonas Thody and Peter Richardson as followeth

	£	s	d
in the hall			
Imprimis a litle square table and a frame to it		iij	iiij
Item an old table bord & an old [*?*]penne		ij	
Item a tubb & 2 old chaires			xij
Item a pott a kettle a candelstick and xj smale peeces of pewter		viij	
Item a spitt, a paire of pothangers a paire of pothookes & a paire of tonges		ij	
in the loft over the hall			
Item an old borded bedd a bushell a kymnell & other trashe		vj	viij
in the Chamber			
Item a standing bedd with the bedd to it		xxiij	iiij
Item a trundle bedd		iij	
Item iij paire of sheetes		xiij	iiij
Item an old cupbord & chest		x	
Item 2 cofferes & other thinges		iiij	
Item his apparell		xx	

in the yard			
Item an old cart & wheeles & other thinges in the yard		xx	
Item vij bushelles of pease		xiij	iiij
Item 2 acres of beach land		x	
Summa totall	vij		

George Smithe his marke, Jonas Thody, Peter Richardson
[*Exhibited by the executrix at Bedford on 15 May 1621*]

Notes: John Storer was buried at Eaton Socon on 1 March 1621. He made his will on 20 February 1621, describing himself as a husbandman. He gave his wife Elizabeth and her heirs a cottage and pightle; and the house and land where he dwelt for life, then to his son John on condition that he paid £6 to the testator's son Luke. He left £6 to his son William. He appointed his wife residual legatee and executrix and she was granted probate by John Smyth at Bedford on 15 May 1621 (Lincs Archives, LCC WILLS/1621/ii/64).

315 John Francke of Wyboston, Eaton Socon, husbandman made 19 March 1621

Lincolnshire Archives, INV/124/56

A true Inventory of all the goods & Cattels moveable & unmoveable late John Franckes of Wyboston in the parishe of Eaton Socon in the County of Bedford Husbandman deceased, made the xix[th] day of March anno domini 1620 aprasyed by William Levat, Robert Bunde, Leonard Wright and Richard Wright

	£	s	d
Inprimus in the Hall one Cuberd a framde table & two Joyned Formes and foure fliches of bacon with other things there	iij	x	
Item in the buttery one barell one bottell a drinke stall and two shelves with other small things there		v	
Item in the best Chamber a Joyned bed with all that belong to it three Coffers one Cheare & other things there	v		
Item in an other chamber one bed & other things there		xiij	iiij
Item in an other roome a kimnell a barell & other things there		x	
Item in the milke house a cheze presse two tubs & other things there		xxv	
Item all the brasse and all the pewter		xl	
Item all the hempe all the sheets & the other small Linen		l	
Item a new peece of woolen Clothe		xxiiij	
Item all his Apparrill	iij	x	
Item ij horsses iiij Cowes & iij bullocks	xiiij	x	
Item three sheepe foure hogs & sixe pigs		l	
Item all the Grayne unsowne	ix		
Item all the wheat & rye Sowne	vj	x	
Item all the Tilthe unsowne	vj		
Item all the pease and oates sowne	vj		
Item all the Cheezes & all the pullin		xx	
Item a plough & plough geares & a grinston		v	
Item all the wood about the yarde		xiij	iiij

Item all the compas in the yarde		xiij	iiij
Item yf any things not thought on or unnamed		ij	
Summa Totalis	67	11	

signum p[rae]dic[*ti*] William Levat [*mark*], signum p[rae]dict[*i*] Leonard Wright [*mark*], Robert Bundye [*signature*], Richard Wright [*signature*]
[*Exhibited by the executrix at Bedford on 15 May 1621*]

Notes: John Francke was buried at Eaton Socon on 11 March 1621. He made his will on 6 March 1621, leaving his house and land to his son John at the age of 21, after the death of the testator's parents and £6 13s 4d at the age of 18. He gave his wife Anne his barn next to the street, his horses and cattle, all his grain and an acre of land to bring up his son. She was the residual legatee and executrix and was granted probate by John Smythe at Bedford on 15 May 1621 (Lincs Archives, LCC WILLS/1621/ii/65).

316 Gilyon Enterdwse of Kempston

made 8 April 1621

Lincolnshire Archives, INV/124/55

An Inventorie of all the goodes and Cattels that weare of Gilyon Enterdwse late of Kempston decessed made and preysed by James Spencer, Gregarie Paton and John Allen the Eight daye of April 1621 as followeth

	£	s	d
Inprimis one beddsteed preysed at		xij	
Item a penn at		viij	
Item one trunke and a Cofor at		v	
Item thrie stockes of bees at		xv	
Item one Ewe at		vij	
Item tow Chusshinges and other ymplementes at		iij	
Item all hir apperell at		xx	
monye dew by obligacons from Thomas Smyth and William Newold	xxxvj	xvj	
Summa totalis of all is	xl	vj	

[*Exhibited by the executrix at Bedford on 15 May 1621*]

Notes: Gilyon Enterdwse was buried at Kempston on 10 March 1621. She made her will on 28 December 1620, calling herself Jelion Barber alias Enterduse. She left £6 to her brother Thomas when it was received from the bond due from William Newold; her stock of bees and a penne to her sister-in-law Alice Enteduse and her ewe for a stock for her first child; small sums to nine people; and the residue to her mother Elizabeth, who was her executrix and to whom probate was granted by John Smith at Bedford on 15 May 1621 (Lincs Archives, LCC WILLS 1621/ii/20). She was mentioned in the will of her father Bartholomew Barber alias Enterdewce (Beds Archives, ABP/W1617/337), whose inventory is in BHRS, vol. 20, p. 101. Both Gilyon and her father consulted Dr Napier. Her consultation in 1620 recorded that she was 46 (Forman and Napier, case no. 50352).

317 John Rickett of Elstow, labourer made April 1621

Lincolnshire Archives, LCC ADMONS 1621/128

The top of the document is damaged and words in the heading are missing. Obvious words have been inserted in italics in square brackets.

Beddf 1621. An Inventory of the goodes and Chatteles of John R[*ic*]ket of Elstow Laborer decessed taken [...] Aprill and aprissed by us whose [*name*]s are under written

	£	s	d
Imprimis in the hall a tabell and a forme a old Cubard a Coffer and a Cradell and ij old Cheires at		viij	vj
Item one brase pot ij Cetteles a scillit a frying panne and a scomer at		vj	viij
Item three pewter dishes one pint pot two sausers a potinger one Candell stick and a aquavita botell		iij	vj
Item a payer of Cobiornes a payer of ~~bell~~ pot hangers a gridiorn a spit apayer of bellows [...] [*?*]linn wheell [*word deleted and illegible*] other od thinges to the value of		iij	iiij
Item in the Chamber one borden bedsteed one Chest ij Coffers at		v	x
Item one Cuverlet one blanket one matris one bolster and a pillow at		vj	viij
Item one payer of tayer hemp sheetes iij payer of harden ij payer of pillowbers ij napkines at		x	
Item in the yard on hovell and Compas at		vj	viij
Item a Cow and vij sheep at		xl	
Item a Cuk and a henn at			xij
Item his warringe a parell at		vj	viij
Item one old hirdell gat and some small thinges for gotten to the valeue of			viij
Sum is	iiij	xix	vj

John Whitbreade, Will Jaques, William Waddopp

[*Exhibited by Margaret Rickett, relict, at Bedford on 15 May 1621*]

Notes: John Rickett was buried at Elstow on 11 April 1621 as John Rickard. Administration was granted to his widow Margaret by John Smith on 18 May 1621 and a bond was taken (Lincs Archives, Act Book A/x/54 and LCC ADMONS 1621/128).

318 Robert Austin of Tilsworth, husbandman undated; 1621

Lincolnshire Archives, INV/124/63

The inventary Indented of all and singular goodes Cattells and chattells and howsehold-stuffe of Robert Austin of Tylsworth in the Com' of Bedfs husband-man deceased taken and praysed by Richard Theede, Thomas Crawley, Richard Hawkins, John Gerney: as followeth

	£	s	d
In primis his apparell		xxx	
Item one boorded-bead, one Coverlett one blankett one boulster two pillowes and one matize		xx	
Item another boorded-bead, one boulster two blankets and matize		xvj	

	£	s	d
Item five payre of sheetes and one table clothe		xx	
Item five pillowe-beeres		x	
Item three yeards of woolen-clothe		vj	
Item five Coffers and all other thinges in the chamber		xx	
Item one Coobboord and one chayre		xx	
Item one table and one ~~ioy~~ yoiunte stoole and Certayne other thinges in the hall		v	
Item brasse and pewter		xxx	
Item one barrell, bowles, tubes and other wooden vessells		vj	viij
Item one spitt, handyron one frieinge panne and all other old yron		iij	iiij
Item certayne boordes & sythes and linen wheele and other thinges in the lofte		*[value missing]*	
Item one fleets of bacon and one store pigge		vj	viij
Item Heay in the barren		xxxiiij	
Item the woode and the ladder		xiij	iiij
Item one kowe and two bullockes		lij	viij
Item hens and bees		x	
Item two acres of grayne in the field		l	
Item in money owinge	lxx		
Summa Totalis	88	3	viij

[*Exhibited by the executrix at Dunstable on 12 May 1621*]

Notes: Robert Austin was buried at Tilsworth on 20 April 1621. He made his will on 16 April 1621, giving his house and land and £20 to his elder son Thomas and £40 to his son John, when they reached the age of 21. The residue was left to his wife Elizabeth, who was appointed executrix. Probate was granted by John Smith to the executrix at Dunstable on 12 May 1621 (Beds Archives, ABP/W1621/171 and Lincs Archives, LCC WILLS/1621/ii/63).

319 Thomas Roffe of Shelton, husbandman — made 18 April 1621

Lincolnshire Archives, INV/124/58

A true Inventary of all the goods & Chattles of Thomas Roffe late of Shelton in the County of Bedff husbandman decessed valued and priced the xviij[th] day of Aprill 1621 by Richard Laye, Thomas Morris & Richard Mee of the same towne & County as hereafter followeth

	£	s	d
In the hall			
Imprimis 2 cupbords 2 tables 3 formes ij chayres, a bench bord a settle with other implementes	iij		
In the house next the hall			
Twoo coffers 4 wheeles, j cherne j cheesepresse with other ymplementes		x	

In the little milk house

4 gallons of liquor 6 shelves with other implementes		viij	

In the little parlor

Twoo borden bedstedds 2 mattrices & the rest of the bedding & j Coffer, paynted Clothes with other implementes		xlvj	viij

In the loft over the parlor

One bord bedsted with the bedding & the paynted Clothes		iij	iiij
2 bolting tunnes		ij	
Item j old coffer, j old trunck j wheele with other implementes		vj	[?]viij

In the parlor next the kytchin

two trusse bedds, iiij fetherbedds j mattrice, ij bolsters 12 pillowes ij blanketts, iij coverings ij quiltes with the Curtaynes	x		
Item one cupbord, j presse j little table 4 coffers j chayre, j little box with other implementes		xxx	
Item viij payre of flexen sheetes, xij payre of harden sheetes j dozen of napkyns, iij flexen table Clothes, iij hollan pillow beares, iij flexen pillow beares vj harden pillow beares, ij long towells, iij table clothes	ix	vj	viij
Item his wearing apparell	v		

In the kytchin

Imprimis one table, ij chayres, one settle, iij formes, ij stooles, one trough, ij shelves, j salt barrell j glasse case		xiij	iiij
Item j brasse pan, vj kettles, ij brasse potts, ij spitts with hookes hangers, cobyrons & other yron worke for the fyre with other ymplementes there	iiij	iij	4
Item vij bacon flitches	iij	vj	viij
Item dishes spoones trenchers pailes & other implementes		iij	iiij

In the buttery

vj little barrells v kymnells v tubbes, ij beare stalles, wooll yarne bottles & other trash		xxxiij	4

In the milke house

One long kymnell, iiij shelves ij formes, j cherne, xij boles iij creame potts with other implements		xx	

In the loft over the milkhouse			
One Cheese rack, j warpe of fysh		iij	iiij
Also in the milkhouse			
xxx^{tie} peyces of pewter		xl	
In the stable			
Eight horses	xxxv		
In the garden			
vj stockes of bees		xl	
In the yard			
Imprimis ij draggs, ij sythes		viij	
Item axes, hatchetts & j barre of yron		vj	viij
bease & bullockes – xxiiij	xl		
iij hovells, ij moveable howses	viij	x	
Item v rackes, iiij plowes, with cart geares & plow geares, ~~h~~ harrowes, role, & other necessary things for husbandry	xj		
Item xvj hoggs & piggs	v		
In the barne			
barly thresht & unthresht	xiiij		
In the wheate barne			
iij quarter of wheat		xlvj	viij
Item forkes flayles skuttles sieves skeene fanne & sackes		xxj	4
Item v shiprackes v troughes		x	
Item ladders		x	
Att Undyes house			
Imprimis j trust bed, j trundle bed & j Chest		xxx	
malt xx^{tie} quarter	xiij	vj	8
iij coffers, j table		v	
wood, tymber, & plow tymber att home, att Kings house & att Undyes with 12 hurdles	xx		
Item iij fatts, j garner, j maltmill j hayre cloth, & j brasse panne	iij	x	
In the Feild			
Imprimis lxiiij sheepe	xxiiij ~~xliiij~~		
Item wheat barly oates & pease fower score Acars	lxxx		
Item Cockes henns capons & Chickens		xv	
Item the lease of his house	C		
Item the lease of one close att Keyston	xviij		
Item all other things not valued & pryced		iij	iiij
Debtes due to him att the tyme of his death	xv		

	£	s	d
Item in ready money	v		
Sum total	447	19	7
[*Corrected total*	*£447*	*19s*	*4d*]

[*No exhibition clause*]

Notes: Thomas Roffe was buried at Shelton on 18 April 1621. He made his will on 15 April 1621. He gave a cottage and six acres, animals and eighteen sheep to his son Peter; £60, £40 and £50 to two sons and a daughter; ewes and lambs to grandchildren. He gave Undyes cottage with the profits to his wife Mary for life, stipulating that she should live with son Robert until he married, then she should move to Undyes cottage. He also gave her furniture and £10. His son Robert was residual legatee and executor, and was granted probate by John Smith on 15 May 1621 (Lincs Archives, LCC WILLS/1621/ii/93).

320 Robert Feild of Studham, yeoman made 4 May 1621

Lincolnshire Archives, INV/124/61

A true Inventory of all the goodes Cattells & Chattelles of Robert Feild late of Studham in the Countie of Hertford yeoman deceased taken & prized on Friday the 4th day of May 1621 by John Sibley, Anthonie Belfeild, John Payce, Richard Beamond, William Paice & Edward Slow

	£	s	d
Inprimis all his apparrell & monnie in his purse	iiij		
Item in the hall a long table & frame with 8 ioyd stooles with a settle under the window & a Cupbord	ij	x	
Item 4 Chayres & ix Cushions		xv	
Item in the Chamber over the hall one standing bedsted with ij fetherbedes & ij boulsters j blankett iiij pillowes & ij Coverlydes	viij		
Item ix silver spoones & two silvered Cuppes	iiij	x	
Item one Large presse		xv	
Item a round table v Chestes iij stooles & a Chayre	j	x	
Item all the lynnen as sheetes table Clothes napkins & other small parcelles	vj	xiij	iiij
Item in the Chamber over the kitchin ij standing bedstedes	ij		
Item j trundle bed ij fetherbedes a flockbed iij boulsters vij pillowes j Coverlyd v blankettes	v		
Item ij Chestes & a trunke		xiij	iiij
Item in the next Chamber ij playne bedes with the beding belonging unto them, a parcell of woll & som other odd ymplementes there	vj		
Item in ij garrett loftes a parcell of hemp, sithes peasehookes & other odd ymplementes there	j		
Item in the kitchin a table & frame with a fourme an ould Cupbord dresser bordes & shelves	j		
Item the iij best brasse pottes	iij		
Item all the other brasse	iij		
Item all the pewter	iij	x	
Item all the panns & spittes with all the Chimnie yrons about the howse	j		

	£	s	d
Item in the butterie all the barrelles & other odd lumbar there	j		
Item in an other ould roome the salting troughes & other odd lumbar there	j		
Item all the bacon in the ruffe	iij		
Item all the Wheate Oates pease & other grayne in the barnes	xxv		
Item all the horses & harnes	xxx		
Item all the kine	xij		
Item all the swine	v		
Item all the sheepe	xx		
Item all the poultrie	j		
Item all the Cartes & ploughes wheeles & other ymplementes belonging unto them	xv		
Item all the grayne groweing on the ground	Cx		
Item all the fire wood & Compost in the yarde	iiij		
Item a mault quearne & other odd ymplementes	j		
Item the Lease of the farme	L		
Summa totalis	332	16	8

[*Exhibited by Joanna Feild, relict and executrix, at Dunstable on 12 May 1621*]

Notes: Robert Feild was buried at Studham on 1 May 1621. He made his will on 6 April 1621, giving £20, household goods and a silver spoon to each of his four daughters, the money payable when they reached the age of 20. Daughter Martha was also given a silver mazer. His son Robert was given the other silver mazer, furniture in the hall and the large press in the chamber over the hall. After other bequests, he gave his wife Joan the residue of his moveable goods. The remaining years of the lease of his farm were given equally to Joan and his son Robert who were appointed joint executors. Probate was granted to the widow Joan by John Smith at Dunstable on 12 May 1621, power reserved to Robert Feild, a minor (Beds Archives, ABP/W1621/170). Robert Feild consulted Dr Napier three weeks before his death, who recorded that he was 60 and 'canot make water, very little, much payne about his chest' (Forman and Napier, case no. 52256).

321 Nicholas Gates of Dunstable, weaver — made 7 May 1621

Lincolnshire Archives, LCC ADMONS 1621/120

The seaventh day of Maij 1621
An Inventorey of all the goodes & Chattelles of Nicholas Gates late of Dunstable in the county of Bedd weaver who dyed intestate the xx[th] daie of Januarij laste or there aboutes and prised by William Medcalf of Dunstable aforsayd, Richard Heath & William Marshe of the same towne gen [*gentleman*] the day and yeere above said

	£	s	d
Inprimis his wearinge Apparell		xiij	iiij
Item in the hall a long table 2 old cubbordes certeine old painted clothes a pare of cobierons & other small thinges of little value		xx	

	£	s	d
Item in another rome One loome & the furniture		xxvj	viij
Item all the brasse & pewter		xl	
Item the Cowprey ware		v	
Item in a little chamber an old bed sted an old Fetherbed an old coverlet & other thinges belonging to itt & other small parcelles		xxvj	viij
In another chamber 2 bedstedes 2 coverlettes j fetherbedd one woollbeed a round table i Carpett 4 formes & other furniture belonging to the said beddes, one of the foure bedstedes beinge a truckle bedd		xlvj	viij
In another chamber one truckle bedd One wooll bedd & blanckett one old table and an old forme		vj	viij
Item in another chamber 4 old chestes		vij	
Item x paire of sheetes with the reste of the lynnen	iij		
Item 5 shepe and one lambe		xxxiij	iiij
Item a lynnen & a woollen wheele		iij	iiij
Item all the wood in the yard		xlvj	viij
Item ~~one~~ 2 quarte pottes 3 stone Jugges & 3 black pottes & 2 little earthen dishes		iij	
Item one Ieoren dripping pan & 2 little spittes		ij	
Summa	xvij	0	iiij

signum dicti William Medcalfe, Richard Heath [*signature*] et mei Willimi Marshe [*signature*]
[*Exhibited at Dunstable on 12 May 1621*]

Notes: Nicholas Gates was buried at Dunstable on 17 January 1621. Administration was granted to his widow Loverie at Dunstable by John Farmer (probably Farmerie) on 12 May 1621 and a bond was taken, Simon Pickles being notary public (Lincs Archives, Act Book A/x/53 and LCC ADMONS 1621/120). William Marsh, one of the appraisers, was the schoolmaster (CCEd).

322 William Whootton of Harrold, shepherd — made on 14 May 1621

Lincolnshire Archives, INV/124/59
Slight damage down the right side with loss of one figure.

Harrold Com Bedd maie the 14 1621. An Inventorye of the goodes Cattels & Chattels of William Whootton shepehearde lately decessed taken by us Roberte Paull Clerke, Thomas Islapp weaver, George Reade husb, and John Brewer husb the day & yeare aforesayde

	£	s	d
In the haull			
Imprimis in the haull an olde short framed table, an olde Joyned Cubbard, an olde Pen with other sorrye olde trash & lombar in the sayde haull		xx	

In the Chamber

	£	s	d
Item in the Chamber, One olde bedsteede, vj olde Coffers litle & greate, one olde Forme, iij barrels, a woole bedd with painted Clothes		xx	
Item viij payer of sorrye olde sheetes with all other Linnen		xlvj	viij
Item ij° Coverlettes one of a better sorte & thother a sorrye olde one, iij blancketes, one better & thother twoe verye sorrye ones, ij° olde bowlsters, iij sorrye Pillowes with other sorrye thinges		xxvj	viij
Item iij peeces of Coarse woollen Cloth for blancketing		xxvj	viij
Item his weareing Apparrell woollen & Linnen		xxvj	viij
In the little Chamber			
Item in thother Chamber ij° sorrye rotten bedsteedes, a Croe of yron, a mattock with other sorrye rotten trashe		xiij	iiij
Item brasse & pewter with an olde fryeing pan a spitt and a payer of Andyrons		xxx	
In the milke howse			
Item in the milke howse, a salting trooffe, tubbes, and all other sorrye treene ware		xiij	iiij
Item a hovell with woode on it, & all other woode		xxvj	[*?viij*]
Item a Lyve store hogg with twoe flitches of bacon		xxiij	iiij
Item v beasse & bullockes	x		
Item vj sheepe		xl	
Item a hen & a Cock			xij
Item all other thinges unnamed & unpryzed		ij	
Summa	xxv	xvj	iiij

[*Exhibited by the executrix at Bedford on 15 May 1621*]

Notes: William Whootton was buried at Harrold on 11 May 1621. Robert Paull, the appraiser, was vicar of Harrold 1585–1625 (CCEd). William Whootton made his will on 10 May 1621, giving small sums of money to sisters and their children and distributing many of the items listed in his inventory to nearly a dozen people, including the hovell and a third of the wood to a brother-in-law and the pied bullock to William Covington, providing that the testator's wife was to have the milk and calf until Michaelmas. There was no mention of the residue or maintenance for his (unnamed) wife, who was nevertheless appointed his executrix and was granted probate by John Smith at Bedford on 15 May 1621 (Lincs Archives, LCC WILLS/1621/ii/21).

323 Silvester Taverner of Marston Moretaine, gentleman

undated; made between March and May 1621

Lincolnshire Archives, INV/124/62

The handwriting is cramped and difficult to read.

A perfect inventorie of all the goodes and chatles of Master Silvester Tavener of Marston Morten in the County of Bedford taken by us whose names are underwritten

	£	s	d
Imprimis Nicholas Lockey of Marson Morten oweth him the said Master Tavenor			

[*?*]~~vjli~~ [*illeg.*] ~~wherof ther is paid xxxs Sum remayneth~~ [*illeg.*][68]	ij	xvj	viij
Item vj beaste	xvj		
Item on mare on colt and on filli	v		
Item nine silver spoones		xlv	
Item iiij hogges		xl	
Item [*?*]iij fetherbedds and iiij pillows & iij boulser	iij		
Item nine payre of sheetes		xxx	
Item ij payre of pillowbeers		iiij	
Item v blanckettes		x	
Item iij coverliddes		xx	
Item vj cushins		xx	
Item iiij standing beddes	iij	vj	viij
Item all the wood lying in [*?*]yard & [*?*]grond	ix		
Item pewter		xx	
Item spittes, pothuokes dripping pan and Cobirons tonges [*?*]fireshule		vj	viij
Item brasse, pottes, pans, [*?*]bottles	iij		
Item Tables stooles and Chayres		xxx	
Item Tubbs barrelles and Cimnils		x	
Item his Apparrell	iij		
Summa totalis	lvj	xix	

Samuel [*?*]Faye his mark, Thomas Shepherd his mark, Nicholas Locklye his mark, John Wodell his mark

[*Exhibited by the executor at Hitchin on 14 May 1621*]

Notes: Silvester Taverner was buried at Willian in Hertfordshire on 18 March 1621. He made his will on 6 January 1621, describing himself as a gentleman and requesting burial in the parish church. He left his copyhold in Lidlington to his daughter Elizabeth Fage as long as her husband Thomas paid £80 to their daughter Elizabeth when she was 21. He left his house and lands in Marston Moretaine to Elizabeth and Thomas Fage on condition that he paid £60 to the testator's daughter Lucy; £40 to testator's daughter Anne Bigg; and £30 to testator's grandson Thomas Taverner (son of John Taverner, deceased). These sums were to be paid in the south porch of Willian church at specified times. He left items of furniture and household goods to his granddaughter Elizabeth Fage, daughters Lucy and Anne Bigg and other small bequests. He appointed his son-in-law Thomas Fage executor. Probate was granted before Thomas Willson at Hitchin on 14 May 1621 (original will, Beds Archives, ABP/W1620–1621/159; copy, Lincs Archives, LCC WILLS 1621/ii/198). Silvester Taverner and members of his family consulted Dr Napier in the early 1600s but not in the months before his death (Forman and Napier, *Casebooks*).

324 William Edwardes of Nether Dean, Dean, tailor undated; made between January and May 1622

Lincolnshire Archives, INV/126/168

A true inventory of all the goodes and Chattelles of William Edwardes of Neither Deane [*in*] the countie of Bedford whoe departed this liffe in the yeare of our Lord [*blank*] taken by us

68 This line has been heavily deleted and is barely legible.

John Bisby, William Eston, Robert Kinge and Francis Ostler inhabetantes of the same towne in maner and forme as followeth

	£	s	d
Innprimis his wares and his debte booke	xlv		
Item his waring aparell	vj		
Item tenn paier of sheetes	iiij	x	
Item ten eles of flaxen clothe		xiij	iiij
Item ten pillowbeeres sixten napkins tow towelles	ij		
Item one bearing cloth		x	
Item the best bede with all the bedding and furnituer	viij		
Item one other Bede with the furnituer one pound ten shillinges	[*1*	*10*	*0*]
Item serten provision in a chese chamber	ij	vj	viij
Item three bareles and serten other Implimentes in the buttry		x	
Item brasse & pewter	ij	x	
Item Tubes and other woodden ware	j	x	
Item formes cheares and stooles in the haule	j		
Item his bookes	j	v	
Item spitt anneyrones tonges fier shoule and pothangins		x	
Item a chest and a coffer and three boxes & three cusshenes and serten boardes		xx	
Item tow bease and a bullacke	v		
Item twelfe sheepe	iij		
Item one hogge	j		
Item one aker of tilth and one aker of pease land with seed to sow them with	j	xiij	iiij
Item barley	j	x	
Item woode	ij		
Item chesse and bacon	j	vj	
[*Total*	*£94*	*4s*	*4d*]

Will Eston [*signature*], Francis Ostler [*signature*], John Bisbey [*signature*], Robert Kinge [*signature*]
[*Exhibited by the executrix at Bedford on 23 May 1622*]

Notes: William Edwardes was buried at Dean on 26 January 1622. In his will, which was undated, he described himself as a tailor. He left £6 13s 8d to each of his three children at the age of 21. He left 40s to his mother as long as she left her goods that were in his house to his children; otherwise, 10s. His wife Bridget was residual legatee and executrix. She was granted probate by John Farmerie at Bedford on 23 May 1622 (Lincs Archives, LCC WILLS1622/i/193). She married Richard Thurnebacke in Dean on 11 April 1630.

325 Richard Hall of Pertenhall, labourer — made 22 March 1622

Lincolnshire Archives, INV/126/166

The Inventorye of Richard Hall of Partensell taken the 22 of March in the yeare of our lord ~~1622~~ 1621

	£	s	d
Item all his aparell		22	

In the hall			
on cuborde with six peeces of pewlter on penn on table with cheares cradle and other smale thinges		30	
Linen			
Three flexen sheetes three harden sheetes and other linen		44	
in the chamber			
on bedd on matryce tow bowlsteres on coverled on blankett one chest towe coferes with othere smale thinges		33	4
in the laught			
on bedd pease and corne a kimnell on spininge whelle with some other thinges		23	4
in the milke house			
five smale brasse kettles tow tubes on barrell a frynge panne with other thinges		33	4
in the barne pease and haye		40	8
in the yarde			
Woode on cowe on sowe tow stores	3	6	8
Sheepe			
sixe couples forwe shsharhoges on ewe fowre lamhoges	5		
Pullen			
Teenn hennes three capones on coke		10	
In money		40	
Summa totalis	22	9	4
[*Corrected total*	*£22*	*3s*	*4d*]

Oliver Freeman, William Mashall
[*No exhibition clause*]

Notes: Richard Hall was buried at Pertenhall on 8 March 1622. He made his will on 7 March 1622, describing himself as a labourer. He left his house and tenement to his son Richard when he reached the age of 21, or to his wife Elizabeth for life if the son died before reaching 21. His wife was residual legatee and executrix and was granted probate by John Farmerie at Bedford on 23 May 1622 (Lincs Archives, LCC WILLS/1622/i/194).

326 William Peirce of Toddington, yeoman made 30 March 1622
Lincolnshire Archives, INV/126/155

The Inventorie indented of all the goodes and Chattles of William Peirce late of Todington in the Countye of Bed yeoman deceased made and proved the xxx[th] daie of Marche in Anno Domini 1622 by those whose names are hereunder written

	£	s	d
In primis in Redie monye	vj	j	vj
Item his apparrell		xl	
Item xij stooles, iiij Chaires, iij Tables & frames to them Two little tables, one Cupbord, ij Court Cupbordes ij Benchbordes			

One pott shelfe, Two standing beds, one trundle Bed, one forme three chestes, one Cofer, two Boxes & a paire of playeing tables	x		
Item three Feither bedes iiij Boulsters iiij pillowes, iij Coverlides, iij Blankettes, ij Matrisses, & ij paire of Curtaines	xij		
Item seaven paire of sheetes, vj paire of pillow beeres, one dossen of napkins, ij Cupbord clothes, j long towell & vj Cushins	vj		
Item The Brasse pewter and pottes	v		
Item one treble violen & certeine old bookes		xx	
Item the andiornes, spittes, pott hookes, driping pans, pott hangers tongues, Fyer showelles, & other implementes of iorne		xxx	
Item the Two Boles cheese fattes pales & other woden stuffe		xx	
Item the wood & Timber	x		
Item Two Leases	Lx		
Item debtes dew upon spetialties	Cviij		
Sum total is	ijCxxij	xj	vj
The debtes oweing by the Testator are	xv	vj	viij

Cornelius White [*signature*], Christo: England [*signature*], Thomas Dearman [*signature*]
[*Exhibited by the executrix at Dunstable on 22 May 1622*]

Notes: William Peirce was buried at Toddington on 25 March 1622. He made his will on 22 March 1622. He gave £10 each to his daughters Agnes and Elizabeth and sons Robert and Francis; and £6 13s 4d to his son Charles remitting the money Charles owed to the testator. He appointed his wife Agnes as residual legatee and executrix and she was granted probate by John Farmerie at Dunstable on 22 May 1622 (Lincs Archives, LCC WILLS 1622/i/192).

327 Richard Wood, vicar of Flitton

made 26 April 1622

Lincolnshire Archives, INV/126/149

An Inventory of all the moveable goodes of Richard Wood viccar of Flitton deceased as they were pryced by William Lake, William Goodwin & Roger Chapman April 26 1622

	£	s	d
Imprimis his bookes & wearinge Apparel	xiij	vj	viij
Item 4 Cowes & twoe heckfers	xx		
Item 3 sheepe		xxvj	viij
Item 3 hogges		xxx	
Item Geese & powltrye		xvj	
Item Grayne on the grownde	vj	~~x~~	
Item Hempe on the grownde		x	
Summa totalis	xliij	ix	iiij
In the Parloure			
Inprimis one Cupboarde		xx	
Item one standinge bedsteede		l	
Item 2 chestes		xxx	
Item one livery Cupboarde		x	
Item one litle table		v	
Item one truncke		v	
Item 2 cheres & one box		xij	
Item one Trundle bed		iij	iiij
Item one fetherbed & a mattres		l	

Item 2 Coveringes		xxx	
Item 2 bowlsters & 3 pillowes & 4 Cartaynes		xx	
Item 3 other Coveringes		xl	
Item 7 blanketes		xlvj	viij
Item some newe linnen Clothe		viij	
Item 36 payre of sheetes & one od one	xiiij	x	
Item 8 tableclothes		xxiiij	
Item 6 payre of pillowbeeres		xxiiij	
Item 4 dosen & 5 napkins		l	
Item 8 towels		xiij	iiij
Item a warminge pan & other lumber		v	
Summa tot.	xxxvj	xvj	iiij

In the Hall

Inprimis a table & a frame		xx	
Item one Cupboarde		xx	
Item one livery Cupboarde		vij	
Item one litle table		iij	iiij
Item 15 ioyned stooles		xxij	
Item 2 cheyres		v	
Item one Carpette		viij	
Item one potshelfe		iij	iiij
Item waynscote & bencheboard		xx	
Item 2 greate Iron rackes & a bare of Iron		xiij	iiij
Item 2 Cobirons a fyreshovel & payre of toungs		iiij	
Item some paynted clothes & a Curtayne		v	
Item a payre of bellowes potes & glasses		ij	iij
Item Cushions & other lumber		v	
Summa tot.	vj	xviij	iij

In the lofte over the hall

Inprimis one standinge bedsteede		v	
Item another bedsteede		iij	iiij
Item 3 chestes		xxx	
Item 4 cheyres		ix	
Item 2 mattresses 2 blanketes		xx	
Item 2 bowlsters		xvj	
Item 2 shelves & other lumber			xij
Summa tot.	iiij	iiij	iiij

In the lofte over the parloure

Item 4 cheeses		xxx	
Item 2 Cofers		iiij	
Item one Cradle		iij	iiij
Item cheeseracke shelves & other lumber		xx	
Summa tot.	ij	xvij	iiij

In the roome at the stayres heade

Inprimis certayne flitches of bacon		xxx	
Item basketes & other lumber		xx	
Summa tot.	ij	x	

In the lofte over the buttrye

Inprimis one bedsteede		iij	iiij
Item a strawbed		iij	iiij
Item 20 skaynes of yarne & newe clothe		xxij	

Item a sacke & pannel		iij	iiij
Item 6 wheeles		xij	
Item a hotchel 2 payre of skales		iij	iiij
Item one litle Cofer a shelfe and other lumber		ij	
Summa tot.	ij	ix	iiij

In the lower Chamber

Inprimis one standinge bedsteede		xxx	
Item a Courte Cubboarde		x	
Item a litle table & a box		viij	
Item one chest		x	
Item a fether bed & mattresse	iij		
Item one bowlster & 2 pillowes		xv	
Item a blanket 2 Curtaynes & other lumber		iij	iiij
Summa tot.	vj	xvj	iiij

In the Buttery

Inprimis in Pewter		xxxv	
Item in brasse		xxvj	viij
Item one saltingtroughe with a Cover		vj	viij
Item 5 barrels 2 kimnels & a churme		xvj	
Item one powldringe tubbe & 7 chesfates		iiij	vj
Item one frying pan shelves & other lumber		x	
Summa tot.	iiij	xviij	x

In the kitchen

Inprimis one potte twoe kettles & 4 spites		xxj	
Item one payre of Andirons & a racke		ij	
Item 2 tubbes 3 payles & one bowle		vij	
Item 3 formes a dresser board & other lumber		xij	
Summa tot.		xxxxij	

In the milhowse[69]

Inprimis one malt querne		x	
Item a boltinge hutche & a chesepresse		iiij	
Item a knedinge troughe & other lumber		iij	
Summa tot.		xvij	

In the yarde

Inprimis wood & tymber	iij		
Item one bucket a cheyne & a rope		iij	
Item boardes	v		
Item a litle strawe & other lumber			xij
Summa tot.	viij	iiij	

In an other yarde

Inprimis some tymber & troughes		xij	
Item dounge Cowrackes & other lumber		xij	
Summa tot.		xxiiij	

In the barne

Imprimis haye	iij	x	
Item one Calfe		x	
Item one draught rake		iij	
Item hurdles wood & lumber		xij	
Summa tot.	iiij	xv	

69 Probably milk house.

In the new howse

Inprimis in the parloure one bedsteede			xl	
Item in the lofte over the parlour a bedsteede			x	
Item in the halle 2 tables a trevet a skuttle & chafinge dishe			xiij	iiij
Item in the buttrye 2 tubbes a kettle a panne a bowle a drinkestall & other lumber			xlv	
Item in the kitchen 2 pothangers one payle 2 shelves & other lumber			v	
Item in the garner wheate malt barly & rye		viij		
Item in another old howse some wood & lumber			v	
Item in the barne hempe ladders bushel fanne bucket & other lumber			xxxvj	
Item in other out howses hay wood & other lumber			xxx	
Item in the yarde one hovel loaden with woode dounge & lumber		iiij	vj	
	Summa	xxj	x	iiij
Item in ready monye		viij		
Item bondes & debtes		xxx		
Item 5 silver spoones			xxx	
	Summa	xxxix	x	
	Summa totalis	189	j	v
	[*Corrected total*	*£189*	*2s*	*5d*]

[*Exhibited by the executrix at Dunstable on 22 May 1622*]

Notes: Richard Wood was buried at Flitton on 25 April 1622. He was instituted vicar of Flitton on 9 February 1600 and became a licensed preacher in 1612 (CCEd). The patron of Flitton was the Dean and Chapter of Christ Church, Oxford, and Wood is likely to have been an Oxford graduate, although it is difficult to identify him conclusively in *Alumni Oxon*. He made his will on 21 November 1621, requesting burial in the chancel of Flitton church. He made provision for his seven children born between 1602 and 1614 leaving them goods, land or money, including the cupboard or press containing his books to his daughter Marie. His house and close at Warde hedges (a hamlet in the parish) was left to his eldest children (Beds Archives, L5/462). He gave the residue to his wife Katherine and appointed her executrix, desiring her to have a care for the children's education. Probate was granted to his wife at Dunstable on 22 May 1622 (Lincs Archives, LCC WILLS/1622/i/183). The 1607 glebe terrier described the vicarage as of five bays, built with timber and covered with tiles (Beds Archives, ABE1). Two bays had chambers over and were boarded. There were seven rooms: a hall, three chambers, a kitchen and a buttery. There was also an old, thatched, timber barn of three small bays. However, the Bedfordshire Archives Community History page for Flitton vicarage records that the vicarage was not much inhabited by the vicar in the early seventeenth century and the house described in this inventory may not be the vicarage. The new house at the end of the inventory has not been identified.

328 Samuel Fulke of Barton in the Clay, rector made 30 April 1622

Lincolnshire Archives, INV/126/169

A true Inventorie of all the goodes and Chatteles of Samewell Fulke Parson of Barton made the last day of Apriell 1622 as they were praysed by John Crouch, John Dearmer and Frances Carter

	£	s	d
Inprimis			
Item in the hall one longe table with a frame 3 litle tables 2 formes		xx	
Item in the parler 2 tables 4 Chares 11 stoules and 6 Cushins	iij		
Item one Courte Cubert 3 bench bordes Certayne Cutchins & other things	ij		
Item in the iner parler 2 Chares 2 fourmes 2 litele tables 2 stoules one box and other thinges		xx	
Item in the litle Chamber one bedsted 2 litle Chares one table one stoule		xx	
Item in the loaft over the iner parler one bedsted one trundle bed 2 Chestes	ij		
Item in the loaft over the parler 3 standing bedes 5 Chestes	xj		
one Chare one deske 2 Cobirons apaier of tonges and fiershovell		xiij	4
Item 4 feather bedes 9 matterises 10 blankets 8 Coverlides	xxj		
Item one Rugg one quilt 10 Curtains with other thinges	iij	vj	viij
Item in the loaft over the hall one standing bed one Chest & other things		xiij	4
Item in the sadlehouse one stonne morter & a feaue bordes		v	
Item in the seller 6 barrilles 2 shelves 3 drinkstales		xiij	4
Item one Carpitt and 3 Cushins		xx	
Item silver and guilte plate	xxx		
Item 2 gounds and all his wearing appariell	xiij	vj	viij
Item in the kitchin all the brase and peuter	vij	x	
Item in the butterie one Cass one safe one table 4 spites tow driping panes 2 frieng pans with other implements		xl	
Item in another house one Cass 2 tables one fourme & other things		xx	
Item in the milkehouse one table 2 Churmes a boulting hutch & other things	ij		
Item in the 2 loaftes 3 tables 4 fourmes with benches & other things	ij		
Item in the bruhouse one salting trofe 3 fates 2 boules & other things		xx	
Item in the neather kitchin one furnise one mault quarne [*valued with the next line*]			
Item one Chesepres 2 iron rackes a pele & other implements		xxxiij	4
Item fierwood in the maulthouse and in the yard		xxxiij	4
Item 3 laders and halfe a loade of haye		xv	
Item 2 bease and 4 quarters of maulte and other things	ix		
Item in the wagin house 2 wagins		xx	
Item 12 paier of shetes one od sheete 13 pillowbears 7 tablecloathes	vj		
Item 2 douzen of Napkins 4 toweles		xx	
Item 6 boulsters and 6 pillowes	4		
Item in the studdie 2 Chares 2 deskes and all The booukes and other thinges	lxxx		
Item 18 bushelles and a halfe of wheate	4	x	
Item Rent and Readie mony in the house	xxvij		
Item one flitch of Bakon		x	
[*Total*	*£244*	*10s*	*0d*]

[*Exhibited by Maria and Phebe, the two executrices, at Hitchin on 27 May 1622*]

Notes: Samuel Fulke was buried at Barton on 29 April 1622. He was rector of Barton for 52 years, from 1570 until his death (CCEd). Although listed as MA he is not in Venn ACAD nor *Alumni Oxon.* His wife Susan, who consulted Dr Napier in 1618, when her age of 62 was noted, was buried there in 1618 (Forman and Napier, case no. 47447). Samuel Fulke made his will on 30 July 1621 leaving money, silverware and some household goods to his daughters, Mary, Phebe and Susan who were appointed joint executrices. He left money to two grandchildren and appointed his two sons-in-law as overseers. Mary and Phebe were granted probate at Hitchin on 22 May 1622 (Lincs Archives, LCC WILLS 1622 i, 180).

The 1607 glebe terrier (Beds Archives, ABE1) described the parsonage house as timber-built, covered with tiles and having four bays. It had two floors and was 'lofted' and glazed. It had 30 rooms of varying sizes, some of which may have been outbuildings: a hall, two parlours (boarded and ceiled), two butteries (boarded and ceiled), a cellar, a study, a milkhouse (boarded and ceiled), two kitchens (one boarded and ceiled), a store house and a furnace house (ceiled), two strawhouses, a duck house (unceiled), a brewhouse (unceiled), a larder house, a pantry and a boulting house (ceiled); and over these rooms were five bed chambers (ceiled), a drying chamber (not ceiled), a closet (ceiled), a garret, a corn loft, an apple loft (not ceiled), and a house of office (not ceiled). There were also cow houses and hogs houses. The survey was made by Samuel Fulke and the churchwardens. They reported that the house was in good repair and that Samuel Fulke had spent £361 6s 8d of his own money on it. The building is likely to be the rectory constructed in 1575, now listed Grade II and described in a 2004 sales catalogue (Beds Archives, Z449/1/38). He was mentioned in the will of his brother William Fulke, theologian, Hebraicist and Master of Pembroke College, Cambridge, who died in 1589 (TNA, PROB 11/74/422).

329 William Hardinge of Eaton Bray, ploughwright made 7 May 1622
Lincolnshire Archives, LCC ADMONS 1622/110

A true Inventarie of all the goodes and Cattell of William Hardinge, late of Eyton within the Countie of Bedforde, plowghwright, deceased, taken and prised by William Mackereth gentleman, Edmonde Buckmaster, John Welles, Cutbert George and Edmonde Cooke, the vij[th] day of May, Anno Domini 1622

	£	s	d
In a lower chamber			
Imprimis his wearinge apparaile prised at		xiij	iiij
Item two boarded bedsteades, two matterisses, foure coverlattes, fyve blankettes, foure boulsters, & one pillowe prised at		xxx	
Item sixxe paire of sheetes, one pillowebeere, a table cloath, and other lynnin, prised at		xxvj	viij
Item three coaffers, olde painted cloathes and other implementes prised at		v	
In the upper loaft			
Item woll, one coafer, two tubbes, one woollen wheele, a busshell, boardes and other implementes, prised at		xv	
In the Hall			
Item one table, a Cubborde, a benche and a benchboarde stooles and painted cloathes prised at		vj	viij
Item pewter prised at		vj	
Item one brasse pan, fyve brasse kettles a skymmer, and two brasse candlestickes prised at		xvj	

	£	s	d
Item one iron spit, two pothangers, a paire of bellowes a frienge pan, and other implementes, prised at		iij	iiij
In the butterie and the entrie			
Item one saltinge trough, a kneadinge trough, an olde Cupborde one tubbe, a mault querne and other implementes prised at		x	
Item one mattocke, a draught rake, & his worckinge tooles prised at		viij	
Without doare			
Item one Grinston two ladders and certaine lumber prised at		iij	iiij
Item two geaste beastes and one bullocke prised at	iiij	vj	viij
Item fyve sheepe and two lambes prised at		xxvj	viij
Item one pigge prised at		ij	
Item foure hennes and a cocke prised at		ij	vj
Item two landes of pease prised at		x	
Item soile in the yearde prised at		iij	
Summa totalis	xiij	xiiij	ij

[*Exhibited by the administratrix at Dunstable on 22 May 1622*]

Notes: William Hardinge was buried at Eaton Bray on 30 April 1622. Administration was granted to his widow Elizabeth on 22 May 1622 and a bond was taken (Lincs Archives, Act Book A/x/62 and LCC ADMONS 1622/110).

330 John Hoddle of Elstow, yeoman

made 9 May 1622

Lincolnshire Archives, INV/126/159

An Inventory of all the goodes And Chattles of John Hoddll late of Elstowe in the Countie of Bedford decesed taken and Aprised this nineth day of maye in the yere of our lord god 1622 by thos whos names ar hearunder writen

	£	s	d
In primis in the hall on ~~framed~~ longe table with A frame two short tables ij formes And other thinges ther to the vallue of		vj	viij
Item in the parler on long table with A frame on short table with a fram on Chere And v stoulles with other thinges ther to the vallue of		xxiij	iiij
Item in the Chamber tow Joyned bedes with eche of them A testor over it to the value of		xx	
Item moor ther Towe great Chestes to the vallu of		xiij	4
Item allso ther on Cobard to the vallue		v	
Item likwies ther on littell table with a frame		ij	vj
Item more ther on litell Coffer on chere on band box And diveres other thinges ther to the vallu of		v	
Item in the Buttery ij drink barilles vj boles And diveres other Treen war ther to the vallue of		x	
Item in the kitchin on great bruing kettell ij bras pottes vj great peutter dishes with diveres other bras And peuter ther to the vallue of		xxvj	viij
Item on fetherbed And Certain other beding		xxvj	8
Item for sheetes and other naperry to the vallue of	vj		
Item in the yard Certain wood to the vallue of		xxxiij	iiij
Item in the stabll Certain haye And strawe to the vallue of		xij	

Item in the feild of Tilth barly v rodes			xxx	
Item of peason in another fild on ac' di [*one acre and a half*]			xx	
Item for the leas of [*word deleted and illegible*] Wm Hardinges house and land And Wm Cranfildes land		xiij	vj	8
Item in Redy mony	~~xxxxvj lxxxvj~~	xlvj	vj	8
Item the waring repill of the said John Hoddll worth		iij		
Item: All other lombr in the yard forgot			ij	
	[*Total*	*£80*	*9s*	*10d*]

John Bellie minister, The mark of William Hardinge, John Whitbreade, William Jayes
[*No exhibition clause*]

Notes: John Hoddle was buried at Elstow on 27 April 1622. He made his will on 8 June 1615, describing himself as a yeoman. He gave everything to his wife, Marie, whom he appointed his executrix. She was granted probate by John Farmerie at Bedford on 23 May 1622 (Lincs Archives, LCC WILLS/1622/i/187). John Bellie, one of the appraisers, was not the minister at Elstow and has not been identified.

331 John Willson of Warden Abbey, gentleman

made 9 May 1622

Lincolnshire Archives, INV126/174–177

The inventory is on seventeen sheets of paper. There is some damage and creasing and a few letters or words are missing. All the totals and a few items, as indicated, have been written in a different hand from the list.

[*first sheet*]
A true Inventorye of all my linnen taken the ix[th] daye of Maye in the yeare of our Lord 1622

£ s d

Sheetes

Imprimis
One fine holland sheete of three bredethes
Item one payer of new fine holland sheetes with towe bredthes and halfe
Item one payer of holland sheetes with towe bredthes and seeming lace in the middest
Item towe payer of little thin holland sheetes
Item one payer of course shepheards holland sheetes
Item three payer of fine flaxen sheetes ell wide
Item towe payer of new fine flaxen sheetes ell wide
Item towe payer of fine flaxen sheetes yard ~~ell~~ wide
Item one payer of little flaxen sheetes yarde wide
Item towe payer of pleate broad flaxen sheetes
Item one payer of new flaxen sheetes yard wide
Item towe payer of fine tare of hemp sheetes pleate broad
Item five payer of fine tare of hemp sheetes yard wide
Item three payer of fine new tare of hemp sheetes yard wide
Item five payer of fine flax towe sheetes
Item fouer payer of course flax towe sheetes
Item three payer of fine hemp towe sheetes
Item a payre of teare of hempe sheetes

Pillowbeers

Imprimis three fine holland Pillowbeers seamed ~~& sticked~~ with lace and stitched
Item towe payer of fine holland ones with playn seames
Item one payer of holland ones with layed worke
Item towe payer of fine holland ones stitched and purled
Item three payer of fine holland pillowbers with playne seames
Item three payer of fine flaxen pillowbeers
Item towe payer of tare of hemp ones
[*second sheet*]

Towells

Imprimis towe fine holland laced ones
Item three fine flaxen towells fouer yardes longe
Item towe short flaxen towells
Item six long tare of hemp towells
Item three short tare of hemp towells
Item halfe a dozen of short hemp toe towells

Napkins

Imprimis fouerteen fine flaxen napkins wrought with layed worke
Item three dozen of very fine flaxen napkins done with blue
Item three dozen of flaxen napkins somewhat courser
Item seaven dozen of fine tare of hemp napkins
Item towe dozen of new tare of hemp napkins

A note of childe bed linnen

Inprimis a lane sheete with three breadthes hemmed & stitched round about
Item twoe great double lane pillowbeeres
Item five halfe lane pillowbeeres
Item a lane cushion cloth of cutworke lased round about
Item a drawne worke cushion cloth wrought with blacke silke & three pillowbeeres to it
Item a lane face cloth
Item a cradle heade cloth
Item a wrought cradle head cloth
Item a cradle head cloth wrought with cut worke
Item twoe wrought pillowbeeres for the cradle
Item six fine holland cradle heade clothes
Item one lane cutworke cloth for the childes mantle
[*third sheet*]
Item twoe playne lane ones
Item foure holland ones
Item foure lane bibes
Item five lane bandes
Item six lane crossclothes
Item twoe lane handkercheifes for the childes face
Item one wrought handkercheife
Item a tiffeny vale a stomacher & a band wrought

to it
Item a lane vale
Item nine lased holland crossclothes
Item fourteene playne holland crossclothes
Item twelve litle shirtes
Item thirteene bedes wherof six are of
holland
Item twelve lased biggines
Item ten head bandes
Item seven long holland bibes
Item six neckclothes
Item eight kercheifes
Item three wrought bibes
Item ~~6~~ six duzen of double clothes
Item six payre of litle shag sleeves
Item five payre of playne ones
Item seven white blankhits
Item three payre of knit sleeves
Item a mantle of crimson taffety
with twoe broade silver lases
Item one of stammell with silke
and silver lase
Item twoe mantles of pennystonne
bounde about with a silke lace
[*the next five lines are in a different hand*]
[*in the right margin*] All thes praysed at £128
Item for Lynnen yarne
Item his wearing ~~Cl~~ apparell £xx
Item his Armor £v
Item his Bookes £4
[*fourth sheet*]

Table Cloethes of Diaper and Dammaske

Imprimis one fine diaper table Cloeth six yardes longe
and three yardes wide
Item twentye fine diaper napkins to yt dobble stitched
Item a diaper towell of fouer yardes longe to the tablecloeth
Item three longe diaper table Cloethes
Item one diaper towell and Cobberd cloeth
Item one side boord table Cloeth of diaper
Item towe short dammeske table Cloethes
Item one dozen of fine diaper napkins
Item towe dozen of new diaper napkins

Flaxen table Cloethes

Item eight fine long flaxen boord Cloethes seaven yards long
and towe yardes wide
Item six fine flaxen table Cloethes somwhat shorter
Item fouer long tare of hemp table Cloethes
Item towe fine flaxen square boord table Cloethes
Item fouer fine tare of hemp table cloethes for a square
boord
Item three new tare of hemp table cloethes

Item eight short hemp toe table cloethes

Cubbord Cloethes

Imprimis fouer verre fine holland Cubbord Cloethes one of them dobble stitched the other three laced round about
Item one fine holland Cubbord Cloeth somewhat shorter laced and fringed
Item one fine flaxen Cubbord cloeth
Item towe flaxen cubbord cloethes somewhat courser
Item towe more flaxen Cubbord Cloethes somewhat worne
Item fouer tare of hemp cubbord cloethes
[*fifth sheet. Badly damaged at the top left. Parts of several lines are missing.*]

[*n*]ote of the plate

Inprimis a great gilt standing cup with a kiver
Item a gilt bole with a kiver
Item a silver beere bole
[...] silver wine boles
[...] [*?*]pounce [...]oade gilt boale
Item [...] a silver bole
Item a litle gilt bole
Item a double gilt salt with a kiver
Item a great silver salt
Item a litle gilt trencher salt
Item a duzen of silver spoones
Item three great gilt spoones
Item twoe litle silver spoones
Item a ~~litle~~ sugar box of silver & a spoone to it
Item a silver pot
Item a silver porringer
Item a litle silver botle
Item a silver teaster for hot water
Item twoe pots tipt with silver
[*two lines in a different hand*]
Item two silver bootes
[*in the right margin*] the plate praysed at £liij
[*sixth sheet*]

In the great chamber and long entry

Inprimis a large chest lined for linen, barred with iron with twoe lockes
Item a large waynscot wrought chest, twoe draweres & lockes to them
Item a great trunke
Item two chestes wherof one fur & the other of waynscote
Item three large deskes

Item an iron grate for a
cole fier
[*in the right margin in a different hand*] The goodes praysed at £iiij xs

In the closet

Inprimis one trunke
Item a cellar of glasses
Item foure litle boxes
Item a windowe curtayne
[*in the right margin in a different hand*] Thes praysd at xls
[*seventh sheet*]
[*at the top of the page in a different hand*] CCClxxxxiiij xiij 8
Item in reddy monye 200

~~**The debtes appeare that the testator did owe at the time of his death**~~

~~Imprimis for Rent~~ ~~53~~ ~~0~~ ~~0~~
~~Item to his neece Mistress Susan Spouner~~ ~~50~~ ~~0~~ ~~0~~
~~Item to his Cousen Pigott of London~~ ~~xxij~~ ~~0~~ ~~0~~
~~Item more in London~~ ~~x~~ ~~0~~ ~~0~~
[*eighth sheet*]

In the dary

Inprimis a cheese presse
Item twoe churmes
Item three tubbes
Item thirteene kimnels
Item eight booles
Item sixteene cheese [*fats*]
Item twoe sutors
Item twoe side dishes
Item a payre of butter scalls
Item five creame pots
Item twoe milke payles
Item a trenell
Item pot hangers
Item a kurde siffe
Item a payre of bellowes
Item three baskets
Item foure butter clothes
Item three strayners
Item three wash tubes
Item twoe wash peales
Item twoe cheese rackes
Item eight cheese boardes
Item a tub to put in cheeses
[*in the right margin in a different hand*] all thes praysede at ls [*50s*]
[*ninth sheet*]

A note of my pealter

Inprimis a greate charger and
a plate for a pasty
Item a bason and ewer
Item two spout pots for wine
Item five payre of peulter

candlestickes
Item twoe payre of latin
candlestickes
Item three duzen and ~~a ha~~
nine of peulter platters
Item twoe duzen of plates
Item a duzen and halfe of
saceres
Item a duzen of porringers
Item a greate bason
Item one pye plate
Item five chamber pots
Item six litle peulter pots
with kivers
[*in the right margin in a different hand*] The pewter praysed at £vj
[*tenth sheet*]

In the larder

Inprimis twoe powdering troffes
Item a powdering tub
Item a hare safe
Item foure vargis barrels
Item three rundlets
[*in the right margin in a different hand*] praysed at xxxiijs 4d

In the backhouse

Inprimis a kneading troffe
Item twoe litle kimnels
Item a boulting arke
Item twoe tubbes for meale
Item three peckes for flower
Item peeles & cole rackes of iron
Item twoe wooden hand peeles
Item twoe grist sackes
Item twoe sarcing siffes
[*in the right margin in a different hand*] praysed at xxvjs viijd

In the brewehouse

Inprimis a copper
Item a mashing fat
A yeilding fat
Item twoe lesser fats to coole
wort in
Item foure tubbes
[*in the right margin in a different hand*] Thes goodes praysed at £viij
Item three litle barrells
Item a malt Querne xxs
[*eleventh sheet*]
Inprimis a feild bedsteade of wallnut tree
the top & vallums of fugurato with a
deepe fringe of silke & curtaynes of
greene sea fringed with greene and
oringe silke
Item towe fetherbedds

Item twoe boulsters
Item twoe pillowes
Item twoe blankhits
Item A greene rug with five breadthes
Item A bed mat
Item Eight gild knobs for the bed top
Item A large ioyned cubbarde
Item A carsy greene cubbard cloth with a silke frindge
Item A windowe cushion ~~cloth em~~ of vellet embroadered with flowers
Item Foure needle worke cushions
Item Three great cheares whereof on of fugurato with silke frindge the other twoe of satin fringed with silke
Item One lower cheare of needle worke
Item Foure high stooles of fugurato fringed
Item Twoe lowe stooles of fugurato fringed
Item A large looking glasse
Item A payre of handirons
Item Fier shovell, and tonges with brasse topes
Item A necessary stoole
Item Three windowe curtaynes & rodes
[*in the right margin in a different hand*] All the goodes in this chamber praysed at £xxv xs

In the blewe chamber

Inprimis a feilde bedsteade of wallnut tree with the top vallums & curtaynes of crimson mockado & greene silke fringe with five gilt knobs
Item a fether bed
Item twoe boulsters
Item twoe pillowes
Item one blanckhit
Item one greene rug of foure breadths
Item a bed mat
Item a court cubbarde
Item a cubbarde cloth fringed of noridge stuffe
Item a lowe square table
Item a high chayre of silke carfa fringed
Item a lowe [*c*]hayre

and t[*woe*] lowe stooles
of the same stuffe fringed
Item three high stooles of
the same stuffe fringed
Item a long windowe cushion
of needle worke fringed
Item a windowe curtayne
with the rod
Item a necessary stoole
Item a payre of handirons
fier shovell, & tonges
[*in a different hand*] The goodes in this chamber praysed at £xv
[*twelfth sheet*]

In the parler

Inprimis a table with a frame
Item a court cubbarde
Item a large greene carpet
of broade cloth with a
fayre border of needle
worke the most part of
silke coulers
Item a cubbarde ~~cloth~~ carpet
Item a carpet for the
square borde
Item a large chayre of carsey
lased & fringed
Item twoe backe chayres of
greene carsey fringed
Item a lowe chayre of
needle worke
Item one lowe stoole of fu-
garato fringed with silke
Item five high ioynt stooles
with carsey lased & fringed
Item six turky worke
cushions
Item two windowe curtaynes
& rods
Item a payre of andirons
fiershovell & tonges
Item a payre of bellowes
Item a map
[*in the right margin in a different hand*] Thes goodes praysed at £xij
[*thirteenth sheet*]
Item twoe warming pannes [*this item may be included in the total at the foot of the twelfth sheet*]

In the nursery chamber

Imprimis a fetherbed
Item twoe boulsters
Item twoe bed mats
Item one pillowe

Item one blanckit
Item a greene rug
Item a canopy of darnix with two curtaynes
Item a trundle bedsteede
Item a matresse and twoe bed mats
Item a boulster
Item one blanckit
Item a yellowe coverlid
Item twoe broade waynscote boxes
Item three cradles

[*in the right margin in a different hand*] The goodes in this Chamber praysed at	£vij	xs

In the maydes chamber

Inprimis a matresse
Item a boulster
Item a blanckit
Item a yellowe coverlid

[*in the right margin in a different hand*] The goodes praysed at		xxs

In the mens chamber

Inprimis a matresse
Item a boulster and pillowe
Item a blanckit
Item a coverlid

[*in the right margin in a different hand*] The goodes praysed at		xxs

[*fourteenth sheet*]

In the hall

Inprimis a long drawing table with a frame
Item a square table with a frame
Item a waynscot cubbarde
Item a waynscot chayre
Item a waynscot forme
Item fifteene ioynt stooles
Item a childes chayre
Item foure small turned chayres
Item six cushions
Item twoe lowe waynscot stooles
Item a payre of Andirons Fiershovell & tonges
Item a halberde
Item a browne bill

[*in the margin in a different hand*] praysed at	£iiij	

In the buttery

Inprimis three hogsheades
Item three great barrells

Item three great stone iugges
Item a peaulter flagon
Item a peulter pot & bole
Item three peulter saltes
Item twoe peaulter basons
Item twoe cannes and a Jagck
Item a great wooden botle
Item a lether botle
Item a voyder with the knife
Item a buttery basket
[*in the right margin in a different hand*] praysed at xls
[*fifteenth sheet*]

In the courte parler

Inprimis a fether bed
Item twoe boulsters
Item a pillowe
Item one blanckhit
Item a large tapestry
coverlid
Item a bed mat
Item a livery cubbarde
[*in a different hand*] The goodes in this Chamber praysed at £vij

In his owne chamber

Inprimis a waynscot bedsteede
with curtaynes & vallums
greene and yeallowe
Item a fetherbed
Item a matresse & a bed
mat
Item twoe boulsters
Item twoe pillowes
Item a payre of blanckhits
Item a greene rug of
foure breadthes
Item a tawny irish mantle
Item a trundle bed
Item a matresse
Item a fether boulster
Item a blanckit
Item a coverlid
Item ~~foure~~ three trunkes
Item a waynscot chest
Item twoe band boxes
Item twoe windoe curtaynes with rods
Item a payre of andirons fier shovel & tonges
Item twoe chayres
[*in the right margin in a different hand*] The goodes in this
chamber praysed at £xj xs
[*sixteenth sheet*]

A note of the sheepe and other cattell ~~praysed at xxx^{li}~~

Inprimis sixty six sheepe of praysed at

all kindes	xxx		
Item eighteene cowes	liiij		
Item ~~twoe~~ three mares	xij		
Item twoe old geldinges	iiij		
Item twoe sowes and a bore		xxx	
Item six young store hoges		xxx	
Item for Cartes plowes etc		xl	
Somma Totalis	442	10	
[*Corrected total*	*£682*	*10s*	*0d*]

~~Item for monye and bondes owing~~

Nicho[las] Spencer [*signature*], Oliver Boteler [*signature*], Andrew Denys [*signature*], Mathew Eaton [*signature*]

[*at foot of page on the left*] 442^{li} 10^{s}

[*seventeenth sheet*]

Bandes due to the testator at the time of his death

By Martyne Skinner	xxxiij[70]	iij	4
By Christopher Pepper and Christopher Buttolfe	xix	x	
By Thomas Buttolfe and Christophor Buttolfe	xix	iiij	
By Christopher Thursby esqer	liiij	iij	4
By Richard Skinner and John Kinge	viij	0	0
By Thomas Wilbore thelder John Wilbore and Ralph Harrison	liij	xv	0
By John Veare and John Nevill	j	xviij	0
By Thomas Buttolfe upon a Bill	v	0	0
[*Total of money owing to the deceased*	*£194*	*13s*	*8d*]
[*Total for goods and money owed*	*£877*	*3s*	*8d*]

[*in a different hand*] memorandum ther doeth appeare in the lue of a ioynter of 80^{li} per annum a band of a 1000^{li}

[*No exhibition clause*]

Notes: John Willson was buried at Warden on 27 April 1622. He made his will on 16 April 1622, describing himself as a gentleman. He left £300 to each of his three children; his lands in Braintree, Essex, to his wife Bridget for life and £20 from each of the children's portions to bring them up. Other legacies were listed in a schedule, which has not survived. His wife was the residual legatee. The executors were his wife and father-in-law Thomas Wynn, gentleman. Probate was granted to his widow on 10 July 1622, with power reserved for the other executor (TNA, PROB11/140, and Lincs Archives, LCC WILLS/1622/i/99). Master John Willson, gentleman, married Mistress Bridget Winne, gentlewoman, in Warden on 7 July 1614. She was from an Old Warden family. Their three children were baptised in Old Warden in 1615, 1617 and 1618 and a fourth child, described as the daughter of Mistress Wilsone, was baptised in 1622, but there was no provision for her in John Willson's will. Bridget Wilsone, widow, married Thomas Wine of the Charterhouse, London, gentleman in Warden on 12 May 1626. They lived in Old Warden for some years. John Willson consulted Dr Napier in 1615 when his age was given as 24, and in 1617 and 1622 when he was diagnosed with dropsy and consumption (Forman and Napier, case nos 43272, 44367 and 53765).

70 This figure has been substituted for xxij.

332 Anthony Hawkynes of Houghton Regis made 14 May 1622
Lincolnshire Archives, INV/126/150

Anno domini 1622 Regis Jacobi nunc Regis Anglie vicesimo etc Scotld quinquagesimo quint A true Inventorie indented and made the fourtentes day of Maye in the yeare abovewritten of all such goodes and Chattells which were Anthony Hawkynes of Houghton Regis in the com' of Bedd lately decessed a prised by us whose names are hereunto subscribed vizt

	£	s	d
Inprimis in his purse		x	
Item his wairing apparell	iij		
In the Hale			
One table and frame, and xij ioyne stooles		xxx	
Item one Cubbord two Chaires & a square table		xx	
Item two dozen & dmi of pewter		xl	
Item thre Candlestickes two saltes two pewter pottes on spicemorter one brazen Chaffindishe: a warming pann:		vj	viij
In the Parlour			
Twoe Bedsteedes		xxxiij	iiij
two Fetherbeds two materices thre boulsters	iij		
Item thre Coverlides two blankettes		xl	
Item on Table, on chest, & eight cushions		xxvj	viij
In the Chamber over the haule:			
One bedsted, 4 chestes, one Cubbord two boxes		L	
Item one fetherbed one matterice five pillowes, on boulster two Coverlettes: & two blankettes	iiij		
Item twelve paire of sheetes: & six pillowbears	vj		
Item five table cloth & a dozen & halfe of napkins		xxxiij	iiij
Item thre brasse pottes, five kettles, thre posnettes		xl	
Item two andirons, two dog irons, thre spits, five shovell pott hangers, two driping pannes: fire tongues		xx	
Item all the barrells, bruing vessells boules and dishes and other implementes about the house		xx	
Item fower horses	x		
Item two beast, two hogges, & the poultry in the yard	v		
Item two longe cartes one doung cart & 3 pair of wheeles	v		
Item ploughe with ploughe geres with the horse harnes		xiij	iiij
Item the hay and stray, wood and tymber	v		
Item the Compasse about the yarde		xx	
Item thre and thirty acres of graine in the field being wheate barley and pease with other graine about the yeard	40		
Summa totalis	101	3	4

Thomas Wallis, John Wheeler his marke, Thomas Tompkyns minister
[*Exhibited by the executor at Dunstable on 22 May 1622*]

Notes: Anthony Hawkynes was buried at Houghton Regis on 28 April 1622. The appraiser, Thomas Tompkins, was vicar of Houghton Regis 1607–1640/41 (CCEd, Beds Archives, Fasti/1/HouR).

333 John Killingworth of Wilshamstead, yeoman made 16 May 1622
Lincolnshire Archives, INV/126/156
This is a fair copy of the inventory, beautifully written.

A trew Inventorie of all the goodes & cattelles of John Killingworth late of Willshamsted in the countie of Beddf yeoman deceased taken the sixtene day of Maye in the yeres of the Raigne of our dread soverraigne Lord James by the grace of god of England France & Ireland Kinge Defender of the Fayth etc the twenteth and of Scotland the five & fifteth 1622 praysed by Thomas Beeche [*signature*], Peter Taylor, Richard Hedling, Walter Williams

	£	s	d
Inprimis in the halle a table with a frame a forme & twoe Joyned stooles twoe Cuphoords & a litle liverey table	iij		
Twoe brasse pannes – x^s A brass pott – x^s a ketle & brass pot – xv^s			
A great ketle – xv^s A skymmer a posnet a frying pan & a litle ketle – v^s		[*55*]	
Three spitts – v^s twoe chayres – v^s potthookes a girdiron two pothangers a paire of bellowes a firefork a fire pan – v^s		[*15*]	
Item fowertene peices of pewter a saucer a candlstick a salt seller with a spice morter & a pestell & a basting ladle		xxij	
Item twoe potshelves a lanthorne twoe cushons & painted cloathes & a hand baskett & a paire of sheeres		iiij	
In the litle Chamber			
Item a bedsted a chest a barrell with other lumber		xx	
In the great chamber			
Item twoe sidebeds with there beding a cofer & other lumber		xxx	
In the lofte over the chambers			
Item a standing bed with a fetherbed thre boltsters thre pillowes	iij		
Item five paire of flexen seamed sheets & a paire of huswiffe clotes	iij		
Item two boorde clothes fower pillowe beares twoe faced cloaths And other lynnen		xxiiij	
Item a coverlett & a blanket		xij	
Item twoe chests & a cofer – xx^s. A woollen wheele and painted cloathes a fan cheese shelves & other lumber – xij^s		[*32*]	
In the kitchin			
Item a kneading troughe a kneading boorde a tub a barrell a milke cherme a coope a drinkstale shelves & other lumber		xxiiij	
In the butterie			
Item a fatt a chespresse ij milkchermes a tub & other lumber & ij wheels		xx	
In the milkhouse			
Item a litle table iij chese shelves ij baskets & other lumber		xij	
In the lofte over the halle			
Item certaine hemp a parcell of woolle stockcards & other lumber		xl	

In the yarde

	£	s	d
Item iij kyne – vij^{li} x^{s} the dunge – xxij^{s} iij piggs x^{s} all the woode in the yard & twoe hovelles in the yard – xxx^{s}	[*10*	*12*]	
In the Feilds			
Item half an acre of barley & iij roodes of pease		xxxiij	iiij
Item all his weareing Apparrell		xl	
totalis Summa est	38	15	4

[*Exhibited by the executor at Bedford on 23 May 1622*]

Notes: John Killingworth was buried at Wilshamstead on 18 March 1622.

334 John Bellamie, vicar of Chalgrave made 19 May 1622

Lincolnshire Archives, INV/126/138

A true Inventorie of all the goodes and chatels of John Bellamie clerk late vicar of Chalgrave in the countie of Bedford, made and prised by us whose names are hereunder written the xixth daie of maie Anno domini 1622

	£	s	d
First his bookes	vij		
Item two kine	vj		
Item his horse		xxv	
Item two sheepe		xij	
Item iiij stockes of bees		xl	
Item his firewood		xx	
Item one table, five stoles, ij chaires, j paire of pothangers,[71] one paire of andyrons, j paire of pothookes, one fire shovell, one paire of tonges and j litle table		xxij	
Item one malt mill		vij	
Item one pigg		ij	vj
Item vj bowles and ij pales		iiij	
Item brasse and Pewtar		lij	
Item j churne iij tubs and other lummerie in the scholehouse		xvj	
one paire of staires			xvj
Item one wainscote bedsted		xxxiij	iiij
Item one trucklebed		v	
Item fetherbed and a bowlster	iiij		
Item one white rugg		xiij	iiij
Item ij blankettes		xiij	iiij
Item one darnix covering & one other covering		xxiij	iiij
Item cupbord and a presse		xx	
Item two chestes, one table, ij stoles, ij chaires and two boxes in the parlour		xij	

71 *pothangers* has been written over *pothooks*.

Item one sword, one dagger, and a murrion		v	
Item iij flockbedes, iij bowlsters, and iiij pillowes		l	
Item ten paire of sheetes, iij tableclothes, Five pillowebeares, ten handtowels, and napkins ij doson	iiij	xv	
Item ij coverlettes and ij blankettes		x	
Item j wainscott bed and one other bed		xxvj	viij
Item iiij chestes, j chaire, j box & one deske		xiij	iiij
Item certaine bordes		viij	
Item one washing bowle		iij	
Item certaine quarters, plankes and other lummerie		vj	viij
Item ij old bedstedes, & one pitchfork and a bill		ij	vj
Item his wooll		lvj	
Item certaine lummerie in the cheesechamber			xij
Item haie, strawe, j ladder & plankes in the barne		xv	
Item lime and brickes		iiij	
Item his apparrell	iiij		
Item monie in his purse	ij	vj	viij
Item certaine debtes in his Easter book uncertaine what he oweth as yet uncertaine			
sum totalis	liiij	xvj	
[*Corrected total*	*£55*	*5s*	*0d*]

signum Gyles Pearce, Raphe Dolle [*signature*]
[*Exhibited at Bedford on 17 September 1622*]

Notes: John Bellamie was buried at Chalgrave on 12 May 1622. He was vicar of Chalgrave 1582–1622, and was appointed licensed preacher in Chalgrave in 1605 (CCEd; Beds Archives, Fasti/1/Chal). A month before his death, John Bellamie aged 80 consulted Dr Napier (Forman and Napier, case nos 53923 and 53958). He made his will on 2 May 1622, making several small bequests and leaving the residue to his wife Margaret, who was appointed executrix. She was granted probate at Bedford on 17 September 1622 (Lincs Archives, LCC WILLS 1622/i/97).

335 William Hinde of Cardington, singleman made 21 May 1622
Lincolnshire Archives, INV/126/165

An Inventory of the goods and chattells of William Hinde, Late of Cardington in the County of Beddford singleman Deceased prized by those whose names are heere under written The 21 daye of Maie Anno Domini 1622

	£	s	d
Imprimis one coffer		2	6
Item a peice of lether		1	10
Item Moneye Indebted to him	3	11	2
Item his Apparell		6	8
Summa	4	2	2

The names of the prizers Thomas Wattson, William Cranfeilld his marke
[*Exhibited by the executor at Bedford on 23 May 1622*]

Notes: William Hinde was buried at Cardington on 31 March 1622. He made a nuncupative will on 20 March 1622, giving a coffer to his brother, a piece of leather to a friend and the residue to be divided among his brother's children. The friend, Clement Laine, was appointed executor and was granted probate by J. Farmerie at Bedford, undated (Lincs Archives, LCC WILLS/1622/i/199).

336 John Cooper or Cowper of Tempsford, husbandman

undated; made between May 1617 and November 1622

Lincolnshire Archives, INV/126/146

This is a list of the deceased's goods sold by the administrator. It is not a standard inventory nor a probate account.

A note of such of the goodes of John Cooper late of Temsford deceased as were sold by John Cooper of Barkford admi[ni]strator of the same as followeth viz

	£	s	d
Inprimis 3 hogges solde to Edward Armes		xxxij	
Item one cowe sold to Thomas Rogers		xlvj	viij
Item twoe weaninge calves		xxij	
Item xiij sheepe	iij	xvij	ij
Item twoe beastes sold to Rich Thorneley	iiij	ix	iiij
Item twoe drie bullockes sold to Thomas Staploe	iij	vj	viij
Item one horse for		l	
Item one other horse sold for		liij	iiij
Item extrees plow timber & other trashe in the hay howse sold to Thomas Staploe for		x	
Item 3 old plowes plow geares & twoe tawe trees sold to him for		vij	
Item an old dung carte bodie & an old longe cart bodie sold to him for		vj	
Item a tub a bolster & a basket sold to him for		viij	vj
Item iiij ducke & vij ducklinges sold to him for		ij	
Item a paire of rackes sold to Master Adams for			xx
Item a pitch kettle sold to Henrie ~~Fem~~ Finche for			xviij
Item a quarte kettle a paire of potthangers & 4 dishes sold to Thomas Thornley for		ij	viij
Item a ioyned bedd a borded bedstead sold to Eliz [?]Cac[*illeg.*]		xxj	
Item a Cubbord		xvj	
Item ij old Flockbedes		viij	
Item a litle old table a chaire stoole & a buffet stoole		iij	
Item six peeces of pewter a bason a pewter candlesticke & a brasen candlesticke		vij	
Item a brasse pott & pothookes & hangers & a kettle		viij	
Item ij barrells iiij milkbowles iiij cheesfates 6 cheese bordes a salting troughe a kimnell a fryenge pan & other implementes		xiiij	
Item a tub & a kitle		iij	
Item one blanket		iiij	
Item a bolting arke & a cheese presse		viij	
Item a molding bord & a forme		iiij	
Item a ioyned bedstead sold to Edw Langley for		xj	
Item a borded bedstead			xij

Item a hatchet			viij
Item 2 old kettles an old pan & a lattin basin			
sold to the brasier of St Neotes		xij	iiij
Item one kettle sold to Rich Stacie		vij	vj
Item a tread & a gridiron sold to John Wall		iij	viij
Item an old fetherbed sold to Abell Cooper		ix	
Item a long carte a dung carte bodie a barrell			
a rowle & certaine wood sold to Hellen Finche		xlj	
Item 2 old coverletes & an old blanket		vj	viij
Item a bushell & a riddle			xvj
Item a litle table			xij
Item a pair of horse gears a cart saddle & fill			
straps sold to Hen Tingey		iiij	
Item a paire of horse gears a carte saddle fill gears			
sold to Edw Frem [*sic, Freman?*] for		iij	iiij
Item grasse sold to him for		v	
Item grasse sold to Hen Thorneley for		iij	viij
Item a close of grasse sold to John Butler for		xxiiij	vj
Item a hempland & a seeding plowe sold to Thomas			
Thorneley for		xij	
Item a hovell sold to Hen Thornely for		xx	
Item a mattrisse & a woollen wheele sold to him for		ij	
Item a long ladder a grindstone with the spindle &			
certaine wood sold to old Bailie		xiiij	
Item a cubbord & painted clothes sold to Hen Thorne		vij	
Item old iron sold to Tho Staploe		v	
Item old iron a mattock head & a washbarrell			
sold to Hen Edwardes for		iij	
Item iiij strakes of iron sold to Hen: Rayner for		iij	iiij
Item a kneading troughe sold to John Walls for			xx
Item a folding table sold to Robte Abbot for		xj	
Item received of Leonard Wright for debte		xl	
Item received of Edw: Cooper for debte		xx	
Item received of Edw: Freshwater for a debte of xxvj^{s} viij^{d}			
for a horse sold to him being decayed but onelie		vij	
Item an old cubbord sold to Frauncis Parkin		iij	
Item a close & dung sold to Hen: Parkin		xlvj	viij
Item lockes fetters & other old iron sold to Tho: Pattinson		ix	iij
Item a bolster sold to Edw Gale for		x	
Item wood sold to him for		xx	
Item a coverlet sold to him for		iij	
Item the croppe of graine	liij	j	
Item an old dublet a Jerkin a hat & a pair of shos sold to			
Thomas Springe for		iiij	viij
Summa	C	xj	ix

Theis parcells following are yet unsold

Inprimis xx^{tie} paire of sheets with other lynnen	viij		
Item vij coffers		xx	
Item vij pillowes		vij	
Item iiij forkes & a crowe of iron		ij	

	£	s	d
Item an old table & a forme remaininge at Temsford		iij	iiij
Summa	ix	xij	iiij
Summa totalis huius Inventarij	Cx	iiij	j

[*Exhibited by the executor at Buckden on 8 November 1622*]

Notes: John Cooper was buried at Tempsford on 17 May 1617. This document is a draft account of the administration of the estate. Although it was made five years after his death, the identification of the deceased with John Cooper or Cowper, husbandman, who was buried at Tempsford on 17 May 1617, has been made because his was the only appropriate death in the area in a likely time span. John Cooper from Tempsford made his will on 13 May 1617. He gave his tenements in Upper Caldecote (Northill) and Tempsford, 40s, a coffer, a slate gate with hooks and hinges and a hurdle gate to his son Thomas. He gave varying sums of money, bedding and a coffer to each of his seven daughters when they reached the age of 21. The residue was to be divided amongst his children and his son Thomas was appointed executor. He also directed that the hemp tow and tare in the house should be spun and woven into clothes for the children. Probate was granted to John Cowper's brother at Biggleswade on 12 July 1617, during the minority of the executor (Beds Archives, ABP/W1617/314).

337 Nicholas Luke of Begwary, Eaton Socon, esquire — made 4 October 1622

Lincolnshire Archives, INV/126/148

The inventory is a fair copy, well written, with a full exhibition clause.

A true and perfecte Inventary of all & singler the goodes & chattells moveable & imoveable of Nicholas Luke late of Begwary in the parish of Eaton Soocon in the County of Bedd Esquier deceased made & taken the fourth day of October Anno domini 1622 viewed & appraised by William Block, John Harrison & Thomas Carre

	£	s	d
Inprimis his apparell appraised at		xl	
Summa p3			
In the parlor			
Item one table one liverie cubbord one lether chaire twoe lether stooles one litle wrought chaire twoe greene stooles [*?*]sixe ioyned stooles twoe paire of andirons one fire shovell one paire of tonges one carpet foure cushions one wicker chaire one longe cushion & other thinges there	iij		
Summa p3			
In the hall			
Item two tables one forme one livery cubbord two chaires		xxx	
Summa p3			
In the kitchin			
Item one iacke one table three spittes one cheespresse three stooles two chaires one paire of tonges one paire of andirons the barre & pothookes & other implementes there		xl	
Item foure brasse pots twoe kettles one litle brasse panne one table foure boles twoe tubbs the fryeing panne & other implementes		xl	
Summa	iiij		

		£	s	d
In the milke house				
Item foure tubbs & one furnace			xx	
	Summa p3			
In the buttery				
Item two hogsheades & two barrells			vij	
	Summa p3			
In the larder house				
Item one table one truncke one salting trough one woollen wheele one powdring tub one safe & other thinges there			x	
Item 32 peeces of pewter & pewter spoones one still & the warming panne			xl	
Item one cubbord & one truncke			xij	
	Summa	iij	ij	
In the chamber at the west end of the house				
Item one bedstead one fetherbed one bolster two pillowes five curtaines & the valence one coverlet & a blanket one liverie table one cheste one chaire & other implements there			liij	iiij
	Summa p3			
In a little chamber				
Item one bedstead one fetherbed twoe blanketes twoe bolsters twoe pillowes three curtaines one livery table & one chaire			l	
Item one bedstead one fetherbed & a coffer			x	
Item one bedstead one livery table one cofer one chaire one fetherbed one trundlebed twoe blankets & twoe coverletes & other thinges there			xx	
Item j bed j fetherbed j mattris j blanketes & a coverlet			x	
	Summa	iiij	x	
In the closet				
Item certaine thinges there			x	
Item seaven paire of flaxen sheetes nine paire of other sheetes foure bordclothes 3 cubbord clothes foure dozen of napkins tenne pillowbeares		v		
	Summa	v	x	
In the folkes chamber				
Item one bedstead one fetherbed one bolster one blanket one coverlet & other thinges there			x	
	Summa p3			
Item sixe beastes & a bull & a horse		ix		
Item one sowe & piges & five shotes			xxvj	viij
Item all the plate appraised at		x		
Item xiiij geese xj turkies twoe hens & a cocke			xx	
	Summa	xxj	vj	viij
	Summa totalis huius Inventarij	xlix	ix	

[*Exhibited by William Stirropp, notary public, for the executor at Stamford on 18 March 1624*]

Notes: Nicholas Luke was buried at Eaton Socon on 18 May 1622. He made a short will on 11 May 1622, leaving £400 to his daughters Amye and Olive Luke and property arrangements as a guarantee of payment. Also mentioned are his son Nicholas and his daughter Anne Collins. His 'son' William Francis was appointed executor. On 1 July 1622 a commission was granted to his daughter Anne Collins to administer the estate until his executor sought probate. William Francis was granted letters of administration with will annexed on 19 September 1622 (TNA, PROB 11/140).

338 Miles Horne of Whipsnade

made 22 October 1622

Lincolnshire Archives, INV/126/135

A true Inmitarie of the goodes of Myles Horne of Whipsnaid Deceaced the 22th of October 1622

	£	s	d
Inprimis his Reparrell & his money in his purse		xxv	
Item in the Hall a table 1 Cubbard & the stoles		x	
Item the brasse & peuter		xx	
Item other Impell		iij	iiij
In the Chamber			
Item a bedsted with the furniture		xx	
Item 1 other bede		v	
Item 3 Chestes		x	
Item 3 par of sheetes		x	
In the Lofte			
Item i bede with the furniture		vj	viij
Item 2 Chestes		ij	vj
Item 30 poundes of Wolle		xv	
Item his working Towles		x	
~~**The Corne in the barne**~~			
Item the Corne in the barn		xl	
Item the tymber & fyer wood		x	
Item 4 stockes of beese		xx	
Item the heaye		xx	
Item the grynstone			xviij
Item 1 hogge		viij	
Item i Cowe & a bulleck		xxxiij	iiij
Item 24 sheepes		liij	iiij
Item 2 akers of wheate sode [*sown*]		xl	
Item 4 akers of tylthe		xxvj	viij
[*this line is in a different hand*] Item all the Poultrie		ij	vj
Some is	19	12[72]	10

John Horne & Allexsander Goodall praysers & John Dobson skryvenner
[*Exhibited by the executors at Dunstable on 11 November 1622*]

Notes: Miles Horne was buried at Whipsnade on 28 August 1622.

72 12 has been written over 10.

339 William White of Biddenham, teler[73] made on 15 May 1623

Bedfordshire Archives, ABP4/194

There are two copies of this inventory. They are identical except for a few minor spelling variations. The transcription has been made from the more legible copy.

An Inventory of the goodes and cattelle of Willyam White of Biddenham in the countie of Bedford teler decesed the xv daye of Maye 1623

	£	s	d
Item in the halle ij cobardes		xiij	
Item a tabelle with a frame ij tabelle bordes ij stolles a forme acheare apenne with other Impelle mentes		xij	
Item iij kettelles a brase pot a friinge pan		x	
Item iij peuter dishies and iij salltes		iij	
Item pothookes and pot hangienes a spite a pare of andiernes with other Impelle mentes			xviij
Item in the chamber ij Joinde bedes		xx	
Item ij coferes and other Impelle mentes		iij	
Item in the boltinge house j bed and a trundell bed		xvj	
Item ij barilles a wollinne whelle a linnine whelle and wother [*other, or with other*] Impelle mentes		iiij	
Item in the buttery a salltinge trofe ij barilles a tube a chirme a paille dishies and j bolle with other Impelle mentes		x	
Item a flocke bede a bolster ij pillowes		v	
Item ij coverlides		viij	
Item iij pare of sheetes		xij	
Item waringe a parille		x	
Item ij bease	iiij	x	
Item iiij shipe		xx	
Item iij henes and a coke		ij	
Item ij gese and a gander		j	
Item in the yarde iiij baye of hovillinge with a hoogge stie		xliij	
Item wod and palles		xx	
Item compas			xviij
Item iij landes of barlie and iij of pease		xxxiij	iiij
Item glasse			xviij
Som	xvj	xix	x

praysed by John Wodward and Willyam Emrye

[*No exhibition clause*]

Notes: William White was buried at Biddenham on 5 May 1623. His wife Joan was buried on 27 March 1623.

73 This occupation has not been identified. Possibly it is a tailor or tiler.

340 Laurence Gerie of Potton and Great Stukeley, Hunts made 7 June 1623

Huntingdonshire Archives, AH18/7/31

This is the section of the inventory dealing with Potton. The inventory is on parchment. There are some holes, damage from staining and faded text.

A true & perfecte Inventarie of all the moveable [*go*]ods of Laurence [*Ge*]rie aforesaid which were at Potton in the countie of Bedd & were taken and praised the vij[th] day of June Anno Domini 1623 by [*?*]Richard [*?*]Cullicke & William Plomer as followeth

	£	s	d
In the lofte at Thomas Perritts			
Inprimis one bedstead		xxvj	viij
Item one fetherbed a bolster & a pillowe	iij		
Item a coverlet a blanket & a strawebed		xiij	iiij
Item a great cheste		viij	
Item five paire of sheets & one sheete twoe board clothes twoe pillowbeares & halfe a dozen of table napkin	iij		
Item viij peeces of pewter		xvj	
Item a face cloth & a [*illeg.*]		x	
Summa	ix	xiiij	
In the parlour			
Inprimis a ioyned table & a forme		xiiij	
Summa p3			
In the hall			
Inprimis one table & one forme & one old table in the lofte		xvj	vj
Item a [*?*]puter [*?*]cubbord		iij	
Item a molding board a kneading troughe with a cover & a bolting arke		x	
Summa		xxix	vj
In the lofte in the yearde			
Inprimis an old bedstead a litle kneading troughe with the old iron and boardes & other trashe		xij	
Item vij bushells pease		xiiij	
Summa		xxvj	
In the Barne			
Inprimis a parcell of haye certaine chaffe twoe bordes a fanne a ladder with other thinges		xxj	iiij
Summa p3			
At [*illeg.*]			
Inprimis one ioyned [*ta*]ble twoe ioyned formes & an old b[...]		x	
Summa p3			
At Childes howse			
Inprimis one halfe headed ioyned bed & a [*?*]painted clothe		vj	viij
Item one hovell with the rafters on yt one [*?*]old carte & shod wheeles & twoe plowes		L	
Item twoe peeces of [*?*]oak in the yeard & a peece of ashe		[*value illeg.*]	

Item the plowgeare in the stable & a seedlep with other thinges there & a harrowe			[?]iij	[?]iiij
	Summa	iij	x	

At [?]Carters

Inprimis a presse & board			xviij	
	Summa [*p3*]			

The document is torn off and nothing more remains

	[*Total*	*£19*	*2s*	*6d*]

[*No exhibition clause*]

Notes: Laurence Gerie's burial has not been found. His wife Sarah was buried at Potton on 6 November 1620 (see Beds Archives, X222/19 for the identity of his wife; *BPR*, vol. 61, p. 118 for their marriage in 1607, p. 173 for her burial). People called Parrett, Child and Carter lived in Potton in 1623 (*BPR*, vol. 61).

341 William Throstle of Swineshead made in August 1623

Huntingdonshire Archives, AH18/20/27

The inventory is severely damaged. Most of the heading and the exhibition clause are missing. Some of the values are almost illegible and may not have been correctly transcribed.

[...] August 1623 [...]

	£	s	d
Imprimis his wearing apparel		5	0
In the hall			
Imprimis on table with a frame on forme with a bench board	0	[?]10	0
Item one cubboad three chayres [*illeg.*] on [?]payre of bellowes four board [...] payre of [?]pot [?]hangles five painted clothes	0	6	8
Item five kettles on brasse pott, [?]seaven [?]pieces of pewter a [?]tubb, on payle [*inserted above the line*] a candlesticke on salt	1	10	0
In the chamber			
Item fyve coffers, two boarded bedsteedes with the painted clothes	1	3	4
Item two old coverlets, two blankets [*illeg.*] pillowes	0	13	4
Item four flexen sheetes eight harden sheetes [*illeg.*] [?]pillowbears	1	10	0
In the loft			
Item two wheeles, a troffe, with other lumber [*illeg.*]	0	10	0
Item in good dettes	10	0	0
Item in despperat dettes	[?]2	0	0
Item in wood in the yard	0	3	0
[*Total*]	18	16	4

Signum Jo[han]is [?]Gurrie [*mark*], Signum John Cooke [*mark*]

[*All that remains of the exhibition clause is the statement that it was exhibited by the executrix in 1623 and the signature of John Jackson, notary public*]

Notes: William Throstle was buried at Swineshead on 19 June 1623.

342 Stephen Mumforde of Clapham, labourer or cottager made 5 March 1624
Bedfordshire Archives, ABP4/288

Cou[n]t[y] Bedd. The 5th day of March 1623. A true and perfect Iventory of all the goodes and Chattelles of Stephen Mumforde of Clapham laborer deceassed vewed valued & priced by John Selbey, William Fynch the day above wrighten

	£	s	d
Imprimis in the halle			
A table a benchborde and 2 formes		v	0
Item 3 kettelles & a skillet		x	0
Item a Fryinge pann matdock showell spade bill & houfe		iij	vj
Item 3 tubes 2 payles		v	0
Item boles dishes & other Impellment		ij	0
Item a grediron & 2 wheeles		iij	iiij
In the chamber			
Item Cubberd cheest & 3 coffers		xvj	viij
Item a bedsteed with mattris and 2 boulsters		xv	iiij
Item all the pewter		vj	viij
Item 6 pare of sheetes 2 pare of pillowes bears & other linnen		xxvj	viij
Item x elles of linenen cloth		x	0
Item wooll & hemptow		xvij	0
Item a truckell bed & 2 olde barreles		iiij	0
Item 4 buslles of barley		x	0
Item 2 Fliches of bakon		x	0
Item Cheese		vj	~~viij~~
Item his apparill		xxvj	viij
In the yard			
Item hay		xiij	iiij
Item a greanston		0	xij
Item 2 beastes & 2 caulfes	v	iij	iiij
Item part of lease of his for rent for 7 years		xx	
Item a old hovell		v	
Item for other thinges and not particulerly nominated		ij	vj
Sum	16	3	6
[*Corrected total*	*£16*	*3s*	*4d*]

John Selbey [*signature*], William Finch his marke
[*No exhibition clause*]

Notes: Stephen Mumforde was buried at Clapham on 18 February 1624. He made his will on 16 February 1624, describing himself as a cottager. He forgave his brother a debt of 30s; made two small pecuniary bequests; and appointed his wife Elizabeth residual legatee and executrix. She was granted probate at Bromham on 5 March 1624 (Beds Archives, ABP/W1623–4/86).

343 Roger Throstle of Swineshead, labourer made between February and July 1624
Huntingdonshire Archives, AH18/20/31
The document is damaged along the top right and down the right side. It is also faded and stained. Some words are missing or illegible.

An Inventory of the [...] Chattles of Roger Throsle late whilst he lived of Swynshed in the County of Hunt laborer deceased praysed [*?*]indifferently by Thomas Dauson of the same place Clarke [*an*]d John [*Port*]soyle the [*illeg.*]

	£	s	d
Imprimis his weareing Apparell and Bedding		xx	
Item due by Thomas Throsle his sonne	iiij		
Summa	v		

[*Exhibited by Thomas Throstle executor on 3 July 1624*]

Notes: Roger Throstle was buried at Swineshead on 1 February 1624. The appraiser, Thomas Dawson, was rector of Swineshead 1594–1639 (Venn ACAD; CCED).

344 Henry Linnis of Meppershall, tailor undated; made August or September 1624
Bedfordshire Archives, ABP/W1624–1625/67

A true Invitory of the moveable goods of Henry Linnis 1624

	£	s	d
Imprimis two milsh kine	iiij		
Item the wood and the haye a hovel & a litelhouse	iij		
Item in the Chamber the bedding and other trash		xxx	
Item in the Hale a table and two brascittels & halfe a doosen of peuttor & other trashe		xxx	
Item his aparell		v	
Item an Ewe & lam		v	
Item a pigge		x	
Item the pullin and all other Impelments		iij	
[*Total*	*£11*	*3s*	*0d*]

the names of those that praised the goods Robert Mathew, William Fann
[*Exhibited by the executrix on 30 September 1624*]

Notes: Henry Linnis was buried in Meppershall on 7 August 1624. He made his will on 12 (sic) August 1624, describing himself as a tailor. He gave 4d each to the three children of his first marriage; the value of a cow to be shared by the two sons of his second marriage who also received his best suit and their mother's linen; and a ewe and lamb to the son of his third marriage. He appointed his wife Mary as his executrix and she was granted probate on 30 September 1624 (Beds Archives, ABP/W1624/67). She married Edmund Feild of Maulden in September 1625.

345 Peter Musgrave of Swineshead, yeoman made 16 October 1624
Huntingdonshire Archives, AH18/13/53
The top and bottom quarters of the inventory are damaged and stained.

[...] Invetorie of the goodes, chattelles [...] dettes of Peter Musgrave [*la*]te of Swyneshed deceased in the Countie of Hunt yeoman praysed [*words missing*] xvj[th] day of October 1624 [...] J[...] Parsoyle & Gibbes

	£	s	d
In the Hall			
[...] one cubboard, one table, one bench & bench board, [*illeg.*] [*?*]great Coffer, all [...] fyve ch[...]	1	13	[...]
[*Line damaged and only a few letters are legible*]			
[*Line damaged and only a few letters are legible*]		xv	?
[*Line damaged and only a few letters are legible*]			
[*Line damaged and only a few letters are legible*] a [*?*]frying pan [...] & potho[*illeg.*]	0	iij	[*?*]iiij
[...] one brasse pan, [...] [*gr*]eat kettels [...] [*l*]esser kettels, two frying [...] brasse lad[*dle?*] [...] weyghing six[...] poundes	ij	[...]	[...]
[...] [*br*]asse pottes [*weig*]hing xl[...]	j	[...]	[...]
Item [...] peeces of [*pe*]wter weighing xxxiij [li]	j	[...]	[...]
Item [...] [*?*]basin xv pottingers xiiij spoones, [*?*]three saucers, two butterdishes, three pewter candlestickes, one pewter pott, two chamber pottes, three saltes, a little pewter pott, one little platter, one peece of old pewter	0	xviij	0
In the chamber			
Imprimis one fetherbed weighing liiij[li]	j	xiij	iiij
Item, three balsters, vij pillowes weighing four score & three poundes	ij	v	0
Item on new darnix coverlett, a red blankett a greene blankett, two yardes of black cloth	ij	0	0
Item three old darnix coverlettes, two blankettes, one matteris	j	iij	iiij
Item four flexen seamed sheetes, & on holland seamed sheete	j	xiij	iiij
Item eight flexen sheetes	ij	0	0
Item ten payre of harden sheetes	ij	0	0
Item three flaxen boardclothes, four yardes a peece	0	xij	0
Item harden boardclothes	0	iij	0
Item eleven table napkins	0	v	vj
Item one holland seamed pillowbeer	0	v	0
Item four flexen pillowbeers & a face cloth	0	iiij	vj
Item six harden pillowbeers	0	iij	0
Item a neew cloake & safegard	j	xiiij	0
Item a neew skirt of a petticoate, lace sylke & greene bayes	0	xij	0
Item Ellens gowne	j	x	0
Item Ellens best petticoate & best wastcoate	0	xiij	iiij
Item an old petticoate, & a stuffe wastcoate	0	iiij	0

Item [*illeg.*] bandes, three white aprons, a green apro[*n*]	0	xvj	0
[*Item*] ~~four~~ two playne bandes, neckclothes, hedcloths, [*?*]cuffes	0	ij	vj
[*Item*] fyve yardes of neew cloth	0	[*?*]xvj	0
Item three yardes & three [*quar*]ters of course cloth	0	[*illeg.*]	0
Item [*?*]a [*?*]gown, a petticoate, an old gow[*n*]	j	[*?*]x	[...]
[...]ing lynen [...] [...]ves & tw[...] [...]tes	j	[...]	[...]
[*Item*] [*?*]her wear[*ing*] [*appar*]ell	j	x	0
Item in readie mo[*ney*]	v	ix	0
[*Item*] Ellens hatte	0	iij	iiij
[...] two bedsteedes, [...]			
[...] vj [...]elles			[*illeg.*]
[*line damaged*]	?	iij	[...]
[*line damaged*]	?	viij	[...]
[*line damaged*]	j	x	[...]
[*illeg.*] coverlett two blanketes, two matterisses	0	xiij	iiij
[*illeg.*] flytch of bacon	0		[*illeg.*]
[*illeg.*] iij [*?*]bucketes iij syves, a payre of stockcardes			
[...] [*?*]ij coffers, a troffe, a cloth-			
[...] iij boardes			[*value missing*]
[...] beame, scales, & weightes	0 [*damaged, missing*]		
[...] kytching malt querne a bolting arke			
[*illeg.*] [*?*]chese [*?*]pres, a troffe [*illeg.*]			[...]
[...] iiij payles, a kymnell, a [*?*]chern [*illeg.*] [...]			
[...] andirons, an axe, a [*?*]hatchet, a bar[...]			
[*missing or illeg.*] a scuttell, viij cheese fattes [*illeg.*] [...]			
[*second side of the paper*]			
[...]tholes in the yard			[*value missing*]
[...] rest[*?ing*] upon it			[*value missing*]
[...] [*p*]ullen in the ya[...] a bushell & a drag			[*value missing*]
[...] j swyne, A so[*w*] [...] piges			[*value missing*]
[...] [*?*]x kyne & two heyfers			[*value missing*]
[...] [*?*]wheat in the barnes	x	[*illeg.*]	
[...] of pease	iij	[*?*]xij	
[...] two hayreckes & haye in the barne	v	[...]	[...]
[...] [*illeg.*]ntye& seaven sheep	[*?*]xxiij[74]	[...]	[...]
[*missing or illeg.*]	lxvj	xv	[...]

[*money owed to him*]

[*Jh*]on Col[*illeg.*]	xxij	0	
[*Th*]omas [*D*]awson	xj	0	
Jhon Lavender	xj	0	
[Christofer] Fox	xxvj	xiij	[*?4*]
Thomas Sylke	v	x	0
[...] Bromsall	xvj	x	0
Henry Brigges	xj	0	0
[*T*]homas Gurrie	vij	0	0
William Byworth	xj	0	0

74 This value might be shillings.

Jhon Parsoyle	vij	x	0
Robert Lankaster	iij	0	0
Roger Gyles	j	0	0
Thomas Boone	v	0	0
Thomas Hooll	iij	x	0
William Bromsall	iij	xiij	iiij
Thomas Peete	iiij	x	0
Olliver Ghostloe	ij	xiij	iiij
Walter Moore	0	x	0
	Cliij	0	0

The totall summe of the invitorie is two hundred three score & seaven poundes, eight shyllinges & two pence	CClxvij	viij	ij

Jhon Parsoyle [*mark*], Jhon Gibbes [*mark*]
[*Most of the exhibition clause is missing or illegible. Exhibited in January 1626.*]

Notes: Peter Musgrave was buried at Swineshead on 17 September 1624. His wife Margaret was buried there on 29 August and daughter Ellen on 12 September 1624. The introduction to Swineshead parish register transcriptions suggests that the unusually high number of burials from the Musgrave and other families in a seven week period might indicate plague deaths (*BPR*, vol. 7, p. Fii). Almost on his deathbed, he consulted Dr Napier who recorded his age as 72 and drew up an astrological chart for him (Forman and Napier, case no. 59088). His daughter Ellen, aged 21, consulted Napier on 6 September, who noted 'exteme sick' and a 'pestilent loosenes' (Forman and Napier, case no. 59056).

346 John Tounesend of Billington, yeoman

made 8 November 1624

Lincolnshire Archives, INV/129/371

A true Inventorie of all the goodes and cattels moveables & immoveables of John Tounesend late of Billingdon in the parish of Layton Bussard als Groveberrie yeoman deceased praysed the eight of November Anno 1624

	£	s	d
Imprimis his wearing apparrell		xxxiij	iiij
Three horses	xj		
one cowe		xl	
wheat Barley beanes & hay in the barne	x		
Nine Achers of tilth & wheate	ix		
Two achers of tilth and ~~acher~~ a roode of wheat with iij achers of Beaneland in Standbridge feild	iiij		
Lumber The cart & wheeles & other necessaries aboute the house	iij		
Twentie Sheepe	iij		
Beanes threshed		xx	
In money		lij	viij
Hurdels			xxj
One Sack		ij	
Summa	xlvij	viij	ix
[*Corrected total*	*£47*	*9s*	*9d*]

Praysers William Hogge, Richard Woodstock, witnessesse Henrie Waterhouse

	£	s	d
More for rent for his one land from Michaelmas to alhallon day		xiij	iiij

[*Exhibited by the executor at Leighton Buzzard on 16 May 1625*]

Notes: John Tounesend's burial has not been found. He made his will on 31 October 1624. He gave 10s or 20s each to his brother's and sisters' children, except one; and 6s 8d each to his three sisters and two brothers. He gave his five acres and a rood of freehold in Stanbridge Field to his mother for life and then to his niece. The crop in the bean land bequeathed to his mother should be used to pay his debts. Thomas Capon, who was residual legatee and executor, was granted probate by William Dalbie at Leighton Buzzard on 16 May 1625 (Lincs Archives, LCC WILLS/1624–25/539).

347 Johan Everett of Sandy, widow made 29 November 1624

Lincolnshire Archives, INV/129/336

November the 29th Anno domini 1624. A trew inventary of all the goodes and chattles of Johan Everett of Sandey Widdowe late deceased prized by us John Underwood and Edward Rawley as followeth

	£	s	d
Inprimis in the Hall five Kettles and one chayer one payer of bellowes and other lumber		xiij	iiij
In the Chamber one Coffer		iiij	
Item two Coverlettes, two boulsters two pillowes & one Flockbedd one blankett		xx	
Item two payre of harden sheets		v	
Item one kneadinge troffe and certaine boards and other Lumber		ij	
Item two Laddles		ij	
Item her wearinge apparrell		xx	
Item ~~her~~ two smocks and other wearing lynnin		v	
Item due to the Testatrix upon specialty			
Edward Fickis	iiij		
Edward Springes handes	iiij		
In the handes of William Bromsall	ix	v	
due without specialty in the handes of Symon Ward	vij	xiiij	
In the handes of Thomas Person		vj	
In the handes of Roberte Clarke		vj	
Summa totalis	xxix	iiij	iiij
[*Corrected total*	*£29*	*2s*	*4d*]

[*Exhibited at Bedford on 21 May 1625*]

Notes: Johan Everett's burial has not been found. She made her will on 12 November 1624, leaving a 'lader' each to a daughter and son (possibly the ladles of the inventory) and the money held by Simon Ward, Edward Fike and Edward Spring to her son John, who had to recover it at his own expense and allow his brother William 6s 8d a year during his apprenticeship. Her daughter Alice was residual legatee and executrix and was granted probate by William Dalbie at Bedford on 21 May 1625. A note in a different hand after the witnesses' signatures lists her money in the hands of Bromsall, Person and Clarke although the amounts are not the same as appear in the inventory (Lincs Archives, LCC WILLS/1624–25/538).

348 David Towler of Odell, blacksmith — made 10 February 1625

Lincolnshire Archives, INV/129/343A

A True & perfect Inventorye of all the Goodes & Chattels of David Towler in the parish of Woodhill in the County of Bedford Black-smithe taken & made February the xth

	£	s	d
Imprimis one milch cowe & a bullocke	4		
Item foure sheepe		20	
Item Corne, pease, & Haye		34	
Item Tilthe & pease lande		15	
Item two flitches of Bacon		x	
In the Hall a Table, one fourme		4	
Item two Chayres, a stoole & an old fourme			18
Item an ould Court Cubbarde		4	
Item two ould kettles, a skillit & a skimmer		7	
Item foure Pewter Platters		3	6
Item a fire-forke, one spit, a paire of Bellowes, a paire of pot hangers		2	
Item sixe pewter spoones, an old Candlesticke, & an old frying pan			6
Item a spinninge Wheele			xij
In the Chamber a standing Bed		7	
Item a Coverlet & Blanket		6	
Item an old feather bed, on boulster, a pillow & a Mattrise		25	
Item three little barrells & two ould Tubbes		3	
Item three Coffers & a fourme		3	2
Item an ould Curtaine			xij
Item an ould sive			ij
Item his wearing Apparell		13	4
Item an ould watch Bill			6
Item foure Paire of Sheetes		15	
~~Item his Debt~~			
Item for ould trash as a troffe, a ladder etc			6
Memorandum: he owethe	4		
Summa totalis	xij	18	0
[*Corrected total*	*£12*	*17s*	*2d*]
~~deduct 4 lib Remaining~~	8	~~18~~	

In the presence of us signum John Bradforde [*mark*], Thomas Savage [*signature*], signum Thomas Balle [*mark*], John Sheffeilde [*signature*]
[*Exhibited by the executrix at Bedford on 21 May 1625*]

Notes: David Towler was buried at Odell on 2 January 1625. He made a nuncupative will, giving his house to his youngest son after the death of the testator's wife Agnes. He gave a bullock to his grandson; and 12d each to his five children. He appointed his wife executrix and she was granted probate by William Dalbie at Bedford on 21 May 1625 (Lincs Archives, LCC WILLS/1624–25/442).

349 Francis Dillyngham rector of Wilden, clerk made 24 February 1625
Lincolnshire Archives, INV/129/343

A true and perfect Inventorye Indented of all & singuler the goodes and Chattells of Frauncys Dillyngham late of Wylden in the Countye of Bedford Clarke decessed made the xxiiij[th] daye of Februarye Anno domini 1624 viewed and Appraised by John Fitzhugh gent, Henrye Wagstaffe, Edmond Crowe and John Fowler as followeth

	£	s	d
Inprimis in the hall two tables one Cubbord two chayres sixe ioyned stooles the waynscote & benches and other lumber there	3		
Item in the parlor A table one Cubbord one Chayre eight ioyned stooles with the waynscote there		50	
Item in the buttrye sixe barrells all the brasse & pewter with the spittes & other Implementes there	6		
Item in the mylkhouse A saltyngtroffe A cheese presse the payles mylke boles sixe flitches of bacon with other lumber there	4		
Item in the hall chamber two beddes with the beddyng on them three chestes A Chayre with the boardes in the floore	12		
Item in the Chamber over the parlor two beddes with the beddyng on them one table A Chayre one Chest one deske & the waynscote there	6		
Item in the Studdye all his bookes A stoole with other implementes there	70		
Item in the Cheese lofte the Racke & cheese		12	
Item in the next chamber two borded beddes with the beddyng		10	
Item in the boultyng house one tubb one kymnell with other implementes there		12	
Item in the backhouse A furnace A maltmyll plowe tymber & carte tymber with bordes & other implementes there		40	
Item in the stable sixe horses with plowe geares & Carte geares & other implementes there	28		
Item in the yarde seaven bease three bullockes and one yearlynge	20		
Item in the chamber over the buttrye two beddes with the beddyng on them	3		
Item all the naperye & lynnen viz of table napkyns foure dosen & A halfe, of pillowbeeres eight of borde clothes nyne & of sheetes 60 payre	27		
Item the wheate in the barne and pease	30		
Item the barley and malte	37		
Item in the yarde nyneteene hogges & stores	15	10	
Item the two hovells in the yarde		42	

Item the Inner palyng & wheate barne with other Implementes	13		
Item the haye and strawe	14		
Item the Cartes & plowes & the furnyture to them	6		
Item the Compasse in the yarde	3		
Item the fire woode		20	
Item of wheate sowne in the field eleaven Acres	22		
Item of pease three Acres & of oates three Acres	3		
Item all the poultrey in the yarde		10	
Item all in plate	32		
Item of debtes owing by specialtye	37	10	
Item in readye money	19		
Item of debtes owing without specialtye	22		
Item the Chaffe		25	
Item his wearyng Apparell	34		
Item three Cupboardes		30	
Item Foure tables three stooles		30	
Item three bedsteedes one Chest		20	
~~Sume total huius Inventarij~~			
Item A malt mill a Cheese presse		6	8
Item two Fattes		6	8
Item one Hovell		10	
Item viij peeces of pewter vj porringers with other small peeces		10	
Item one Furnace, one Chest		20	
Item two kettles two pottes		10	
Item one Chest with two paire of flexen sheetes		10	
Item one Bedsteed with furniture upon it		40	
Item one Carpett, one Coverlett with other Implementes		20	
Item three Chaires six stooles one Cupbord		10	
Item one garner		20	
Item one powdering troughe three spittes a paire of Andirons with other Implementes		10	
Summa huius Inventarij			[*blank*]
[*Total*	*£490*	*14s*	*4d*]
[*at the foot of the next page*]	478	1	
	12	13	4
[*Total*]	490	14	4

[*Exhibited by the executor at Bedford on 21 May 1625*]

Notes: Francis Dillingham was buried at Wilden on 24 February 1625. He was a Fellow of Christ's College, Cambridge, 1594–1601 (Venn ACAD); rector of Wilden 1600–25 (CCEd; Beds Archives, Fasti/1/Wilden); and one of the translators of the King James Bible, 1611 (Venn ACAD; *ODNB*). He made his will on 14 January 1625. He gave £5 each to his four sisters; £80 each to three Selby relations and £50 to another; and sums to other family and servants. He gave his freehold land to his brother Thomas, who was residual legatee and executor. Probate was granted at Bedford on 21 May 1625 (Beds Archives, ABP/W 1625/204). The 1607 glebe terrier describes the parsonage house as having five 'neyther' rooms covered with tile and all having chambers over; a bakehouse covered with straw; a stable with three rooms, covered with straw; a great barn of five bays, covered with straw; a small barn of three bays, covered with straw; a house covered with tile (Beds Archives, ABE 1). He consulted Dr Napier on 17 February 1625, who recorded that he was 51, had a chill and cold and prescribed for him (Forman and Napier, case no. 59804).

350 Peter Hunnilove of Bedford, tailor made 7 March 1625
Lincolnshire Archives, INV/129/347

A true Inventorie of all & singular the goods & Chattels of Peter Hunnilove late of the towne & county of Bedford Taylor praysed by Robert Goodhall, Richard Flint & Richard Crafts this 7th of March 1624

	£	s	d
Inprimis 3 beasts	5	0	0
Item Hay	0	6	8
Item Wood	0	6	8
Item in the Hall one Table & a frame & a forme & six stoles 4 Cushions 2 spits one payre of bellowes & all yron about the fyre	0	12	0
Item three & twenty ~~shillings~~ peeces of pewter, & eleven spoones a brush & a black jack & all the brasse	1	6	8
Item in the butterie two cubbarts & other old trash	0	15	0
Item in the Chamber one standing bed & a trundlebed with all the furniture belonging to them	2	0	0
Item three chests a chaire a forme & a box	0	13	0
Item nyne payre of sheets six napkins two bord Cloaths	2	0	0
Item in an other Chamber two borded beds & the furniture to them and eight pillow beares & two coffers	1	0	0
Item in the shop one bed & certayne paynted cloaths there & in other parts of the howse	0	3	4
Item his wearing apparrell	2	0	0
Debts			
Item a bond	1	5	0
Item an other bond	3	3	0
Item a bill	1	10	0
Item a bill	10	8	8
[*Total*	*£32*	*10*	*0d*]

Robert Goodhall [*signature*], Richard Flinte [*signature*], Richard Crafts marke
[*Exhibited by the executrices at Bedford on 21 May 1625*]

Notes: Peter Hunnilove was buried at Bedford St Paul's on 6 March 1625. There was no total on the inventory and the debts were not specified as owed to or by Peter Hunnilove. The total supplied here has assumed that the debts were money owed to him. He made his will on 4 March 1625. He gave his house and orchard to his son Thomas. He ordered that the terms of a bond (to leave his wife Elizabeth all the goods she had brought to the marriage and £5) should be carried out. He gave small sums of money and goods to his children, step-children and grandchildren. He appointed his three daughters, Elizabeth, Jane and Sarah as his executrices and they were granted probate by William Dalbie at Bedford on 21 May 1625 (Lincs Archives, LCC WILLS/1624–25/440).

351 John Holloway of Cople, husbandman made 7 March 1625
Lincolnshire Archives, INV/129/341

Anno 1624 March 7. A True Inventory of all the Goodes and Chattelles of John Holloway late of Cople in this County of Bedfford husbandman, deceased: Made by those whose names are here under written the seaventh day of March in the yeare of our Lord God 1624 as followeth

	£	s	d
In the Hall			
Inprimis. One Longe Table, with a Frame: A Bench Boarde, and a Foarme	0	8	0
Item One Cupboarde, one Penn, one Cheere and two stooles	0	10	0
Item One Brasse pott, three kettles, one Sckellet one possnett, one Chafeindish, & one Candlsticke	0	18	0
Item Eight pewter platters, three Cuppes, one pewter Candlesticke, two podingers, and one Salte	0	7	0
In the Buttery & Milke-house			
Inprimis Three Barrells, three Tubbes, two Payles, with a Beere staule	0	9	4
Item Five Bowles, one Tunnill, six earthen pottes, with other small Trash	0	5	0
Item One salteing trough, one small Table with two shellves	0	3	4
Item The dishes, trenchers, spoones pothookes, pothangers, with other trumpery	0	1	4
In the Chamber within the house			
Inprimis One Bed-stead, one Mattrisse, two Blanquettes, one Coverlecte, one Boulstar with two pillowes	1	6	8
Item One Coaffer, one Cheere with a small old Cupboarde and the painted cloathes there	0	8	0
Item all the Linnen in the house [*this line has been inserted in a different hand*]	1	14	8
In a Lofte over the sayd Chamber			
Inprimis A quantitie of yarne, a parcell of Hemp, with a Hetchell, & a shelffe	0	6	0
In the Chamer without the house			
Inprimis One Bedstead, one fetherbed, one straw			

bedd, two Blanquetes, one Coverlecte one Boulstar, and three pillowes	2	10	8
Item One Chist, one Boxe and the painted cloathes there	0	11	0
In the shoppe, & the Boulting-house			
Inprimis One Bedstead, one shop-board, one old Coaffer, two boardes, & two hemp-brakes	0	5	0
Item One kimnell, three Binges, one Boultinge Arke, with two Bushells & a halffe of wheate	0	19	0
In the Store-house, & Chaff-house			
Inprimis Three Forkes, three Rakes with certaine old Iron, & other trumpery	0	4	0
Item Certaine Chaffe, & dragge Rake & other thinges	0	4	0
Item one spitt one Grydyron a Brush & painted cloathes [*this line has been inserted in a different hand*]	0	3	4
Item in the Backhouse			
Inprimis. A woollen wheele, a Linnen wheele, & a Reele	0	2	0
In the Barne			
Inprimis. The Haye	1	0	0
Item. The Barly ~~being in straw~~ mislyn & wheat	2	[*illeg.*]	0
~~Item The wheate unthreshed~~	0	~~12~~	0
Item The winnowinge cloath, one Hand-riddle, one Seeve with other thinges	0	1	0
In the yarde			
Inprimis One Cowe	2	6	8
Item Two store-hogges	0	14	0
Item Fower flitches of Bacon	1	6	8
Item Nine stockes of Bees	2	5	0
Item The Hovell there	0	4	0
Item The Compasse	0	4	8
Item The Pullen	0	4	6
Item for goods forgotten [*this line has been inserted in a different hand*]	0	1	0
In the feilde			
[*line deleted*]			
Last of all his wayringe Apparell	2	10	0
Summa totius	24	13	10

The names of us which were the pricers hereof the day & yeare above mentioned Richard Purser [*signature*], William Barker [*mark*], Rodger Merill [*mark*], Thomas Smith [*mark*]
[*Exhibited by the executors at Bedford on 21 May 1625*]

Notes: John Holloway was buried at Cople on 2 February 1625, described as 'senior et pater-familias'. He made his will on 12 April 1624. He gave his cottage with 10 acres of arable to his wife Margaret for life, then to his son John. He divided his household goods among his sons, daughters and grandchildren after his and his wife's death. He appointed John Negoose and Thomas Smith, his sons-in-law, as his executors, to whom probate was granted by William Dalbie at Bedford on 21 May 1625 (Lincs Archives, LCC WILLS/1624–25/194).

352 Henry Foster of Thurleigh, yeoman made 7 March 1625
Lincolnshire Archives, INV/129/342

A true Inventory of all the goods & Chattells of Henry Foster late of Thurligh in the County of Bedfford yeoman deceased taken the seventh day of March 1624 by Thomas Lloid Clerke, William Foster & Richard Cadwell

	£	s	d
Imprimis wee prize the horses & the plow & Cart & implements of husbandry at	x		
Item the Tilth & wheat & peaseland at	vj		
Item the three Acres & half & xij pole of underwood new fallen in Burnewood	x		
Item the swine at	ij	v	
Item the two oxen & foure bullocks	ix		
Item the sheepe at	xiiij		
Item the xij milchbeasts at	xxxvj		
Item the hay at	ij	x	
Item the barley pease & oates	iij		
Item the malt mill & hovells & firewood at	ij	x	
Item the lease of the Farme at		x	
Item the tables & Chaires in the hall		xx	
Item the Andirons & spitt & bellowes		v	
Item the safe & fire shovall & grediron & other stuff in kitchin at		xx	
Item the brasse & pewter		xxx	
Item the goods in the milkhouse		xl	
Item the money	vj		
Item the standing bedd & bedding & the coffers in the chamber over the hall at	v		
Item the bed & bedding & other householdstuff in the chamber over the kitchin	iiij		
Item his books & apparell	vj	xiij	viij
Item things forgotten at			xij
Summa totalis	Cxxiij	iiij	viij

[*Exhibited by the executrix at Bedford on 21 May 1625*]

Notes: Henry Foster was buried at Thurleigh on 27 February 1625. One of the appraisers was the deceased's father William Foster; another was Thomas Lloyd, the vicar of Thurleigh. Henry Foster made his will on 11 February 1625. He gave £40 to Katherine Parsell of Swinshead, whom he had intended to marry, on condition that she returned the deeds setting up her jointure. He gave 10s or 20s to several family and friends to buy rings. His lands were to pass according to the terms of a deed between himself and his father. The residual legatee and executrix was sister Elizabeth Foster, to whom probate was granted by William Dalbie at Bedford in May 1625 (Lincs Archives, LCC WILLS/1624–25/196).

353 Thomas Rozell of Willington made 11 March 1625
Lincolnshire Archives, INV/129/351

March the xj 1624. A true Inventorie of all the goods and Chattells of Thomas Rozell late of Willington deceased

	£	s	d
In the Halle			
Imprimis one table with a frame 4 ioynt stooles on Cupboord 2 Chussions a glasse shelfe one litle table certaine benches and other thing	1	vj	8
In the Parler			
one Beddstead aframe bedd abolster a Coverlett one Cupboord one litle presse for Cloase one Coffer two boxes and a looking glasse	i	10	
In the lowe Parler			
one Beddsteed one fetherbedd one flock bedd one bolster two blanketts one Coverlett, one Cupboord two Chests and two Boxes and certaine painted Cloathes one Matris two old blanquetts	3	0	0
In the Drink house			
4 Barrells 6 tubbs one penne one salting trough vj boules one cherme and other trashe	1	10	
In the lofte			
one Cheese racke one trundle Bedd two paire of wooll cards two stone of Hempe one wicker baskett two bushells of unions and other implements	0	xiij	iiij
two lynnen wheeles and one woollen wheele		iij	4
Lynen			
Six pair of sheetes two pillowe beares two boord Cloathes six napkins one towell	ij	0	0
Pewter and Brasse			
20 peesses of pewter of all sorts 4 brasen ketles two posnetts one brasse pott one warming Panne two brazen candlesticks a morttr one driping panne one spitt a paire of hand Irons tongs and fire shovell a pair of pott hookes and a pair of Bellowes	ij	10	
All his wearing apparell	i	10	
In the yard			
Wood Planckes broken boords and 3 ladders		xv	
one HoggsCoat and a leane too		10	
one Canch of Haye	1	0	0
one litle mayre	j	0	0
In the Backhouse			
one mault myll two steks to putt grayne in on kneeding trowgh and other implements	i	10	

Pailes and gates about the yard	0	v	0
one dragg rake 3 sacks two pitchforks	0	v	0
Aples and old Iron	0	v	
posts sommertrees and Boords for 4 lofts	iiij		
Certaine Plowe greere [*sic*] and Cart grare and two pannells	0	iij	4
Graine in the feild			
one Acree of wheat, one Acre o[*f*] maseldine one Acree of tylth to sowe with barley	iij	0	0
3 Acres of Bratch Land	j	0	0
Some	27	15	8
[*Corrected total*	*£27*	*16s*	*8d*]

John Osmond [*signature*], William Hill [*signature*], Wyllyam Fadlutt [*signature*]
[*Exhibited by the executor at Bedford on 21 May 1625*]

Notes: Thomas Rozell was buried at Willington on 4 March 1625.

354 Susan Underwood of Sandy, widow made 16 March 1625
Lincolnshire Archives, INV/129/334

A trewe and perfect Inventary of all and singuler the goodes and Chattles which were late Susan Underwood of Sandey in the County of Bed widdowe deceased valued & indifferently prized the xvj[th] day of March Anno domini 1624 by John Underwood thelder and Richard Allen both of Sandey aforesaid yomen as followeth

	£	s	d
In the Hall			
Imprimis one ioyned table with a frame one side table, one forme, viij ioyned stooles ~~and~~ iiij Cheares and three pott shelves		xxxvj	
Item three brasse pottes fower kettles two possenettes one Cheffendish one brasse Candlesticke & one morter		xlj	
Item Eleaven pewter platters, three smale pewter dishes, two pewter Candlestickes fower porringers and one Chamberpott		xviij	
Item one payre of Andirons one spitt & one drippinge pann		iiij	
In the Chamber			
Item two Cubberdes		xxvj	
Item two Chestes one truncke two boxes & one little table		xxv	
Item one bedsteed, one Featherbedd three Coverringes, one blanckett, two bowlsteres and one pillowe	iij	x	
Item Nyne payre of Sheetes, one odd Sheete & three table Cloathes	v		

In the lofte over the Chamber			
Item one bourded bedd, one trundle bedd ~~one~~ two flocke beddes, two boulsteres, three pillowes, two payre of sheetes two Coveringes & two blanckettes		xxx	
Item two Coffers, one Saltinge troughe one Cradle with other lumber		xx	
Item her wearinge Apparrell		xl	
In the lofte over the Hall			
Item two Coffers, seaven pillowe beares, two speare Cloathes, Nyne-teene table Napkins, three pillowes one blanckett with other lumber		xl	
In the Buttery			
Item two barrells, two Tubbs with hempe and other lumber		xx	
In the Hay Howse			
Item the Hay there		xiij	iiij
In the yard			
Item one Cowe		xl	
Item [*?*]burnige Wood and Ferne		vj	viij
Debtes due to the Testatrix			
Item in the handes of Theophilus Cater by bond	iiij		
Item in the handes of Agnesse Swetman Widdowe by bill	iiij		
Item in the handes of William Allen by bond	v	x	
Debtes due to the Testatrix without specialty			
Item in the handes of Thomas Peirson		xij	
Item in the handes of Anthony Swetman		x	
Item in the handes of John Larkin		ix	
Item in the handes of the said John Larkyn	v		
Item in the possession of the said John Larkyn one Cowe		xl	
Item one silver spoone in the handes of the said John		v	
Summa totalis	xlviij	xvj	

Signum John Underwood, Richard Allin [*signature*]
[*Exhibited by the executor at Bedford on 21 May 1625*]

Notes: Susan Underwood was buried at Sandy on 13 March 1625. She made her will on 3 January 1621. She left £10 and the bulk of the furniture, linen and household goods listed in the inventory to her daughter Agnes including a silver spoon and a cradle; a pair of sheets to her daughter Elizabeth; £4 and some household items to Henry, her younger son. She appointed her elder son John residual legatee and executor. He was granted probate by William Dalbie at Bedford on 21 May 1625 (Lincs Archives, LCC WILLS/1624–25/37).

355 John Wye of Broome, Southill, yeoman made 16 March 1625
Lincolnshire Archives, INV/129/366
The inventory is beautifully written. The inventory of goods at Southill is on both sides of the main sheet. A second sheet has been sewn to its foot and lists his goods at Biggleswade. This list is at the foot of the first side of the main sheet but has been transcribed here at the end of the inventory for clarity.

An Inventorye of all the goodes and Chattelles of John Wye late of Broome in the parishe of Southeill in the Countye of Bedf yeoman deceassed taken by us John Raymonte and Anthony Renolde of the parishe of Southeill aforesayd gent and William Goldsmythe of Shefford in the Countye of Bedf aforesayd yeoman the sixtenthe daye of Marche in the Yeares of the Reigne of our moste dread soveraigne Lord James by the grace of god of England Fraunce & Ireland kinge defendor of the Faythe etc the twoe and twentythe & of Scotland the eighte & Fivetyth 1624 in manner followeinge

	£	s	d
In the haule			
Inprimis in the haule a longe table with a Frame and twoe ioyned Formes		xx	
Item one Cubberde with the presse in yt and a deske uppon yt with the Cubberd Clothe and a pott shelfes		xiij	iiij
Item the Muskett with the Furniture		xxvj	viij
Item twoe Chaffeinge dishes a pestell a morter and a Warmeinge pann		viij	
Item a payre of Iron Jackes a longe pitche forke		ij	iiij
In the kytchin			
Item a Fyer shovell a payre of tounges a payre of Iyron Cobyrons a payre of pott hangers and twoe spyttes and twoe drippinge pannes		xiij	iiij
Item a shorte table by the Fyer side a gyrdyron a skymmer and other trashe aboute the kytchin		iij	
Item one payre of Carte roopes and a payre of bellowes		ij	viij
In the chamber over the haule			
Item one Joyned Bedstead with a trundell bedd twoe Feather beddes twoe Coveringes and Fower Blankettes and a mattryce with twoe boulsteres of Feathers and one pillowe	v	j	iiij
Item Five Curtaynes and three Curtayne roddes Fower ioyned stooles & a chayre & a Cloathe baskett		xv	
Item Five Candellstickes of pewter a quarte pott twenty nyne peeces of pewter a brasse morter twoe pewter Cuppes twoe saltes Fowerteene pewter spoones & twoe lattyn Candelstickes and a warmeinge pann		xlvj	
Item Fower greate Chestes twoe Coffers a little table and twoe highe ioyned stooles and a Box		xlvij	
Item twelve payre of sheetes and one sheete of hempe tare and hempe towe and one Childbedd sheete of Lokarum twoe table boarde Cloathes twoe Cubberd Cloathes & twoe payre of pillowe beares	v	iij	iiij
Item twoe dozen of table napkyns and eighte payre			

of sheetes and an odd sheete of hempe tare and hempe towe Fower handtowelles a payre of pillowebeares	iij	x	
Item Fower payre of harden sheetes and twoe handtowelles of harden		xvj	viij
In the lofte over the buttery			
Item three Flytches of Bacon and twoe Flytches in the troughe		l	
Item certayne Fleeces of Wooll	iij		
Item three Coffers and Fower cheeses and other trashe and some old Iron		xiiij	iiij
In the chamber over the kytchin			
Item a boarded bedstead with a mattryce a pillowe and a coveringe and a wicker chayre a payre of Iron rackes and a payre of Stocke Cardel' a woollen wheele & a Cradle & other trashe there		xxiij	
In the parlour			
Item one Bedstead		x	
In the Folkes chamber			
Item one boarded bedsteade and twoe linnen wheeles		v	
Item a rideinge pillion for a woman and Fower Cushions		vij	
Item his wareinge apparell		xxx	
Item nyne henns and a Cocke		viij	
Item dewe unto this testator by billes and bondes	CCxviij	viij	
In the Feilde			
Item eleven acres of wheate and Rye in the Feildes of Broome	xvj	x	
Item twoe acres and a halfe of pease		xl	
In the stable			
Item Five horses one beinge blinde and one other lame	xiij	iij	iiij
Item the Carte geares and plowe geares for Five horse		xx	
Item one Fleake			vj
In the yard			
Item seaven Cowes or beastes	xviij	xiij	iiij
Item one yoake of draughte steares	v	x	
Item Five drye bullockes beinge twoe yeares old	viij	x	
Item one sowe and Fower stoores		xlv	
Item one Fatt hogg		xx	
Item seaven Cowe rackes		v	x
Item three sheepe rackes		vij	vj
Item three ploughes with there coulteres and shares and three foote teames and twoe longe teames with three whiple trees		xviij	
Item one Hovell		xx	
Item three woodden harrowes		iiij	
Item an olde payre of yron harrowes		v	
Item twoe dozen and a halfe of [?]slate hyrdelles		vij	vj
Item the Compasse in the yard	iij	vj	viij

Item three hogges troughes			xvj
Item Fortey Couples of Ewes & lambes	xvij		
Item Five & Fortey drye sheepe	xiij	x	
Item old wheeles aboute the yarde and an olde ploughe and other Fier wood		v	
Item three ploughe beames		ij	vj
Item a dozen and a halfe of ploughe Coppes and some small ploughe timber		v	
Item twoe draughte rakes and one broken one		v	
In the barne			
Item one Kanche of Rye to threshe	x	xiij	iiij
Item twoe peeces of mowes of barley to threshe and some threshed	xxv		
Item an Ile of Haye in the Barne		xl	
Item the Chaffe in the barne & Chaffe howse		xxx	
Item a skreene a dounge Rake and twoe Fannes a shovell and twoe pytche forkes		viij	
In another barne			
Item twoe peeces of Mowes of haye	vj	xiij	iiij
Item Fower payre of shoed wheeles three Carte bodyes & one Tumbrell with there carte laddere & false raves	vij		
In the bake howse			
Item one Fornace with the Curbe	iij		
Item a Querne and a Cheese presse		xv	iiij
Item a swill tub and a seedecoate		ij	
Item two kneadinge kymnelles and a mouldinge boarde and other trashe in the Bake howse		v	vj
In the maulte howse			
Item Fower ladders	[*value illegible*]		
Item three ox yoakes and a newe carte bodye and other trashe there	[*value illegible*]		
Item three tubbes and a hempe stocke	[*value illegible*]		
In the lofte over the maultehowse			
Item twentye bushelles of whyte pease		xl	
Item three quarteres of gray pease		xlviij	
Item a quarter of horse Corne		xij	
Item twoe quarteres of wheate	iiij		
Item three bushelles of Rye		ix	
Item a bushell and a strike and a castinge shovell & twoe skeppes & Fower meade rakes and twoe ridles		vj	viij
Item eighte ploughe beames & twoe new axell trees		vj	viij
Item thyrtey neckes & sheathes of ploughe timber a dozen of wrystes and seaven ploughe beames		x	
Item a Gryndstone with an Iron spyndell		ij	vj
In the milke howse			
Item a salteinge troughe and Five shelves and three plankes		vj	

In the buttery

Item Five barrelles and a greate tubb and a charme and six milke booles		xiij	iiij
Item eighte kettelles and one pann		xxx	
Item Fower brasse pottes and a brasse posnett		xxiiij	
[Total at Southill, less the illegible values	*£431*	*15s*	*2d]*

[*A second sheet of parchment has been sewn to the bottom of the first. It is faded and badly damaged. Some words are illegible or missing.*]

Item his goodes att Bigleswade apprysed by Thomas [*?*]Notthe and Edwarde Braye as followeth			
Item one table and one Cuberde and a liverye cobberd and a pott Shelfe and other thinges		xx	
Item [*illeg.*] table in the parlour and other [*?*]smale thinges there		x	
Item in the [*?Bu*]tterye and the milke howse [*illeg.*] Shelfes and other thinges		v	
Item in [*the ki*]tchyn a troughe to knead[...] in and a payre of Cobyrons		iij	iiij
[Total at Biggleswade		*38s*	*4d]*
[Total of all his goods, except for missing values	*£433*	*13s*	*6d]*

[*Exhibited at Bedford. The exhibition clause is at the foot of the list of goods at Biggleswade. The document at this point is crumpled and torn and the exhibition clause is largely illegible.*]

Notes: John Wye was buried at Southill on 10 March 1625, as John Wye senior. He made his will on 5 March 1625. He gave £70, five couples of sheep, a chest, a little coffer and six pieces of pewter to his two daughters, Frances Hunt and Anne Wye; £70, five couples of sheep, and a lease of 20 acres to his son Thomas; 40s a year to his son William; 12d to his eldest son John; and 5 couples of sheep to his godson John Wye. He gave the residue to his wife Alice who was also appointed executrix. A codicil sets out that if 'the bonds which I have will not reach unto this money here bequeathe then all my Childrens portions shalbe deducted according to the rate that the bonds amount unto'. (This provision may have been invoked as his bills and bonds amounted to £218 and he made gifts of £210 and required a further £20 to produce interest of 40s a year for his son William.) Probate was granted to his wife Alice by William Dalbie at Bedford on 21 May 1625 (Lincs Archives, LCC WILLS/1624–25/197).

356 William Greene of Husborne Crawley, weaver — made 18 March 1625

Lincolnshire Archives, INV/129/319

Husborne Crawley. A True Inventorie of all the Goodes of William Greene weaver late of Husborne Crawley deceased seene and prised the xviij of March Anno domini 1624 by Henrie Kettle, Thomas Brotherton & Sollomon Greene as Followethe

	£	s	d
in the Hall			
Inprimis an old Table & Benche & Forme		iij	iiij
Item foure Cheares		ij	
Item one old Cubbord and a pen		iij	iiij
Item a Brasse pot iij° kettles & ij postnets		x	

	£	s	d
Item a Tubb and a Barrell		ij	vj
Item a Brasse Chaffendishe one Candlesticke one skimmer and a fryinge pan		ij	
Item Three pewter dishes		ij	
Item dishes ij boules one payle a woodden morter ij little Stooles and all other odde Implementes in the hall			xij

In the Chamber

	£	s	d
Item five payre of Sheetes ij pillowbeares ij napkins & one board Clothe		xxij	
Item Two blanketes Two kiverlides		xiij	iiij
Item Three Bedsteades		v	
Item one Chest one Coffer & ij Boxes		vj	viij
Item his wearinge apparrell		xx	
Item money owinge to him	xxxv		
The Some	xxxix	xiij	ij

[*Exhibited by the executrix at Dunstable on 17 May 1625*]

Notes: William Greene was buried at Husborne Crawley on 7 March 1625. He made a nuncupative will on 6 March 1625. He gave £3 each to his two elder sons for apprenticeships; 40s each to his two elder daughters; his house and grounds to his wife Margaret for life then to his youngest son, him paying 50s each to the two younger daughters. His wife Margaret was residual legatee and executrix. There is no probate clause (Lincs Archives, LCC WILLS/1624–25/238).

357 Thomas Grene of Bedford St Paul, baker made 18 March 1625

Lincolnshire Archives, INV/129/354

A True Inventorye of all the goodes and Chattells moveables & howshouldstuffe of Thomas Grene late of the towne of Bedford Baker deceased made the eighteenth daye of March Anno Domini 1624 and appraysed by those whose name are here under written as followeth

	£	s	d
Inprimis Twoe geldinges one blacke and thother dunn valued at	iij	x	
Item Twoe other geldings ones white price xxx^{s} and thother browne baye price fyve poundes both att	vj	x	
Item fyve quarters & a halfe of Rye & barley	v	x	
Item fyve quarters of Rye valued at	v	x	
Item twoe quarters of the best wheate	iiij		
Item one quarter & a halfe of the worst wheate		xl	
Item Twoe bushells of wheate & Rye		vj	
Item wood and haye valued at		xl	
Item Sadles and pannyers & brydles		x	
Item in the backhowse mouldingboardes & Arkes at [*sic*] and one troffe & other thinges valued		xiij	iiij
Item in the hall one Table fowre stoles twoe Chayres one little Cubberd & other smale thinges at		~~xxxiij~~ xl	
Item one other Table one Chest & ~~one~~ other thinges at		v	
Item ~~brasse and~~ pewter valued at [*bracketted with the next line*] Rackes spittes & pannes & other yron at [*this line inserted*]		l	

Item in the Seller barrells & tubbes & other thinges at		xx	
Item in the best Chamber one Table one bedstedd with the furnyture thereto belonginge att	x		
Item one trundle bedd & the furnyture thereto belonginge att	iiij		
Item Twoe Chayrers twoe Chestes one Trunck & other smale boxes & little stoles ~~valued att~~ att & other smale thinges in the Chamber valued att		xl	
Item in the next chamber one standinge bedsteed & one trundle bedd with the furnyture & other thinges at		xx	
Item in thother chamber over the hall One standinge bedsteed with the furnyture one little table one presse one Chest & one Coffer at	v		
Item one standinge bedstedd & one trundle bedd with the furnyture upon one bedd at		xx	
Item twentye payre of sheetes valued at	viij		
Item three dozen of table napkyns & table clothes valued att		xl	
Item halfe a dozen of pillowe beeres valued		x	
Item one Carpett, one Coverlett & Cushyons att	vj		
Item One Furnys twoe brasse pottes three kettles & other brasse		xxx	
Item One great kettle valued att		xiij	iiij
Item One gowne valued att	vij		
Item Twoe Cloakes and other apparell at	iiij	x	
Item One silver salt one silver Cupp sixe silver spones & twoe other little silver Cupp at	vj		
Item One greene Rugge & Certen Curteynes att		l	
Item Certen bookes valued att		xxvj	
Item Fishe and apples valued att		xv	
Summa	99	18	8

Richard Joye [*signature*], Jonas Androwe [*signature*], Richard Gale [*signature*]
[*Exhibited by the executor at Bedford on 21 May 1625*]

Notes: Thomas Grene was buried at Bedford St Paul's on 20 February 1625. The appraiser, Richard Joye, of Staple Inn, London, bought property in Bedford in 1611 (Beds Archives, Z2/1) and witnessed transactions in and around Bedford after that date.

358 Henry Raulins of Thurleigh, yeoman made 22 March 1625
Lincolnshire Archives, INV/129/335

A true Inventory of all the goods & Chattalls of Henry Raulins late of Thurligh in the County & Archd[eaco]nry of Bedfford deceased taken the xxij[th] day of March 1624 by Edward Bull, William [*?*]Allen & Nicholas Browne

	£	s	d
Imprimis wee price the three horses at	7		
The 2 beasts at	4		
The cartbody & plow & cart timber at	1		
The plow & Cart geares at		10	
The five piggs at		15	

The hovell at		13	
The hay at		6	8
The wood at		5	
Thirty bushells of barly at	3		
one quarter of wheat at	1	4	
[*?*]Foure Acres of tilth at	2		
Five Acres of pease at	2	10	
Three Acres of pease land at		12	
The stuff in kitchin & milkhouse at		12	
The stuff in Buttery at		2	
The pease & pease straw at			20
The Rowle & harrowes & plow at		5	
The pitchforkes & staves at		2	
The hempe & flaxe at		5	
The skreene & sieves & sedlip at		6	
The Fetherbedd & bedding belonging to it	1	10	
The sheets & other linen at	1		
The table & coffers & chaire & stooles at		6	
The geese & pullen at		3	
The grindstone at		1	
The bacon at		8	
The painted cloathes at		5	
The sackes at		3	
The brasse & pewter at		6	
his Apparell at	2	10	
The dung in the yard at		5	
The pailes at			8
The barr of iron & other tooles at		3	
All things forgotten at		1	
[*Total*]	34	1	8
[*Corrected total*	*£32*	*11s*	*0d*]

[*Exhibited by the executor at Bedford on 21 May 1625*]

Notes: Henry Raulins was buried at Thurleigh on 21 March 1625. He made his will on 9 March 1625, describing himself as a yeoman. He gave his house and lands to his brother Edward Raulins on condition that he look after their father John Raulins. He gave small sums to his brothers and a sister and £3 each to his widowed sister and his niece. The residual legatee and executor was his brother Edward, to whom probate was granted by William Dalbie at Bedford on 21 May 1625 (Lincs Archives, LCC WILLS/1624–25/232).

359 John Chamberlayne of Bedford St Paul made 23 March 1625

Lincolnshire Archives, INV/129/349

An inventarie of the goods & Chattells of John Chamberlayne late of St Paules in Bedford deceased Taken the 23th daie of March 1624 by John Richardson & Henrie Angell

	£	s	d
Inprimis in the shopp the cutting board			
an ould bed with other implements there		6	8
In the kitchen an oulde cubbard & other trash		ij	

	£	s	d
In the chamber over the shopp			
ij little tables vj stools ij barells			
4 kettles one [*?*]fanne & other [*?*]gear			
as a great chadger & [*?*]sum small			
pewter & a wheele		xv	
In the hall chamber xj platters			
& other small pewter v kandlestikes		xij	
one pres cubbard		xvj	
one bedsteed one trukle bed with			
the bedding		xl	
iiij ould koffers		x	
iij boxes & a chayre & ij little			
buffett stooles		v	
vj pare of course sheets 12 napkins			
a pare of pillow bears one boardcloth			
& ij pillowes		33	4
All his wearing apparell		xx	
[*Total*]	viij		
John Richardson [*signature*], Henre Angell his mark			
the debtts of the partie dceasted			
comes to	v	xvij	
[*Exhibited at Bedford on 21 May 1625*]			
Allocant' per iurum Dalby etc			

Notes: John Chamberlayne was buried at Bedford St Paul's on 11 March 1625, as John Chamberlin.

360 Simon Dickenson of Leighton Buzzard, miller made 24 March 1625

Lincolnshire Archives, INV/129/331

A true and perfect Inventary of all the goods Chattells and Cattalls of Simon Dickenson late of Leighton deceased taken and apprised by William Hogg, William Nash, Edmund Tommes & Thomas Stevens March 24 1624

	£	s	d
In the Hall			
Inprimis A Table with a frame & seven ioynd stooles		16	
Item Two chayres		2	
Item two payre of pothangers a payr of creepers a barre of Iron Fireshovell Tongs & bellows		6	8
Item a warming pan a brasen skimer brasen ladle a brush		4	
Item fifteen peeces of pewter a quart pott a pint pott a chamberpott an aquavita bottle two Candlesticks with potts & glasses		12	
Item foure Cushions		1	
In the kitching			
Inprimis five kettles brasse, two pottage potts, a possnet brass two dripping panns a frying pann a gridiron a brasen ladle a chafing dish		50	

Item two payre of potthangers two spitts, two payre of pott hookes, two bushells, three old barrels, three Tubbs two kivers two seives two Bole dishes a halfe pecke, an old Lanterne ~~two~~ foure payles a seattle		30	
Item a salting trough a boulting Hutch five shelveboords foure woodden Candlesticks nine ropes of onions		4	
In the parlour			
Inprimis two bedsteeds a chest and a deske ~~a litle Lanterne~~ three shelve boords a baskett		8	
Item five blanketts Nyne coverings two bolsters a flockbed, a strawbed		26	8
In the chamber over the Hall			
Inprimis Two ioynd Bedsteds, a fetherbed a fether bolster a strawbed, two fether pillowes a payre of blankettes, a Covering five Curtaynes, 3 iron rodds	6	13	4
Item a mattrice a bolster a pillow a payre of blanketts a Covering		30	
Item a Table with the frame ~~fou~~ six stooles, a cheste a Cofer a litle Table with a box		30	
Item a wicker chayre seven Cushions a payre of Andirons		10	
Item in linnen ten payre of sheets three table clothes, a doossen & three napkins seven towells five pillow beers		50	
Item a saddle a Bible, another table		8	
Item a cradle a mattock an ax 3 forkes a forrest bill and other lumber		10	
Item in the little parlour			
Inprimis a Table with a frame two stooles		6	
Item a Cupboord		[*?13*]	4
Item eight platters three salts foure Cupps a candlestick pewter, with a woodden Candlestick		20	
In the Barne			
Inprimis foure ladders a hutch wood and strawe	6		
In the celler			
Item foure barrells two drink stalles		8	
Item in bonds	10		
Item his wearing apparrell		40	
Summa	41	19	

William Hogg [*signature*], Ed. Tommes [*mark*], Thomas Stevens [*signature*], William Nashe [*signature*]
[*Exhibited by the executrix at Leighton Buzzard on 16 May 1625*]

Notes: Simon Dickenson's burial has not been found. He made his will on 20 February 1625, describing himself as a miller. He gave half his household goods to his five children, who were under 21, and the residue to his wife Katherine, who was appointed executrix and was granted probate by William Dalbye at Leighton Buzzard on 16 May 1625 (Lincs Archives, LCC WILLS/1624–25/536).

361 Elizabeth Purratt of Fancot, Toddington, widow made in 1625
Lincolnshire Archives, INV/129/326

The Inventorie of all the goodes Chattles debtes and Credittes of Elizabeth Purratt Late of Fancote in the parishe of Todington in the Countye of Bedd widowe deceased made proved and prysed the [*blank*] daie of [*blank*] 1625 by those whose names are hereunder written

	£	s	d
In primis her Apparrill		xiij	iiij
Item one Bedd & certeine Bedding		xiiij	
Item in Linen		xij	
Item one Little Table, fowre stooles, two Cofers and two tubbs		xij	iiij
Item one Morter, two little kittles, one Chafing dyshe, Three Candlestickes, Two Platters & a pewter dyshe		viij	
Item in debtes oweing unto her upon spetialtie	xlj		
Somma totalis is	xliij	xix	viij

William Marbles his marke, Richard Gurney his marke
[*Exhibited by the executor at Dunstable on 9 May 1625*]

Notes: Elizabeth Purratt was buried at Toddington on 5 March 1625. She was possibly the widow of William Purratt or Parrott of Fancot, labourer who died in 1619 and whose inventory valued at £143 8s 6d is in BHRS, vol. 20, p. 130 (Beds Archives, ABP/W1618–1619/208, I 4/141). She made her will on 9 March 1625. She gave £6 to one grandchild and small sums to five people. She appointed her son-in-law Thomas Scrivener (and his wife Elizabeth) residual legatee and executor, to whom probate was granted by William Dalbie at Dunstable on 2 May 1625 (Lincs Archives, LCC WILLS/1624–25/532).

362 John Vincent of Toddington, yeoman made 28 March 1625
Lincolnshire Archives, INV/129/325

The Inventorie of all the goodes Chattles debtes & Credittes of John Vincent late of Todington in the Countye of Bedd yeoman deceased made proved & prysed the xxviij° daie of March 1625 By those whose names are hereunder written

	£	s	d
In primis his apparrill		l	
Item one gould Ringe		xix	
Item in the parlour one old bedsteed, one truckle Bedd one Table & Frame, one Chest, one trunke two boxes two Formes & the Furniture to one of the Beddes	iij	x	
Item the Linen	iij	x	
Item in the haull one Cupborde, one Table & frame Two Chaires, Nyne stooles, and other implementes		xl	
Item in the Chamber over the haull one Fether Bedd		xxx	
Item in the Chamber over the parlour one half hedded Bedd one deske, one Table and Frame, one old trunke and certeyne Bedding	iiij	x	
Item the Basse, Iorne workes pott mettle & pewter	iij		
Item the Brewing vesselles and other implementes		x	

Item two hogges and two Flitches of Bacone		xl	
Item the wood muck & strawe		x	
Debtes oweing upon spetialties, By George Batt gent	xvij		
by George Impey	x		
by Thomas Spufferd	v		
by Richard Eames	x		
Debtes owing without spetialties, By Thomas Webbe		xx	
by Anne Presser widow		v	
by Raphe Johnsonn		x	
by George Joanes		xx	
by John Feild	vij	x	
by William Rose		v	
by Edward Lillye		xij	
by Thomas Jacksonn			xiiij
Somma totalis is	Lxxviij	iij	ij
[*Corrected total*	*£77*	*12s*	*2d*]
Debtes oweing by the said John Vincent, To Elizabeth Farie		v	
To James Mathew		xl	
To Cornelius White	iiij	x	
To James Coolverhowse		xxx	
To Barnabie Blackwell		vij	
To John Baker		xiiij	
To Thomas Spufford for woodd		x	
Somme of his debtes is	ix	xvj	
which being taken out of the lxxviij^{li} iij^{s} ij^{d} Restes	lxxviij	vij	ij
[*Corrected total*	*£67*	*16s*	*2d*]

Thomas Pottes, Thomas Mathew, Cornelius White
[*Exhibited by the executors at Dunstable on 6 May 1625*]

Notes: John Vincent was buried at Toddington on 29 March 1625. He made his will on 21 March 1625. He gave £50 to his daughter Mary; and 10s each to his landlord, Henry Smith, and six family members. He gave the residue to his daughter Mary and appointed her and his landlord Henry Smith executors (Lincs Archives, LCC WILLS/1624–25/276).

363 John Brittan of Silsoe, Flitton, husbandman made between March and May 1625
Lincolnshire Archives, INV/129/318

A true Inventory of all the goods Chattells and Cattell of John Brittan deceased vewed and praysed by them whose names are under whritten: Anno Domini 1625

	£	s	d
Imprimis his wearinge apparell	2	0	0
within the hall house			
One Table & frame, seaven ioynd stooles	0	15	0
One Cubbarde, a little Chayre, one deske, Two shelves, two formes two woodden candlesticks	1	3	3
Two tubbs, one payle, foure Cheesfats dishes, woodden spoones, & trenchers	0	5	4
One payre of scales foure small weights	0	0	8
Two kettles, one brasse pot, one posnet, one frying pan	0	12	0

Ten pewter platters, five pewter spoones,			
one pewter salt, one pewter Candlesticke			
one pewter sawcer, one pewter pallenger [*pottinger*?]			
one pewter pot, one brasse Candlesticke	0	12	0
One spit, one gridiron, one payre of pothookes			
One payre of pothangers; one fire shevill a payre of tongs	0	3	6
One payre of bellowes, one woodden mortis & pestill	[...]	[*?*]10	4
One flitch & a halfe of bacon	0	8	0
One mole-staffe, one shevill, one bill, one fan	0	2	6
One mattock, one hoe, one axe, one banking iron			
two peas-hookes, one dogget	0	5	0
One thetching rake, one hobiron, one hammer, two forkes	0	2	0
within the low chamber			
One Cubbard, five Coffers	0	13	0
Two borded beds, one stoole, two formes one barrell	0	4	0
Two coverlids, three blankets one matteris			
three pillowes, one boulster	1	0	0
Six payre of sheetes, three table napkins			
one towell, one pillowbeer one table cloth one wallet	1	0	0
Linnen yarne, rough hempe, wooll	1	2	0
A clothe-basket, two hand-baskets, one sive	0	1	6
within the Butterie			
Seaven milke-boles, one powdringe trough			
three barrells, five shelfes	0	7	6
Butter & cheese and one Cherme	0	2	6
One smoothing steele, one settinge steele, one barking iron	0	1	0
In the Lofte			
Wheate, Rye, and barley	1	2	0
One woollen wheele, two linnen wheeles, one reele	0	3	0
one Cheese-racke	0	0	6
In the barne			
One fanne, one wheelebarrow, one hay hooke	0	2	0
In the yarde			
Two kine, one yearlinge calfe	5	13	4
Hay, wood, hempe in the ground	0	15	4
Dunge	0	4	0
In the orchard			
Bees and Bee-hives	6	0	0
In the feilds			
Foure sheepe	1	5	0
Three half-acres of barley	2	10	0
Fives roodes of pease	1	13	4
The whole summe in all is Thirtie pound ten shillings six pence	[*30*	*10*	*6*]
[*Corrected total*	*£30*	*19s*	*7d*]

Renolde Cole [*signature*], William Gamble his marke, Robert Moore [*signature*]
[*Exhibited by the executrix at Dunstable on 17 May 1625*]

Notes: John Brittan was buried at Flitton on 22 March 1625; this must be a mistake in the register or in its transcription (*BPR*, vol. 18, p. B63) as he made his will on 16 April 1625. He described himself as a husbandman. He left a house, clothes and working tools to his son William. He gave the grounds, house in which he lived and his goods to his wife Temperance for life, then to son William. He appointed his wife executrix and she was granted probate by W. Dalbie at Dunstable on 17 May 1625 (Lincs Archives, LCC WILLS/1624–25/540).

364 Thomas Symons alias Seaman of Eversholt, yeoman made 4 April 1625
Lincolnshire Archives, INV/129/328

An Inventorye of the goodes and Chattelles late Thomas Symons late of Eversholte in the Countie of Bedd deceased praysed the Fowerth daie of Aprill Anno Domini 1625 by William Gregorye the'lder, Raph Whittamore, Richard Redell and Richard Tomlyn

	£	s	d
The goodes being within the dwelling howse of the saide Thomas Symons deceased			
In the hall			
Inprimis One Cubbard one long table with a Frame Two Chaires one litle table two pott shelves one Forme and other lomber		xxx	
In the parlour			
Item one bedsteed one Fether bedd one Rugg two blanckettes and Curtaynes to the bedd	iij		
Item one Trundle bedd one Coffer one Chest one Chaire and one litle round table		xv	
In the litle Chamber next the Kitchen			
Item one Bedsteed one Fetherbedd One Covering two blanckettes one Chaire one pott shelfe and other lomber	iij		
In the Kitchen			
Item two kettles two Tubbs one Iron dripingpann one Frying pan one parre of Rackes one Cheesepresse		xx	
In the milkhouse			
Item six milck boles iij barrelles		v	
In the loft over the parlour			
Item 2 bourded beddes one Fetherbedd and other Furniture about them		xx	
In the loft over the hall			
Item one bedsteed one round table Fower Cofers and one litle boxe		xxiij	iiij
Item xviij[en] parre of sheetes and th'other lynen	v		
In the loft over the Entry			
Item one brasse pott one brasse pann one hanging shelfe and other lomber		xiij	iiij
In the yarde and about the house			
Item Fower bease and a Calfe	~~iiij~~ x		
Item one parcell of haye		xx	
Item divers parcelles of Fyer woode		xxx	
Item the Compasse & dung about the yard		x	
Item one ladder		ij	
Item his wareing apparell		xl	
~~Item one tenement which Robert Fountayne dwelles in of lease hold~~			

William Gregorie senior [*signature*], the marke of Richard Tomlyn, Raffe Whittam [*signature*], Richeard Reddell [*signature*]

on the verso

	£	s	d
Item on Tenement and other Lease Land	17		
Item Debtes due by specialtie	72	4	
Item debtes due without specialtie		34	6
Item more Debtes due by specialtie	17		
Sum total	140	7	2

[*Exhibited by the executrix at Dunstable on 17 May 1625*]

Notes: Thomas Symons was buried at Eversholt on 27 March 1625. He was a churchwarden in 1619–20 and 1620–21 with William Gregorie senior (*BPR*, vol. 75, p. 118). He made his will on 20 March 1625, calling himself Thomas Simons alias Seaman, yeoman. He left money or land to his sons and daughter and gave the rest of his leasehold houses to his wife Isabell for life, then to son William. He gave the residue to his wife and appointed her executrix (Lincs Archives, LCC WILLS/1624–25/284).

365 Thomas Harbert of Leighton Buzzard, butcher made 4 April 1625

Lincolnshire Archives, INV/129/332

Slight damage on the right side of the first page. Some values may be missing.

A true and perfect Inventary of all the goods Cattells and chattels of Thomas Harbert late of Leighton deceased taken and apprized by Thomas Leech, Roger Wynton & Thomas Paynton Apprill 4 1625

	£	s	d
In the Hall			
Inprimis A Long table with a frame, & seven high stooles, two low stooles		18	
Item foure chayrs great and litle		4	
Item two benches & a back of waynscott		8	
Item a Cupboard		20	
Item two litle safes		3	
Item in pewter, of pote pewter 28 – of saucars one dossen, seven salts double & single, 3 pewter Candlesticks, spoones one dosen & an halfe two pewter Cups, a pint pott an aquavita pottle two pewter pottengers, a beaker, 2 chamber potts	3		
Item a Jacke turnbroche, three payre of hangers, three spitts a morter & pestle, a skymer & litle ladle brasse, a beefe fork, two andirons, a fire showell, payr of tongs a payr of bellowes, an Iron for the fire		35	
Item two shelves, a lether buckett, a leading staffe		3	
Item a fleetch and an halfe of Bacon		15	
Item a litle Table, & an Iron barre in the chimnye		4	[...]
In the shopp			
Inprimis two vates, a boulting Hutch, five cooking kivers two Boles & a Bushell		26	
Item five Cleavers		5	
Item a payre of skales brasse with weights		2	

	£	s	d
Item 3 wheeles		6	
In the Buttrye			
Inprimis 3 brass potts two possenetts		20	
Item 3 dripping pans; one of iron, a frying pan		5	
Item in stone potts & treen dishes		6	8
Item a Table with a frame shelves & benches		5	
In the kitching			
Imprimis a Furnace & 3 kettles brasse two pothookes a Trevett		43	4
Item certayn old payles with other woodden lumber		10	
Item in a room over the sellar			
Imprimis A table with a frame ~~fowr~~ five stooles, an old [?]churn a moulding boord, & certeyn Benches		20	
In the sellar			
Inprimis ~~twelve~~ twenty Barrells small & great foure Tubbs two tunnells, foure stalls one dussen black potts, a quart pott of pewter		50	
Item in Ale ready brued		40	
In the Chamber over the Hall			
Imprimis A Table with a frame seven stooles, lettices & benches		30	
Item two standing ioynd Bedsteeds, with a Trundle Bedd	3		
Item three fetherbeds, fower fether bolsters, five pillowes three strawbeds 3 matts	15		
Item foure Coverleds foure Blanketts, ten Cushions	5		
Item in another Loft			
Item ~~sixtene qrter~~ in malt & other Lumber	16		
In the chamber over the Entrye			
Item an old Bedstead with a mattrice & bolster a [?]flockbed ~~two~~ a chests, a salting trough, masline, & pease with other lumber		50	
In the Parlour			
Imprimis A standing bed & [?]fether Bed with all the furniture, a warming pann three chests & two boxes	10		
Item in Linnen, twenty payre of sheets, twelve pillowberes a doosen of Table clothes, four dossen Napkins, halfe a doosen towells, 2 payre of pack sheets	20		
In the stable & Back house			
Inprimis one Horse, three Hoggs	4	10	
Item in wood for fire a hovell two ladders	3		
Item in payles about the garden		10	
Item Two stable hoases standing upon pattens, two litle Barnes of foure Bay standing upon pattens, with a slaughter house standing upon pattens & a stable of two bayes	40		
Item in haye	3		
Item in poultrye		5	
Item two acres of wheat on the ground		40	
Item one acre & halfe of oats		20	
Item one halfe acre of beans		10	
Item tilth		20	

Item his wearing apparrell	5		
Summa	154	4	4

Chr Sclater [*signature*], Thomas Leech [*signature*], Roger Wynton [*signature*], Thomas Poynton Junior [*signature*]
[*Exhibited by the executrix at Leighton Buzzard on 16 May 1625*]

Notes: Thomas Harbert's burial has not been found. He made his will on 15 March 1625, describing himself as a butcher. He gave £10 each to his son and two daughters at the ages of 21 and 18 respectively. He gave five freehold acres and the residue of his goods to his wife Rebecca and appointed her executrix. She was granted probate by William Dalbie at Leighton Buzzard on 16 May 1625 (Lincs Archives, LCC WILLS/1624–25/535).

366 William Jeayse of Colmworth, husbandman made 8 April 1625
Lincolnshire Archives, INV/129/353

A true and perfect Inmitorie of all the goods and Chattles of Willyam Jeayse of Colmorth in the Countie of Bedd husbandman late disceased Taken and prized the 8th day of Aprill Anno Domini 1625

	£	s	d
Imprimis his Apparrill	2	0	0
Item 3 feather bedds 4 Pillowes	3	0	0
Item 7 bolsters 3 Coverringes	5	0	0
Item 6 blanckites	2	0	0
Item 3 beddsteeds and the hanginges	1	10	0
Item sheetes and other Linnen	12	0	0
Item 4 chestes and a Cubbard and A presse and a Cofer	3	0	0
Item 3 Cheares 5 buffitt stooles	0	10	0
Item A Table a forme & a Cubbord	1	0	0
Item Painted Clothes & Cushinges		10	0
Item spittes and Cobbiornes	1	0	0
Item Peiuter and brasse	4	10	0
Item the Come of iorn and a mattocke a payre of tonges and 2 treads and the potthangles A bile and A hatchatt	0	13	0
Item 4 barriles a Saltinge troufe a saffe And A Arke	2	0	0
Item 25 Sheepe	9	0	0
Item 7 Cowes 7 bulluckes	21	0	0
Item 5 horses and the harnises	15	0	0
Item hoges and piges	1	15	0
Item Cartes & wheeles	4	0	0
Item one Houevell & wood	5	0	0
Item A haye Cocke	2	0	0
Item Chafe and Claver	2	0	0
Item fattes and Hurdles	1	0	0
Item wheat Corne Peayse and oytes	23	0	0

Item bordes and A Role and more fates	2	0	0
Item Another houevill and other thinges in itt	5	0	0
Item 3 stockes of bees	1	0	0
Item the wheate and tilth	26	0	0
Item the peayse Land	13	0	0
Item the Compas	2	0	0
Item 2 hogges of bacon and butter and Chese and other Smale untilles	5	0	0
Some Totallis	176	8	4
[*Corrected total*	*£176*	*8s*	*0d*]

Taken and prized the day and yeare above written by Willyam More and John Goodman [*Exhibited by the executor at Bedford on 21 May 1625*]

Notes: William Jeayse was buried at Colmworth on 5 March 1625.

367 Robert Woodward of Cranfield, yeoman made 9 April 1625

Lincolnshire Archives, INV/129/352

An Inventorie of all the goodes and cattell Moveable and in moveable of Robert Woodward of Cranfeilde yeoman lately decessed made and apprised the ix day of Aprill 1625 by us Thomas Basterfeilde Abraham Odle

	£	s	d
Inprimis one horse price		xl	
one hovel one maultmill one binge one chesepresse price		xx	
one boulting hutch one saultinge trough one chese racke price		iiij	
Item three tubs one kimnel two payles price		iiij ~~xx~~	
Item two cubberts two tables two formes foure cheirs one pene price		xxiiij	
Item foure stooles price		ij	
one barrell price		ij	
Item in the chamber one standinge bedstede one fether bed one Coverlet two blanckets one boulster two pillowes one paire of sheets price	iiij		
two chestes one coffer price		x	
Item brasse one poot three cettels one posnet price		xx	
Item in pewter xj platters one porringer one sauser one saulte price		x	
Item one smale bible price		vj	viij
Item ix payre of sheetes price		xxx	

Item vj pillowbeares vj table napkines two table cloathes price		xx	
Item blanckets six yardes of wollen cloath price		xx	
Item peoose [*pease?*] threshed and unthreshed in the barne price		xxx	
Item one payre of iron Rackes one spitt with other olde iron price		x	
Item two hundereth of oken bordes		xiij	iiij
Item viij stockes of beese price		xxvj	viij
Item in redie money in the house	xij		
Item of money oweinge by bondes	lxxxx		
Item one cloake with his other wareinge apparell price	iij	vj	viij
Summa totalis	Cxxiij	xix	iiij

[*Exhibited by the executor at Bedford on 21 May 1625*]

Notes: Robert Woodward was buried at Cranfield on 6 April 1625. He made his will on 5 April 1625. He gave the use of specified items (including the malt mill and bin, and some furniture) and £20 to his wife Joan during her life, then to his son Robert. He also gave Joan the brass, pewter and linen, which she could dispose of as she wished. He gave the agricultural implements to son Robert; £25 to one son-in-law; and forgave a debt of £20 owed by another son-in-law, Roger Pearse, on condition that he paid 10s a year to Joan, and also gave him £20. He gave several items of furniture or bedding to his son, daughters and grandchildren, either immediately or after Joan's death. He appointed his son-in-law Roger Pearse as executor, to whom probate was granted by William Dalbie at Bedford in May 1625 (Lincs Archives, LCC WILLS/1624–25/190).

368 Abraham Barber of Pulloxhill, yeoman made 14 April 1625

Lincolnshire Archives, INV/129/315

The inventory is badly damaged at the bottom.

A true Inventary of the goodes & Chattles of Abraham Barbar taken Aprill the 14th 1625

	£	s	d
In the Parlour			
Imprimis one table with a frame & 6 ioynestooles	1	3	4
Item 2 fourmes 2 chaires	0	8	0
Item 7 lowe ioynestooles	0	5	0
Item one Court cubboard a great chest & a wicker chaire	1	6	8
Item one standing bedsteed one trundle bed	1	13	4
Item Curtaines & curtaine rods with fringe	0	13	4
Item one fethebed 2 boulsters one coverlid 2 blancketts & one strawe bed	3	10	0
Item 7 chushions one cubboard cloath & a deske a pere of bellowes, fiershoule & a parre of litle doggs	0	13	4
In the Haule			
Item one table with a frame, one litle square table 5 ioynestooles one cubboard 2 chaires with other implements	2	10	0

In the Kitchen

Item one table & a frame 2 tubbs 3 pailes a morter & a pestle	0	10	0
Item 2 brasse potts 2 great kettles one brasse pann, 5 litle kettles 2 drippinge pans & 3 spitts	3	6	8
Item 2 parire of potthanges 2 parire of pothookes one frying pan 3 skilletts one parire of andirons bacon & other implements	2	0	0
In the boultinghouse			
Item one boultinge hutch 2 kimnells & other implements	0	5	0
In the milkehouse			
Item 7 bowles 2 litle kimnels 2 barrells 2 churnes & other lumber	1	0	0
In the Buttery			
Item one safe 2 hodgsheads a messhing fatt & other implements	0	16	0
In the millhouse			
Item one maultquerne one boarded bed a mattres 2 blankets a boulster & other lumber	1	0	0
Item one saltinge trough 3 shelves 2 wheeles & other smale thinges	0	6	8
In the Chamber over the milhouse			
Item one standinge bed with curtaines & curtainerodes	1	6	8
Item one featherbed one boulster 2 blankets & a coverlid	1	10	0
Item one trundle bed a mattresse 2 blankets & a boulster	0	10	0
Item one square table with a frame 3 chests & one coffer	1	5	0
Item covers for stooles & chaires a chushion [...] cloath	1	6	8
Item [...] bedticke 2 blankets	1	13	8
Item [...] [*?woo*]llen cloath	0	14	[...]
[*The remainder of the inventory is missing*]			
[*Total to this point*	*£29*	*13s*	*4d*]

[*No exhibition clause*]

Notes: Abraham Barber was buried at Westoning on 21 March 1625. He made his will on 4 March 1622, calling himself a yeoman and requesting burial in the chancel of Pulloxhill or Westoning. He gave freehold land in Stopsley after his wife Margaret's death to his son William who also received the testator's part of the parsonage of Pulloxhill at the age of 21. He gave his wife £20 a year from the parsonage to bring up his children, reduced to £10 a year for the upbringing of his two daughters after William reached 21. William was to have the other £10 a year. The remaining income from the parsonage was to be used by his overseers for William and for portions for his daughters. Among the household goods left to his daughters were joined stools and a chair with stammell covers, perhaps the 'covers for stools and chairs' listed in the chamber over the milhouse. He appointed six overseers to deal with his property bequests and appointed his wife Margaret as executrix. A nuncupative codicil was made on 18 March 1625 stating that if his goods were not sufficient to pay his debts, his daughters' income from the parsonage would be deferred until the debts were paid (Lincs Archives, LCC

WILLS/1624–25/274). There is no grant of probate on the copy of the will. See Beds Archives, ABCP21–27 for an account of the Pulloxhill parsonage. Note the discrepancy between the small household value of the inventory and the property interests in his will.

369 William Bennitt of Potton, shoemaker undated; c. 1625

Lincolnshire Archives, INV/129/333

An Inventory of the goodes and Chatells of William Bennitt of Potton Shoemaker deceased

	£	s	d
Speratt debptes oweing to him	v	x	
Despatt debptes oweing to him	iiij		
The parler chamber			
The furniture in that Chamber is valued at	vij	13	4
Sheetes lynnen and woollen cloath	vj	13	4
The Hall			
The furniture in the Hall valued at		40	
The Buttery			
a saltin troff with other Trash at		x	
The Kitchin			
Pewter Brass Tubbs & other Trash at	iiij	xvj	
The Boltinghowse			
A Fatt barrells & other Trash at		xx	
The Chamber over the kitchin			
A Boorded Bedsteed with other Trash at		xx	
The Chamber over the Hall			
Bacon and lath with other Trash at		xxx	
The chamber over the Parlor			
Hamps grayne lyme & other Trash at		xxv	
In the yarde			
Tymber fier wood and other Trash		xlvj	viij
Strawe and Hay		vj	
A Cowe 3 Ewes 2 lambs & 2 piggs at	iiij		
2 Acres of Rye		xxx	
of Reddy mony	iiij	iij	
In the Shop			
Shoes leather & other necessaries	xxvij		
His weareing apparrell	iij		
Summa totalis	78	3	4
[*Corrected total*	*£77*	*3s*	*4d*]

the praisors names Samuel Moulton [*signature*], Mathew Thorne [*signature*], Jho Sympson [*signature*], Willyam Robinsonn [*signature*], Edward Breuton [*mark*], Thomas Comptonn [*signature*]

[*No exhibition clause*]

Notes: William Bennitt was buried at Potton on 15 April 1625. His will was undated. He left his two houses and goods to his wife Alice for her life then to his sister Margaret Goodered. He made bequests to family and others, including £5 to his mother Margaret Bennett. His wife, who was appointed his executrix, was granted probate by William Dalbie on 21 May 1625 (Lincs Archives, LCC WILLS/1624–25/39).

370 William Hammond of Shillington, weaver made 18 April 1625
Lincolnshire Archives, INV/129/317

Decimo octavo die Aprilis anno domini 1625. A true Inventorie indented of all the goods & Chattels of William Hammond late of Shitlington in the Countie of Bedford ~~deceased~~ Weaver deceased as followeth

	£	s	d
Imprimis one Cofer & one boxe		x	vj
Item one Cowe and one sheepe		xlvj	viij
Item one Loome one warping fatt & the barrs		xl	
Item Certayne slayes of Woollen Linnen & other implements in the shoppe		xxx	
Item in bonds and readye monye	lxv		
Item his waringe aparell	iij	x	
Summa totalis	74	17	2

The aprisers of the aforesaid goods & Chattels are theise Vidz Michaell Ancell & Richard Glover
[*Exhibited by the executor at Dunstable on 17 May 1625*]

Notes: William Hammond was buried at Shillington on 22 March 1625.

371 John Squier of Ampthill, tailor made 22 April 1625
Lincolnshire Archives, INV/129/323

An Inventorie Indented & Taken the xxij day of Aprill 1625 of all the Goodes & Cattelles of John Squier late of Ampthill in the County of Bedf deceased praysed by Thomas Arnald & Solomon Spring as followeth

	£	s	d
Inprimis in the hall one Cobbord a table and frame one old cheare & other lumbr price		x	
In the Chambr 2 borded bedes 2 old coverledes 2 old blankettes 2 boulsters ij old flockbedes		viij	
Item 2 Coffers one box 3 parie of hempen sheetes 2 pillowbeares 2 old bord clothes & half a dozen of napkins		xiij	
In the loft over the Chambr one borded bed j old Tubb			xij
Item 8 peeces of pewter a dozen of spounes a morter Two pottes & 2 old kettelles		x	
Item one Cowe & a yearling bulock		l	
Item one pigg		ij	
Item 2 ewes & 2 lames & one dry sheepe		x	
Item his wearing Aparell		v	
The whole some is			[*blank*]
[*Total*	*£5*	*9s*	*0d*]

debts owing by the said John Squier at the time of his death

Inprimis to Richard Fuller	iij		xij
Item to Johane Squier		xviij	
~~Item to Robert Squier~~		~~xv~~	
[*Total of debts*	*£3*	*19s*	*0d*]

Thomas Arnald, the marke of Solomon Springe
[*Exhibited by the executrix at Dunstable on 17 May 1625*]

Notes: John Squier was buried at Ampthill on 8 April 1625. He made his will on 3 April 1625, describing himself as a tailor and reciting the sale of a house in Bedford jointly with his eldest son, who retained the proceeds. He gave another son a three-bay house, currently let, next to the one he lived in. He gave his wife the house where he lived for her life then to another son on condition that he paid legacies amounting to £16 to ten other brothers and sisters. He appointed his wife Mary executrix (Lincs Archives, LCC WILLS/1624–25/284). The terms of this will are difficult to reconcile with the low value and paucity of contents of the inventory. The appraiser Thomas Arnald was a witness to the will and was mentioned in it as a good friend.

372 Thomas Puddiphat alias Hille of Studham, husbandman made 23 April 1625
Lincolnshire Archives, INV/129/324

The Inventory of the goodes & Chattelles of Thomas Puddiphatt alias Hille of Studham in the countye of Bedford made the xxiij[th] day of Aprille in the yeare of our lorde 1625 praised by us John Sibley, Nicholas Palmer, John Paine & Thomas Paine

	£	s	d
Inprimis for his wearinge apparrell and money in his purse		30	
Item in other money and bondes	36	8	
Item for one table and a frame and cupborde and chaire two formes & other small Implementes in the halle		30	
Item for brasse and Peuter		30	
Item for one spitte one drippinge panne and other Irons about the fire		4	
Item for one bedsteede one fether bed with a boulster and pillowe and other furniture thereto belonginge in the chamber belowe		33	4
Item for four chestes in the same chamber		x	
Item for one bedsteed with a fether bed and other furniture to it belonginge In the chamber over the halle		33	4
Item for sixe paire of sheetes three table cloathes and other linnen		32	
Item for bedding in another roome		x	
Item for bacon		x	
Item for tubbes barrelles & other lumber aboute the house		5	
Item for wheate and other graine readye thresthe in the house	3		
Item for the wheate and other graine growing on the grounde	x		
Item for two milch kine	4		
Item for seventeene sheepe	5	13	4
Item for one hogge		x	
Item the woode in the yarde		x	
Item for the Poultry		3	4

The whole summe amountes to three scoare and eleven poundes twelve shillinges O [*sic*] foure pence	[71	12	4]

[*Exhibited by the executor at Dunstable on 3 May 1625*]

Notes: Thomas Puddiphat alias Hille was buried at Studham on 20 April 1625. He made his will on 20 February 1621, giving household items and 40s a year to his wife Agnes, who died in September of that year (*BPR*, vol. 77, p. 79). He gave sums amounting to about £50 to the children of family, kinsmen and others. He left his house and lands in Studham to his kinsman William Smith of Hemel Hempstead, who was also given the residue and appointed executor. He was granted probate by William Dalbie at Dunstable on 17 May 1625 (Lincs Archives, LCC WILLS/1624–25/542).

373 Jane Barnet of Stotfold, widow — made 3 May 1625

Lincolnshire Archives, INV/129/321

A true Inmitorie of all the goods and cattels of Jane Barnet Widdo of Statfould in the Countie of Beddeford late deseased praysed by us whose nanes [*sic*] are under named the third daye of Maye in the year of our lord god 1625

	£	s	d
Imprimes in the halle j tabel a bench and a bench board		ij	
Item v stooles			xij
Item j Cubbard		ij	
Item j Casse		iiij	
Item j pott shelfe			xij
Item ij kettels j posnit and j scimmer		iij	iiij
Item j payer of Andyrons			xij
Item j gridyron j driping pann j poot hanger ~~and j driping pan~~ and j fring panne j spit			xvj
Item painted clothes			x
Item dishes wodden platers and tre[*n*]chers and other Impelmentes			xij
Item in the ~~middel~~ Chambers iij Coffers and j boxe		x	
Item ij bedd steeds and ij foormes		ix	
Item j presse cubburd		xiiij	
Item j Chayer and j pot shelfe j barrill and the painted clothes		ij	vj
Item j boule ij tubes			xij
~~Item j feather bed ij pillowes ij boulsters j blanket~~			
Item the bedding		iij	
Item j paye of sheetes and iiij pillobeears and other linin		x	
Item iij pewter dishes ij poots vj spoones iij sasers		v	
Item hur waring parrill		x	
Item ij wheeles j barsket and othe impelments			xij
[*Total*	*£4*	*3s*	*0d*]

Jeames Castill his mark, John Elmer his marke
[*Exhibited by the beneficiaries at Dunstable on 17 May 1625*]

Notes: Jane Barnet was buried at Stotfold on 3 May 1625.

374 Robert Hanscombe of Meppershall, yeoman undated; between March and May 1625

Lincolnshire Archives, INV/129/316

The Inventorie of all the goods Chattels & Cattels of Robert Hanscombe of Sct Thomas Chappell in the parish of Mepershall in the Countie of Hartf yeoman deceased made & valewed by Thomas Bownest, William Hanscombe & Thomas Morris the [*blank*]

	£	s	d
In primis in the hall one long table, one square table ij Cubbards, ij formes, ij Chayres		xxvj	viij
In the parlour			
One bedsted, one fetherbed one [*word deleted and illeg.*] pillowe, one Coverlett, one mattrice, ij blanketts, & one boulster	v		
Item ij Cofers, & one Chayre		x	
In the Chamber over the parlor			
One bedsted ~~bedsted~~, one fetherbed [*word deleted and illeg.*] one mattrice, one boulster & a Coverlett	iiij		
Item vj Cofers & a potshelfe		xx	
Item in the maids Chamber ij bedsteds & bedding		xx	
Item in the roome over the entrie ij bedsteds and bedding		xxx	
Item in the folkes Chamber iiij bedsteds with the bedding		xl	
Item in the butterie vj hogsheads & one trough		xx	
Item in the kytchyn brasse & pewter	v		
Item other Lumbar there		x	
Item in the larder x flytches of bacon		l	
Item one trough & a tubb		x	
Item in the mylkehouse milkevessells and other ymplements there		xl	
Item butter and Cheese	vij		
Item in the brewhouse the bruing vessels	iij		
Item a mault querne		xx	
Item lynnen in the house	vij		
Item in the barnes & yard Corne and grayne to thresh	Cx		
Item xx quarters barley ~~barley~~ ready drest	xx		
Item viij quarters peaze & oates	v	vj	viij
Item Carts & Cart geares, plough & plough geares	xx		
Item xv[teene] horses	lx		
Item xxij mylch beaze	lx		
Item x yearling bullocks	xij		
Item CC sheepe	lxxx		
Item xxx hoggs	xx		
Item hay	vj		
Item wheat sowen xxx acres	lxxx		
Item edge sowen C acres	Cxx		
Item tylth unsowen xCviij acres	Cxl		
Item forcks, rakes cowracks & other ymplements in the yard		xl	

Item ready money	x		
Item his a[*pare*]ll	vj	xiij	iiij
Summa totalis	799	13	4
[*Corrected total*	*£797*	*16s*	*8d*]

Debts

In primis by Roger Person		xxxiiij	
Item by Henry Hodge		xxxiij	iiij
Item by John Ravens	vj		
Item by Richard Ravens		xl	
Item Edmond Master		xxvj	viij
Summa debit	ix	xiiij	
[*Corrected total of debts*	*£12*	*14s*	*0d*]

[*Exhibited by the executor at Dunstable on 6 May 1625*]

Notes: Robert Hanscombe of Meppershall was buried at Holwell, Herts on 21 March 1625. St Thomas's Chapel in Meppershall, now a Grade II listed building, is to the south of Chapel Farm. It was leased from the Earls of Kent by the end of the sixteenth century. See Beds Archives, Community History pages on St Thomas Chapel Meppershall and for an account of St Thomas's chapel, manor and farm.

375 John Cockine of Westoning, husbandman made 11 May 1625

Lincolnshire Archives, INV/129/320

A true Inventary of the goodes & Chatles of John Cockine taken the 11th of May 1625

	£	s	d
In the Haule			
Imprimis one Cubboard one table & frame a square table a fourme a henpen	0	10	0
Item one iron pott 3 kettles 6 pewter dishes one spitt & other lumber	0	13	4
Item one flitch of bacon a fiershovel a parir of tonges a grediron	0	5	0
In the Chamber			
Item one boarded bedsteed a fetherbed one boulster a mattresse 2 pillowes one Coverlid one blanckett	2	0	0
Item 6 parire of sheetes 3 pillowbeares one tablecloath & other linnen	1	15	0
Item 2 Coffers & other lumber	0	5	0
In the loft over the Camber			
Item old boards towe old blanckets of barley & rie 3 bussheles	0	10	0
In the yard			
Item 2 tubbs 2 old cartes a parire of wheeles wood & other smale thinges	0	6	8
Item 3 hens	0	1	6
In the barne			
Item hey & strawe a fann & busshell	0	6	8
Item one store pigge	0	5	0

Item his wearinge apparrell	1	0	0
Item in rough hemp 30 pounds	0	2	6
Item dunge in the yard	0	3	4
Item in the field 3 halfe acres of wheat	2	0	0
Item one acre of barley	1	0	0
Item 3 halfe acres of pease one of oates	1	10	0
Item 6 norfolk lambes	0	15	0
Item one calfe	0	10	0
[*Total*	*£13*	*19s*	*0d*]

[*Exhibited by the executrix at Dunstable on 17 May 1625*]

Notes: John Cockine was buried at Westoning on 8 April 1625. He made his will on 6 April 1625 calling himself a husbandman. He gave each of his children 1s; two Norfolk lambs to his son Henry and one to a grandson (listed in his inventory). He gave the residue to his wife Maudlen and appointed her executrix. She was granted probate by William Dalbie at Dunstable on 17 May 1625 (Lincs Archives, LCC WILLS/1624–25/174).

376 George Farye of Toddington, cordwainer made 12 May 1625

Lincolnshire Archives, INV/129/322

The Inventorie of all the goodes Chattles debtes and Credittes of George Farye late of Todington in the Countye of Bedd Cordwinder deceased made proved & pryced the xij^{o} daie of Maye 1625 by those whose names are hereunder written

	£	s	d
Imprimis his apparrell		xxxiij	iiij
Item in redie monyes	xxxiij		
Item in debtes due ~~upon~~ with out spetialties	xxiiij	vj	x
Item debtes ~~with out~~ upon spetialties	lxxxviij		
Item in Corne & grayne	xviij	x	
Item the woodd boardes poles & tresselles		l	
Item In the haul one cupboard, one table & Frame one pott shelf, one little Table, three stooles, one Forme iiij little stooles, one Chaire, and other small implementes		xxx	
Item the Brasse pottes, pewter and Iorne workes	iiij		
Item two Flitches of Bacone		xv	
Item the Cooperie wares & certeine other small implementes		xxij	vj
Item xiij^{ten} paires of sheetes iij table Clothes xx^{tie} napkins 7 pillowe beeres and other Linen	v	x	
Item the Bedes & bedding and Joynes stuff in the Chamberes	v	x	
Somma totales	Clxxxvj	vij	viij

Thomas Pottes [*signature*], Thomas Mathew [*signature*], Cornelius White [*signature*]
[*Exhibited by the executrix at Dunstable on 17 May 1625*]

Notes: George Farye was buried at Toddington on 28 February 1625. He made his will on 2 November 1624. He gave £60 in money to his wife Elizabeth and varying sums to his son, two daughters and a grandson. He gave debts, owed by named people, to his daughters. He gave the residue to his wife who was appointed executrix and was granted probate by William Dalbie at Dunstable on 17 May 1625 (Lincs Archives, LCC WILLS/1624–25/487).

377 Thomas Osmond of Willington made 12 May 1625
Lincolnshire Archives, INV/129/365

May the 12th 1625. The true Inventary Indented of all the good and Chattelles of Thomas Osmond of Willington late deceased

	£	s	d
In the Hale			
Inprimis ij Tables ij formes v stooles ij Cubbordes one Chest one Saltinge Trough with some other Implementes	iij	vj	
In a lowe Chamber			
Item Two Bedsteedes one feather bed [...] Matresses iij bolsters ij pillowes ij Coverlettes ij Blankettes iiij Chestes certaine painted Cloathes with some other Implements	iiij	vj	viij
In an Inner chamber			
Item one bedstead one Mattres one boulster ij blankettes one Coverlett one chest with Certaine painted Cloathes	ij	x	
Item Certaine Hempe iij barrelles one Bushell iiij sackes iiij bottelles ij wheeles & other Implementes	j	x	
Item Brasse and Pewter	v	xiij	iiij
Item Certaine Boardes and Joystes	j	0	0
Item certaine Woole one Woollen wheele and other Shelves		x	
In the Kitchine a boultinge howse			
Item one Cheese presse v Tubbes ij Barrelles two chermes a Boultinge Tubb Two Kymnelles x Milkebowles an Henne Penne and other Implementes	iij		
Lynnen			
Item three Table Cloathes xj paire of sheetes viij Napkyns iij Pyllowbeares iij Towelles xiiij Elles of new Cloath	iiij		
His wearinge apparrell	ij	vj	viij
Item Grayne in the feild one acre of Barley one acre of Pease	iij	vj	viij
Item Grayne Ready Threshed		viij	
Item in the barne Barly and Hay	ij	x	
Item Wood in the yard	j		
Item ij Hovelles and a Hodgscoate	vj	xiij	iiij
Item Mylch beastes and a bullocke	ix	x	
Item Twenty Pownde of Hempe tare		xiij	iiij
Item two Pigges		viij	
Item one Hempeland		x	
Item iiij Bondes billes and ready money	xviij	x	
Item in Pullen		v	
Item Baccon		iij	
Summa totalis	lxxj		
[*Corrected total*	*£72*	*1s*	*0d*]

Praysers William Selby, John Osmond, Richard Morgayne
[*at the foot of the page*] Ingrosse & indent another with this & returne
[*Exhibited by the executor at Bedford on 21 May 1625*]

Notes: Thomas Osmond's burial has not been found.

378 Thomas Meanord or Maynard of Bedford, bachelor made 13 May 1625
Lincolnshire Archives, INV/129/348

An Invetorye of the goods of Thomas Meanord the younger sone to Thomas Meanord the elder taken the 13 daye of May 1625 by Thomas Spengle and Richard Smithe as folouth

	£	s	d
Item all his waringe parell		xx	
Item on [*?*]shiepe		vj	
Item in detes to him dewe	vij		
some	8	vj	

Richard Smithe, Thomas [*?*]Sencle
[*Exhibited by the legatees at Bedford on 21 May 1625*]

Notes: Thomas Meanord was buried in Bedford St John's on 18 April 1625. He made an undated nuncupative will, being described as a bachelor. He gave 40s to Marie Audlye and everything else to his parents, Thomas and Susan Maynard. Probate was granted by William Dalbie at Bedford on 21 May 1625 but it is not clear to which legatee the grant was made (Lincs Archives, LCC WILLS/1624–25/199).

379 Phoebe Horne of Houghton Regis, widow made 17 May 1625
Lincolnshire Archives, INV/129/329

Anno domini 1625. A true Inventorie of all such goodes & chattells which were the proper goodes of Phebey Horne of Houghton Regis in the com' of Bedd widdowe lately decessed Indented & made the 17th day of Maye the yeare abovewritten

	£	s	d
Inprimis all her weareing apparell		xl	
Item William Hoge doth owe unto the said decessed	20		
Suma totalis	22		

per me Tho: Tompkins vic[*ar*] ibidem [*signature*], Daniell Fossey [*signature*]
[*Exhibited by the executor at Dunstable on 17 May 1625*]

Notes: Phoebe Horne was buried at Houghton Regis on 6 April 1625. She made her will on 6 March 1625. She forgave £5 of the £20 owed to her by her son William Hoge and directed him to give the other £15 to her executor. She gave £14 or clothes to her daughters and grandchildren. She gave the residue to her son-in-law William Fossey, who was appointed executor. He was granted probate by W. Dalbie at Dunstable on 17 May 1625 (Lincs Archives, LCC WILLS/1624–25/541).

380 Henry Merrill of Cople, labourer made 18 May 1625
Lincolnshire Archives, INV/129/350

The Copie of A True Inventory of all the goodes of Henry Merrill of Cople in the County of Bedfford Labourer, made by Thomas Chuball, Thomas Eaton & others of the same Towne the 18th day of May 1625 as followeth

	£	s	d
In the Hall			
Inprimis One Table, one foarme, & two boardes	0	5	0

Item One Cup-boarde	0	6	8
Item Six peeces of small pewter with one Salte	0	4	0
Item One chafeing-dish, & two small Candlestickes	0	1	2
Item One Kettle, one Skellet, & an old Brasse-pot	0	5	0
Item One Pen, one cheare with other trash	0	1	0
In the Chamber			
Inprimis Three Coaffers in the Chamber	0	8	0
Item One boarded Bed-stead	0	1	8
Item One Coverlette, one Blanquett with two old pillowes	0	5	0
Item One payre of sheetes with three course sheetes	0	7	6
Item One Speere cloath, one Towell, & one pillow-beere	0	3	0
Item All the painted Cloathes	0	3	4
Item All his wayringe Apparell	0	5	0
Summa totalis	2	16	4

The prisers were William Greenough vicar there, Thomas Chuball, Thomas Eaton
[*Exhibited by William Palmer one of the beneficiaries at Bedford on 21 May 1625*]

Notes: Henry Merrill was buried at Cople on 1 May 1625, described as 'paterfamilias'. The writing of the inventory used elaborate capital letters and his surname has been interpreted in indexes as Wherrill. The parish register records his burial, the baptism of children and the burial of his wife Eleanor under the surname Merrill (*BPR*, vol 10, pp. B2, B3 and B37).

381 John Durrant of Cockayne Hatley, rector — made 19 May 1625

Lincolnshire Archives, INV/129/337

There are two copies of the inventory, one on paper, the other on parchment. They are identical except for the signatures of the appraisers, the list of debts, the note of allocation signed by W. Dalby and the exhibition clause which are on the parchment copy. The transcription has been made from the paper copy with the addition of these extra items.

A true and perfect Inventarie of all & singuler the goodes Debtes rightes and Chattelles of John Durrant late Parson of Hatley Port in the countie of Bedf clerke deceased made the ~~twenteth~~ nyneteenth day of Maie Anno Domini 1625 by us whose names are hereunto subscribed vizt

	£	s	d
Inprimis in the Parlour two Tables fowre ioyned stooles five Chaires, two coverd stooles, a Cupboard and seaven Cushions, One Bedsteade with all manner of furniture thereunto, three Formes one Callyver & headepiece one paire of Andyrons a pott shelfe a Carpett and other smalle thinges	vj	xiij	iiij
Item in the Lofte over the Parlour one greate Chest, one Table, two Formes, three chaires, two stooles a Footepresse fowre Curtens with curten rods and other thinges		xx	

Item in the Lofte over the Milkehouse one standeing bedsteade and another without a tester with all furniture & beddeing belongeing unto them, two Cupboardes, three Chestes, a Trunke two Trundle bedsteades, two ioyned stooles, a Hamper All the rest of the Lynnen besides that which was upon the beddes with other trashe	v		
Item in the Stodie certayne bookes and other thinges	viij		
Item in the Cheeselofte certayne Cheeses with two wheeles certayne woolle and other trashe		v	
Item in the Kitchen All the brasse & Iron a Chaire, a ioyned stoole, a Cupboard, a dresser board, a pott shelfe, a nest of Boxes with other trashe there		xxx	
Item in the Buttrie one Cupboard three chermes, a Chaire, a Tubb a table three hoggesheades, two barrelles, a warmeing panne certayne pewter with other trashe		xl	
Item in the Milkehouse a Table a safe with certayne cheeses, milke vesselles and other trashe there		v	
Item in the Brew house certayne breweing vesselles one haire safe, a bushell a Copper ~~furnace~~[75] a kneadeing Troffe a powthering Troffe with other trashe		xxx	
Item in the yarde Five Cowes two bullockes one Sowe & a shoate	xviij		
Item a Hovell rofte & boarded with certayne strawe and woode and other trashe there Allso a Manger a Racke and plankes in the stable	v		
Item certaine Dunge & woode in the yarde and other trashe		xxvj	viij
Item all his apparell	iiij		
Item two silver booles and two silver spones	iiij		
Item a horse		xxvj	
Item oweing unto the said deceased the summe of	Cxviij		
Summa Totalis	Clxxvij	xvj	

From the parchment copy and in a different hand:
The names of the Praysers Oliver Bowles [*signature*], Sa: Bradstrete [*signature*] [*Samuel in the parchment copy*], Sa: Moulton [*signature*] [*Samuel in the parchment copy*], Oliver Freeman [*signature*], Nicholas Rennoldes [*signature*]

[75] *furnace* is only in the paper copy.

Debts owing by John Durrant late Parson of Hatley Port in the Countie of Bedf deceased viz

To Elizabeth Crabtree	lx		
To Benimine Crabtree	lx		
To Zipporah Crabtree	xiij	vj	iiij
To Silvester Crabtree	ij		
To William Keifford	xxj		
To Thomas Dad	x	x	
To Robert Collins	v		
[*Total of his debts*	*£171*	*16s*	*4d*]

Allocantar huiusmodo debita iusq[ue] Executrix etc W Dalbye [*signature*]
[*Exhibited by Martha Durrant, relict and executrix, on 21 May 1625*]

Notes: John Durrant was buried at Cockayne Hatley on 13 May 1625. He was vicar of Potton 1618–21, succeeding Thomas Crabtree (*301*) and being succeeded by Samuel Moulton, one of the appraisers; and rector of Cockayne Hatley 1621–25 (CCEd; Beds Archives, Fasti/1/Pott and Fasti/1/HatC). He was the executor of Thomas Crabtree's widow Alice, and also her son-in-law, having married their daughter Martha (Beds Archives, ABP/W1618–19/25). John Durrant made his will on 3 May 1625, leaving all his goods to his wife Martha, who was appointed executrix and granted probate by William Dalbie at Bedford on 21 May 1625 (Lincs Archives, LCC WILLS/1624–25/478). At her death in 1618 Alice Crabtree had probably not completed administering her husband Thomas's will and John Durrant would have taken it over, which might explain the sums listed in his inventory as owing to Elizabeth, Benjamin, Zipporah and Silvester Crabtree.

382 Henry Squire of Thurleigh

made 20 May 1625
Lincolnshire Archives, INV/129/355

A true Inventory of all the goods & Chattells of Henry Squire late of Thurligh in the County & Archd[eaco]nry of Bedfford deceased taken the 20th day of May 1625 by Christopher Dawson, Richard Cadwell, Thomas Darling & Hugh Sharpe

	£	s	d
The stuff in the hall at		iij	4
The bedds & bedding & coffers in the chamber		xiij	4
The trogh in the litle howse			xij
The wood in the yard at		ij	
The ready money	ij	ix	
his wearing Apparell		iij	4
Things forgotten at			ij
Summa totalis	3	12	2

[*Exhibited before Dalby at Bedford St Paul's on 21 May 1625*]

Notes: Henry Squire's burial has not been found.

383 William Foxcroft, senior, rector of Bedford St Cuthbert made 10 June 1625
Lincolnshire Archives, INV/130/477
The inventory is on velum. It is creased and holed and some text has rubbed away. Missing letters or words, where obvious, have been supplied in italics.

A true Inventoryr of all the go[*ods catte*]lls and Chatt[*ell*]s of William Foxcroft sen. Clarke, late Rector of St Cutberds in Bedford, deceased taken and appr[*ai*]sed by us who on testymony [*wh*]ereof, have here unto subscribed our hands this Tenth daye of June, Anno domini 1625, as followeth [*vizt*]

	£	s	d
Imprimis one old [...] dublett a pare of breeches, [*and*] other old apparrell, bootes lynn[*en*], wollen and shooes		xxx	
Item Calvins Harmonye uppon [*the*] fower Evangelists,[76] Mus [...] his common places,[77] and Urs [...] Catechesme[78] with other old bookes		xxx	
Item three old tables, [*one*] forme, five old chayres, one old [*cupb*]ard, and one sorrye press		xxij	
Item twoe old beds[*teads*], one truckelbedd three old coffers, with [*other*] implements		xviij	
Item three old Mattr[*esses*] [...] [*o*]ne old Fetherbed, three old Co[...] [*?Coverletes*], six pare of sheets, with other old lynnen and woollen	iij		
Item twoe brass potts, one kettell [*illeg.*] other old [*illeg.*]		xxij	
Item [*illeg.*] peces of p[*illeg.*] tynn Co[...] [*faded*] one pare of [*And*]irons, one pare [*of*] [*be*]llowes, one pare of tongues, one fyer shovell with other old Ironn		xxiiij	viij
Item a little linnen yar[*n*]e [*?with*] a little wooll, and flax		xiij	[*iiij*]
Item a little canch of [*whea*]t and rye with a little undressed [*bar*]ley	iij		
Item twoe old bese	iij		
Item one hefer, and h[*er*] [*c*]alfe		xl	
Item eigh[*t*] henns [*a*]nd [*on*]e Cocke		vj	
Item three little barrells twoe tubbes			

76 Jean Calvin published commentaries on the harmony of the three synoptic gospels, Mathew, Mark and Luke.
77 Wolfgang Musculus, *Common places of Christian religion*. Originally published in 1560 and published in London in 1563 and 1578.
78 Zacharias Ursinus, *The summe of Christian religion: delivered in lectures upon the catechism*, translated by H. Parrie. Oxford, 1587. Later editions in Oxford or London in 1589, 1591, 1601, 1611, 1617.

three boles [*t*]woe [*illeg.*] [...] [*wi*]th other woodden and ear[*th*]en s[*tu*]ff		xiij	iiij
Item a little wood with other impleme[*nts*]		x	
Somma tota[*lis*]	xx	ix	iiij

Debts owing by the sayd Deceased vizt

Imprimis to his son Thomas Foxcrof[*t*]	iij		
Item toe his sonn William Foxcroft		xl	
Item owing to Thomas [*illeg.*]eward		l	
Item to the Churchwardens of St Cutberds		xliiij	
Item to John Bowstred		xl	
Item to Master John Richards[*on*]		xl	
Item to Nickholas East		xl	
Item to Edward Turner		xj	
Item to Master Parradine		[*illeg.*]	vij
Item to Master Luxfo[*illeg*]		[*illeg.*]	
Item to Henrye [*An*]gell		[...]	viij
Item to John Bea[*r*]d		[...]	
Summa totalis	xviij	[...]	[...]

Theodore Crowley [*signature*], Thomas Croote sen [*signature*], John Richardson [*signature*]
[*No exhibition clause*]

Notes: William Foxcroft was buried at Bedford St Cuthbert's on 20 March 1625. He matriculated at St John's College, Cambridge, in 1579, was vicar of Clapham in 1601 and rector of Bedford St Cuthbert's 1585–1624 (Venn ACAD; CCEd; Beds Archives, Fasti/1/BedSCu). Administration was granted to his son Thomas Foxcroft, vicar of Stagsden, by Dr Farmerie at Dunstable on 13 June 1625, his widow Anne having renounced administration (Lincs Archives, Act Book A/x/93). A bond for good administration was taken (Lincs Archives, LCC ADMONS 1625/73).

384 Thomas Hawkynes of Houghton Regis, yeoman made 24 June 1625

Lincolnshire Archives, INV/129/426

The top right edge of the paper is folded. Missing letters have been supplied.

A true Inventorie of all such goods and chattels which were Thomas Hawkynes of Houghton Regis in the com' of Bedd ye[*oman*] lately decessed indented & made the Fower and twentith day [*of*] June Anno domini 1625, being valued and prized by us whose nam[*es*] are hereunto subscribed:

	£	s	d
Imprimis all his apparell	1	10	0
Item money in his purse	0	3	0
Item all the tylth & composse	5	0	0
Item Barley, pease, in the fieldes	16	0	0
Item certain plankes	0	10	0
Item on pilch	0	4	0
Item one fetherbed, on boulster, a pillowe on paire of sheets & curtaines, on blankett	2	1	2
Item on Candlestick a slice, dog-yrons and on paire of tongues	0	3	0
Item one horse	2	0	0

Item oweing unto him the decessed by Anthony Hawkynes his brother as by a note may appeare	11	9	0
Item parte of a lease from Master[79] ~~Skibbinges~~ William Phillips	5	0	0
Summa totalis	44	2	2
[*Corrected total*	*£44*	*0s*	*2d*]

per me Thomas Tompkins vicar, Thomas Wallys
[*Exhibited by the executor at Dunstable on 25 July 1625*]

Notes: Thomas Hawkynes was buried at Houghton Regis on 18 June 1625, described as Thomas, son of Thomas Hawkins. He made his will on 16 June 1625, describing himself as Thomas Hawkynes the younger, son of Thomas Hawkyns. He gave his property (his lease of half a messuage or tenement in Houghton Regis called Davies alias Brigge, his term of years in land called the Nine Acres and the rents from twelve acres of freehold in Houghton Regis) to his father Thomas Hawkyns for three years. This land was to be sold at the end of three years by his friend Ragland Vaughan of St Giles in the Fields, Middlesex, and his brother-in-law John Whitley of Luton and the proceeds distributed to his brother and two sisters. His brother Anthony who owed him money had died in 1622 (*332*). He gave the residue to his father who was also appointed executor and to whom probate was granted by Edward Hills surrogate for John Farmerie at Dunstable on 25 July 1625 (Lincs Archives, LCC WILLS/1624–25/87).

385 Robert Austin of Potton, barber — made 28 April 1626

Bedfordshire Archives, ABP 4/195

A true ~~Imnytorye~~ Inventorie of all the goodes and Chattels as well moveable as unmoveable of Robart Austin of Potton late deceased as they were prized and valued by Henry Wallis, Thomas Langhorne, John Compton, Richard Paratt and John Langhorne the 28th of Aprill 1626

	£	s	d
Imprimis in the Hall house a table with a forme two bench boardes fower chaires sixe stooles a cupboard a shelfe two andirons a side table two pothangers a bar of iron a paire of bellowes a gridiron and a paire of tonges with other utensils		xxiij	
Item in the parlour one ioyned standing bed with a featherbed a mattresse two boulsters, two pillowes two blankets and three coverlids	v	vj	viij
Item one cupboard a table with a frame one stoole a benchboard two formes [*?*]two chaires five coffers a shelfe with other implements		l	
Item 24 paire of sheetes, sixe table clothes, three dozen and fower napkins ~~sixe table clothes~~ sixe towels twentie pillowberes tenne shaving cloathes two long towels fower shirts nine bandes three aprons and three handkerchers	x	x	
Item three peeces of linnen cloth		xiij	iiij
Item three peeces of woollen cloth	v		

[79] Changed from Mrs.

Item in the little chamber one halfe ioyned bed steed and a boarded bedsteed two coverlids two blankets a featherbed a mattresse three bolsters and two pillowes two coffers and painted cloathes	iij	x	
Item in the buttery eight barrels and a tunnell and a cupboard		xv	
Item in the chambers over the parlour one boarded bedsteed a round table a coffer and painted cloathes a warping fate and barres a paire of stock cardes two linnen wheeles with other trash		xvij	
Item in the chamber over the buttery one standing ioyned bedsteede with two boarded bedsteedes a featherbed a strawe bed a bolster a pillowe two coverliddes		xxxiij	iiij
Item three coverlids a blankett two mattresses two pillowes and two boulsters		43	
Item in the chamber over the Hall sixe bushels of Rye two bushels of barly two bushels of wheate one bushell of malt a cradle with other utensils		40	
Item eight skore pound of wooll dyed	viij		
Item a bible		vj	viij
Item a birding peece		vj	viij
Item in the Kitchin a Copper a moulding board a boulting arke with other utensils		xx	
Item in the milkehouse one hutch one churne five shelves one kimnell earthen pottes and pannes and cheesefates with other thinges		viij	
Item in the little buttery one brasse panne five kettles a dripping pan two skummers two spitts a luver fower brasse pots one salting trough two booles a mustard querne a bushell and halfe of salt	iiij		
Item tenne candlestickes three chaffingdishes two morters two basins a colinder and a warming panne and five kettles		xxxiij	iiij
Item sixteene platters two basins halfe a dozen of saucers seaven porringers two aquavitae bottles one chamber pot and a little sweete water pott and two other pottes one quart pott a dozen and halfe of spoones and three saltsellers		xxxiij	iiij
Item fower cushions and eight earthen pots		iiij	
Item his barbing toolcs		xiij	4
Item in the shoppe fower loomes with their severall furnitures three hundred of boardes a cutting knife two sawes two iron wedges a woollen wheele and a paire of scales with weightes and two tubbes with other utensils	xij		
Item in the garner two bushels and two skreenes a kilne heare three shovels, one plancke and other things		xxxx	

Item in the malthouse fower sithes, one poplar, three boardes and two ladders with other trashe		xiij	iiij
Item in the yard timber and wood		40	
Item woode lying abroad		40	
Item the Haye	iij	vj	viij
Item the grayne on the grond betweene eight and nine acres	x		
Item one manngie horse		vj	viij
Item one cowe and three bullocks	viij		
Item threescore and seaven guest sheepe and eighteene couples and three lambes	xxiij		
Item sixe hogges	iij		
Item two hennes and a cocke			xx
Item nine sheepe skinnes		viij	
Item his wearing apparrell	iiij		
Item readie money in his purse		v	vj
Item in desperate debts		xx	
[*Total*	*£126*	*8s*	*6d*]

[*No exhibition clause*]

Notes: Robert Austin was buried at Potton on 25 April 1626. He made his will on 23 April 1626, describing himself as a barber. He left £30 and household linen to daughter Edith; the house he (John) lived in to son John until his brother Robert who was John's apprentice finished his apprenticeship, and then the house to Robert; £10, a loom, a warping fatt and a pair of bars to son Edward; £20 and a double loom to son Henry; and £20 each to daughters Saba, Anna and Rebecca. The residual legatees and executors were his wife Saba and son Francis, to whom probate was granted on 9 May 1626 (Beds Archives, ABP/W1626/111).

386 William Gore of Swineshead made 31 May 1626

Huntingdonshire Archives, AH18/7/41

Some damage from holes and smudging.

A true invit[*ory of all the*] goodes & chattels of Wm Gore of Swyneshed late of [*Swy*]neshed deceased prysed by Jhon Parsoyle & Richard Bromsall the last of maye 1626

	£	s	d
Imprimis his wearing apparell and readie monie	2	0	0
In the hall			
One table, on forme, on stoole, one chayre	0	16	0
[...] chamber			
One bedsteed one cubboard, One little table, two coffers one boxe, on cradle, one lynen wheele, on stoole	2	3	4
One fetherbed, on bolster, 3 pillowes, on coverlet, on blanket [...]	3	0	0
Item [...] saucers one peuter candlesticke, 2 saltes 3 pottengers, 4 spoones, on chamberpot, one warmeing pan, one peuter cup, a smoothingyron		13	4
[*In*] the [*b*]utt[*ry*]			
Three kettles, on skillett, on brasse pott	1	0	0
Item 2 barrells, one cherne, 4 boles, 2 tubbes, one kymnell 2 stoppes a kneading troff, with other implementes	1	0	0

In the loft

Fyve flexen sheetes, seaven harden sheetes, 3 pillowbeers			
4 boardclothes, 6 table napkins, One towell	2	13	4
Two bybles	0	10	0
One boarded bedsteed on flockbed bolster[80] 3 pillowes 2 old coverlettes			
on matteris on blankett[81]			
10 [*?*]pounds of flaxe the workeing tooles with other implementes	2	10	0
A fyre shovell, a payre of tonges, pothangers & a saltbox	0	3	4
In the [*?*]yard			
boards tymber fyre wood, hay & compas	5	0	0
A mylch cowe on yearing bullocke, a weaning calfe			
one hogge, 4 hens	4	13	4
[*Total*]	26	2	8

Jhon Parsoyle [*mark*], Richard Bromsall [*mark*]

[*Exhibited by Anne Gore, relict and executrix, on 31 May 1626. The exhibition clause was signed by R. Furley, deputy registrar.*]

Notes: William Gore was buried at Swineshead on 27 May 1626.

387 Alice Rose of Cople, widow made 19 January 1627

Bedfordshire Archives, ABP/W1626–1627/25

January 19 Anno 1626. A True Inventory of all the goodes of Alce Rose of Cople in this Countie of Bedfford widow made, & taken by those whose names are subscribed, the 19 of Januar[*y*] etc

	£	s	d
Inprimis in the Hall			
One Cupboard, two pewter platters			
and one Candlesticke		v	
Item one Possnet, & a little kettle			xviij
Item three old shelves			viij
Item A bigger kettle		ij	
Item A Cheare, a forme [...] fower small stooles			xviij
Item A Hathet, & an Iro[*n*] [...] wedge			x
Item A Grate-yron, a frying-pan, & pot-hangers			xij
Item Two old firkins, 3 old basketes, & a Seeve		ij	vj
Item The painted cloathes there, a paire			
of Bellowes with other trash			xvj
Item in the Chamber			
Two boarded Bedes with certaine			
Beddinge belonging to them		xxvj	viij
Item Three Coaffers there		vj	viij
Item five sheetes two table cloathes,			
three pillow-beers, & 3 napkins		xiij	iiij
Item certaine painted clothes there			xij

80 The word *bolster* has been inserted above the line.

81 This line has been inserted between the one above and below.

	£	s	d
Item in an Out-house			
One old penn, one Arke with other trash		iiij	vj
Item Two forkes, a pease hooke			
a Cobyron, & a meale seeve			xviij
Item a linnen wheele, and a			
woollen wheele there		ij	
Item Certaine old Boardes		iij	iiij
Item Two Tubbs one payle			
and one stoope		iiij	
Item A Ladder			vj
Item All her Apparell		xiij	iiij
Summa totius	iiij	xiij	ij

The names of the prizers are these John Harrison, John Davy [*mark*], Thomas Turpin [*mark*]
[*Exhibited by George Rose on 20 February 1627. The signature of the registrar at the end of the exhibition clause is illegible.*]

Notes: Alice Rose was buried at Cople on 18 January 1627. Her nuncupative will was made on 15 January 1627. Amongst small bequests of money or goods to her sons and grandchildren, she gave the boards over her milk-house to her son George. Possibly this is the outhouse of the inventory. She did not appoint an executor and administration was granted to her son George on 20 February 1627. The witnesses included William Greenough, vicar of Cople.

388 Lucy Marshall of Everton, widow made in or after April 1627

Huntingdonshire Archives, AH18/13/109

The document is badly damaged and only the section down the centre of the inventory remains. There are also holes, stains and fading in this remaining section. A varying amount of most lines is missing or illegible.

[...] of … the goodes and Chatteles [...] as personale of Lucy [...] of Everton in County [...] deceased widdowe veiwe[*d*] [...] by us whose na[*m*]es are [...] as follow [...]

	£	s	d
Imprimis her weareinge [*appar*]rell	[*value missing*]		
In the upper chamber			
An old bedsteed a old blankett a matteris [...]			
a pillowe a paire of Andirons a wheele [...]	[*value missing*]		
In the lowe chamber			
Imprimis an Bedsteed one Fetherbedd on[...]			
[*m*]atteris tow boulsters iij pillowes [...]			
[*illeg.*] Alone Coverledds	[*value missing*]		
Item an other bedsteed a matteris ij boulsters			
a Coverledd painted cloths a hudge		[*?*]xx	
In the Hall			
Imprimis one table and Frame iiij			
old chaires a livery Cubbord a [*?*]lattene			
ij paire of potthooks a forme ij stooles		xvij	
Item 8 paire of old sheettes and a odd sheete		xvij	
Item one wallett iij pillowbeeres			
one boardcloath		v	
Item ij peices of New cloath		xv	

In the butterye			
Imprimis iiij barreles ~~iij old ketteles~~			
ij old panns an old bason ~~a Chaff dish~~			
ij tubbs a bushell a Churme a Chaffindishe			
bowles with divirs other Lumber		xvj	
Item five kettles a chaffindish		[*value illegible*]	
Item vj Flitches of bacon and the			
saltinge trough		[*?*]xxx	
In the Chamber over the but[*tery*]			
Imprimis a fetherbedd vj ells of cl[*oth*]		[*value missing*]	
Item a quarter of barly		[*value missing*]	
Item a bushell of whea[*t*] & [*illeg.*] xvj peices			
of pewter aqua vita bottle ix spones			
ij saltes v candelstickes ij morters one			
pestell ij gredyrons a [*?*]warming pan		[*value missing*]	
Item a Chest a forme a Ch[*air*]e with			
[*di*]vers o[*the*]r lumber and [*illeg.*]		[*value missing*]	
In the Bakehowse			
[*Im*]primis a quarter barly		[*value missing*]	
[...] a trough ij [...] a tread iij [...]			
[...] [*k*]neadinge trough a ~~kneading~~ [...]			
old pann with other lumber		[*value missing*]	
In the kitchin loft			
[...] busheles oat [...]		[*value missing*]	
the first side ends here; one or more lines may be missing			
In the stable			
[*Impr*]imis iij stone horse		[*value missing*]	
[...] plowe geares and cart geares [...]			
[...] [*?*]horses a Fam a yoake			
[...]ames a draught a [*?*]crowe of			
[*ir*]on [...] arke with other lumber		[*value missing*]	
In the Hay howse			
Imprimis Hay in the howse		[*value missing*]	
In the barne			
Imprimis a Canch of graine		[*value missing*]	
Item a canch of hay a parcele of [*?*]chaff			
a [*?*]Riddle a [*?*]~~skrene~~ a skreene a la[...]			
3 forkes ij sackes a gosse yoake xi [...]			
[*hu*]rdles [*illeg.*] rake		[*value missing*]	
Item a canch of teares		[*value missing*]	
In the yard			
Imprimis vj bease iij yearelinges	xviij		
Item a paire of oxen	ix		
Item iij Calves		[*?*]xxx	
Item iiij stoares ij pigges a sowe		xxxxvj	
Item sheepe v couples v guest sheepe		liij	4
Item ij carts ij paire of wheeles ij			
plowes ij paire of harrowes	iiij		
Item ij old hovells ij troughes wood			
furzear a[n]d [*?*]brume a Role		xxvj	8

	£	s	d
Item pullen in the yard 8 henns a cocke 4 ducks a drake, iij capons ij [*sto*]cks of Bees		xvj	
Item the Compasse in the yard		x	
Item tilth and breach sowen and unsowen	xxxv		
Item in ready mony		xxxxx	
Somma totalis	112	~~18~~ 17	[...]

[*pray*]sers Thomas Bolnest [*signature*], signum [...] Watts, signum [...] Punn[...]
[*Only a fragment of the exhibition clause remains, containing the name Geo Barnardi (i.e. George Barnardiston). The exhibition clause was signed by Jacksonne, notary public.*]

Notes: Lucy Marshall was buried at Everton on 2 April 1627.

389 Mary Onslow of Everton, Hunts, spinster made 28 August 1627
Huntingdonshire Archives, AH18/7/48
Slight damage to the right side.

A true and perfitt Inventory of all the goodes and Chatteles of Mistress Mary Onslow late of Everton in the County of Huntingdon Spinster taken veiwed and praised by us whose names are underwritten this eight and twentieth day of August in the third yeare of the Raigne of our Soveraigne Lord Charles of England Scotland Fraunce and Ireland Kinge defender of the faith Annoque Domini 1627

	£	s	d
Imprimis her weareinge apparrell	xx	0	0
Item iij paire of flaxen sheettes ij payre of seamed sheettes iiij paire of hemptare sheettes ij paire of pillowbeares	ij	xiij	4
Item A dozen of damaske Napkins	0	xvj	0
Item five peices of Flaxen ij ells and a halfe in a peice ij short fringed cloathes and a flaxen table cloath a dozen of hemptare Napkins	0	xx	0
Item a Cubberdcloath a table cloath a diaper towell	0	xiij	0
Item iiij brasse pottes one brasse pann one posnett with other trash	j	xiij	4
Item a dozen of pewter platters	0	xiij	4
Item vj Cushions of Turkye worke a Chaire a Chest	0	xiij	4
Item in debtes oweing by good specialty	CC	0	0
Item in readye monye	x	0	0
Item more in monye	x	0	0
Somma total:	CCxxxxvijj	[*illeg.*]	[*illeg.*]
	248	2	4

George Barnardiston [*signature*], Richard Amps [*signature*]
[*Exhibited by Cecily Winch and Dorothea Scott, executrices, and in the presence of John Jackson, notary public, on 31 January 1628*]

Notes: Mary Onslow was buried at Everton on 11 June 1627. She made her will on 30 March 1627, making bequests of around £650 to family and godchildren (Hunts Archives, AH60/22/803 and summarised in BHRS, vol. 2, p. 58). She was the daughter of Richard Onslow of Knowle, Surrey Solicitor General to Elizabeth I and Speaker of the House of Commons who died in 1571. The executrix Cecily Winch was her sister and the wife of Sir Humphrey Winch of Everton, who had been an MP, held judicial appointments in Ireland and as Justice of Common Pleas in England. The other executrix was Cecily Winch's daughter ('Richard Onslow 1527/8–1571' *ODNB*; *The Visitations of the County of Surrey*, London, Harleian Society, 1899, pp. 154–5; 'Sir Humphrey Winch 1555?-1625' *ODNB*). George Barnardiston, one of the appraisers, is probably the man who died in 1628 and was described as a gentleman of Everton in his will made soon after Mary Onslow's death.

390 John Gurrie of Swineshead, husbandman made 27 December 1627

Huntingdonshire Archives, AH18/7/50

The inventory has several holes, resulting in the loss of words in three places. It is torn across, below the exhibition clause.

A true invitorie of the goodes & chattels of Jhon Gurrie late of Swyneshed husb. prysed the 27 daye of December 1627 by Larance Foster & Jhon Gibbes

	£	s	d
Inprimis his wearing apparell	2	0	0
In the hall			
Imprimis a framed table, a benchboard, and settle iij chayres two lynnen wheeles iiij cushens	1	6	8
Item iij peeces of peuter, one chamber pott, on chafindish two brasse candlestickes, on little salte [*?*]seler	0	5	0
In the chamber			
Item on trusbedsted iiij coffers, two boxes two little barrels	1	6	8
Item one matteris, two bolsters four pillowes, two coverlettes two blankettes	1	16	8
Item two paire of flexen sheetes, four paire of harden [*she*]etes, two boardclothes, three pillowbeers, vj [*ta*]blenapkins, two towels	2	10	0
Item xvj ells of harden, two ells of tilliwillie	0	13	4
In the loft over the hall			
Item two tubs, a wollen wheele & other trash	0	10	0
In the kytchin			
Item fyve kettles, one brasse pot, a paire of andirons two pot hangers, on spitte, a cheespresse a molding table, tubs payles & other trash	2	0	0
Item grayne of all sortes in the yard & haye	4	10	0
Item four melch kine three bullockes, three calves, one horse	16	0	0
Item swyne in the yard	1	10	0
Item twentie sheepe	5	0	0
Item one colt & part of another	2	10	0
Item tymber & fyer [...] the yard	1	0	0
[*w*]heat sowen	0	16	0
Item in redie mon[*ey*] [...]	13	10	0

Item for the moitie & [...] [*illeg.*] ten sheepe & vij pigges	1	18	4
Summa	58	17	8
[*At the foot of the page are the figures*	*59*	*6*	*8*]
[*Corrected total*	*£59*	*2s*	*8d*]

Laurence Foster [*signature*], Jhon Gibbes [*mark*]
[*Exhibited by Robert Gurrey, one of the executors, on 9 February 1628. The exhibition clause was signed by R. Furley, deputy registrar.*]

Notes: John Gurrie was buried at Swineshead on 17 October 1627.

391 John Coxe of Stagsden, yeoman made 19 February 1628
Lincolnshire Archives, LCC ADMONS 1628/33
There is slight creasing. Words have been supplied, where obvious.

A true Inventory Indented of all the moveable goods Cattells and Chattells of John Coxe of Stachden in the County of Bedd yeoman late deceased, made and praised the Nyneteeneth daye of February [...] Anno Domini 1627 by us George Nichols and [*Lewes*] Stonebridge

	£	s	d
Inprimis his Apparrell	iij		
Item all the Beddinge praised at	viij		
Item one Bedsteede and two Borddedbeds		xx	
Item all the Lynnen	v	xiij	iiij
Item one Presse fower Coffers & Chests		xx	
Item two Cubbords, one Table, one forme one Table bord with all other Cheares formes and stooles		l	
Item three barrells, three tubbs with all other woodden Ware		xlv	
Item all the Brasse and Pewter		xxx	
Item one spitt one barre of Iron with all other Iron Ware		x	
Item Three Kyne, one Caulfe fower Sheepe and two Lambes	viij		
Item two Hovells with all the wood	iij	x	
Item all the Haye, Strawe and Chaffe		xxvj	viij
Item all the Grayne theshed & unthreshed		xxvj	viij
Item sixe Henes and one Cocke		iiij	vj
Item one Sowe		x	
Item one dragge Rake, one Ladder with all other Implements		v	
Item in money due by bonnd	xx		
Item two acres and three Roods of Tylth and two of Brach		xlvj	viij
Item in Howsehold Provision		xv	
The summe totall is	lxiij	xij	x

George Nicols [*signature*], signum Le: Stanbredg
[*A brief note of exhibition records that the administrator was sworn*]

Notes: John Coxe was buried at Stagsden on 9 February 1628.

392 Richard Wasse of Ampthill, labourer made 21 March 1628
Lincolnshire Archives, LCC ADMONS 1628/154

An Inventarye of all the goodes & Chattells of Richard Wasse late of Ampthill in the County of Bedd Laborer deceased taken & praised by Ambross Sam and Edw: Smith the xxj[th] daie of March in the yeare of the Raigne of our soveraigne lord king Charles of England Scotland France & Ireland the third 1627 as followeth

	£	s	d
In the parlor			
Inprimis one bedsted a flockbedd a matrice two pillowes two boulsters an old blankett & an old Coverlett praised att		x	
Item fowre paier of course sheetes five pillowbeeres & fowre napkines praised at		v	
Item pewter dishes six, one saltseller and a sawcer praised at		v	
Item one press Cubberd one chaire one table one forme and two chestes praised at		x	
Item his apparrell praised at		vj	
In the Loft			
Item one boarded bed a flockbed a boulster & one Coverlett praised at		iij	iiij
Item three Chestes an old trundlebed--steed & a parcell of ferne praised at		iiij	
In the halle			
Item two tables two formes one Chaire with other Lumber praised at		iiij	
Item two spittes a bankeing iron a potthanger & a paire of potthookes praised at			xviij
Item iij kettles a posnett a porridg pott iij barrells a tub & two kymneles a paire of Andirons frying pan & a tunnell a skimmer a smoothing iron & a pint pott & an old safe praised at		xiij	iiij
Item iij old tubs certayne wood in the yard iij skeene of yarne five bordes an old bedsteed & a dung rake & a table at Goodman Sayes praised at		x	
Item one sow hog praised at		vij	
Item oweing him in monie by William Kerbie		vij	
Item oweing by Edward Kerbie in monie		xx	
Item oweing by John Piggott		ij	vj

	£	s	d
Item oweing for Rent			
Goodman Cason		xvj	viij
The totall of this Inventarye is	vj	v	iiij

[*Exhibited by the administrator at Ampthill on 13 June 1628*]

Notes: Ampthill's parish register records the burial of *Thomas* Wasse on 5 February 1628, probably a mistake for *Richard* Wasse. This is supported by the family relationship between the deceased and the Kirbies, who owed him money, as Richard Wasse married Mary Kirbie in March 1617 (*BPR*, vol. 17, pp. A79 and A51); but if the burial entry for Thomas Wasse is correct, Richard Wasse was not buried at Ampthill and his burial has not been found elsewhere.

393 Thomas Stanbridge of Wootton, yeoman made 21 April 1628
Lincolnshire Archives, LCC ADMONS 1628/144

The Imventory of the goodes and cattles of Thomas Stanbridge Lait of Wotton in the county of Bedford yoeman deacesed, prased by George Gam[b]ell, Francis Cannon and John Calbeck, the 21[th] of Aprill, 1628.

	£	s	d
First in the hail house, A Longe table, one Round table, A forme, fyve			
little Buiffytes, A pott Shelfe, and a chayre, pryce		xvij	vj
Item a pair of Bellows, A pair of and Irons, 2 spittes			
with other Iron workes		vij	vj
Item 3 Brass kittles, one Brass pott, one Little posnyt		xx	
In the parler			
One court cobbert, A table stoile, A Bible, xj queshones		xviij	
In the Buttre, 3 Barrels with other husslement[82]			
In the other Buttre, A Salting trough with other Bourdes		xvij	
In the Kitchings, all the wodden stoufe		xij	
In the Lowe parlor, one stand bed, one mattres			
A coverlitt, 3 Blankettes with a bouster, & 2 pillows		xl	
Item one credle, one trunk, one coffer, with A flask		vij	
In the great cham[*be*]r			
one stan[d]inge Bed, A fether bed, A coverlit, one Blankit			
4 pillowes, a Bouster	v		
Item one Lange table, 6 Joynt stoyls		xl	
Item one chayre, tow chestes, & a Box			
And 4 Queshens		xxx	
In A other cham[*be*]r			
One stan[d]ynge Bed, a coverlit, A mattres, & A flockbed			
4 pillowes		xl	
Item all the pewder		xx	
Item ~~xij~~ viij pair of Sheites, 2 dussan of napkins			
4 Bordes clothes		xl	
Item other Lynnen		xx	

82 The value of these items has been included with the value of the next line.

		£	s
Item in the stable, & other out houses, & tow hoggstyes			xx
	Sum ys	xxij	ix

George Gamble [*signature*], Francis Cannons marke
[*Exhibited by the administrator at Ampthill on 24 April 1628. A note at the foot of the sheet records that Master Reeve took the administrator's oath.*]

Notes: Thomas Stanbridge's burial has not been found.

394 Dionisia Norton of Sharpenhoe, Streatley, widow and gentlewoman made 6 May 1628
Lincolnshire Archives, LCC ADMONS 1628/118
There is slight damage and a few words are illegible.

The Inventory Indented of all and singuler the goodes debtes and Creddittes of Mistress Dionis Nortons late of Sharpenhoe in the Countie of Bedf deceased taken prized and valued by John Peppiatt of Sharpenhoe aforesaid yeoman and Francis Pruddon of Streatley the Sixt of May Anno Domini 1628 as followeth vizt

	£	s	d
Inprimis in the hall three tables one little forme, two little chaire and fower stooles		xx	
Item in the kitchin five pottes foure skellettes foure pannes two brasen Candlestickes, one morter two dripping pannes, one fryinge pann foure spittes three spott [sic, *pot*] hangers one paire of Cobirons and a fire shovell	vij		
Item one cupbord two chaires seaven stooles one side table twelve pound of yarne, twelve [*?*]theales shelves and other Implementes	ij		
Item two basons thirteene platters twentie small dishes one quart pott two beakers	j	xvj	
Item in the milkhouse two churnes tenn trayes two bowles two pewter dishes one plate six shelves and other Implementes	j		
In the Chamber where she lay			
Inprimis one standing bedd with a featherbed one paire of sheetes three boulsters three pillowes, two Blankettes one Rugg & curtaines	iiij		
Item sixteene paire of sheetes, one fine sheet two Table Clothes two Cubbord Clothes one paire of pillowberes, twelve table napkins & one other sheet	iiij		
Item one other bedd with a feather bedd one paire of sheetes a pillowe & two bolsters	j		
Item one Trunke with five Cushions one Carpett and a copper Coverlaid	j	iij	
Item three Trunckes, five coffers one cubbord a sheete three boxes one coffer box	j		
Item in money	ix	xiij	

Item one bible and other Bookes		vj	viij
Item Eight silver spoones one little ringe and a tooth and eare pickers	ij	v	
Item one paire of Troy waightes			xij
Item in the studie boxes and other Implementes		vj	viij
Item Mistress Dionis Nortons apparrell	iiij		

Other Chambers

Inprimis in the Chamber over the kitchin one bedd with beddinge another old bedd 3 old Coffers and other implementes	j	vj	
Item in another chamber one bedd and beddinge a paire of iron rackes a Coffer	j		
Item in the milkhouse chamber one bedd one Trunke and a Table	j	iij	
Item in another Chamber apples woole waightes an Iron Crowe and other implementes	ij		
Item a side saddle and a pinnion clothe		xiij	
Item a guilded salt seller	ij	x	
Item in the Chamber over the seller a saltinge trough a drie fatt, a cheese racke a forme and other Lumber		viij	
Item in the new loft a cradle bordes and other Lumber		v	
Item in the brew house and bolting house a quearne and other Lumber		x	
Item in the shopp by the gatehouse one salting trough, tiles broad [*?*] ~~Rhestes~~ [*?*]Rystes and other Lumber	j		
Item in the stable & yard one forme axetrees two hogg troughes two ladders and one Cow rack		vj	viij
Item strawe in the barne		vj	viij
Item certaine wicker bottles			xij
Item a Cover of a salt and a pi[*illeg.*][83]		v	

In the feild

Inprimis nine acres of wheat three of barley five acres & a rood of pease thirteene acres of oates whereof the one halfe is valued at	xvj		
Item five & Twentie Ewes and lambes & three & fiftie drie sheepe	xxiiij		
Item a sowe and piggs	j	xiij	iiij
Item three Cowes	vij		
Item a horse	j	xiij	iiij
Item two stockes of bees		x	

83 This line has been inserted in a different hand. The last word is obscured by the letters of the word *feild* in the next line.

In the Barne

Item the wheate & barley j

Sume totall is Ciiij xv viij

Ciiij^{li} xv^{s} viij^{d}

[*Corrected total £104 2s 4d*]

[*Exhibited by the administrator at Ampthill on 2 June 1628. The exhibition clause was signed by J. Walker, notary public. A note at the foot of the inventory refers to later proceedings.*]

Notes: Dionisia Norton was buried at Streatley on 7 May 1628, described as a gentlewoman. Her husband, William Norton, gentleman, died in 1622. His will identifies two daughters by his first wife and Dionisia as his second wife and mother of seven children. He gave her a featherbed, bedstead and the furniture to go with it. The residue was divided among all his children. He appointed her and his friend Master Hale, vicar of Westoning, executors. They renounced executorship and administration was granted to his son Thomas (TNA, PROB11/140). Dionisia Norton did not leave a will. Her son Richard Norton of London, citizen and fishmonger, was bound (with John Peppiatt of Sharpenhoe) in the sum of £204 on 24 June 1628 to administer her estate (Lincs Archives, LCC ADMONS 1628/118).

395 Christopher Crouch of Potton, innholder made 16 September 1630

Bedfordshire Archives, T49/2

The inventory is stained, badly faded and rubbed. It was published in Bedfordshire Notes and Queries, *1893, vol. 3, pp. 276–8, when far more was legible. The 1893 transcription is reproduced here with a few minor corrections.*

A true Inventorie Indented of all the goods and Chattells as well moveable as unmoveable of Christopher Crouch of Potten Inholder late deceased weare prised and valewed by Richard Paratt, Edward Waller and Richard Ampes the xvjth daye of September Anno Domini 1630

£ s d

In the [*illeg.*]

Inprimis one table with a frame
one bench board with a backe 6 ioyned
stooles 3 Chaires one Cubboard 2 pott
[*illeg.*] 4 Cushions one shelfe one fliche
of bacon 2 paire of potthangers a fire
shovell and tonges a paire of bellowes 2 lowe
stooles 2 cobiorns and a fier iron a payer
of tables a curteyne and a hower glass xxvj viij

In the great parlor

Item one table with a frame one forme
2 bench boards 3 [*?*]Chares one standinge
bedd and beddinge one curteyne one
lowe chaire and 3 shelfes iij

In the little parlor

Item one table with a frame one bench &
forme one standinge bed and beddinge one
truklle bed & beddinge i Cubbert 2 little
curteyns on box 1 stoole & cushions
one curteyne and a halfe iiij

In the chamber over the great parlor			
Item one table with a frame 2 chayres one bench boarde 1 forme 4 stooles one standinge bedd with beddinge & curteyns one trundle [*illeg.*] one frame bedd one little table with 3 cushions	v	x	
In the chamber over the kitchyne			
Item one little table one lowe stoole one standing bedd and beddinge		xxiij	iv
In the chamber over the brewhouse			
Item one saddle 2 shelfes i cradle 1 [*?*]chaire 5 cheeses and other ymplementes		xvj	
In the little lofte			
Item one board bedd & beddinge a pillion and cloath with other ymplements		xiij	iiij
In the Cocke lofte			
Item a bushell and stricke a casting shovell six piecies of newe yron & other ymplements theire		xxx	
In the kitcheyne			
Item seaventeene peeice of pewter 6 porringers 6 sawcers [*illeg.*] Candlestickes 4 brasse kettles and other ymplements theire	iij	v	
In the brewhouse			
Item one Copper one Mash fatt one yeildinge fatt 2 great tubes 6 kymnells and other ymplements theire	iij		
In the Seller			
Item 2 barrells of beare 3 kylderkyns 1 runlett 2 drinkinge stooles and other ymplements		l	
In the great parlor			
Item 13 paire of sheetes x towells 3 board cloathes 2 dosen & a halfe of Napkyns 10 pillowebeares one face cloath	vj		
In the stable			
Item 3 horses 7 rackes 6 mangers 2 ploughes Cartes & other ymplements	xij	x	
In the yarde			
Item the wood and timber with hogges troughes and other ymplementes	v		
In the Garner			
Item the Malte screene and castinge shovell	xv	vj	viij
In the Malthouse in the towne			
Item wheat Pease Rye bushell Fann and a ladder	iij	13	iiij
In the yard in the towne			
Item one Hovell 2 rackes and woode		xiij	iiij
In the barne in the towne			
Item barley Oates haye & other ymplementes	xxvj	vj	viij

	£	s	d
In the barne att home			
Item wheate Rye barlye and strawe a quarne & a Fanne	xvj		
In the haye house att home			
Item Haye and Pease	vj		
In the yarde att home			
Item 4 Cowes 3 bullockes	x		
Item one paire of Steers	[*?*]j	x	
Item Threescore and 15 sheepe & Lambes	xvj		
Item Capons and Pullyn		xv	
Item in readie money	xviij		
Item the tylth and [*arr*]able	vj	viij	
Item his wearinge apparell	iij	vj	viij
Item Money in his purse		iij	
[*Total is at least*	*£174*	*7s*	*0d*]

Richard Paratt [*signature*], Edward Waller [*signature*], Richard Ampes
[*Exhibited by the executrix in October 1630*]

Notes: Christopher Crouch was buried at Potton on 13 September 1630. His widow Dorothy was buried there on 18 July 1639. He made his will on 20 March 1630 asking to be buried in the church of Potton (the word *yard* was crossed out). He gave his 'capital messuage' in Potton called the Bell where he lived to his wife Dorothy for life, then to his son Oliver Crowche who was to pay £20 to each of the testator's younger daughters Mary, Joan and Catherine (who also received one hempland and one rood of arable) when they reached 21. He gave his animals and crops to his wife, on condition that she paid £40 each to his daughters Dorothy and Alice. His household stuff was left to his wife for life then to his daughters. The residual legatee and executrix was his wife, who was granted probate on 12 October 1630 (Beds Archives, ABP/W1630/71). A week before his death, he consulted Dr Napier who noted that he was 58 and drew up an astrological chart (Forman and Napier, case no. 22892).

396 Thomas Cranfild of Tempsford

undated; January–June 1631

Lincolnshire Archives, LCC ADMONS 1631/39

A trew inventory of all the goodes and Chateles of Thomas Cranfild of Temsford late decesed vewed and praysed by those whose names are heare under Written

	£	s	d
Imprimus in the haule one old tabull and a fourme a Cubburd a penne towe old arkes one Cheare and Cartaine other trash		xx	
Item in the Cheching one brase pote and three Cetteles towe panes and Cartaine other Impellmentes		xxvj	viij
Item the pewter [*word rubbed out*] nyne dysses one sault		viij	
Item in the Chamber one borded bedsted with a fether beed a materes a Ceverled a blanket towe boulsteres one pellow one Chest towe Coferes and Cartaine other Impelmentes		xl	
Item in the laft on borded bedsted one Cofer a Wollin Whele a linen Whele one bottel and Cartain other Impellmentes at		xiij	iiij

Item in the buttere towe bareles three tubes one Sauling trowef and Cartain other trash at		x	
Item the Lining seven payre of shetes and one shete towe bourd Clathes one spere Clath three pelobeares towe napkines		xl	
Item his wairing aparell		xx	
Item in the yard one horse		xxxiij	iiij
Item one Cowe and one bullack at three [*sic*]		[*?*]lxvj	viij
Item tow piges at		viij	
Item the grayne in the barne		L	
Item the haye and the stra at		xxxiij	iiij
Item towe Rouft [*roofed*] houfelles at	3	x	
Item the woode at		vj	viij
Item a Coke foure henes		ij	vj
Item in the fild towe aceres three Roudes of Wheate and Rey at	5		
Item fyve Roudes of tylth at		xiij	iiij
Item foure aceres of breach land at		xiij	iiij
the hole Sume is	xxx	xv	2
[*Corrected total*	*£28*	*15s*	*2d*]

Thomas Sexten his marke, Richard Pufforde [*signature*], Henrye Wallis [*signature*]
[*Exhibited by the administratrix at Bedford on 14 June 1631. A note on the back of the inventory records that his widow Katherine and Richard Bestoe of Gamlingay, Cambridgeshire, husbandman, were bound to administer the estate. The amount of the bond is not stated.*]

Notes: Thomas Cranfild was buried at Tempsford on 10 January 1631. Administration was granted to his widow Katherine at Bedford on 14 June 1631 (Lincs Archives, Act Book A/x/128).

397 Evans Kinge of Stotfold

made 11 March 1631

Lincolnshire Archives, LCC ADMONS 1631/235

A true Inventory of the goodes & Chatles of Evins Kinge Late of Statfold now disceased vewed and praised by those whose names are under written. March xj[th] 1630

	£	s	d
Imprimis in the haall a table a frame a forme two litle chears and littell stolles		xv	
Item a Cradle		ij	vj
Item in the Chamber one standing Bed one halfe headed bed a trundle Bed		xxxvj	viij
Item one Cubard one Chest a boxe and a Cofer		xxvj	viij
Item three barrells two Tubes five boulles and a Cimnell		xij	vj
Item two payles six dishes a dosen of trenchers		ij	vj
Item a peeke a payer of skealles			xij
Item on payer of flexen shetes		x	
Item six payre of hempe tayr shetes		xxx	
Item six pillow bears ten napkins and a table Clothe		xij	iiij
Item thre matterises two old Coverings and thre blankates		xxviij	
Item thre bolsters four pillowes		xiij	iiij

	£	s	d
Item two Collers two payer of harnise two Cart sadelles		xv	
Item Iron in the lofte a harow and other trosh in the lofte		xx	
Item an old plowe a sher and a Colter a payre of sling tres and two Roolles		xij	
Item thre bottels		v	
Item six peeces of pewter and a pewter pote		viij	
Item a payer of pothokes a gridgiron a friinge pane a skimmer and a payer of pot hangers		iiij	
Item a brase pote two posnetes and two kettels		xxx	
Item a wollen whell and a lining whelle		iiij	
Item thre bease	vj	xiij	iiij
Item sixtene shepe	iiij		
Item barley in the straw	ij	x	
Item thre bushils of [*?*]linti[...]lls		xv	
Item two bushels of ottes		vj	
Item xj bushill pease	ij	vj	viij
Item two bushell of tayrs		vij	viij
Item six sakes and a bage			xij
Item viij henes and a Coke		iij	
Item his waring aperill	iij		
Item the dounge		x	
Item a screene		vj	viij
Item thre forkes			xviij
Item twelve pound of linen yarne		viij	
Item five yeardes of wollen Cloth		xv	
Item one draft Rake		iij	iiij
The some is	xxxj	ix	ij
[*Corrected total*	*£36*	*15s*	*8d*]

Willyam Allyn [*signature*], the marke of Willyam Ford

[*Exhibited by the administratrix at Ampthill on 15 June 1631. A note at the foot of the page records that the inventory was sworn before John Walker and that a bond was taken from the relict, Joan King and Thomas Rogers of Stotfold, a tailor.*]

Notes: Evans Kinge was buried at Stotfold on 27 February 1631. Administration was granted to his widow Joan King by John Walker at Ampthill on 15 June 1631 and a bond was taken (Lincs Archives, Act Book A/x/128 and LCC ADMONS 1631/235).

398 Elizabeth Witt of Wootton, widow made 31 March 1631

Lincolnshire Archives, INV/137/422

The inventory is damaged at the bottom of the page and the last lines of the exhibition clause are missing.

A true Inventorie of all the goodes Chattles & moveables of Elizabeth Witt late of Wotton deceased taken & prized by the persons here under written the laste daye of March 1631

	£	s	d
In the hall			
Imprimis a Cubboard a table & a frame & 6 ioyned stooles three chaires with other smale thinges		xl	

	£	s	d
in the parlour			
Item one standinge bedsteed with all the furniture	iiij		
Item a table, a chest, a cubboard a chaire		xxxiij	iiij
in the buttrie			
Item the brasse and pewter there	iij		
Item an iron barr 2 paire of pothangers 2 paire of anyrons 2 spittes a paire of tonges & a drippinge pan		xij	
in the milke house			
Item 2 tubbes, 3 barrells 2 troughes with a charme 8 bowels and other trashe		xxvj	
in the kitchin			
Item a cheese presse a boultinge arke & divers other smale thinges there		vj	viij
in the chamber over the parlour			
Item 2 bedsteedes, a chest & an old coffer		xxiiij	
Item the beddinge to the 2 bedsteedes belongeinge		l	
in the chamber over the hall			
Item 2 bedsteedes 2 coffers with their furniture		xlvij	
in the chamber over the kitchin			
Item the yarne and woule		xx	
Item the linnen yarne with other smale thinges		xiij	iiij
in the roome over the milke house			
Item 2 wheeles a longe cart rope, 6 pound of towe with other smale thinges		vj	viij
Item all the linnon	vij	vj	viij
Item all hir apparrell		l	
in the stable			
Item 4 horse with cartes and Cartgeeres plowe & plowegeers with other implementes of husbandrie	xj		
In the yard			
Item 2 beastes & 4 bullockes	xiij		
Item in the feildes 10 acres of wheate & barley	xxv		
Item 14 acres of pease	xxj		
Item a debt upon bond of	xxx		
Summa totalis	130	15	8

Pryzers Humphrey Cottenham, Richard Impey, Henry Witt
[*Exhibited by Henry Witt, executor, on 14 June 1631*]

Notes: Elizabeth Witt was buried at Wootton on 17 April 1631, as the widow of John Witt, who had been buried on 6 November 1630. John Witt, husbandman, made his will on 30 October 1630, leaving his messuage and tenement with eight acres of land to his son Henry Witt after the death of his wife Elizabeth, on condition that Henry pay varying sums of money to his brothers and sisters. He gave the bedstead in the parlour with its bedding to his daughter Alice after his wife's death; £5 and the framed hovel in the yard to his daughter Elizabeth; and 40s to his daughter Anne. He gave the residue to his wife Elizabeth and appointed her executrix. The will was proved on 20 November 1630 (Beds Archives, ABP/W1630–1/90). Elizabeth Witt made her will on 22 March 1631. She gave between £5 and £7 to six of her children, except her eldest son John who received 12d and her son Henry. Many of her household goods were left principally to her daughters Elizabeth Orton, including 8lb of wool and 5lb of dressed flax, and Alice Witt. She made some adjustments to her husband's dispositions. She gave the residue to her son Henry Witt, whom she appointed executor. He was granted probate by John Walker surrogate for John Farmerie at Bedford on 14 June 1631 (Lincs Archives, LCC WILLS/1631/352).

399 William Barre of Tempsford, butcher made 12 April 1631

Lincolnshire Archives, INV/137/418

The inventory is damaged at the bottom and the end of the inventory is missing.

The Inventary off the goodes and Chattels off William Barre off Tempsford in the Countie off Bedfford Bucher desecid the 3 daye off Aprill 1631 and praysed the xij daye off the said Aprell followinge by the praisers whose names are under written

	£	s	d
In the halle			
Inprimos a Cobbard	0	16	0
A tabell with the Frame and Forme and bench	0	12	0
A littell tabell a Cheeste and 3 Cheares	0	5	0
A greate Brase pane v Cattelles 3 potes a gose pane and Tow pare off Cobeyarnes with the pothangers and hockes and grideyarn and Fringe pane and all other Impellmentes	2	10	0
In the Chamber			
A staninge Joyne badested ꝑ a Flocke bade	1	3	4
3 pillows a Coverlide 3 Cheestes one boxe one tabell 6 Joyne stowles	1	10	0
and 15 putter dishes v poringars 3 puters bolles 2 Candellstickes a salte and xij spones	0	18	0
In the littell Buttre 3 baskates and shelffes and the other Impellmentes	0	3	4
In the littell Chamber			
A Bordded beade and a Cradell ~~a flocke~~ a blancat and an under Cloth	0	4	0
In the Chamber over the halle			
on halffe headed beade a old Coverlide and a Casting shovell		6	8
the lasste Chamber			
A Joyne bead a Father beade a bolster 2 pillows and a Coverlide a trundelbad a mattris a blancat and a pillow on Cheste	2	6	8
Tow pare off Flexsone shetes 2 pare hemptar shetes on Flexson on hallan shete and 6 pillowbares and 17 tabell napkines on tabell Cloth and 6 pare off Corse shetes	4	0	0
A bascate and v^{li} off woole	0	5	0
In the buttre			
3 barelles wheles a old huch a busell 2 Riddelles	0	10	0
In the milke house			
3 shelffes a Tabell 2 tankardes a Churne 2 boles with the potes and panes and other Impelments	0	8	0
In the Chichinge			
4 tubes 2 pales 2 spetes an old pane a Cattel the Chese prese v slipes off Lining yarne and the other Impellmentes	1	10	0
In the stabell			
2 horse	2	10	0
2 Cowes on bullockes	7	0	0

A Chaff house the plow geares and Carte geares	0	6	8
2 Cartes with showed wheles 2 plowes	3	[...]	4
Cartane [*certain*] plo[...]			
2 mead [...]			

[*the page is torn and the remainder of the inventory is missing*]

[*Total to this point* *£30* *5s* *0d*]

[*No exhibition clause*]

Notes: William Barre's burial has not been found.

400 Thomas Wallin alias Poulter of Shillington, yeoman made 22 April 1631
Lincolnshire Archives, INV/137/394

A true Inventarie indented of all the goo[*ds*] [*&*] Chattells of Thomas Wallin alias Poulter la[*te*] of Shitlington in the Countie of Bedf yeoman deceased Valued & prised the xxij[th] day of Aprill Anno domini 1631 By those whose names are heare under written

	£	s	d
Imprimis in the Halle one Cupboord one table & frame, two fourmes one Chare stooles with other implementes	1	10	0
Item in the Parlour one standing bed with the furniture thereunto belonging with two Chestes two Chares one little table & two stooles	9	0	0
Item in the Chamber over the parlour one bed with the furniture & one Chest	2	0	0
Item in another Chamber one halfe headed bed two Cofers with other stuffe	0	8	0
Item in the milke house boles dishes potts pans with other small implementes	0	5	0
Item in the Kitchin one siftinge arke one bolting arke one Cheese presse tubbs pailes & other small implementes	1	10	0
Item in the Butterie three barrells & one drinke stall	0	4	0
Item Linnen & woollen Cloth	6	13	4
Item brasse & pewter	1	10	0
Item three bease	8	0	0
Item fire woode & boord	4	10	0
Item threshing planks	0	10	0
Item Hay & straw	1	0	0
Item wheate barly malt pease & oates	29	0	0
Item graine in the feild	8	0	0
Item sheepe	3	0	0
Item one store & two flitches of bacon	1	10	0
Item in ready money & owinge upon specialtie	63	0	0
Item his waringe Apparell	5	0	0
Sum is	146	10	4

William Fowler [*sen*], William Fowler Jun, William Elmer, Matthew Hare [*signature*]
[*No exhibition clause*]

Notes: Thomas Wallin was buried at Shillington on 21 April 1631. He made his will on 15 April 1631. He gave his timber to his brother and the residue to his wife Elizabeth, who was appointed executrix (Lincs Archives, LCC WILLS/1631/381).

401 Elizabeth Kidgell of Eaton Bray, singlewoman made 29 April 1631
Lincolnshire Archives, INV/137/396

The Inventarie Indented of the moveable goods and Chattells of Elizabeth Kidgell late of Eyton in the Cownty of Bedford singell woman deceased made and prized by Jhon George and Richard Atkins the Nyne and Twenty daie of Aprill: Anno Domini 1631

		£	s	d
Imprimis in Ready money		15	0	0
Item One littell Coffer prized at		0	3	4
Item her wareing apparell prized at		0	10	0
	Some ys	15	13	4

John George his marke, Richard Atkins
[*No exhibition clause*]

Notes: Elizabeth Kidgell was buried at Eaton Bray on 3 March 1631.

402 William Pearson of Shillington, yeoman made 3 May 1631
Lincolnshire Archives, INV/137/393
The document is fragile, creased and has holes near the end. Some words and values are missing.

A true Inventorie of all the goodes and chattells aswell mooveable as immooveable of William Pearson late of Shitlington in the countie of Bedf: yeoman valued & prised the third daie of Maie anno domini 1631 by John Paratt, Thomas Asheton and William Goodale

	£	s	d
In the Halle			
Imprimis on table & frame on foorme and on cubboord		30	
Item two chaires two stooles on paire of andirons two hookes a pottshelve and on shelve		10	
In the parlor			
Item on ioynened bed with the furniture to it	3		
Item on table on chest foure stooles and thre cusshions		34	
In the chamber			
Item on bedd with the furniture five pillowes & foure cofers		40	
Item on boorded bed and the furniture to it		13	4
Item on moulding boorde and on kneadding trough		3	4

	£	s	d
Item eleaven paire of sheetes sixe pillowbears eight napkins foure table cloothes & two towells	7	10	
Item on furnace		20	
Item brasse and peuter		50	
Item on salting trough on fatt and three kimnells		20	
Item on cheese presse tubbes boolles pailes pottes disshes spoones trenchers [*illeg.*]		40	
Item on horse and foure bease		[*value missing*]	
Item two sheppe & two hogges		50	
Item graine	13		
Item the graine in the feild	76		
Item cartes and cart gears and plowes and plow gears	4	10	
Item boordes planckes forkes rakes & other implements		27	
Item on paire of harrowes & a hovil		30	
Item fire woode & compasse	4		
Item in readie monies & monie owing	24		
Item in bacon		30	
Item pullin		6	8
Item his apparrill	3		
Su[*mma*] tota[*lis*]	[...]	4	4
[*Corrected total: at least*	*£155*	*4s*	*4d*]

John Pa[*rr*]att [*signature*], Thomas [*A*]shton [*signature*], William Goodale [*mark*]
[*No exhibition clause*]

Notes: William Pearson was buried at Shillington on 19 April 1631. He made his will on 15 April 1631. He gave one acre of arable to his wife Agnes and her heirs and all his household goods, except a furnace, a bed and a table. He gave his interest in the lands of his brother Edward in Orford Darcy, Huntingdonshire, to son George. His son John was appointed residual legatee and executor (Lincs Archives, LCC WILLS/1631/394).

403 Edmund Randell of Clifton made 6 May [*?*]1631

Lincolnshire Archives, INV/137/443

Slight damage and a hole; missing letters have been supplied where obvious.

A true Inventorye of all the goodes of Edmund Randell late of Clifton in the Countye of Bedf deceassed, mad the sixt day of Maye [*blank*] in the yeare of our Lord and prized by us whose names are subscribed.

	£	s	d
Imprimis in the hall one Cobert		13	4
Item a table, a forme and one Joyned stole		6	8
Item for all the pewter on [*the*] Coberts head		20	
Item all the brasse		11	
Item two barrells & a tub & a Coffer, dishes & all oth[*er*] things in the buttery		7	

Item in th[*e*] Chamber two beddes & the bedding		35	
Item for [...] [*c*]offers [...]		10	
Item for the linnen in the [*h*]ouse as sheets, pillowbeers boord cloathes and napkins		53	4
Item for fyve yardes of woollen Cloath		12	6
for all his apparell		26	8
Item for a woollen whele a Cradle, a hatchell and other old implementes		5	
Item halfe a quarter of barlye		20	
Item two Chaires, two pailes, a hobingyron, & all other odde implemetes		6	8
Item foure ells of lynnen Cloath		3	4
Item for two acres of tylth ground and fyve rodes of brach	7	10	
Item for a Cowe and a bullocke	3		
for six henns		6	
for all the dongue in the yard		6	
for all the wood in the yard		10	
for the loome and the furniture thereof		50	
for the hempland		6	8
Summa totalis	25	19	2

Richard Same his marke, Christofer Sheffeild his mark, Mordicay Randell [*signature*]

Debtes

Inprimis owing [*?*]to Wyllyam Wallys of Longford	4		
Item to Wyddow [*?*]Hawn[*es*] of Clyfton	3		
Item to Master Rolt of Clifton for a [*word deleted and illegible*] [*?*]Fyne	2	13	4
Item to Master Badferd & Richard Same	0	13	4
Sum	10	6	4
[*Corrected total of debts*	*£10*	*6s*	*8d*]
so that hur [*sic*] goodes is	15	13	2
[*Corrected total of goods less debts*	*£15*	*12s*	*6d*]

[*No note of exhibition*]

Notes: Edmund Randell was buried at Clifton on 24 March 1631. The appraiser Mordecai Randall was not Edmund Randell's son. The creditor Master Rolt was Walter Rolt, Lord of the manors of Lacies and Clifton; and Master Badferd was Isaac Bedford, vicar of Clifton. Edmund Randell made his will on 28 July 1628. He gave his eldest daughter Elizabeth his house and lands in Clifton and Langford at the age of 21 on condition that she paid £16 to her sister Christian. He gave his wife Anne the benefit of his land in Langford for her life; and the house, sharing with Elizabeth; and all his moveable goods, paying 26s 8d which he owed to Elizabeth Campkyn. His wife was appointed executrix (Lincs Archives, LCC WILLS/1631/354).

404 William Bundey of Chawston, Roxton, yeoman — made 27 May 1631

Lincolnshire Archives, INV/137/421

Damaged, much faded and the foot of the inventory is missing.

A true and perfect Inventarie of all the goods Chattell and Cattell of William Bundeys of Chalverston wthin the parishe of Roxton, and countie of Bedf yeo[man] lately deceased, and o[n] the 27th day of May Anno Domini 1631 by Leonard Feild, John Bundey, William Childe, and Thomas Swift yeomen the prisers and valewers therof

	£	s	d
Inprimis In the hall. A penne, a glasse case, a spitt A paire of hand yrons A paire of pott han gers, a cradle, with other smale necessaries		13	4
Item about a dosen peeces of pewter with salt cellers pottes, spoones, a candlesticke and the rest of the pewter		13	4
Item Two brasse pottes Two ketles, Two posnets, a great brasse pan, a chafinge dishe, a fryinge pan, a morter, a warminge pan a skimmer Two candlestickes, with the rest of the brasse		50	
Item a Furnace		20	
Item In the parlour a standinge bedsteed another bedsteed A longe Table with the frame, a Cupbord, A litle Table, a Chest, Three Coffers, a Trunke, certaine stooles and other smale necessaries	5		
Item a Flock bed, Three bolsters Foure pillowes, Foure blankettes, a Coverlett with the rest of the beddinge with certaine quishions, and painted clothes		50	
Item All his Apparell	3	6	8
Item Eight paire of sheetes, Foure Table clothes, about Eighteene Table nabkins, with the rest of the linnen		50	
Item Foure barrels, Two bolles and such like necessaries		10	
Item A cheese presse, Three milke bowles, Three chees Fattes, pails, bowles, dishes, spoones, tren chers, woodden candlestickes, and other such like necessaries		8	
Item his halfe part of all the Tubbes, kimnels, Trough of a grindlestone, of a racke, and of all the wood		10	
Item his halfe part of about Three quarters and a halfe of barley	3		
Item his halfe part of all the sackes, winnowe clothes bagers, skuttels, baskets, ladders, of a Fanne, of a bushell and such like necessaries		4	
Item Two horses and theer furniture	10		
Item Two bease, and Three bullockes	9	10	
Item Two hogges		22	8
Item Twelve sheepe, and Fyve lambes	4	10	
Item all his duckes and hennes		6	
Item his halfe part of certaine hovelles, with theer rafters and strawe	5	6	8
Item his halfe part of all cartes and wheeles	3	6	8
Item his halfe part of all the ploughes with their yrons, and other their necessaries, and of all harrowes		15	
Item his halfe part of all sithes, draggrakes, other rakes, forkes, spades, shovels, mattockes, and other such like necessaries		6	8
Item his halfe part of all the composse, of certaine hurdles, hatchets, rowles, hand sawes, wimbles, of an exe, and of other such like necessaries		20	

	£	s	d
Item certaine hempe, with a hempe land		2	6
Item his halfe part of all the bacon		6	8
Item his halfe part of about Twentie and Foure Akers of wheat, Rie, and Barley in the [?]Tilly Feildes	24		
Item his halfe part of about Fifteene Akers of Barley, Pease, Oates and Lintels in the Brach Feild	5		
[...] owinge to the said deceased for b[...] and bu[...]		2	8
[*The document is damaged and the remainder is missing*]			
[*Total to this point*	*£88*	*10s*	*10d*]

[*No exhibition clause*]

Notes: William Bundey was buried at Roxton on 26 May 1631. He made a nuncupative will on 13 May 1631, giving his son Robert a great brass pan and £15 at the age of 21; and a chest and £15 to his daughter Jane at the age of 21. His wife Marie was residual legatee and executrix. She was granted probate by John Walker on 13 June 1631 (Lincs Archives, LCC WILLS/1631/391).

405 Robert Jones of Steppingley, gentleman — made 31 May 1631

Lincolnshire Archives, INV/137/392

The inventory is written on three sides of the two sheets and is damaged on the outside lower corners. There is also some fading on the top right side. Some words and values are missing.

An Inventory of all the movable goodes & Cattels of Robarte Jones of Steppingley in the County of Bedford gent deceased as they were pryced by Gilberte Browne & William Emmerton May 31 1631

	£	s	d
In the Hall			
A table with a frame		iij	iiij
Item a hanginge shelfe and 2 boardes			xij
Item a payre of Bellowes			iiij
Item a payre of tounge			iiij
Item a fyreshover			ij
Item a payre of Andyrons			vj
Item a payre of Rackes		v	
Item 2 payre of pothangers			xviij
Item a payre of pothookes			vj
Item one fryinge pan			xvj
Item a gridiron			xij
Item 2 porridge potts		x	
Item 3 kettles		x	
Item one brasen chafingdishe		ij	
Item a warminge panne		ij	
Item a morter & pestill		ij	
Item one brasen Candlesticke			vj
Item 4 pewter Candlestickes		iiij	
Item a bowle			xij
Item a hanginge Candlestick			xij
Item a pewter goblet			viij

Item a litle ewre			vj
Item a quarte & pynte potes			vj
Item a flagon		vj	viij
Item 4 ioyned stooles		ij	
Item 2 pewter saltes			viij
Item 14 peeces of pewter		x	
Item 2 basons 2 p ewres		v	
Item one other brasen chafingdishe with a foote			vj
Item 4 plates		v	
Item a Coffin of pewter			xij
Item 18 plate trenchers		iiij	vj
Item 10 sawsers		ij	
Item 8 knobes & perfuminge panne			xij
Item 2 aquavita bottles		ij	
summa	iiij	[*?*]iij	vj
[*Corrected sub-total*	*£4*	*9s*	*6d*]

In the Parloure

A table and frame	[*value missing*]
Item 8 stooles	[*value missing*]
Item 2 Cupboardes	[*value missing*]
Item 4 Covered [...]	[*value missing*]
Item 3 cheyre [...]	[*value missing*]

[*the foot of this page is damaged*; one or more lines may be missing]
[*second page*]

In another roome

One Cubboarde		xvj	
Item 2 chestes		v	
Item a bedsteede		xvj	
Item a trundle bed		iij	vj
Item a fether bedd		xx	
Item a Coveringe and blankette		ij	
Item a bowlster		iij	
Item a lookinge glasse			xij
Item a longe deske		ij	
Item a close stoole			vj
Item 3 pewter chamber pottes		ij	
Item 4 payre of sheetes		xiij	iiij
Item 8 napkins		iiij	
Item 2 shirts		v	
Item his wayringe apparel	iij	vj	viij
summa	viij		vj
[*Corrected sub-total*	*£8*	*0s*	*0d*]

In the studdye

A table		ij	
Item a deske		ij	
Item a litle cheste			xvj
Item one cheyre		iij	iiij
Item his bookes		xl	
summa		xlvij	viij
[*Corrected sub-total*	*£2*	*8s*	*8d*]

In the greene Chamber

	£	s	d
A bedsteed with Curtaynes & vallons		xxx	
Item a halfe hedded bedsteede		iij	
Item a rugge		ij	
Item a fether bed		xx	
Item a fayre Coveringe		xxx	
Item a Carpett		x	
Item one greate chest		vj	viij
Item one Iron chest		v	
Item one dosen of napkins		xx	
Item 2 pilloweberes		iij	
Item 2 holland tableclothes		x	
Item 2 towels of dyaper		v	
Item 2 payre of fyne sheetes		xx	
Item 2 dyaper tableclothes		x	
summa	viij	xviij	viij
[*Corrected sub-total*	*£8*	*14s*	*8d*]

In the [...]

	£	s	d
[...]		v	
[...]			xx
[...]		ij	
[...]		ij	vj

[*damage at the foot of the page; one or more lines may be missing*]

[*third page*]

In the Milk howse

	£	s	d
Twoe kimmels			xx
Item 3 chesefates			vj
Item a [*?*]ch[*eese*] racke			xij
summa		iij	ij

In the buttry over the seller

	£	s	d
A cheste		ij	
Item barrels and tubbes		x	
Item a grater & 2 dosen of trenchers			xij
Item a payre of goldwayghtes			xvj
summa		xiiij	iiij

In the yard

	£	s	d
Inprimis woode		x	
Item 2 horse	v		
Item one hecfer		xl	
Item a longe Carte & wheeles & dounge carte		xl	
Item 9 sheepe		xliiij	
Item a payre of harrowes		x	
summa	xij	iiij	

In the feylde

	£	s	d
One Acre of barly		xx	
Item one acre of oates		x	
summa		xxx	
Summa totalis	xlv	xv	iiij

[*No exhibition clause*]

Notes: Robert Jones was buried at Steppingley on 3 June 1631. He made his will on 16 May 1631, giving household goods to his sons and daughters and lambs or 12d each to his grand-children. His wife Elizabeth was residual legatee and executrix (Lincs Archives, LCC WILLS/1631/399).

406 William Same of Millbrook made 7 June 1631

Lincolnshire Archives, LCC ADMONS 1631/154

Slight damage at the top and down the right side. Some words at the top are missing and a few pence values may be missing.

An Inventory of [...] the goodes and Ch[...] late of William Sames of Milbrocke in the County of Bedd: deseased taken the vij[th] day of June by William Brace and John Dunkin 1631

	£	s	d
Imprimis his apparell		xiij	iiij
In the hall			
Item one Cobbard one table one frame one forme one penn seven peeces of pewter and a salt a pewter beker and a sawcer		xxvj	
Item ij brasse kettells one brasse pott and a brasse pann and iij brassen Candlestickes		xvj	
In the Chamber			
Item one bedsteede a matteris a blanckett and a Coverlitt and two Coffers		xiij	
Item of linnin iij pare and a halfe of sheetes one pare of pillowbeares and ij little bord Clothes		xvj	
In the loft			
Item one parcell of oates dressed up		viij	
Item more ij Coffers one bedsteed one pare of shetes and a blanckett with other small triffeeles		vj	viij
In the Buttery			
Item one barrell iij milkbooles and a strayner		iij	iiij
In the Barne			
Item one parcell of Rye in the straw		xiij	iiij
Item in the yard one parcell of wood		iij	iiij
Item in the Feeld ij acars of oates		xx	
Item more in the Feeldes ij Cowes and xj sheepe and a lame	vj		
Item of spades scuppootes and other old stufe and trash		ij	
Summe is	xiij	ij	
[*Corrected total*	*£13*	*1s*	*0d*]

William Brace [*signature*], John Dunkin [*signature*]

[*Exhibited by the administratrix at Ampthill on 15 June 1631*]

Notes: William Same was buried at Millbrook on 29 May 1631. Administration was granted to his widow Alice by John Walker, surrogate for John Farmer, at Ampthill on 15 June 1631 to administer the estate during the minority of William Samme, his son and executor, and a bond was taken (Lincs Archives, Act Book A/x/128 and LCC ADMONS 1631/154).

407 John Phillippes of Shefford, Campton, innkeeper made 11 June 1631
Lincolnshire Archives, LCC ADMONS 1631/124

An Inventorye of all the Goodes and Chattells of John Phillippes of Shefford in the Countie of Bedf Innekeeper latelie diseased taken the xj[th] daye of Jone 1631 by William Gouldsmithe of Campton Clerke, William Gouldsmithe of Shefford Tanner, and John Patenham of Shefford Butcher a[*s*] [*fo*]lloweth

	£	s	d
In the Parlour			
Inprimis in the Parlour one longe Table and eight ioynid stooles		xxv	
One Courte cupbourd with the cloathe and a Cushion on yt		xx	
Fower Chayres		xv	
Thre Cushions			xviij
One payre of Copyrons			xij
Summa	iij	ij	vj
In the Hall			
One Table and halfe a dozen of stooles		xx	
One Round Table and the Benches		viij	
One Cuppbourd and a glasse shelfe		xxiij	4
One Chayre and a Cushion a payre of Cobbeyrones fier shovell and Tonges with other implementes		x	
Twoo buffette stooles			xx
Summa	iij	ij	
[*Corrected sub-total*	*£3*	*3s*	*0d*]
In the lyttle Parlour			
One standinge Bedde with the Beddinge	iiij		
One Trundle Bedde with the Beddinge		xx	
A Table with the Benches a smale Chayre and three lyttle Boxes		xiiij	
Summa	v	xiiij	
In the Buttrye			
Sixe hoggesheades with the Beere and Brewstalles and other thinges belonginge to the buttrye	iij	xiij	4
In the kitchin and the Brewehouse a Copper with the brewinge vessell and some other thinges	iiij	x	
In the Chamber over the Hall			
One Standinge Bedde		xxx	
One Round Table Fower stooles a Cheste and a Forme		xxvj	viij
In the Chamber over the Parlour			
One standinge Bedde with a featherbed and a Rugge and the Curtaynes	jx		
One Table seaven stooles and a Chayre		xx	
One Courte Cuppbourd		v	
A payre of Cobbeyrones and Tonges		viij	
Summa	x	xviij	
In the Chamber over the lyttle Parlour and the Entrye			
One Standinge Bedde with a fatherbedd a Redde Rugge and Redde Curtaynes	x		

One greate drawinge Table and seaven stooles		l	
A Courte cuppbourd and Cupbourd cloathe and a Bason and Ewer		xxv	
One Chayre a Cheste and a Truncke		xx	
Halfe a dossen of Cushions		xxx	
Three Carpettes	v		
A payre of Cobbeyrons fyer shovell and Tonges		x	
Summa	xxj	xv	

Lynnen

Twoo payre of holland sheetes	iij		
Nyne payre of Flaxen sheetes	vj		
Thre payre of hempe tare sheetes and three payre of Toe sheetes		liiij	
Tenne holland pyllowbeeres		xxv	
Syxe Flaxen pyllowebeeres		viij	
Fyve hempe tare pyllowbeeres		v	x
Twoo dyapar bourd Cloathes with two dossen and three dyapar Napkyns	iij		
Three flaxen Bourd Cloathes and 2 dossen of flaxen napkyns		xxxij	
Three tare bourd Cloathes and a dossen of napkyns		xxij	
Twoo dyapar Towells, Twoo holland Towells and Twoo tare Towells with a Flaxen one		xvj	
Summa	xx	iij	
[*Corrected sub-total*	*£20*	*2s*	*10d*]
Pewter and Brasse	iij	xiij	iiij
His waringe apparell	v		
The woode in the yeard	iij	xiij	4
Two Hoggescoates		xiij	4
Haye		x	
A lease of howse and Lande in Buckingham shyre	lx		
The whole Summe of this Inventorye commes to a hundred Fortye eight powndes Twelfe shyllinges and vj[d]	[148	12	6]
[*Corrected total*	*£149*	*5s*	*4d*]

William Gouldsmithe [*signature*], The marke of William Gouldsmithe, John Pateman [*signature*]

[*No exhibition clause. A note at the foot of the inventory records that John Patenham, yeoman, and Richard Worsley, innholder, both of Shefford, were bound in the sum of £300 to administer the estate.*]

Notes: John Phillippes was buried at Campton on 3 April 1631. Administration was granted to his widow Anne in the presence of Francis Carr, notary public, at Bedford on 13 June 1631 and a bond was taken (Lincs Archives, Act Book A/x/128 and LCC ADMONS 1631/124). The signature of William Gouldsmithe, the rector of Campton and one of the appraisers, matches the handwriting of the inventory, which is distinctive and poor. Richard Worsley, one of the bondsmen, was a grocer living at The Cock in Waterend, Shefford, in the 1630s (Beds Archives, O/66).

408 John Keppest of Eaton Socon made 13 June 1631
Lincolnshire Archives, INV/137/420

The 13 daye of June 1631. An Inventorye of all suche goodes as John Keppest had at his deathe

	£	s	d
Im primest all his weringe Aparell lenenge and wolen at		xx	
In the hall one Cheare one forme and one warminge pane at		v	
one pare of pote hockes at		j	ij
Item in the parler one Chest at		vj	
one small boxe and A Cheare at		j	
Item in the Chamber over the parler one trundell bedsted at		iij	iiij
one borded bedsted one matres towe pelowes one old Coverled one blanket and one pare of shetes at		x	
Item in the Chamber over the hall one Joyned bedsted one fetherbed one boulster towe pelowes one Coverled and one blancket at		xx	
Item one hallfe accare of wheate at		xx	
one pelobeare at		ij	
Some is	iiij	viij	vj

Thomas Goodsonn, Richard Tingay, Thomas Warde
[*Exhibited by the executor on 13 June 1631*]

Notes: The Eaton Socon parish register records the burial of Joan Kippest on 25 May 1631, possibly a mistake in transcription for John (*BPR*, vol. 74, part 2, p. 261).

409 Elizabeth Anglesey of Keysoe, widow made 13 June 1631
Lincolnshire Archives, INV/137/419

A iust and true Iventory of all the goodes and Chattelles wherof Elizabeth Anglesey late of Keyshooe in the County of Bedd Wydowe deceassed died seized of had made taken prized and valued the Thirteinth daye of June Annoque domini 1631 by these whose names are underwritten

	£	s	d
Imprimis her wareinge apparell	vj	xiij	iiij
Item money in her pursse	iiij	xiij	viij
Item money oweing of her	lij	x	
In her bedd Chamber			
Imprimis one bedsteede with a footepasse Twoe Featherbeddes, Twoe Matrisses, Five boulsters, Seaven Pillowes, Three Coverlettes one Quilt, Twoe Karpettes, one Cupbord cloath Fyfteine blanckettes, and Seaven Cushcons	xiiij		
Item Foure Chestes wherof Twoe are barred with Iron, one Coffer, Five boxes, one Little Table,			

	£	s	d
Three Cheiares twoe wherof are wicker, Three Stooles and other utencilles	ij	x	
Item one paire of hollan sheetes, Eleaven paire and a sheete of flexen sheetes, Eleaven paire of Hearden sheetes, Three and Twenty pillowbeares, sixe boardcloathes, Five long Towelles and eight shorte Towelles, and Foure dozen of Table napkynes	ix		
Item one Bason and Ewer, Thirteyne platters, one bason, one Cullender Seaven pewter dishes and sawsers, Seaven pewter pottes, Twoe pewter Candlestickes, and other peeces of pewter and alsoe certeyne Stone Jugges	ij		
Item one brasse pott, one possnet, one little kettle, one Latten bason, Twoe latten Candlestickes Twoe brason Ladles, one chaffingdish one morter and other utencilles	j	vj	viij
Summa totalis	xCij	xiij	viij

Thomas Folbigg, Henry Slade, Robert Gowler, Henry Moawd
[*Exhibited at Bedford by the executor on 14 June 1631*]

Notes: Elizabeth Anglesey was buried at Keysoe on 2 June 1631. The appraisers, Thomas Folbigg and Henry Slade, were churchwardens in Keysoe in the 1620s and 30s.

410 John Gybson of Swineshead

made 12 March 1633

Bedfordshire Archives, PA 181

March 12: 1632 A true Inventarie of the goodes of John Gybson late of Swaynshead in the Countie of Hunt deceased taken the day and yeare above written and prised by Thomas Dawson Clarke, Laurence Foster and John Tyler

	£	s	d
Inprimis his wearing Apparrell		l	
Item in readie money in his purse			[*blank*]
In the Hall			
One Table one Forme two ioy-ned Stooles a Bench and Bench-board		xij	
One Cupbord one Arke one Coffer one glasse Case		xv	
Two peices of wainscote one wheele three Chayres three lesser stooles two Cushions		x	
Five kettles one brasse pott one Posnett a Chafeingdish a Skimmer		xx	
Sixe peices of pewter a pewter Bole two Salt sellers two Candle-stickes		xiiij	
A payre of Tonges Pothangers a Trevett a grydyron a fryinge Pann two yron hookes		iij	vj
Foure boardes and other lumber		iij	iiij

In the Buttrye			
Three Tubbs two Barrells one Chirne one Cheese presse two boles three Cheese fattes and other lumber		xiij	
In the loft over the Hall			
Two boarded Bedsteades two Chestes and three Coffers a little Table a Chayre painted Clothes and other lumber		xx	
Two Mattresses, two Bolsters two Pillowes two Coverlettes & one blankett		xxxiij	iiij
Five flaxon Sheetes nineteene harden sheetes	iij	xij	
Two flaxen Pillow beers sixe harden Table Napkins a harden board Cloth two hand Towells	ix		
Two flitches of Bacon a stone of Cheese		xx	
Three yardes and halfe of woollen Cloth and two yardes of grey Cloth		xv	
Sixe Slipps of harden yarne		ij	
In the Barn			
Wheate and Barlye threshed and unthresht		xl	
Haie wood and Compasse		xviij	
Three Milch kine two yearlinges	xj		
Tenn Couples and eight guest Sheepe	iiij	x	
One Sowe and three Pigges		xiij	iiij
Three Acres of Pease two Acres of Tylth	iiij		
Summa	xxxviij	xv	vj
[*Corrected total*	*£47*	*4s*	*6d*]

[*Exhibited by Agnes Gybson, widow and administratrix, on 26 March 1633. The exhibition clause was signed by R. Furley, deputy registrar.*]

Notes: John Gybson was buried at Swineshead on 1 March 1633.

411 John Moxe of Dean

made 18 October 1633

Bedfordshire Archives, ABP/W1633/174

A true Inventary of all suche goodes & Chatles that of late appertayned to John Moxe late of Deane in the Countie of Bedd deceassed, praised & indifferently vallued by Thomas Twigden & Gamaliel Hale the xviij[th] of October 1633 as Followeth:

	£	s	d
Imprimis All his apparell	2	0	0
Item in the Chamber next the Hall, One Bedsted with a matris			

& a boulster & pillowes, with ij blankettes & ij Coverlettes	1	13	4
Item One Cheste, & iij Coffers with other implementes	0	19	6
Item Eight pare of sheetes, two bord clothes, with some other small lyninge	3	6	8
Item in the Hall, one Table One Coberd, one Chare & other Implementes	0	18	9
Item three kettles, one brasse pott, a skellet & a warming pan	0	13	4
Item iiij peeces of Pewter & a Candlestick	0	2	6
Item one ould Bedsted with a Mattres, & an ould Covering	0	10	4
Item ij barrelles with other implementes	0	1	10
Item in the next roome to the Hall, One Arke for graine, one kymnell, one Tubb, with some other Implementes	0	9	8
Item in the Barne, Three lodes of Haye	1	3	4
Item Wheate, Barley, & Pease	3	0	0
Item All the woode aboute the yeard	0	6	8
Item One Cowe, on Bulluck & a Calfe	3	6	8
Item Eight Hyves of Beese	1	0	0
Item Fyve sheepe	0	10	0
Item one Hogg	0	6	8
Item Six Henns & a Cock	0	2	6
Item the Muck in the yeard	0	5	0
Sum	20	16	9

Gamaliel Hale [*signature*], The marke of Thomas Twigden
[*Exhibited by the executrix on 16 November 1633*]

Notes: John Moxe was buried at Dean on 14 October 1633. He made his will on 31 May 1633, giving small sums of money, a stock of bees and furniture to family members. He appointed his wife Olive executrix. A commission was issued to Thomas Dillingham vicar and John Moore curate of Dean on 9 November 1633 to administer the oath to her, which was done on 13 November and probate was granted to her on 16 November 1633 (Beds Archives, ABP/W1633/174).

412 William Porter of Brach Mill, Luton, miller made 7 October 1634
Bedfordshire Archives, ABP4/196

The Inventary of all and singuler the moveable goodes Cattelles and Chattells of William Porter Late of Brach mill in the parishe of Luton in the Countye of Bedford miller deceased vallued and praysed the Seventh day of October Anno Domini 1634 by Henry Higbey, Richard Crawley, George Slow Junior, Edward Crawley all of Luton yemen as followeth

	£	s	d
In the hall			
Imprimis a Cobard		x	
Item, a poridge pott, 5 kettilles, 2 posnates		xxvj	viij
Item a longe table and frame 2 Joyned stoles, a form and 2 old Cheares & 3 old Coshins		x	
Item a Frying pann, 2 hangers, a pare of Bellowes 2 pott hangers a pare of Bayardes, a Fire shovell, a vice with Two wheles and 4 hookes a par of Tonges a spitt a pott-shelfe with other ymplementes		x	
In the Buttrey			
Imprimis 3 Tubes a peck a bole a boshell wayte a half boshell waite, a peck waite 2 little bariles 2 knedinges troffes a Cloth Baskett a Form, a hatchett and a Saw		xx	
In the Chamber over the hall			
Imprimis 8 pewter dishis, a [*?*]Bazen 3 drinking Cups, 2 Saltes 2 Saseres a porringer & 4 spones		xiij	iiij
Item a Table & Frame 3 Coffers a presse a bede stede a linnan whele		xvj	
Item 6 par of shettes 6 napkins a Table Cloth & other linnan		xxx	
Item a woole Beade, 4 Feather pillowes 4 Flock pillowes: 3 blankettes 2 Coverlides with other Bedding		xxx	
Item in the hay loft hay		xxx	
Item ~~woodes~~ wood and ~~hay~~ hirdles in the yard		x	
Item a hogge		v	
Item 2 horses and Flaggye haye	iij		
Item in the mill a par of Scales and Beame, a mattuck a spade and other ymplementes		iij	
Sum is	xiiij	iiij	
[*Corrected total*	*£14*	*14s*	*0d*]

The marke of Henry Higbey, Richard Crawley [*signature*], The marke of Georg Slow, Edward Crawley [*signature*]
[*No exhibition clause*]

Notes: William Porter was buried at Luton on 18 July 1634.

413 Raphe Pratchett of Flitwick, husbandman made July or August 1635
Lincolnshire Archives, INV/143/29A

A True Invetary of the goods & Chattles of Raphe Pratchett Latte of Flittweck deceased And prysed By Ambros Sam & Mathew Allen

	£	s	d
Item towe acres of Rye & seven Roods of Oattes	v	vij	
one other acer of Rye prysed at		xxxvj	viij
three Rodes of pease & tharches		xxx	
towe Rodes of Rye & halfe a Rod of thecthes		xxxij	
Halfe ann acer & Halfe a Rode of grass		xxv	
one other Acer of Rye		xxx	
three Roods of thecthes		vj	viij
towe parselles of hay		lv	
towe Cowes & towe Bullockes	v	x	
towe store piges		xiij	iiij
one Ewe & lambe		v	
three Horses	iij	x	
towe longe Cartes & one dung cart	iij		
one plowe & horse harnes & other Impellment		vj	viij
wood Hempe & Apelles		xx	
polltry		ij	vj
In the Halle			
Item Ruffe Hempe			vj
towe pottage pottes		x	
foure ketteles		xvj	
five platters		vj	
one table & frame & forme		x	
one Chayer & Cubard		iij	iiij
ould lumber In the Halle		v	
In the Chamber			
Item five pare of sheetes		xx	
three pillowe beares		v	
towe table Clothes		ij	
one flockbed vj pillowes and A boulster		x	
towe Blanckettes & one Coverled		vj	
five Cofers & one box		vj	viij
three borded Bedd steedes		v	
In the Buttry			
Item sixe tubes & one Churme		x	
one penn			xij
one dusen pownd of lyneen yarne		x	
towe pownde of wollon yearne		ij	
five yards of wollen Cloth		xv	
towe Elles of lincy wollcye		ij	
one littell Barrell			x
three spineing wheeles		iij	
ould Iyorne		iij	iiij
Other lumber theire		v	

In Another Rome

Item one pearsell of Cheeses		vj	viij
his wareing Clothes		x	
In mony		iiij	
Lumber theire			xviij

Debtes oweinge the deseaced

Thomas Webbe		xx	
Geo: Webbe		xviij	
Henry Sufeild		v	
Fra: Armestronge		xij	
Rich Welchman		iij	iiij
Ambros Sam		iij	
Arther Boone			xiiij
John Bentley		ij	iiij
[*in the left margin and in a different hand*] Summa totalis	39	15	1
[*Corrected total*	[*£42*	*4s*	*6d*]

Debtes that the deceased oweth

Mistres Halfepeny	v		
Martins Cooke	iij		
Master Honyewood	iij		
William Jactson [*sic*]		xiij	
Geo: Crypsus		xj	
Master Collopp		xx	
Ambros Sam		iij	
Tho: Cooper		vj	viij
Arnold Scarrott			xvj
[*Total of debts*	*£13*	*15s*	*0d*]

[*Exhibited by the executrix at Ampthill on 17 August 1635*]

Notes: Raphe Pratchett was buried at Flitwick on 5 July 1635. He made his will on 8 September 1634, describing himself as a husbandman. He gave an acre of meadow to his grandson and £11 among his sons and daughters. He gave his house, lands and goods to his wife Joan and appointed her executrix (Lincs Archives, MISC WILLS/F/77).

414 George Gale of Husborne Crawley, yeoman made 4 August 1635

Lincolnshire Archives, INV/143/27

A Trwe Inventorie of all the Goods and Chattels of George Gale late of Husband Crawley in the countie of Bedford yeaman seene & prised the forthe day of August 1635 by George Kinge, Michaell Cavill, Robert Crowch & John Ball as folloeth

	£	s	d
in the hall			
Imprimis one Cobbord one table with a frame one forme one chaire one Joyned stowle	1	0	0
Item all the Bras & Peuter	1	6	8
Item two pothangers one trevet disshes stownes Gridiron and all other lomber in that Roome	0	6	8

in the chamber			
two Bedsteds five Coffers	0	16	0
Item one Civerlid fore Blankets one fetherbed tow Bolsters 3 pilloes	2	3	4
Item ten paiar of sheetes five pilloberes 2 napkines 2 table cloathes	2	10	0
Item 3 painted cloathes one old Borded pres	0	3	4
in the citchen			
Item one malt quarne one cheespres 2 Barrels 4 tubbes 3 pailes one kimnell one saltinge trofe 4 boles with all other lomber	1	0	0
Item 3 horsses & one Colte	9	10	0
Item plowes cartes harrowes harnese with all other thinges for husbandrie	3	3	4
Item six Beas 4 Bullockes	14	0	0
Item 14 sheepe & vi lambes	2	6	8
Item ix aceres of wheate Rie & Barley with som other dressed Graine	18	0	0
Item 4 aceres of Oates & 4 aceres of peas	8	0	0
Item one old hovill with a little timber som hurdles Cowrackes sheeprackes fierwod & all other lomber whatsoever	2	0	0
Item one loade of hay	1	0	0
Item his wearinge Aparrell	3	0	0
Item the hogges & poltrie	1	6	8
the Som is	~~60~~ ~~13~~	~~12~~	~~8~~
[*This revised sum is written in a different hand*]	73	12	8
[*Corrected total*	*£71*	*12s*	*8d*]

[*Exhibited at Ampthill on 18th day of an unnamed month in 1635*]

Notes: George Gale was buried at Husborne Crawley on 29 July 1635. He made his will on 28 July 1635. After small bequests to family and kin, he left everything to his wife Anne, whom he appointed executrix (Lincs Archives, LCC WILLS/1635/ii/151).

415 John Tybball of Everton, husbandman — made 6 December 1636

Huntingdonshire Archives, AH18/20/67

The page is stained at the top right side and damaged lower on that side. Some values may be lost or incorrectly transcribed.

An Inventarye of the goodes and Chattells of John Tybball of Everton in the Countye of Beds husbandman made this six[84] day of December 1636

	£	s	d
Imprimis six Acres & a halfe of wheate 2 Acres 3 Roodes of tylth 3 halfe Acres of Rye one halfe acre of [*?*]brache	xij		

[84] The writing is badly faded and the date might be 16 not 6 December.

Item the grayne in the barne	5	x	
Item the grayne & haye in the yarde	vj		
Item a hovell		40	
Item a Carte & other ymplements		xxvj	viij
Item 2 horse		xlvj	viij
Item 5 Beastes	ix		
Item his weareinge Apparrell		xxx	
Item In his Chamber 2 bedsteedes 4 Cofers & one Cheast with other ymplements		xx	
Item 5 paire of sheetes 2 pillowe beares & one table cloath		[*?*]xx	
Item In the kitchyn one Cubbert one Table with other ymplements		xxj	
Item 4 kettells & one brasse [*?*]po[*tt*]		xxiij	iiij
Item 2 pewter dishes		ij	
Item Twenty six pullyn in the yarde		xiij	iiij
Sum is	xlv	iij	
[*Corrected total*	*£44*	*13s*	*0d*]

debtes oweinge

To Richard Tybball		xxxv	
To John Fisher		xxvij	
Monye oweinge		xl	
[*Total debts*	*£5*	*2s*	*0d*]

praysed by us whose names are hereunder written [*?*]Geo [*?*]Cawcott, Thomas [*illeg.*], Thomas [*?*]Bolnest
[*No exhibition clause*]

Notes: John Tybball's burial has not been found.

416 Alice Cadwell of Everton, widow made 23 January 1637
Huntingdonshire Archives, AH18/3/156
The document is damaged down the right side and some values are missing.

Everton xxiij[th] of January 1636. A true Inventary of the goodes and Chatteles of Alylce [*sic*] Cadwell Deceased

	£	s	d
Imprimis on Cobbord on table on Forme		x	
Item three Cettels		x	
Item on Caske		[...]	
Item peuter plater on Charme tow tubes on barrell tow payles on butter basket	[*value missing*]		
Item tow lomes on fatt and stockcards	[*value missing*]		
Item on bedstede with bedding on Coffer		xxij	
Item on Cowch with other lomber		v	
Item on parssell of hemp		j	iiij
Item on paire of flaxson sheetes with a towell and on paire of harden sheetes		xij	
Item on bedsted and fower bordes with a paire of scoles		v	
Item tow frying pan and pott hangers with other lombe[*r*]	[*value missing*]		
Item tow Cowes five sheepe with haye	vj	[...]	[...]

Item hir waring aparrell		xx	
the some totall is ~~x^{l} xix^{s}~~	xij		j

prisers John Laftis [*mark*], the marke of Edward Basse, the marke of Thymoty Banes, Richard Amps [*signature*], the marke of Robbert Cadwell

[*Exhibited by Robert Cadwell uncle of Margaret Cadwell, daughter of the deceased, administrator during her minority on 30 January 1637. The exhibition clause was signed by R. Furley, deputy registrar*]

Notes: Alice Cadwell's burial has not been found.

417 Alice Goody of Goldington made between 10 and 26 April 1638

Bedfordshire Archives, ABP4/199

Some damage on the right side. Some pence values may be missing.

The will of Alce Goody

	£	s	d
The Emitary of hur woolinge and linning		30	
And A standing Beed	1		
And A chest and A Cofer		7	6
and A brase pan att		15	0
A plater givne to Alce Aseldine		1	
John Alderman owt to Alce Goody	10		
so Alce Goody ~~give~~ Gave to Mary			
Goody this	10		
John Fox Owt Alce Goody	3		
Alc Goody Gave that 3^{li} Umphiry			
Fox her Brother			
[*Sum*	*£16*	*13s*	*6d*]

That is hur last will and Testament

[*No exhibition clause*]

Notes: Alice Goody was buried at Goldington on 10 April 1638. Her nuncupative will was made while she lay sick in William Grante's house in mid-March. She made small bequests of household goods and clothing to her brother and sister William and Mary Goody and her brother Humphrey Fox and other bequests as listed in the inventory. John Fox was described as her father-in-law. She appointed William Grant the younger as her executor but he renounced. The will was proved on 26 April 1638 and administration granted to her sister Mary Goody (Beds Archives, ABP/W1630/243, i.e. 1638). It has not been possible to ascertain whether John and Humphrey Fox were her step family or related by marriage.

418 Jeffery Philipes of Nether Dean, Dean, shepherd died 22 December 1640

Bedfordshire Archives, ABP/W1641/141

A true inventory of all the goodes & chateles of Jeffery Philipes of Nether Deane in the county of Bedford sheepherd whoe departed this liffe the 22th day of Decomber 1640

	£	s	d
Imprimis one Cow	2	0	0

	£	s	d
Item seaven sheepe	2	0	0
Item in the halle one cubbord one tabell and the pewter upon it and four litell keteles	2	0	0
Item in the parlor one beed with the fourniture & cofferes with other lumber	2	0	0
Item the chamber over the parlor twentie poundes of woole serten boardes with other lumber	1	0	0
Item in the midell chamber one beed one chest with other lumber	1	0	0
Item 2 paier of flaxen shetes five paier of harden shetes five pillowbeers 2 board clothes 3 napkines	1	10	0
Item in the dayrie howse 2 shelfes a chese prese & other lumber	0	13	4
Item the woode & compas in the yarde	0	13	4
Item one aker of pease one aker of wheat & Barly	2	0	0
Item his Aparell	0	10	0
The sume is	15	8	0
[*Corrected total*	*£15*	*6s*	*8d*]

William [*?*]Ston [*signature*], Robert Kinge
[*Exhibited by the executrix on 1 July 1641*]

Notes: Jeffery Philipes was buried at Dean on 27 December 1640. His will was probably nuncupative and made on 22 December 1640. He gave a sheep to his daughter Martha and made his unnamed wife residual legatee and executrix, to whom probate was granted on 1 July 1641 (Beds Archives, ABP/W1641/141).

419 Edward Edwyn of Dunstable, maltster made September 1641
The National Archives, PROB2/431C
The inventory is faded and some values and text are illegible.

A true and perfect Inventory of all and singuler the Good[*s*] chattells Rights [*&*] credittes of Ed[*ward*] Edwyn late of [*illeg.*] Dunstable [*in the*] Countie of [*Beds*] Maultster [*illeg.*] taken val[*ued and*] appraised the [*illeg.*] daie of September In the yeare of [*our*] Lord god 1641 [*by*] [*the names of the four appraisers are partly illegible. They might be William Mee*[...], *Richard Chester, William Fossey and Richard Hawk*[...] as followeth Vizt

	£	s	d

In the Hall

Inprimis twoe tables
one cupboard 4 Stooles

2 Chaires and other woodden Implementes	[*value illegible*]		
Item in pewter and Brasse	[*value illegible*]		
Item Bacon	[*value illegible*]		
Item Andirons, hookes spittes [*and*] other Im[*ple*] ments	[*value illegible*]		

In the Chamber where hee did lodge

Item all the deceaseds weareing apparrell	[*value illegible*]		
Item one new [*illeg.*] woollen cloth		xl	
Item one Featherbed two bolsters 2 pillowes Two blanckettes [*?*]j [*?*]Coverlidd j standing bedd steed and curteines to the same and matterice, bolster trundle beadsteed, and [*illeg,*] to that Bedd	[*value illegible*]		
Item 12 paire of shetes 4 Table clothes and some other lynnen	[*value illegible*]		
Item 4 Chests one trunck one Table [*illeg.*] chaire, A Box 2 stooles with other Implementes		xl	

[*illeg.*] Chamber

Item one half headed bed steed, a Flockbedd a bolster pillow and other thinges belonginge to the Bedd	[*value illegible*]		
Item Barr table and other lumber		xiij	

In the Mault Chamber

Item in M[*illeg.*] [*three lines faded and illegible*]	xiij		

In the Chamber below

Item in Barley	vij	v	
Item the Sackes		xxx	

In the Barne

Item the Grayne [*?and haie*] in the same	vj		
Item the straw		xxx	

In the yard

Item all the [*?*]Wood	iij	iiij	

In the Mault Shopp

Item all the woodden Im plementes		xiij	iiij

	£	s	d
Item the Tilth of 2 acres [*of*] ground in the Feild		l	
Item in ready mony		xx	
Item good debtes owing for Mault and other thinges	lxxj	vj	
Item delivered in goods since his death	xix	iiij	
Summa Totalis[85]	3Cxlv	xij	ij

[*A name above the exhibition clause is mainly illegible. It might be John Marche.*]
[*The exhibition clause is largely illegible. Exhibition was in 1641.*]

Notes: Edward Edwyn was buried as Edward Edden at Dunstable on 22 August 1641.

420 John Harding of Henlow

undated; made March–July 1643

Bedfordshire Archives, ABP4/289

The document is creased, damaged, badly stained and faded. Some of the values are illegible. It was repaired by the record office in 1925.

A true Emytory of John Hardinges goods lately deseassed

	£	s	d
Item in the hall A table & a kubberd two fourms with other things		[...]	
Item for a fether bed and bedsteed with the bedinge tat [*to it*] and a table and a form In the parler	ij	vj	viij
Item for two bedsteeds and a flock bed and a blanket & a huch		x	
In the Chamber			
Item for tw ~~beds~~ borded beds with the bedinge and two old Cofers	j	vj	viij
Item for seven pare of shits and two pare of pilebers	j	x	
Item for two table Cloes with a doussen of Napkins		xij	
Item for woollen weele and two [*word deleted and illeg.*] linnin weels		iij	
Item for his Reparel	j	x	
Item for nine peulter disshes		x	
Item for the bras and a spit and a pare of Cobirons with other smal things		ij	
Item for barrels and bruing vesels		xx	
Item for two beas and a wening Kafe	iiij	x	
Item for two stores and a sow and pigs		xx	
Item for a Coke and two hens		ij	
Item for wood		x	
Item for hemp		x	
Item for three akers [*?*]brach grene	[*iij*]		
Sum	xxij [*deleted*]		iiij

85 The total of £3Cxlv (£345) is clear but is incompatible with the goods described in the inventory. A sum of £145 would be more consistent.

[*The following is on a separate sheet, badly faded, damaged and mainly illegible. It looks like a draft account of money paid out by the executrix.*]

John Hardinge of Hawes

[*illeg.*]	Inve[*nto*]ry [*total*]	22		4
To [*?*]Roger [*illeg.*] of [*?*]Campton		v	x	
To Tho [*?*]Hind of Bedf[*ord*]			xij	
To John B[*illeg.*] for wood			xxx	
[*illeg.*] of [*?*]Clopwell [*?Clophill*] for wood			xx	
To Edward [*?*]Pincke of Luton			x	
To Tho Goodcheap of Shefforde			[*?*]vj	
To Ri [*?*]Carter de ead[*em*]			viij	
	[*Total debts of at least*	*£9*	*16s*	*0d*]

[*No exhibition clause*]

Notes: John Harding was buried at Henlow on 16 March 1643. He made his will on 6 November 1640, leaving his freehold and copyhold land in Henlow to his wife Elizabeth for life, then to kinsman Henry Moorton with remainder to the testator's brothers and nephews. He made pecuniary bequests exceeding £45 to family members. His wife was the residual legatee and executrix and probate was granted to her in 1643, the oath having been administered on 4 July 1643 (Beds Archives, ABP/W1643/53). (The will is damaged and the full date of probate is missing.)

421 Jonas Offam of Everton, husbandman made 28 April 1645

Huntingdonshire Archives, AH18/15/18

There is some fading and the right side is stained; some values are illegible and many are very difficult to read.

A true Inventerie of all the goodes and Chattelles of Jonas Offam late of Everton in the Countie of Bedford Husban man deseased praised by Thomas Bolnest and Paul Luke the 28th Apill 1645

	£	s	d
Inprimis in his pursse	[*value illegible*]		
Item his aparill	[*value illegible*]		
In the halle			
Item two cubberdes and a table on brass pot three little brass Cetles [*illeg.*] pewter platers an Irne pott and other Implementes	[*value illegible*]		
Item in the butteree two barelles a tub a powdering troffe	[*value illegible*]		
Item in the Chamber above stares on Joyne bed and the beding and other Implimentes	[*value illegible*]		
Item in the parlor a coorse fetherbed and a bollster a blancket six peaire of sheetes and three Coofers and other lumber		5	
Item in the milck house a cheese presse foure boweles two bottles and other Implimentes		xx	
Item In the backe house a brewing furnesse boorde plowtimber and other Implimentes		xxxj	
Item the grayne in the greate barne a [*?*]skrene a bushell and planckes and other Implementes	x		

Item in the litle barne		xvj	
Item five horse with plowe geares and Cartgeeres			[*value illegible*]
Item six milkein Cowes			[*value illegible*]
Item six litle bullockes			[*value illegible*]
Item two hoffelles with a passell of peese [*illeg.*]	[*?*]iij	[*?*]x	
Item two Cartes and tow paire of wheele and plowes in the hofell [*?and other lumber there*]			[*value illegible*]
Item the Compas in the yarde		xxxiij	
Item thirtie sheepe	vij		
Item two hogges a sow and seven pigges			[*value illegible*]
Item the fire woode			[*value illegible*]
Item twelfe henes and on Cocke		vj	viij
Item the grayne growinge in the feilde	[*illeg.*]	lx	
Item a leasse	x	[*illeg.*]	
Item the hempe growinge		[*?*]vij	
[*illeg.*]			
Summa totalis huius Inventij	Cxxxiij	[*?*]xix	viij

Thomas Bolnest [*signature*], Paul Luke [*signature*]

[*Exhibited by Alice Offham, widow and executrix, on 10 June 1645. The exhibition clause was signed by John Crosse, registrar.*]

Notes: Jonas Offam's burial has not been found.

422 Phinees Leveridge of Swineshead made 24 September 1647

Huntingdonshire Archives, AH18/12/98

The inventory is split vertically through the centre of the heading and stained along the vertical fold down the whole document. The ink has bled through the page.

A true & perfect [*Inven*]tory of all the goods & chattels which were [...] Phinees Leveridge of Swineshead deceased [*ind*]ifferently valued by Thomas Par[*so*]yle, John Cook, Thomas Bromsayle & Henry Fox of the same town Sept: 24 1647

	£	s	d
In the yard			
Imprimis 16 sheep & lambs	3	0	0
Two cowes	4	13	4
A sow & 6 pigs	1	6	8
4 Calves	2	0	0
Wood	1	0	0
In the barn			
Wheate corn & pease	5	0	0
In the close			
One hovill 4 racks a frame for a gigge	0	13	4
Hay	3	0	0
In the brewhouse			
A malt mill a mashing fatt & some other brewing vessels & lumber	1	0	0
In the cheese chamber			
Cheese, apples, 3 botles shelves etc	1	0	0

In the outre chamber			
A boarded bed 3 forks a rying seive a ridle & other odde implements	0	6	8
In the kitchin			
Brasse & pewter A cupboard a table a cheese presse spits pot hookes 2 dripping potts & othre odde lumber	2	0	0
In the milk house			
A powdering trough a churm milk vessels & othre odde implementes	0	13	4
In the boltinghouse			
A bolting ark a kneading trough & other odde thinges	0	5	0
In the hall			
One table one cupboard one form halfe a dozen chayres & stooles andirons fireshovell & tongs cushions curtaynes & other small matters	2	0	0
In the parlour			
One livery cupboard one table ~~halfe a dosen~~ 3 [*?*]leather chayres & [*?*]8 stooles a carpet halfe a dosen cushions a [*?*]curtay[*ne*] a cupboard cloth a [*?*]bason ewer	1	13	4
In the buttrey			
6 barels one safe a glassecase a coffer drinck stals with some lumber	0	16	0
In the hall chamber			
Two bedsteds one presse 1 trunck 2 coffers One featherbed 3 blanckets a coverleyd a bolster a pillow a box	3	0	0
His wearing apparrell	1	10	0
Item money in his purse[86]	1	10	0
In the best chamber			
One ioyned bed one [*?*]enther bed one bolster one pillow on blancket one rugge 5 curtaynes 3 chests 2 chayers 2 stools 3 cushions	5	0	0
In the litle chamber			
1 flock bed one matterice 2 blanckets one bedsted on coffer	0	10	0
seven payer of sheets 6 pillowbeeres 1 dozen napkins 3 table clothes & other small linen	2	0	0
Summa totalis[87]	43	17	8

86 This line has been inserted in a different hand.
87 This line has been written in the same hand as the previous insertion.

Debts owe[*ing*][88] by the deceased[89]

Imprimis oweing [*to*] Francis Barber of Alcunberry	5	0	0
Item to John Richards of Risely by bond	2	0	0
Item to Thomas Tapp of Brampton	3	0	0
Item to Rachell Peck	2	0	0
Item spent att the funerall of the deceased	4	1	6
Summa	16	1	6

[*Exhibited by Sarah Levericke, relict and executrix, at Huntingdon on 23 October 1647, and signed by John Crosse, registrar. On the cover is a note of the exhibition by Sara Leverick, relict, on 25 September 1647.*]

Notes: Phinees Leveridge's burial has not been found.

423 William Rechford of Oakley, husbandman undated; c.1648

Bedfordshire Archives, ABP4/287

Very poor writing and spelling. The words and *and* one *are almost indistinguishable.*

A note of the goods and cattell of Wellam Rechford lat deseced Item in primis decessed the xj day [*illeg*] 164[...]

	£	s	d
in the shope a pare of belloes and a anfeld and coles and hammeres with others workinges towles	iij		
Item in yard for a melle for tember one hovell[90] and other burning wood		xxx	
Item in the hall one cubbard and iij tabeles and one forme and cheare and iiij stowels and cheast and iiij cussengs & a potsheaIf weth x pecses of pauter prased		xxxv	
Item in the chamber nexte the hall one staningbad a trundell bad a presse a tabell and ij [*?*]coffers and cheare with the furnetere belonging to the bades prsed weth xj pecsseds of pauter and ij candldell [*sic*] steckes one chamber pot		xl	
Item in the next chamber one staning bad and one trondell bad weth the furnetuer belonging to them and cheare and iiij cofferes and pot shelfe and one tabell and one lettell boyx and form prased	iij	x	
Item for his waring a parell – ij Dublates and ij gerkeins and ij klokes and ij pare of breches and ij pare of [*?*]hous and ij pare of shuwes and ij hates and iij shurtes p[*r*]assed	iij		

88 The paper is split and the end of this word and a word on the next line are missing. The syllable *ing* has been inserted here and *to* inserted in the next line as the most likely readings.
89 This section is in a different hand and has been lightly crossed out with an X through the whole section.
90 *ffe* has been inserted above *v*.

Item of lenning – xvj pare of shets – ij dossun of napkenes – iiij bords Cloth – xij pellobeares prassed at		iiij	x
Item in the lofft over the hall – ij badstades and ~~ij blanekeds~~ and the furnituer belonging to them and coffer and forme and forme [*sic*] and par of stockards prassed			xl
Item in the next loft – ij stone of hemp and matteres and boster and cofferled prassed			xv
Item in the chechene – ij brass potes and cubbarde and ij catteles and one cradell and iiij bowles and fring pane and deches and trenshers and tonges prassed			xxxij
Item in the butrer – ij panes and iij catteles and iij tubes and iij bareles and iij welles prassed		iij	
	Summa	xxv	xij
[*on the verso*]			
Item a cowe and ij steres ~~and~~ prassed			xl
Item and iij akeres grain prassed		v	
	the holle some is or tharabouts	xxxiij	xij

prassed By Henry Carter [*signature*], Thomas Strenger mark, George Northe [*signature*]
[*No exhibition clause*]

Notes: William Retchford 'husband of Elizabeth' was buried at Oakley on 11 August 1648. He made his will on 8 August 1648, giving £40 and a bullock to his daughter Elizabeth at the age of 21. The residual legatee and executrix was his wife Elizabeth (Beds Archives, ABP/W1649–50/139).

424 Michael Beament of Wrestlingworth, yeoman made 19 November 1651
Bedfordshire Archives, X222/31

An Inventary of all and singuler the goods and Chattells and debts of Mihell Beament late of Wreslingworth in the County of Bedford yeaman deceased taken and valued the ninetene day of November 1651 by Henry Randall and Henry Wynne as Folloeth vix [sic]

	£	s	d
Imprimas his money in his perse and parell 10^{li}	10	00	00
Item in the hall house one tabull & sixe stoules & three Cheares	1	0	0
Item in the parlor tow tabulles & tow Koberdes & other nessetares	1	10	0
Item in the milckhouse one Ches pres one troffe and other nesse tares	0	16	0
Item in the Chiching brase and pewter and other lomber	7	00	0
Item in the buttere fife barelles with other lumber	0	13	4
Item in the Chamber over the pa rlor one Inebed fernised & one Cuberd tow Chestes fower Cheares [?]~~tow~~ fife sto			

ules with other nessesareyes	6	00	0
Item in the Chamber over the hole one Ine bed & one trundell bed with the beddinge three Chest with other nessesareye	4	10	0
Item in the Chamber over the mil cke house one borded bed with some appulles	0	13	4
Item in the Chamber over the but tere one borded bed with other nesse careye	0	18	0
Item in the Chamber over the Chi chinge some Cheses some woole & some hempe with other thinges	2	10	0
Item fower horses with thare geares	32	0	0
Item sixe ~~Co~~ koues	15	0	0
Item three hoges & fife stores	4	10	0
Item twenty shepe	6	00	0
	93	00	8

[*second page*]

Item we finde in the yard fower Cartes tow pare of wheles & plowes & harroes & wood & kow racke	5	10	0
Item in the barne one mowe of whete & the rest barley	75[91]	0	0
Item in the malt house some pease	10	0	0
Item in the heahouse some heay & some owtes	6	0	0
Item for the whole tilth and brach	80	0	0
Item in desperate detes	10	0	0
[*carried over from the first page*]	93	0	8
Some is	279	10	8

Henry Randall [*signature*], Henry Wynne [*signature*]
[*No exhibition clause*]

Notes: Michael Beament's burial has not been found. He made his will on 10 November 1651, leaving everything to his wife Elizabeth to bring up their children; his land to his son Michael at the age of 21, on condition that he paid his daughter Elizabeth £200; and £10 per annum to the testator's mother Joan. There is no grant of probate (Beds Archives, X222/30). From the handwriting, it appears that the inventory and will were written by the appraiser, Henry Wynne.

425 Susan Carter of Bedford, widow of Thomas Carter, glover 14 May 1652
Bedfordshire Archives, ABP/W1638/116
See the notes at the end of this schedule for an explanation of the document.

A scedule indented of all the goodes and chattelles sold by the sayd John Carter unto the sayd William Carter his unckle according to the tenor of the deed annexed according to theire

91 Above 75 is a smudged number, possibly 65.

valuasion as they stand in the now dwelling howse of the sayd John Carter situate in Bedford called or knowen by the name of the Sunne as followeth

	£	s	d
In the chamber over the Entry one bedsted	01	15	00
two chests one chayre and a forme	00	14	00
one fetherbedd One boulster three downe pillowes	02	10	00
one coverlett two blankettes	01	13	04
Curtaynes vallens curtaine Rods	00	13	04
five cushyns	00	10	00
two flexen board clothes & two harden ones	00	11	00
two payre of flexen sheetes	00	15	00
five payer harden sheetes	00	10	00
two pillowbeares	00	02	00
one cupboard cushion	00	15	00
In the chamber over the hall one Rug one yellowe blankett one flocke boulster one fether boulster one fether pillow one wooll bed one straw bed one bedsted one table one forme	01	18	04
In the hall as followeth one bedsted one presse cupboard one court cupboard one table and forme one chayre one glasse Case	04	05	00
One fether bedd two boulsters one pillowe a straw bedd one coverlett one blankett three Curtaynes	01	06	08
In the butterrie fower hogsheades	00	14	00
one poudering tubb one Tunnyll	00	03	00
In the parlour one table one forme tenne stooles	01	00	00
fower chayres	00	08	00
two ketles one pann one pott one warmeing pann one skillett one Candlesticke	01	17	00
fower pewter platters three chamber potts and one quart pott	00	08	00
one skymmer	00	01	00
two spitts a payre of andyrons			

a payre of ways two foorkes			
a payre of bellowes	00	08	06
The whole valuasion is	22	18	02

Sealed and delivered by the sayd John Carter In presence of [*no witnesses*], the marke of John Carter
[*There is no exhibition clause*]

Notes: Thomas Carter was buried at Bedford St Paul's on 8 April 1638. His widow, Susan Carter, was buried there on 30 April 1652. Thomas Carter made his will on 17 October 1637, describing himself as a glover. He directed that his two houses in St Paul's were to be held in trust by Theodore Crowley, minister of St John's Bedford, and William Hawkyns then of Tilbrook, Bedfordshire, and to be sold to pay his debts and legacies. He left 20 nobles each to three children; £5 to another; and the remainder from the sale of the house to his wife Susan to bring up the three youngest children. Susan was to have his household goods during her lifetime, and after her death they were to be sold and 20 nobles given to each of the three youngest children; any remaining was to be divided equally among all his children. His wife Susan was his executrix and was granted probate on 8 October 1638. Susan died intestate in 1652. On 6 May 1652, her eldest son Thomas Carter, gentleman, of Sandy, renounced administration in favour of his brother John. By deed of May 1652 (in draft only) John, Joan and Elizabeth Carter, three of the children of Thomas Carter glover 'long since deceased' recited that Thomas Carter in his will gave his two houses in the parish of St Paul's Bedford in trust for them to be sold to pay his debts and legacies. They acknowledged that their brother Thomas Carter had tendered payment of £80 to Carter of Bletsoe, gentleman, for the two houses; and paid them 20 nobles each and that they had no claim on the houses. By bond of 11 May 1652, John Carter, fellmonger of Bedford, and William Carter silkweaver of Bedford, bound themselves to Theodore Crowley (in his capacity as surrogate to the archdeacon of Bedford) in the sum of £50 on condition that John Carter administered Susan Carter's goods, because his brother Thomas had renounced administration. On the same day a formal grant of administration was made to John Carter. By deed of 14 May 1652, John Carter, fellmonger, of the Sun in Bedford sold Susan's goods, as listed in a schedule, to his uncle William Carter, silkweaver of Bedford, for the payment of her debts. Any amount remaining was to be 'restored' to John Carter. The deed said that the goods had been symbolically transferred by the delivery of one pewter salt by way of seisin. *The document transcribed here is the schedule to the deed.* By an agreement on 8 June 1652 between John Carter and Simon Beckett, brewer of Bedford, John Carter undertook to pay Beckett £11 10s 4d within six weeks and Beckett would acquit him of the debts of Susan Carter.

The inventory is listed in indexes under the name of Thomas Carter. It has been assigned here to Susan Carter because of the gap of twelve years between their deaths.

426 Stephen Cox of Kempston, weaver — made 5 May 1654

Bedfordshire Archives, AD164

An Inventorie of the goodes and Chattells of Stephen Cox late of Kempston in the County of Bedford deceased taken and prized the Fift day of May in the yeare of Our Lord One Thousand Six hundred Fiftie and foure by us Richard Morton, Thomas Money and John Mouse

	£	s	d
Imprimis in the hall One Table Three ioyned stooles one Forme One chaire Two other Stooles one salt box	00	10	00

Item one bedsteade, Two Chestes One Trunck with other ymplements	01	06	08
Item in the further Chamber one bedsteade one Cubbard one box, one Coffer one Chaire one fetherbedd Tick Two blanckettes one bolster Two pillow ticks and Coverlidd Two Cushions	06	00	00
Item in the milkehowse five pewter-dishes, one pewter Cupp One salt, Three pewter-spoones Two brasse pottes, foure brasse kettles One Tinn-pann one fire-Shovell and tonges Two paire of pott hangers one dripping-pann one paire of Cobirons one spitt one warmeing pann one brasse back pann one pewter Candlestick One gridiron one frying pann	3	17	4
Item in the loft one borded bedd one Coffer Two blanckettes one pillow one strawbedd Two bushell bagges, one sack one hand-baskett one butter baskett one Coverlidd	01	10	00
Item more in the milkhowse Three barrelles Three Tubbs Five bowles Two kimnelles one boulting-trough One salting-trough one Churme Three Cheese fattes and suter Foure dishes Foure spoanes with other implementes	02	10	00
Item in linnen Five paire of sheetes Two pillow-beers a flexen and a hollon one, Two napkins	02	10	00
Item his weareing apparrell & money in his purse	5	00	00
Item in the Shopp one Loome with other furniture	2	00	00
Item Three Cowes One bullock price	7	10	00
Item Three quarters of mault price	2	08	00
Item Wood in the yard Timber and other wood	3	00	00
Item in the barne Two ladders Three forkes one shovell and spade one mattocke, and a houe, one drag-rake Three sheepe, Three Lambes	01	14	00
Item money due upon deede bond and otherwise	48	10	00
Summe totall of this Inventary is	88	06	00

Richard Morton, John Mouse, Thomas Money

[*Exhibited by Francis Flanders for the executor in London on 25 November 1654. The exhibition clause was signed by Mark Cottle, who was the registrar of the Court of Probates.*]

Notes: Stephen Cox was buried at Kempston on 2 May 1654. He made his will on 20 April 1654, describing himself as a weaver. He gave his messuage and closes to his son Stephen; 50s a year to his wife Rebecca during her life and the moveables in the house and one cow; and small bequests to his mother-in-law, daughter and niece. Son Stephen was appointed his residual legatee and executor and obtained probate in London on 23 November 1654 (TNA, PROB 11/238/461).

427 Ann Fisher of Carlton, widow made 20 July 1655

The National Archives, PROB2/432B

An Inventary of all & singular the goodes ch[att]ells of Ann Fisher late of Carlton in the County of Bedford wid[*ow*] dec[ease] Taken vallued & appraized the Twentieth day of July In the yeare of our Lord God 1655 by us Thomas White & Paul Payroll as Followeth vizt

	£	s	d
Inprimis her Purse & apparell	v		
In the Hall			
Item Two Tables one Court Cupbord Fower-teene high Chayers & Sixe Lowe one payr of Andirons with other small Implements	vij	x	
In the Kitchinge			
Item One Cupbord one table, dresser box Two brasse potts, Five brasse panns Two dripping panns one Jacke Three spitts one payre of racke one payre of Andirons with other small Implements	vj		
Item Two [?]Quernes	j		
Item Peuter great & small, two dozen Candlestickes & other Lumber	iij		
In the Brewhouse			
Item One Furnace & Mashing fatt tubbs & other Lumber	ij		
In the Milke house			
Item One Cheese presse & Churne & other Lumber		x	
In the Butterie			
Item Fower Hoggsheads & other old Lumber	j	x	
In the Studdy			
Item One Joined bedstead one feather bed one feather bolster one pillow one Coverlett one blanckett & Curtaines	iij		
In the Buttery Chamber			
Item One High & lowe bedstead one feather bed & other Lumber	iij		
In the Parlour Chamber			
Item Flaxen sheets tenne payre hempe teare sheetes tenne payre napkines fower dozen Two table cloathes one damaske one diaper, Two other table clothes Fower pillow beeres & other small lyninge & Lumber	xiij	vj	viij
In the Hall Chamber			
Item One Court Cupbord Two Chayre Curtaine vallence one chest & other small things	j	x	
In the Kitchinge Chamber			
Item One Jointed bedstead one feather bedd one feather bolster one Pillow Curtaine & vallence one Court Cupbord and Coverlett three chayres one paire of Andirons & other Implements	ix		

In the little Parlour Chamber

Item One Joined bedstead, one feather bedd, one bolster, one Pillow Curtaines & vallence and Chayre & other Implementes	iiij		

In the Gallerie

Item One presse & bedstead & other Lumber		v	
Item desperate debts upon bond	Cxxiij		
Item Another debt upon an Article which is	xx		
Item One Table, one chayre Two Trunckes and Plate & other Implementes	x		
The Totall Sume of this Inventary is	CClxiiij	xj	viij
[*Corrected total*	*£213*	*0s*	*8d*]

Rob Cottle [*signature*]
[*Exhibited by Robert Cottle for the administratrix on 10 January 1661*]

Notes: Ann Fisher's burial has not been found. She made a nuncupative will on 4 February 1655, leaving everything and the bonds to her daughter Frances, to whom administration was granted on 10 January 1661 under the name Frances King alias Fisher, the wife of John King (TNA, PROB11/303).

428 Robert Staunton of Birchmore, Woburn and London, esquire made 29 December 1656
The National Archives, PROB2/562
The handwriting is irregular and faded in places.

A true & perfect Inventary of all & singular the goodes Chattles and Debts of Robert Staunton Esq[ui]er late of Birchmore in the county of Bedford deceased but for these two yeares last past of Gr[*illeg.*] the Evangelist in Watling streete Lond[on][92] taken & appraised the 29th day of December1656 by Henry Hill, John Shemeld, Richard Houghton & Henry Budd as followeth vizt

	£	s	d
Inprimis the wearing apparrell of the said dec[ease]d	10		

In the greate Chamber

Item one feather bed and boulster two pillows one flocke bed	2	3	4
Item one rugge a covering 3 blankets & 3 Curtains and rodds	1	10	
Item a Bedsteed the vallence & 14 Curtaines	1	15	
Item 4 Chaires & 2 stooles		x	
Item a table a Covering cloth 4 curtains and rodds		5	
Item 2 creepers 2 brasse andirons one fire shovell & 2 pictures		9	

92 The church of St John the Evangelist, Friday Street was on the corner of Friday Street and Watling Street. It was destroyed in the fire of London and not rebuilt.

In the blew Chamber

Item one featherbed 3 feather boulsters and one pillow	2	10	
Item one rugge & 2 blankets		15	
Item one blew covering 4 Curtains and vallence with curtaine rodds	2		
Item one bedsteed 4 stooles & other Lumber		10	
Item one carpett & the hangings		18	
Item in the garrett next the garden one flocke bed two feather boulsters and one pillow		10	
Item one Coverlett one blankett 5 Curtains & 2 curtaine rodds		12	
Item one bedsteed matt & cord		6	
Item one Table & carpett 2 settle benches 3 chaires & other Lumber		20	

In the greene Chamber

Item one feather bed one flocke bed 2 feather boulsters & one pillow	2		
Item one coverlett 2 blanketts five curtaines three curtaine rodde & an old bedsteed		10	
Item two stooles one cheste & other Lumber		5	

In the garrett next the garden

Item 2 flocke beds one feather boulster one flocke boulster and one feather pillow		18	
Item two blankets & one coverlett		8	
Item one ioined bedsteed		9	
Item two Cushians & 4 small cushians		12	
Item one Carpett		15	
Item one Tapestry Coverlett & vallence and one Cushian		15	
Item one greate chest a Beame and scales & other Lumber		10	

In the Closett next the greene chamber

Item an old bedsteed & other Lumber		5	

In the Hall chamber

Item one featherbed 2 feather boulsters & 2 feather pillows	2	13	4
Item one Coverlett one Quilt and two Blankets	1		
Item one Bedsteed 5 Curtaines and vallence 3 curtaine rodds & a matt	1	10	
Item one Couch & four chaires		16	
Item a table 2 carpetts three curtaines & two curtaine rodds	1	2	

Item one paire of Andirons a par of tongs & a fire shovell		5	
In the Kitchin chamber			
Item one featherbed two feather boulsters & 2 feather pillows	2	6	8
Item one rugge & two blankets	1	2	
Item one bedstead one flockbedd foure curtaines & vallence three curtaine rodds & a corde		2	
Item one chaire 5 stooles & a couch		18	
Item 3 window curtaines & two rodds		[?]6	
Item one par of andirons a fire shovell & a par of tongs		5	
Item two Truncks		3	
In the new Chamber			
Item one feather bed one feather boulster & 2 downe pillows		2	
Item 3 blankets & 2 counterpanes		20	
Item one bedsteed five curtains & vallence & 2 rodds	2	10	
Item 2 window curtaines & 2 rodds		5	
Item one Chaire & 2 stooles		7	
Item one little iron grate one par of brasse andirons a par of tonges & a par of bellows		8	
Item the hangings & 2 pictures		10	
In the maids chamber			
Item one feather bed 2 feather boulsters & a feather pillow	2	1	
Item 2 blankets & a Rugge		10	
Item a Bedsteed 3 Curtaines two curtaine rodds a matt & cord		13	
Item a featherbed 2 feather boulsters a flocke boulster & a feather pillow	2		
Item 3 blankets & a rugge		9	
Item a halfe headed bedsteed two curtaines 2 rodds a matt & corde		5	
Item one halfe Cupboard & one presse		10	
Item a little Truncke 2 deskes one chaire & other Lumber		6	
In the maid's Garrett			
Item 2 flockebeds & 2 flocke bolsters		x	
Item one Coverlett & one blanket		5	
Item one bedsteed 3 sheets & other Lumber		10	
Item one Chest & one stoole		4	6
In the greate Parlour			
Item one drawing Table & one sidetable	1	1	
Item one courte cupboard 14 chairs & 2 stooles	2	10	
Item six chaires & 3 carpetts		18	
Item 5 Curtaines & 4 rodds		6	

Item one brasse pair of Andirons one brasse paire of Creepers one par of Tongs & one fire shovell	1		
In the little Parlour			
Item one drawing Table		6	
Item 9 high chaires & seaven low Chaires		16	6
Item one Courte Cupboard one carpett one cupboard cloth		20	
Item two ioint stooles and five Cushions		4	
Item two creepers a paire of Tongs & a fireshovell		3	4
Item one Clocke		x	
In the Hall			
Item one Table		10	
Item two chaires & six stooles		5	
Item one side boarde & cloath		3	4
Item one par of Andirons & Lumber		13	4
In the Larder			
Item one Table one chest a safe & other Lumber		7	
In the Kitchen			
Item one Jacke five spitts 3 racks one grate one iron barre & 2 potthangers	1	6	8
Item one Table & Cupboard		8	
Item 3 Chaires		2	
Item 3 brasse kettles 3 brasse pannes & one brasse posnett	2	6	8
Item one par of brasses for Andirons		13	4
Item 3 iron dripping panns		9	
Item two warming pannes		4	
Item three Flaggons forty pewter dishes 2 basons & a Cullender		6	
Item Sixty Plates		21	
Item 9 Candlesticks		ix	
Item 4 Chamberpotts		3	
Item one brasse fish [*?*]plate one brasse ladle & two brasse skummers		5	
Item one Cleaver one chopping knife one steele & other Lumber		8	
Item two suites of Armes 3 muskets one fouling gunne & one Carabine	1	10	
Item six brasse potts & 5 skelletts	2	10	
In the garden Chamber			
Item one bedsteed one par of andirons and one old stoole		4	
In the Washhouse			
Item one par of Coleirons		3	

Item four Tubbs one washer one Table one par of tressles & lumber		13	4
In the brewhouse			
Item one Furnace one Cooler one Mashing vate		2	
Item one malte mill one iron grate one cheese presse one salting Trough	1	5	
Item one Kneading trough and other Lumber		3	4
In the Granary			
Item one par of Harrows one oxe chaine 9 plough beames with other Lumber		15	
In the Chamber next the Hay loft			
Item one Binne 2 boarded bedsteds one little Table one chest & lumber		10	
In the tyled Barne			
Item one leaden cesterne one long Ladder & Lumber		12	
In the long Hovell			
Item two old carts & 2 par of wheeles		20	
In the greate Barne			
Item 2 [?]speers		5	
In the Coach house			
Item one old coach		15	
In the greate yarde			
Item one Leaden Cesterne	1	x	
In the Seller			
Item 3 hogsheads 2 tearses 4 Rundlets & 3 drinckstalls	1	13	4
[*sub-total*	*£91*	*1s*	*0d*]
Att Thomas Turney's house at Crawley[93]			
Item one long Damaske Table clothe 3 dozen & 2 napkins one long Towell 2 side board cloathes & one cupboard cloth all of Damaske		6	
Item 13 holland pillowbeeres and one wrought pillow beere	1	x	
Item 3 dyaper Tableclothes & three sideboard clothes	2	3	
Item 9 holland sheetes	2	5	
Item one flaxen table cloth 3 holland tablelothes 3 cupboard clothes	2	10	
Item one paire of wrought Dimity Pillowbeers		4	
Item one dozen of layd worke napkins & Towell		15	

93 This is likely to be Husborne Crawley, where the Turney family lived.

Item 13 holland napkins stitched at the ends		12	
Item 4 callico curtaines & 4 peeces for a bedd		15	
Item one red carpett & one red curtaine		13	4
Item one red mantle one white mantle & one tufted holland cloak	1	10	
Item one white wrought wastcoate & 2 pinne cushions		2	6
Item 2 flaxen short tablecloathes		3	
Item 2 sugar dishes & 2 salts	2		
Item furniture for a woman's horse	1	10	
Item two Damaske Tableclothes	1	2	
Item 3 old pillowbeeres & one old sheete		4	
Item 2 old cupboard cloathes 13 course sheetes & one course tablecloathe	1	6	8
Item one Taffata furniture for a Chamber	x		
Item 2 Chests & 2 truncks		x	
[*sub-total*	*£30*	*1s*	*6d*]

At Birchmore

Item one greate silver salte one [*?*]kettle one Tankred & 6 spoones	10		
Item one par of flaxen sheetes & one par of pillowbeeres		15	6
Item two par of Hempen sheetes		10	
Item 2 course table cloathes		2	6
Item 10 Dyaper napkins		10	
Item 7 flaxen napkins		3	6
Item Bookes	2	1	
[*sub-total*	*£14*	*2s*	*6d*]

At Crawley sent backe from Birchmore

Item 2 par of Holland sheetes	1		
Item one Dyaper tablecloth		8	
Item 18 dyaper napkins		18	
Item 2 holland Cupboard cloathes		9	
Item one flaxen tablecloth		2	6
Item one hempen Tablecloth		1	6
[*sub-total*	*£2*	*10s*	*0d*]

An inventory of his goods at the Blackboy in Watlingstreete Lond[on] appraised by Gabriell Holland, Andrew Rowley & William Staunton the 23th of Jan[uar]y 1656 [*illeg.*]

In the deceased's lodging chamber one chest of Drawers		5	
Item in the Space by the chamber doore one chest of drawers		6	

In the long chamber

Item one feather bed and feather boulster 1 feather pillow two flocke boulsters 1 flockebed one rugge & an old blankett	2		

	£	s	d
Item two Ruggs two Coverledds an old Cushion & blankett		12	
Item eight deale boxes		2	6
Item one nest of Drawer		1	6
Item one Deske one Boxe both of Wainscott		3	
Item 3 Truncks		4	
Item one peece of hangings		13	4
In the Nursery			
Item one feather bed one bolster & two blankets all old		16	
[*sub-total*	*£5*	*3s*	*4d*]
Debts due to the Deceased			
Imprimis from Sir Francis & Sir Anthony Vincent per bond[94]	100		
Item from William Jenney or Cheney & William Farre	57		
Item from William Taylor	50		
Item from Sir Henry Mildmay[95]	60		
Item from Sir Algernon Peyton[96]	96		
Item from the Lady [*?*]Savauge & others	85		
Item from William & George Shuttlewood	24		
Item from Edward Cooke & J[*a*]c[*o*]b Coleman	18		
Item from Robert Byway	[*?*]4		
Item from John Cowley	17		
Item from Steeven Durrant & Laurence Coles	13		
Item from John Greene & William Woster	5		
Item from Alexander Gurney	2		
Item from Leonard & Richard Yates	[*?*]2		
Item from William Kirke[97]	3	6	8
Item from Charles Rutten & others	8		
Item from Steephen Smith[98]	4		
Item from John or George Leech	8		
Item from William Cradocke[99]	20		
Item from Robert Munns	122	16	
Item from Thomas Rutton	3		
Item from William Stone	9		
Item from William Huffe	2	7	

94 Possibly Sir Anthony Vincent of Stoke D'Abernon in Surrey, one of the Committee for Surrey, and his son Sir Francis who was caught in July 1648, allegedly conspiring to betray the garrison at Oxford. Father and son had to provide a bond of £200 for Sir Francis's appearance before the Derby House Committee (*Cal. SP Dom: Charles I, 1648–9*, vol. 22, p. 217; article on Sir Francis Vincent in *The History of Parliament: the House of Commons 1660–1690*, https://www.historyofparliamentonline.org/volume/1660-1690/member/vincent-sir-francis-1621-70).

95 Possibly Sir Henry Mildmay, MP for Maldon, Essex, active in Parliament during the 1640s and a commissioner for the trial of Charles I (*ODNB*).

96 Probably Sir Algernon Peyton of Doddington, Cambs. where he was also rector. With his brother, he sought an Act of Parliament in 1653 to sell lands to pay debts (*Journal of the House of Commons: Volume 7, 1651–1660* (London, 1802), p. 347).

97 Staunton's will mentions rent of 6s 8d for Kirke's farm at Cawcott.

98 Staunton's will lists Stephen Smith as a tenant in Woburn.

99 Staunton's will lists William Craddock as a tenant in Somerset.

	£	s	d
Item from William [?]Hix	60		
Item from the Earle of Anglesey[100]	60		
Item from Henry Budd[101]	9		
Item from Joell Byworth	2		
Item from Thomas Blinkarne[102]	130		
Item from [*blank*] Clethrow		10	
Item from William Coward[103]	74	10	
Item from [*blank*] Chaplin	5	6	
Item from [*blank*] Ganden & [*blank*] [?]Dawcra	103		
Item from Thomas Dutton	2		
Item from Samuell Fenner	3	8	
Item from [*blank*] [?]Dawson & [*blank*] Farrow	2	16	8
Item for Haddam for Farme Rents	115	10	3
Item from Robert Hangham & William Sedgwicke	100		
Item from William [?]Nashe	4		
Item from [*blank*] [?]Janney	2		
Item from [*blank*] Kent & [*blank*] Shorter	103	6	
Item from John Lodgingham	4		
Item from [*blank*] Lush	4		
Item from George Purefoy	106	13	
Item from [*blank*] Parker[104] & others	39		
Item from George Potter[105]	20		
Item from [*blank*] Byland & [*blank*] Marry	5	4	
Item from Richard Stone	50		
Item from [*blank*] Saunders & [*blank*] Lee	104		
Item from Thomas Turney[106] for Rents by [*illeg.*]	72		
Item from Michaell [?]Tilcocke	18		
Item from [*blank*] Tennant & [*blank*] Kerby	106		
Item from [*blank*] [?]Whiteing	2	10	
Item from John [?]Wolcox for Rent	7	10	
Item from [*blank*] Worall	1	10	
Item from Laurence Cole	13		
Item from Ambrose Whatmore	5	10	
Item from [*blank*] Ball	2		
Item in Cashe at the testators death	50	17	
[*Sub-total of money owed to the deceased*	*£2102*	*19s*	*7d*]
Summa	2275	[*illeg.*]	[*illeg.*]
[*Corrected total*	*£2245*	*18s*	*11d*]

100 Charles Villiers, 2nd Earl of Anglesey, died 1661.
101 Staunton's will lists Henry Budd as a tenant in Aspley Guise.
102 Staunton's will details financial transactions with Master Thomas Blinkarne and also left him money for a mourning ring.
103 Staunton left him money for a mourning ring.
104 Possibly Master Parker, mentioned in his will and possibly his agent or lawyer.
105 He was mentioned in Staunton's will and given money for a mourning ring. He became rector at Simpson, Bucks, in 1661 (CCEd).
106 Referred to in his will. Possibly the same as Thomas Turner, who was one of the overseers.

[*At the foot of the last sheet there is an almost illegible text that repeats the date of probate.*]

	165		
	2088	5	1
	20	10	0
[*Total*]	2273	15	1

[*These figures are not explained.*]

[*Exhibited by Master Clements, notary public, for the executor at London on 8 June 1666. The exhibition clause was signed by Clements.*]

Notes: Robert Staunton was buried at Woburn on 24 December 1656. He made his will on 20 April 1653, requesting burial near his wife or father in the chancel of Woburn church. He provided for his sons and daughters and listed property in Woburn, Aspley Guise, Bromham, Southill, Stagsden, North Crawley (Buckinghamshire, sold by 1653), elsewhere in Buckinghamshire and in Kent, London, Somerset and Surrey. He had business interests in Deptford, the Fens and elsewhere. Some of the seventy or more people mentioned in his will are also listed in the inventory as owing him money. The will was proved in London on 27 January 1657 (TNA, PROB11/261). Robert Staunton was one of the Bedfordshire members of the committees set up by Parliament in 1642 and 1643 to administer Bedfordshire and collect weekly assessments. Birchmore House was plundered by Royalist forces in 1645.[107]

429 Thomas Curfey of Lidlington, labourer made 22 August 1657

Bedfordshire Archives, CH442

The inventory has been written on a long thin strip of parchment.

A true and perfect Inventary of all and Singuler the goodes chattles cattles and debtes of Thomas Curfey thelder late of Littleington in the County of Bedford Labourer deceased Taken and valued the two and twentieth day of August in the yeare of our Lord God one thousand Six hundred Fiftie Seaven by Edward [*?*]Harry, William [*?*]Nute[108] and John Crouch as Followeth vizt

	£	s	d
Inprimis his wearing Apparrell	ij		
Item in the Hall one presse one forme two chaires and two boordes		viij	
Item in the said roome three kettles one brase pott three pewter platters and one candlesticke		xvj	
Item in the little chamber one boorded bed with one woolbed thereon one bolster two pillows two blancketts one peece of cloth		xxv	
Item in the same roome tenne boordes three barrells			

107 Beds Archives, Community Histories, Woburn, where there is also an account of the Staunton family's occupation of Birchmore House.

108 Or Mute, i.e. Mote. The writing is difficult to read.

with other lumber		x	
Item in the great chamber one boorded bed two blancketts one pillowe		x	
Item in the same Roome one cheese presse one kneading trough seaven boordes seaven Fleeces of woole two wheeles with other lumber		xx	
Item one paire of Andirons two paire of pott hangers one fire shovell one paire of tonges		v	
Item six paire of sheets two pillowbears one boordcloth		xxiiij	
Item for rye in the house		xxj	
Item for oates in the barne and hay	iij	vj	viij
Item for wood and hurdles in the yard		xliij	iiij
Item two bullocks		liij	iiij
Item eight sheepe and two lambes		xl	
Item one store hogge		xiij	iiij
Summe totall is	19	15	8

[*Exhibited by John Watson for the executrix at London on 6 October 1657. The exhibition clause was signed by Thomas Southwood.*]

Notes: Thomas Curfey died on 10 August and was buried at Lidlington on 12 August 1657. He made his will on 6 December 1655, leaving his house and lands to his wife Alice for life and then the land to his son William on condition that he paid £5 to each of his brothers and one sister (the other received 12d) on successive years after their mother's death. Alice was granted probate on 2 October 1657 (Beds Archives, CH441, will and separate document granting administration).

430 William Newold of Kempston, yeoman made between August and October 1657
The National Archives, PROB2/566
The inventory is badly damaged, stained and faded at the top and down the left side of the first sheet. Some text is missing or illegible.

[*?A True*] Inventory of all the goods and Chattells of William Newold late of [...] County of Bedf [...]man deceased taken and app[*raised*] the 14th day of [*illeg.*] of our Lord [*illeg.*] fifty seaven by us [*illeg.*] names are [*illeg.*] written

	£	s	d
[*In the*] Hall			
[*four lines illeg.*]	02	[...]	[...]
[*three lines illeg.*]	02	[...]	[...]
One paire of Andirons book [*sic*] [*illeg.*] other small thinges here att	00	[...]	[...]

In [*illeg.*] Chambers

Item two standing bedsteds one feather bedd two Mattresses two straw bedds fower blanketts one Coverlidd one Rugg three bolsters fower pillowes Curtines and vallence att	07	03	04
Item one feather bedd two Chests two [*illeg.*] three boxes two Chayres and a little table	05	06	08

In the upper Chambers

Item one standing beddstedde and a bedforme one flocke bed one strawe bedd one feather bolster and two blankettes att	01	13	[*?*]04
Item one Cheste one Coffer two [*?*]bings and oth[*er*] [*s*]mall thinges at	01	00	00
Item one standing bedstedd one bedforme one strawe bed one Coverlidd a little Coffer two stooles and other small things att	02	05	00
Item a little parcell of wooll and a parcell of Cheeses att	02	16	08
Item fifteene paire of sheetes and one odd sheet att	05	06	08
Item three board cloathes and a dozen and halfe of napkins at	01	15	00
Item fowerteene pillowbers hand towells and other small lynnen at	01	10	00
Item all his wearing apparell at	06	10	00

In the kitchin

Item one old table a little falling table two formes two stooles tw[*o*] Chayres a pare of bellowes a grediron pott hangers hookes fire [*?*]shovell fire forke and other Lu[*mber*] there att	01	05	00
Item two Flitches of bacon and a halfe att	01	10	06
Item one Furnace with the Iron belonging to itt and other ould Iron att	02	00	00
Item five [*illeg.*] kettles two porridge potts two possnettes one Chaffindish two skymmers two dripping panns and one warmeing pann att	04	03	00
Item fifteene pewter dishes one pewter flaggon one pewter bason three pewter porringers two			

pewter potts one fruite dish one pewter Candlesticke one pewter salt one pewter bowle and a tynn Candlesticke att	01	016	00
Item one pewter Chamber pott and twelve pewter spoones att	00	03	00
In the [?]buttrey			
Item eight barrells three drinke stoles and other lumber here att	02	00	00
In the bolting house			
Item one bolting arke one Doe Troffe two brewing fattes five tubbes three kymnelles a wash barrell and other lumber there att	03	00	00
Item two boarded beddes one flocke bedd one flocke bolster one fether bolster three blankettes and two Coverliddes att	01	16	08
In the Milkhouse			
Item milke vessell 2 churmes one Cheese presse shelves and other Lumber there att	01	10	00
In the Loft over the milkhouse			
Item three bushelles of woates a skreene a bushell a pecke and a halfe pecke two wyre sives three riddles nine sackes two baggs two lynnen wheeles A sedcord and other lumber there at	02	12	00
Item a parcell of Coales att	00	10	00
Without doores			
Item three horses horse harnes and other Lumber in the stable att	16	00	00
Item three long Cartes three dung Cartes and fower payre of Cart wheeles att	17	00	00
Item fower plowes and shares three Colters plow tymber plow Chaines Extryes and other Implementes belonging to husbandry att	04	00	00
Item two pare of harrowes at	00	16	00
Item seaven Cowes att	20	00	00
Item fower score & ten sheepe at	22	10	00
Item fower hoggs att	05	00	00
Item wheate and barley to thresh and thresht att	75	00	00
Item pease and oates to thresh and thresht att	30	00	00
Item hay att	15	00	00

Item one borded ruft hovell at	08	00	00
Item another ruft hovell att	02	00	00
Item three other hovells att	05	10	00
Item a sheephouse and hurdles at	01	10	00
Item three Fannes and two draggrakes att	00	15	00
Item a parcell of boardes at	00	10	00
Item ladders forkes wood and other lumber about the yard att	03	10	00
Item three and twenty acres of Tilth att	23	00	00
Item a Lease att	57	00	00
Item poltery about the yard att	00	13	04
Item moneys lent to John Sharp	15	00	00
Item moneys due payd to Mr William Blocke for Jo: Sharpe	40	00	00
Item in other desperate debtes	05	00	00
Item in the house in ready Cash	03	00	00
Total	643	19	–
[*Corrected total*	*£432*	*7s*	*2d*]

The marke of John Marryott sen., Tho Amps
[*Exhibited at London in October 1657. The exhibition clause was signed by Thomas Price.*]

Notes: William Newold was buried at Kempston on 26 August 1657. He made his will on 24 July 1657, leaving his freehold land to his son Thomas; £60 to his son-in-law William Sharpe; small sums to his brother and his brother's younger children; and the residue to his wife Grace who was appointed executrix and to whom probate was granted on 30 May 1657 (TNA, PROB 11/267).

431 Thomas Kent of Pulloxhill, yeoman made 8 September 1657
The National Archives, PROB2/437
The inventory is stained and badly damaged on the lower right side. Much of the heading is also illegible.

An In[*ventory*] [...] and singuler the [...] Debts of Thomas [...] Pulloxhill in the [*County*] of Bedd yeoman dec[eas]ed t[*aken*] [...] the 8th day of September [*illeg.*] by John Cooper and Henry Baker

	£	s	d
In the Hall			
Imprimis one Table with a frame, a forme 6 stooles an Arke shelves 3 brasse potts [...] Kettles 3 skillets 2 pannes a brazen Ladle a morter a driping pann a fire shovell Andirons tonges a warminge pann jj peeces of pewter tenn poringers 6 saucers 2 Dozen and a halfe of spoones a fla[*gon*]			

2 pinte potts 3 Candlestickes a[*nd*] other thinges there	x
In the parlor	
Item one Joyned bedsteade [...] Curtaines vallence & beding [...] thereon one Court Cupbor[*d*] [...] 2 Chests 3 boxes a Cheare a square Table a glasse Cas[*e*] and other thinges there	[*value missing*]
In the Dary house	
Item 3 Tubbs 5 barrells [...] Cheesepresses 4 kimnell[*s*] [...] Chearne shelves boules [...] Cheesefattes a salting [...] and other Lumber there	[*value missing*]
Item [...] wearinge appar[*rell*]	[*value missing*]
In the Chamber over [...]	
Item one standing bed with [...] bedinge one little bed & beding [...] one Truncke 2 Coffers 3 [...] apereell of Woole [*?*]9 [*?*]pair [...] sheetes 5 paire of [...] beeres 2 dozen and hal[*f*] [...] napkins 4 board Cloat[*hes*] [...] Towells boxes & other [...]	[*value missing*]
In the D[...]	
[*Two lines damaged and text missing*]	
[...] 13 Cowes and [...]	[*value missing*]
Item 8 pigges & 2 [...]	[*value missing*]
Item five stockes [...]	[*value missing*]
[*?*]Item Hay Wooll [...]	[*value missing*]
[*illeg.*] and yard	[*value missing*]
The sume totall [*of this*] Inventary is	[*value missing*]

[*Exhibited in September but the day of the month and the year are illegible*]

Notes: Thomas Kent was buried at Pulloxhill on 24 August 1657. A word appears below the total that might be *wande*, possibly the name of the notary public. The year used in this transcription was ascribed to the inventory by The National Archives and corresponds with his date of burial.

432 Joan Hewett of Knotting, widow — made 5 October 1659

The National Archives, PROB2/578

The Inventary of all & singuler the goods chattells & debts of Joane Hewett late of Knotting in the County of Bedford widdow dec[ease]d taken and prized the fifth day of October in the yeare of our Lord God 1659 by Thomas Savage th'elder and William Hale as [*illeg.*] followeth viz[t]

	£	s	d
Inprimis one bedstead one featherbed, two coverlidds			

and one blanckett	v	x	
Item one cupboard two chestes and one boxe Coffer	ij	v	
Item three kettles two brasse potts and one warmeing pann	iij	xvj	viij
Item eight pewter dishes, one quarte pott and three pewter candle stickes		xviij	vj
Item one long table one little table and two formes	j	xiij	iiij
Item one bedstead and five paire of sheetes	ij	vij	
Item one spitt twoe paire of potthangers one paire of andirons one gridiron and a paire of bellowes		ix	vj
Summa totalis huius Inventarij	xvij		

[*Exhibited by John Allen for the administrator at London on 30 May 1661. John Allen's name appears above the exhibition clause.*]

Notes: Joan Hewett's burial has not been found. Her husband, Edmund Hewett, left her £10 a year in his will in 1656 (TNA, PROB11/262).

Glossary

The aim of the glossary is two-fold. It focusses on terms that are little used today or had a different or specialised meaning in the sixteenth and seventeenth centuries. It also includes unusual spellings and some variant spellings of common words. Many phonetic and unusual spellings can be worked out by slowly reading the word aloud and remembering that:

- some words were run on from the preceding article, e.g. as 'acase' instead of 'a case'; it will be listed here as 'case';
- *c* and *k* were often interchangeable;
- *c* was often omitted before *k* or added where it would not be used today;
- *e* was often added to, or omitted from, the end of a word;
- *i* and *j* were often interchangeable, mainly at the beginning of words;
- *s* and *c* were often interchangeable;
- *y* was often used instead of *i*;
- letters were often doubled

Many less demanding variant spellings have been included for readers unaccustomed to sixteenth and seventeenth century terms and spelling.

* see the word asterisked for the definition.

Definitions without a source are based on the *Oxford English Dictionary*. Definitions beginning *possibly* or *probably* or ending *(editorial)* have not been found in dictionaries and are editorial conjecture.

Other sources:

Bailey, N. and J. Worlidge, *Dictionarium Rusticum, Urbanicum & Botanicum: or A dictionary of Husbandry*, 3rd ed. (London, 1726), 2 vols

Batchelor, Thomas, *An orthoëpical analysis of the English language ... dialect of Bedfordshire* (1809). Reprinted 1974 as *Lund Studies in English* vol. 45

Chinnery, Victor and Val, *Names for things: A Description of Household Stuff, Furniture and Interiors 1500–1700* (Wetherby, 2016)

Cox, Nancy and Karin Dannehl, *Dictionary of Traded Goods and Commodities 1550–1820*. University of Wolverhampton, 2007. British History Online

Cumming, Valerie and C. W. and P. E. Cunnington, *The Dictionary of Fashion History* (London, 2017), 2nd ed.

Holme, Randle, *The Academy of Armory, or, A Storehouse of Armory and Blazon* (Chester, 1688)

Raymond, Stuart A., *Words from Wills and other probate records* (Bury, 2004). A useful modern resource but lacks sources

Wharton, J. J. S., *The Law Lexicon ... explaining all the technical words and phrases employed in the several departments of English Law ...* (London, Spettigue and Farrance, 1848)

Wright, Joseph, *The English dialect dictionary, being the complete vocabulary of all dialect words still in use, or known to have been in use during the last two hundred years* (London, 1895–1905), 6 vols

Yaxley, David, *A researcher's glossary of words found in historical documents of East Anglia* (Dereham, 2003)

achauendish: a chafing dish*

acre: an acre is about 0.4047 hectares

addes: adze

alestall: stall*

Alhallon day: All Hallows' day, 1 November

***allocantur dicta debita*; *allocantur huiusmodo debita*:** these debts have been allowed

allome: alum: an astringent mineral salt used as a mordant for dyeing and in tanning

almery: aumbry*

alone: probably holland*

ambery: aumbry*

ambulyng: ambling

an Irons: andirons*

andfeild, anfeld, anfilde, anvile: anvil

andirons: a pair of iron stands with a bar at right angles, placed either side of a fire with logs balanced on the bars, providing a flow of air under the logs to encourage burning. They were often decorated.

angars: hangers*

angel: a gold coin issued in England between 1465 and c1642, bearing the image of the archangel Michael killing a dragon. Its value varied from 10s to 6s during this period. In the 1550s it was worth 10s (Yaxley).

***anno salutis*:** in the year of salvation, AD

anyarne: an iron

anyrons: andirons*

aperne, apern ware: apron; napery* ware

apparitor: an ecclesiastical court official appointed to keep order, serve notices and inform the court of activities within its jurisdiction

appraiser: a person appointed by the executor or administrator to value the decedent's property

appulles: apples

appurtinances: appurtenances: a legal term meaning the accessories; usually used for land and rights but also as a general term for fittings

apryns, apry ware: apron; napery* ware

***apud*:** at

aquavita, aquavitae, aquavite: aqua-vitae: a strong alcohol distilled from the lees of wine

arine: yarn*

ark: chest*, box*, coffer*, or similar for storing dry goods. In these inventories, it is often the container used in bolting* or sifting* flour.

armory for a horseman: possibly the harness, saddle and weapons that were required under the 1558 legislation in case of war (4 & 5 Ph. & M., c. 2, *Statutes* *of the Realm*, vol. 4, p. 316). The Act did not list what the harness and weapons comprised. It was repealed in 1605.

arndeyreons: andirons*

aster croppe: probably grain sown at Easter

augers, augars: auger: 1. a carpenter's hand tool for boring holes in wood; 2. a metal bit attached to a carpenter's brace

aumbry: a cupboard, locker, safe or press, especially for storing food

aundiorne, aundirons: andirons*

awgers: augers*

awmbre: aumbry*

axetree, axeetres, axell trees, axeltrees: ax-tree or axletree: the axle of a set of wheels for a cart or plough (Yaxley)

back bord: a board at the back of furniture, distinguishing it from furniture without a back. In these inventories, applied to benches, chairs and stools. The back might be made of wainscot*.

back howse: 1. a bake house; 2. a back house: the rear portion of a house often used for domestic chores or storage

back pan: possibly a baking pan

backside: premises belonging to a house or farm situated behind the main building, including gardens, fields, outbuildings, etc.; a backyard

baies: bay*

bake chers: chairs with backs

bakehouse: 1. bake house; 2. back house

balans, pair of: a pair of scales for weighing, comprising a horizontal beam balanced on a central pivot with a pan at each end

ballrybb: bald-rib: a joint of pork cut from nearer the rump than the spare-rib

balsters: bolster*

banckir: banker*

band box: probably a box to hold bonds*

bandes: 1. a neck-band or collar of a shirt, originally to make it fit closely round the neck, afterwards often ornamented. In the sixteenth and seventeenth centuries, a collar or ruff worn round the neck by a man or woman; 2. swaddling bands: narrow lengths of bandage wrapped round a new-born infant's limbs to prevent free movement

bankate: blanket*

banker, bankecar: 1. a fabric covering for a bench or chair, typically of tapestry; 2. an ornamental hanging or tapestry for a bed or the walls of a room

banking iron: unknown; possibly a barking* iron

bar: 1. in the chimney to hang pots on; 2. a warping* bar in a loom. It was usually of iron.

bard chest: probably a chest with iron bands or bars

bare cart: a cart without iron tyres (Yaxley)

bare keyne: probably a barren cow, or one not bearing a calf in that year

bare welys, pair of: wheels without iron tyres

baringe clouth: bearing* cloth

barke: bark was used in the tanning process

barking iron: a tool for stripping bark from trees
barleape, barlepp: bearleep: a large basket
barleyge, barleyghe: barley
barlype, barlyppe: barleape*
barrel, barilles, barrlls, baryles: a wooden barrel or cask. The standard capacity was 32 gallons for ale and 36 gallons for beer (see Yaxley for a summary of barrel capacities)
barren: barn
barse: brass
baryng shete: bearing* cloth
bascate: basket*
bashn: probably a basin
basket: usually of wicker but in these inventories sometimes made of cloth
basse: brass
basting ladle: a ladle used to baste meat, i.e. pour fat, cooking juices or other liquid over roasting meat, in order to prevent it from drying out during cooking
bawlls: bowls
bay, baies, baye, bayes: 1. bay: the division of a house, or other building, generally from fifteen to twenty feet in breadth; 2. bay: a horse of a reddish-brown colour; 3. baize: a woollen cloth resembling a thin serge introduced by Walloon refugees in the 1560s (Cumming)
bayard: a hand barrow used for heavy loads. In these inventories, usually listed with fire shovels, tongs and other fire equipment and sometimes as a pair
baylife: bailiff: the agent or steward of a landowner, who collected rents and managed the estate for its owner or tenant
baylywicke: bailiwick: the office of Bailiwick of Dunstable with tolls and profits of three annual fairs held on Ash Wednesday, 2 May and Lammas Day and of a weekly market held on Wednesdays was let by James I by letters patent of 30 October 1605 for 40 years (Bedfordshire Archives)
baynede: bayard*
bazen: basin
bdsted: bedstead*
beach: breach*
beakers: a drinking vessel with a wide mouth
beakhorne: bickern: an anvil with two projecting taper ends, later only one taper end
beams: 1. part of a set of scales*; 2. part of a plough* or cart
beaneland: land upon which beans were grown
beare stales, stalles, tubs: stall*, tubs* for beer
bearing cloth, sheet, blanket: 1. a piece of cloth, typically of high quality, used to wrap a baby in at baptism; 2. more generally, a piece of cloth for wrapping a young or newborn baby
bearinge byll: specific purpose is unknown; probably an agricultural implement. See bill*
beas, beace, bease, beasse, bees, beese, beesse: beasts*
beasts: 1. cows; 2. horned cattle (Batchelor)
beattell: a wooden club or hammer used for driving wedges or pegs

bed: a sack or mattress stuffed with something soft or springy, placed on a bedstead, and covered with sheets, blankets, etc. In these inventories, normally filled with feathers, flock*, straw or wool

bed cord: cord threaded between the holes in the bed frame and pulled tight to support the bed or mattress (Yaxley)

bed mat: a thin, strong mat laid over bed cords and under a mattress or bed (Yaxley)

bedding: a collective term for mattresses (also called beds), pillows, bolsters, blankets and other covers making up a bed, but excluding sheets and pillow cases

bedforme: unknown; possibly a bed frame

bedpan: 1. a warming* pan. 2. a chamber pot for bed-ridden people (Chinnery; not recorded in *OED* before 1654)

bedstaves: rods about 16 inches long and 1 inch in diameter that fitted into holes in the bedframe and kept the bedding in place (see Chinnery for a detailed explanation)

bedstead: the wooden frame of a bed. In these inventories, bedsteads are described as framed*, joined*, boarded*, field*, girth*, plaine*, seeled*, sidebeds*, standing*, truckle* and trundle.

bedstedd flees: unknown

bedstydyes, bedstydles: bedstead*

bedticke: tick*

beefe fork: a long-handled, two or three pronged fork for handling meat on a spit or in the pot

beene house: probably a building or place for storing beans or vetches

beere, beare: 1. beer: made with hops, in contrast with ale which was not; 2. pillowbear*

beerestalls, beere staule: stall*

beers: pillowbear*

bees, beese, beeze: 1. beasts*; 2. bees

beffe, beife: probably preserved beef

beheses: probably bee hives

beker: beaker*

bell candelstykes: a candlestick with a bell-shaped base

bell salt: a salt cellar with a bell-like profile

bellies, bellostes, bellouse, bellowes/se, bellowys: bellows, often as a pair

belly bands: part of a cart harness passing round the belly of a horse, to check the play of the shafts

beme: beam*

bench board, bence bord: a long wood or stone seat, with or without a back and sometimes for more than one person; or a board which forms a bench, or part of a bench

benche settle: long wooden bench, usually with arms and a high back (often extending to the ground), and having a locker or box under the seat

bencher: possibly a banker* or a bench*

beneigh: beneath

benys: beans

berdes: bed*

berynge byll: bearing* bill

berynge shette: bearing* cloth

bese, besse, bestes, beys, beysse, beyste: beasts*
bgards: bayard*
bibes: a child's bib
biggin: a child's cap
bill, bile, byll: 1. a tool for pruning or cutting wood, lopping trees, hedges etc. In these inventories, used for bearinge* bills, forest* bills and hedginge* bills; 2. a promissory note or bill of exchange; 3. a type of halberde*, in these inventories called black*, browne* and watch* bills. See also mill* bills
binge: possibly bin
birding peece: a gun for fowling (Yaxley)
black bill, byll: a type of halberde* with a black head
black jack: a large, tar-coated leather jug for beer
blades, pair of: windinge* blades
blankets, blaketes: 1. a bed covering; 2. undyed woollen cloth used for a bed covering or clothes
boalsturs: bolster*
boardcloths: a cloth, usually of linen, to cover a table or cupboard
boarded beds or bedsteads: a bed with boarded or panelled sides, possibly with slats instead of cords, into which the bed* was fitted
boards: a piece of sawn timber, more than 4 inches wide and less than 2½ inches thick, distinguished from a plank which was thicker
bodey trases, pair of: traces*
bodyes: 1. an inner garment for the upper part of the body, quilted and strengthened with whalebone (worn chiefly by women, but also by men); a corset, stays; frequently called a pair of bodies (bodice); 2. cart* bodies
bofett stoles: buffet* stools
bolackes, bolak: bullock*
bole-dishes: a bowl-shaped dish
boles, bollys: bowl
boll: bull
bolock, boloxke: bullock*
bolster, bollssteres, bolste, bolstres: a long, stuffed pillow usually the width of the bed and placed under individual pillows
bolting: bolting or boulting: sifting bran or coarse meal in the process of producing flour. In these inventories, the process is carried out in an ark*, barrel*, hutch*, trough*, tub*, tun* or vessel and sometimes in a separate bolting house.
boltings, pair of: unknown
bonds: a written obligation under seal, binding a person to pay an agreed sum or perform an act. When the obligation is fulfilled, the bond is void (Wharton). Bonds for administering a deceased's property were usually for a sum twice the value of the estate and had several bondsmen, who were bound to the court official to administer the property.
booe: long bow
boolookes: bullock*
boolster, booulsteres: bolster*
boorded stool: unknown
boordenbed, boordyd bedstid: boarded* bed

boorels: barrels*
boosshells: bushel*
boote, bottes: 1. boats; 2. silver boat as table ware
bostares, bosters: probably bolsters*
bote hose: boot-hose: an over-stocking covering the leg and protecting finer stockings from contact with the boot
botlsters: bolster*
bottams: bottoms or balls of yarn (*Dictionarium Rusticum*)
boulockes: bullock*
boultils: probably bottles
boulting: bolting*
boultinge pype: part of the equipment for processing meal into flour for baking (*Dictionarium Rusticum*)
boundes: bonds*
bowells, bowels, bowlles: bowls
bowlester, bowlsteres, bowlstrs: bolster*
bowletylles, a pair: unknown
bowletyng arke: bolting* ark*
bowllty howsshe: bolting* house
bowltar: unknown
box coffer: probably a cross between a coffer* and a box*
boxes, boxseyes: a small lidded chest, generally without feet, and therefore intended to rest upon a table; sometimes noted as containing documents or valuables
boyls: bowls
brach, brache: breach*
bracly whyeat: unknown; probably breach* wheat
brake: 1. a toothed implement for breaking hemp or flax; 2. a wooden mill to crush green fruits and hops; 3. a heavy harrow for crushing clods; 4. a tool resembling a pair of scissors used for peeling bark from willows for basket-making; 5. a lever or handle for working a machine, e.g. a pump; 6. a cage or trap; 7. a framework to hold something steady
braley: barley
brand: unknown; possibly a branding iron
branderd: unknown; possibly a brandiron*
brandiron, bryndyren: 1. a gridiron*; 2. andiron*, a stand for a kettle, a trivet; 3. a iron for branding cattle (Wright)
brandlett: unknown; possibly the same as a brandreth: 1. brandiron* 1; 2. a stand for a cask or hayrick; 3. an iron framework on which to rest utensils in cooking (Wright)
brascittles: brass kettles
brasepayes: brass pans
brasier: brazier: someone who works with brass
bratch: breach*
brawe: unknown
brayse: brass
breach: 1. land newly broken up from grass; 2. land prepared for seed. In these inventories, applied to fields and land (Wright).

breach barlye, breach grene: breach grain: includes all the leguminous crops such as beans, peas, and tares (Batchelor)
bread grater, grate, gratte: a grater for hard bread or crusts to make breadcrumbs
breadthes, bredethes: the breadth of cloth was laid down in legislation. For broad* cloth it was set at 63 inches (160cm) in 1535, reduced to 58½ inches (148.6cm) in 1584.
bredere: probably a breeder, or animal ready for breeding
breeches, briches, pair of: a pair of breeches reaching just below the knee
brest wimbell, wimble: gimlet or auger* upon which the chest is pressed to exert greater force
brewing: the process of making ale and beer. In these inventories, brewing was carried out in coppers*, kettles* and vessels
brewing furnesse: furnace*
brewstalles: stall*
brindlett: brandlett*
broad cloth: a fine, double width, woollen cloth of plain weave, used mainly for men's clothes
broad reshes, rystes: wrystes*
broches: broach: a spit
browne bill: a type of halberde* painted brown, formerly used by foot-soldiers and watchmen
bruehousse, bruhouse, bruyng house, brwinghowse: brewhouse
brume: broom; a plant used for thatching (*Dictionarium Rusticum*)
brundlett: brandlett*
brydelles, brydles: bridle
bryndyren: brandiron*
buckinge tubbe, buck tubs: a tub for cleaning yarn, cloth, or clothes by steeping or boiling them in a lye of wood ashes (*OED*, Wright)
bucks: box*
buffet, buffit, buffytt stool: a low stool, often three-legged
buffet forme: probably a low form
buffyn: buffin: 1. a coarse cloth in use for the gowns of the Elizabethan middle classes; 2. a garment made of that material
buiffyttes: probably buffet* stool
bulchin: bull calf
bullock, bulloxkes, bulluckes: 1. a young bull or an ox; 2. cattle of either sex (Wright)
bullocks breeders: cows
bullting howce: bolting* house
bullymonge: bullimong: 1. a mixture of grains grown together e.g. oats, peas, and vetches; 2. buck-wheat; also called maslin (*Dictionarium Rusticum*). Used for feeding cattle (*OED*).
bus: abbreviation for a bushel*
bushel, bushell, busell, bussylls: 1. a measure of capacity equal to 8 gallons (36.4 litres), used in these inventories for barley, malt, oats, rye, vetches and wheat; 2. the standard container in which a bushel was measured
buttery: a cool storeroom for provisions, especially ale, food and kitchen utensils

by-: see bi-
bȝ: bus: a bushel*

cab irnes: cobirons*
caddes, a pair: cards*
caffa, caffey: caffa: a rich silk cloth, similar to damask, much used in the sixteenth century; coarse taffetta (Cumming)
cake peele: peele*
caldelstekes: candlesticks*
calderne: cauldron (cawdron*)
calleter: probably a caliver (callyver*)
callico: calico: cotton cloth, imported from the East, often plain white and bleached or unbleached; cotton weft and linen warp (Cumming)
callyver: caliver: a light musket or arquebus, introduced during the sixteenth century. It was the lightest portable firearm, except for the pistol, and fired without a rest.
cambar, camber: chamber
cammil: kimnel*
canch, cansche, canth: a small rick adjoining another (Batchelor)
candlestick, canstikes, canstkes, canstyckes: a stand for a candle. It could be a simple plate or an elaborate holder, and made of wood or metal (Chinnery).
cannes: containers for liquid
canopy, cannope: covering or hangings suspended over a piece of furniture. In these inventories, it was suspended over beds.
canvase: canvas: a strong, unbleached, hemp* or flax* cloth used for stout clothing and bedding
capcasse: cap-case: 1. a travelling-case, bag or wallet; 2. a receptacle of any kind, e.g. a box, chest, cask or case.
cappes, capps: 1. a head covering; 2. cap-like cover on an object; 3. a closed wooden vessel
carabine: carbine: a firearm, shorter than the musket, used by the cavalry and other troops
carchaffes: kerchiefe*
cards, cardes: cards, often as a pair. 1. set with metal or wire teeth and used to separate and align the fibres of wool, etc.; 2. an implement used for raising a nap on cloth. In these inventories, used for preparing flock*, hemp*, tow*. See also stock cards*
careseye: kersey*
carfa: caffa*
carpet: a thick fabric, commonly of wool and often decorated with needlework or Turkey work, used to cover beds, cupboards, tables etc. Not a floor covering.
carsey, carsy: kersey*
cart boddes, bodyes: a cart was a two wheeled vehicle, without springs, used in farming and for carrying heavy goods. The body was the part which held the load.
cart boott: cart-bote: an allowance of wood to a tenant for making and repairing carts
cart cloutes: an iron plate to protect the axle-tree from wear
cart gear, gerys, pairs of: a general term for the harness with which horses were attached to the cart

cart harnes, carthernis: probably the same as cart gear

cart saddles: a small saddle placed on the back of a cart-horse to support the shafts

cart timber: beams, heads, sheaths, hales, spindles, shelboards, bodies and rings for wheels (*OED*)

cart traces, pair of: ropes, chains or leather straps by which the collar of a draught-animal was connected with the splinter-bar or swingletree

cartaine, cartane: certain

cartaynes: curtain*

cartlades: cart loades*

case, cass, casse: 1. a box or chest; 2. a container for items for safe keeping, transportation or display; 3. a hen hutch. The meaning is unclear in several inventories.

casement: 1. a window; 2. a hinged frame containing glass, forming part of a window

caske: similar to a barrel and containing standard quantities of ale, beer or wine

casokes: cassock: 1. a long, loose coat or gown; 2. a cloak or long coat worn by soldiers in the sixteenth and seventeenth centuries

cassaddell: probably a cart* saddle

cast nett: 1. a fishing net for sweeping the bottom of the river; 2. unknown (see *199*)

casting shovell: a large shovel for casting grain in winnowing

casy: kersey*

cateles, cattel, cattelles: kettle*

caules: calves

cawcers: saucers*

cawdron: cauldron: a large vessel for boiling, with handles or something to stand it on or suspend it over a fire

cearchowes: kerchiefe*

ceatle: kettle*

ceffates: unknown

cellar, celler: 1. a storage room, above or below ground; 2. salt* cellar

cellar of glasses: a box for holding drinks and glasses

cemnles: kimnel*

cestern: cistern: 1. a tank for storing water; 2. applied to different types of large containers for holding liquid or food; 3. the water tank in which grain was soaked in malting. The earliest example in *OED* for the third definition post-dates these inventories but is consistent with the inventory usage.

ceteles, cetles, cetteles, cettels, cettles: kettles*

ceverled: coverlet*

chadger: charger*

chafer, chaffer: a vessel for heating water or food

chaffe: 1. cut hay and straw used for feeding cattle; 2. husks of grain, peas or beans separated by threshing or winnowing

chaffe house: probably a place in which chaff in sense 1. was stored

chafing dish: a small brazier to hold burning charcoal used to keep food warm or to heat anything placed upon it

chaire stoole: a stool with a back but no arms (Yaxley)

chamer: chamber

chanendish, chanlffing dyshes: chafing* dish

chappingknyffs: choping* knyfe

charcoole: charcoal: a fuel prepared from wood and used for cooking before the widespread availability of coal
charger, chardger: a large plate or flat dish for carrying a joint of meat
charme, charne: churn*
chasse: unknown; possibly an error for casse (case*) as both occurrences of the word are in inventories with the same handwriting
chattels, chattayles, chattelles, chattles, chattls: moveable and immoveable goods. They include leases, rent for a term of years, and an interest in an advowson but do not include freehold land (Wharton).
chauendish, chaulffing dyshes: chafing* dish
chaver: chafer*
chaving dish: chafing* dish
cheachests: chairchest: a chair with a chest beneath the seat (Yaxley)
cheafinge dishe: chafing* dish
chearme: churn*
cheaste: chest*
chechene, cheching: kitchen*
cheese bord, ches bord: a circular, wooden board used in cheese-making. It was placed on the curd to press out the whey.
cheese presse: an apparatus for pressing the curd in cheese-making
cheese racke, wrack: a rack or frame for drying or storing newly made cheese
cheesfats: the vessel or mould used in cheese-making to press the curd and shape the cheese
cheffendish, chefingdishies, chefyn dyshe: chafing* dish
cheis molles: moulds in which cheese is pressed
cherchew: kercher, kerchiefe*
cherffendish: chafing* dish
cherme, cherne: churn*
chesfat: cheesfats*
chest: a wooden, joined container, with a flat lid, used for storage
chettell: uncertain; possibly a kettle
cheyers: chairs
cheyne, cheyns: chains
chichin, chiching: kitchen*
child bed linnen, lynninge: the bedding used by women when giving birth and the clothes for the baby
chimnie yrons: possibly the same as fire irons: implements for tending a fire, usually comprising a shovel, tongs and poker
chirm, chirme, chirne: churn*
chisfates: cheesfats*
chist: chest*
choping knyfe: a cleaver or chopper
chosse chare: close* chayre
chreesete: cresset: an iron lamp
churn, churm: a container in which butter is made
chushions, chushyns, chusshinges, chussins, chussions: cushions
chychyn, chykchen, chytchen: kitchen*

chyne: chine: the backbone and immediately adjoining flesh of a bacon-pig, remaining when the sides are cut off for bacon-curing
chyrme: churn*
cimnel, cimneles, cimnell: kimnels*
cittell: kettle*
civerlid: coverlet*
cives: sieves*
ckafe: calf
clake: cloak*
clarke: clerk*
claver: possibly clover
cleansinge dyshe: probably used for removing impurities from liquid. In these inventories, found in the context of dairying and brewing.
cleates, clettes: wedges. In these inventories, occurring with wood and other items in a yard.
cleaver, clever: a tool for chopping, especially a butcher's chopper for cutting up carcases
clerk, clerque: a cleric
cloak: a loose outer garment worn by men and women. See also livery* cloak.
cloase: clothes
cloath: 1. cloth; 2. clothes; 3. cloths
cloes, clooes, cloothes, clowes: cloths
cloke, clookes: cloak*
clooke bag: a bag for carrying a cloak* or other clothes
close: 1. an enclosed field; 2. clothes or cloths
close chair, chayre, stole: a chair or stool containing a chamber pot
closet, clossit: in these inventories, a room for storage
cloth basket: basket*
coale: 1. charcoal (charcoole*); 2. seacoal (seacoles*)
cobb: cob: a small, sturdy horse
cobbaod, cobbardes: cupboard*
cobbarnes, cobbeiernes, cobbeyrons, cobbournes: cobirons*
cobert: cupboard*
cobirons, cobeyarnes, cobhyerns: a pair of upright iron bars, either free-standing or leaning against the back of the hearth, with hooks at intervals to support spits across the fire (Yaxley)
cocke loft: a small, upper loft directly under the ridge of a roof, usually accessed by a ladder
cocke of hay: haycock
coet: coat
coffer, cofare, coferre: a storage chest or box with a curved lid, in contrast to the flat lid of a chest (Yaxley)
coffer box: probably a cross between a coffer* and a box*; maybe a box with a curved lid
cofferled: coverlet*
coffin: a pie-dish or mould, made of pewter
coke, cokk: cock

cole, coles: charcoole*, seacoles*
cole fier: probably a coal fire
cole pan: probably a container for coale*
cole rack, rake: for raking ashes from an oven, furnace or fire
coleirons: andirons adapted for use with coal fires by fixing horizontal bars to hold the coal (Yaxley)
colendre, colinder: colander: a container, usually of metal, closely perforated at the bottom with small holes, and used as a sieve or strainer in cooking
coleurs, collarres, collers: collar: part of a horse's harness, made of leather and canvas stuffed with straw or wool, to be put around the neck of a draught animal or carthorse (*Dictionarium Rusticum*)
colter: coulter*
***com', comitatus*:** county
come of iorn: unknown; possibly a currycomb or main comb, tools used in barns and stables (*Dictionarium Rusticum*)
come of whete: coomb: a weight of 4 bushels of grain
commodytyes: commodity: a benefit or convenience to a person
common feilde: the open fields
compas: compost, manure
coobbard, coobbert, coobord: cupboard*
coofers, cooffer: coffer*
cooking kivers: kiver*
cooler: a container for cooling liquids e.g. milk, or the wort in brewing
coolorde: cupboard*
coopery, cooperie: wooden vessels such as casks*, buckets and tubs*, made or repaired by a cooper
cooples: couples*
coosschyns: cushions
cooverlets: coverlet*
copfer: coffer*
***copia concordat*:** copy agreed
copirons: cobirons*
coples: couples*
copper: a large copper or bronze vessel, hanging on chains over a fire or fixed in a masonry stand with a grate under it and used for heating water, boiling clothes and brewing etc. (Yaxley)
copper coverlaid: a copper-coloured coverlet*
copper ware: 1. vessels made of copper; or 2. coopery* ware
coppes: part of the plough gear; unknown. Possibly the same as copsies*.
copples: couples*
coppord: cupboard*
copsies: copsole, copsil: a wedge for keeping the coulter* of a wooden plough in place at an appropriate angle to the beam
copyrons: cobirons*
corded: bed* cords
cordes: a quantity of wood cut for fuel c.8ft x 4ft x 4ft (c.2.4m x 1.2m x 1.2m)
cordwinder: cordwainer: a shoemaker

cortaynes: curtains*
corte cupborde, table: court* cupboard, table
coshines, coshins: cushions
cote, cotte: coat
couberte: cupboard*
couch: 1. furniture for sitting or reclining on; 2. a bed without hangings
coulters: coulter: the iron blade fixed in front of the share* in a plough; it makes a vertical cut in the soil, which is sliced horizontally by the share
coultes: colts
counter: originally a board with squares used for accounting purposes. In these inventories, probably a board or working surface in a workshop or a counter* table.
counter table, cownter table: a table incorporating an accounting counter. See Yaxley for a description of how a counter table was used.
counterpane: the outer covering* of a bed, a coverlet*
couples: a ewe with a lamb
courackes: cow rack*
court cupboard: 1. a movable sideboard or cabinet used to display plate; 2. an open shelved sideboard featuring display shelves (Chinnery)
court dishes: a drinking cup (Chinnery)
court parlour: unknown
court table: unknown
courtaine: curtain*
coushens, coushings: cushions
coverlet: the uppermost covering of a bed
covering, coverringes, coverynges: a covering for a bed, hardly distinguishable from a coverlet
cow bullocke: bullocks: horned cattle of either sex (Wright)
cow racks: rack*
cow standardes: in these inventories, an upright timber in a cow house
cowbard, cowber: cupboard*
cowch: couch*
cowfars: coffer*
cowler: cooler*
cowleteres, cowlter: coulters*
cowpery, cowprey ware: coopery*
cowples: couples*
cowse: cows
cowse rackes: rack*
coysshins, cozons: cushions
cradell clothe: unknown
cradle, cradell, credle: 1. a frame for carrying or holding something; 2. a baby's cradle
cradle head cloth: head* cloth
crape: crop
creepers, creeps, crepers: a small dog* iron for supporting logs, a pair of which were placed on a hearth between the andirons*; often in pairs
crewse: cruse*

cribbes: crib: a manger, or barred holder for animal fodder. In these inventories, used for cows and sheep.
croawne, croune: crown: a gold coin worth 5s
crossclothes: a linen cloth worn across the forehead or as a head covering, especially by women
crow of iron, croe of iron: a crowbar or other iron bar
cruettes: cruet: a small container for liquids
cruse: 1. a small earthen or stoneware vessel for liquids; 2. a pot or a drinking vessel
cubberd with a presse: probably a closed cupboard, usually shelved, to keep clothes in (Yaxley)
cubberdcloath: cupboard* cloth
cubburd: cupboard*
cuhshins, cuisheins: cushions
cuk: cock
cullander, cullender: colander (colendre*)
cullter, cultors: coulter*
cumberd: cupboard*
cumpas: compost; manure
cupboard: 1. originally a 'board' for displaying cups and dishes, pewter or plate; 2. a cabinet with shelves, for keeping cups, dishes, etc., and provisions ready for use
cupboard cloth: a cloth used to cover a cupboard
cupbord carpet: carpet*
cup-dishes: unknown
cupples: couples*
curbe: the framing around the top of a brewer's copper or furnace
curry: a small cart; the earliest example in *OED* is from 1682
currycombe: curry-comb: a comb or metal instrument used for currying or grooming horses
curtaine rods: rods for curtains around a bed or window
curtains, curten, curtines, curtyns: 1. hung around a bed; 2. covering a window
curtells: kirtle*
cuschins, cushcons, cushell, cusians, cussengs, cussens, cusshenes, cusshines, cusshinges, cusshins, cusshyns, cussions, cussyn, cussyones, cutchins, cutshens: cushions
cutworke: openwork embroidery or lace worn in the late sixteenth and seventeenth centuries
cuverletes: coverlet*
cuverynges: covering*
cuyssions: cushions
cypres: cypress: a thin, transparent material usually of silk and linen mix, sometimes with a crepe weave, used for linings, hat bands and, especially in black, for mourning

damask, danaske: a rich, silk fabric woven with elaborate designs and figures, often of a variety of colours (*OED*); a monochrome figured fabric of silk, linen or wool (Cumming). In these inventories, used to describe napkins* and testers*.
darnacles, darnix: dornix*

dary, dayrye: dairy

day howse, dayrie howsse: dairy

***de eadem*:** of the same (place)

deale: 1. a portion or an amount; 2. a plank of wood 9in x 3in x 6ft; originally of fir or pine

debpts: debts*

debte booke: an account-book in which debts are recorded

debts desperate: desperate debts: bad debts, unlikely to be recovered

debts sperat: debts which it was anticipated would be recovered

deed of gift: a gift made by a deed in writing and signed

defeasaunce: defeasance: a collateral deed or other document expressing a condition which, if fulfilled, renders the deed or contract null and void; a clause or condition having this function

deseborde: unknown; possibly a board used as a desk for writing

deske, desckes: 1. a table or board on which to write; 2. possibly a separate freestanding desk box which could be placed on a table

desperate, desperatt dettes, despatt debptes, desprat: debts*

detts sperat: debts*

***di, dimd, dmi*:** dimidium: half

diaper, diapre, dieper, dyaper, dyeper, dyoper: a linen fabric with a diamond pattern and the spaces filled by parallel lines, a central leaf or dot, etc. In these inventories, used to describe cloths, napkins* and towels.

dicker: a quantity of ten hides or skins

dimity: stout cotton fabric, woven with raised stripes or fancy figures; usually used undyed for beds and bedroom hangings, and sometimes for garments (*OED*); a fine fustian* (Cumming)

dishborde: probably a shelf for storing dishes

doblett: doublet*

dobnetes: small cooking pots

doe trough: trough* for dough

dog irons, yron dogges, pair of dogges: iron supports for the logs of an open hearth, usually in pairs, consisting of a bar with a pair of legs at each end placed on either side of the centre of the hearth (Yaxley)

dogget: unknown

doggne: dung, compost

donge: for items beginning with dong see dung*

dore: doors would only be listed if they were treated as moveable

dornix, dorniskes, dornyx: a silk, worstedd*, woollen, or partly woollen fabric, originally manufactured in Tournai (*OED*), and in the sixteenth century, made in Norfolk copying Flemish silk or worsted fabrics (Cumming). In these inventories, used for carpets*, coverlets*, cushions and canopies*.

double clothes: unknown; in the context of baby clothes, possibly nappies (editorial)

double gilt: gilded with a double coating of gold (Cox)

doublet: a close-fitting body-garment, with or without sleeves, worn by men from the fourteenth to the eighteenth centuries; a doublet and hose was typical male attire

dounge: for items beginning with dounge see dung*

downe: the fine, soft feathers forming the inner layer of a bird's plumage, used in these inventories for stuffing beds (bed*), bolsters* and pillows

dradge: dredge: mixture of various kinds of grain, especially of oats and barley, sown together

drafftes: as a pair of iron drafftes: unknown

drag, dragge: a heavy harrow* used for breaking up ground or clods of earth

drag raak, racke, raikes, rake, rockes: a hand tool, a long shaft with a wide head having wooden or iron teeth, used to gather corn, hay, wood, etc. (Yaxley)

dragg nett: unknown in this context

drak rake: drag*

draughes for a cart, iron: unknown

draught rake: drag*

draughtes, pair of: unknown

draweng, drawght, drawinge, drawte rake: possibly the same as drag* rakes

drawers: a sliding, open-topped box within the frame of a larger piece of furniture which could be pulled out, rare until the late sixteenth century (Chinnery)

drawing steares: probably steers used as draught animals

drawing table: a table that may be extended by drawing out leaves

drawingknyfe: a blade with a handle at each end, used for shaving or scraping a surface; a farrier's knife

drawne work: ornamental work done in textile fabrics by drawing out some of the threads to form patterns, with or without the addition of needlework. In these inventories, used for cushions.

dressed, drest: 1. to prepare something for consumption or use; 2. to separate corn from chaff (Batchelor). In these inventories, applied to crops and leather.

dresser: 1. a sideboard used for storing crockery, glasses, cutlery and other dining items; 2. a dresser* board

dresser board, dressyng bourde: a board used for dressing or preparing something, in particular a kitchen table or surface on which food is prepared before serving

dresser box: unknown; some type of storage container

drie sheepe, dry ship, drye shepe: unknown; probably sheep without lambs

driinge rake: a rack for drying something, e.g. cheese

drincke tunnell: tunnell*

drink stall, stoles: stall*

drinke barilles, barrells: barrel*

drinking cloth, drincking clothe: unknown

drinkinge stooles: stall*

dripping panne: a pan used to catch the dripping from meat roasting on a spit

dripping pot: presumably a pot to hold dripping

dry, drie, drye, fatt, trough, tub: a large vessel for dry goods, as opposed to liquids

drynck buttrye: buttery*

dryngkyn tub, drynke tubbs: tubs*

dubblettes, dublates: doublet*

dublas: probably dowlais, a coarse linen

dukes: ducks

dung cart: a cart for carrying dung, earth, refuse, etc.; especially one with a tilting body

dung forke: a large, long-handled fork, typically with three or four tines, used for lifting, turning or spreading dung, compost

dung hokes: dung hook: unknown, but differs from a dung fork which is listed with it in the same inventory

dung raake: dung rake: a long-handled tool with downward-curving tines, used to rake up, spread or turn dung

dunn: dun: a horse of a dull, greyish-brown colour

durance: a stout, durable, closely woven worstedd*

dy-: see di- except for word below

dyehowse: the building in which a dyer carried on his trade

ear pickers: an instrument for cleaning wax from the ear

eares: pan with ears, a stean*

earthen, erthen: earthenware, pottery made of clay. In these inventories, applied to cruses*, dishes, pans, pitchers (picheres*), platters*, pots* and steans*.

Easter book: a vicar's account book for recording Easter dues

edge graine, edge sowen: 1. grain that ripens irregularly due to lack of rain or damage by bad weather (Wright); 2. grain grown on headlands, which were initially unploughed, then ploughed at right angles and sown

ekes: unknown

ell, eles, elles, ells, elnes: a cloth width of 45 inches (1.14m)

elyng tub: yealding*

enterrer: unknown

enther bed: unknown

entry, entrye, entrey, entrie: an area or lobby (usually small) between the entrance of a house and the chimney stack, with rooms either side (editorial)

ere: year

esquire: a member of the gentry, ranking below a knight

Eton: Eaton Socon. Eton and Eaton are the spellings most often recorded by A. Mawer and F. M. Stenton, *The Place-Names of Bedfordshire & Huntingdonshire*, p. 54.

eve: ewe

eveslath: laths used in a roof

ewer, ewre: a pitcher with a wide spout, used to hold water for washing the hands. Often listed with a basin.

exe, exses: axe

exe trees, exteryes, extries: axetree*

extry pynnes: linch pins: to keep the wheel on the axetree* (*Dictionarium Rusticum*)

Eyton: Eaton Bray. Eiton and Eyton are the spellings most often recorded by A. Mawer and F. M. Stenton, *The Place-Names of Bedfordshire & Huntingdonshire*, p. 121.

face cloth: probably a faced* cloth

faced cloathe: a woollen cloth with a smooth nap (*OED*); a cloth with different finishes on front and back (Cumming)

fagattes, faggot: a bundle of sticks, twigs or brushwood tied together for use as fuel

fall cowe: in this context, possibly a cow which has just given birth

falling, falinge table: a type of folding table in which the leaf or leaves are hinged from a fixed central board, and hang down when not in use (Chinnery)

falling yates: a gate at the entrance to an enclosure for livestock

fallinge band: broad band of fabric fastened at the neck and lying flat against the body; a form of collar or neckerchief (Chinnery)

false raves: rails or boards added to the sides of a cart to enable a greater load to be carried

fan, fam: a basket used for winnowing threshed corn from the chaff by throwing it into the air

fare chest: either a fair chest or a fir chest

farges baryll: barrel of verjuice (verges*)

fassyll: vessel

fat, fates, fatt: vat*

fatting keene: cows being fattened

feather bed, fatherbedd: a bed* or mattress* filled with feathers

feches, fecthes: vetches*

feddare: feather

fele: foal

fell wouII: wool pulled from a sheepskin, rather than shorn from a live animal

felles: the skin or hide of an animal with the hair or wool

ferkyn: firkin*

ferne: ferns: used for fuel

fernised: furnished

ferr, chest of: probably a chest made from fir

fetches: vetches*

fetherbed matteris: featherbed* or mattress*

fetherbed ticke: tick*

fetters, fettars, fetteres: fetters, especially for hobbling horses; often described as a pair

field bed, bedsteade: a portable or folding bed, originally used by soldiers in the field. Later, also a bed with an arched canopy and covered sides.

fill geares, straps, stroppes: thill*

fils: in this context, probably files used by a blacksmith

fire, fyer stick: a poker

fire pan: a pan for holding or carrying burning fuel

fire shovell, fireshule: fire shovel. In these inventories, often with tongs and a fire fork in the context of gridirons* and pothangers*.

fire slyce: 1. a fire shovel; 2. a tool for clearing clinker etc. from the bars of a furnace

firefork, fyreforke: a pronged instrument for tending a fire

firkins: a small cask for liquids, fish, butter, etc., originally containing a quarter of a barrel or half a kilderkin*

fitches: vetches*

flaggye: limp, drooping

flagon, flaggon: a large bottle for holding wine

flask: a container made of horn, leather or metal for carrying liquid

flasket: a long, shallow basket, made of osiers or cloth

flax: the plant *Linum usitatissimum* bearing blue flowers which are succeeded by pods containing the seeds commonly known as linseed. It is cultivated for its textile fibre and for its seeds. In these inventories, it occurs extensively as a material in different qualities (harden*, tare* and tow*) for clothing and household linen, such as cloths, napkins*, pillowbears*, sheets and towels.

flaxen, flaxin, flaxson, flaxyn: a linen made from flax. In these inventories, it is used for household and bed linen.

flayles: flail: an implement for threshing grain

fleake: flake: 1. a wattle hurdle; 2. a temporary gate; 3. a frame or rack for storing or drying provisions, hung on the wall to reduce the chance of depredation from rats and mice (Cox)

fleaked howse: unknown

flease of wolle: fleece

fleccon, flecson, flexen, flexon, flexson, flexsyn: flaxen*

fleeches, fleet, fleetch: flitch*

flees, fleses, flesses: fleece

fletcher: a maker of bows and arrows

flitch, fletches, fliche, flicke, flicthes, flitches, flittches: flitch of bacon: the salted and cured side of a pig or hog

flock, flockis: coarse tufts and refuse of wool. In these inventories, used to stuff beds*, bolsters* and pillows.

flower: 1. flour; 2. flower

flyches, flycke, flyshe, flytches, flythe: flitch*

folding table, folded, folden: a table with a folding top with a separate leaf or leaves hinged from a fixed top board, folding over and lying on top of it when closed (Chinnery). Different from a falling* table.

foldinge cloth: unknown

folio: a book of the largest size

folkes chamber: folks: retainers, servants, workpeople; a servants' room

followe plowes: unknown

folow grond: probably fallow ground

folte table: folding* table

foole, foolles: foals

foot pace, footpasse: 1. a raised platform or step; 2. a fixed or portable wooden step. In these inventories, often associated with beds.

foote presse: unknown; possibly another name for a foot pace. In these inventories, less likely to be associated with beds than foot paces.

foote teames: a short chain connected to a plough or harrow

footestole: a low stool, usually joined, and associated with a chair (Chinnery)

forcer: 1. a chest*, coffer* or casket; 2. a small box* or chest* often for important papers, valuables or money and sometimes strengthened with iron bands (Chinnery)

foreyard: the yard or court in front of a building

forke steales: the handle of a fork

form: a long seat without a back, a bench

fornace: furnace*

fornitudde: furniture*

forrest bill: a woodman's bill-hook, for lopping trees

forser, forster, foser, fossar, fosser: forcer*

foulded, foulden, foulding, foult table: folding* table

fouling gun: fowling piece: a light gun for shooting wild fowl
fowldyd, fowlte table: folding* table
frame, framed, fraime, fram: furniture and buildings made with a frame, distinct from a boarded or solid construction. In these inventories, applied to bedsteads*, forms*, hovels*, tables* and trestles*.
frendg, freng: fringed*
frese, frice, friese: frieze: a coarse woollen cloth with a nap usually on one side only. In these inventories, used for coats.
freute: fruit
frieing, frieng pan: frying* pan
frieshovell: fire shovel
friing, friinge fring pann, fringpane: frying* pan
fringed, frindge: decorated with a fringe. In these inventories, applied to chairs, cupboards* clothes, curtains*, stools*, valances*, window cushions.
friyng, friynge panne, fruinge pan: frying* pan
frwite: fruit
fryeing, fryeng panne: frying* pan
frying pan: a shallow pan, usually of iron, with a long handle, for frying food
fryjnge, fryng pane: frying* pan
fryse: frieze (frese*)
fugurato: figuretto: a figured material (*OED*); a costly flowered material, possibly woven with metalic threads (Cumming)
fuller: a person whose occupation is fulling* cloth
fullers earth: a fine-grained clay used by a fuller in cleaning woollen cloth
fullers handilles: possibly a pair of handles in which teasels were fixed to raise the nap on woollen cloth; or the handles of shears
fullers nyppars: unknown; probably pincers or pliers used by a fuller
fulling: the process of beating cloth to clean and then thickening it
fulling, fullenge troughe: presumably the trough in which cloth is steeped for fulling
fulling myll: a mill in which cloth is fulled. In the earliest fulling mills, which were usually water-driven, the cloth was beaten with wooden mallets.
fur chest: probably a chest made from fir
furme: form*
furnace, furnase, furnasse, furnes, furnice, furnis/e, furnys: 1. a cauldron (cawdron*); 2. a heat source, either free-standing or built-in, and found in kitchens, backhouses (bakehouses?), brewhouses, milkhouses, and woad- and dyehouses. The term is clearly applied to apparatus of varied size and complexity.
furnished: equipped with whatever was appropriate to the item being described
furniture: 1. furniture for a bed, e.g. mattress*, pillows, bolsters*, etc.; 2. furniture belonging to husbandry, e.g. the gear for ploughs and carts, collars and harnesses for horses; 3. parts of a loom
furse, furzeas: furze or gorse, used for fuel
fustian, fuschane, fustyan: a coarse cloth made of cotton and flax
fy-: for words beginning fy-, see fi- except as below
fypes: unknown
fyreshover: fire* shovel

gable roope: the rope running in the gable wheel mechanism in a mill to hoist sacks (http://goldenwindmill.org/training/wheels.pdf)
gaires: gears*
gallerie: a long narrow room, sometimes serving as a passage to other parts of a house
gallon: a liquid measure of 8 pints (4.55 litres)
garner, gardner: garner: a storehouse or container for grain
garrett: garret: a room at the top of a house
gat, gates: a gate or a hurdle used as a gate
gears, gayers, geeres, geres: in these inventories, used as a general term for the apparatus of carts*, looms*, mills and ploughs* and harness for animals pulling carts and ploughs
geaste: gest*
geeis: geese
gentleman: a member of the gentry, entitled to bear arms, though not ranking among the nobility
gerdle: girdle: 1. a belt worn round the waist; 2. used to carry light articles
gerkeins, gerkens: jerkins*
gese: geese
gest: 1. geason: barren, unproductive. In these inventories, applied to cattle and sheep; 2. a guest room
geyse: geese
gient: joined*
gig, gige, gigge: 1. a winnowing fan (Wright); 2. possibly a larger piece of equipment for the same purpose
gilt: coated with gold leaf
gin, gynne: 1. a trap; 2. an apparatus for hoisting heavy weights
girkyns, gyrkyn: jerkins*
girth, girte, gyrt, gyrthe: 1. a girth: a leather or cloth band, drawn tightly round the body of a horse to secure a saddle or pack; 2. great (Batchelor); 3. in the context of a bed, webbing laid straight or diagonally across the frame of a bedstead (Holme)
glasscase, cupbord or shelf: an item of furniture to hold or display glasses (Chinnery)
glasseyes: glasses
goblet: a bowl-shaped metal or glass drinking cup, without handles, usually with a foot and sometimes a cover
going geares: a combination of wheels and levers to make a mill work
goldwayghts: scales for weighing gold
golins: goslings
gooddee: goody: a courtesy form of address for a woman, usually a married woman of low social status
gose, gosse pan, gostpan: a pan for cooking a goose
gosse yoake: probably a yoke for geese
gown: a loose, flowing outer garment, often indicating status
gowse penne: 1. a pen for a goose (cf. hen* pen); 2. a pan for cooking a goose
grate iron, grate-yron: possibly the same as an iron grate
gray pease: a variety of peas, suited to cold, wet, clay soils, sown in February at the rate of 2 bushels of seed to the acre (*Dictionarium Rusticum*)
graye pleyn: a type of cloth

grdiorne: gridiron*
greane: grain
greanstone: grindstone*
gredeyron, gredyer, gredyrons: gridiron*
greene, grene: grain
greid-eiorne: gridiron*
grend stone, grenstone: grindstone*
gresse: grease: the rendered fat of animals, used as an ingredient in soap and remedies for injuries to animals and humans (*Dictionarium Rusticum*). In these inventories, kept in churns*, pots* or cupboards*.
greydyoren, greyron: gridiron*
gridiron, griddirne, grideyarn, gridgiron: a cooking device formed of parallel bars of iron or other metal in a frame, usually supported on short legs, and used for broiling flesh or fish over a fire
grindle stone: grindstone* (Batchelor)
grindstone: a thick disc of stone revolving on an axle (or spindle), and used for grinding, sharpening or polishing
grist sackes: sacks of corn to be ground
gritts: oats that have been husked but not ground (or only coarsely); coarse oatmeal
grograyne, grogen: grogram: a coarse fabric of silk or silk and wool
grydarne, gryddyorne, grydirne: gridiron*
grydyll ston: grindstone*
grynding stone, gryndston, grynstone: grindstone*
guedlinges: geldings
guest: gest*
guilded, guilt, guilte, gylte: gilded, gilt*
***Gulielmus*:** William
gy-: for words beginning gy-, see gi-, except for words below
gyes: geese
gyned: joined*
gyntell: gentleman*
gyrdlyerne: gridiron*
gyst: gest*

hackney stable: a stable for horses
hadges: hogs*
hail house: hall-house: the principal living-room in a farm-house
haire cloth: cloth made of hair. In these inventories, it is found in outbuildings but it is not clear what it was used for; possibly the same as a haire* sive or a kiln* haire
haire safe: 1. possibly the same as haire* sive; 2. possibly a safe or cupboard lined with haircloth (to keep out insects) in which food was stored
haire sives: hair sieve: a sieve made of hair cloth stretched over a circular wooden frame, used for sifting and cleaning meal before use (Chinnery)
halberde: a weapon with a spearhead or spike above an axe blade and a hooked back, on a pole of around 1.8 metres long
hale: hall
half boshell wait: a measure or weight of half a bushel (c. 18.2 litres)

half headed bed (and bedstead): definitions vary. All agree that it was a bed with short corner posts; some add without a tester canopy, and others that it had a canopy over the head of the bed only.
half peck: a unit of capacity for dry goods, one-eighth of a bushel (approx. 4.55 litres)
halfe inche bordes: boards or planks of half an inch thickness (1.27cm)
hallan, hallon sheet: holland*
halling, hallyn, hallyng: a tapestry* or painted* cloth for the walls of a hall
halter, halltares: a rope to go over the head of animals to lead or fasten them
hame: haulm (haume*)
hamper: a large, covered basket often of wickerwork, generally used as a packing-case
hamps: unknown
hand basket: a small basket to be carried in the hand
hand giorns: andirons*
hand Ieornes, hand Irons, handdiernes, handirons: andirons*
hand mill: a hand-operated mill for grinding corn, etc., consisting of two stones, the upper of which is rotated on the lower; a quern
hande peeles: peele*
handells, handills: fullers* handills, plough* handells
handkerchers: handkerchiefs
hand-riddle: a hand-held sieve
handyron: andirons*
hangenges, hanges: hangings (hangines*)
hangers, hanggares: pot* hangers
hangines, hangyng: hangings: 1. wall hangings; 2. bed curtains; 3. painted* cloths. Sometimes described as a pair.
hanginge candlestick: probably attached to a wall
hangles, hangeles of iron: an iron chain for suspending a cooking pot over the fire (Chinnery)
hankyns: hangings (hangines*)
happharlett: hapharlot: a coarse bedcovering or coverlet*
hardells: hurdles*
harden, harten: coarse linen made from the hard fibres of flax* or hemp* (Yaxley). In these inventories, used for household linen and wearing linen.
hare safe: haire* safe
hare syfe, syffe: haire* sieve
hareclothe, hayre cloth: haire* cloth
harneis, harnes: harness for horses or other animals
harrow, harow, harroes, harroos: harrow: a heavy timber or iron frame set with teeth, which is dragged over ploughed land to break clods, root up weeds or cover seeds. Sometimes made in two halves, and then called harrows or a pair of harrows.
harrow sleed: a sledge on which harrows were transported (Yaxley)
hatchell, hattchelles: hatchel: a tool with sharp teeth for combing out flax* and hemp*
hatchet, hachat, hacthet, hatched, hathct: a small, short-handled axe designed to be used with one hand
haulters: halter*

haume: haulm: the straw from various crops; might be used for thatching
havill: hovel*
hawe: probably a hoe
hawling, hawlyng: halling*
hay hooke: for pulling hay from a rick or stack
hayffers: heifers*
hayre cupbord: possibly a haire* safe
hayre for the kill: kiln* haire
hea: hay
head bandes: a strip of material worn round the head; also called a cross cloth (Cumming)
head cloth: 1. a covering for the head; 2. cloth hung over the head of a bed, in these inventories, over a baby's cradle
head peese: headpiece: a helmet or armour for a person's or horse's head
headborough: parish officer having the same role as a petty constable
heahouse: hayhouse
hearden, heardyn: harden*
hearst of velvet: unknown; possibly a hearse cloth or funeral pall for covering a bier or coffin
hearsyve: haire* sive
heay: hay
hecfer, hecforsse, hecforth, heckffordes, heckforth: heifer*
hechyll, heckles: a tool for combing prepared hemp* fibres
hedginge bill: a bill with a long handle used in cutting and trimming hedges
hegsheds: hogshead*
heifer, heiforde, hekefers: a young cow, especially one that is over one year but has not yet calved
heire clothe: haire* cloth
hemblocke: unknown; possibly the same as hempe* stock
hemp: an annual herbaceous plant, *Cannabis sativa*, cultivated for its fibre, which was used for household linen and clothing. See Cox for a description of its preparation for spinning and weaving. In these inventories, it may be used interchangeably with flax*.
hemp brake: an instrument for bruising or breaking hemp*, more specifically for peeling the outer skin of hemp from its core (Cox)
hemp tow, hemptoo: tow*
hempe hards: the hard fibre of flax* or hemp*
hempe land: land used to grow hemp*
hempe stock, hemstock: perhaps a wooden frame for drying hemp* (the only source is Joy Bristow, *The Local Historian's Glossary of Words and Terms*, Newbury, 2001)
hempe teare, teere, hemptar, hemptare: tare*
hempe tresels: possibly the frame to lay hemp* on for drying (*Dictionarium Rusticum*)
hen casse: a hen* pen
hen pen, henpe: a hen coop or enclosure for poultry, often in the house
hengles: hangles* or hangeles*

heor for a kylne: kilne* haire
heowe: ewe
heoy: hay
herden: harden*
herrowes: harrows*
hetch: hutch*
hetchele, hetchell: hatchell*
hettchett: hatchet*
hevell: hovel*
heycoke: haycock
heyfer, heyfor, heyford, heyghforthe: heifers*
hiche land: hitched land: part of the common field withdrawn by common consent from the customary rotation (especially in the fallow year) and used for a particular crop such as vetches* (Wright)
hillings: coverings*, a bed quilt
hirdles: hurdles*
hoases: in this context, probably a stable or hovel*
hobbing iron, hobingyron, hobiron: 1. part of a grate or fireplace; 2. a shoemaker's tool, possibly a last (Wright). Neither of these definitions are satisfactory in the context. Possibly the same as hobbing scythe, used for mowing high tufts of grass (Wright).
hode: unknown
hodes, hodges: hogs*
hodgtroufe: hogstrough*
hoffels, hoffelles: hovel*
hoggescoates, hodgscoate, hoggs coats: hog cote: a pigsty
hoggesetroughes, hoggestroves, hoggestrowes, hoggs trowgh: hogstrough*
hoggetubbe: hogstrough*
hoggrell: hoggerel: a young sheep, especially one in its second year
hogherd: a person who tends hogs
hogs, hogges: 1. a domestic pig reared for slaughter; 2. a young sheep from the time it is weaned until its first shearing
hogshead, hodgsheads, hogeshedd, hogges hed: hogshead: a large cask, especially for storing liquids, containing 54 gallons of ale or beer (c. 245.5 litres) or 52½ gallons of wine (c. 238 litres)
hogstrough: a trough from which hogs* or pigs eat
hogstye, hoogge stie: a pigsty
holland, hollan, hollon, holonte: a good quality linen used for clothing such as shirts and smocks* and for sheets, napkins* and towels
hoppes, hopps: hops
horse corn: beans and oats
horse lockis, loke, horselock: a hobble or shackle for a horse's feet
horse racke: a container or manger for holding fodder, either fixed to a wall or moveable
hose, hosen, hosse, pair of: 1. men's clothing for the legs, sometimes only reaching down to the ankle, sometimes also covering the foot; 2. breeches

hostlery: stable
hotchel: hatchell*
houche: hutch*
houe, hooves, hoves, howe: hoe
houevell, houfelles: hovel*
houfe: unknown; possibly a hoe
hous, pair of: hose*
house of office: outside privy
hovel, hoviles, hovyls, howell, howfeildes: an outhouse used as a shelter for cattle, or storage for grain or tools; an open shed. As temporary structures, they could be included in inventories.
hower glass: an hour glass: a sand-glass that runs for an hour
howsen: houses
hoycke: hook
hudge: probably a hutch*
hurden: harden*
hurdles, hurdell, hyrdles: a portable rectangular frame, with interwoven infill of hazel, willow, etc., used to make temporary fences, sheep-pens or gates
husbandman, husbonne man: a farmer, below the status of a yeoman; a man who cultivated a small tenement*
husbandrie, husbandrye, husbanry: the business of farming
husslement: hustlement: odds and ends, a miscellaneous collection
huswiffe clotes: housewife's cloths: linen cloths of a quality suitable for domestic use
hutch, hutche, huch: 1. a chest or coffer for storage; 2. a box or pen for an animal
hynes: hens
hynges: hinges
hyve: bee hive

iack: jack*
ieoren, ierne, ierons: iron
ierkyns: jerkin*
ile: aisle
immoveables, immoveabell, imoveable: a legal term applied to property, such as land, things on it and rights over it, e.g. trees, buildings, servitudes
impell, impelle mentes: implements
***Imprimis*:** firstly
inboed: inbowed: concave
indented: the wavy edge to a document, where two copies written on the same sheet were separated. The counterparts were kept by different people (or the court and the executors or administrators) and could be fitted together to verify the document.
ine: probably joined*
inebed: probably a joined* bedstead
Ingles croune: an English crown: from 1544, a gold coin worth 5s
inneholder: defined as synonymous with innkeeper. In these inventories, the term innholder is used more frequently than innkeeper.

inner palyng: probably a paling or fence

***Institucion of Christian religion*:** either: 1. Jean Calvin, *The institution of Christian religion*, published in 1536 and first published in English in London in 1561; or 2. Alexander Nowell, A *cathechisme, or institution of Christian religion: to be learned of all youth next after the little cathechisme, appointed in the Booke of common prayer*, London, 1577.

intestate: a person who died without making a will

inwarde hedges: possibly the hedges nearest the house

ioke: yoke*

iorne: iron

ioyd, ioynde, ioynened, ioynid, ioynte: joined*

ioynter: jointure: an estate limited to the life of a widow, providing maintenance for her after the death of her husband

iren, irn, irne, iyron: iron

irish mantle: a blanket or plaid made in Ireland and worn by all levels of society; it was also exported to England (Cox)

iugges: jug

jack, jagcke: 1. a device for turning a spit for roasting meat over an open fire, sometimes described as a pair of jacks; 2. a drinking vessel, a black* jack; 3. a shortened form of the term jacket (jakett*); 4. a device for lifting heavy weights

jack stufe: unknown

jakett: jacket: an outer garment, with or without sleeves, worn over the doublet

jerkin, jerkyn, jearkyne: a man's close-fitting jacket, often of leather, with or without sleeves and having a short skirt; worn over the doublet* (Cumming)

jine, jynn: gin*

joggell: jogget, jobbet or jubbet, a small load, especially of hay (Wright)

joined, joinde, joine, joyned: wooden furniture made by a joiner, rather than a carpenter, and fitted together with joints. In these inventories, applied to bedsteads*, frames*, stools*, tables and other furniture.

joyces, joystes, joysts: the timbers on which the boards of a floor or the laths* of a ceiling were nailed

june: joined*

kafe, kave: calf

kanche of rye: canch*

kans: canne*

kanstyc: candlesticks*

karchers: kerchiefe*

kauffer: coffer*

keachyn, kechyn, kechyng: kitchen*

keateles: kettle*

keercher: kerchiefe*

kemneles: kimnel*

kene: kine*

kercheif, kercher, kerchewes: kerchiefe*

kerchiefe, kyrcheyffes: 1. cloth used to cover the head, formerly a woman's head-dress; 2. a covering for the breast, neck, or shoulders. Short for neckerchief (Cumming).

kersey: coarse cloth, woven from long wool and usually ribbed

kettle, kettell, kettilles, kettls, kettylles: a round, copper alloy or iron vessel, widening at the top and having a looped handle attached to the upper rim to suspend it over a fire. It did not have a spout as modern kettles do.

keverledes, keverlets, keverlettes, keverlletes: coverlet*

keverryn, keverynge, keveryns: coverings*

key, keyne, kien: kine*

kilderkin: a cask for liquids, fish, etc. set in 1532 at 18 gallons* for beer and 16 gallons for ale (see Yaxley for a summary of barrel capacities.)

kill: kiln*

kiln: furnace or oven for burning, baking or drying items. In these inventories, used for making malt*.

kiln haire/hare/hayre/heare: a cloth of hair or fine thread, laid on the floor of a malt* kiln, for spreading sprouted barley on so that it could be dried by hot air from a furnace

kiln howse: a building containing a furnace for drying grain, hops, etc. or for making malt*

kimnel, kimbnill, kimmel, kimmill, kimnailes, kimnyles, kinelles, kinmell, kymmelles, kymnyllys: 1. a tub used for brewing, kneading, salting meat and other household purposes; 2. a shallow, wooden vessel for milk to set in (Batchelor)

kine, kye, kyen: cow

kirtle, kyrtylles: a woman's gown, skirt or outer petticoat* (*OED*). A full kirtle comprised a skirt and bodice (bodyes*); a half kirtle was the skirt only (Cumming).

kishin: kitchen*

kitchen, kiching, kytchenne, kytchin: a room in which food was prepared or cooked

kitchinor: kitchen*

kitle, kittelles: kettle*

kiver: 1. a cover; 2. a shallow, wooden vessel or tub; 3. such a vessel used for setting milk (Batchelor) or cooking

kiverlets, kiverlides: coverlets*

klokes: cloak

kneading: preparing dough for making bread. In these inventories, kneading was done on boards, in kimnels*, troughs* and tubs*.

knobes: 1. a small rounded ball, often as decoration at the end of an item; 2. with a perfuming panne: meaning unknown

koberdes: cupboard*

kocke: cock

kofers: coffer*

kolte: colt

kosshyns: cushions

koverges: coverings*

koverled: coverlet*

kowe: cow

kowlle: cooler*

kubberd, kubbord: cupboard*
kurde siffe: curd sieve
kushinns: cushions
ky-: see ki- except for items below
kylet: unknown; possibly a skillet*
kyll, kylle, kylne: kiln*
kymlyns: probably kimnel*
kyssynges: cushion
kytte: possibly kettle*
kyttle, kyttylles: kettle*
kyverleds: coverlet*
kyyn: kine*

l: li*
lace, lased: 1. sewn or fastened with laces; 2. trimmed with ornamental work or braid
laine: lamb
lam hog, lambe hooges: a lamb of the second year
lammes: lambs
landes, lands: 1. a strip in the common fields; 2. a yardland; also hempe* land
landirons, lanndirons: andirons*
lane: lawn: fine linen, resembling cambric
larder house, lardry: a room or closet for storing meat and other provisions
lastes: 1. a wooden or metal model of the foot on which boots and shoes were shaped; 2. a measure of volume or weight, e.g. a last of wool was 12 sacks and a last of hides was 12 dozen
lath: a thin, narrow strip of wood used to form a groundwork upon which to fasten slates or tiles on a roof or the plaster on a wall or ceiling
latten, latteyne, lattin, laton, latyn: latten: a yellow alloy of copper, tin and a little lead, resembling brass (Yaxley). In these inventories, used for basins, candlesticks*, dishes, ladles, lavers*, mortar* and other cooking ware.
lattices, lattese: lattice: an open structure made of laths*, wood or metal crossed and fastened together, used as a screen, e.g. in window openings
laught: loft
laver, lavor: a basin, or cistern for washing
layd, layed worke: couched work or embroidery
lb: a pound weight (c. 453.6 g)
leace: lease
lead: 1. a large, open vessel made or lined with lead and, in these inventories, used in brewing; 2. a milk cooler; 3. weights used with scales; 4. a metal
leading staffe: unknown
lease in possession: a lease currently held
lease in reversion: a lease that begins when an existing lease has ended
leashe: lease
leastaves: unknown
leather jackes: jack* 2.
led, ledde, leden: lead* 4.
legge-wood: logs cut from trees, typically for use as firewood

leistow: laystow, laystall: burial place
lenan, lenenge, lenning: linen*
lentils, lentels: lentils: 'the least of all pulses', they thrive in ordinary ground and give a good yield; a sweet fodder good for calves and other young animals (*Dictionarium Rusticum*)
lether barke: oak bark used in the process of tanning leather
lettices: lattice*
levarie cubbart: livery* cupboard*
li: libra, a pound: used for both a pound weight and a pound in money (£)
lime, lyme: a solution of lime was used 1. to remove the hair from hides; 2. in cement and plaster; 3. in whitewash
lincy wollcye, lynsye woollsy: linsey-woolsey: a loosely woven cloth with a linen* warp and wool weft (Cumming)
linen, linan, lining, lyneen: cloth woven from flax*. In these inventories, possibly also used for hemp* cloth.
linen wheel: a wheel operated by hand or foot to spin flax or hemp
linne, linninie, lynneon, lynninge, lynnyng: linen*
lintels: lentils*
listes, lystes: 1. strips of cloth; 2. covers or garments made from lists
lithe: soft. In these inventories, used to describe grograyne*
livery, liverey, liverie, liverye: 1. food, clothing or accommodation provided for a retainer; 2. furniture that might be used for these purposes or generally. In these inventories, used to describe cloaks*, bedsteads*, cupboards* and tables.
loades, lodes: a unit of measure for some items: e.g. a load of hay was 36 trusses (18 cwt, c.900kg); used in these inventories for hay, vetches* and wood
lockeram, lokarum: linen* fabric of various grades used for household linen
lockes: horse* lockis
lockine glase: looking* glass
lodging, loginge chamber: in these inventories, used for the chamber where the deceased slept
lomber: lumber*
lomes: looms*
long cart: unknown; it may merely be a long cart
longe bill: hedginge bill* (*Dictionarium Rusticum*)
longe teames: unknown
longes therto, longtherto: belonging
lonngingc: belonging
lookes: locks
looking glass: a mirror
loom, lomes, loumes, lowmes: 1. in these inventories, used for weaving wool, hemp* or flax*; 2. a loom was also a tub or other vessel, but does not seem to have been used with this meaning in these inventories
loppe: lop: smaller branches and twigs of trees; faggot-wood not timber*
loves: unknown; possibly a laver*
loyde: load*
lugg wheeles: unknown

lugges: 1. a long stick or pole; the branch or limb of a tree; 2. a heavy piece of wood fastened to an animal's leg, to impede movement; 3. a pole used in thatching (Wright)

lumber, lumberdes, lumberdy, lumbery, lummerie: 1. disused articles of furniture; 2. useless odds and ends

luver: possibly a laver*

ly-: see li-

made: used to describe an ark*: meaning unknown

maingers: manger*

malt: barley or other grain prepared for brewing, distilling or vinegar-making, by steeping, germinating and kiln-drying

malt howse: a building where malt* is prepared and stored and also, more generally, a brewhouse

malt mill: a mill for grinding or crushing malt*

malt querne, quarne, qwerne: a hand-mill for grinding malt*, usually consisting of two circular stones; (in *plural*) the quern stones themselves

malte screene: a large sieve for sifting malt*

maltster, malster, maltman: a person whose occupation is making malt*

manger: a long, open box or trough in a stable or barn for fodder for horses and cattle

manngie: mangy: a horse suffering from mange, a skin disease

mantle, mantell: a loose, sleeveless cloak worn by men, women and children

mark: a monetary unit of two-thirds of a pound sterling (13s 4d), but not a coin

marter: unknown; possibly martell, a hammer

marys: mares

maser, masser: mazer: a bowl or drinking cup, usually without a foot, made from a burr or knot of a maple tree and frequently mounted with silver or silver-gilt bands at the lip and base

mashe, mashing, masshinge, masshyng: the process of mixing ground malt with hot water in a vat* or tub* to form wort*

mashing stall: stall*

masline, maseldine: maslin: 1. a mixture of several kinds of grain, grown together, especially rye mixed with wheat; 2. a mixture of grain and pulses, especially oats mixed with peas

master: 1. a man who employs another; 2. a term of respect to a social superior; 3. a title used towards men of status or certain professions (editorial)

matdock: mattock*

matize: mattress*

matrices, matterice: mattress*

matt: mat: 1. an underlay for a bed made of woven or plaited straw (Holme) or a coarse piece of sacking (*OED*) on which a feather bed was laid; frequently described as a mat and cord; 2. a piece of a coarse material used as a protective covering for floors, walls and furniture

matt and cord: bed* cord, bed* mat

matted chair: a chair formed from woven or plaited rushes

matterce: mattress*

mattock, mattuck: a tool similar to a pick, having a point or chisel edge at one end of the head and an adze-like blade at the other, used for breaking up hard ground or grubbing up trees

mattress, mattras, matterewys, mattrice: a quilted straw or flock bed (Holme); a large rectangular case of strong fabric, filled with yielding but resilient material such as straw, hair, etc., usually forming part of a bed (*OED*). In these inventories, filled with feathers, flock*, straw or wool.

mault: malt*

maun, maund: a basket of wicker* or other woven material, or occasionally made of wooden slats, with a handle

maunger: manger*

mawlt: malt*

mawngers: manger*

mayles: unknown; possibly a mistake for railes*

meade rakes: unknown; possibly a hay rake for use in meadows

meal, meeles, mele: 1. ground grain; 2. a container for meal. In these inventories, used on its own or to describe bowls, kimnels*, sieves* and tubs*.

melch: milch*

melle: possibly a hammer or maul

messhing, meyshinge fatt, tub: mashe*

messuage: a dwelling house together with its outbuildings and the adjacent land

meswers: measures

meylle: meal*

Michaelmas: 29 September

milch, milsh, mylch, myllch, myltche: milk: applied to cows in milk or bred or kept for milk, and described as cattle, beasts* and kine*

milckehowse, mylck hows, mylke howse, mylkehouse, myke house: milk house, dairy

milhowse: 1. mill house, or 2. milk house

milkchermes: milk churns*: a container for making butter

milkein cowes: milkers

mill bills: a steel adze fixed in a wooden handle, used for dressing and cracking millstones

mill horses: a horse used for working a mill

mill stones, milston: a pair of circular stones which grind corn by the rotation of the upper stone on the lower one

millions: melons

mislin, mislyn: masline*

mistress: a courtesy title for women of the status corresponding to that of men addressed as Master. It was applied to both married and unmarried women (editorial).

mockado: fabric resembling velvet, much used for garments and trimmings in the sixteenth and seventeenth centuries

moe: more

moitie: moiety: half

moldingboord, moldeinge boarde: moulding board: a board or table on which dough or pastry was kneaded and shaped

mole staffe: a staff used to club moles

molestapple: unknown; possibly the same as mole* staffe

mortar, morter, mortis, morttr: mortar: a cup-shaped container of a hard material (e.g. marble, brass, wood) in which ingredients used in cookery were pounding with a pestle*

mottocke: mattocke*

moulding boordes: moldingboord*

moult quarne: malt* quern*

mourning ring: ring worn as a memorial for a deceased person

moveable, movabelles, moveabell: personal property; goods as opposed to immoveables*

moveable howses: probably a type of hovel* or shed that could be dismantled and moved

mowe: mow: a quantity of hay, corn, beans, peas, etc., especially a heap of grain or hay in a barn

mowledyng, mowlding bord: moldingboord*

moyne: money

muck: compost, manure

muckcart body: dung* cart

mukforkes: dung* forke

mullyn halters: mullen: a headstall or bridle for a horse

murrion: morion: a brimmed helmet, worn chiefly by foot soldiers in the sixteenth and seventeenth centuries

musket: a gun with a long barrel, typically smooth-bored and firing a large calibre muzzle-loaded ball, used by infantry and usually aimed from the shoulder or mounted on a forked stand

mustard, musterd querne: quern*

mustarde myll, musterd mill: a mill for grinding mustard seeds

my-: see mi-

nabkins: napkins*

nacar, naker: an acre*

nage, nagg: a small riding horse or pony

naperne: an apron

napery, naprye ware: linen used for household purposes, especially table linen

napkins, napkeins, napkings: 1. table napkins; 2. other napkins or small pieces of linen

neat: an ox or bullock*, cow or heifer*

neate stall: a cattle stall*

neates house: cattle house or shed

necarchers: neckercheifes*

necessary stoole: close* chair or stool

neck bandes: bandes*

neckclothes: normally a cloth worn round the neck (usually by a man), but in these inventories listed with childbed linen. See bandes*

neckercheifes, neckercher: a linen cloth worn about the neck. Also called a kerchiefe*

neckes: wooden connecting parts of a plough, illustrated in *Dictionarium Rusticum*
needle, needel worke: stitched work entirely covering a surface
nessecareys, nessesareyes, nessetares: necessaries, necessities
nest of boxes: a small cupboard, usually with a single door, containing a nest of small drawers
nest of drawers: a chest of drawers
neu: an ewe
nold, nolde, nolld: an old
norfolk lambes: Norfolk sheep: 1. described as hardy and agile, producing good meat although not much wool (N. Kent, *General View of the Agriculture of Norfolk*, 1794, p. 102); 2. renowned in 1541 for producing wool suitable for weaving worstedd* cloth (Cox)
noridge stuffe: Norwich stuff: fustian*, grograyne* or satin cloth made in Norwich (Cumming)
notary public: a person authorised by the Faculty Office to carry out certain legal formalities; in these inventories, acting in probate matters before a court
nould: an old
***nunc regis*:** of the current king.
nuncupative will: a will declared orally
nywe: new

oats, oetes: used as a food for people and animals, especially horses
oken: oak, used for furniture
olstoules: old stools*
on: one
ootes: oats*
orase: arras: a rich tapestry* fabric, in which figures and scenes are woven in colours
orchatt: orchard
otes, ottes, outtes: oats*
ovir howce: a room above another
owt: owed
ox yoakes, oxe yokes: yokes*
oxe chaine: chains used to secure oxen to a cart (*Dictionarium Rusticum*)
oxe teames, teamys: a piece of equipment (in later use especially a chain) used to harness horses or oxen to a plough, harrow or cart
oxen: used for 1. ploughing; 2. fattening for meat (*Dictionarium Rusticum*)
oytes: oats*

pack sheets, pair of: sheets for packing goods
paiell, paile, paille, pale, palles: 1. pail: a bucket; 2. paling: rails or fence
painted cloths: a wall hanging, painted with images or text
pallatte: pallet: a straw bed or mattress; an inferior bed or sleeping place
pallenger: unknown; possibly a porringer* or pottinger*
palse: unknown; probably palings
pan with two eares: steane*
panelles, pannell, pannylls: panel: 1. a piece of cloth placed under a saddle to protect the horse's back; a saddle pad; 2. a saddle, especially a simple frameless pad to which loads may be fastened; 3. panniers (pannyers*) (Yaxley)

pannyers: pannier: a basket or container attached either side of an animal to carry goods

parcell, parsell: 1. a portion or piece of land; 2. an amount or quantity of something; 3. a bundle or load

parcell guilt: parcel gilt: partly gilded, especially on the inner surface only

parer: a knife or implement for paring something or cutting away grass and roots

paring: apparel

partable: able to be separated or divided

partere: probably pewter*

paryter: apparitor*

pashell: pestle*

pastrye: 1. a room where pastry was made; 2. a store room for food or utensils (Yaxley)

pasty plate: a plate or dish in which pasties were cooked (Cox)

***patet*:** the sum as it appears, applied to sub-totals

pattens: probably stones on which a hovel rested to bring it above ground level, similar to staddle stones (Wright)

pauter: pewter*

payels, payles, paylles, payls: pails, buckets

paynted, payneted, paynited, paynted, payntyde clothes/cloythys: painted* cloths

paynted tester: similar to painted cloths; see tester*

payre of tables: playing* tables (Yaxley)

payringe iron: paring iron: an iron implement for pruning or trimming (Yaxley)

payted: painted

peac, peace, peaces: 1. piece; 2. pease*

peachell: unknown; listed with a searchell* so possibly a different type of sieve*

peale: peele*

pealter: pewter*

peantid cloth: painted* cloth

pearche: perch: 1. a fuller's* staff; a heavy stick used to beat cloth in the fulling process; 2. wooden bars, over which pieces of cloth were pulled to inspect or dress them

pease: peas: a pulse having varieties suitable for all types of soil. See *Dictionarium Rusticum* for a description of cultivation.

pease hookes: 1. a hook for reaping peas; 2. hooks with a crooked iron head on a long handle used to pull up pea plants (Yaxley)

peaseland: land on which peas were grown

peason: pease*

peaudre: pewter

pec, pece, peces, pecis: piece, pieces

peck waite: peck weight: a standard measuring vessel for a peck, a unit of capacity for dry goods equal to a quarter of a bushel* (9.09 litres)

peckhorne: unknown; probably a beakhorne*

pecses, pecsseds: piece, pieces

pedecote: petticoat*

pedge: probably a pig

peece, peeces: 1. pease*; 2. pieces

peele: peel: 1. a pole with a broad, flat disc at one end, for placing loaves in an oven; a baker's shovel; 2. a shovel or shovel-shaped implement, especially a fire shovel. It could be of wood or iron.
peelowe beares: pillowbear*
peen: pen*
pees, peese, peesse: pease*
peese, peess, peices: pieces
peisse land: peaseland*
peiuter: pewter*
pello bere, pelobeare, peloberys, pelow beares, pelowbeares, pelowbers, pelowberys: pillowbears*
pelts: the hide or skin of an animal with the wool or hair still on
pen, penn: 1. a moveable chicken coop, which might be kept in the kitchen*; 2. a hanging trencher* rack or shelf for storing dishes (Chinnery)
pennie: penny: one twelfth of a shilling; abbreviated to d
pennystonne: penistone: a coarse, freize (frese*) cloth used for garments and linings
pented, penteyd cloth: painted* cloths
peper quyrns, a pair: pepper quern* or mill: a hand mill for grinding pepper
percell: parcell*
perfuminge panne: a pan for holding burning perfumed pastels (Chinnery)
pese: 1. piece, or 2. pease*
pesehokes, pesehookes: pease* hooke
peseland: peaseland*
peses, pesies, pesys: pieces
peson: pease*
pesse, pesses: 1. piece; 2. pease*
pestle, pestell, pestill: a club-shaped tool used to crush ingredients such as herbs and spices in a mortar*
petticoat, peticoate, petticote, petycotes: petticoat: 1. a woman's underskirt worn to be seen, showing beneath a gown; 2. a man's tight-fitting undercoat, usually padded and worn between the shirt and doublet*
pewlowes: pillows
pewter: a grey alloy of tin and lead, and sometimes other elements. In these inventories, it was used for dishes and tableware and was sometimes valued according to its weight because it could be melted down and re-used. It might be displayed on a cupboard*
peyce, peyes: pease*
peyncted, peynted: painted* cloths
peys, peyse, peyson, peysse: pease*
peysses: pieces
peze: pease*
picheres: pitcher: a jug
pickforkes: pitchfork*
piggen: piggin: 1. a small pail especially of wood with one stave longer than the others to serve as a handle; sometimes used as a milking pail; 2. a wooden drinking vessel
pightell: pightle: a small field, close or enclosure
pilch, pylche: a rug or pad laid on a saddle

pillion, pillioorn: 1. a light saddle used by women; 2. a pad or cushion attached behind a saddle, on which a second person could ride, or to which luggage might be fastened

pillion cloth: a cloth placed under a pillion on a horse, usually to protect clothing from wear

pillowbear, pillowbeer, pillober: pillow cases: a removable fabric covering for a pillow

pillowes ticke: tick*

pinnion, pynnyan: probably pillion*

pinsons, pair of: pincers

pint: a liquid measure of one eighth of a gallon (0.57 litres)

pipkin: 1. a small pot or pan, usually of earthenware; 2. a drinking vessel; 3. a bottle

pitch kettle, pitch pan: a container for heating pitch

pitchfork, pith forkes: 1. a long-handled fork with two sharp prongs, for lifting and pitching hay, straw or sheaves; 2. also occasionally a short-handled fork for lifting dung or breaking clods

pitoll: unknown

plaine bed or bedsteade: probably what it says, a bed or bedstead which was plain in appearance

plate, playte: gold or silver vessels

platters, plattirs: a large, flat dish or plate

playing, playeng tables, pair of: a table on which games are played, especially one which has a playing board inlaid on its surface

playner: 1. a tool for smoothing the surface of sand or clay in a mould; 2. a tool for smoothing a hard surface such as wood

plene trases, pair of: trace*

plough, plloe, ploo, plooes, plos, ploues, plouges, plought, plow, ploweght, plowgh: an implement drawn by horses or oxen to turn the soil and cut furrows in preparation for planting seeds. Illustrations of types of ploughs with their component parts labelled appear in *Dictionarium Rusticum*, and in Yaxley, although Bedfordshire terminology may not be the same. The inventories include plough parts that have not been identified from these sources. Compounds beginning with variant spellings of plough have been simplified below to begin with plough.

plough beames: the central, long beam of timber or iron in a plough, to which the other principal parts were attached

plough boott: ploughbote: wood or timber which a tenant was entitled to cut for making and repairing ploughs and other agricultural implements

plough chains: a chain used as the trace* connecting the draught animal to the plough (Cox)

plough coppes: unknown; possibly the same as copsies*

plough gears: a collective term used for items needed for a plough. They are listed separately in some inventories. See the other entries here and also beams,* copsies*, neckes* & sheaths, tyes* & teathers

plough handells: probably the handle of the plough, illustrated in *Dictionarium Rusticum*

plough harnes, harnis: a general term for the traces, chains etc. used to fasten animals to a plough (Cox)

plough horse gayres: probably the harness and straps fastening horses to the plough
plough shares: the pointed, iron blade in a plough that cut the soil horizontally
plough team, teme: 1. piece of equipment (a rope or chain) used to harness horses or oxen to a plough, harrow* or cart; 2. the main beam of the plough (Yaxley)
plough timber, tymber: wood used for making or repairing ploughs
plough traces, pair of: trace*
plough woode: unknown; possibly the same as plough timber or plough bote
ploughwright: a person who makes ploughs
pocte: pot*
podinger: pottingers*
pole: 1. newly fallen underwood; 2. poles for market stalls
pollen, pollin, poltery: pullen*
pond: pound*
pones: pans
poot: pot*
poplar: unknown; possibly a felled poplar tree; poplar was used in building
poridge pott: a pot for cooking porridge, a thick soup made with vegetables, herbs or meat, often thickened with barley or pulses
porringer, porren gers: a bowl or pot, of metal, earthenware or wood, used to hold soup, stew; also called a pottinger
portale: portal: 1. space within the doorway of a room, partitioned off by an inner door; 2. the inner door to such a space (sometimes forming a movable piece of furniture)
posinghe: unknown; probably a cooking pot
posnet, posnit, porsnet, postnet: a small, metal pot or vessel for boiling, having a handle and three feet
pot: 1. a drinking vessel; 2. a cooking pot, usually large, made of earthenware or metal, and often with three feet for standing by a fire or with handles for hanging over a fire
pothangeles, pot hangells, pothangilles, pothangles, pott hangylles, pott hengles, pottehangle: pot* hangers
pothangers, pott hangges, pott hangres: devices from which a cooking pot, kettle, etc., could be hung; especially 1. a bar with a series of holes or teeth on which to attach a pot-hook at various heights; 2. a pot* hook
pothangings, pot haynges, pote hangyn, pote hanings, poot hankyns: pot* hooks, often in pairs
pothookes, pot hooks, pot huckes: hooks suspended over a fire on which to hang a pot* or kettle*. Sometimes described as a pair.
potnyger: pottinger, see porringer*
pott mettle. 1. metal used for making pots, containing alloys of copper and lead, and often including zinc and tin; 2. a low-grade type of brass
pottage pot: the pot used to cook a thick soup or stew, typically made from vegetables, pulses, meat, etc.
pottinger, potynger: porringer*
pottle, pottel: 1. a pot, tankard or similar container for drinking; 2. a container or quantity of wine or other drink; 3. a unit of capacity of half a gallon (2.3 litres)
poudering, pouldring: powdering*

pouldes: pound*
pound: 1. a unit of weight of 16 ounces (0.45kg); 14 pounds made one stone (6.35kg); 2. an English monetary unit, originally a pound weight of silver, divided into 20 shillings (abbreviated to s); each shilling was divided into 12 pence (abbreviated to d); also equal to one and a half marks*
pouwte: pewter*
powdering, powthering: salting or pickling meat, which took place in a trough*, trunk*, tub* or vessel
powlltre, powltreey, powltrey: poultry
powltreey ware: unknown; possibly equipment used in the care of poultry
powter: pewter*
prayeseres, praysers: appraisers*
preese, preesse: press*
prefescacion: unknown; probably either from prefestinate (to act too hastily) or prefixion (to fix or arrange something in advance)
presentment: the submission of an inventory to the church court
press: 1. a large cupboard, usually shelved, often in a recess, for holding linen, clothes, books, etc., or food, plates, dishes and other kitchen items; 2. a device in which materials such as linen* might be compressed between boards to create a pattern of neatly creased folds (Yaxley); 3. also a cheese* presse
presse of bordes: press* 2
pressing ierons: a flat iron or smoothing iron for pressing clothes
preysement: appraisement: estimating the monetary value of goods
prezes: appraisers*
pricers: appraisers*
procurator: an agent or attorney acting for executors or administrators in the church courts
puater, puder: pewter*
pullen, pullane, pullayne, pulleine, pullin, pullyn: poultry
pullet: a young hen
purled: to decorate or edge with small loops
puter, pweter, pwtar: pewter*
py-: see pi- except for words below
pyche: unknown; possibly 1. beehive, but this usage is in the north of England; 2. piche, a small basket or fish trap
pȝ: patet*

qishions: cushions
qt: quarter*
quart, qwart: a liquid measure of a quarter of a gallon, i.e. 2 pints (1.14 litres)
quarter: a dry goods measure of eight bushels* (Yaxley)
quarters: a piece of wood four inches wide by two or four inches thick, used as an upright stud or short cross-beam in partitions and other framing
quern, quarne, quearn, querene: a hand-operated device for grinding corn, etc., consisting of two stones, the upper of which rotated on the lower; also a small hand-mill for grinding pepper, mustard, etc.
querne house: a building in which a quern* or querns were kept or operated

quesheis, queshens, queshones: cushions
quilt, quylt: a bed covering consisting of two joined pieces of fabric enclosing a layer of soft material (such as wool or down) which acted as padding or insulation
quishens, quishinges, quishins, quishions, quisshins, quisshions, quooshions, quyshen, quyshones, quyshynges, quyshyons, quysons, quysshens, quysshyns, quyssyns: cushions
quoffers: coffer*
qwerne: quern*

rack: 1. a frame for holding animal fodder, either fixed to a wall or capable of being moved where required in a field or farmyard; 2. a frame on which cloth, etc., was stretched, usually before drying; 3. a rake
railes: 1. a bar forming part of the sides of a cart or wagon; 2. a horizontal bar for hanging things on; 3. a fence or railing
rake: usually a rake but sometimes meaning a rack*
randlet, ranlett: rundlet*
range to hold up the coles: probably a grate for coal or charcoal
rapier: a long, thin, sharp-pointed sword, worn by gentlemen with ordinary dress
ravelles: unknown; possibly railes*
rawe maulte, moulte: malt* that is almost ready to go to the kiln (*OED*)
rayles: rail: a piece of linen or other cloth worn by women around the neck
reele: reel: a device on which yarn or thread is wound
reke: rick*
reparel, reparill, reparrell, repill: apparel
repynge hoyke: reaping hook: a curved, sharp-edged, cutting tool used for reaping
reshes: wrystes*
rey: rye
rick: a stack of hay, wood, corn, peas etc., sometimes built on a frame and thatched to keep it dry
rickeyard: farmyard or similar enclosure containing ricks*
riddle, riddell: coarse-meshed sieve for separating seed from corn, ashes from cinders, etc., generally with a circular rim and a base of strong wires crossing at right angles
rideing pillion: pillion*
rideing thrum: probably a riding* cloth with a shaggy surface or fringed. See thrum*
riding cloth: a cloth placed underneath, or used in place of, a saddle
ridinge pannell: panelle*
ridle: riddle*
rie: rye
rieing syve, ryeing syle, rying seive, ryeinge seves: a sieve used to ree, i.e. to clean grain, pulses, etc. especially by sifting in a circular motion so that the chaff collects in the centre
rige wythes, rydge wythes: rigwiddie: a band, rope or chain running across the cart-saddle on the back of a draught-horse and supporting the shafts of a cart or carriage
ringe, ringges: 1. a ring for the finger; 2. curtain rings; 3. a wooden part in a windmill that contains the corn between the stones when grinding (*Dictionarium Rusticum*, describing a windmill)

riouls: rial: a gold coin worth 10s when issued in 1465 and worth 15s from 1553

rised backen: unknown; possibly refers to hogs* fattened for bacon or bacon hung up to cure

rocks: a distaff or part of a spinning* wheel

rod, rodd, rood: 1. rails for bed curtains or window curtains; 2. an area of land of a quarter of an acre (Yaxley)

rofte: roofed

rogge: rug*

role, rolle, roole, rooll: a roller used for levelling soil or crushing clods of earth

rood: rod* 2.

rootes: unknown in this context

rosett: russet*

roufed, rowffed: roofed

rowle: role*

ruffe: roof

ruffes, roffes, pair of: a ruffle or frill around the wrist of a sleeve

ruft: roofed

rug: 1. a thick, woollen blanket used as a bed covering; 2. a coarse, woollen cloth. Not a floor covering.

rulle: unknown; possibly a role*

rundlet, runlet: the same as a kilderkin* or half barrel; a vessel of varying capacity often for wine. Large rundlets varied from 15 to 18½ gallons (approx. 68 to 84 litres), small ones from one pint to 6 gallons (approx. 0.6 to 27 litres) (see Yaxley for a summary of barrel capacities)

running bede: unknown; possibly the same as a truckle* bed

russet, ruset, russett: a coarse woollen cloth of a reddish-brown or subdued colour, worn by country people, especially the poor. Russet might refer to the cloth, the clothes or the colour.

ry-: see ri-, except for the following

rybes: unknown

rydyn iron: unknown; possibly an implement for riddling or sifting ashes from a fire, later called a riddling pan

rystes: unknown; possibly a rest or trestle* or wrystes*

sacer: saucer*

sacken clothe: a hemp* material, coarser than canvas* used by poor people for outer garments (Cumming)

sadlehouse: a building in which saddlery is kept

safe, saffe: 1. a well-ventilated cupboard for protecting provisions from insects and rodents; 2. a secure container with elaborate locks for money, deeds and other valuables

sakes: sacks

sallett dishes: salad dishes

salseller: salt* cellar (sellers)

salt box: a wooden box to hold salt for cooking (Yaxley)

salt sellers: salt cellar: a small vessel used on the table for holding salt. It might have a single bowl or two joined together.

salting, sauling, saulting: curing meat or fish to preserve it. In these inventories, the process is carried out in troughs*
saltinghe: unknown
salttrowe: salting* trough*
sarcing siffes: unknown; possibly a serse*
saucers, sawcers: a receptacle, usually of metal, for holding sauces at a meal
sault, sawltes: a salt* cellar (seller)
savegard: safeguard: an outer skirt worn by women to protect their clothing, especially when riding
say, saye, sayes: a light, twilled, woollen fabric resembling serge, used for aprons, bedding, curtains, etc., and from the seventeenth century commonly green in colour
scacke: sack
scales, scalls: for weighing, consisting of a beam centrally pivotted, with a pan at each end and weights; usually referred to as a pair of scales
scaltes: a salt* cellar (seller)
sceased of: seised of: possessing
schares: chairs
schoode wheeles: wheels with metal rims
schore: a score, twenty
scillit: skillet*
scimmer: skimmer*
sckellett: skillet*
scoales, scoles: scales*
scomer, scommer: skimmer*
scooles and beame, pair of: scales*
score, scores: 1. twenty; 2. an account for goods obtained on credit by a customer
scottelles: scuttle*
screene, scrine, scryen: a large sieve*
scunder: unknown; possibly a skimmer*
scuppootes, scuppott: scuppet: 1. a spade used for trenching and making ditches; 2. a similar instrument used for turning hops while drying
scuttle, scuttell: 1. a basket for winnowing corn; 2. a casting shovel, a large shovel to cast grain in winnowing; 3. a large open basket, usually of wicker, used for carrying corn, earth, vegetables, etc.; 4. a dish or trencher*
scythe: a tool for mowing grass or other crops, having a long, thin, curving blade fastened at an angle with the handle and wielded with both hands with a long, sweeping stroke
sea: say*
seacoles: the contemporary name for coal as distinguished from charcoal (charcoole*, cole*)
sead cod: sedlip*
seamed: 1. an embellished seaming used in joining costly fabrics; 2. an ornamental strip of material inserted in, or laid over, a seam. Used in these inventories to describe sheets, and pillowbears* and sometimes seams in black.
searchell: unknown; possibly a serse*
seare: thin, worn

seassed of: seized of; possessed of

seches: sacks

sedcod, sedcord: sedlip*

sedlip: a basket for carrying seed, when sowing by hand

sedyng plowghe, seeding plow: the *OED* definition of a plough adapted to sow seed into the furrow has no examples before 1767. It may be the three-in-one plough, harrow and seed dropping plough referred to by Walter Blith (*The English improver* 3rd ed. 1652, p. 220), by John Worlidge (in *Systema Agriculturae*, 4th ed. 1687, p. 230) and in *Dictionarium Rusticum* (1704). Worlidge was dismissive of its utility.

see: say*

seed cod, seedecoate: sedlip*

seedlep: sedlip*

seeled bedstead: ceiled bedstead*: one with a canopy

seeming lace: a strip of lace of cut work or needlework used instead of a seam to join the edges of linen (Cumming)

seeve, seive: sieve*

seized of: possessed of

sellar, seller, sellor: 1. a cellar; 2. a soller*

sellares, sellowrs, sellers, sillers, celler: salt* cellar (seller)

sere: seare*

serse: a searce or searcer: a sieve* or strainer, used for sifting flour or in the dairy

settinge steele: unknown

settle, settel, settill, setyll: 1. a wooden bench, usually with arms and a high back, often with a locker or box under the seat; 2. a raised shelf or rack of brick or wood to support barrels (Wright)

settle bench: settle*

seve: sieve*

shacke forkes, shackforkes: shake fork: a wooden fork with two tines or prongs used by threshers to shake and remove the straw from the grain; also, a pitchfork

shaerge: probably shear* hog

shaftes: arrows; the long, slender rod of an arrow

shag sleeves: sleeves made of shag, a cloth having a velvet nap on one side, usually of worsted (worstedd*), but sometimes of silk

share, shares: plough* shares

sharog: shear* hog

sharre, sharrs: plough* shares

shear hog: 1. a lamb between its first and second shearing; 2. a male lamb after first shearing (Batchelor)

shearbord: shear board: a padded board, used in the fulling process, over which cloth was stretched for cropping with hand-shears

shearman: a man who shears woollen cloth

shears: 1. a pair of wedge-shaped blades, used by fullers*, tailors and sheep-shearers; 2. a plough* share

sheathes of plough timber: one of the connecting timbers in a plough

sheddcod: sedlip*

sheepe brande: probably a branding iron for sheep

sheepe coate: sheepcote: a building for sheltering sheep
sheepe hooke: sheep hook: a shepherd's crook
sheepe rackes: a rack from which sheep feed
sheephouse: covered pen for housing sheep
sheers: shears*
sheeve: possibly a sieve*
sheites: sheets
shepheards holland sheets: unknown
sher: plough* share
sherehogges: shear* hog
shetys: sheets
shevells: possibly shelves or shovels
shevill: shovel
shilfe, shilves: shelf, shelves
ship chist: a chest for travelling aboard ship (Yaxley)
shipe: sheep
shipp trenchers: probably trenchers* used on ships
shirte bands: neck bande*, collar or wrist bands of a shirt
shoat: 1. a young, weaned pig; 2. an ill-grown ewe
shod, shoed: edged or sheathed with metal; in these inventories, applied to cart wheels and shovels
shoit: shoat*
sholve: probably a shovel
shooinge horne: in these inventories, probably a tool for shoeing a wheel or animal
shooters: used in the context of woad making; unknown, probably a chute
shootes, shoott: shoat*
shop: 1. a room where goods were made or sold; 2. a workroom
shop boord: 1. a counter; 2. a work bench or work table, in a shop or workshop
shorllings skynes: the sheepskin after the fleece has been shorn (*Dictionarium Rusticum*)
shotchill: shuttle: used in weaving for passing the thread of the weft between the threads of the warp
shotes, shott, shotys, shoutes: shoat*
shouse: shoes
showd wheles, showde whelles, showed wheles: shod*
showing horne: shooinge* horne
shoyd cart: shod* cart
shrene: screene*
shsharhoges: shear* hog
shude: 1. shod*; 2. shed
shulf: shovel
shuyd carte: shod* cart
shyetes: sheets
shythes: scythe*
sickin: possibly silken
sickle, sykelles: an agricultural tool similar to a reaping-hook (repynge* hoyke), but distinguished from it by a serrated cutting-edge

side board: generally synonymous with side* table

side saddel: a saddle on which the rider sits with both legs on the same side of the horse (usually the left), used by a female rider wearing a skirt

side table: a table placed at the side of a room or to the side of the main table. It might be used for holding food and drink before serving, for dining or for displaying tableware.

sidebeds: a bedstead* which fitted against the wall and had only two posts (Raymond)

sideleape: sedlip*

sieve, syfes, syves: a sieve having a finer mesh than a riddle*. It had a round frame and fine mesh for sieving. In these inventories, described as hair or wire sieves, and used for meal* and ryeing*

siftinge, syfting: in these inventories, used to describe arks* and troughs* into which meal or flour was sifted

***signum*:** the mark of a person, not his signature

***signum dicti, praedicti*:** the mark of the said or aforesaid person

silver nut, sylver nutte: a cup made from a coconut shell mounted in silver

sincke howse: a building containing a sink and used for washing and the disposal of waste water

sithe, sithes: scythe*

siules: unknown; probably a milk strainer

sives, syves: sieves*

skaines, skaynes: skein*

skale, skaeles, skealles, pair of: scales*

skanstexkes: candlestick*

skciller: probably a skillet*

skeene: skein*, screene*

skein, skeynes: a quantity of thread or yarn, wound to a certain length upon a reel

skeletes, skellet: skillet*

skemer, skemmer, skemmor: skimmer*

skep, skeppis: 1. a basket* or hamper, usually for holding grain; 2. a beehive

skillet, skyllet: a cooking utensil of brass, copper or other metal, usually having three or four feet and a long handle, used for boiling liquids, stewing meat, etc.

skimmer: a shallow ladle or sieve*, usually perforated, used to skim liquids

skoles, skools: scales*

skomer: skimmer*

skoppett: scuppootes*

skore: a score, twenty

skreen, skreyne, skryne: screene*

skryvenner: scrivener: a person employed to draw up contracts, deeds and other legal documents

skummer: skimmer*

skuttle, skuttels, skuttell: scuttle*

skymer: skimmer*

skyps: skep*

slabbes: unknown; probably the rough, outside plank of timber cut from a log or a tree-trunk preparatory to squaring the main portion

slate hyrdelles: unknown; possibly hurdles for carrying slates

slayes: the part of a loom* used to beat up the weft
sleeves, sleves: separate items of clothing that could be worn with any body-garment; often called a pair
sleidg: probably a sledge hammer
sleppe: slip*
slice, slyce: 1. a flattish utensil (sometimes perforated) used in cookery; 2. a fire-shovel; 3. an instrument for clearing the bars of a furnace when choked with clinkers
sling tres, pair of: swingletrees: a crossbar on a plough*, pivoted at the middle, to which the traces* are fastened, giving freedom of movement to the shoulders of the draught-animal
slip, sliyppe: a quantity of hemp* or linen* yarn
slyngers: possibly swingletrees (sling* tres)
slynges, pair of: a device or chain used for moving heavy weights (Wright)
slype, slypp/e: slip*
smock, smokes: smocks: a woman's undergarment. In these inventories, often made of harden* or flax*.
smoothing iron, smoothingyron: a flat-iron; an iron slicker used for smoothing fabrics or leather
smoothing steele: unknown; probably a smoothing iron
snaffle: a simple form of bridle-bit for a horse
snathe: snaithe: the pole or shaft of a scythe*
soller, sollar: a room on an upper floor, providing more privacy than the hall
soltinge: salting*
somertrees: summer-tree: a horizontal, load-bearing beam in a building
sonne in law: son-in-law or stepson
sorrelled: a bright chestnut colour, reddish brown
sorrie, sorry: of little account or value
soultes: salt* cellar (seller)
sowehogge: female pig
soywe: sow
spanish leather: a fine leather originally made in Cordoba (Cox)
spars: 1. one of the rafters of a roof; 2. a wooden bar to secure a gate or door; 3. a piece of timber
speare, speere: spere* cloth
speates: spit*
specialty, specialte, spetialti, spetialtie: a contract by deed; bonds*, mortgages and debts, secured by writing under seal (Wharton)
speers: spars*, spere* cloth
speet, speit: spit*
sperat debptes, dettes: debts*
spere cloth: unknown; the description is applied to cloths and towels; possibly a cloth covering a short partition projecting into a room and providing draught protection
spet, spete, spett: spit*
speyre: spere* cloth
spice mortar: a small mortar in which spices were ground
spindle: an iron rod acting as an axle. In these inventories, used with grindstones.

spinge wheles: in the context, unclear and probably not spinning wheels

spinninge wheel: a wheel worked either by the hand or foot for spinning hemp, linen or wool. In these inventories, often designated as linen* wheels or woollen wheels or simply as wheels.

spirecloth: spere* cloth

spires, spyres: 1. spars*; 2. a fixed wooden screen

spit: an iron rod for skewering meat or poultry for roasting in front of a fire. The spit was usually supported on cobirons (Yaxley).

splentes: splint: the upright laths* used in a wall

spout pots: a jug with a spout, used for wine

spruse: spruce tree, used for furniture. In these inventories, used for chests* and coffers*.

spyndle, spyndell, spyndyll: spindle*

stacke: a rick of hay, pease*, straw, fodder, etc., sometimes thatched to protect it from the weather

staires, pair of: possibly a step ladder

stall: 1. a stand for a cask. In these inventories, used for containers for preparing and storing ale, beer and drink; 2. a standing place for animals in a stable or shed or a division for one animal. In these inventories, used for neats*; 3. a moveable market stall

stammell: a coarse, woollen cloth, or linsey-woolsey (lincy* wollcye), usually dyed red (*OED*); or a good quality worsted or linsey-woolsey (Cumming)

standers: standard: a permanent fixture in the house and thus omitted from the inventory (editorial)

standing, staninge: resting on a base or feet, as distinguished from hanging or leaning. In these inventories, used to describe cups, field* beds, pens*, stools* and tables.

standing bed: a high bedstead*, as distinguished from a truckle* bed

standish: 1. a stand containing ink, pens and other writing materials; 2. an inkpot

stantte: unknown; possibly a tub* or container or a stand on which to place items

stapp, stappe: unknown; possibly stop*

stares: stairs

staule: stall*

staves: 1. the plural of staff; 2. wood used for bows; 3. the long handle of an implement; 4. bedstave*

stayles: stail: the shaft of an arrow or spear

steanes, stenes, staynes: stean: a vessel for liquid, usually of clay with two handles or ears

steele with a brasse cover to warm a bed: warming* pan

steeles: 1. a handle or shaft; 2. a tool for sharpening knives

steeres, steares, steres, sterys: a bullock or young ox (*Dictionarium Rusticum*)

steks: unknown; possibly sacks

steping, steypyng: steeping: a container in which grain etc. was soaked or steeped; in these inventories, applied to vats*.

sticke: 1. part of the handle of a breast plough (Wright); 2. possibly staves or stakes

still: an apparatus for distilling

stoare: store*

stock, stokes of bees: a swarm in May, or June, is called a stock at Michaelmas (*OED* quoting 1679)

stock cards, stockards, stocke cardel: a large wool-card fixed to a stock or support, with the carding or combing action being performed by another, smaller, two-handed card (Yaxley). In these inventories, often described as a pair of stock cards.

stockings: 1. a close-fitting garment covering the foot, the leg and often the knee; 2. leggings or long boots, a 'boot-hose' or 'boot-stocking' (bote* hose)

stoile, stole, stolle: stool*, stall*

stomacher: 1. an ornamental covering for the chest and front of the body worn by women under the lacing of the bodice; 2. a man's waistcoat

stone: 1. a weight of 14lbs (6.35kg); 2. mill* stones

stone bottles, jugges, pots: stoneware: a hard, dense pottery ware

stone horse, stonded horse: a stallion (*Dictionarium Rusticum*)

stool: 1. usually a single seat with three or four legs but the term was loose and a stool could seat more than one person, or have a back or arms. Some were joined*. See also back* bord, buffet*, chaire* stoole, close* chayre or stole, necessary* stool (see Yaxley for a description of different designs of stool); 2. stall*

stop, stoope: a pail or bucket

store, stoorres, storse, storys: animals kept for fattening. In these inventories, usually applied to hogs* and pigs and also to bullocks*.

stoules, stowels, stowles: stool*

stower: store*

stownes: unknown in this context

stoyles, stoylle: stool*

strakes, straaks of iron: the iron rim of a cart wheel (*Dictionarium Rusticum*)

straw, strawen, strave bed: a bed* or mattress* filled with straw

straw chaire: a chair made of straw or wicker* (Chinnery)

strike, stricke, stryke: 1. a dry measure usually identical with the bushel*, but could vary between half a bushel and four bushels; 2. the cylindrical wooden measuring vessel containing this quantity

stringer: a person who makes bow strings

studds: upright posts for a timber-framed wall

stuffe: woven material of any kind, but often worsted (worstedd*)

styll: still*

suites of armes: a set of armour and weapons, the composition of which is unknown (editorial)

***summa huius inventarij*:** the total of this inventory

***summa patet*:** the total is evident. Used for the sub-total where only one value is shown for the items listed in that section.

***summa totalis, totaliter, totalitur*:** final total

***summa totalis huius inventorii*:** final total of this inventory

surplisse: surplice: vestment worn by clergy

suter, sutor: suiter: a round board placed between two cheeses in a press

sutes: a man's suit of clothing, described as a matching doublet* and breeches* or hose*

swarme of bees: a swarm in May, or June, is called a stock at Michaelmas (*OED* quoting 1679)
sweet worte: in brewing, the wort* before adding hops
sweete water: a sweet-smelling liquid preparation, used for sprinkling on clothes or washing hands
swill tub: tub for kitchen refuse fed to swine
swilling trough: possibly 1. a trough containing swill for pigs; 2. a trough for washing things
swinele: swingel: the part of a flail that strikes the corn (Batchelor)
swynetroffes: trough*
sy-: see si- except for words below
syle: sieve*
sypers: cypress: a tree from the Mediterranean, whose wood was used for furniture
syth, syythys: scythe*
syve: sieve*
syvinge dishe: possibly a dish or container for holding something that has been sieved

table bords: a board forming the top of a table, supported on a frame or trestles
table carpet: carpet*
table stoile: unknown; possibly a stool table, listed in *OED* and described as a table on trestles
taffata, taffety: a fine, crisp and usually lustrous fabric of a plain weave in which the weft threads are thicker than those of the warp, originally of silk and later also of a silk mix
tallow: hard animal fat; used for making candles and soap, and dressing leather
tankard, tankred: 1. a tall drinking vessel; 2. a large open wooden tub*, used in the dairy
tapestry, tapstery: a fabric decorated with painted, embroidered or woven designs. In these inventories, used for coverings*, coverlets* and cushions.
tare, taire: 1. tares: vetch*; 2. hemp tare: a quality of hemp*. In these inventories, used for household linen.
taster: a small, shallow cup for tasting wine
tawe trees: tawtree 1. the stretcher between the traces* of a cart horse; 2. the swingle tree of a horse-drawn plough harness (Wright)
tawny, tayney: a composite colour, brown with a preponderance of yellow or orange
tayer, tayrs: tare*
teame, teamys: plough* team
teare, teares: tare*
tearse: tierce: 1. one third of a pipe (42 gallons of wine); 2. a cask or vessel holding this quantity, usually of wine but also of provisions or other goods
teaster: tester* or taster*
teeme: plough* teeme
teere: tare*
tegg: teg: 1. yearling sheep before first shearing; 2. lambs of about six months old (Batchelor)
teike: tick*

teler: unknown; possibly tailor or tiler
telth: tilth*
teme, temes: plough* teame
tenante, tennan, tennannt, tennon, tennre, tenor sawe: tenon saw: a fine saw for making tenons, having a thin blade, a thick back and small teeth
tenement, tennyment: both the house and the land in a holding
tenters, tenter tymber: a wooden framework on which cloth is stretched after being milled, so that it may set or dry evenly and without shrinking
teres, teris: tare*
tester, testerne, testor: a canopy, usually over a bed supported on the posts of the bedstead* or suspended from the ceiling
teyler: unknown; possibly tailor or tiler
tharches: vetches*
theale, thele: a board, plank or joist
theave sheape: a ewe 1. usually a ewe in its first or second year, that has not yet borne a lamb; 2. a female lamb after first shearing (Batchelor)
theches, thecthes, thetches: vetches*
thetching: thatching
theylle: theale*
thill: the shaft or pair of shafts of a cart or wagon. The draught animals were attached to either side of a single shaft or in line between a pair (Yaxley).
thill geares: harness used to attach the horse next to the cart to the thill
thillstrapps, thillstroppes, pair of: unknown; probably part of the thill gear
thone: the one
thother: the other
thromcloth: a coarse, woollen cloth with a rough, tufted surface (Wright)
thrum, thrumbd, thrombe: thrum: 1. the ends, or short pieces, of waste wool or yarn; 2. loose ends of thread projecting from the surface of a woven fabric, shaggy; 3. covered, made or fringed with thrums. In these inventories, applied to cloth, coverlets* and testers*.
thrundell bedd: trundle or truckle* bed
tick, tycke, tyke: the case for a mattress or pillow; from the sixteenth century also applied to the strong, hard linen used for making them. In these inventories, used for bolsters*, feather* beds and pillows.
tiffeny: tiffany: a transparent, gauze muslin; cobweb lawn; or thin transparent silk
tills, tilles: lentil*
tillige, tylleg: tillage: land under cultivation
tilliwillie: cloth made of worsted (worstedd*)
tilth, tylth: 1. cultivated ground, which has been loosened by the plough (Batchelor); 2. the tilling, manuring or improving of land (*Dictionarium Rusticum)*; 3. a ploughing; 4. land lying fallow (Wright); 5. land under cultivation, as distinct from pasture, forest or waste land; tilled or arable land
tilthe corne, grayne: possibly a crop grown on fallow land
tilthe unsowne: possibly unsown land, either fallow or ploughed
timber: 1. growing trees on land forming part of the freehold, especially oak, ash and elm, of twenty years or more old; 2. trees felled for building or similar use (Wharton). Distinct from wood.

tinne, tyne, tynn: made of tin
tire: tyer*
toah: tow*
tobe, tobee: tub*
tod, todd: 28lb of wool (12.7kg)
toe: 1. two; 2. to; 3. hemp tow*
toelles: tools
toggwithe: tugg* withes
tonges, tongues: tongs, often as a pair. In these inventories, usually associated with fires.
too, tooe, tooen: 1. tow* towen*: a grade of hemp* 2. two
tooth and eare pickers: toothpicks and ear pickers of bone were recorded as being imported from 1545
toowbe: tub*
topes: possibly top; or knobe*: a small rounded ball, often used as decoration
tornyd: turned*
tortrees: tawe* trees
tosting iron: possibly a fork used for toasting bread or other food
tostinge plate: unknown
toubes, toubs: tub*
touel, touell, touwells: towel
tounges, pair of: tonges*
tow, towe, towen: fibrous stems of flax* and hemp*, raw or prepared; tow was the short fibres separated by heckling from the fine and long fibres; used to describe hemp products generally. In these inventories used for household linen.
tow cardes: cards*
towen, toowen, touwen: 1. fabrics made of hemp* or flax* linen tow; 2. two
towls: tools
trace, trases, pair of: the rope or leather straps connecting a draught animal to the cart or plough*. In these inventories, sometimes described as a pair of body traces or a pair of plain traces.
trash, trasche, trase, trayse: anything of little or no value
trayes: tray: a shallow, open vessel
tread, treadde, treade, treads: unknown; see p. lxiii of the Introduction
trean: treen*
treas: unknown; possibly trayes*
trecher: trenchers*
tred, tredd, tredde, treddes, tredds, trede, tredes, treed: tread*
treen, treene, trene, treing: made of wood. In these inventories, treen ware often referred to dishes
trefittes, treavitt: trivet*
trencher, trenches, trenschers, trenshers: 1. a square or circular, flat piece of wood on which meat was served; 2. a plate of wood, metal or earthenware for food
trencll: unknown
trestle, tresles, tressell, tressylles, trestelles, trestills: a frame, e.g. to support boards to form a table

treveat, trevet, trevit, trevytt: trivet*

trifles, trifeles, trifells, triffeeles, triffels, triffles, triffls: trifles: small articles of little intrinsic value

trincher: trencher*

trivet: 1. a three-footed stand or support; 2. a stand for a pot, kettle, or other vessel placed over a fire for cooking or heating

troaffe: trough*

troch: trash*

trockle bedstead: truckle* bed

trodde: unknown

trofe, troff/es, trogh/es, trohe, troofe, trophe: trough*

trosh: trash*

trough, troues, trought, trouth: 1. a narrow, open, box-like container made of wood or stone for liquid. In these inventories, used for drinking troughs for animals; 2. a tank or vat*. In these inventories used for fulling*, kneading*, powdering*, salting*, sifting*, swilling* and yoting*.

trounke: trunk*

troundell bed: trundle, see truckle* bed

troves, trovis: trough*

trowef, trowes, trowfe, trowffe, trowgh, trowthe: trough*

Troy waightes: the standard system of weights used for precious metals and stones

truckle bed: a low bed running on truckles or wheels, usually pushed beneath a high or standing bed when not in use; also called a trundle bed

trumpery: something of no value

trunchin coffer: unknown

trundle bed: truckle* bed; also referred to as a trundle bedstead*

trunk, trunke, trunck: a chest*, coffer*, or box with a rounded top, for carrying clothes and other personal items when travelling; originally covered with leather

trunsures: trenchers*

truss, trusse, trusbed, trusbedsted, trust bed: trussing bed: one that could be dismantled for travelling

trusse: a close-fitting garment worn by men and women

tryen, tryn: treen*

tryfelles, tryffles: trifles*

tryffatt, tryvet: trivet*

tub, tubes: a wide-bodied, flat-bottomed, open-topped wooden vessel, usually formed of staves and hoops. In these inventories, used for holding dry goods and liquid and for carrying out processes such as buckinge* and washing.

tugg withes: a strap or tie used to attach the swingle-tree to the head of the plough*, harrow* or cart

tumbrel, tumbrell, tumbrils: a cart constructed so that the body tilts backwards to empty out the load; especially a dung-cart

tunell, tunnell, tunnill, tunnyll: 1. a funnel; 2. in some inventories, possibly used for a tun or other container

tunninge, tunnynge: storage containers. In these inventories, used for tubs* and vessels for ale or beer.

tuns, tunes, tunnes: 1. a cup; 2. a large cask or barrel* for liquids or provisions; 3. a vat or container used for bolting*, mashing* or yealding*; 4. a cask for wine or oil of 252 gallons (4 hogsheads)

turkes, turkies: turkeys were introduced into England during the sixteenth century

turkey, Turkye worke: an imitation of Turkish tapestry work; in these inventories, used for cushions and coverlets*.

turnbroche: turnbroach: a turnspit

turned, turnyed: wooden items produced by a turner on a lathe

twells: unknown

twobes: probably tubs*

twoels: towels

ty-: see ti-, except for words below

tye, iron: unknown

tyer, tyre: a tyre: an iron plate, called strakes or streaks, with which cart and carriage wheels were shod. In these inventories, often referred to as shod wheels.

tyes & teathers: unknown; probably ropes with which the leg of a horse or other animal is tied, to maintain grazing within a designated space

tylfylde: a tilled field

tymber stickes: felled trees left to become seasoned (Wright)

tyth barn: a barn for storing grain given to the parson as tithe

tythe: tithe: a tenth of annual produce, taken as a tax in kind for the support of the church and clergy

under cloth: a sheet or cloth for a bed*. The material from which it was made is not mentioned in any of these inventories.

underwood: small trees or shrubs, coppice-wood or brush-wood, growing beneath higher timber trees

undressd: not having been prepared for use; in these inventories, it is applied to flax* and barley

unions: onions

unmooveable, unmovable: immoveables*

unthresht: not threshed

ure: ewer*

utencilles, untilles: utensils: a general term for household articles

valance, valence, vallens, vallons, vallums: valance: drapery hanging round the canopy of a bed; in later use, a short curtain around the frame of a bedstead

vale: veil: fabric covering for the head; in these inventories, it was made of lawn or tiffany*

vantage: advantage, benefit, profit, gain; in these inventories, used in the context of the return from animals e.g. their milk or calves or hiring them out

vargis: verges*

vat: a cask*, tun*, or other container usually large, used for fermenting ale, beer*, verjuice (verges*) or other liquid or for storing them. In these inventories, usually called a fat.

velvet, vellet: a silk fabric having a short, dense, smooth pile, imported from Spain, Italy and France

venecyans: venetians: hose* or knee breeches* originally introduced from Venice and fashionable c.1570–1620
vened: weaned
verges, vergis, veriuce: verjuice: the acid juice of green or unripe grapes, crab-apples or other sour fruit, made into a liquor and stored in barrels; much used in cooking
vetches, vetshes, vitches: vetches: leguminous plants of the genus *Vicia*, cultivated as a source of food for livestock
***vic ibidem*:** vicar of the same place
vice, vyse: a tool with two jaws to grip and hold a piece of work in position while it is being filed, sawn, etc.
***videlt, vidlet, vidz, viz, vz, vzt, vȝ*:** abbreviations for *vedelicet*: that is to say
***vidua*:** widow
voyder: voider: a tray, basket or other vessel in which dirty dishes or utensils, fragments of food, etc., were placed when clearing the table or during a meal

wagins: wagon: a vehicle for carrying hay, corn, etc., distinguished from a cart because it had four wheels
wainscot: a superior quality of foreign oak imported from Russia, Germany and Holland, chiefly used for fine panel-work on walls and furniture. In these inventories, used for bedsteads*, chairs*, chests*, cupboards*, forms*, presses*, stools* and the back of a table.
wallet: a bag for holding provisions, clothing, books, etc., especially on a journey
wallnut tree: in these inventories, its wood was used for some bedsteads and chests
wardens: a variety of pear
warming pan: a long-handled covered pan of metal (usually brass) containing hot coals, used to warm beds
warpe of fysh: a quantity of four fish
warping barrs: a bar used in weaving to measure the length of warp required to weave a piece of cloth (Cox)
warping fate, fatt: probably the container in which the thread or yarn to be used for the warp in weaving was sized before use (Cox)
warren: a piece of enclosed land for breeding game
wash, washing: in these inventories, the process of washing was carried out in bowls, barrels and tubs* but it is not clear from the context what was being washed; several were in the dairy or other service areas
wash peales: unknown; in these inventories, associated with wash tubs* and probably a stirring paddle
waste coate, wast cote, wastcoates: waistcoat: a garment covering the upper body down to the waist and often decorated, worn by both men and women (*OED*); a waist-length under doublet also called a petticoat* (Cumming)
watch bill; watchyng byll: a watchman's bill* or halberde*; the earliest *OED* example is from 1665
water carte: a cart, usually a barrel or tank on wheels, for carrying water
wayners, wayning: weaners, young animals
waynescotte, waynscot, waynskott: wainscot*
ways, pair of: possibly weights (waytes*)
waytes, wayts: weights, part of the mechanism of a jack* to turn a spit* for cooking

weathers: wethers*
wedges, wedgys: in some of the inventories used in splitting logs
wedwe: widow
welles: wheels*
wenchcoate: wainscot*
wendling, wenell cavles: weaning calves
wenscote, wenskott: wainscot*
wenyinge: weaning; applied to calves
wethers: a ram, especially castrated (*OED*); a male sheep of two years or more (Batchelor)
wette: wheat
wevers wayte: weights for cloth were set out in An Act for the Making of Wollen Cloth 1551, 5 & 6 Edward VI c.6 (*Statutes of the Realm*, vol. 4, p. 136)
weynscott: wainscot*
whaled bone bodyes: bodyes*
what: wheat
wheel: 1. cart wheels; 2. spinning* wheels for flax*, hemp* or wool
whiple trees, whipletres: a crossbar, pivoted at the middle, to which the traces* of a plough* or harrow* were fastened, giving freedom of movement to the shoulders of the horse or other draught-animal. *OED* equates it to a swingle tree, which is not referred to in these inventories.
whipp saw: a narrow-bladed saw set in a frame and used in a sawpit by two men
white grayne: 1. oats sown in April (*Dictionarium Rusticum*); 2. wheat, barley and oats (Raymond)
whitlether: a soft, pliant leather of a natural, light colour, produced by dressing with alum (allome*) and salt
whyte pease: a variety of pease*, suited to a light, rich soil (*Dictionarium Rusticum*)
wicker, wickar, wiker, wycher, wyckar, wycker, wyker: a pliant twig or small rod, usually of willow. In these inventories, used for making baskets*, chairs, cradles*, hampers*, maunds*, riddles* and scuttles*.
wimble, wymble: 1. a gimlet, auger or brace for boring holes; 2. a hay trusser's tool for twisting and plaiting ropes of straw
windinge blades: a pair of blades on which to wind yarn
window cloth: 1. curtain; 2. winnowing* cloth
windscot: wainscot*
winnow, winnowing: the process of separating grain from chaff by tossing it in the air. The grain is caught in a winnowing cloth or sheet.
without specialty: specialty*
woade fatte: a vat* or tub* in which woad was fermented and prepared for use as a dye, or in which wool or cloth was dyed using woad
woadehouse: a building in which woad was prepared for use as a dye
woates: oats
woatmill: possibly oatmeal
woatmill house: possibly where oatmeal was stored or where the mill for grinding oats was kept
woll sheep: probably the same as woolled* sheep
wollbed, woole beade, woollbeed: probably a bed* (i.e. mattress*) stuffed with wool

wollen wheele, wheill, wooland wyyll: a wheel worked by hand or foot to spin wool
wood dragge: drag*
wool, wolen, woll cardes: cards*
woolled sheep: unshorn sheep
wootes: oats
worminge pann: warming* pan
worstedd: worsted: a fine, smooth fabric made from closely-twisted yarn spun of long-staple wool combed to lay the fibres parallel
wort: a sweet liquid produced by steeping ground malt or other grain in hot water, which was then fermented in tuns*, tubs* or vats* to produce ale or beer
woule, woulling: wool, woollen
wrought: a fabric, furnishing, garment or household linen decorated with needlework or cutwork*
wrystes: the part of a plough* that turns up the earth in furrows (Wright)
wy-: see wi- except for word below
wynmelles: unknown; possibly a wimble*

yard: a measurement of three feet (91.44cm)
yarn: spun fibre of flax*, hemp*, silk or wool
yates: gates; see falling* yates
yealding, yealyng, yeeldinge, yeeling, yeilding, yelding, yelinge: the fermenting part of the brewing process. In these inventories, the process was carried out in vats*, tubs* or tuns*.
yeard: yard*
yeareling, yearing, yearlyng, yearyng, yerlynges, yeryng: an animal in its second year
yearne: yarn*
yelyng boule: a bowl used in the fermenting process
yelyng hous: a room or outhouse where fermentation was carried out; a brewhouse
yemen: yeomen
yerengers: yeareling*
yerkynge: jerkin*
yerne: yarn*
yewis: ewes
yewre: ewer*
yinde: joined*
yoiunte: joined*
yokes, yoake, yockes: 1. a device fitted to the neck of a pair of animals, usually draught animals, to enable them to pull a plough*, cart, etc.; 2. the draft animals themselves
yoting troughe: the trough used for steeping grain in water in brewing
yoyned: joined*
yurn: yarn*

Bibliography

Manuscripts

Bedfordshire Archives Service

ABC	Court books of the Archdeaconry of Bedford
ABE	Archdeaconry of Bedford, estate terriers
ABP/W	Archdeaconry of Bedford, probate
AD	Ancient deeds or deposits
CH	Chester muniments
DW	Deeds and papers relating to the Luton Hoo Estates deposited by Daniel Watney, Eilouart, Inman & Nunn of London (architects)
F	Documents deposited by Dr Fowler
Fasti	A list of incumbents of Bedfordshire parishes compiled in the 1950s and 60s
FN	Francklin of Great Barford and Bolnhurst
OR	Orlebar manuscripts
PA	Parsons deposit: Boswell & Dillingham of Dean
PM	Pym Archive
T	Page-Turner Muniments and Manuscripts
X	small deposited documents or collections
Z	small donations

Hertfordshire Archives and Local Studies

A	Archdeaconry of St Albans

Huntingdonshire Archives

AH	Archdeaconry of Huntingdon

Lincolnshire Archives

DIOC	records of the Diocese of Lincoln
INV	Lincoln Consistory Court inventories
LCC ADMONS	Lincoln Consistory Court administrations (and inventories)
MISC WILLS	Lincoln Wills, administrations and inventories

The National Archives

PROB 2	Prerogative Court of Canterbury, inventories compiled before 1661
PROB 11	Prerogative Court of Canterbury, will registers

Online resources

Bedfordshire Archives, Community Histories https://bedsarchives.bedford.gov.uk

British History Online https://www.british-history.ac.uk

Cambridge Group for the History of Population & Social Structure, 'Ogilby's Principal Roads, 1675: After A map of XVIIth century England, Ordnance Survey 1930 with additions' https://www.campop.geog.cam.ac.uk (accessed on 1 November 2019)

Civil War Petitions database https://www.civilwarpetitions.ac.uk

Clergy of the Church of England database https://theclergydatabase.org.uk

Forman and Napier Casebooks https://casebooks.lib.cam.ac.uk and https://cudl.lib.cam.ac.uk/collections/casebooks/1

Historic England https://historicengland.org.uk

History of Parliament Trust https://www.historyofparliamentonline.org

Office for National Statistics, Census 2021 https://www.ons.gov.uk/visualisations/censuspopulationchange

Venn, J. A., *Alumni cantabrigienses: a biographical list of all known students, graduates and holders of office at the University of Cambridge, from the earliest times to 1900* (Cambridge, 1922–1954), 10 vols. Online as A Cambridge Alumni Database https://venn.lib.cam.ac.uk

Primary sources

For early sources used in the Glossary, see the Glossary

Acts and Ordinances of the Interregnum, 1642–1660, ed. by C. H. Firth and R. S. Rait (London, HMSO, 1911), 3 vols

Batchelor, Thomas, *General View of the Agriculture of the County of Bedford drawn up by order of the Board of Agriculture and internal improvement* (London, 1808)

Blith, Walter, *The English improver improved or the survey of husbandry surveyed*, 3rd ed. (London, 1652)

Camden, William, *The abridgement of Camden's Britannia with maps of the severall shires of England and Wales* (London, 1626)

Constitutions and Canons Ecclesiastical of the Church of England 1604 no. 125 and 92 (https://www.anglican.net/doctrines/1604-canon-law/)

Cowell, John, *The Interpreter or booke containing the Signification of Words ... as are mentioned in the Law Writers of Statutes of this ... Kingdom ...* (Cambridge, 1607)

Grafton, Richard, *A Briefe Treatise Conteinyng Many Proper Tables and Easy Rules, very necessary and needeful, for the use and commoditie of all people ...* (London, 1573)

Harrison's Description of England in Shakespere's Youth: being the second and third books of his Description of Britaine and England; ed. by Frederick J. Furnivall (London, 1877)

Journal of the House of Lords (London, 1767–1830), 42 vols

Lyndwood, William, *Provinciale Constitutions p[ro]uincialles, and of Otho, and Octhobone, translated in to Englyshe* (London, 1534)

A short, yet a true and faithfull narration of the fearefull fire that fell in the towne of Wooburne, in the countie of Bedford, on Saturday the 13 of September last, Anno. 1595 Together with a Christian admonition as to the particular people of that place (London, 1595)

Statutes of the Realm (London, Record Commission, 1817), 11 vols

Swinburne, Henry, *A briefe treatise of testaments and last wills* … (London, 1591, 1611)

The Visitations of Bedfordshire annis domini 1566, 1582 and 1634, Publications of the Harleian Society vol. 21 (London, 1884)

Wentworth, Thomas, *The Office and Dutie of executors, or, A treatise of wills and executors, directed to testators in the choise of their executors and contrivance of their wills, with direction for Executors in the execution of their Office, according to the law* … (London, 1641 and later editions)

West, William, *Symboleography which may bee termed the art, description or image of instruments, extra-judicial, as covenants, contracts, obligations, conditions, feffements, graunts, wills, etc Or the paterne of presidents. Or the notarie or scrivener. … The first part, newly corrected and augmented by William West of the Inner Temple gentleman* (London, 1592 and 1598 editions)

Books and articles

For sources used in the Glossary, see the Glossary

'A Sixteenth Century Inventory' and 'An Inventory of the XVIIth Century', *Bedfordshire Notes & Queries* vol. 3 (1893), pp. 252–4 and 276–8

Arkell, Tom, 'Interpreting probate inventories', in Arkell, *When Death Do Us Part*, Chapter 4

Arkell, Tom, and others, *When Death Do Us Part: understanding and interpreting the probate records of early modern England* (Oxford, 2000)

Bailey, J. M., 'Rowe's Cottage: a 'Wealden' House at Little Barford, Bedfordshire', *Bedfordshire Archaeological Journal* vol. 12 (1977), pp. 85–98

Bailey, J. M., 'Lower Roxhill Farm, Marston Moretaine: a measured survey of a timber-framed building', *Bedfordshire Archaeological Journal* vol. 12 (1977), pp. 99–106

Bailey, John, *Timber Framed Buildings: a study of medieval timber buildings in Bedfordshire and adjoining counties* (np, 1979). Published by Buckinghamshire and Cambridgeshire Historic Building Research Group

Bevan, Kitrina, 'Legal Education in Late Medieval England: how did provincial scriveners learn their law?', in M. Korpiola, ed., *Legal Literacy in Premodern European Societies* (Basingstoke, 2018), pp. 19–41

Bowden, Peter J., ed., *Chapters from The Agrarian History of England and Wales volume 1: Economic Change: prices, wages, profits and rents 1500–1750* (Cambridge, 1990)

Bowker, Margaret, 'Some Archdeacons' Court Books and the Commons' Supplication against the Ordinaries', in D. A. Bulloch and R. L. Storey, *The Study of Medieval Records: Essays in Honour of Kathleen Major* (Oxford, 1971), pp. 282–316

Brown, Rev. J. E., 'An Inventory of Household Goods, 1612', *The Antiquary* vol. 42 (1906), pp. 27–9

Brown, Maureen and Paul, *Leighton Buzzard's Tudor House: the story of 17 to 21a Hockliffe Street* (Leighton Buzzard?, 2016?)

Buck, Anne, 'Clothing and textiles in Bedfordshire inventories, 1617–1620', *Costume* no. 34 (2000), pp. 26–38

Burgess, J. H., *The Social Structure of Bedfordshire and Northamptonshire 1524–1674* (University of York, Ph.D. thesis, 1978), 2 vols

Chartres, John, ed., *Chapters from the Agrarian History of England and Wales, volume 4: Agricultural Markets and Trade 1500–1750* (Cambridge, 1990)

Cirkett, A. F., ed., 'English Wills 1498–1526', BHRS vol. 37 (Streatley, 1957), pp. 1–82

Clay, Christopher, ed., *Chapters from the Agrarian History of England and Wales volume 2: Rural society: landowners, peasants and labourers* (Cambridge, 1990)

Collett-White, James, *Inventories of Bedfordshire Country Houses 1714–1830*, BHRS vol. 74 (Bedford, 1995)

Cox, Alan, *Brickmaking: a history and gazetteer* (Bedford, 1979), Survey of Bedfordshire [A joint publication of Bedfordshire County Council and the Royal Commission on Historical Monuments, England]

Cox, Nancy and Jeff, 'Probate inventories: the legal background – Part 1', *The Local Historian* vol. 16 (1984), pp. 133–45; Part 2 *The Local Historian* vol. 16 (1984), pp. 217–27

Davidson, Caroline, *A Woman's Work is Never Done: a history of housework in the British Isles 1650–1950* (London, 1982)

Dils, Joan, 'The books of the clergy in Elizabethan and Early Stuart Berkshire', *The Local Historian* vol. 36 (2006), pp. 92–105

Drury, J. Linda, 'Inventories in the Probate Records of the Diocese of Durham', *Archaeologia Aeliana* vol. 28 (2000), pp. 177–91

Dyer, A. and D. M. Palliser, eds, *The Diocesan Population Returns for 1563 and 1603* (Oxford, 2005) Records of social and economic history, new series, 31

Emmison, F. G., 'Jacobean Household Inventories', BHRS vol. 20 (Aspley Guise, 1938), pp. 1–143

Evans, Vivienne, *Historic Inns of Dunstable* (Dunstable, 2002)

Falvey, Heather, 'The probate process in medieval England and Wales and the documents which it generated', *The Local Historian* vol. 52 (2022) pp. 8–26

Fisher, F. J., 'The London Food Market, 1540–1640', *The Economic History Review* vol. 5 (April 1935), pp. 46–64

Foster, Joseph, *Alumni Oxonienses 1500–1740* (Oxford, 1891), 4 vols

Freeman, C. E., 'Elizabethan Inventories' in *Harrold Priory: a Twelfth Century Dispute and other articles*, BHRS vol. 32 (Streatley, 1952), pp. 92–107

Gay, Edwin F., 'The Midland Revolt and the Inquisitions of Depopulation of 1607', *Transactions of the Royal Historical Society* vol. 18 (n.s.) (1904), pp. 195–244

Godber, J., *History of Bedfordshire 1066–1888* (Bedford, 1969)

Havinden, M. A., ed., *Household and Farm Inventories in Oxfordshire, 1550–1590*, Oxfordshire Record Society vol. 44 (London, 1965)

Heal, Felicity and Clive Holmes, *The Gentry in England and Wales, 1500–1700* (London, 1994)

Hindle, Steve, 'Persuasion and Protest in the Caddington Common Enclosure Dispute 1635–1639', *Past & Present* no. 158 (1998), pp. 37–78

Howard-Drake, Jack, *Oxfordshire Church Court Deposition 1570–1574* and *1609–1616* (Oxford, 1993, 2003)

Howe, Pat and Jane Harris, eds, *Wills, inventories and probate accounts from St Albans, 1600–1615*, Hertfordshire Record Society vol. 32 (np, 2019)

Hughes, Annabelle, ed., *Sussex Clergy Inventories, 1660–1750*, Sussex Record Society vol. 91 (Lewis, 2009)

Index of Bedfordshire Probate Records 1484–1858, ed. by Chris Pickford. British Record Society, *Index Library*, vols 104, 105 (London, 1993, 1994)

Jurkowski, M., C. L. Smith and D. Crook, *Lay Taxes in England and Wales 1188–1688*, PRO Publications, 1998. Public Record Office Handbook no. 31

Kassell, Lauren and others, eds, *The casebooks of Simon Forman and Richard Napier, 1596–1634: a digital edition*, https://casebooks.lib.cam.ac.uk

Kennett, David H. and Terence Paul Smith, 'Crowhill Farm, Bolnhurst, Bedfordshire: a timber-framed building and its history', *Bedfordshire Archaeological Journal* vol. 12 (1977), pp. 57–84

Lee, Ross, *Law and Local Society in the time of Charles I: Bedfordshire and the Civil War*, BHRS vol. 65 (np, 1986)

Lewington, Honor, *Stoke Mandeville wills and inventories 1552–1853*, Buckinghamshire Record Society vol. 38 (Aylesbury, 2019)

Lovell, Mary S., *Bess of Hardwick: first lady of Chatsworth, 1527–1608* (London, 2005)

Lutt, Nigel, ed., *Bedfordshire Muster Rolls 1539–1831*, BHRS vol. 71 (np, 1992)

McGregor, Margaret, ed., *Bedfordshire Wills proved in the Prerogative Court of Canterbury 1383–1548*, BHRS vol. 58 (np, 1979)

Mander, Nicholas, 'Painted Cloths', in *The Cambridge Guide to the Worlds of Shakespeare* (Cambridge, 2015), pp. 461–70

Marshall, Lydia M., *The Bedfordshire Hearth Tax Returns for 1671*, BHRS vol. 16 (Aspley Guise, 1934, repr. 1990)

Munby, L., *Hertfordshire Population Statistics 1563–1801*, 2nd ed. by Heather Falvey (np, 2019), Hertfordshire Record Society

Munby, L., *How Much is that Worth?* (Chichester, 1989) The Local Historian at Work, 4

Munby, Lionel M., ed. *Life & Death in Kings Langley, Wills and Inventories 1498–1659* (King's Langley, 1981)

Orlin, Lena Cowen, 'Fictions of the early modern English probate inventory', in Henry Turner, ed., *The Culture of Capital: Property, Cities, and Knowledge in early modern England* (New York, London, 2002), pp. 51–83

Outhwaite, R. B., *The Rise and Fall of the English Ecclesiatical Courts 1500–1860* (Cambridge, 2006)

Overton, Mark, *Agricultural Revolution in England: the Transformation of the Agrarian Economy, 1500–1850* (Cambridge, 1996)

Overton, Mark and others, *Production and Consumption in English Households 1600–1750* (London, 2004)

Peters, Robert, *Oculus episcopi: administration in the Archdeaconry of St Albans 1580–1625* (Manchester, 1963)

Porter, Stephen, 'The Making of Probate Inventories', *The Local Historian* vol. 12 (1976), pp. 36–7

The Register of Henry Chichele, Archbishop of Canterbury, 1414–1443, ed. by E. F. Jacob, Canterbury and York Society vol. 42 (Oxford, 1937), vol. 2

Schneider, Joan, 'An Inventory of 1612/1613: a Luton Brewer' and J. J. Hayes 'The Malting and Brewing Process', *Manshead Archaeological Society Journal* no. 19 (1969), pp. 30–41

Simpson, Richard, compiler, *Memorials of St John at Hackney, Part III* (Guildford, 1882, privately printed)

Spaeth, D., '"Orderly made": re-appraising household inventories in seventeenth-century England', *Social History* vol. 41 (2016), pp. 417–35

Spicksley, Judith M., '"Fly with a duck in thy mouth": single women as sources of credit in seventeenth-century England', *Social History* vol. 32 (2007), pp. 187–207

Spufford, Margaret, 'The limitations of the probate inventory', in John Chartres and David Hey, eds., *English Rural Society 1500–1800: Essays in Honour of Joan Thirsk* (Cambridge, 1990), pp. 139–74.

Spufford, Peter, 'Long-term Rural Credit in Sixteenth- and Seventeenth-century England: the Evidence of Probate Accounts', in Arkell, *When Death Do Us Part*, pp. 213–28

Stratton, J. M., *Agricultural records AD220–1968*, ed. by Ralph Whitlock (London, 1969)

Tearle, Barbara, *The Accounts of the Guild of the Holy Trinity, Luton 1526/7–1546/7*, BHRS vol. 91 (Woodbridge, 2012)

Thirsk, Joan, ed., *The Agrarian History of England and Wales volume 5, part 1 Regional Farming systems* (Cambridge, 1984)

Weaver, John, 'The Building Accounts of Harrold Hall', in *Miscellanea*, BHRS vol. 49 (np, 1970), pp. 56–80

Welch, Edwin, 'The Geography of Dissent in Bedfordshire', in *Bedfordshire Historical Miscellany: Essays in Honour of Patricia Bell*, BHRS vol. 72 (np, 1993), pp. 54–60

West, Bernard B., 'A note on the post suppression remains at Warden Abbey Farm', *Bedfordshire Archaeological Journal* vol. 2 (1964), p. 69

Whiteman, Anne, and Mary Clapinson, eds, *The Compton Census of 1676: a critical edition* (London, 1986)

Wrightson, Keith, *Earthly Necessities: economic lives in early modern Britain, 1470–1750* (Penguin, 2002)

Wrightson, Keith, *Ralph Tailor's Summer: a scrivener, his city and the plague* (New Haven, 2011)

Youngs, Frederic A., *Proclamations of the Tudor Queens* (Cambridge, 1976)

Name Index

Roman numerals are references to pages in the Introduction and Appendices. Arabic numerals refer to inventory numbers.
Many surnames have variant spellings. They are listed under the nearest to the modern version. A name may occur several times, often with different spelling, in some inventories. Missing or illegible letters in the original documents are shown as [...].

Abbreviations

Christopher	Chris	Katherine	Kath
Edmund (Edmond)	Edm	Margaret	Margt
Edward	Edw	Nicholas, Nicolas	Nic
Elizabeth	Eliz	Richard	Rich
George	Geo	Robert	Rob
Henry	Hy	Roger	Rog
Humphrey, Humfrey	Hum	Thomas	Thos
James	Jas	widow	wid
John	Jn	William	Wm

Place Index

Roman numerals are references to pages in the Introduction and Appendices. Arabic numerals refer to inventory numbers. All the Bedfordshire parishes are listed alphabetically in Appendix 1; they have not been indexed here.
Place names are listed under their modern spelling unless unidentified, when the original spelling and any possible identification have been added. Missing or illegible letters in the original documents are shown as [...].

County abbreviations:

Bucks	Buckinghamshire	Leics	Leicestershire
Cambs	Cambridgeshire	Mddx	Middlesex
Herts	Hertfordshire	Northants	Northamptonshire
Hunts	Huntingdonshire	Oxon	Oxfordshire

Subject Index

References in Roman numerals are to pages in the Introduction and Appendices. References in Arabic are to inventory numbers.
Words in brackets in the headings are explanations of the coverage of the term, unusual spellings or alternative terms used in the inventories.

Unknown or uncertain terms

The following words have not been satisfactorily identified. They are listed separately to bring them to readers' attention. Possible explanations have been provided for some.

Printed and bound by CPI Group (UK) Ltd, Croydon, CR0 4YY

16/04/2025

14658568-0001